Computers, Technology, and Society

Second Edition

COMPREHENSIVE

Includes CD-ROM with Videos, Animations, Labs, and the Entire Text!

June Jamrich Parsons

Dan Oja

Stephanie Low

COURSE
TECHNOLOGY

ONE MAIN STREET, CAMBRIDGE, MA 02142

an International Thomson Publishing company I(T)P®

Cambridge • Albany • Bonn • Boston • Cincinnati • London • Madrid • Melbourne • Mexico City
New York • Paris • San Francisco • Singapore • Tokyo • Toronto • Washington

New Perspectives on Computers, Technology, and Society Second Edition—Comprehensive
is published by Course Technology.

Associate Publisher	Mac Mendelsohn
Series Consulting Editor	Susan Solomon
Senior Product Manager	Donna Gridley
Product Manager	Rachel Crapser
Production Editor	Debbie Masi
Text Designer	Ann Turley
Cover Illustrator	Douglas Goodman
Photo and Video Researcher	Abby Reip
Video Editor	Jeanne Busemeyer, Hyde Park Publishing Services, Planet Interactive
CD-ROM Development	MediaTechnics Corporation
Animations	Planet Interactive
Composition	GEX, Inc.

© 1999 by Course Technology—I(T)P®

For more information contact:

Course Technology
One Main Street
Cambridge, MA 02142

ITP Europe
Berkshire House 168-173
High Holborn
London WCIV 7AA
England

Nelson ITP, Australia
102 Dodds Street
South Melbourne, 3205
Victoria, Australia

ITP Nelson Canada
1120 Birchmount Road
Scarborough, Ontario
Canada M1K 5G4

International Thomson Editores
Seneca, 53
Colonia Polanco
11560 Mexico D.F. Mexico

ITP GmbH
Königswinterer Strasse 418
53227 Bonn
Germany

ITP Asia
60 Albert Street, #15-01
Albert Complex
Singapore 189969

ITP Japan
Hirakawacho Kyowa Building, 3F
2-2-1 Hirakawacho
Chiyoda-ku, Tokyo 102
Japan

ISBN 0-7600-7022-9

Printed in the United States of America

3 4 5 6 7 8 9 10 BM 03 02 01 00 99

Preface to Students and Instructors

Presenting *Computers, Technology, and Society Second Edition*

The New Perspectives Series is pleased to present *Computers, Technology, and Society Second Edition*; as we call it, CTS. It's a book. It's a CD-ROM. It's either or it's both. If you've used a New Perspectives book before, you've come to expect the best in content accuracy, timeliness, and the latest technology to teach technology. And CTS will not disappoint you. If you've never used a New Perspectives book before, you're in for a treat.

What's the Same?

We've retained the hallmark features that contributed to the great success of *Computers, Technology, and Society First Edition*: large, clear illustrations with many helpful, detailed labels; Focus Questions attached to the major headings that are designed to engage, pique interest, and motivate the relevance of the material that follows; and a rich collection of interesting and entertaining Review Questions and Projects.

What's New?

Every book now includes a CD, which contains the entire book as well as animations, videos, links to the Web, Labs, and three ways for interactive self-assessment. The content has been thoroughly updated and we've added new art and photographs. Also, *Computers, Technology, and Society Second Edition* is now available in two versions: Brief and Comprehensive. The Brief version of this book contains four chapters: The Impact of Computers on Your Life; Computers and Privacy; Computers, Intellectual Property, and Ethics; and Computers and Intelligence. The Comprehensive version contains Chapters 1–9 of our *Computer Concepts 3rd Edition* text plus these four societal chapters.

The popular first edition of *New Perspectives on Computers, Technology, and Society* was one of the first textbooks to include essential computer concepts along with comprehensive coverage of related societal and ethical issues. This second edition continues in that tradition. Our revised and updated chapters will lead students to a better understanding of the legal and ethical implications of a technology-based society. The new InfoWeb feature included in each chapter is especially valuable because the suggested Web links and resources will lead students to the latest information about current laws and research on important issues. Here is a brief overview of what you will find in the four societal chapters:

- **The Impact of Computers on Your Life** explores the impact of technology on the way we live, learn, and work. This chapter includes full discussion of job market trends and computer-based education, as well as the political and social use of the Internet and the World Wide Web.

- **Computers and Privacy** discusses technology-related issues of personal privacy and freedom. Students will learn how personal information is stored and shared electronically, and how to safeguard their own personal information. The security of communicating via the Internet using cryptography is explained. Also included is a discussion of electronic commercial transactions and government concerns about the unrestricted use of the Internet.
- **Computers, Intellectual Property, and Ethics** describes how intellectual property laws such as copyright, patents, and trademarks are being adapted to protect creative works in digital format. Throughout this chapter, students examine when and how to ask for permission to use digital works like graphics, Web page elements, software, and e-mail, and learn methods for protecting their own digital work.
- **Computers and Intelligence** discusses the latest research on human intelligence and whether electronic devices can achieve some simulation of intelligence or intelligent behavior. Several models of artificial intelligence are examined. The chapter concludes with an overview of current applications of artificial intelligence—software agents, biometrics, expert systems, robotics and virtual reality.

Quick Checks

At the end of each section you will find a Quick Check section designed to help make sure key concepts have been grasped. Answers to the Quick Checks are at the end of the book, or, if you are using the CD, you can click the "Check Answers" button.

Key Word Practice and Practice Test

Both the Key Word Practice and Practice Test are available if you are using the CD. Both have tracking disk capability for student/instructor feedback, printing capability, and study guide generation to guide the re-study of incorrect answers.

InfoWebs

The InfoWeb icon connects you to Web links, film, video, TV, print, and electronic resources. InfoWebs keep you up-to-date and solve the problem of constantly changing URLs. If you're using the CD and have Internet access, you can click the InfoWeb icon and be linked directly to resources on the Internet using your browser of choice. If you are using the CD and do not have Internet access, you will be linked to the InfoWeb section at the end of the chapter. Refer to the InfoWeb number in the chapter to find its place in the InfoWeb section at the end of each chapter.

CD Connections

If you are the using the CD-ROM, you'll love clicking these icons. They reveal videos, animations, screen tours, and other treasures to enhance learning and retention of key concepts.

Labs

Concepts come to life with the Labs—highly interactive tutorials that combine illustrations, animations, digital images, and simulations. The Labs guide you step-by-step through a topic, present you with Quick Checks, let you explore on your own, test comprehension, and provide printed feedback. Lab icons at the beginning of the chapters and in the text's margins indicate when a topic has a corresponding Lab. Lab Assignments are included at the end of each relevant chapter. If you are using the CD, you can launch a Lab from any Lab icon.

Supplements

Online Companions: Dedicated to Keeping You Up-To-Date at www.course.com As with the first edition of CTS, we will continue to offer you a dedicated Web site for *CTS Second Edition*. Instructors can browse the password-protected Faculty Online Companion to obtain an online Instructor's Manual and more. Students can access this text's Student Online Companion, which contains the InfoWebs and other useful materials.

Course Presenter Course Presenter is a lecture presentation tool providing instructors a replacement for overhead transparencies. It includes a predesigned presentation for each chapter of the textbook, including the video clips, animations, and Labs. Instructors can also customize this presentation to their own preferences.

Course Test Manager: Testing and Practice at the Computer or on Paper Course Test Manager is cutting-edge, Windows-based testing software that helps instructors design and administer practice tests and actual examinations. Course Test Manager can automatically grade the tests students take at the computer and can generate statistical information on individual as well as group performance.

Instructor's Manual This all new enhanced Instructor's Manual offers an outline for each chapter; suggestion for instruction on chapter content, including how to effectively use and integrate the InfoWebs, the CD connections, and the Labs; answers to all end of chapter materials; and numerous teaching tips.

Application Software Instruction *CTS Second Edition* is part of the New Perspectives Series, which includes microcomputer applications textbooks and Internet titles. These textbooks include Quick Checks, Labs and Lab Assignments, Student and Faculty Online Companions, Figure files, Course Test Manager, and more. You'll find that either the text-based or the computer-based instructional materials fit perfectly with *CTS Second Edition*.

Custom Books The New Perspectives Series offers instructors two ways to customize a New Perspectives text to fit their courses exactly: CourseKits®, two or more texts packaged together, and Custom Editions™, your choice of books bound together. Custom Editions offer unparalleled flexibility in designing concepts and applications courses. Instructors can build their own book by ordering a combination of titles bound together to cover only the topics they want. Students save because they buy only the materials they need. There is no minimum order, and books are spiral bound. CourseKits offer significant price discounts.

Acknowledgments

This edition was a major undertaking for all the people who worked on it. Everyone made sacrifices, offered their creative talents, stayed on schedule, and was dedicated to making this book and CD the best it could be. The dedication and commitment they exhibited made us proud to be a part of the New Perspectives team. So, our thanks and deep appreciation go to the entire staff at GEX Inc., Planet Interactive, the many student testers and beta testers, Donna Schuch, Jeremy Gaboury, Sue Oja, John Reynolds, John Zeanchock, Ann Turley, Doug Goodman, Susanne Walker, Abby Reip, Jeanne Busemeyer, Joe Myers, Marilyn Freedman, Fatima Nicholls, Mac Mendelsohn, and especially to the triumvirate of Debbie Masi, Donna Gridley, and Susan Solomon.

June Jamrich Parsons
Dan Oja

Being part of the New Perspectives team is an exciting and rewarding experience. Researching the current legal and ethical issues has been interesting and beneficial to myself, to my colleagues at The College of Charleston, and most of all to my students. Thanks to all of them who asked the brilliant questions that ushered my search for answers! With the advice and assistance of the entire New Perspectives team, especially Pam Conrad, Abby Reip, Rachel Crapser, and Marilyn Freedman, I was able to explore a surprising level of depth on a wide variety of current issues. My deepest appreciation to all of them for their dedication and to June Parsons, Dan Oja, and Mac Mendelsohn for giving me the opportunity to work on this project.

Stephanie Low

BRIEF CONTENTS

CONTENTS

COURSE LABS

Course Labs offer the absolute best when it comes to interactive learning reinforcement.
The Labs offer:

- Steps, which guide students step-by-step as they learn/review basic concepts.

- Quick Checks, which appear as students work through the Steps and which draw attention to key points.

- Quick Check Summary Reports, which can be printed as homework and as validation that students have completed the Steps.

- Explore, in which students can experiment, practice skills, and complete the Lab Assignments at the end of each chapter.

Chapter 1

Using a Mouse
This Lab guides students through basic mouse functions and operations, Interactive exercises using dialog boxes allow students to practice mouse skills by creating posters.

Using a Keyboard
Students learn the parts of the keyboard and basic keyboard operations. They practice basic keyboarding with interactive typing exercises, including a self-paced typing tutor that helps improve speed and accuracy.

User Interface
Students are presented with user interfaces on a general/conceptual level, and then have the opportunity to interact with menu driven, prompted dialog, command line, graphical, and combination interfaces.

DOS Command-Line Interface
This Lab presents students with concepts and basic skills associated with the DOS command line, and provides hands-on practice entering commands at a live DOS prompt.

Peripheral Devices
Descriptions, drawings, and animations explain the functions of many popular peripheral devices.

Chapter 2

Computer History Hypermedia
This dynamic Lab has been updated and contains descriptions, drawings and photos related to the history and development of computing devices. Students learn to use hypertext links to research historical events and trends.

Multimedia
This Lab shows students what it's like to work with multimedia and see what it might be like to design some aspects of multimedia projects.

Chapter 3

Word Processing
This Lab guides students through essential word processing skills, such as typing and editing text, formatting, saving, and opening a document. They interact with a word processing program, specially designed for this Lab, that offers a hands-on introduction to word processors.

Spreadsheets

Students are introduced to essential spreadsheet skills. A spreadsheet program, specially designed for this Lab, allows students to practice and explore these skills on their own.

Database

After learning essential database concepts, students learn to use query by example to search a visual database for specific records.

Chapter 4

Using Files

Students see what happens on the screen, in RAM, and on the disk when they save, open, revise, and delete files.

Defragmentation and Disk Operation

In this Lab, students interact with simulated disks, files, and FATs to discover how the computer physically stores files. This Lab demonstrates how files become fragmented and how defragmentation utilities work.

Windows Directories, Folders, and Files

Students work with a directory tree to learn basic concepts of directory hierarchies and file types.

DOS Directories and File Management

Students learn the basics of DOS file management, including subdirectories, copying, and moving files.

Chapter 5

Troubleshooting

Students use a simulated computer to step through the boot process. They learn to identify and troubleshoot the most common boot-related problems.

Binary Numbers

This Lab introduces students to binary numbers, demonstrates how data is stored electronically using 1s and 0s, and provides practice converting between binary and decimal.

CPU Simulator

Students use a microprocessor simulation to see what happens in the ALU, control unit, and register during execution of simple assembly language programs. They can run prepared programs or write their own to see how a microprocessor actually works.

Chapter 6

Buying a Computer

Completely updated for this edition, this Lab is ever more helpful to students. An online glossary helps students interpret the technical specifications and advertisements to compare features and make purchase decisions.

Chapter 7

E-mail

Students use a simple e-mail simulation to learn essential e-mail skills including creating, sending, forwarding, replying, printing and saving mail.

Chapter 8

The Internet: World Wide Web
Students interact with a simulated Web browser to explore home pages, URLs, linking, and hypertext. You can assign this Lab even if an Internet connection is not available.

Web Pages & HTML
This Lab is a primer on HTML basics and shows how HTML is used to create pages. Students then see how they can modify these pages and view them in a browser.

Chapter 9

Data Backup
Using a simulated business environment, this Lab teaches basic backup procedures. Students experience data loss, attempt to restore lost data, and learn first-hand the value of regular backup procedures.

Videos and Animations

Chapter 1

Chapter 2

Chapter 3

Chapter 4

Chapter 5

Chapter 6

Chapter 7

Chapter 8

Chapter 9

Chapter LIF

Chapter PRV

Chapter IPE

Chapter INT

Credits

Chapter One: Chapter Opener: Courtesy of Photofest. Figure 1-1: Courtesy of Corbis-Bettmann. Figure 1-3a: Courtesy of Hewlett-Packard. Figure 1-3b: Courtesy of Digital Equipment Corporation. Figure 1-3c: Courtesy of IBM Corporation. Figure 1-3d: Courtesy of US Robotics. Figure 1-3e: Courtesy of Casio. Figure 1-4: Courtesy of IBM Corporation. Figure 1-5: Courtesy of Royal Caribbean Cruises Ltd. Figure 1-6: Courtesy of IBM Corporation. Figure 1-7: Courtesy of American Airlines. Figure 1-8: Courtesy of Cray Research. Figure 1-9: Video courtesy of Synchromic Studios Inc. Figure 1-11a: Courtesy of David Young Wolff/Tony Stone Images. Figure 1-11b: Courtesy of Caere Corporation. Figure 1-11c: Courtesy of 3M Visual Systems Division. Figure 1-11d: Courtesy of Hewlett-Packard Company. Figure 1-11e: Used by permission © Logitech 1997. Figure 1-11f: Courtesy of Dragon Systems. Figure 1-13g: Courtesy of Creative Labs, Inc. Figure 1-13h: Used by permission © Logitech 1997. Figure 1-11i: Courtesy of Hewlett-Packard Company. Figure 1-11j: Courtesy of Epson America, Inc. Figure 1-11k: Courtesy of Epson America, Inc. Figure 1-11l: Courtesy of Hewlett-Packard Company. Figure 1-11m: Courtesy of PictureTel Corporation. Figure 1-11n: ©1997 Wacom Technology Corporation. Figure 1-14: Video courtesy of Microsoft Corporation. Figure 1-23: Screen tour courtesy of Microsoft Corporation, video images from Bergwall Productions. IW1: Courtesy of Photofest. IW2: Courtesy of AP/Wide World Photos. IW3: Courtesy of Microsoft Corporation. IW4: Courtesy of Dragon Systems.

Chapter Two: Chapter Opener: Courtesy of AP/Wide World Photos. Figure 2-2: Courtesy of Shelly R. Harrison. Figure 2-5: Courtesy of Durvin & Co. Photography. Figure 2-17: Courtesy of CompUSA, Inc. Figure 2-18: Courtesy of Shelly R. Harrison. Figure 2-21: Photo provided courtesy of Proxima Corporation. Figure 2-22: Courtesy of SAS Institute. Figure 2-24: Courtesy of ProCD, Inc. Figure 2-26: ©PC-TV. Figure 2-27: Courtesy of Virgin Interactive Entertainment. Figure 2-28: Courtesy of Intuit. Figure 2-29: Courtesy of Joe Baraban/The Stock Market. Figure 2-30: Courtesy of Microsoft Corporation. Figure 2-31: Courtesy of Shelly R. Harrison. Figure 2-33: Courtesy of Microsoft Corporation. Figure 2-35: Courtesy of Creative Labs, Inc. Figure 2-36: Courtesy of Intel Corporation. Figure 2-39: Video images courtesy of Bergwall Productions, screenshots courtesy of Microsoft Corporation. IW1: Courtesy of CompUSA, Inc. IW2: Courtesy of Shelly R. Harrison. IW3: Courtesy of Intuit.

Chapter Three: Chapter Opener: Courtesy of USGS. Figure 3-1: Still shots courtesy of Corbis-Bettman and North Wind Picture Archives, video images from Real to Reel Productions. Figure 3-4: Courtesy of Gamma Liaison. Figure 3-7: Courtesy of Vatican Library. Figure 3-13: Courtesy of National Archives and Records. Figure 3-16: Courtesy of Jacques m. Chenet/Gamma Liaison. Figure 3-18a-b: Courtesy of Smith Corona Corporation. Figure 3-18c: Courtesy of Hewlett-Packard Company. Figure 3-19: Courtesy of Robert Frerck/Odyssey Productions. Figure 3-28: Courtesy of AP/Wide World Photos. Figure 3-30: Courtesy of Rodale Press and Jerry O'Brien. Figure 3-31: ©Jeff Lowenthal/Chicago. Figure 3-39: Courtesy of Stewart Cohen/Tony Stone Images. Figure 3-40: Photo provided courtesy of Proxima Corporation. IW1: Courtesy of North Wind Picture Archives. IW2: Courtesy of Gamma Liaison.

Chapter Four: Chapter Opener: Courtesy of Dilip Mehta/Contact Press Images, Inc. Figure 4-14: Courtesy of IBM Corporation, Research Division, Almaden Research Center. Figure 4-18a-d: Courtesy of Shelly R. Harrison. Figure 4-18e: Courtesy of Iomega. Figure 4-19a: Courtesy of Shelly R. Harrison. Figure 4-19b: Courtesy of Iomega. Figure 4-20: Video courtesy of Western Digital Corporation. Figure 4-26: Courtesy of Iomega. Endnote: Courtesy of IBM Research. IW1: Courtesy of Iomega. IW2: Courtesy of IBM Archives.

Chapter Five: Chapter Opener: Courtesy of James Kaczman. Figure 5-2: Video segments courtesy of Motorola Semiconductor Products Sector, ©1997 SEMATECH, INC., Portions of Silicon Magic used with permission of Semiconductor Equipment and Materials International, ©1991. Figure 5-3a-b: Courtesy of Texas Instruments. Figure 5-3c-d: Courtesy of Intel Corporation. Figure 5-14: Courtesy of Smithsonian Institution. Figure 5-15: Photo courtesy of Intel Corporation, video segments courtesy of Motorola Semiconductor Products Sector, ©1997 SEMATECH, INC., Portions of Silicon Magic used with permission of Semiconductor Equipment and Materials International, ©1991. IW1: Courtesy of Intel Corporation.

Chapter Six: Chapter Opener: Courtesy of Mobile Communications Division of U.S. Robotics. Figure 6-9: Courtesy of IBM Corporation. Figure 6-10: Courtesy of Microsoft Corporation. Figure 6-11a: Courtesy of IBM Corporation. Figure 6-11b: Courtesy of Sharp Electronics Corporation. Figure 6-11c: Courtesy of Toshiba America Information Systems, Inc. Figure 6-12: Courtesy of IBM Corporation. Figure 6-15: Courtesy of ©1997 Gateway 2000, Inc., reprinted with permission. Figure 6-16a: Courtesy of James P. Dawson/NYT Pictures. Figure 16-b: Courtesy of Microsoft Corporation. Figure 6-16c: Video courtesy of Microsoft Corporation. Figure 6-19: Courtesy of Shelly R. Harrison. Figure 6-21: Courtesy of Shelly R. Harrison. Figure 6-21: ©PC-TV. Figure 6-22: Courtesy of INFOWORLD Magazine/Illustration: Gene Grief. Figure 6-23: Courtesy of Reed Rahn; Digital Imaging: Slim Films. Figure 6-24: Video segments courtesy of Motorola Semiconductor Products Sector, ©1997 SEMATECH, INC. IW1: Courtesy of Altec Lansing Technologies, Inc. IW2: Courtesy of Shelly R. Harrison.

Chapter Seven: Chapter Opener: Courtesy of Spencer Jones 1995/FPG International. Figure 7-5: Courtesy of Bruce Ayers/Tony Stone Images. Figure 7-10a-b: Courtesy of SMC. Figure 7-12: Courtesy of Proxim, Inc. Figure 7-17: Courtesy of Novell.

Chapter Eight: Chapter Opener: Created by Dan Oja. Figure 8-1: Courtesy of NCSA/UIUC. Figure 8-8: Courtesy of Theodor Holm Nelson, Project Xanadu. Figure 8-15: Courtesy of Microsoft Corporation. Figure 8-27: © PC-TV. Project 5: Drawing by P. Steiner, © 1993 from The New Yorker Collection. All rights reserved.

Chapter Nine: Chapter Opener: Courtesy of Stock Montage/SuperStock. Figure 9-2: video © PC-TV. Figure 9-13: Courtesy of AP/Wide World Photos. Figure 9-14: Courtesy of Fischer International Systems Corporation. Figure 9-16: © PC-TV. Figure 9-24: Courtesy of Western Digital Corporation. IW2: Courtesy of Chuck Savage/The Stock Market.

Chapter LIF: Chapter Opener: Video © 1998 Cochran Communications. Figure 1: Courtesy of PAR Technology Corporation. Figure 3: Courtesy of Hewlett-Packard Company. Figure 9: Courtesy of Apple Computer, Inc. Figure 10: Courtesy of Hewlett-Packard Company. Figure 11: Courtesy of AP/Wide World Photos/Denis Paquin. Figure 12: Courtesy of 3M Visual Systems Division. Figure 13: Courtesy of A.D.A.M. Software, Inc. Figure 14: Courtesy of Northeastern University. Photo: J. Levine. Figure 22: Courtesy of Don and Pat Valenti/Tony Stone Images. Figure 24: Reprinted with special permission of King Features Syndicate.

Chapter PRV: Figure 2: Courtesy of Cerulean Technology, Inc. Figure 5: Courtesy of UPI/Corbis-Bettman. Figure 8: Courtesy of Charles Thatcher/Tony Stone Images. Figure 9: Photo: Ken Heinen, Collection of the Supreme Court of the United States. Figure 13: Courtesy of Sensormatic Electronics Corporation. Figure 20: Courtesy of Jeffrey Aaronson/Network Aspen. Figure 22: Courtesy of Mykotronx, Inc.

Chapter IPE: Figure 1c: Courtesy of the United States Patent and Trademark Office. Figure 1f: Courtesy of the United States Patent and Trademark Office. Figure 2: Courtesy of The Gamma Liaison Network. Figure 3: Kleenex is a Registered Trademark of Kimberly-Clark Corporation and reproduced with their permission. Figure 5: Courtesy of Hewlett-Packard Company. Figure 7: Courtesy of W.W. Norton & Company. Figure 11: Courtesy of the Wall Street Journal Interactive Edition. Figure 14: Courtesy of Corbis-Bettmann. Figure 20: Courtesy of Thomas R. Karlo. Figure 22: Corel is a trademark of Corel Corporation. Courtesy of United Airlines. Used by permission: AT&T©1998. Courtesy of Underwriters Laboratories. Courtesy of the American Association for Retired Persons.

Chapter INT: Chapter Opener: Courtesy of Photofest. Figure 2: Courtesy of the Association for Computing Machinery. Figure 4: Courtesy of AP/Wide World Photos. Figure 13: Courtesy of Dr. Victor Johnston, NMSU. Figure 16: Video courtesy of Miros, Inc. Wellesley, MA. Photo reprinted with permission from CNET, Inc. Copyright 1998. Figure 18: Courtesy of Lucas Film Ltd. Figure 19: Courtesy of PhotoDisc, Inc. ©1997. Figure 20: Courtesy of the California Institute of Technology, Jet Propulsion Laboratory and NASA. Figure 21: Courtesy of Maurice Smith and Andrew Syred, Microscopy-UK 1997/1998. Figure 23: Courtesy of the California Institute of Technology. Figure 24: Courtesy of Rene Ertzinger. Figure 26: Photograph by Ken Heinen; National Museum of African Art, Eliot Elisofon Photographic Archives, Smithsonian Institution.

USING COMPUTERS:
ESSENTIAL CONCEPTS

Peripheral
Devices

User Interfaces

DOS
Command-Line
User Interface

Using a
Mouse

Using a
Keyboard

LABS

InfoWeb

2001
1

In the classic science-fiction film *2001: A Space Odyssey*, astronaut Dave Bowman and four crew members depart on a mission to Jupiter. The mission objective: to discover the source of a mysterious object from space. Midway through the mission, the onboard computer, named HAL, begins to exhibit strange behavior. Dave leaves the spacecraft to make some external repairs. When he is ready to reboard, he speaks to the computer, "Open the pod bay door, HAL." HAL's reply is chilling, "I'm sorry, Dave, I'm afraid I can't do that."

This dialog between a human and a computer raises some intriguing questions. How realistic is it? Can humans and computers communicate this fluently? What went wrong with the communication? Why won't the computer let Dave back into the spaceship?

To use a computer effectively, you must communicate tasks to the computer and accurately interpret the information the computer provides to you. The means by which humans and computers communicate is referred to as the user interface, and this is the central theme of Chapter 1.

In this chapter you will learn which computer components are necessary for communication between humans and computers. You will also learn about the user interfaces typically found on today's computer systems and how to respond to what you see on the computer screen. This chapter concludes with a discussion about manuals, reference guides, and tutorials that will help you learn how to interact with a specific computer system or software package.

CHAPTER**PREVIEW**

This chapter is a practical introduction to computers that you can immediately apply in the Lab component of this course: starting a computer, logging into a network, starting programs, and using a variety of user interfaces. When you have completed this chapter you should be able to:

- Define the term "computer"
- Describe the relationship between computer hardware and software
- Identify the parts of a typical microcomputer system
- List the peripheral devices that are typically found on microcomputer systems
- Define the term "user interface"
- Describe how you use interface elements such as prompts, commands, menus, and graphical objects
- Describe the resources you can use to learn how to use computers and software

A Computers: Mind Tools

Computers have been called "mind tools" because they enhance our ability to perform tasks that require mental activity. Computers are adept at performing activities such as making calculations quickly, sorting large lists, and searching through vast information libraries. Humans can do all these activities, but a computer can often accomplish them much faster and more accurately. Our ability to use a computer complements our mental capabilities and makes us more productive. The key to making effective use of the computer as a tool is to know what a computer does, how it works, and how you can use it. That is the focus of this book.

Von Neumann's Definition

What is a computer? If you look in a dictionary printed before 1940, you might be surprised to find a computer defined as a person who performs calculations! Machines also performed calculations back then, but they were referred to as calculators, not computers. The modern definition and use of the term "computer" emerged in the 1940s when the first electronic computing devices were developed as a response to World War II military needs.

InfoWeb

von
Neumann
2

In 1945, a team of engineers began working on a secret military project to construct the Electronic Discrete Variable Automatic Computer, referred to by the acronym EDVAC. At the time, only one other functioning computer had been built in the United States. Plans for the EDVAC were described in a report by the eminent mathematician John von Neumann, pictured in Figure 1-1.

The InfoWeb icon connects you to Web links, film, video, TV, print, and electronic resources. If you're using the CD and have Internet access, click the InfoWeb icon to go directly to resources on the Internet. Otherwise, refer to the InfoWeb section at the end of each chapter.

Figure 1-1

When this photo was published in 1947, the caption read, "Dr. John von Neumann stands in front of a new Electronic 'Brain,' the fastest computing machine for its degree of precision yet made. The machine which can do 2,000 multiplications in one second and add or subtract 100,000 times in the same period was displayed today for the first time at the Institute for Advanced Study. Its fabulous memory can store 1,024 numbers of 12 decimal places each. Dr. von Neumann was one of the designers of the wonder machine."

Von Neumann's report has been described as "the most influential paper in the history of computer science." It was one of the earliest documents to specifically define the components of a computer and describe their functions. In the report, von Neumann used the term "automatic computing system." Today, popular usage has abandoned this cumbersome terminology in favor of the shorter terms "computer" or "computer system." Based on the concepts presented in von Neumann's paper, we can define a **computer** as a device that accepts input, processes data, stores data, and produces output. Let's look more closely at the elements of this definition.

A Computer Accepts Input

What kinds of input can a computer use? Computer **input** is whatever is put into a computer system. "Input" is also used as a verb that means to feed information into a computer. Input can be supplied by a person, by the environment, or by another computer. Some examples of the kinds of input a computer can process are the words and symbols in a document, numbers for a calculation, instructions for completing a process, pictures, audio signals from a microphone, and temperatures from a thermostat.

An **input device** gathers and translates input into a form that the computer can process. As a computer user you will probably use the keyboard as your main input device.

A Computer Processes Data

In what ways can a computer process data? **Data** refers to the symbols that describe people, events, things, and ideas. Computers manipulate data in many ways, and we call this manipulation "processing." Some of the ways a computer can process data include performing calculations, sorting lists of words or numbers, modifying documents and pictures according to user instructions, and drawing graphs. In the context of computers, then, we can define a **process** as a systematic series of actions a computer uses to manipulate data. A computer processes data in a device called the **central processing unit** or **CPU**.

A Computer Stores Data

Why does a computer store data? A computer must store data so it is available for processing. The places a computer puts data are referred to as storage. Most computers have more than one location for storing data. The place where the computer stores data depends on how the data is being used. The computer puts data in one place while it is waiting to be processed and another place when it is not needed for immediate processing. **Memory** is an area that holds data that is waiting to be processed. **Storage** is the area where data can be left on a permanent basis while it is not needed for processing.

A Computer Produces Output

What kinds of output does a computer produce? Computer **output** is the results produced by a computer. "Output" is also used as a verb that means the process of producing output. Some examples of computer output include reports, documents, music, graphs, and pictures. An **output device** displays, prints, or transfers the results of processing from the computer memory.

Study Figure 1-2 to make sure you understand fundamental computer functions and see if you recognize the modern devices that help the computer accomplish each function.

Figure 1-2

Basic computer functions

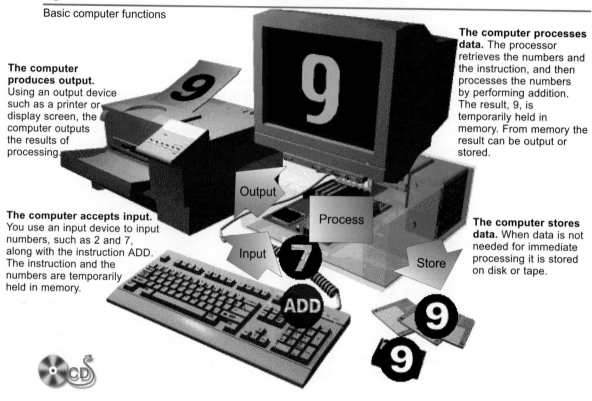

The computer produces output. Using an output device such as a printer or display screen, the computer outputs the results of processing.

The computer processes data. The processor retrieves the numbers and the instruction, and then processes the numbers by performing addition. The result, 9, is temporarily held in memory. From memory the result can be output or stored.

The computer accepts input. You use an input device to input numbers, such as 2 and 7, along with the instruction ADD. The instruction and the numbers are temporarily held in memory.

The computer stores data. When data is not needed for immediate processing it is stored on disk or tape.

Output

Process

Input

Store

ADD

At the end of each section in this book, you will find a "Quick Check" designed so you can make sure you understand what you have read before you continue. The answers to the Quick Checks are at the end of the book, just before the Index.

QuickCheck A

1. The four functions performed by a computer are input, storage, output, and _____.

2. _____ refers to the symbols processed by a computer.

3. A computer processes data in a device called the _____ processing unit.

4. The computer puts data temporarily in _____ while the data is waiting to be processed.

5. When data is not needed for processing, the computer puts it in _____.

ⓑ Computer System Basics

A computer system includes a computer, peripheral devices, and software. The electric, electronic, and mechanical devices used for processing data are referred to as **hardware**. In addition to the computer itself, the term "hardware" refers to components called **peripheral devices** that expand the computer's input, output, and storage capabilities. Computer hardware in and of itself does not provide a particularly useful mind tool. To be useful, a computer requires a set of instructions, called **software** or a **computer program**, which tells the computer how to perform a particular task. Computers become even more effective when connected to other computers in a **network** so users can share information.

Software

Why does a computer need software? A computer without software is like a record player without any records; a tape player without any tapes; or a CD-player without any CDs. Without software, a computer is just a useless gadget with a power switch. Fortunately, software is plentiful and available for an astonishing number of tasks. Walk into a large computer store and you will see shelves full of software, including software for producing resumes, software for managing a small business, software to help you study for the Graduate Record Examination, software that teaches you Spanish, software to help you plan your diet, software for composing music, and software that takes you on an adventure through a dangerous labyrinth.

Software sets up a computer to do a particular task then tells the computer how to interact with the user and how to process the user's data. For example, music composition software sets up the computer to show you a musical staff. It tells the computer to let you input notes from your keyboard or synthesizer. Then the software tells the computer how to process this input into electrical signals that will play your music through a speaker.

One of the best things about using computers is browsing through a computer store or a computer software catalog to find just the right software to make your life easier and more interesting.

Categories of Computers

How is using a microcomputer different from using a mainframe? Computers traditionally have been divided into four categories, based on their technology, function, physical size, cost, and performance. These categories, however, evolve with the technology. The lines that divide the different computer categories are fuzzy and tend to shift as more powerful computers become available.

Because the characteristics of each computer category shift and change as technology advances, it is difficult to categorize a particular computer unless you have up-to-date technical expertise. So, if you want to categorize a particular computer, look at the sales literature to find out how the manufacturer classifies it.

InfoWeb

Microcomputers
3

Microcomputers, also known as personal computers, are the computers you typically find in homes and small businesses. A microcomputer usually costs about $2,000, and its processor performs about 200 million operations per second. The microcomputer you use might be a stand-alone unit, or it might be connected to other computers so you can share data and software with other users. However, even when your computer is connected to others, it will generally carry out processing tasks for only one user. Microcomputers come in many shapes and sizes, as you can see in Figure 1-3.

Figure 1-3

Microcomputers

A standard **desktop microcomputer** fits on a desk and runs on power from an electrical wall outlet. The display screen is usually placed on top of the horizontal desktop case.

A microcomputer with a **tower case** contains the same basic components as a standard desktop microcomputer, but the vertically-oriented case is large and allows more room for expansion. The tower unit can be placed on the floor to save desk space.

A **notebook computer** is small and light, giving it the advantage of portability that standard desktop computers do not have. A notebook computer can run on power from an electrical outlet or batteries.

A **personal digital assistant (PDA)**, or **palm-top computer** achieves even more portability than a notebook computer by shrinking or eliminating some standard components, such as the keyboard. On a keyboardless PDA, a touch-sensitive screen accepts characters drawn with your finger. PDAs easily connect to desktop computers to exchange and update information.

Figure 1-4

A typical minicomputer handles processing tasks for multiple users.

Terminals act as each user's main input and output device. The terminal has a keyboard for input and a display screen for output, but it does not process the user's data. Instead, processing requests must be transmitted from the terminal to the minicomputer.

The minicomputer stores data for all the users in one centralized location.

InfoWeb

Minicomputers
4

A **minicomputer** is somewhat larger than a microcomputer and can carry out the processing tasks for many users. If you are using a minicomputer system, you use a terminal to input your processing requests and view the results. A **terminal** is a device with a keyboard and screen used for input and output, but not for processing. Although a terminal resembles a microcomputer because it has a keyboard and screen, a terminal does not have any processing power of its own.

When you input a processing request, your terminal transmits it to the minicomputer. The minicomputer sends back results to your terminal when the processing is complete. The minicomputer system in Figure 1-4 is fairly typical of minicomputers that cost between $20,000 and $250,000.

Minicomputer systems typically help small and medium-sized businesses perform specific tasks such as accounting, payroll, and shipping. For example, the main office of Royal Caribbean Cruises uses a minicomputer to track passenger bookings (Figure 1-5).

Figure 1-5

Stop in at any Caribbean port and you'll see ships emblazoned with the distinctive blue-anchor logo of Royal Caribbean Cruises, Ltd. With a fleet of ten ships and over five million passengers a year, the company uses IBM minicomputers to keep track of passenger bookings and corporate accounting.

InfoWeb

Mainframes
5

Mainframes are large, fast, and fairly expensive computers, generally used by business or government to provide centralized storage, processing, and management for large amounts of data. As with a minicomputer, one mainframe computer carries out processing tasks for multiple users who input processing requests using a terminal. However, a mainframe generally services more users than a minicomputer. To process large amounts of data, mainframes often include more than one processing unit. One of these processing units directs overall operations. A second processing unit handles communication with all the users requesting data. A third processing unit finds the data requested by users.

Mainframes remain the computer of choice in situations where reliability, data security, and centralized control are necessary. The price of a mainframe computer system is typically several hundred thousand dollars. A mainframe computer is housed in a closet-size cabinet, as shown in Figure 1-6 and its peripheral devices are contained in separate cabinets.

Figure 1-6

The closet-sized system unit for the IBM S/390 G4 mainframe computer contains the processing unit, memory, and circuitry to support multiple terminals.

When you use a mainframe, your processing requests are transmitted from your terminal to the computer. At the same time, other users may also transmit requests. The computer processes each request in turn and transmits back the results. Mainframes service user requests quickly. Even though there might be 200 people submitting processing requests, the speed of the computer's response makes it seem as if you are the only user (Figure 1-7).

Figure 1-7

During a recent airline fare war, an American Airlines mainframe handled over 4,000 reservation transactions per second.

InfoWeb

Supercomputers
6

Supercomputers are the fastest and most expensive type of computer. The cost of a supercomputer such as the one in Figure 1-8, ranges from $500,000 to $35 million.

Originally designed for "compute-intensive" tasks such as weather prediction, molecular modeling, and code-breaking, supercomputers today have also expanded into business markets where the sheer volume of data would cause lengthy processing delays in a traditional mainframe environment. For example, MCI uses supercomputer technology to manage a huge pool of customer data. Queries that once took over two hours, now take about a minute of supercomputer time.

The speed of a supercomputer can reach one trillion instructions per second, making it possible to perform complex tasks such as modeling the movement of thousands of particles in a tornado or creating realistic animations (Figure 1-9).

Figure 1-8

The Cray T3E supercomputer, configurable with six to 2,048 processors, provides the computing power to tackle the world's most challenging computing problems.

Figure 1-9

To create the animated dinosaur skeleton for the McDonald's commercial that aired during Super Bowl XXX, each frame typically takes one hour of computer time on a very fast microcomputer. With 24 frames per second, it would take 24 hours to complete one second of animation. The animators at Synchromics used the power of the supercomputer at the Maui High Performance Computing Center to reduce the time from 24 hours to 2 hours.

System Components

When I use a computer system, what hardware components will it include? This book focuses on microcomputers because that is the category of computers you are likely to use. Although the focus is on microcomputers, most of the concepts you will learn apply to the other categories of computers as well.

Microcomputer, minicomputer, mainframe, and supercomputer systems include devices to input, output, process, and store data. Study Figure 1-10 to learn about the hardware components you are likely to use on a typical microcomputer system.

Figure 1-10

Microcomputer system components

The **system unit** is the case or box that contains the power supply, storage devices, and the main circuit board with the computer's main processor and memory.

Storage media are physical materials that provide long-term storage for computer data. **Floppy disks** are popular microcomputer storage media. A **CD-ROM** is a high-capacity storage medium with a capacity of up to 680 million characters. Most CD-ROMs contain information when you purchase them and do not allow you to add or change the information they contain.

The primary output device on a microcomputer is the **monitor**; a display device that forms an image by converting electrical signals from the computer into points of colored light on the screen.

A **floppy disk drive** is a storage device that writes data on floppy disks. A typical microcomputer system has a 3½-inch floppy disk drive that stores up to 1.44 million characters of data on a single floppy disk. A light indicates when the floppy disk drive is in use—a warning not to remove your disk until the light goes out.

A **CD-ROM drive** is a storage device that uses laser technology to read data from a CD-ROM.

A **hard disk drive** can store billions of characters on a non-removable disk platter. A hard disk drive is mounted inside the system unit; an external light indicates when the hard disk drive is in use.

A **mouse** is an input device that you use to manipulate objects on the screen.

Most computers are equipped with a **keyboard** as the primary input device. A computer keyboard includes the letter and number keys, as well as several additional keys that control computer-specific tasks.

Microcomputer Compatibility

Can all computers use the same software? Hundreds of companies manufacture microcomputers, but there are only a small number of microcomputer designs or **platforms**. Today there are two major microcomputer platforms, popularly called PCs and Macs. **PCs** are based on the architecture of the first IBM microcomputers. PCs are manufactured by IBM, Compaq, Dell, Gateway, and hundreds of other companies. **Macs** are based on the Macintosh computer, manufactured by Apple Computer, Inc. Because about 80% of the microcomputers in use today are PCs, the examples in this book focus on the PC platform.

Computers that operate in essentially the same way are said to be **compatible**. Two computers are compatible if they can share the same software and use the same peripheral devices.

Not all microcomputers are compatible with each other. PCs and Macs are not regarded as compatible because they cannot use the same hardware devices or use the same programs without hardware or software to translate between them. In the past, sharing data between platforms was often difficult, and sometimes impossible. However, sharing data between these two platforms is inconvenient, but not impossible.

Peripheral Devices

LAB

Peripheral
Devices

Is it possible to expand or modify a basic computer system? The term **peripheral device** designates equipment that might be added to a computer system to enhance its functionality. For example, a printer is a popular peripheral device used with micro, mini, and mainframe computers. Keyboards, monitors, mice, and disk drives are sometimes classified as peripheral devices, even though they are included with most basic computer systems.

Peripheral devices allow you to expand and modify a basic computer system. For example, you might purchase a computer that includes a mouse, but you might prefer to use a trackball. You might want to expand your computer's capabilities by adding a scanner so you can input photographs. If you're an artist, you might want to add a graphics tablet, so you can sketch pictures using a pencil-like stylus. A peripheral device called a modem connects your computer to the telephone system so you can access information stored on other computers.

Most microcomputer peripheral devices are designed for installation by users without technical expertise. When you buy a peripheral device it usually comes with installation instructions and specially designed software. You should carefully follow the instructions to install the device and its software. Also make sure the computer is turned off before you attempt to connect a peripheral device so you don't damage your computer system. Figure 1-11 on the next page shows some of the peripheral devices that are typically added to microcomputer systems.

Figure 1-11

Peripheral devices

A **bar code reader** gathers input data by reading bar codes from product labels or price tags.

A **dot matrix printer** creates characters and graphics by printing a fine pattern of dots using a 9-pin or 24-pin print mechanism.

An **LCD projection panel** is placed on an overhead projector to produce a large display of the information shown on the computer screen.

A **color ink-jet printer** creates characters and graphics by spraying ink onto paper.

A **sheet scanner** converts a page of text or images into an electronic format that the computer can display, print and store. A hand scanner converts a 4-inch section of a page.

A **plotter** uses pens to draw an image on paper.

A **sound card** can be installed inside a computer system unit to give a computer the capability to accept audio input from a microphone, play sound files stored on disks and CD-ROMs, and produce audio output through speakers or headphones.

A **computer video camera** records an image of the person sitting at a computer or of a small group. Special digitizing hardware and software convert the image into a signal a computer can store and transmit.

A **trackball** is a pointing device that you might use as an alternative to a mouse. You roll the ball to position the pointer on the screen.

A **graphics tablet** accepts input from a pressure-sensitive stylus, converting pen strokes into images on the screen.

A **laser printer** uses the same technology as a photocopier to print professional-quality text and graphics.

Computer Networks

What's different about using a network? A **computer network** is a collection of computers and other devices connected to share data, hardware, and software. Network users can send messages to others on the network and retrieve data from a centralized storage device. Using a computer on a network is not much different from using a stand-alone computer except that you have access to more data, the ability to communicate with others, and you'll have to follow security procedures.

A network must be secured against unauthorized access to protect the data it stores. Most organizations restrict access to the software and data on a network by requiring users to log in with a unique user ID and password.

A **user ID** is a combination of letters and numbers that serve as your "call sign" or "identification." Your user ID is public—it is usually part of the address someone would need to send you messages over the network. You can let people know your user ID, but you should never reveal your password.

A **password** is a special set of symbols known only to you and the person who supervises the network. You should not reveal your password because it would violate your responsibility to help maintain network security. Also, you should understand that if someone logs into a network using your user ID and sends offensive messages or erases important files, it will look as if you did it. Figure 1-12 shows you what to do when a computer asks you to log in.

Figure 1-12

A network log in screen

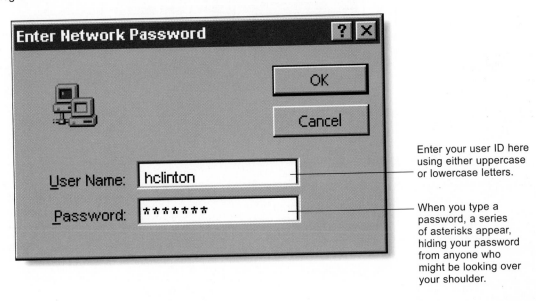

Enter your user ID here using either uppercase or lowercase letters.

When you type a password, a series of asterisks appear, hiding your password from anyone who might be looking over your shoulder.

A network can connect microcomputers, minicomputers, and mainframes. Small networks connect a few computers within a building, whereas larger networks can stretch across the country. The world's largest computer network, the **Internet**, provides connections for millions of computers all over the globe. The Internet provides many information services, but the most popular is the **World Wide Web**, often referred to as the **Web**.

The Web is a sort of "flea market" for information. Computer sites all over the world store data of various sorts, such as weather maps, census data, product information, course syllabi, music, and images. When you connect your computer to the Web, you can access this information. Search engines, like the one shown in Figure 1-13 help you find the information you want from among the millions of sites and the thousands of pages on each site.

Figure 1-13

Lycos is a popular search engine that helps you find information on the Web

To use this search engine, type in the keyword(s) for your search or select a category.

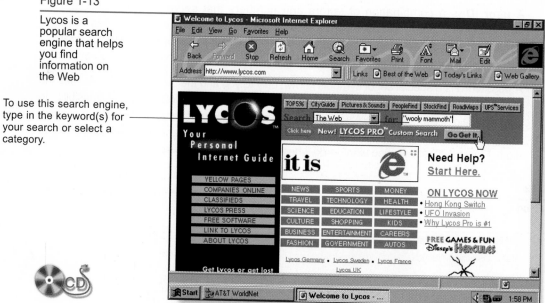

QuickCheck B

1 Most microcomputers are equipped with a(n) _____ as the primary input device and a(n) _____ as the primary output device.

2 A(n) _____ is generally devoted to carrying out the processing tasks of only one user, even when it is connected to other computers.

3 A(n) _____ is a device that resembles a microcomputer but does not have any processing capability.

4 If an organization wants to provide processing for more than 200 users and reliability, security, and centralized control are necessary, a(n) _____ computer would best meet its needs.

5 An IBM computer is _____ with a Compaq computer because it operates in essentially the same way.

6 A computer _____ allows you to send messages to other computer users and access data from a centralized storage device.

C The User Interface

User
Interfaces
7

To effectively use the computer as a mind tool, you must communicate with it; you must tell the computer what tasks to perform, and you must accurately interpret the information the computer provides. The means by which humans and computers communicate is referred to as the **user interface**. Through the user interface, the computer accepts your input and presents you with output. This output provides you with the results of processing, confirms the completion of the processing, or indicates that data was stored.

Ideally, a good user interface makes a computer easy to use, intuitive, and unobtrusive. However, this ideal is not always the reality. Donald Norman, a well-known cognitive scientist, wrote a delightful book called *The Psychology of Everyday Things* in which he says, "Well-designed objects are easy to interpret and understand. They contain visible clues to their operation. Poorly designed objects can be difficult and frustrating to use. They provide no clues—or sometimes false clues. They trap the user and thwart the normal process of interpretation and understanding."

As with many objects in everyday life, some computer user interfaces are not well conceived, and using them is frustrating. User interfaces are still evolving in response to the needs of a rapidly growing community of computer users that includes children, as shown in Figure 1-14.

Figure 1-14

User interfaces are
supposed to be intuitive.

Interacting with the Computer

Is the user interface hardware or software? The user interface is a combination of software and hardware. The software that controls the user interface defines its characteristics. For example, software controls whether you accomplish tasks by manipulating graphical objects or typing commands. The hardware controls the way you physically manipulate the computer to establish communication, for example, whether you use a keyboard or your voice to input commands. After you have a general understanding of user interfaces, you will be able to quickly figure out how to make the computer do what you want it to do.

LAB

User
Interfaces

The software interface elements you'll typically encounter include prompts, wizards, commands, menus, dialog boxes, and graphical objects. The hardware interface elements you'll use include pointing devices, keyboards, and monitors.

Prompts

Why is it sometimes hard to figure out what the computer wants me to do? A **prompt** is a message displayed by the computer that asks for input from the user. In response to a computer prompt, you enter the requested information or follow the instruction. Some prompts, such as "Enter your name:", are helpful and easy to understand, even for beginners. Other prompts, like A:\>, are less helpful.

A sequence of prompts is sometimes used to develop a user interface called a **prompted dialog**. In a prompted dialog, a conversation of sorts takes place between the computer and user. In the following example of a prompted dialog, the computer's prompts are in uppercase; the user's responses are in bold.

HOW MUCH MONEY IS CURRENTLY IN YOUR ACCOUNT?
1000
HOW MUCH MONEY WILL YOU DEPOSIT EACH MONTH?
100
WHAT IS THE YEARLY INTEREST RATE PERCENT?
6
WHAT IS THE LENGTH OF THE SAVINGS PERIOD IN MONTHS?
36
O.K. AFTER 36 MONTHS YOU WILL HAVE $5149.96 IN YOUR SAVINGS ACCOUNT.

A prompted dialog is rarely found in commercial software packages. There are two reasons why. First, the process of interacting with such a dialog is very linear. You must start at the beginning of the dialog and respond sequentially to each prompt. It is difficult to back up if you make an error.

The second reason that a prompted dialog is difficult to use is due to the ambiguity of human language. If a prompt is not clear and you respond to it with something unexpected, the dialog will not function correctly. In Figure 1-15 you can see an example of this difficulty in the dialog with a computer-based library card catalog system.

Figure 1-15

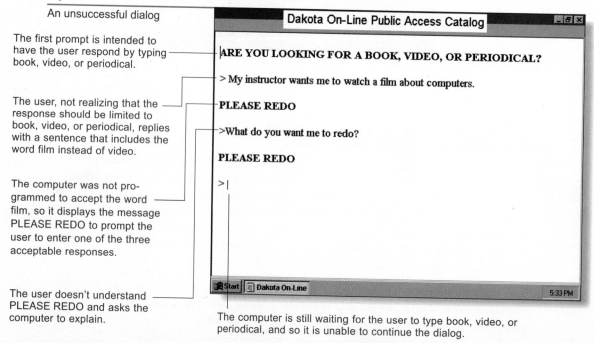

An unsuccessful dialog

The first prompt is intended to have the user respond by typing book, video, or periodical.

The user, not realizing that the response should be limited to book, video, or periodical, replies with a sentence that includes the word film instead of video.

The computer was not programmed to accept the word film, so it displays the message PLEASE REDO to prompt the user to enter one of the three acceptable responses.

The user doesn't understand PLEASE REDO and asks the computer to explain.

Dakota On-Line Public Access Catalog

ARE YOU LOOKING FOR A BOOK, VIDEO, OR PERIODICAL?

> My instructor wants me to watch a film about computers.

PLEASE REDO

>What do you want me to redo?

PLEASE REDO

>|

Start | Dakota On-Line | 5:33 PM

The computer is still waiting for the user to type book, video, or periodical, and so it is unable to continue the dialog.

The difficulty with the dialog in Figure 1-15 was not necessarily the fault of the user. The prompts should have provided more specific instructions, and the computer program should have accepted a wider vocabulary. Unfortunately, if this were the interface on your online library card catalog, you would need to learn how to work within its limitations.

Today's commercial software tends to use "wizards" instead of prompted dialogs. A **wizard** is a sequence of screens that direct you through multi-step software tasks such as creating a graph, a list of business contacts, or a fax cover sheet. Wizards, like the one in Figure 1-16, use graphics to help explain the prompts and allow users to back up and change their responses.

Figure 1-16

Using a wizard

The Business Card Wizard helps you create business cards that you can print on a laser printer.

The wizard prompts you at each step. First, you enter the information you want printed on the card.

Next you decide what style you'd like for your business card. The wizard lets you move forward, or backward to change your responses until the business card is set up to your satisfaction.

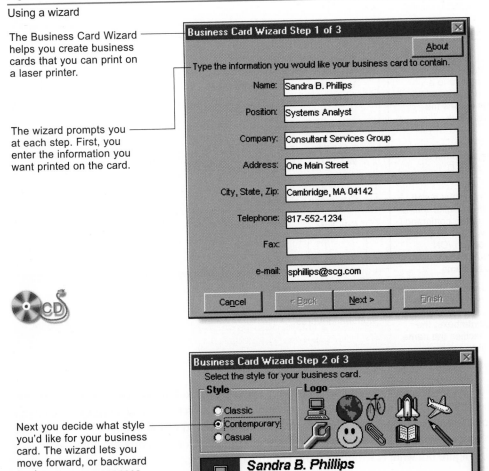

Commands

Is it true that I have to memorize lots of commands to use a computer? A **command** is an instruction you input to tell the computer to carry out a task. When you use older microcomputer interfaces and many mainframe interfaces, you must type commands, then press the Enter key to indicate that the computer should now carry out the command. Each word in a command results in a specific action by the computer. Command words are often English words, such as *print*, *begin*, *save*, and *erase*, but command words can also be more cryptic and might even use special symbols. Some examples of cryptic command words include *ls*, which means list; *cls*, which means clear the screen; and *!*, which means quit. Figure 1-17 shows how you might use a command to find out what is on your disk.

Figure 1-17

Using commands

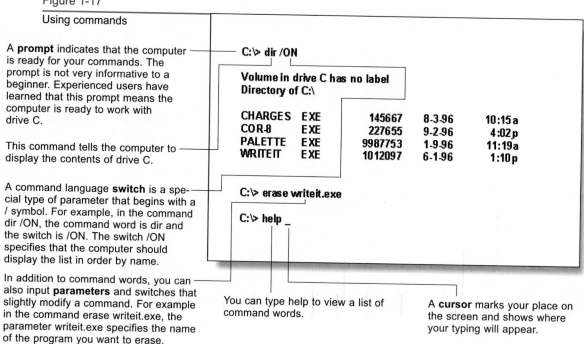

A **prompt** indicates that the computer is ready for your commands. The prompt is not very informative to a beginner. Experienced users have learned that this prompt means the computer is ready to work with drive C.

This command tells the computer to display the contents of drive C.

A command language **switch** is a special type of parameter that begins with a / symbol. For example, in the command dir /ON, the command word is dir and the switch is /ON. The switch /ON specifies that the computer should display the list in order by name.

In addition to command words, you can also input **parameters** and switches that slightly modify a command. For example in the command erase writeit.exe, the parameter writeit.exe specifies the name of the program you want to erase.

You can type help to view a list of command words.

A **cursor** marks your place on the screen and shows where your typing will appear.

```
C:\> dir /ON

Volume in drive C has no label
Directory of C:\

CHARGES   EXE        145667    8-3-96    10:15a
COR-8     EXE        227655    9-2-96     4:02p
PALETTE   EXE       9987753    1-9-96    11:19a
WRITEIT   EXE       1012097    6-1-96     1:10p

C:\> erase writeit.exe

C:\> help _
```

The commands you input must conform to a specific syntax. **Syntax** specifies the sequence and punctuation for command words, parameters, and switches. If you misspell a command word, leave out required punctuation, or type the command words out of order, you will get an **error message** or **syntax error**. When you get an error message or syntax error, you must figure out what is wrong with the command and retype it correctly.

An interface that requires the user to type in commands is referred to as a **command-line user interface**. Learning to use a command-line user interface is not easy. You must memorize the command words and know what they mean. To make the situation even more difficult, there is no single set of commands that you can use for every computer and every software package. If you forget the correct command word or punctuation, or if you find yourself using an unfamiliar command-line user interface, you can usually enter the Help command. If online help is not available, you'll need to use a reference manual.

LAB

DOS
Command-Line
User Interface

Menus and Dialog Boxes

Are menus easier to use than commands? Menus were developed as a response to the difficulties many people experienced trying to remember the command words and syntax for command-line user interfaces. A **menu** displays a list of commands or options. Each line of the menu is referred to as a **menu option** or a **menu item**. Figure 1-18 shows you how to use a menu.

Figure 1-18

Using a menu

Most of today's software includes a **menu bar** with a list of **menu titles** such as File, Edit, and View. Clicking a menu title displays the menu.

A menu shows you a list of **menu options**. You can select an option using the mouse.

Some menu options lead to a **submenu** that gives an additional set of command choices.

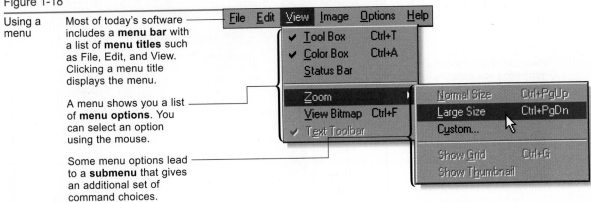

Menus are popular because when you use them, you do not have to remember command words. You just choose the command you want from a list. Also, because all the commands on the list are valid commands, it is not possible to make syntax errors.

You might wonder how a menu can present all the commands you might want to input. Obviously, there are many possibilities for combining command words, so there could be hundreds of menu options. Two methods are generally used to present a reasonably sized list of menu options, submenus, and dialog boxes.

A **submenu** is an additional set of commands that that the computer displays after you make a selection from the main menu. Sometimes a submenu displays another submenu providing even more command choices.

Instead of leading to a submenu, some menu options lead to a dialog box. A **dialog box** displays the options associated with a command. You fill in the dialog box to indicate specifically how you want the command carried out, as shown in Figure 1-19.

Figure 1-19

Using a dialog box

The Print option displays three dots to indicate that this menu leads to a dialog box.

When you select Print, the Print dialog box appears. The dialog box prompts you to enter specifications about how the computer should carry out the print task.

Click this button to display a list of printers you can use.

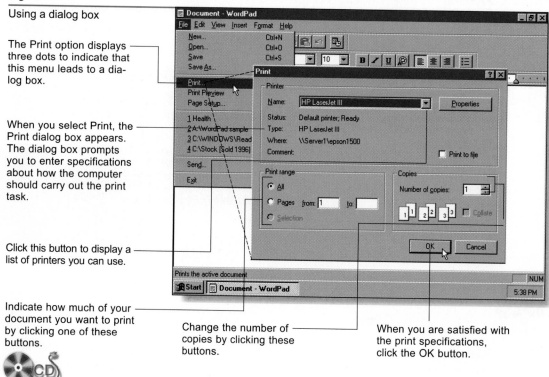

Indicate how much of your document you want to print by clicking one of these buttons.

Change the number of copies by clicking these buttons.

When you are satisfied with the print specifications, click the OK button.

Dialog boxes display controls that you manipulate with the mouse to specify settings and other command parameters. Figure 1-20 explains how to use some of the dialog box controls that you are likely to encounter.

Figure 1-20

Dialog box controls

Round **option buttons** allow you to select one of the options. Square **check boxes** allow you to select any or all of the options.

Drop-down lists display a list of options when you click the arrow button.

Spin boxes let you increase or decrease a number by clicking the arrow buttons. You can also type a number in the box.

Graphical Objects

Why are GUIs so popular? A **graphical object** is a small picture on the screen that you can manipulate using a mouse or other input device. Each graphical object represents a computer task, command, or a real-world object. You show the computer what you want it to do by manipulating an object instead of entering commands or selecting menu options. Graphical objects include icons, buttons, tools, and windows, as explained in Figure 1-21.

Figure 1-21

Graphical objects

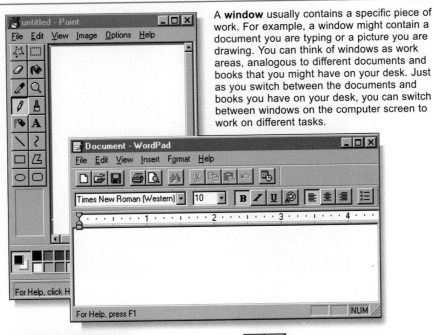

A **window** usually contains a specific piece of work. For example, a window might contain a document you are typing or a picture you are drawing. You can think of windows as work areas, analogous to different documents and books that you might have on your desk. Just as you switch between the documents and books you have on your desk, you can switch between windows on the computer screen to work on different tasks.

An **icon** is a small picture that represents an object. When you select an icon, you indicate to the computer that you want to manipulate the object. A selected object is highlighted. The My Computer icon on the right is selected, so it is highlighted with dark blue.

A **button** helps you make a selection. When you select a button, its appearance changes to indicate that it has been activated. The Paintbrush button is selected and it appears to be pushed in. Buttons are sometimes referred to as **tools**.

An example of manipulating on-screen objects is the way you delete a document using Windows software. The documents you create are represented by icons that look like sheets of paper. A Recycle Bin icon represents the place where you put documents you no longer want. Suppose you used your computer to write a report named "Sport Statistics," but you no longer need the report stored on your computer system. You use the mouse to drag the Sport Statistics icon to the Recycle Bin and erase the report from your computer system, as shown in Figure 1-22.

Figure 1-22

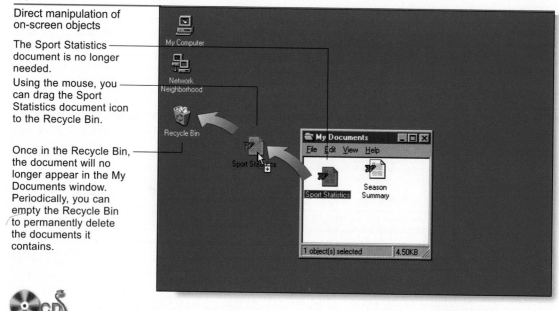

Direct manipulation of on-screen objects

The Sport Statistics document is no longer needed.

Using the mouse, you can drag the Sport Statistics document icon to the Recycle Bin.

Once in the Recycle Bin, the document will no longer appear in the My Documents window. Periodically, you can empty the Recycle Bin to permanently delete the documents it contains.

Graphical objects are a key element of **graphical user interfaces** or GUIs (pronounced "gooies") found on most of today's microcomputers. GUIs are based on the philosophy that people can use computers intuitively—that is, with minimal training—if they can manipulate on-screen objects that represent tasks or commands.

Graphical user interfaces often contain menus and prompts in addition to graphical objects because graphical user interface designers found it difficult to design icons and tools for every possible task.

Most graphical user interfaces are based on a metaphor in which computer components are represented by real-world objects. For example, a user interface with a **desktop metaphor** might represent documents as pages of paper and storage as a filing cabinet. Metaphors are intended to make the tasks you perform with computers more concrete, easier to explore, and more intuitive.

LAB

Using a Mouse

Pointing Devices

Some mice have three buttons, while others have only one or two—why? A **pointing device** such as a mouse, trackball, or lightpen helps you manipulate objects and select menu options. The most popular pointing device is the mouse. The mouse was developed by Douglas Engelbart in the early 1970s to provide an input method more efficient than the keyboard. Englebart's work coincided with efforts to construct graphical user interfaces. The popularity of the mouse and graphical user interfaces grew slowly, until Apple Computer, Inc. produced the Macintosh computer in 1983. Now virtually every computer is equipped with a mouse.

When you move the mouse on your desk, a **pointer**—usually shaped like an arrow—moves on the screen in a way that corresponds to how you move the mouse. You select an object on the screen by pressing the left mouse button a single time. This is referred to as **clicking**. Some operations require you to click the mouse twice in rapid succession. This is referred to as **double-clicking**. You can also use the mouse to **drag** objects from one screen location to another by pointing to the object, holding down the mouse button, and moving the mouse to the new location for the object. When the object is in its new location, you release the mouse button. Figure 1-23 shows you how to hold a mouse and use it to manipulate graphical objects.

Figure 1-23

Using a mouse — A pointer on the screen, usually shaped like an arrow, moves as you move the mouse.

To hold the mouse, rest the palm of your right hand on the mouse so your index finger is positioned over the left mouse button. Lightly grasp the mouse using your thumb and ring finger.

To select an object, use the mouse to position the pointer on the object, then click the left mouse button.

If you move the mouse to the right on your desk, the pointer moves to the right on your screen. When you pull the mouse toward you, the pointer moves toward the bottom of the screen.

The mouse moves the pointer only when the mouse is in contact with a hard surface like a desk. If you pick up the mouse and move it, the pointer will not move. This is handy to know. Suppose you are dragging an object, but your mouse runs into an obstacle on your desk. You can just pick up the mouse, move it to a clear space, and continue dragging.

The mouse you use with a Macintosh computer only has one button. PCs use either a two- or three-button mouse. A two-button mouse allows you to **right-click** an object and provides another way of manipulating it. For example, if clicking the left button selects an object, clicking the right button might bring up a menu of actions you can do with the object. On a three-button mouse you rarely use the third button. Some three-button mice, however, allow you to click the middle button once instead of double-clicking the left mouse button. This feature is useful for people who have trouble double-clicking. It also helps prevent some muscular stress injuries that result from excessive clicking.

Keyboard

Do I need to be a good typist to use a computer? Virtually every computer user interface requires you to use a keyboard. You don't have to be a great typist, but to use a computer effectively you should be familiar with the computer keyboard because it contains special keys to manipulate the user interface. Study Figure 1-24 before you read the rest of this section.

LAB

Using a Keyboard

You use the typing keys to input commands, respond to prompts, and type the text of documents. A cursor or an insertion point indicates where the characters you type will appear. The **cursor** appears on the screen as a flashing underline. The **insertion point** appears on the screen as a flashing vertical bar. You can change the location of the cursor or insertion point using the arrow keys or the mouse.

The **numeric keypad** provides you with a calculator-style input device for numbers and arithmetic symbols. You can type numbers using either the set of number keys at the top of the typing keypad or the keys on the numeric keypad. However, notice that some keys on the numeric keypad contain two symbols. When the Num Lock key is activated, the numeric keypad produces numbers. When the Num Lock key is not activated, the keys on the numeric keypad move the cursor in the direction indicated by the arrows on the keys.

The Num Lock key is an example of something called a toggle key. A **toggle key** switches back and forth between two modes. The Caps Lock key is also a toggle. When you press the Caps Lock key you switch or "toggle" into uppercase mode. When you press the Caps Lock key again you toggle back into lowercase mode.

Now here's an interesting problem that faced the designers for word processors that use command-line interfaces. Suppose someone is typing in the text of a document and wants to issue a command to save the document on a disk. If the user types SAVE, it will just appear as another word in the document. How does the computer know that SAVE is supposed to be a command and not just part of a sentence such as "Save your money." Interface designers solved this problem by introducing function keys, control keys, and Alt keys.

Function keys, like those numbered F1 through F12, are located at the top of your keyboard. They do not exist on the keyboard of a standard typewriter but were added to computer keyboards to initiate commands. For example, with many software packages F1 is the key you press to get help. The problem with function keys is that they are not standardized. In one program, you press F7 to save a document, but in another program, you press F5.

The Alt and Ctrl keys work in conjunction with the letter keys. If you see <Ctrl X>, Ctrl+X, [Ctrl X], Ctrl-X, or Ctrl X on the screen or in an instruction manual, it means to hold down the Ctrl key while you press X. Ctrl+X is a **keyboard shortcut** for clicking the Edit menu, then clicking the Cut option.

Figure 1-24

The computer keyboard

☐ Editing Keypad   ☐ Typing Keypad
☐ Numeric Keypad   ☐ Function Key Array

The **Esc** or "escape" key cancels an operation.

The function of the **Scroll Lock** key depends on the software you are using. This key is rarely used with today's software.

Indicator lights show you the status of each toggle key: Num Lock, Caps Lock, and Scroll Lock. The Power light indicates whether the computer is on or off.

The **Caps Lock** key capitalizes all the letters you type when it is engaged, but does not produce the top symbol on keys that contain two symbols. This key is a **toggle key**, which means that each time you press it, you switch between uppercase and lowercase modes. There is usually an indicator light on the keyboard to show which mode you are in.

The **function keys** execute commands, such as centering a line of text or boldfacing text. The command associated with each function key depends on the software you are using.

Each time you press the **Backspace** key, one character to the left of the cursor is deleted. If you hold down the Backspace key, multiple characters to the left are deleted one by one until you release it.

The **Print Screen** key prints the contents of the screen when you use some software. With other software, the Print Screen key stores a copy of your screen in memory that you can manipulate or print with graphics software.

The **Pause** key stops the current task your computer is performing. You might need to hold down both the Ctrl key and the Pause key to stop the task.

Page Up displays the previous screen of information. **Page Down** displays the next screen of information.

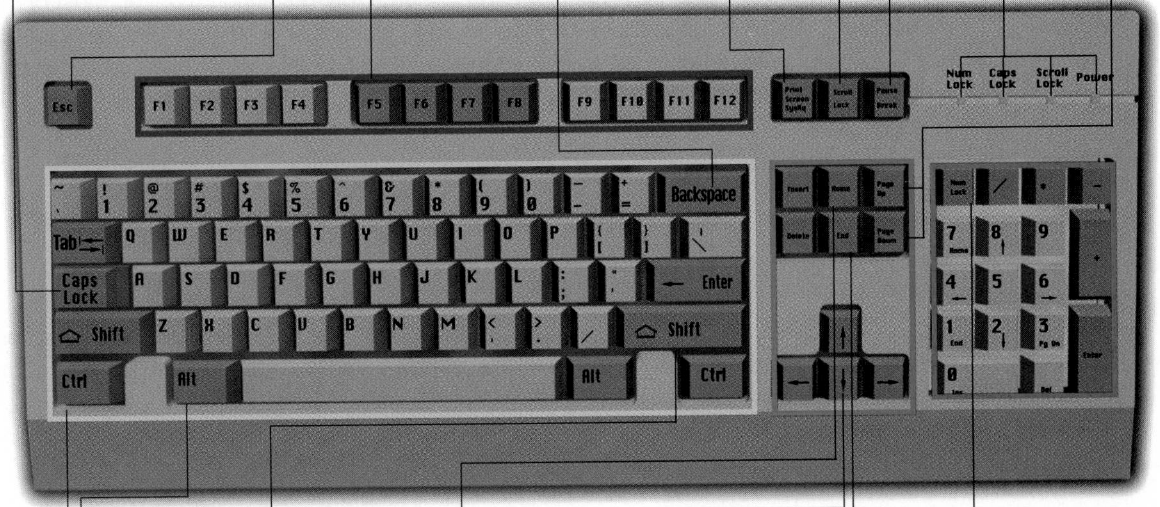

The **Num Lock** key is a toggle key that switches between number keys and arrow keys on the numeric keypad.

You hold down the **Alt** key while you press another key. The result of Alt key combinations depends on the software you are using.

You hold down the **Ctrl** key while you press another key. The result of Ctrl key combinations depends on the software you are using.

You hold down the **Shift** key while you press another key. The Shift key capitalizes letters and produces the top symbol on keys that contain two symbols.

Home takes you to the beginning of a line or the beginning of a document, depending on the software you are using.

The **arrow keys** move your position on the screen up, down, right, or left.

End takes you to the end of the line or the end of a document, depending on the software you are using.

Monitor

How are the monitor and user interface related? A monitor is a required output device for just about every computer user interface. Whereas you manipulate the keyboard and mouse to communicate with the computer, the monitor is what the computer manipulates to communicate with you by displaying results, prompts, menus, and graphical objects. Monitor display technology determines whether the interface designer can include color and graphical objects.

The first microcomputer monitors and the displays on many mainframe terminals still in use today were character-based. A **character-based display** divides the screen into a grid of rectangles, which can each display a single character. The set of characters that the screen can display is not modifiable; therefore, it is not possible to display different sizes or styles of characters. The only graphics possible on character-based displays are those composed of underlines, exclamation points, and other symbols that already exist in the character set. One of the reasons that mainframes rarely support graphical user interfaces is because of the legacy of character-based terminals connected to mainframe systems.

A **graphics display** or **bit-map display** divides the screen into a matrix of small dots called **pixels**. Any characters or graphics the computer displays on the screen must be constructed of dot patterns within the screen matrix. The more dots your screen displays in the matrix, the higher the **resolution**. A high-resolution monitor can produce complex graphical images and text that is easier to read than a low-resolution monitor. Most of the monitors on microcomputers have bit-map display capabilities. This provides the flexibility to display characters in different sizes and styles as well as the graphical objects needed for GUIs. Monochrome or gray-scale monitors display text and graphics in shades of gray. Color monitors allow the interface designer to use the impact of color to create pleasing screen designs and use color as a cue to direct the user's attention to important screen elements.

User Interface Comparison

What's it like using different types of user interfaces? Now that you have learned about user-interface elements, let's see how they work for a typical computer activity. One of the most frequent computer activities is starting a program. Figure 1-25 illustrates the different ways you could start a program—using commands, using graphical objects, and using a menu.

Figure 1-25

Starting programs
with different types
of user interfaces

To start Microsoft Works using the
DOS command-line user interface, you need to know the name
the computer has given the program. In this case the computer
calls Microsoft Works "works". At
the C:> prompt, type **works** then
press the Enter key.

C:>works

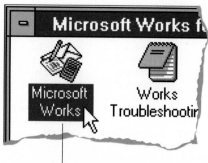

To start Microsoft Works using a graphical
object, you must move the pointer to the
Microsoft Works graphical object and double-
click the left mouse button.

Figure 1-25

Starting programs
with different types
of user interfaces
continued

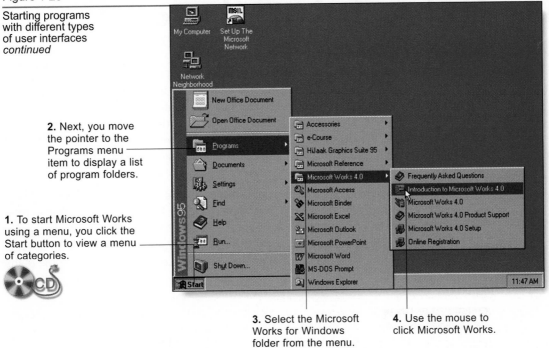

2. Next, you move
the pointer to the
Programs menu
item to display a list
of program folders.

1. To start Microsoft Works
using a menu, you click the
Start button to view a menu
of categories.

3. Select the Microsoft
Works for Windows
folder from the menu.

4. Use the mouse to
click Microsoft Works.

QuickCheck C

1. A(n) _____, such as "Enter your name:", is one way a computer can tell the user what to do.

2. Instead of prompted dialogs, today's software tends to use _____ to direct a user through multi-step software tasks, such as creating a graph or creating a fax cover sheet.

3. When you use a command-line interface, you press _____ when you are done typing a command.

4. If you type a command, but leave out a required space, you have made a(n) _____ error.

5. When you make a menu selection, a(n) _____ or a dialog box might appear to let you enter more details on how you want the computer to do a task.

6. Most _____ are based on a metaphor, such as a desktop metaphor in which documents are represented by folder icons.

7. The flashing underline that marks your place on the screen is called the _____; the flashing vertical bar is called the _____.

8. You can use the _____ key and the Alt key in conjunction with letter keys instead of using the mouse to control menus.

9. _____ are work areas on the screen analogous to different documents and books you might have open on your desk. (Hint: Don't forget to read the figure captions!)

User Focus

Ⓓ Help, Tutorials, and Manuals

InfoWeb

Computer
Terms
8

No class can ever teach you all you need to know about using computers or everything about one software package. You should not feel frustrated if you don't "know" how something on your computer works. One of the most important skills you can develop as a computer user is the ability to figure out how to do new computing tasks. But don't expect to figure things out in a flash of inspiration! You usually have to get some additional information.

You can find information about installing computer hardware and using computer software in books, on your computer screen, on videotapes, and on audio cassettes. We can refer to these books, tapes, and so forth as "resources." To use these resources effectively, you need to know they exist, you need to know where to find them, and you need to develop some strategies for applying the information they contain. Let's take a look at some of the resources you can use to do this.

Online Help

If I'm using a program and I "get stuck," what help can I get from the computer? The term "online" refers to resources that are immediately available on your computer screen. Reference information is frequently available as online help, accessible from a Help menu or by typing HELP at a command-line prompt. Figure 1-26 shows how you access online Help for the Microsoft Office 97 software.

Figure 1-26

Using the Office Assistant to get online help

The Office Assistant provides help in response to questions you type.

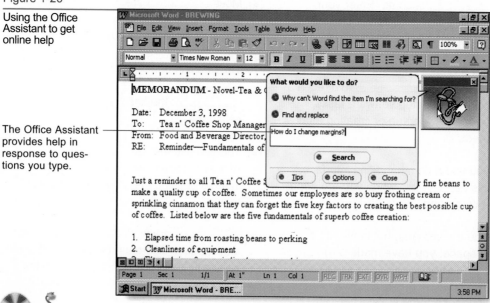

Tutorials

How can I get the most out of a tutorial? A **tutorial** is a guided, step-by-step learning experience. Usually this learning experience teaches you the generic skills you need to use specific hardware or software. For example, suppose you purchase CorelDRAW software, and the first thing you want to draw is your company logo. When you use a tutorial that teaches you how to use CorelDRAW, you learn how to do such things as draw straight lines and wavy lines, use color in the drawing, and change the sizes of the pictures you draw. The tutorial does not teach you exactly how to draw your company logo. To get the most out of a tutorial, therefore, you need to think about how you can generalize the skills you are learning so you can apply them to other tasks.

When you use a tutorial, don't try to cover too much ground at once. Two 60-minute sessions each day are probably sufficient. As you work on a tutorial, take notes on those techniques you expect to apply to your own projects. When you have completed enough of the tutorial to do your own project, put the tutorial aside. You can complete the rest of the tutorial later if you need to learn more. Tutorials come in a variety of forms, as shown in Figure 1-27.

Figure 1-27

Tutorials and reference resources

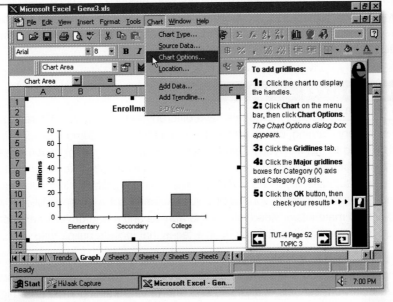

Computer-based **tutorials** display step-by-step instructions in boxes or windows on the screen. Computer-based tutorials have an advantage over their printed counterparts because they can demonstrate procedures using computer animation.

Audio tutorials on cassette verbally walk you through the steps of the tutorial. An advantage to this type of tutorial is that you do not have to read instructions. However, you must stop the tutorial and rewind, if you do not hear or understand the instructions. You might like audio tutorials if you easily retain information presented in lectures.

Video tutorials on videotape visually illustrate how the software or hardware works. Some video tutorials are designed so that you watch them, take notes, then try the steps on the computer later. Other video tutorials are designed to be used while you are sitting at the computer. As with audio tutorials, you can stop and rewind video tutorials if you miss something.

Printed tutorials are very popular. To use a printed tutorial, you read how to do a step, then you try to do it on the computer.

Reference Manuals

When should I use a reference manual instead of a tutorial? **Reference manuals** are usually printed books or online resources that describe each feature of a hardware device or software package. They might also include examples of how to use these features. A reference manual is organized by features, rather than by lesson.

Think of reference manuals as encyclopedias, containing descriptions of all features of the software. Do not assume that you should read a reference manual from cover to cover. Instead, leaf through it to get a quick overview of all the features. A reference manual can be quite long, sometimes thousands of pages.

You should use a reference manual to find out if a feature exists or to find out how to use a feature. When you use a reference manual, first check the index to locate the information you need, then turn to the appropriate section and read it carefully.

Reference manuals are usually included with the hardware or software that you buy. Most often, reference manuals are printed documents, but a recent trend is to provide computer-based reference manuals that you can read on the computer screen. Computer-based reference manuals are extensive and are often distributed on CD-ROMs.

You can usually find independent publishers who produce reference manuals for popular hardware and, particularly, for popular software. You might want to purchase one of these reference manuals if it is easier to understand or better organized than the manual included with the hardware or software you purchased.

InfoWeb

Learning
Styles
9

Other Sources of Information

Who needs a manual? Individuals have different learning styles. Whereas some people enjoy discovery learning, others prefer structured lectures or demonstrations. Your learning style is related to the way you'll best learn how to use a computer. If you like reading and easily remember the things you read in books, you will probably like using printed reference manuals and tutorials. If you are a visual learner, you will probably like video tutorials. If you are an adventurous learner, you might enjoy exploring software applications without referring to printed materials or video tutorials. Graphical and menu-driven user interfaces make this sort of exploration possible, as do interfaces that include online help.

Another approach to learning how to use computers is to take a course. Because you're reading this book, you are probably enrolled in an introductory computer course. Courses are available from schools, manufacturers, and private training firms and might last from several hours to several months. Courses about software packages tend to be laboratory-based with an instructor leading you through steps. Some courses might be lecture only, however; you might want to ask about the course format before you register.

If you run into a problem and are pressed for time, ask an expert. You might have a friend who knows a lot about computers, or on the job you might know a computer "guru." These are both good sources of information, as long as you don't overuse them.

You might also seek help from the support line of a software or hardware company. A **support line** is a service offered over the phone by a hardware manufacturer or software publisher to customers who have questions about how to use a software or hardware product. Sometimes these support line calls are toll-free; sometimes they are not. In addition to paying for the phone call, you might also pay a fee for the time it takes the support person to answer your question.

EndNote

Artificial Intelligence (AI) is the ability of a machine to simulate or surpass intelligent human behavior. Science fiction usually depicts computers as intelligent devices. HAL, though dangerous, certainly seemed to think for himself. Can computers have intelligence? This is a debate that has been raging among computer scientists and philosophers for half a decade. In 1950, British mathematician Alan Turing proposed a "test" of machine intelligence. The Turing test, as it is now called, is somewhat like a TV game show. It pits a contestant against two backstage opponents—one a computer and one a human. The contestant asks questions to try to identify the computer. Turing suggested that if the computer could not be identified, then it was acting just as intelligently as the human.

InfoWeb

Artificial
Intelligence
10

In Turing's original test, the questions and responses were typed out because computers could not understand or output speech. Today, it would be difficult to envision an intelligent computer that could not talk. We've all watched the Star Trek crew converse easily with the on-board computer. Most computers today are equipped to record and play sounds—most computers can play your regular music CDs in the CD-ROM drive—but your dialog with the computer remains silent, carried out with a mouse and keyboard. Will future user interfaces be conversational?

For a computer to understand spoken commands, it must be able to interpret human language, a process called **speech recognition**. Developers have run into problems, however, programming computers to understand different voices and different accents—an added complication in the ambiguity of human language. Suppose you tell your computer, "Open the Financial document, highlight the September data, then print it." Do you mean to print the entire document or only the September data?

Researchers are making progress solving speech recognition problems. The next time you encounter an automated telephone operator, for example, you might have the option of speaking instead of pushing the buttons on your phone.

InfoWeb

Chapter
Links

The InfoWeb is your guide to print, film, television, and electronic resources. Use it to obtain updates on quickly changing technical information and to locate information for research papers. If you're using the New Perspectives CD-ROM, click the InfoWeb icon on the left side of this paragraph to access the online InfoWeb links. Otherwise, use your Web browser and type in the address of the New Perspectives site: www.cciw.com/np3. At the New Perspectives site you'll find up-to-date links to the topics covered in this chapter.

1 2001: A Space Odyssey

One of the themes in the 1968 science fiction classic, *2001: A Space Odyssey*, is the relationship between humans and computers. Written by scientist and novelist Arthur C. Clarke, the book *2001: A Space Odyssey* (New York: New American Library, 1968) was the basis for a movie directed by Stanley Kubrick. The film *2001: A Space Odyssey* (MGM, 1968) is thought-provoking, and its special effects are still pretty impressive, even after 30 years. Perhaps Clarke's vision of the future is so powerful because of his strong background in science and research. Clarke is well known for his theoretical contribution to the invention of the communications satellite. For soundtracks and images from the film, critical commentary, and essays by Arthur C. Clarke, visit the 2001 Internet Resource Archive, at **www.design.no/2001**.

2 John von Neumann

Perhaps the greatest mathematician of his time, John von Neumann (1903–1957) had a photographic memory and a superhuman ability to perform mental calculations. Von Neumann's security clearance allowed him access to ENIAC and EDVAC, the first large scale digital computers developed in the United States. Find out more about von Neumann at **ei.cs.vt.edu/~history/VonNeumann.html**. His 1945 paper, "First Draft of a Report on the EDVAC" is reprinted in Nancy Stern's book **From ENIAC to UNIVAC: An Appraisal of the Eckert Mauchly Computers** (Digital Press, 1981).

For information about the exciting early days of computing, visit the Computer Museum's Web-based timeline **www.tcm.org/history/timeline/** and look at the years 1945–1952. If you'd like more information, check your library for the video, **The Machine That Changed the World, Episode 1: Giant Brains** (WGBH Television in cooperation with the British Broadcasting Corp., 1991).

3 Microcomputers

In 1977, Digital Equipment Corporation CEO Ken Olsen proclaimed, "There is no reason for any individual to have a computer in their home." It was a statement he would later regret. Microcomputer technology and the vision of pioneers like Apple Computer's Steve Jobs made personal computers a reality. A detailed history of Apple Computers is on the Web at **www.hypermall.com/History**. For more information about the heady days of the microcomputer industry, read the fast-paced book **Accidental Empires: How the Boys of Silicon Valley Make Their Millions, Battle Foreign Competition, and Still Can't Get a Date** by Robert X. Cringely (Published by HarperCollins, 1996).

4 Minicomputers

In 1957 Kenneth Olsen and Harland Anderson formed a company called Digital Equipment Corporation (DEC). Their original objective was to grab a slice of IBM's business market and sell million-dollar mainframes. Financial realities prevailed, however, and a new plan emerged—build a slightly scaled down computer and sell it for $125,000 to scientific and engineering markets. DEC computers proved successful even in other markets and by 1969, the era of miniskirts and miniseries, these computers were universally referred to as "minicomputers."

The book **Computer: A History of the Information Machine** by Campbell-Kelly and Aspray (Basic Books, 1996) contains a good history of minicomputers. On the Web, you can tour Carl Friend's mini-computer museum at **www.ultranet.com/~engelbrt/carl/museum**.

Today's minicomputer vendors include IBM, DEC, and Hewlett Packard. For an update on what's new about minicomputers, visit DEC's Web site at **www.digital.com**.

5 Mainframe Computers

IBM is synonymous with mainframe computers. The company traces its lineage back to the Tabulating Machine Company built around an 1890's card punch device invented by Herman Hollerith. IBM did not dominate the computer market until 1964 when it introduced the IBM System/360 mainframes that were to be the staple of business computing for a quarter of a century. The history of IBM is expertly chronicled in **Building IBM: Shaping an Industry and its Technology** by Emerson W. Pugh (MIT Press, 1995), and the video **The Computer Revolution: Birth of the Computer** (available from Films for the Humanities and Sciences).

IBM is not the only mainframe vendor, but its Web site at **www.ibm.com** is a good place to find information on the latest mainframe technology.

6 Supercomputers

It takes a supercomputer to beat the World's best chess player. In 1997, Gary Kasparov admitted defeat to IBM's Deep Blue supercomputer. IBM has an excellent Web site devoted to the match, at **www.chess.ibm.com**.

In the past three years, supercomputer technology and applications have changed remarkably. Today, supercomputer technology is largely based on "super" versions of the same processors that you find in microcomputers. Although supercomputers have not abandoned their specialized markets, they frequently perform the same tasks as mainframes. Seymour Cray was the well-known pioneer of supercomputer technology. You can read a 1994 interview with Cray from the Smithsonian archives at **www.si.edu/resource/tours/comphist/cray.htm** or an excellent book, **The Supermen: The Story of Seymour Cray and the Technical Wizards Behind the Supercomputer** by Charles J. Murray (John Wiley & Sons, 1997). Cray's company, Cray Research, was purchased by Silicon Graphics in 1996.

The World's Fastest Computers (*Byte*, January 1996) is an excellent article on supercomputers, accessible on the Web at **www.byte.com/art/9601/SEC6/ART1.HTM**. For an update on supercomputer technology, visit the sites of supercomputer vendors using the Web link **www.cs.cmu.edu/ ~scandal/vendors/htm**.

7 User Interfaces

In the film *2001: A Space Odyssey*, HAL wouldn't open the pod bay door, but users every day run into examples of computers that stubbornly refuse to open a particular file, locate a Web site, or carry out a requested command. Why does this happen? Although hardware and software bugs account for some user frustrations, many problems are due to miscommunication—a breakdown in the human-computer interface. Donald Norman's **Things That Make Us Smart: Defending Human Attributes in the Age of the Computer** (Addison-Wesley, 1994) is a book about how technology should enhance human intelligence, but only if it is user-friendly.

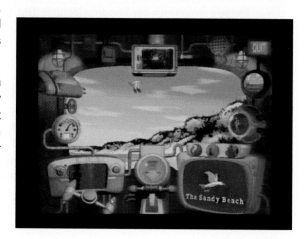

Today's graphical user interfaces have come a long way to making computers usable. Many people believe that GUIs were "invented" at Apple computers, because Apple's Macintosh was the first commercially successful computer with a GUI. However, GUIs evolved from Alan Kay's 1970 vision of the "Dynabook"—a portable, personal computer much like today's notebook computers and PDAs. The Web site **http://www.acm.org/sigchi/hci-sites/** is a good gateway to links on user interfaces.

8 Computer Terminology

Whether you're learning about computers for the first time or you're a computer pro, an up-to-date computer dictionary is always a handy companion to help you read computer magazines or look at computer ads. **The Computer Desktop Encyclopedia** by Alan Freedman (American Management Association, 1996) is one of the best references available today. You'll find the Web version at **www.techweb.com/encyclopedia/defineterm.cgi**. Another excellent Web-based compendium of computer terms is the *Webopedia* at **www.webopedia.com**. At **wfn-shop.princeton.edu/foldoc/** you can quickly look up any computer term you type at the "ever-expanding dictionary of computing." Users keep this Web dictionary up-to-date by adding new terms.

Check your library for a more in-depth reference, **The Encyclopedia of Computer Science** by Anthony Ralston (Van Nostrand Reinhold, 4th ed. 1997). Microsoft's Multimedia encyclopedia, **Encarta 97** (Microsoft Home, 1997) also provides a good assortment of computer definitions.

9 Learning Styles

What's the best way for you to learn? Do you absorb more information from a lecture than a book? Would you rather watch a demonstration or do it yourself? Educators agree that people learn in different ways, including auditory (hear it), kinesthetic (do it), and visual (see it). Take a quick inventory of your learning style at **www.howtolearn.com/personal.html**. Your personality also seems to affect the way you learn—extroverts succeed in different learning environments than introverts. You can fill out a question-naire to find out your personality type at **www.keirsey.com**.

10 **Artificial Intelligence**

In the film *2001: A Space Odyssey*, the computer HAL became operational on January 12, 1997. At the film's 1968 release, computer scientists were not altogether uncomfortable with the prediction that a computer like HAL might be achievable in 30 or so years. The science of artificial intelligence (AI) was in its infancy, but technology and software were developing at a dizzying pace.

The question "Can computers think?" is still under debate. Alan Turing and Marvin Minsky would argue "Yes!" Alan Turing's paper, **Computing Machinery and Intelligence** (*Mind 59*, 1950) got the discussion rolling and describes the famous Turing Test of machine intelligence. For an expanded perspective on the argument, read Minsky's paper, "Why People Think Computers Can't" at **ww.ai.mit.edu/people/minsky/papers/ComputersCantThink.txt**.

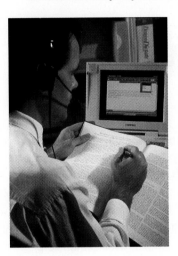

On the computers-can't-think side of the argument are John Searle and Hubert Dreyfus. A "must read" is **What Computers Still Can't Do: A Critique of Artificial Reason** by Hubert L. Dreyfus (MIT Press, 1992). Another classic in this continuing argument is **Minds, Brains, and Programs** by John Searle (Behavioral and Brain Sciences 3, 1980). The fourth episode of **The Machine that Changed the World: The Thinking Machine** sums up the arguments for and against machine intelligence and describes the challenges still in the forefront of artificial intelligence research.

It would be hard nowadays to envision an "intelligent" computer that couldn't understand human speech. So what's the current status of speech recognition and speech synthesis? Check out "An Introduction to Speech Recognition" at **www.speech.be.philips.com/intro.htm** at the Philips Speech Processing Web site.

Review

1 Using your own words, write out the answers to the questions below each heading in the chapter.

2 List each of the boldface terms used in this chapter, then use your own words to write a short definition of each term. If you would like clarification of one or more terms, refer to a computer dictionary or a computer science encyclopedia such as those listed in the InfoWeb section of this chapter. You can also refer to the Glossary/Index at the back of this book.

3 At the top of a sheet of paper write "Definition of the term computer," then make a list of important words, names, and phrases that are related to your list.

4 Use lines to divide a sheet of paper into four equal sections. In the top-left corner write "microcomputer." Write "minicomputer" in the top-right corner, "mainframe" in the bottom-left corner, and "supercomputer" in the bottom right corner. Place words, phrases, and definitions in each section that describe and differentiate each type of computer.

5 Draw a sketch of a microcomputer system, without referring to this book. Then label as many components as you can. When you have finished, look at Figure 1-10 to see if you omitted anything.

6 List as many peripheral devices as you can, without referring to this book. Indicate whether each peripheral is an input device, an output device, or both. When you have finished, refer to Figure 1-11 and review any devices you omitted.

7 Make a list of the user interface elements covered in this chapter. Write at least three terms or phrases associated with each. For example, user interface element: prompt. Associated terms and phrases: (a) prompted dialog, (b) wizards, (c) can be ambiguous or confusing.

8 Make a list of information resources that might help you install hardware and learn to use software. Write a one-sentence description of each resource.

9 Use the New Perspectives CD-ROM to take a practice test or to review the terms presented in this chapter.

Projects

1 **Your Computer** Draw a sketch of a computer system in your computer lab, home, or office and do the following:

a. Title the sketch appropriately, for example, "My Computer at Home."

b. List its brand name and model number, for example, "Dell Dimension."

c. Label the following parts, if applicable:

monitor	screen
keyboard	3½-inch disk drive
5¼-inch disk drive	hard drive light
CD-ROM drive	power switch
power light	system unit
mouse	printer

2 **Getting Started on Your Network** Do this project only if your school has a computer network for student use. If the network requires a user ID and password, get them. Learn how to log in. Write a one- to two-page step-by-step tutorial on how to log into the network. Your tutorial should include the following:

a. A title

b. An introductory paragraph explaining where the network is located, who can access it, and how students can get a user ID and password

c. Numbered steps to log into the network (if your lab policy requires that you turn on the computer each time you log in, you should include instructions for doing this in your tutorial)

d. Numbered steps for logging out of the network

3 **Evaluate a User Interface** Select a computer interface with which you are familiar. For example, you might select your bank's ATM machine or your favorite arcade game. Using the terminology you learned in this chapter, write a complete description of the user interface and its features. Your description might answer questions such as: Does the interface use menus? If so, what type? What hardware elements are required for the user interface? Is the interface intuitive? Does the interface use a metaphor? If so, what? Don't limit yourself to answering just these questions.

4 **Your Library Card Catalog** Find out if your library has a computerized card catalog. If it does, use it to answer the following questions:

a. What is the name of the software your library uses for its computerized card catalog?

b. What type of user interface does it have?

c. Explain the steps you would take to find the call number for the book *War and Peace*.

d. Is the computerized card catalog efficient to use, or do you need to enter a lot of extra information to find a book?

e. What kind of online help is available?

f. Is the computerized card catalog easy to learn and to use?

g. How much had you used the computerized card catalog before this assignment?

5 **Research Tool: The Internet** Do this project only if you have access to the Internet. The Internet is a worldwide computer network that provides access to a wealth of information including a World Wide Web site designed to accompany this textbook. Although the Internet

is the main topic of Chapter 8, using the Internet can come in handy even as you begin using this book. Several of the end-of-chapter projects refer you to information resources on the Internet. If you would like to use the Internet for these projects, this is a good time to get started.

There are several software tools to help you use the Internet, such as Netscape Navigator and Microsoft Internet Explorer. It is not possible to cover these software tools here. Therefore, this is an exploratory project that you can accomplish with the help of your instructor or with a tutorial prepared by your school or Internet service provider. Find out how to use the Internet and then answer the following questions:

a. What is the name of the software tool you use to access the Internet?

b. How do you access the "home page" for your school?

c. Use your Internet software to access the World Wide Web site **http://www.cciw.com/np3**. How can the information at this site help you with the end-of-chapter projects in this textbook?

d. List at least five other locations or "sites" that are available from your home page. How do you get to these other sites?

e. How can you keep track of where you have been on the Internet? (In other words, is there a way to backtrack to sites?)

f. When you are finished browsing on the Internet, how do you quit?

6 **Micros, Minis, Mainframes, and Supercomputers** In this chapter you read about several organizations and the computers they use. Use your library and Internet resources to find case studies that describe how computers are used in specific organizations or businesses and what category of computer (micro, mini, mainframe, or supercomputer) is used. Write a one-paragraph summary of your findings. Remember to include citations for the resources you used.

7 Reference Manuals Locate a software reference manual in your computer lab, home, or library; then answer the following questions:

a. What is the title of the reference manual?

b. How many pages does it have?

c. What are the titles of each section of the manual? For example, there might be a "Getting Started" section or an "Installation" section, and so on.

d. Does the reference manual include an index? If so, does it look complete? You should be suspicious of a large reference manual with a short index—it might be difficult to find the information you need.

e. Does the reference manual contain a list of features? If so, is this list arranged alphabetically? If not, how is it arranged?

f. Read a few pages of the reference manual. Write one or two sentences describing what you read. Does the reference manual seem to be well written and easy to follow? Why or why not?

8 **Identify Your Learning Style** In this chapter, you learned that you can take many approaches to learning how to use hardware and software. For this project, think about your own learning style and how it might affect the resources you select for learning about computers and software. Use the resources in InfoWeb #9 to assess your learning style. Write a one-page paper and include the following:

a. Describe the way you like to learn things in general—do you like to read about them, take a class, listen to a cassette, watch a video, think about them, do library research, or take a different approach?

b. If you have access to the Internet, provide the results of your learning style assessments. Do these seem to accurately reflect your learning style?

c. If you had to learn how to use a new software application, which approach would you like best: working through a tutorial, using a reference manual, exploring on your own, taking a class, or asking an expert? Why?

d. How does this relate to the way you like to learn other things?

9 **Practice Tests** Have you mastered the material in this chapter? You can test yourself using the Course Test Manager (CTM). If your instructor has installed the CTM software in your lab and given you a user ID and password, you can take practice tests. To start CTM, use the Course Test Manager icon (Windows 3.1) or the Course Test Manager menu option (Windows 95). When prompted, enter your user ID and password. Click the Practice Test button, then select a chapter. You can take as many tests as you like. CTM selects 20 questions at random from a test bank of thousands of questions.

Take a practice test for Chapter 1 and print your results.

10 Why Not Just Talk to It? Computer scientists have discovered that it is quite difficult to develop a "conversational" user interface that you could use to simply "talk" to a computer. One of the stumbling blocks is the ambiguity of human speech. For example, if someone tells you "My friend was looking at a bicycle in the store window, and she wanted it," you assume that "it" refers to the bicycle, not the store window. But English grammar does not make the meaning of "it" explicit, so a computer would have a hard time understanding what you mean. Hubert Dreyfus discusses this problem in the video *The Machine That Changed the World* and in the book entitled *What Computers Still Can't Do*. To pursue this topic, do one or more of the following activities:

a. With a small group of other students, try to think of other examples of ambiguity in human conversation that a computer would probably have difficulty understanding. You can share your list with the rest of the class or turn it in to your instructor.

b. Use the resources from InfoWeb #10 to research this topic so you more fully understand the problem. Write a term paper summarizing your research.

Lab Assignments

The New Perspectives Labs are designed to help you master some of the key computer concepts and skills presented in each chapter of the text. If you are using your school's lab computers, your instructor or technical support person should have installed the Labs software for you. If you want to use the Labs on your home computer, ask your instructor for the appropriate software.

Each Lab has two parts: Steps and Explore. Use Steps first to learn and review concepts. Read the information on each page and do the numbered steps. As you work through the Lab, you will be asked to answer Quick Check questions about what you have learned. At the end of the Lab, you will see a Summary Report of your answers to the Quick Checks. If your instructor wants you to turn in this Summary Report, click the Print button on the Summary Report screen.

When you have completed Steps, you can click the Explore button to complete the Lab Assignments. You can also use Explore to practice the skills you learned and to explore concepts on your own.

If you're viewing this textbook on screen, just click the icon for the Lab you want to use. Otherwise, use the instructions below. Your instructor or technical support person might help you get started.

If you have your own New Perspectives CD-ROM:

1 Insert the NP3 CD and wait a few seconds. If the program doesn't start automatically:

Windows 95: Click Start, click Run, type d:\start and press Enter.

Windows 3.1: Click File, click Run, type d:\start and press Enter.

If the New Perspectives software has been installed on a network or local hard disk drive:

1 **Windows 95:** Click Start, point to Programs, point to New Perspectives 3/e, click Textbook 3/e.

Windows 3.1: Double-click the New Perspectives 3/e group icon, double-click the Textbook 3/e icon.

To select a Lab:

1 From the Computer Concepts menu bar, click Labs, then click the Lab you want to use.

2 Follow the instructions on the screen to enter your name and class section.

3 Read the instructions for using the Lab by clicking the Instructions button.

4 When you are ready to begin the Lab, click the Steps button.

Peripheral Devices

A wide variety of peripheral devices provide expandability for computer systems and provide users with the equipment necessary to accomplish tasks efficiently. In the Peripheral Devices Lab you will use an online product catalog of peripheral devices.

1 Click the Steps button and begin the Steps. Complete the Steps to find out how to use the online product catalog. As you work through the Steps, answer all of the Quick Check questions. When you complete the Steps, you will see a Summary Report of your performance on the Quick Checks. Follow the directions on the screen to print the Summary Report.

2 After you know how to use the product catalog to look up products, features, and prices, use the catalog to do the following:

a. List the characteristics that differentiate printers.

b. List the factors that differentiate monitors.

c. Describe the factors that determine the appropriate type of scanner for a task.

d. List the peripheral devices in the catalog that are specially designed for notebook computers.

3 Suppose that the company that produces the peripheral devices catalog selected your name from its list of customers for a free scanner. You can select any one of the scanners in the catalog. Assume that you own a notebook computer to which you could attach any one of the scanners. Click the Explore button and use the catalog to help you write a one-page paper explaining which scanner you would select, why you would select it, and how you would use it.

4 Suppose you are in charge of a new college computing lab. The lab will include 25 computers that are used by students from all departments at the college. You have a $3,000 budget for printers. Use the product catalog to decide which printers you would purchase for the lab. Write a one-page memo to your boss that justifies your choice.

5 Suppose you own a basic computer system, such as the one in Figure 1-10 of this textbook. You have an idea that you can earn the money for your college tuition by using your computer to help other students produce spiffy reports with color graphs and scanned images. Your parents have agreed to "loan" you $1,000 to get started. Click the Explore button and look through the online peripheral devices catalog. List any of the devices that might help you with this business venture. Write a one-page paper explaining how you would spend your $1,000 to get the equipment you need to start the business.

User Interfaces

You have learned that the hardware and software for a user interface determine how you interact and communicate with the computer. In the User Interfaces Lab, you will try five different user interfaces to accomplish the same task—creating a graph.

1 Click the Steps button to find out how each interface works. As you work through the Steps, answer all of the Quick Check questions. When you complete the Steps, you will see a Summary Report of your performance on the Quick Checks. Follow the directions on the screen to print the Summary Report.

2 In Explore, use each interface to make a 3-D pie graph using data set 1. Title your graphs "Cycle City Sales." Use the percent style to show the percent of each slice of the pie. Print each of the five graphs (one for each interface).

3 In Explore, select one of the user interfaces. Write a step-by-step set of instructions for how to produce a line graph using data set 2. This line graph should show lines and symbols, and have the title "Widget Production."

4 Using the user interface terminology you learned in this Lab and in Chapter 1 of this textbook, write a description of each of the interfaces you used in the Lab. Then, suppose you worked for a software publisher

and you were going to create a software package for producing line, bar, column, and pie graphs. Which user interface would you use for the software? Why?

DOS Command-Line User Interface

The DOS command-line user interface provides a typical example of the advantages and disadvantages of command-line user interfaces. DOS was included with the original IBM PC computers to provide users with a way to accomplish system tasks such as listing, moving, and deleting files on disk. Although today's typical computer user prefers to use a graphical user interface such as Windows, DOS commands still function on most IBM-compatible computers.

1 Click the Steps button to learn how to use the DOS command-line interface. As you work through the Steps, answer all of the Quick Check questions that appear. When you complete the Steps, you will see a Summary Report that summarizes your performance on the Quick Checks. Follow the directions on the screen to print the Summary Report. Remember to use the EXIT command to close the DOS window when you're ready to quit.

2 In Explore, write out your answers to a through d.

   a. Explain the different results you get when you use the commands DIR, DIR /p, and DIR /w.

   b. What happens if you make a typing error and enter the command DIT instead of DIR? What procedure must you follow to correct your error?

   c. Enter the command, DIR /? and explain what happens. Enter the command VER /? and explain what happens. What generalization can you make about the /? command parameter?

   d. Enter the command VER /w. Why do you think /w does not work with the VER command word, but it works with DIR?

3 Write a one-page paper summarizing what you know about command-line user interfaces and answering the following questions:

   a. Which DOS commands do you now know how to use?

   b. How do you know which commands to use to accomplish a task?

   c. How do you know what parameters work with each command?

   d. What kinds of mistakes can you make that will produce an error message?

   e. Can you enter valid commands that don't produce the results you want?

Using a Mouse

A mouse is a standard input device on most of today's computers. You need to know how to use a mouse to manipulate graphical user interfaces and to use the rest of the Labs.

1 The Steps for the Using a Mouse Lab show you how to click, double-click, and drag objects using the mouse. Click the Steps button and begin the Steps. As you work through the Steps, answer all of the Quick Check questions that appear. When you complete the Steps, you will see a Summary Report that summarizes your performance on the Quick Checks. Follow the directions on the screen to print the Summary Report.

2 In Explore, demonstrate your ability to use a mouse and to control a Windows program by creating a poster. To create a poster for an upcoming sports event, select a graphic, type the caption for the poster, then select a font, font styles, and a border. Print your completed poster.

Using a Keyboard

To become an effective computer user, you must be familiar with your primary input device—the keyboard.

1 The Steps for the Using a Keyboard Lab provide you with a structured introduction to the keyboard layout and the function of special computer keys. Click the Steps button and begin the Steps. As you work through the Steps, answer all of the Quick Check questions that appear. When you complete the Steps, you will see a Summary Report that summarizes your performance on the Quick Checks. Follow the directions on the screen to print the Summary Report.

2 In Explore, start the typing tutor. You can develop your typing skills using the typing tutor in Explore. Take the typing test and print out your results.

3 In Explore, try to improve your typing speed by 10 words per minute. For example, if you currently type 20 words per minute, your goal would be 30 words per minute. Practice each typing lesson until you see a message that indicates you can proceed to the next lesson. Create a Practice Record as shown here to keep track of how much you practice. When you have reached your goal, print out the results of a typing test to verify your results.

Practice Record

Name: _____

Section: _____

Start Date: _____ Start Typing Speed: _____ wpm

End Date: _____ End Typing Speed: _____ wpm

Lesson #: _____ Date Practiced/Time Practiced _____

SOFTWARE AND MULTIMEDIA APPLICATIONS

2

The quest for multipurpose machines has always enchanted inventors. Soon after the first "horseless carriages" appeared, some inventors dreamed about creating a multipurpose car-boat—a vehicle for both water and land. Car-boats never really caught on. Today, we have a multipurpose machine that is far more useful—the computer.

The computer is the most successful and versatile machine in history. The same computer can produce professionally typeset documents, translate French into English, produce music, diagnose diseases, control machinery, keep track of airline reservations, and much more. A computer's versatility is possible because of software. But what does software do that gives a computer such versatility? What kinds of software can you buy? How do you know what software works with your computer?

In this chapter you will learn how the computer uses software and how you can legally use software. You will learn the difference between system software and application software, and find out about trends in multimedia computing. This chapter ends on a practical note with information about how to install new software on your computer system.

CHAPTER PREVIEW

This chapter contains concepts that help you get started using computer software. Once you understand what kind of software is available, you can select the software that will help you with your work. You can then begin learning how to use it. You also will find out how to use a format utility—an important step if you want to save data on a disk. When you have completed this chapter, you should be able to:

- Determine the legal restrictions placed on your use of software by copyright laws and license agreements
- Describe the purpose of a computer operating system
- Recognize DOS, Windows, UNIX, and Mac OS
- Categorize software as either system software or application software
- Determine the best type of software to use for a specific task
- List the computer equipment you need for multimedia applications
- Determine if a software package is compatible with your computer system

LABS

Multimedia

Computer History Hypermedia

Ⓐ Computer Software Basics

Computer software determines what a computer can do. In a sense, software transforms a computer from one kind of machine to another—from a drafting station to a typesetting machine, from a flight simulator to a calculator, from a filing system to a music studio.

Computer Programs

Do I need to write programs for my computer? A **computer program** is a set of detailed, step-by-step instructions that tells a computer how to solve a problem or carry out a task. Some computer programs handle simple tasks, such as converting feet and inches to centimeters. Longer and more complex computer programs handle very complicated tasks, such as maintaining the accounting records for a business.

The steps in a computer program are written in a language that the computer can interpret and process. As you read through the simple computer program in Figure 2-1, notice the number of steps required to perform a relatively simple calculation.

Figure 2-1

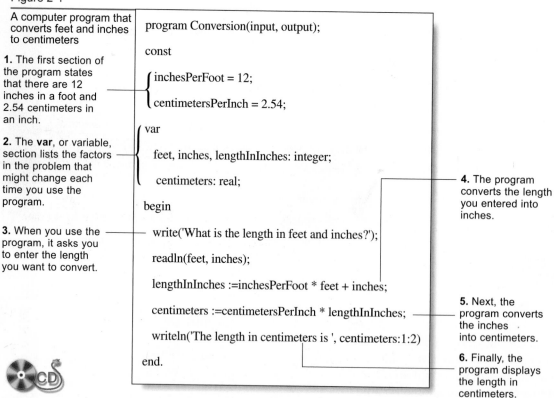

A computer program that converts feet and inches to centimeters

1. The first section of the program states that there are 12 inches in a foot and 2.54 centimeters in an inch.

2. The **var**, or variable, section lists the factors in the problem that might change each time you use the program.

3. When you use the program, it asks you to enter the length you want to convert.

4. The program converts the length you entered into inches.

5. Next, the program converts the inches into centimeters.

6. Finally, the program displays the length in centimeters.

```
program Conversion(input, output);

const
  inchesPerFoot = 12;
  centimetersPerInch = 2.54;

var
  feet, inches, lengthInInches: integer;
  centimeters: real;

begin
  write('What is the length in feet and inches?');
  readln(feet, inches);
  lengthInInches :=inchesPerFoot * feet + inches;
  centimeters :=centimetersPerInch * lengthInInches;
  writeln('The length in centimeters is ', centimeters:1:2)
end.
```

At one time organizations and individuals had to write most of the computer programs they wanted to use, but today most organizations purchase commercially written programs to avoid the time and expense of writing their own. Individuals rarely write computer programs for their personal computers, preferring to select from thousands of commercially written programs, sold as software. Although most computer users do not write their own programs, working as a computer programmer for a business, government agency, or software publisher is a challenging career.

Computer Software

Are computer programs, data, and software the same thing? Software is a basic part of a computer system, but "software" is a term that has more than one definition. In the early days of the computer industry, it became popular to use the term "software" for all the non-hardware components of a computer. In this context, software referred to computer programs and to the data used by the programs.

The U.S. Copyright Act of 1980 defines software as "a set of statements or instructions to be used directly or indirectly in a computer in order to bring about a certain result." This definition implies that computer software is essentially the same as a computer program. It also implies that a collection of data, such as a list of dictionary words, is not software.

In practice, the term "software" is usually used to describe a commercial product, which might include more than a single program and might also include data, as shown in Figure 2-2.

Figure 2-2

A software product

A **software package** contains disks or a CD-ROM and a reference manual.

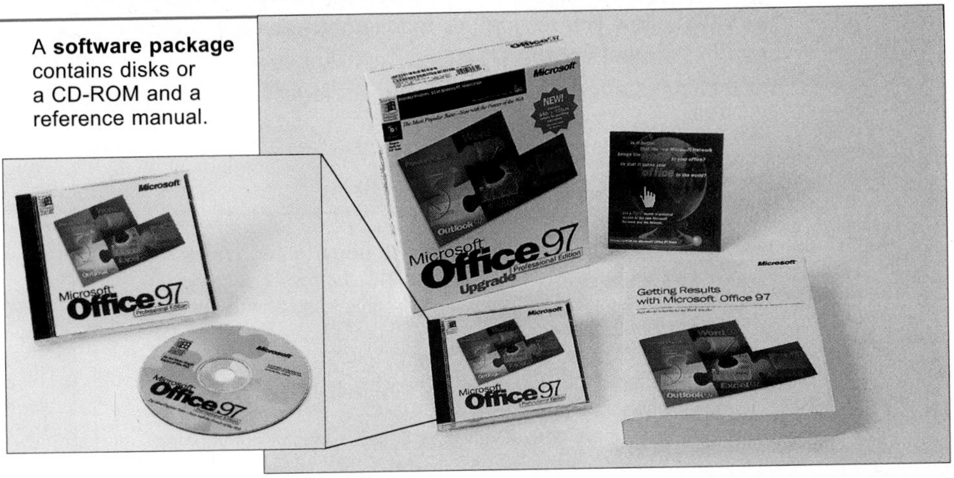

The CD-ROM contains one or more **programs**, and possibly some data. For example, the Microsoft Office 97 software includes programs that help you draw graphics, write documents, and make calculations. The software also includes some data, such as a thesaurus of words and their synonyms.

In this textbook, we define **software** as instructions and associated data, stored in electronic format, that direct the computer to accomplish a task. Under this definition, computer software may include more than one computer program, if those programs work together to carry out a task. Software also can include data, but data alone is not software. For example, word-processing software might include the data for a dictionary, but the data *you create* using a word processor is not called software. Suppose you write a report using a software package, then store the report on a disk. Your report consists of data rather than instructions for the computer to carry out. Because your report does not contain instructions, it is not software.

"Software" is a plural noun, so there is no such thing as "softwares" or "one software." How, then, do we talk about software in the singular? We often use the term "software package" when we want to talk about a particular example of software.

InfoWeb

Copyright
1

Copyrighted Software

Is it illegal to copy software? Just because you can copy software doesn't make it legal to do so. Like books and movies, most computer software is protected by a copyright. A **copyright** is a form of legal protection that grants certain exclusive rights to the author of a program or the owner of the copyright. The owner of the copyright has the exclusive right to copy the software, to distribute or sell the software, and to modify the software.

When you purchase copyrighted software, you do not become the owner of the copyright. Instead, you have purchased only the right to use the software. Your purchase allows you to use the software on your computer, but you cannot make additional copies to give away or sell. People who illegally copy, distribute, or modify software are sometimes called **software pirates**, and the illegal copies they create are referred to as **pirated software**.

Copyrighted software displays a copyright notice such as "© 1998 Course Technology, Inc." When you start a computer program, the copyright notice usually appears on the first screen; it is also usually printed in the reference manual. Most countries have copyright laws that allow you to copy or modify software only under certain circumstances. If you read the sections of the U.S. Copyright Act shown in Figure 2-3, you will discover under what circumstances you can and cannot legally copy copyrighted software.

Figure 2-3

Sections 106 and 117 of the 1980 U.S. Copyright Act

Section 106. Exclusive Rights in Copyrighted Works
Subject to sections 107 through 118, the owner of copyright under this title has the exclusive rights to do and to authorize any of the following:

(1) to reproduce the copyrighted work in copies or phonorecords;
(2) to prepare derivative works based upon the copyrighted work;
(3) to distribute copies or phonorecords of the copyrighted work to the public by sale or other transfer of ownership, or by rental, lease, or lending...

> Only the copyright owner can reproduce, sell, or distribute the copyrighted software.

Section 117 - Right to Copy or Adapt Computer Programs in Limited Circumstances
Notwithstanding the provisions of section 106, it is not an infringement for the owner of a copy of a computer program to make or authorize the making of another copy or adaptation of the computer program provided:

1. that such a new copy or adaptation is created as an essential step in the utilization of the computer program in conjunction with a machine that is used in no other manner; or

2. that such new copy or adaptation is for archival purposes only and that all archival copies are destroyed in the event that continued possession of the computer program should cease to be rightful. Any exact copies prepared in accordance with the provisions of this section may be leased, sold or otherwise transferred, along with the copy from which such copies were prepared, only as part of the lease, sale, or other transfer of all rights in the program. Adaptations so prepared may be transferred only with the authorization of the copyright owner.

> It is legal to copy the software from the distribution disks to the hard disk of your computer.

> It is legal to make an extra copy of the software in case the copy you are using becomes damaged.

> If you give away or sell the software, you cannot legally keep a copy.

> You cannot legally sell or give away modified copies of the software without permission.

Licensed Software

Do I need to read the small print before I buy software? In addition to copyright protection, computer software is often protected by the terms of a software license. A **software license** is a legal contract that defines the ways in which you may use a computer program. For microcomputer software, you will find the license on the outside of the package, on a separate card inside the package, or in the reference manual. Mainframe software licenses are usually a separate legal document, negotiated between the software publisher and a corporate buyer.

A software license often extends the rights given to you by copyright laws. For example, although copyright law makes it illegal to copy software for use on more than one computer, the license for Claris Works software allows you to buy one copy of the software and install it on your home computer and your office computer as long as you are the primary user of both computers.

Software licenses are often lengthy and written in "legalese," but they are generally divided into manageable sections that you can understand by reading them carefully. Your legal right to use the software continues only as long as you abide by the terms of the software license. Therefore, you should understand the software license for any software you use. To become familiar with a typical license agreement, you can read through the "No-Nonsense License Statement" used for software published by Borland International, shown in Figure 2-4.

Figure 2-4

A software license

This section explains that you can use the software "like a book" meaning that more than one person can use it, but only one at a time.

These sections make provisions for multiple users.

Here, Borland essentially says that you use this software at your own risk.

This software is protected by both United States copyright law and international copyright treaty provisions. Therefore, you must treat this software just like a book, except that you may copy it onto a computer to be used and you may make archival copies of the software for the sole purpose of backing-up our software and protecting your investment from loss.

By saying "just like a book," Borland means, for example, that this software may be used by any number of people, and may be freely moved from one computer location to another, so long as there is no possibility of it being used at one location while it's being used at another or on a computer network by more than one user at one location. Just like a book can't be read by two different people in two different places at the same time, neither can the software be used by two different people in two different places at the same time. (Unless, of course, Borland's copyright has been violated or the use is on a computer network by up to the number of users authorized by additional Borland licenses as explained below.)

LAN PACK MULTIPLE-USE NETWORK LICENSE

If this is a LAN Pack package, it allows you to increase the number of authorized users of your copy of the software on a single computer network by up to the number of users specified in the LAN Pack package (per LAN Pack — see LAN Pack serial number).

USE ON A NETWORK

A "computer network" is any electronically linked configuration in which two or more users have common access to software or data. If more than one user wishes to use the software on a computer network at the same time, then you may add authorized users either by (a) paying for a separate software package for each additional user you wish to add or (b) if a LAN Pack is available for this product, paying for the multiple-use license available in the LAN Pack. You may use any combination of regular software packages or LAN Packs to increase the number of authorized users on a computer network. (In no event may the total number of concurrent users on a network exceed one for each

software package plus the number of authorized users installed from the LAN Pack(s) that you have purchased. Otherwise, you are not using the software "just like a book.") The multiple-use network license for the LAN Pack may only be used to increase the number of concurrent permitted users of the software logged onto the network, and not to download copies of the software for local workstation use without being logged onto the network. You must purchase an individual copy of the software for each workstation at which you wish to use the software without being logged onto the network.

FURTHER EXPLANATION OF COPYRIGHT LAW PROVISIONS AND THE SCOPE OF THIS LICENSE STATEMENT

You may not download or transmit the software electronically (either by direct connection or telecommunication transmission) from one computer to another, except as may be specifically allowed in using the software on a computer network. You may transfer all of your rights to use the software to another person, provided that you transfer to that person

(or destroy) all of the software, diskettes and documentation provided in this package, together with all copies, tangible or intangible, including copies in RAM or installed on a disk, as well as all back-up copies. Remember, once you transfer the software, it may only be used at the single location to which it is transferred and, of course, only in accordance with the copyright laws and international treaty provisions. Except as stated in this paragraph, you may not otherwise trans-

fer, rent, lease, sub-license, time-share, or lend the software, diskettes, or documentation. Your use of the software is limited to acts that are essential steps in the use of the software on your computer or computer network as described in the documentation. You may not otherwise modify, alter, adapt, merge, decompile or reverse-engineer the software, and you may not remove or obscure Borland copyright or trademark notices.

LIMITED WARRANTY

Borland International, Inc. ("Borland") warrants the physical diskette(s) and physical documentation enclosed herein (but not any diskettes or documentation distributed by the Paradox Runtime License) to be free of defects in materials and workmanship for a period of sixty days from the purchase date. If Borland receives notification within the warranty period of defects in materials or workmanship, and such notification is determined by Borland to be correct, Borland will replace the defective diskette(s) or documentation. DO NOT RETURN ANY PRODUCT UNTIL YOU HAVE CALLED THE BORLAND CUSTOMER SERVICE DEPARTMENT AND OBTAINED A RETURN AUTHORIZATION NUMBER.

The entire and exclusive liability and remedy for breach of the Limited Warranty shall be limited to replacement of defective diskette(s) or documentation and shall not include or extend to any claim for or right to recover any other damages, including but not limited to, loss of profit, data, or use of the software, or special, incidental, or consequential damages or other similar claims, even if Borland has been specifically advised of the possibility of such damages. In no event will Borland's liability for any damages to you or any other

person ever exceed the lower of suggested list price or actual price paid for the license to use the software, regardless of any form of the claim.

BORLAND INTERNATIONAL, INC. SPECIFICALLY DISCLAIMS ALL OTHER WARRANTIES, EXPRESS OR IMPLIED, INCLUDING BUT NOT LIMITED TO, ANY IMPLIED WARRANTY OF MERCHANTABILITY OR FITNESS FOR A PARTICULAR PURPOSE. Specifically, Borland makes no representation or warranty that the software is fit for any particular purpose and any implied warranty of merchantability is limited to the sixty-day duration of the Limited Warranty covering the physical diskette(s) and physical documentation only (and not the software) and is otherwise expressly and specifically disclaimed.

This limited warranty gives you specific legal rights; you may have others which may vary from state to state. Some states do not allow the exclusion of incidental or consequential damages, or the limitation on how long an implied warranty lasts, so some of the above may not apply to you.

BUSINESS PRODUCTS (With Network Provisions): NO-NONSENSE LICENSE STATEMENT

BUSINESS PRODUCTS (With Network Provisions): NO-NONSENSE LICENSE STATEMENT

This section restates the basic copyright restrictions about transferring software.

Shrink-Wrap Licenses

Do I have to sign a software license for it to be valid? Signing and submitting a license agreement every time you purchase software would be inconvenient, so the computer industry makes extensive use of **shrink-wrap licenses**. When you purchase computer software, the disks or CD-ROM in the package are usually sealed in an envelope or plastic shrink wrapping. A notification, such as the one in Figure 2-5, states that opening the wrapping signifies your agreement to the terms of the software license.

Figure 2-5

When software has a shrink-wrap license, you agree to the terms of the license agreement by opening the package. If you do not agree with the terms, you should return the software unopened.

With a shrink-wrap license, the software publisher avoids the lengthy process of negotiating the terms of the license and obtaining your signature. It is essentially a "take it or leave it" approach to licensing. Court rulings in 1996 and 1997 have upheld the validity of shrink-wrap licensing, one of the most frequently used methods for providing legal protection for computer software.

Licenses for More Than One User

If my company has a computer network, does it still have to pay for a license for each user? Most software publishers offer a variety of license options; some are designed for a single user, others for more than one user. A **single-user license** limits the use of the software to one user at a time. Most commercial software is distributed under a single-user license.

A **multiple-user license** allows more than one person to use a particular software package. This type of license is useful in cases where users each have their own personalized version of the software. An electronic mail program would typically have a multiple-user license because users each have their own mailbox. Multiple-user licenses are generally priced per user, but the price for each user is typically less than the price of a single-user license.

A **concurrent-use license** allows a certain number of copies of the software to be used at the same time. For example, if an organization with a computer network has a concurrent-use license for five copies of a word processor, at any one time as many as five employees may use the software. Concurrent-use licenses are usually priced in increments. For example, a company might be able to purchase a concurrent-use license for up to 50 users for $2,500, or up to 250 users for $10,000.

A **site license** generally allows the software to be used on any and all computers at a specific location, such as within a corporate office building or on a university campus. A site license is priced at a flat rate, for example, $5,000 per site.

Shareware

My friend gave me a copy of something called "shareware." Was that illegal?

InfoWeb

Shareware
2

Shareware is copyrighted software marketed under a "try before you buy" policy. Shareware usually includes a license that allows you to use the software for a trial period. If you want to continue to use it, you must send in a registration fee. A shareware license typically allows you to make copies of the software and distribute them to others. This is a fairly effective marketing strategy that provides low-cost advertising. Unfortunately, registration fee payment relies on the honor system, so many shareware authors collect only a fraction of the payment they deserve for their programming efforts. Take a look at the shareware license in Figure 2-6 and notice the rights it includes.

Figure 2-6

A typical shareware license

You can legally make copies and give them away, but you cannot sell them.

You cannot distribute modified copies.

You can become a registered user for $20.

For $45, you will receive the next update of the software.

License

Copyright (c) 1997, 1998 GuildWare, Inc. All Rights Reserved.

You are free to use, copy and distribute TYPER'S TOOLKIT for noncommercial use IF:

NO FEE IS CHARGED FOR USE, COPYING OR DISTRIBUTION.

IT IS NOT MODIFIED IN ANY WAY.

Clubs and user groups may charge a nominal fee (less than $10) for expenses and handling while distributing TYPER'S TOOLKIT.

Site licenses, commercial licenses and custom versions of TYPER'S TOOLKIT are available. Write to the address below for more information.

This program is provided AS IS without any warranty, expressed or implied, including but not limited to fitness for a particular purpose.

If you find TYPER'S TOOLKIT fast, easy, and convenient to use, a contribution of $20 would be appreciated. With each contribution of $45 or more you will be registered to receive a diskette with the next version of TYPER'S TOOLKIT when available. Please state the current version of TYPER'S TOOLKIT that you have. Send contributions to:

GuildWare, Inc.
Box 391
Glendale, WI 53209

Public Domain Software

Isn't some software free?   Sometimes an author abandons all rights to a particular software title and places it in the public domain, making the program available without restriction. Such software, referred to as **public domain software**, is owned by the public rather than by the author.

Public domain software may be freely copied, distributed, and even resold. The primary restriction on public domain software is that you are not allowed to apply for a copyright on it. Public domain software is fairly rare. It is frequently confused with shareware because it is legal to copy and distribute both public domain software and shareware.

Software Categories

What's the difference between system software and application software?   Because there are so many software titles, categorizing software as either system software or application software is useful. **System software** helps the computer carry out its basic operating tasks. **Application software** helps the human user carry out a task.

System software and application software are further divided into subcategories. As you continue to read this chapter, use Figure 2-7 to help you visualize the hierarchy of software categories.

Figure 2-7

Software categories

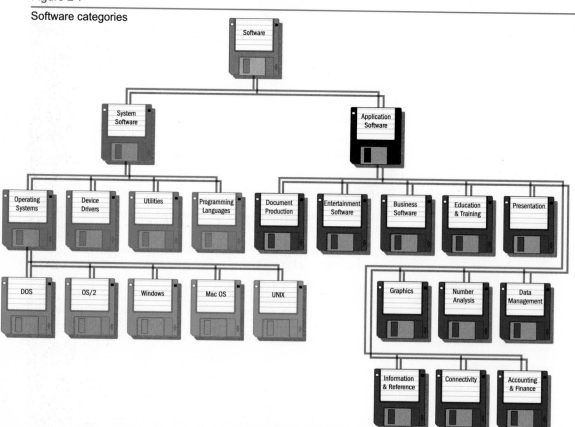

To many computer users, the difference between system software and applications software seems somewhat arbitrary. To clarify the difference, you can generally classify software as system software if the only reason you need that software is because you have a computer. For example, if you didn't have a computer, you would not need an operating system, or device drivers, or computer programming languages.

You would put software in the application software category if it computerizes something you might do even without a computer. For example, you would write letters and papers even if you didn't have a computer, so the software you use to create documents would be classified as application software.

Admittedly, some software is still difficult to classify. For example, the software you use to connect your computer to the Internet is called communications software. You would not be connecting to the Internet if you did not have a computer, and yet communications software has additional features such as voice calls, voice mail, and faxing that you might do without a computer. As you read the next section of this chapter on application software you'll develop a better idea of how it differs from system software.

QuickCheck A

1. If you use a computer to write a report, the report is considered software. True or false? _____

2. To use a computer effectively, you need to be a computer programmer. True or false? _____

3. When you type a report or enter the information for a mailing list, you are creating _____.

4. The instructions that tell a computer how to convert inches to centimeters are a computer _____.

5. To use a computer to write and edit documents, you need word-processing _____.

6. The "try before you buy" policy refers to _____ licenses.

7. A(n) _____ for microcomputer or mainframe software is a contract by which the software publisher grants the buyer permission to use the software.

8. _____ software helps the *computer* carry out its basic operating tasks, whereas _____ software helps a human user carry out tasks.

B System Software

System software is the category of software containing programs that perform tasks essential to the efficient functioning of computer hardware. System software includes the programs that direct the fundamental operations of a computer, such as displaying information on the screen, storing data on disks, sending data to the printer, interpreting commands typed by users, and communicating with peripheral devices.

Let's look at some of the specific functions of the four subcategories of system software: operating systems, utilities, device drivers, and computer programming languages.

Operating Systems

Why does a computer need an operating system? An **operating system** is the software that controls the computer's use of its hardware resources such as memory and disk storage space. You might be familiar with the names of the most popular microcomputer operating systems: Microsoft Windows, DOS, OS/2, and Mac OS. Minicomputer and mainframe operating systems include UNIX, VMS, and MVS.

An operating system works like an air traffic controller to coordinate the activities within the computer. Just as an airport cannot function without air traffic controllers, a computer cannot function without an operating system. When you purchase a microcomputer, the operating system is usually pre-installed on the hard disk and ready to use. You "see" the operating system each time you turn on your computer, and the operating system provides a variety of services that you can use to run programs and manage your data.

If you envision computer hardware as the core of your computer system, then the operating system provides the next layer of functionality by assisting the computer with its basic hardware operations. The operating system also interacts with the next layer—application software—to carry out application tasks such as printing and saving data. Figure 2-8 helps you envision the relationship between your computer hardware, the operating system, and application software.

Figure 2-8

Application software requires the operating system to carry out hardware related tasks such as printing reports and storing data on disks.

The operating system acts as a liaison between the computer hardware and application software.

The computer hardware is the core of the system, but the hardware cannot function without an operating system.

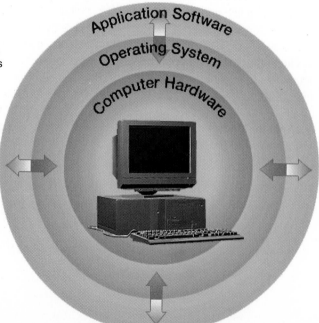

Let's look at a specific example of how the operating system works as a liaison between the computer hardware and application software. Suppose you use application software to write a letter and then you want to print it. The operating system helps the application software communicate with your computer's printer, as shown in Figure 2-9.

Figure 2-9

The operating system helps the application software print a document.

1. The user tells the word-processing application to print the document.

2. The word-processing application signals the operating system that a document must be sent to the printer.

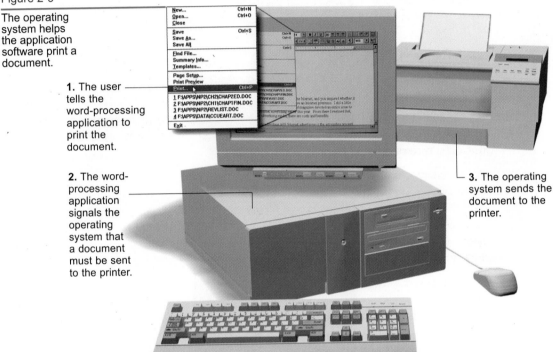

3. The operating system sends the document to the printer.

Operating systems for micro, mini, and mainframe computers perform many similar services. These services can be classified either as "external" or "internal."

The operating system provides **external services** that help users start programs, manage stored data, and maintain security. You, as the computer user, control these external functions. Using a command-line, menu-driven, or GUI user interface, an operating system provides you with a way to select the programs you would like to use. The operating system also helps you find, rename, and delete documents and other data stored on disk or tape. On many, but not all computer systems, the operating system helps you maintain security by checking your user ID and password, as well as protecting your data from unauthorized access and revisions.

The operating system provides **internal services** "behind the scenes" to ensure that the computer system functions efficiently. These internal services are not generally under your control, but instead are controlled by the operating system itself. The operating system controls input and output, allocates system resources, manages the storage space for programs and data, and detects equipment failure without any direction from you. Study Figure 2-10 on the next page to discover more about what an operating system does.

Figure 2-10

Operating system services

Control Basic Input and Output

An operating system controls the flow of data into and out of the computer, as well as the flow of data to and from peripheral devices. It routes input to areas of the computer where it can be processed and routes output to the screen, a printer, or any other output device you request.

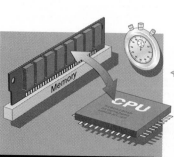

Allocate System Resources

A **system resource** is any part of a computer system, such as a disk drive, memory, printer, or processor time, that can be used by a computer program. The operating system allocates system resources so programs run properly.

For example, each program instruction takes up space inside the computer and each instruction requires a certain amount of time to complete. The operating system ensures that adequate space is available for each program that is running and makes sure the processor quickly performs each program instruction.

The operating system also manages the additional resources required for using multiple programs or for providing services to more than one user at the same time. For example, if you want to run two or more programs at the same time, a process called **multitasking**, the operating system ensures that each program has adequate space and that the computer devotes an appropriate amount of time to the tasks prescribed by each program.

To accommodate more than one user at a time, an operating system must have multiuser capabilities. You typically find **multiuser** operating systems on mainframe and minicomputer systems, where users each have their own terminal but share the processing capability of a single main computer. Multiuser operating systems typically provide speedy service so users each think they are the only ones using the computer.

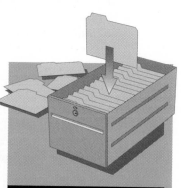

Manage Storage Space

The operating system keeps track of the data stored on disks and CD-ROMs. Think of your disks as filing cabinets, your data as papers stored in file folders, and the operating system as a filing clerk. The filing clerk takes care of filing a folder when you finish using it. When you need something from your filing cabinet, you ask the filing clerk to get it. The filing clerk knows where to find your folder. On your computer system, the operating system stores your data at some location on a disk. Although you might not know exactly where your data is stored on the disk, when you need the data again, you only need to ask the operating system to retrieve it.

Detect Equipment Failure

The operating system monitors the status of critical computer components to detect failures that affect processing. When you turn on your computer, the operating system checks each of the electronic components and takes a quick inventory of the storage devices. For example, if an electrical component inside your computer fails, the operating system displays a message identifying the problem and does not let you continue with the computing session until the problem is fixed.

Maintain Security

The operating system also helps maintain security for the data on the computer system. For example, the operating system might not allow you to access the computer system unless you have a user ID and password.

Microcomputer Operating Systems

Operating
Systems
3

As a computer user, why is it important for me to know which operating system is on my computer? Today's popular operating systems for the PC platform include DOS, Windows, and OS/2. The Macintosh operating system is called Mac OS. UNIX is available for both PCs and Macintosh computers. Versions of UNIX and Windows are also available for minicomputers and mainframes.

You interact directly with your computer's operating system to start programs and manage the data on your disks. You need to know which operating system your computer uses so you can enter the appropriate instructions to accomplish these tasks. How can you tell which operating system your computer uses? Many microcomputer users can recognize an operating system by looking at the first screen that appears when they turn the computer on or by recognizing the operating system prompt. If you study Figures 2-11 through 2-15, you can identify the DOS, Mac OS, Windows 3.1, Windows 95, and UNIX operating systems when you encounter them in the future.

Figure 2-11

DOS

The **DOS prompt** is a distinguishing feature of MS-DOS and PC-DOS.

The **cursor** shows your place on the screen.

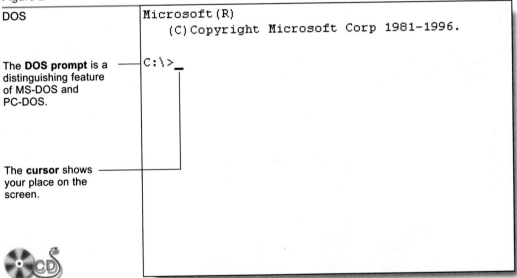

```
Microsoft(R)
     (C)Copyright Microsoft Corp 1981-1996.

C:\>_
```

DOS, which stands for Disk Operating System, is marketed under the trade names PC-DOS and MS-DOS. Both PC-DOS and MS-DOS were developed primarily by Microsoft Corporation and are essentially the same operating system.

DOS was introduced in 1981 with IBM's first personal computer. Since the first version of DOS appeared, this operating system has gone through six major versions.

DOS has been replaced by the Windows operating system on most of today's computers.

Figure 2-12

Microsoft Windows 3.1 operating system

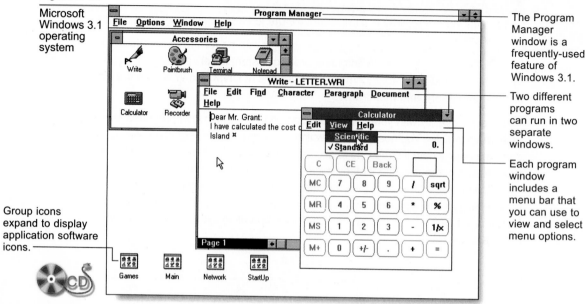

The Program Manager window is a frequently-used feature of Windows 3.1.

Two different programs can run in two separate windows.

Each program window includes a menu bar that you can use to view and select menu options.

Group icons expand to display application software icons.

Microsoft took a more graphical approach to operating systems when it designed Windows. **Microsoft Windows 3.1** provides icons that you can directly manipulate on the screen using a pointing device, and pull-down menus you can use to easily issue a command. The applications you use with Windows 3.1 all have a consistent look, so it is easy to learn how to use new software.

Windows 3.1 also lets you run more than one program at a time in separate windows on the screen, and lets you easily transfer data between them. While using Windows 3.1, you can still run DOS software.

Figure 2-13

Microsoft Windows 95 and Windows 98 operating systems

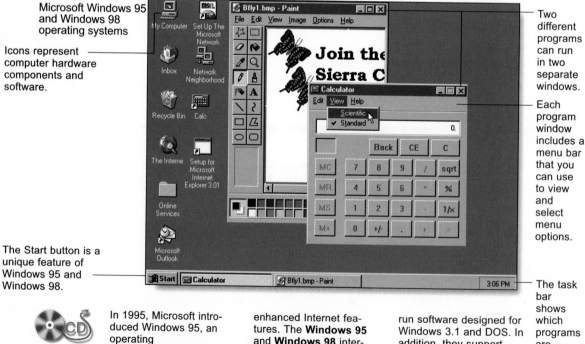

Icons represent computer hardware components and software.

Two different programs can run in two separate windows.

Each program window includes a menu bar that you can use to view and select menu options.

The Start button is a unique feature of Windows 95 and Windows 98.

The task bar shows which programs are running.

In 1995, Microsoft introduced Windows 95, an operating system that offered better operating efficiency than Windows 3.1. In 1998, Microsoft introduced Windows 98 to add enhanced Internet features. The **Windows 95** and **Windows 98** interfaces are similar. They use icons to represent objects such as computers, disk drives, and documents. These operating systems run software designed for Windows 3.1 and DOS. In addition, they support multitasking, networking, and Internet access.

Figure 2-14

Mac OS

Apple icon

Pull down menu

Windows

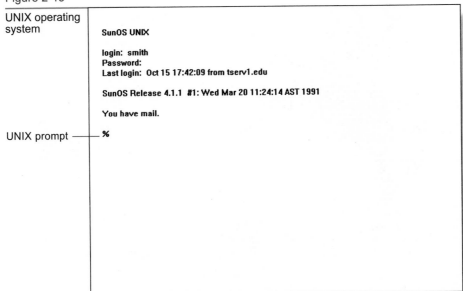

Menu bar

Icons

In 1984, Apple Computer, Inc. took a revolutionary step when it introduced the Apple Lisa computer with a new operating system based on a graphical user interface featuring pull-down menus, icons, and a mouse.

The Lisa computer was not a commercial success, but Apple's next product, the Macintosh computer, was very successful and defined a new direction in operating system user interfaces that became an industry standard.

The **Macintosh operating system** is usually referred to by its version number. For example, version eight of the operating system is called Mac OS 8. The Macintosh operating system has multitasking capability and offers network support.

Figure 2-15

UNIX operating system

UNIX prompt

```
SunOS UNIX

login: smith
Password:
Last login: Oct 15 17:42:09 from tserv1.edu

SunOS Release 4.1.1  #1: Wed Mar 20 11:24:14 AST 1991

You have mail.

%
```

UNIX is an operating system that was developed at AT&T's Bell Laboratories in 1969. UNIX was originally designed for minicomputers, but is now also available for microcomputers and mainframes.

UNIX features a command-line user interface, but you can purchase add-on software that provides a graphical user interface with direct object manipulation and pull-down menus.

UNIX is a multiuser operating system, which means that many users can run programs on a single computer at the same time. UNIX also supports multitasking. UNIX is popular with companies that provide information on the Internet.

Utilities

Does the operating system include all the system software I need? **Utilities** are a sub-category of system software designed to augment the operating system by providing a way for a computer user to control the allocation and use of hardware resources. Some utilities are included with the operating system; they perform tasks such as preparing disks to hold data, providing information about the files on a disk, and copying data from one disk to another. Additional utilities can be purchased separately from software publishers and vendors. For example, Norton Utilities, published by Symantec, is a very popular collection of utility software. It retrieves data from damaged disks, makes your data more secure by encrypting it, and helps you troubleshoot problems with your computer's disk drives. You can also purchase utility software to protect your computer from viruses that could damage or erase your data.

One of the important tasks performed by an operating system utility is formatting a disk. Each disk must be formatted before you can store data on it. Think of formatting as creating the electronic equivalent of storage shelves. Before you can put things on the shelves, you must assemble the shelves. In a similar way, before you can store data on a disk, you must make sure the disk is formatted.

You can buy preformatted disks, but you still might need a disk format utility if you use a disk that has not been preformatted or a disk that was formatted previously for a different type of computer. Figure 2-16 shows how to use the format utility for Windows 95.

Figure 2-16

Using the Windows 95 format utility

1. Insert the disk you want to format and click the **My Computer** icon to select it, then press **Enter**.

3. Click **File** on the menu bar, then click **Format** to open the Format window.

2. Click the 3½ **Floppy (A:)** icon in the My Computer window.

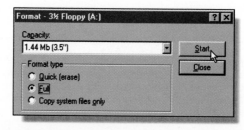

4. Make sure the Capacity box matches the size of the disk you want to format, then click the **Start** button.

Device Drivers

How do I use a device driver? In Chapter 1, you learned that when you purchase a new peripheral device, such as a CD-ROM drive or a mouse, you often need to install software that tells your computer how to use the device. The system software that helps the computer control a peripheral device is called a **device driver**.

When you purchase a new peripheral device, its installation instructions usually tell you how to install both the device and the necessary device drivers. The way you "use" a device driver is to install it according to the instructions. Once the device driver is installed correctly, the computer uses it "behind the scenes" to communicate with the device.

Computer Programming Languages

Is a computer programming language included with a basic computer system? As you know, a computer program is a series of instructions that the computer follows to perform a task. However, the list of instructions written by a human programmer is quite different from the instructions that the computer actually follows. The programmer's instructions must be translated into electrical signals that the computer can manipulate and process.

A **computer programming language** allows a programmer to write programs using English-like instructions, such as those you saw in Figure 2-1. These instructions are translated into a format the computer can interpret and directly process.

As mentioned earlier in this chapter, most computer users do not need to write programs. Therefore, most computers do not include a computer programming language. If you want to write programs, you must purchase programming language software. Today some of the most popular programming languages are BASIC, Visual Basic, C, C++, COBOL, Ada, and FORTRAN. Programming languages such as Java, JavaScript, J++, VBscript, CGI, and Perl are optimized to provide additional interactivity and animations on Web pages.

QuickCheck B

1. If you want to run more than one program at a time, you must use an operating system with _____ capability.

2. _____ is a multiuser operating system.

3. The DOS, Windows, and Mac OS operating systems are typically used on _____ computer systems.

4. The _____ operating system is popular with companies that supply information on the Internet.

5. _____ software helps the computer accomplish such tasks as preparing a disk for data, providing information about the files on a disk, copying data from one disk to another, and retrieving data from damaged disks.

6. You install a(n) _____ to tell the computer how to use a new peripheral device.

7. A(n) _____ allows you to write computer programs using English-like instructions.

C Application Software

Now let's return to the idea presented at the beginning of this chapter—that the computer is a multipurpose machine. Although system software handles internal computer functions and helps the computer use peripheral devices, it doesn't transform the computer into the different kinds of machines you need to write reports, "crunch" numbers, learn how to type, or draw pictures. It is application software that enables the computer to become a multipurpose machine and to perform many different tasks.

Software categorized as **application software** helps you accomplish a specific task using the computer. Application software helps you produce documents, perform calculations, manage financial resources, create graphics, compose music, play games, maintain files of information, and so on. Application software packages are sometimes referred to simply as **applications**.

Software Jargon

What's all this talk about groupware, suites, and productivity software? When you shop for computer software in catalogs or stores, you might encounter terms such as "productivity software," "suites," and "groupware." These terms describe broad categories of applications software.

InfoWeb

Application Software 4

As you might expect from its name, **productivity software** helps you work more effectively. Used by individuals, businesses, or organizations, the most popular types of productivity software include word-processing, spreadsheet, data management, and scheduling. The term **suite** or **office suite** refers to a number of applications that are packaged together and sold as a unit. A typical suite includes software you would use to write documents, work with numbers, create graphics, and keep track of data. **Groupware** provides a way for more than one person to collaborate on a project. It facilitates group document production, scheduling, and communication. Often it maintains a pool of data that can be shared by members of the workgroup.

Software is also categorized by how it is used. For example, document production software helps you create, edit, and publish documents. Software in the connectivity software connects your computer to the Internet, to other computers, and to networks. The names of these functional categories are not consistent. For example, browsing through different software catalogs and perusing the shelves of computer stores, you might notice that connectivity software is sometimes referred to as communications software. As with much of the terminology that is in daily use by non-technical people, software categories might seem somewhat imprecise, but you often can figure out by using common sense.

Figure 2-17

The array of application software is extensive.

How much you use a computer, how much time it helps you save, and how much it improves the quality of your work depends on the software you select and use. The array of software applications is extensive, as you can see from Figure 2-17 and as you read on.

Document Production Software

What software should I use to produce documents? Whether you are writing a 10-page term paper, writing software documentation, designing a brochure for your new start-up company, or laying out the school newspaper, you will probably use some form of document production software. **Document production software** as the term implies, assists you with composing, editing, designing, and printing documents. The three most popular types of document production software are word-processing, desktop publishing, and Web authoring software.

Word-processing software has replaced typewriters for producing documents such as reports, letters, papers, and manuscripts. Individuals use word-processing software for correspondence, students use it to write reports and papers, writers use it for novels, reporters use it to compose news stories, scientists use it to write research reports, and business people use it to write memos, reports, and marketing materials. Because documents are in an electronic format, it is easy to reuse them, share them, and even collaborate on them.

Word-processing software gives you the ability to create, spell check, edit, and format a document on the screen before you commit it to paper. When you are satisfied with the content of your document, you can use formatting and page layout features of your word-processing software to create a professional-looking printout. Today's best-selling word-processing software includes Microsoft Word, Claris WordPerfect, and Lotus Word Pro.

InfoWeb

Desktop
Publishing
5

Desktop publishing software takes word-processing software one step further by helping you use graphic design techniques to enhance the format and appearance of a document. Although many page layout and design features are available in today's word-processing software, desktop publishing software provides more sophisticated features to help you produce professional quality output for newspapers, newsletters, brochures, magazines, and books. Figure 2-18 illustrates the professional results you can achieve with desktop publishing software such as Quark XPress, Adobe Pagemaker, Corel VENTURA, and Microsoft Publisher.

Figure 2-18

For documents with many graphics that will be produced by a professional printer, you should consider using desktop publishing software instead of word-processing software. Desktop publishing software is typically the tool of choice for newspapers, magazines, and books, such as the one you are reading.

Web page authoring software helps you design and develop customized Web pages that you can publish electronically on the Internet. Only a few years ago, creating Web pages was a fairly technical task that required authors to use hypertext markup language (HTML) "tags" such as <A HREF = "contents.htm">. Now, Web page design software helps authors avoid HTML by providing tools to compose the text for a Web page, assemble graphical elements, and automatically generate HTML tags. Best-selling software in this category includes Claris Home Page and Microsoft Front Page.

Graphics Software

What's the best graphics software? **Graphics software** helps you create, edit, and manipulate images. These images could be photographs that you're planning to insert in a real estate brochure, a freehand portrait, a detailed engineering drawing of a Harley-Davidson motorcycle, or a cartoon animation. The graphics software you select depends on the type of image you're creating. Although best-selling graphics packages such as Adobe Illustrator, CorelDRAW, and Micrografx Graphics Suite handle more than one type of image, few graphics packages handle all image types. Once you know the type of image you need, you can read software descriptions and reviews to find the graphics software that's right for you.

Photos. Suppose you want to include photos in a document, brochure, greeting card, poster, or presentation. Photo editing features of graphics software help you crop photos, modify colors, remove red eye, combine elements from more than one photo, and apply special effects.

Paintings. If you have artistic talent and you want to use the computer to create sketches and paintings, you'll be working with a **bitmapped image**. Painting features allow you to create and edit bitmapped images on screen that look like water colors, oil paint, chalk, ink, or charcoal.

InfoWeb

3-D
Graphics
6

Drawings and 3-D objects. Images composed of lines and filled shapes are called **vector graphics**. Their advantage is the relatively small amount of storage space they require. Vector graphics images are easy to manipulate as shown in Figure 2-19.

Figure 2-19

You can create a wireframe drawing of a car, then rotate it to view it from the back, sides, or front. A process called **rendering** creates a 3-D solid image by covering the wireframe and applying computer-generated highlights and shadows.

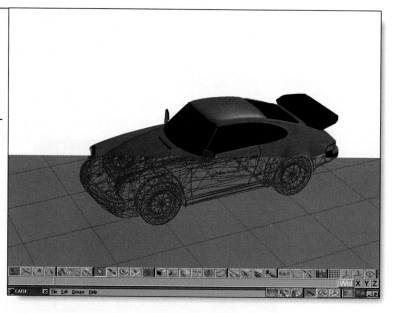

Animations and videos. You can spark up computer presentations by adding animated cartoons or video clips. You can also use animations and videos to illustrate educational tutorials or reference materials. Animation software streamlines the process of creating a series of still frames that produce an animated sequence. You can use graphics software to capture videos from your television, camcorder, or VCR. The software helps you edit the video by cutting out unwanted footage and adding a sound track. The process of converting videos into a format that can be stored on a computer disk is called **digitizing**.

Presentation Software

How do I use the computer to create snazzy speeches and presentations? Suppose you are taking an art history course. Fifty percent of your grade will be based on an in-class presentation. Is there software that can help you? Yes, it's called presentation software. Two of the most popular applications are Microsoft PowerPoint and Lotus Freelance Graphics.

Figure 2-20

A slide typically contains a title, a bulleted list, and a graphic.

PROJECTED INTERNATIONAL SALES

✔AMERICA   3
✔EUROPE   2
✔ASIA   1
✔AFRICA   5
✔AUSTRALIA   4

InfoWeb

Presentations
7

Presentation software provides all the tools you need for combining text, graphics, graphs, animations, and sound into a series of electronic **slides** like the one shown in Figure 2-20. Most presentation software includes collections of graphics and sounds that can enhance your presentation. After you create your slides, use the presentation software to organize them into a compelling visual story for your audience.

You can output the presentation as overhead transparencies, paper copies, or 35mm slides. You can display the slides on a color monitor for a one-on-one presentation or run the slide show for a group using a computer projection device as shown in Figure 2-21.

Figure 2-21

A projection device displays slides on a large wall screen.

Numeric Analysis Software

What kind of software do I use for number crunching? **Numeric analysis software** simplifies tasks such as constructing numeric models of physical and social systems, then analyzing those models to predict trends and understand patterns. Numeric analysis software includes spreadsheets, graphing packages, and statistical packages.

Spreadsheet software performs calculations based on numbers and formulas that you enter. A handy tool for quick or more complex calculations, spreadsheet software also allows you to create graphical views of your data. Spreadsheet software is frequently used by financial analysts to examine investment opportunities, by managers to create budgets, and even by educators to keep track of student grades, and by individuals to track household budgets, analyze retirement investments, and balance checkbooks. Top-selling packages include Microsoft Excel and Lotus 1-2-3.

Graphing software transforms complex data into meaningful graphs that allow you to visualize and explore data. When you put numerical data into a graphical format, you can see patterns and relationships that might not otherwise be apparent. Graphing software performs basic calculations and statistical procedures similar to those in spreadsheet or statistical software, but gives you added formatting flexibility to create more visually attractive graphs. Consider using graphing software if your spreadsheet or statistical package does not produce the kind or quality of graph you require.

Statistical software helps you analyze large sets of data to discover patterns and relationships. It is a helpful tool for summarizing survey results, test scores, experiment results, or population data. Most statistical software includes graphing capability so you can display and explore your data visually. Software such as SPSS, JMP, and Data Desk offer a full line of sophisticated statistical analysis tools (Figure 2-22).

Figure 2-22

To use statistical software, you first enter your data, then select a statistical procedure. The software displays your results as a table or graph.

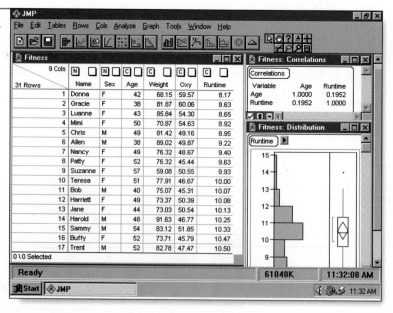

Data Management Software

How can I keep track of information? We live in an information society. We value information and we collect information—tons of it. **Data management software** helps us store, find, update, organize, and report information.

In computer jargon, a **flat file** stores information in records similar to the 3 x 5 cards or Rolodex cards. **File management software** helps you organize these records, find records that match specific criteria, and print lists based on the information. File management software is ideal for working with simple lists of information such as holiday card addresses, doctor visits, and household inventory.

Unlike a single flat file, a **database** is a collection of related files. **Database management software** or **database software** provides a flexible way to join and summarize the information in more than one file. For example, suppose you are the curator for an extensive collection of classic rock videos for MTV. You have a computer file of all the videos. You also have a file of the performers. While looking at the information on Michael Jackson's *Thriller* video, you wonder how old he was when the video was recorded. Instead of closing the video file and opening the performer file, you can use your database software to, in effect, join the two files together so you can see all the information about *Thriller* and Michael Jackson at the same time.

Database software is probably used more frequently by business, government, and education than by individuals. Microsoft Access, Lotus Approach, and Claris File Maker Pro are popular examples of database software for microcomputers. If you're using a database on a mainframe computer, it is likely to be Oracle 7 or IBM's DB2.

A **search engine** helps you find information. File management and database software both include a search engine capable of finding any record you specify in a fraction of a second. You can also purchase separate search engine software that is designed specially to help you find information from the huge pool of documents on the Web. Search engine software that runs on your computer is sometimes dubbed a **personal search engine** to distinguish it from the search engines that are provided at Web sites (Figure 2-23). Popular personal search engines include ForeFront, WebSeeker, and Symantec FastFind.

Figure 2-23

The advantage of a personal search engine is that it can automatically search through more than 20 Web site indexes, delete duplicate results, then provide you with the links you need to go directly to the relevant information.

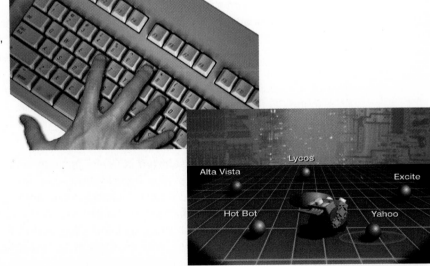

Information and Reference Software

How do I locate facts, figures, and other information? **Information and reference software** provides you with a collection of information and a way to access that information. The fact that this software includes massive amounts of data distinguishes it from data management software, which contains no data. The information and reference software category spans a broad range of applications from encyclopedias to medical reference, from map software to trip planners, and from cookbooks to telephone books. The options are as broad as the full range of human interests.

Information and reference software is generally shipped on a CD-ROM disk because of the quantity of information it includes. With many of these products, links between the CD-ROM and a Web site provide updates to information that has gone out of date. Other software publishers have eliminated the CD-ROM entirely and placed all their reference materials on the Web. Access to that information often requires a fee or a subscription.

Figure 2-24

Listings Deluxe bills itself as the "largest warehouse of reference data ever compiled in a single box." It claims to help you find phone numbers for any home or business in the U.S. or Canada, print street maps of every city in the U.S., look up 450,000 Web addresses, and summarize census data for any region of the U.S.

The most popular software in this category—encyclopedias—contain text, graphics, audio, and video on a full range of topics from apples to zenophobia. Best sellers include Microsoft's Encarta, IBM's World Book encyclopedia, Grolier's encyclopedia, Compton's encyclopedia, and Britannica's CD. All these titles contain the standard information you would expect from an encyclopedia—articles written by experts on various topics, maps, photographs, and timelines. There are several advantages to a CD-ROM encyclopedia over the traditional print versions. Finding the information you are looking for is easier. Also the CD-ROM takes up less space, is more affordable, and includes video and audio clips. The lower cost allows the average person to own a comprehensive encyclopedia, an invaluable resource for research and learning.

Mapping and trip planning software is useful for both individuals and business people. With software like Streetfinder from Rand McNally, you can type an address, and view and print a detailed map. It includes hotel, restaurant, and attraction information; business listings, such as dry cleaners, hair salons, banks, and ATM machines; and links to the Rand McNally Web site, which provides updated information on road construction, weather reports, and seasonal events. With this type of software, you never again need to feel bewildered when you move to or travel to a new city.

Connectivity Software

Do I need special software to connect to other computers and the Internet? By now, most people know that networks and the Internet are the hot technology tickets to an amazing world of information and interaction. **Connectivity software** connects your computer to a local computer network or the Internet and provides you with tools to take advantage of the information and communications they offer. Connectivity software includes basic communications software, remote control software, e-mail, and Web browsers.

Communications software interacts with your computer's modem to dial and establish a connection with a remote computer. Basic communications software is now built into most microcomputer operating systems and is sometimes classified as system utility software.

Suppose you have a computer in your office and a notebook computer at home. You're home one evening and need some information that's stored on your office computer. If both computers have modems and the computer in your office is on, you can use **remote control software** to establish a connection between the two machines. Using the keyboard of your notebook computer, you can control your office computer to locate and view the information you need. Popular remote control applications include Procomm Rapid Remote, pcANYWHERE, ReachOut, LapLink, and Remotely Possible.

E-mail is, perhaps, the heart of Internet activity. It helps you stay in touch with friends, relatives, colleagues, and business associates. **E-mail software** manages your computer mailbox. The preferred e-mail software with over 10 million users, is Eudora from Qualcomm, but Microsoft Internet Mail and Lotus Notes are popular alternatives.

InfoWeb

Web Browsers 8

To access information on the Web, you need communications software and an additional software package called a Web browser. **Web browser software** allows you to view Web pages and manages the links that you use to jump from one document to the next. The two leading Web browsers are Netscape Navigator and Microsoft Internet Explorer. A coming trend, shown in Figure 2-25, is to combine browser-like capabilities with the operating system user interface so you can browse and manage files on your PC in much the same way that you surf through pages on the Web.

Figure 2-25

Microsoft's Internet Explorer 4.0 Web browser turns familiar desktop elements, such as the My Computer icon, into clickable links.

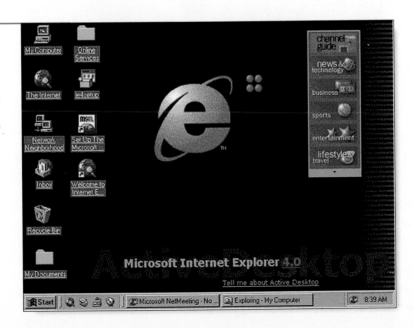

Education and Training Software

| Can I use software to improve my grades? | Do your keyboarding skills need a bit of polish? Do you want to help your children learn and have fun at the same time? Are you the head of human resources and find that your company's managers don't understand all the fuss about diversity? Where will you turn for help? You might very well find your answers in education and training software.

Education and training software helps you learn and perfect new skills. For the youngest ages, educational software, such as The Learning Company's Reader Rabbit and Math Rabbit, teach basic reading and counting skills. Instruction is presented as games that children can play, and different levels of play adapt to the child's age and ability.

For older students and adults, software is available to help learn languages, learn how to play the piano, prepare for standardized tests, improve keyboarding skills, and even learn about managing in a diverse workplace. Exam preparation software is available for standardized tests such as the SAT, GMAT, and LSAT. Although little research is available on the effectiveness of this software, experts believe the results should be similar to those of in-person coaching courses that improve composite SAT scores by about 100 points. Figure 2-26 explains more about exam preparation software.

Figure 2-26

Exam preparation software assesses your skill level, coaches you on your weak skills, and provides test-taking tips.

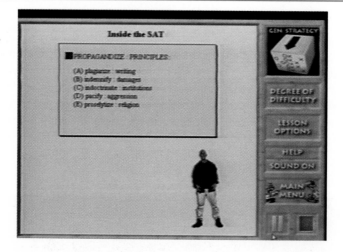

Education and training software is often called **edutainment software** because it blurs some of the lines between learning and game playing. By far, the most active segment of the edutainment industry is childrens' software. In 1996, entertainment and education software titles accounted for about 60 percent of all software sold, and retail sales were about $550 million. There are about 15,000 titles available, and the average price of an edutainment program is $40. Experts expect the edutainment industry to grow to $8 billion worldwide by the year 2000.

Entertainment Software

Are computers changing the way we spend our spare time? Worldwide computer and video game software sales annually exceed $10 billion. Publishers invest 18 months and up to $2 million to create and produce a successful entertainment software title. Overall, the entertainment software industry employs about 90,000 workers and is increasing its employees by 26 percent per year—better than most Fortune 500 companies. Clearly, entertainment software is big business as well as fun business. What is entertainment software? It includes games of all sorts, software toys, simulations, and software designed to help you enjoy hobbies and leisure activities.

Games
Galore
9

Generally, **game software** is divided into six main categories: action, adventure/role playing, classic/puzzle, simulations, and strategy/war games. Many of the most popular games are available in multiple formats. You can play them alone on your PC, in multiplayer environments via the Internet, or on a stand-alone game console such as Sega or Nintendo.

Adventure/role playing software has realistic 3-D graphics, allows players to interact with the environment, and has weapons and monsters galore. Some of the most popular adventure/role playing titles are Duke Nukem, Doom, Diablo, Quake, and Tomb Raider. Games vary in their level of violence, and many new games come with password options that allow parents to reduce the amount of R-rated material. **Action games** like the one shown in Figure 2-27 are similar to arcade games.

Figure 2-27

Guiding an action figure past obstacles requires fast thinking and good reflexes.

Simulation software covers a broad range of interests. With SimCity you develop a city. The computer populates your city with "Simmies" that clog your streets, trash your parks, and threaten to remove you from office if you don't supply better city services. With Nascar Racing 2, you can get in the driver's seat of a stock car and test your driving skills on one of 16 authentic Nascar tracks. You can shoot a round of golf with Tiger Woods, fly fighter planes, attack helicopters, or even strap into the pilot's seat of an X-wing fighter from Star Wars.

With the industry growing at a rapid pace and new technology creating ever more sophisticated multimedia capabilities, the future of entertainment software appears to be limited only by how much money consumers are willing to spend.

Accounting and Finance Software

Can software help me manage my money? If you've been reading the newspapers, then you are probably aware of the predictions that social security is likely to run out of money sometime in the next 50 years. It is never too early to start saving and investing money. The earlier you start, the more likely you will be able to have financial security by the time you are ready to retire. If retirement seems too far away to worry about, you probably have some other short-term financial goals such as earning enough money for next year's tuition, buying a new multimedia PC, or saving $2,000 for a trip to Australia. Without a financial plan, you might never reach these goals. Software can help you keep track of your money and progress toward financial goals.

Money Management 10

Accounting and finance software keeps a record of monetary transactions and investments. In this category, **personal finance software** is geared toward individual finances by helping you keep track of bank accounts, credit cards, investments, and your bills. Some packages support **online banking**—a way to use your computer and modem to download transactions directly from your bank, transfer funds among accounts, and pay bills. The best selling personal finance software program is Intuit's Quicken shown in Figure 2-28.

Figure 2-28

Personal finance software can help you track your money and investments.

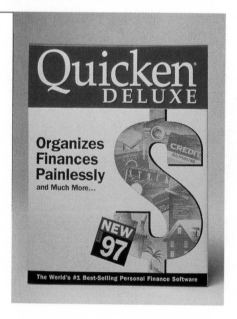

Some accounting and finance software is geared toward business. If you're an entrepreneur— even if you have a small business while you're in college—**small business accounting software** can be a real asset. These programs are easy to use and don't require more than a basic understanding of accounting and finance principles. Best-sellers include Peachtree Complete Accounting, Intuit QuickBooks, and Best!Ware M.Y.O.B. This software helps you invoice customers and keep track of what they owe. It stores additional customer data, such as contact information and purchasing history. Inventory functions keep track of the products you carry. Payroll capabilities automatically calculate wages and deduct federal, state, and local taxes.

Business Software

What's the difference between horizontal-market and vertical-market software? **Business software**, helps organizations efficiently accomplish routine tasks. Often, business software is divided into two categories: horizontal-market software and vertical-market software.

The term "horizontal market" refers to different types of businesses that, despite their differences, have some of the same software needs. **Horizontal-market software** is any generic software package that can be used by many different kinds of businesses. Much of this software comes from other software categories, such as accounting and finance. Payroll software is a good example of horizontal-market software. Almost every business has employees and needs to maintain payroll records. Payroll software keeps track of employee hours and produces the reports required by the government for income tax reporting.

A vertical market is a group of similar businesses that need specialized software. **Vertical-market software** is designed for specialized tasks in a specific market or business. For example, tasks in the construction industry include estimating the cost of labor and materials for a new building and providing the customer with a bid or estimate of the price for the finished building. Vertical-market estimating software for the construction industry would automate the task of gathering labor and materials costs and perform the calculations needed to arrive at an estimate. Other examples of vertical market software include the software that handles billing and insurance for medical practices and software that tracks the amount of time attorneys spend on each case. Advertisements for vertical-market software can be found in trade journals and on the Web.

Figure 2-29

Vertical-market software targets specific businesses and industries.

QuickCheck C

1. If you purchase a software _____, you will get several applications in one package.

2. _____ software provides sophisticated features for producing professional quality newspapers, magazines, and books.

3. You need graphics software that manipulates _____ graphics if you want to create wireframe drawings and rotate them.

4. The main characteristic of data management software such as a search engine is that it contains data. True or false? _____

5. _____ software allows you to browse Web pages and link to other Web documents.

6. _____-market software is designed for specialized tasks in a specific market or business.

D Multimedia

LAB

Multimedia

In the 1960s, a group of mop-haired musicians called the Beatles burst onto the music scene. Millions of screaming fans sent "I Want to Hold Your Hand" rocketing to the top of the charts. The Beatles formed their own record company called Apple Corps, Ltd.

In 1976, two young Californians, Steve Jobs and Steve Wozniak, started a computer company in a garage. Before the decade was out, both Wozniak and Jobs had become millionaires. Their company, Apple Computers, was wildly successful.

Two totally different companies with similar names? Today, the distinction between computer technology and record companies is not so clear. Consumer electronic inventions—radio, telephone, photography, sound recording, television, video recording, and computers—have merged to create a new technology called multimedia.

Multimedia's Roots

Is multimedia the same as CD-ROM? The term "multimedia" isn't new—it refers to the integrated use of multiple media, such as slides, videotapes, audiotapes, records, CD-ROMs, and photos. Now, however, the computer is replacing or controlling the slide projectors, tape recorders, and record players previously used for multimedia presentations. Advances in computer technology have made it possible to combine text, photo images, speech, music, animated sequences, and video into a single interactive computer application. A new definition of multimedia has emerged from this blend of technology. Today, **multimedia** is defined as an integrated collection of computer-based media including text, graphics, sound, animation, photo images, and video.

Envision a multimedia encyclopedia, for example. Like a traditional encyclopedia, it contains articles and pictures on a wide range of topics. But a multimedia encyclopedia has more. Suppose you're writing a research paper on space. You can pull up an article about space exploration, look at photos of spacecraft, and watch a video of the Hubble Space Telescope. As you read the article you can instantly link to related articles as shown in Figure 2-30.

Figure 2-30

A multimedia encyclopedia provides you with a rich selection of text, graphics, sound, animation, and video.

To locate information, use the Find button.

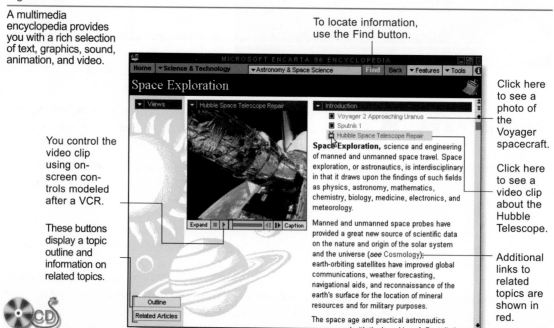

You control the video clip using on-screen controls modeled after a VCR.

These buttons display a topic outline and information on related topics.

Click here to see a photo of the Voyager spacecraft.

Click here to see a video clip about the Hubble Telescope.

Additional links to related topics are shown in red.

Most multimedia applications are shipped on a CD-ROM because the graphics, sound, and video require large amounts of storage space. However, not everything shipped on CD-ROM is multimedia. Many software publishers distribute large data files and non-multimedia software on CD-ROM because one CD-ROM is more convenient and more cost-effective than 20 or 30 floppy disks. For example, the CD-ROM shown in Figure 2-31 contains an archive of articles from back issues of *Visual Basic Programmers Journal*. In this case, the CD-ROM contains data, but no multimedia sounds, video, or animations.

Figure 2-31

Not all CD-ROMs contain multimedia. Some CD-ROMs, such as this one, contain data, but not multimedia elements.

Multimedia Applications

Are multimedia applications better than plain old software? Multimedia technology adds pizzazz to all types of computer applications. For example, a multimedia scheduler might remind you of appointments by displaying a video image of a "personal assistant." "Excuse me," your personal assistant might say, "but I believe you have an appointment in five minutes."

InfoWeb

Multimedia 11

You can use multimedia entertainment applications to have an animated adventure in the far reaches of space. You'll control the animated instrument panel of your spacecraft from your computer keyboard, discuss tactics with video images of your crew members, and hear the sounds of your engines, instrument warnings, and weapons.

You can use multimedia computer-aided instruction to learn a foreign language. You'll watch and listen to a short foreign-language video segment and view a synchronized translation. Then you can practice your pronunciation by speaking into a microphone so the computer can compare your pronunciation with a native speaker's.

You can even create multimedia applications of your own using **multimedia authoring tools** such as Macromedia Director or MicroMedium Digital Trainer Professional. This software helps you create lessons or reference books that include text, videos, animations, and sound tracks.

Multimedia technology opens possibilities for new and creative applications. However, all multimedia products do not necessarily make effective use of multimedia technology. Multimedia product designers have not always considered which technologies would actually enhance their product.

Some multimedia products can be faulted for an incomplete use of multimedia technology. For example, one multimedia product was criticized for including "photos with brief titles but no explanatory text...sketchy text, discontinuity, and almost total lack of sound." On the other hand, overuse of multimedia elements can sometimes detract from the contents. A reviewer pans one multimedia encyclopedia as "big on photos and animations, small on info." So, multimedia has the *potential* to improve an application, if the multimedia product is well designed.

LAB

Computer
History
Hypermedia

Hypertext and Hypermedia

How do hypertext and hypermedia help me use multimedia applications? Hypertext, a key element of many multimedia products, has been used effectively in non-multimedia products as well. Because you are likely to use hypertext with many computer applications and on the Web, it is useful to learn what it's all about. The term **hypertext** was coined by Ted Nelson in 1965 to describe the idea of documents that could be linked to each other. Linked documents make it possible for a reader to jump from a passage in one document to a related passage in another document. Figure 2-32 will help you visualize a hypertext.

Figure 2-32

A hypertext
of linked
documents

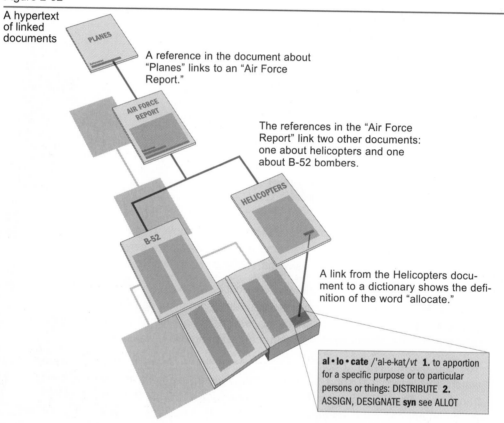

A reference in the document about "Planes" links to an "Air Force Report."

The references in the "Air Force Report" link two other documents: one about helicopters and one about B-52 bombers.

A link from the Helicopters document to a dictionary shows the definition of the word "allocate."

al • lo • cate /'al-e-kat/ *vt* **1.** to apportion for a specific purpose or to particular persons or things: DISTRIBUTE **2.** ASSIGN, DESIGNATE **syn** see ALLOT

InfoWeb

Hypertext
12

Nelson wanted to create a giant hypertext that encompassed virtually every document on library shelves. His goal was not achievable with the technology of the sixties, and little was heard about hypertext for about 20 years. Then in 1987 Apple shipped a software product called Hypercard. It provided a way to create the electronic equivalent of a stack of note cards. Each card could contain text, graphical images, and sounds. Also, the cards could be linked to each other. Users jumped from one card to another by clicking buttons, underlined **links**, or specially marked **hot spots** in the text or graphics. The Hypercard-style implementation of hypertext developed over the next 10 years and became an important element of online help, computer-based learning systems, multimedia applications, and the Web.

The links in today's applications often involve graphics, sound, and video, as well as text. This type of multimedia hypertext is referred to as **hypermedia**. Hypertext and hypermedia are important computer-based tools because they help you easily follow a path that makes sense to you through a large selection of text, graphical, audio, and video information. Figure 2-33 shows you how to use hypermedia links to view film clips, compare critical reviews, and listen to sections of dialog with Microsoft Cinemania software.

Figure 2-33

Using hypermedia

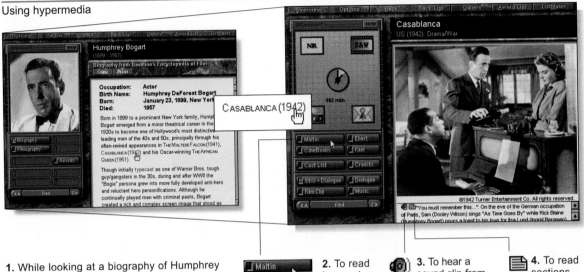

1. While looking at a biography of Humphrey Bogart, you can jump to information about the movie *Casablanca*. The blue lettering used for "Casablanca" indicates it is a link. The hand pointer indicates that you can click the link to jump to the *Casablanca* topic.

2. To read Leonard Maltin's review of the movie, click the Maltin button. Hypermedia buttons such as this help you jump to major sections of the hypermedia.

3. To hear a sound clip from the movie, click the speaker icon. Hypermedia links to sounds are usually indicated by a speaker icon.

4. To read sections of the script, click the document icon.

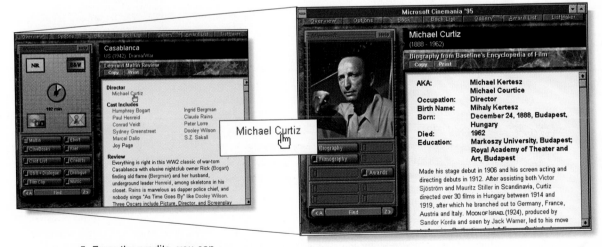

5. From the credits, you can select any topic indicated by blue lettering. For example, select the director's name to see his biography.

Multimedia Equipment

How do I know if my computer can use multimedia applications? Today's multimedia applications require a computer system that can display graphic images, run video clips, and play sounds. Because most multimedia applications are shipped on a CD-ROM disk, your computer needs to have a CD-ROM drive. Your computer system must be able to quickly manipulate and transfer large amounts of data so you need a fast computer with a lot of memory. To display realistic graphical and video images, your computer system must have a high-resolution monitor capable of displaying a wide range of colors. To play realistic sounds, your computer needs a sound card and speakers. Figure 2-34 shows a computer well equipped for multimedia.

Figure 2-34

A multimedia PC

A fast processor and lots of memory can speed up searches and video displays.

A high-resolution color monitor displays graphics, animations, and videos.

Earphones can be used as an alternative to speakers.

Speakers are attached to a sound card for audio playback.

A CD-ROM drive plays the multimedia software.

CD-ROMs contain multimedia software.

Most computer companies produce one or more computer models equipped for multimedia applications. If you are in the market for a new computer, it makes sense to get one equipped for multimedia because of the many excellent multimedia applications available today. If you already have a computer, but it is not equipped for multimedia, you can add multimedia capabilities by purchasing a multimedia kit that contains a CD-ROM drive and sound card.

Figure 2-35

A multimedia kit is designed for non-technical users and usually can be installed in a few hours. Instead of using a multimedia kit, you can purchase a CD-ROM drive and sound card individually, but installing these individual components usually requires more technical expertise.

Speakers

Sound card

CD-ROM drive

Disk containing device drivers

InfoWeb

MMX
13

Multimedia has become so popular that many of today's computers have a Pentium® processor with special multimedia enhancements called **Intel MMX™ technology**. This chip speeds up multimedia features such as sound and video. However, only specially-written software can take advantage of the special multimedia features on the chip. The MMX Logo shown in Figure 2-36 on a software package indicates that the software is optimized for the Intel MMX technology.

Figure 2-36

MMX Logo

QuickCheck D

1 Multimedia is a blend of technologies, such as text, photo images, speech, music, animated sequences, and video. True or false? _____

2 Multimedia is the same as CD-ROM. True or false? _____

3 When you add multimedia to hypertext you get _____.

4 The _____ logo means a software program has been specially designed to handle multimedia commands.

UserFocus

E Installing Software

Many microcomputers are sold with pre-installed system and application software, but eventually most computer users want to install additional software.

Software Compatibility

How do I know what software will work on my computer? Before you install software or a multimedia application, you must make sure it is compatible with your computer system. To be compatible, the software must be written for the type of computer you use and for the operating system installed on your computer. You must also make sure your computer meets or exceeds the system requirements specified by the software. **System requirements** specify the operating system type and minimum hardware capacity needed for a software product to work correctly. The system requirements are usually listed on the outside of a software package, as shown in Figure 2-37. They might also be explained in more detail in the software reference manual.

Figure 2-37

The system requirements on a software package describe the equipment and operating system required to run the software.

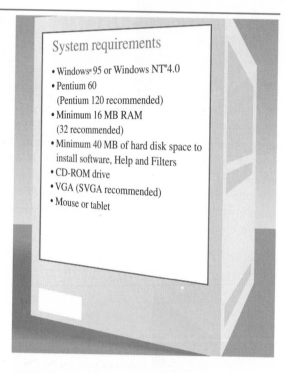

System requirements

- Windows® 95 or Windows NT®4.0
- Pentium 60
  (Pentium 120 recommended)
- Minimum 16 MB RAM
  (32 recommended)
- Minimum 40 MB of hard disk space to install software, Help and Filters
- CD-ROM drive
- VGA (SVGA recommended)
- Mouse or tablet

Determining Compatibility

Does the version of my computer's operating system affect compatibility? Suppose you want to purchase software for your PC. First, you need to make sure the software is written for PCs, rather than for the Apple Macintosh. Sometimes the same software title is available for more than one type of computer. For example, Microsoft Word is available for both PCs and Macs, but these are two distinct versions of the software. You cannot use the Macintosh version of Microsoft Word on your PC.

Once you know the software is compatible with your computer, you must make sure the software will work with your operating system. If your PC uses the DOS operating system, you must select DOS software. If your computer uses the Microsoft Windows operating system, you can select DOS or Windows software because Windows can run software designed for both of these operating systems. If your computer uses OS/2, you can select OS/2, DOS, or Windows software because OS/2 can run software designed for all three operating systems.

Operating systems go through numerous revisions. A higher version number indicates a more recent revision; for example, DOS 6.0 is a more recent version than DOS 5.0. Windows 95 and Windows 98 are more recent versions than Windows 3.1. Operating systems are usually **downwardly compatible**, which means that you can use application software designed for earlier versions of the operating system, but not those designed for later versions. For example, if Windows 95 is installed on your computer, you can generally use software designed for earlier versions of Windows, such as Windows 3.1. However, your software might not work correctly if it requires Windows 95 but you have Windows 3.1 on your computer. If you want to use software that requires a newer version of your operating system, you must first purchase and install an operating system upgrade. Figure 2-38 summarizes the concept of downward compatibility.

Figure 2-38

Downward compatibility

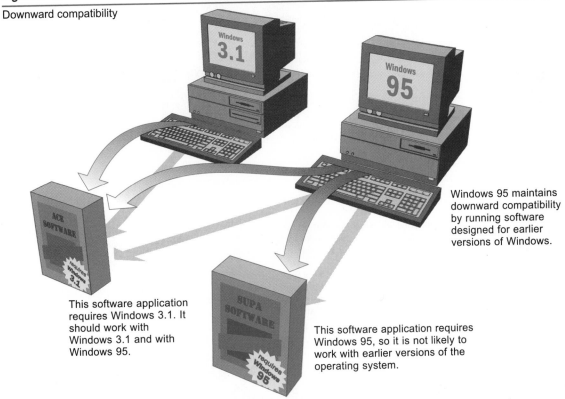

Windows 95 maintains downward compatibility by running software designed for earlier versions of Windows.

This software application requires Windows 3.1. It should work with Windows 3.1 and with Windows 95.

This software application requires Windows 95, so it is not likely to work with earlier versions of the operating system.

Software Setup

When I purchase software, what do I do with the disks? Computer software is usually shipped on floppy disks, called **distribution disks**, or on CD-ROMs. In the years when personal computers first appeared on the market, you could often use the software directly from the distribution disk. Now, that is rarely possible because the programs are so large they take up many disks. Today, instead of using software directly from the distribution disk, you usually install it on your hard disk. During the **installation process**, programs and data for the software are copied to the hard disk of your computer system.

When you install software using a command-line operating system, such as DOS, you should carefully follow the installation instructions provided in the reference manual. There is no consistent installation procedure for DOS software, so each software application might require different steps. On the other hand, for Microsoft Windows applications, the installation process is more consistent and usually much easier. Figure 2-39 shows you how to install Windows applications.

Figure 2-39

The installation process

1. Insert the setup disk and start the setup program.

2. Select full or customized installation. For a full installation, the setup program copies all the files and data from the distribution disks to the hard disk of your computer system. A full installation provides you with access to all the features of the software.

During a customized installation, the setup program displays a list of software features for your selection. After you select the features you want, the setup program copies only the selected program and data files to your hard disk. A customized installation can save space on your hard disk.

☒ **Full Installation**
☐ **Customized Installation**

3. If the software includes multiple disks, insert each disk in the specified drive when the setup program tells you to do so.

4. When the setup program is finished, start the program you have just installed to be sure it works.

5. Fill out the registration card and send it in. When you send in the card, you become a registered user. The perks of being a registered user vary with each software publisher, but they might include receiving free technical support, product information, or discounts on new versions of the software.

When you install non-multimedia applications such as word-processing or accounting software, the computer copies all the program modules from the distribution disks or CD-ROM to the hard disk of your computer. You do not need to insert the disk or CD-ROM every time you want to use the program because everything you need is on your hard disk. For multimedia applications, this is not always the case. You generally copy only a small start-up program to your hard disk, leaving most of the multimedia images, videos, and sounds on the CD-ROM.

Why wouldn't you copy all the multimedia components to your hard disk? The answer is to save hard disk space. Multimedia applications require lots of storage space. For example, Microsoft's Encarta encyclopedia takes up about three times as much space as Microsoft Office 97, which includes word-processing, spreadsheet, presentation, and database software applications. You are likely to have many multimedia applications, but use them infrequently. Rather than devoting a large portion of your hard disk space to a multimedia application, you must insert its CD-ROM into the CD-ROM drive so that you have access to the images, animations, videos, and sound.

InfoWeb

Anti-Piracy
14

EndNote Software is the key to the computer's versatility. System software and application software work together to help you accomplish an incredible variety of tasks. You might think it is "corny" to follow copyright laws and license restrictions, but ethical software use benefits everyone. Software publishers use revenues from software sales to improve current software, provide technical support, and develop new applications. By resisting the temptation to use illegal copies of software, you can help provide software publishers with the resources they need to develop more of the software that makes the computer such a versatile machine.

InfoWeb

InfoWeb

Chapter
Links

The InfoWeb is your guide to print, film, television, and electronic resources. Use it to obtain updates on quickly changing technical information and to locate information for research papers. If you're using the New Perspectives CD-ROM, click the InfoWeb icon on the left side of this paragraph to access the online InfoWeb links. Otherwise, use your Web browser and type in the address of the New Perspectives site: www.cciw.com/np3. At the New Perspectives site you'll find up-to-date links to the topics covered in this chapter.

1 Copyright and Software Law

Software copyright law is the focus of an ongoing discussion among American legal experts, American law makers, software publishers, and consumers' rights advocacy groups. There seems to be general agreement that current laws should be updated. Cornell University provides a hypertext version of the U.S. Copyright Act that is currently in effect at **www.law.cornell.edu/uscode/17**. For Canadian copyright law, connect to **www.perlaw.ca/copyright_index.html**. If you have questions about what's legal and what's not, you'll find Copyright FAQs at the Electronic Frontier Foundation site **eff.org/pub/ Intellectual_property**. For "plain speak" information on the difference between copyrighted, licensed, shareware, and public domain software connect to The Copyright Website at **www.benedict.com**.

2 Shareware:Try Before You Buy

The Internet provides an ideal distribution channel for shareware. You can connect to a shareware site, select the program that you want to try and "download it" by transferring it to your computer. The Shareware Trade Association and Resources' Web site **www.shareware.org** distributes software from over one hundred North American and European programmers. At a similar site, **www.shareware.com** you can search for, browse, and download freeware, shareware, demos, fixes, patches, and upgrades from various software archives and computer vendor sites on the Internet. Before you download shareware, be sure that you understand the copyright and license. Also make sure your shareware source is reputable and guarantees that its software is virus free.

3 Operating Systems

To learn more about operating systems, head for the Web sites of the companies that produce them. DOS and Windows operating systems are at **www.microsoft.com**, the Mac OS is at **www.apple.com**, OS/2 is at **www.ibm.com**, and UNIX is at **www.sco.com**. A good desktop reference if you're using Windows is **Inside Windows 95** by Jim Boyce, et al (New Riders Publishing, 1996) or **Windows 95 Secrets Gold** by Brian Livingston and Davis Straub (IDG Books Worldwide, 1996). Most computer curricula include an operating systems course in which students learn about operating system services and the specific ways an operating system controls computer hardware. One of the standard texts for this course is **Operating Systems: Design and Implementation** by Andrew S. Tanenbaum and Albert S. Woodhull (Prentice Hall, 1997).

4 Shopping for Application Software

These days you can buy software without leaving your house—as long as you have Internet access and a credit card. Egghead Computer is a chain of retail stores that also has a Web site at **www.egghead.com**. Here you will find the descriptions and system requirements for software packages, as well as articles and reviews detailing their strengths and weaknesses. Micro Warehouse Inc. offers catalog sales of hardware and software and also has a Web site at **www.warehouse.com**. At the ComputerESP Web site **www.computeresp.com** you can choose a software package and compare prices from stores and catalogs across the country. Students can often get discounts on software at sites, such as **www.studentdiscount.com** or **www.micromaster.com**.

Computer magazines are good sources of information about software—look for them in your library, on newsstands, or on the Web. Two of the biggest computer magazine publishers are Ziff Davis and CMP. Ziff Davis publications include *PC Week, PC Computing, Mac Week,* and *Computer Shopper.* CMP publishes *Computer Reseller News, Home PC, InformationWeek, NetGuide,* and *Windows Magazine.* You can find their magazines online at the ZDNet Web site, **www.zdnet.com**, and the TechWeb site, **techweb.cmp.com**. *BYTE* magazine at **www.byte.com** has excellent product reviews, but the focus is somewhat technical. *Computerworld* at **www.computerworld.com** has great product comparisons as does *InfoWorld* at **www.infoworld.com**.

5 Desktop Publishing

The popularity of desktop publishing increases every year. Why? Find out how companies save money, improve their image, and publicize their message at **www.adobe.com/studio/casestudies/main.html**, the Web site maintained by the publisher of the popular PageMaker DTP software. You can download your own trial version of the Quark desktop publishing software at **www.quark.com**. The Quark site, home of the highly-rated Quark Xpress software, also contains a detailed list of software features, useful if you want to know what desktop software really does. You'll find links to many DTP sites at **www.teleport.com/~eidos/dtpij/**. For DTP professionals, the online magazine **www.publish.com** is a must read for design tips and the latest on DTP technology.

6 3-D Graphics

One of the most exciting developments in graphics is 3-D rendering. Premier packages include AutoCad and Caligari trueSpace. To find out more about 3-D software, click the Gallery link on the Caligari site at **www.caligari.com**. This site also features a great collection of samples and a free trial version of the software. Persistance of Vision also hosts a site, **www.povray.org/java-index.html**, that contains stunning 3-D samples. While at the site, you can download a well-regarded free ray tracing program. Want to see what kind of graphics you can generate with a supercomputer? Connect to **www.ncsa.uiuc.edu/SDG/DigitalGallery/DG_science_theater.html**.

7 Presentations

Using Microsoft PowerPoint software to create presentations? Your local bookstore might have just the desk reference you need to master all its features. The 400 pages and CD-ROM for **Creating Cool Powerpoint 97 Presentations** by Glenn E. Weadock and Emily Sherrill Weadock (IDG Books Worldwide, 1997) are chock full of great hints. Using presentation software won't guarantee a successful presentation. For tips on how to plan, prepare, and deliver a presentation check your library for books such as **Business Presentations and Public Speaking** by Peter H. Engel (Harvard Business School Press, 1996) and **How to Give A Terrific Presentation** by Karen Kalish (Amacom, 1996). Online you can connect to *Presentations* magazine at **www.presentations.com** for tips on making presentations, selecting presentation hardware and making effective use of presentation software.

8 **Web Browsers**

To access the Web, you need Web browser software. Two companies, Netscape Communications and Microsoft, are in stiff competition to see who can capture and hold the lion's share of the browser market. At the Microsoft site, check out **www.microsoft.com/ie** for a description of the Internet Explorer browser and plug-in Internet tools. Information about Netscape Navigator can be found at **www.netscape.com**.

9 **Games Galore**

Most software publishers give away free playable demos of their game software. A fun site with downloads, including children's games, is **www.happypuppy.com**. "Serious" and more violent game demos are supplied by **www.avault.com**.

10 **Money Management**

Money problems? Personal financial management can't promise to solve them, but can supply the software tools you need to get your finances in order. Visit the Intuit Web site at **www.intuit.com** where you can read about the popular Quicken and QuickBooks software, then download a free trial version. A related site, the Quicken Financial Network at **www.qfn.com**, has articles about retirement planning, managing a stock portfolio, and online banking. Click the Debt Survey link and respond to the questionnaire, then compare your results with others.

11 **Multimedia**

Interacting with multimedia products can be fascinating and will keep you engaged, learning, and having fun for many hours. However, at $50 to $60 a title, you don't want to just browse the titles, read the package copy, and take one home. Fortunately, many magazines review current titles, and some publications and Web sites rate titles. *Publisher's Weekly*, the publishing industry's trade magazine, periodically presents reviews of multimedia titles and a multimedia title bestsellers list, comparable to their book bestsellers lists. You can find their PW Multimedia Directory Web site at **www.bookwire.com/PW/mmd/directory/html**.

12 **Hypertext**

Although Ted Nelson coined the term "hypertext" he claims to have been inspired by an article by Vannevar Bush called "As We May Think" (find it at **www.isg.sfu.ca/~duchier/misc/vbush**) that describes a personal information retrieval device called Memex. Ted Nelson originally envisioned hypertext as the underlying technology for project Xanadu, a vast repository of linked documents that readers could easily peruse and even add their own annotations. You'll find the Xanadu Web site at **www.cinemedia.net/xanadu**. Your library might have Nelson's books, **Literary Machines** (1981) and **Computer Lib** (Microsoft Press, 1987). For information on how hypertext has impacted the Internet and literature, try The Electronic Labyrinth Web site at **jefferson.village.virginia.edu/elab/elab.html**.

13 **MMX**

Multimedia has become so popular that many new computers include a processing chip specially designed to optimize video and sound. However, only specially written software can take advantage of the MMX instruction set. PC Webopaedia at **www.webopaedia.com/MMX.htm** has a definition of MMX and links to related articles.

14 **Anti-Piracy**

According to a May 1995 *Computerworld* survey of information systems professionals, 47 percent of the respondents admitted to copying commercial software illegally, despite the fact that 78 percent agreed it should never be done. Find this and other facts about software piracy at the Business Software Alliance Web site, **www.bsa.org/piracy/diduknow.html**. What should you do if you discover a software pirate? The Software Publisher's Association (SPA) has an Anti-Piracy Hotline at (800) 388-7478. Visit the SPA's Anti-Piracy site for information on software law in U.S. and Canada, answers to your questions about legal copying, and guidelines for schools and businesses at **www.spa.org/piracy/info.htm**.

Review

1. Write a sentence or two explaining the most important concept from each of the five sections of this chapter.

2. Below each heading in this chapter, there is a question. Look back through this chapter and answer each of these questions using your own words.

3. Select 10 terms in this chapter that you believe are most important, then use your own words to write a definition of each term.

4. Under U.S. copyright law, what are the two major rights granted to the copyright holder? What are the three rights granted to the user of copyrighted materials?

5. Complete the following "legal" matrix to clarify the difference between copyrighted software, licensed software, shareware, and public domain software.

Suppose you are not the author of a software package. Is it...	Copyrighted Software	Licensed Software	Shareware	Public Domain Software
Legal to make a backup copy?				
Legal to sell a copy?				
Legal to give a copy to a friend?				
Protected by U.S. Copyright Law?				

6. For each of the following descriptions, indicate whether the software is copyrighted, licensed, shareware, or public domain. For some descriptions, there is more than one answer.

   a. The software does not have a copyright notice

   b. You must send in money to become a registered user

   c. The software is shrink wrapped and there is a message about your rights and responsibilities

   d. When you start the software you see a message "© 1998 Course Technology, Inc."

   e. When you start the program you see a message, "Copyright 1996, 1997 SupRSoft, Inc. All Rights Reserved. You are free to use, copy, and distribute this software for non-commercial use if no fee is charged for use, copying, or distribution, and if the software is not modified in any way."

7. Create a sentence outline of Section B System Software. Your outline should have at least three levels. You can use I., A., and 1. for the outline levels. Be sure that the sentence you write for each outline level focuses on a single, important point.

8. Fill in the following table by using a check mark to indicate which operating systems are available for each type of computer.

Operating System	IBM Compatible	Macintosh	Minicomputer	Mainframe
DOS				
WINDOWS				
OS/2				
MVS				
VMS				
UNIX				

9. Indicate what software tool(s) you could use to accomplish the following tasks. If you could use more than one tool for the task, indicate which you think would be best.

   a. Working with numbers and examining "what-if" scenarios

   b. Producing documents

   c. Working with facts and figures, such as customer names and addresses

d. Drawing pictures, 3-D images, and animations

e. Sending electronic messages between two computers

f. Producing professional-looking brochures and newsletters

g. Creating pie charts, line graphs, and bar graphs

h. Determining times for meetings, tracking special events, and maintaining employee schedules

10 Make a two-column list to summarize multimedia. The left column of the list should include multimedia features such as sound, animation, and so on. The right column should indicate the computer equipment that is needed to implement the features you listed in the left column.

11 Suppose you're thinking of purchasing Microsoft Excel for Windows. The software requires "an IBM-PC/AT, PS/2, or compatible; graphics compatible with Microsoft Windows version 3.0 or later; MS-DOS version 3.1 or later; optional printer; a mouse or compatible pointing device is recommended." You have a Compaq computer with Windows 95, a Hewlett-Packard printer, and a Microsoft mouse. Explain whether you can expect the Microsoft Excel spreadsheet software to work on your computer after you install it.

12 Use the New Perspectives CD-ROM to take a practice test or to review the new terms presented in this chapter.

Projects

1 **Format a Disk** In this chapter you learned how utility software helps you direct the operating system to accomplish tasks such as formatting a disk. This is a good time to try it out. If your lab computers have the Windows 95 operating system, you can do this project on your own by referring to Figure 2-39. Otherwise, your instructor will need to help you.

2 **The Operating System in Your School's Lab** In this chapter you learned how to identify microcomputer operating systems by looking at the main screen and prompt. In this project you will explore more about the operating system in your school computer lab. If you have more than one lab or your computer uses more than one operating system, your instructor should tell you which one to use for this project.

Find out which operating system is used in your school computer lab. Be sure you find out the type and version. You can go into the lab and obtain this information from one of the computers. If you see a command-line user interface, try typing "ver" and then pressing the Enter key. If you see a graphical user interface, try clicking the Apple menu, or click the Help menu, then select Help About. Once you know the operating system used in your school lab, use the operating system reference manual and library resources to answer the following questions:

a. Which operating system and version are used in your school lab?

b. What company publishes the operating system software?

c. When was the first version of this operating system introduced?

d. Does this operating system have a command-line user interface or a graphical user interface?

e. Does this operating system support multitasking?

f. Do you need a password to use the computers in your school lab? Even if you do not need to use a password, does the operating system provide some way to secure access to the computers?

g. What is the anticipated arrival date for the next version of this operating system?

h. How much does the publisher of this operating system usually charge for upgrades if you are a registered user?

3 The Legal Beagle: Analyzing a License Agreement

When you use a software package, it is important to understand the legal restrictions on its use. In this project you have an opportunity to practice reading a real software license agreement and making decisions based on how you interpret what it says. You can do this project on your own or discuss it in a small group, as specified by your instructor. Read the IBM Program License Agreement (on the previous page) then answer these questions:

a. Is this a "shrink wrap" license? Why or why not?

b. After you pay your computer dealer for the program this license covers, who owns the program?

c. Can you legally have one copy of the program on your computer at work and another copy of the program on your computer at home if you use the software only in one place at a time?

d. Can you legally sell the software? Why or why not?

e. Under what conditions can you legally transfer possession of the program to someone else?

f. If you were the owner of a software store, could you legally rent the program to customers if you were sure they did not keep a copy after the rental period was over?

g. Can you legally install this software on one computer, but give more than one user access to it?

h. If you use this program for an important business decision and you later find out that a mistake in the program caused you to lose $500,000, what legal recourse is provided by the license agreement?

International Business Machines Corporation   *Armonk, New York 10504*

IBM Program License Agreement

BEFORE OPENING THIS PACKAGE, YOU SHOULD CAREFULLY READ THE FOLLOWING TERMS AND CONDITIONS. OPENING THIS PACKAGE INDICATES YOUR ACCEPTANCE OF THESE TERMS AND CONDITIONS. IF YOU DO NOT AGREE WITH THEM, YOU SHOULD PROMPTLY RETURN THE PACKAGE UNOPENED AND YOUR MONEY WILL BE REFUNDED.

This is a license agreement and not an agreement for sale. IBM owns, or has licensed from the owner, copyrights in the Program. You obtain no rights other than the license granted you by this Agreement. Title to the enclosed copy of the Program, and any copy made from it, is retained by IBM. IBM licenses your use of the Program in the United States and Puerto Rico. You assume all responsibility for the selection of the Program to achieve your intended results and for the installation of, use of, and results obtained from, the Program.

The Section in the enclosed documentation entitled "License Information" contains additional information concerning the Program and any related Program Services.

LICENSE

You may:
1) use the Program on only one machine at any one time, unless permission to use it on more than one machine at any one time is granted in the License Information (Authorized Use);
2) make a copy of the Program for backup or modification purposes only in support of your Authorized Use. However, Programs marked "Copy Protected" limit copying;
3) modify the Program and/or merge it into another program only in support of your Authorized Use; and
4) transfer possession of copies of the Program to another party by transferring this copy of the IBM Program License Agreement, the License Information, and all other documentation along with at least one complete, unaltered copy of the Program. You must, at the same time, either transfer to such other party or destroy all your other copies of the Program, including modified copies or portions of the Program merged into other programs. Such transfer of possession terminates your license from IBM. Such other party shall be licensed, under the terms of this Agreement, upon acceptance of the Agreement by its initial use of the Program.

You shall reproduce and include the copyright notice(s) on all such copies of the Program, in whole or in part.

You shall not:
1) use, copy, modify, merge, or transfer copies of the program except as provided in this Agreement;
2) reverse assemble or reverse compile the Program; and/or
3) sublicense, rent, lease, or assign the Program or any copy thereof.

LIMITED WARRANTY

Warranty details and limitations are described in the Statement of Limited Warranty which is available upon request from IBM, its Authorized Dealer or its approved supplier and is also contained in the License Information. IBM provides a three-month limited warranty on the media for all Programs. For selected Programs, as indicated on the outside of the package, a limited warranty on the Program is available. The applicable Warranty Period is measured from the date of delivery to the original user as evidenced by a receipt.

Certain Programs, as indicated on the outside of the package, are not warranted and are provided "AS IS."

Z125-3301-02 4/87

SUCH WARRANTIES ARE IN LIEU OF ALL OTHER WARRANTIES, EXPRESS OR IMPLIED, INCLUDING, BUT NOT LIMITED TO, THE IMPLIED WARRANTIES OF MERCHANTABILITY AND FITNESS FOR A PARTICULAR PURPOSE.

Some states do not allow the exclusion of implied warranties, so the above exclusion may not apply to you.

LIMITATION OF REMEDIES

IBM's entire liability and your exclusive remedy shall be as follows:
1) IBM will provide the warranty described in IBM's Statement of Limited Warranty. If IBM does not replace defective media or, if applicable, make the Program operate as warranted or replace the Program with a functionally equivalent program, all as warranted, you may terminate your license and your money will be refunded upon the return of all your copies of the Program.
2) For any claim arising out of IBM's limited warranty, or for any other claim whatsoever related to the subject matter of this Agreement, IBM's liability for actual damages, regardless of the form of action, shall be limited to the greater of $5,000 or the money paid to IBM, its Authorized Dealer or its approved supplier for the license for the Program that caused the damages that is the subject matter of, or is directly related to, the cause of action. This limitation will not apply to claims for personal injury or damages to real or tangible personal property caused by IBM's negligence.
3) In no event will IBM be liable for any lost profits, lost savings, or any incidental damages or other consequential damages, even if IBM, its Authorized Dealer or its approved supplier has been advised of the possibility of such damages, or for any claim by you based on a third party claim.

Some states do not allow the limitation or exclusion of incidental or consequential damages so the above limitation or exclusion may not apply to you.

GENERAL

You may terminate your license at any time by destroying all your copies of the Program or as otherwise described in this Agreement.

IBM may terminate your license if you fail to comply with the terms and conditions of this Agreement. Upon such termination, you agree to destroy all your copies of the Program.

Any attempt to sublicense, rent, lease or assign, or, except as expressly provided herein, to transfer any copy of the Program is void.

You agree that your are responsible for payment of any taxes, including personal property taxes, resulting from this Agreement.

No action, regardless of form, arising out of this Agreement may be brought by either party more than two years after the cause of action has arisen except for the breach of the provisions in the Section entitled "License" in which event four years shall apply.

This agreement will be construed under the Uniform Commercial Code of the State of New York.

4

INTERNET
Optional

Software Applications: What's Available? There are so many software packages that it is difficult to get an idea of what's available unless you take a look through current computer magazines and software catalogs. Use computer magazines and/or the Web to complete the following tasks:

1. Find an ad for a computer vendor that sells a large variety of software. Jot down the name of the vendor and where you found the ad. List the categories the vendor uses to classify software and the number of software packages in each category.

2. Select one type of software from the following categories: operating systems, disk utilities, word-processing, graphics, presentation graphics, electronic mail, desktop publishing, spreadsheets, database, accounting, or scheduling. Read a comparison review of software packages in the category you select. Next locate and photocopy ads for each of the products in the review. Look through the software vendor ads to find the best price for each product. Finally, write a one- or two-page summary explaining your purchase recommendation.

5 **What Software Tool Would You Recommend?** Folk wisdom tells us to use the appropriate tool for a job. This is true for software tools, too. In this project you decide what software tool is most appropriate for a task. You can do this project on your own or discuss it in a small group.

For each of the scenarios that follow, decide which software tool (i.e., word-processing) would accomplish the task most effectively.

a. You want to keep track of your monthly expenses and try to figure out ways to save some money.

b. As the leader of an international team of researchers studying migration patterns of Canadian geese, you want all the team members to communicate their findings to each other quickly.

c. You are the office manager for a department of a large Fortune 500 company. One of your responsibilities is to arrange meetings and schedule facilities for the employees in your department.

d. As a partner in a law firm, you need to draft and modify legal briefs.

e. You are in charge of a fund-raising campaign and you need to track the names, addresses, phone numbers, and donations made by contributors.

f. You are going to design and produce the printed program for a community theater play listing the actors, director, lighting specialists, and so on.

g. A sales manager for a cosmetics company wants to motivate the sales force by graphically showing the increases in consumer spending in each of the past five years.

h. The marketing specialist for a new software company wants to send out announcements to 150 computer magazines.

i. The owners of five golf courses in Jackson County want to design a promotional brochure that can be distributed to tourists in restaurants and hotels.

j. The owner of a small business wants to keep track of ongoing income and expenses and print out monthly profit and loss statements.

k. The superintendent of a local school system wants to prepare a press release explaining why student test scores were 5 percent below the national average.

l. A contractor wants to calculate his cost for materials needed to build a new community center.

m. A college student wants to send out customized letters addressed to 20 prospective employers.

n. The parents of three children want to decide whether they should invest money for their children's education in the stock market or whether they should buy into their state's prepaid tuition plan.

o. The director of fund-raising for a large nonprofit organization wants to keep a list of prospective donors.

6 **Multimedia "Top 10"** In the last two years the multimedia market has exploded. For this project, create your own list of "top 10" multi-media titles. Look in recent editions of computer magazines or on the Web and select the 10 multimedia applications that are most interesting or useful to you. For each multimedia application you select, list its title, publisher, and a short description of what it does. Also list the name of the computer magazine you used and the page on which you found the information about each multimedia application.

7 **Productivity, Suites, and Groupware** Use computer magazines or the Web to find the name or one productivity software package, one office suite package, and one groupware package. For each example, list the title, publisher, and price. Also, write one paragraph about each package describing the kinds of tasks it is designed to accomplish.

8 **Where's the Shareware?** You learned in this chapter that shareware can be less expensive than commercial software; it also lets you try the software before you buy it. But is shareware as available as commercial software? In this project you will find out.

Use computer magazines and/or Internet sites to find a shareware program and a commercial program for each of the categories in the table that follows. For each shareware package, indicate the program name, the name of the retailer

or vendor, and the selling price. In the reference column, indicate the name, date, and page of the magazine, or the Internet site, where you found the information. Shareware vendors frequently advertise in the back pages of computer magazines.

Software Type	Title	Price	Vendor	Reference
Shareware productivity				
Commercial productivity				
Shareware system utility				
Commercial system utility				
Shareware education				
Commercial education				
Shareware games				
Commercial games				

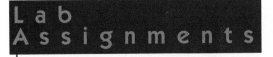

Computer History Hypermedia

The Computer History Hypermedia Lab is an example of a multimedia hypertext, or hypermedia that contains text, pictures, and recordings that trace the origins of computers. This Lab provides you with two benefits: first, you learn how to use hypermedia links, and second, you learn about some of the events that took place as the computer age dawned.

1 Click the Steps button to learn how to use the Computer History Hypermedia Lab. As you proceed through the Steps, answer all the Quick Check questions that appear. After you complete the Steps, you will see a Quick Check Summary Report. Follow the instructions on the screen to print this report.

2 Click the Explore button. Find the name and date for each of the following:

a. First automatic adding machine.

b. First electronic computer.

c. First fully electronic stored-program computer.

d. First widely used high-level programming language.

e. First microprocessor.

f. First microcomputer.

g. First word-processing program.

h. First spreadsheet program.

3 Select one of the following computer pioneers and write a one-page paper about that person's contribution to the computer industry: Grace Hopper, Charles Babbage, Augusta Ada, Jack Kilby, Thomas Watson, or J. Presper Eckert.

4 Use this Lab to research the history of the computer. Based on your research, write a paper explaining how you would respond to the question, "Who invented the computer?"

Multimedia

 Multimedia brings together text, graphics, sound, animation, video, and photo images. If you are using the CD version of this book, you have already seen multimedia in action. In this Lab you will learn how to apply multimedia and then have the chance to see what it might be like to design some aspects of multimedia projects.

1 Click the Steps button to learn about multimedia development. As you proceed through the Steps, answer the Quick Check questions. After you complete the Steps, you will see a Quick Check Report. Follow the instructions on the screen to print this report.

2 In Explore, browse through the STS-79 Multimedia Mission Log. How many videos are included in the Multimedia Mission Log? The image on the Mission Profile page is a vector drawing, what happens when you enlarge it?

3 Listen to the sound track on Day 3. Is this a WAV file or a MIDI file? Why do you think so? Is this a synthesized sound or a digitized sound? Listen to the sound track on page 8. Can you tell if this is a WAV file or a MIDI file?

4 Suppose you were hired as a multimedia designer for a multimedia series on targeting fourth- and fifth-grade students. Describe the changes you would make to the Multimedia Mission Log so it would be suitable for these students. Also, include a sketch showing a screen from your revised design.

5 When you view the Mission Log on your computer, do you see palette flash? Why or why not? If you see palette flash, list the images that flash.

6 Multimedia can be effectively applied to projects such as Encyclopedias, atlases, and animated storybooks; to computer-based training for foreign languages, first aid, or software applications; for games and sports simulations; for business presentations; for personal albums, scrapbooks, and baby books; for product catalogs and Web pages.

Suppose you were hired to create one of these projects. Write a one-paragraph description of the project you would be creating. Describe some of the multimedia elements you would include. For each of the elements indicate its source and whether you would need to obtain permission for its use. Finally, sketch a screen or two showing your completed project.

DOCUMENTS, WORKSHEETS, and DATABASES

The news in 1979 and 1980. The Shah of Iran flees into exile. A partial meltdown at the Three Mile Island nuclear power plant horrifies environmentalists. Members of the U.S embassy in Teheran are taken hostage and will remain in captivity for over a year. The Mount St. Helens volcano erupts, leveling 120 square miles of Washington State forest. John Lennon is murdered.

For microcomputer owners, however, the news in 1979 and 1980 is more positive. Three super software packages arrive on the market. They quickly become best sellers and form the bedrock of microcomputer software. Computer users gladly tackle the complex interface of the WordStar word-processing software so they can create professional-looking documents. VisiCalc, a totally new invention in a category dubbed "spreadsheet software," seems to make it relatively painless for novices to set up complex numerical calculations. A third product, dBase, helps computer users organize their information by creating and maintaining databases. This chapter takes a look at how these software tools affect the computing you do today and how they have affected our society.

CHAPTER**PREVIEW**

This chapter is filled with tips about working with computerized documents, worksheets, and databases. The tips will help you use software to improve the quality of your work, to get better grades, and to enhance your career. The *User Focus* **section explains how to integrate software tools to create great reports and presentations. After you have completed this chapter you should be able to:**

- List examples of how document production software is used in different career fields
- Discuss and demonstrate how document production software can help you improve the quality of your writing and the format of your documents
- Compare and contrast electronic publishing with traditional paper-based publishing
- Discuss some of the ways spreadsheet software affects politics, business, and education in a technologically advanced society
- Describe how spreadsheets work, and how you create, format, and audit a worksheet
- Discuss your responsibilities for creating accurate worksheets and graphs
- Describe the database skills you need to be productive in today's Information Age
- Differentiate between a structured database and a free-form database
- Describe the techniques you can use to search for data in databases
- Describe how to integrate word-processing, spreadsheet, and database software

LABS

Word Processing

Spreadsheets

Databases

A Documents

Word
Processing

Literacy
1

Documents are an integral part of our society and culture. Historical documents such as the Declaration of Independence and the U.S. Constitution promote social and political philosophies. Literary documents, such as *To Kill a Mockingbird* and *War and Peace,* record the issues and dilemmas facing societies and cultures. Fiction entertains. Weekly magazines and daily newspapers provide information on current events. Contracts record agreements for corporations and individuals.

Despite the popularity of radio, television, and film, documents remain an important component of our everyday lives. Historically, growing literacy rates reflect the importance of reading and writing and seem to correspond to social and economic progress.

As literacy increased throughout the world, the tools of document production changed. Hand-copied manuscripts were produced too slowly to satisfy the demands of a literate populace. The printing press, and later the photocopier, made it easy to produce and distribute books, magazines, newspapers, pamphlets, and newsletters. The quill pen was inconvenient because it required the writer to pause every few words to dip the pen into an inkwell. Fountain pens, and later ball-point and felt-tip pens, provided writers with more free-flowing writing tools. The pencil and erasable ink were notable innovations for providing writers with editing capabilities. The typewriter became what might now be called a personal printing device and enabled individuals to produce professional-looking documents without using an expensive printing press (Figure 3-1).

Figure 3-1

Technology has had a significant impact on document production tools.

For most of today's document production tasks, computers with document production software have replaced pencils with chewed-up erasers, smudgy ball-point pens, and clacking typewriters. **Document production software** includes word-processing software, desktop publishing software, e-mail editors, and the software that helps you create home pages and hypertext documents for the Internet's World Wide Web.

Today, it seems that everyone uses computers to produce documents. Using computers, college students write research papers, elementary school students write short essays, secretaries write memos, grandmothers write thank-you notes, executives write corporate reports, job-hunters produce resumes, novelists write books, reporters write news stories, and the list goes on. Should you use a computer for your writing? Check out some good and bad reasons in Figure 3-2.

Figure 3-2

Using a computer for your writing— good and bad reasons

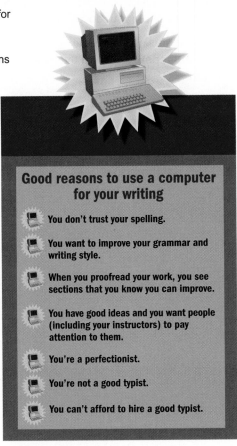

Good reasons to use a computer for your writing

🖥 You don't trust your spelling.

🖥 You want to improve your grammar and writing style.

🖥 When you proofread your work, you see sections that you know you can improve.

🖥 You have good ideas and you want people (including your instructors) to pay attention to them.

🖥 You're a perfectionist.

🖥 You're not a good typist.

🖥 You can't afford to hire a good typist.

Bad reasons to use a computer for your writing

🚫 You never get started until the last minute.

🚫 You're too lazy to proofread your document.

🚫 You want to "borrow" your roommate's report from last semester.

🚫 You hope your readers will be so impressed with your graphics and layout that they don't read what you have written.

A Nation of Typists

Do I really have to know how to type? Typing was once a specialized skill practiced mainly by women in secretarial positions, but it is now a skill possessed to some degree by a sizable percentage of the population in highly literate nations. The pervasiveness of this skill stems from the popularity of computerized document production.

InfoWeb

Typing 2

To use a computer to produce documents, typing on a keyboard is pretty much required. Surprisingly, enrollments in typing classes have not increased. Although there are advantages to being a good keyboarder, you don't need to be an expert typist to create documents. Document production software has a variety of features that help you create error-free documents. In addition, many people are finding that their typing skills quickly improve beyond hunt-and-peck just by using computers from day to day. Typing tutor software can help you quickly increase your typing speed and accuracy without taking a course.

Typically, creating a document requires several steps. To begin, you type the text using a word processor. Next, you edit the document until you are satisfied with the content and writing style. Then, you might use the word-processing software to format and print the document. Alternatively, you might transfer your document to desktop publishing software to complete the layout and printing.

As you type your document, don't get distracted by how your final product will look. Instead, concentrate on expressing your ideas. Later, when you're satisfied with the content of your document, you can shift your focus to the details of how your document will look on paper.

When you use document production software correcting typing and spelling errors is easy. Some word-processing software features **in-line spell checking** that checks the spelling of each word as you type, as shown in Figure 3-3.

Figure 3-3

In-line spell check

A wiggly red line indicates a possible spelling error.

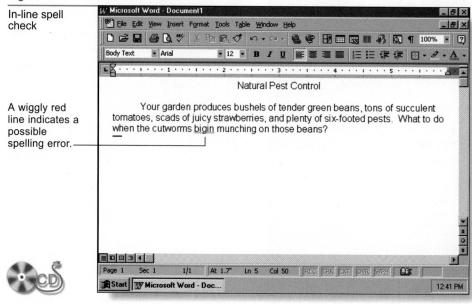

Correcting obvious typographic errors as you're writing is a real benefit, but don't fall into the "tweaking trap." Many writers dither around while writing their first draft, trying to perfect each sentence before continuing. Writing instructors suggest that you can produce better documents faster if you just let your words flow. When you get to a tricky spot, mark the place with a few question marks or asterisks, then continue. You can return to these spots later to select the exact words you want to use.

Word processors make it easy to let your ideas flow because they automatically handle many of the tasks that distracted writers who used typewriters. For example, you don't need to worry about typing off the edge of the paper. With document production software, a feature called **word wrap** takes care of where to break lines. Imagine that the sentences in your document are ribbons of text and word wrap bends the ribbons. Changing margins just means bending the ribbon in different places. Even after you have typed an entire document, adjusting the size of your right, left, top, and bottom margins is simple.

Writing Quality

Does document production software improve writing quality? Computers have been accused of dumping a mountain of poor quality documents into circulation. To anyone who reads electronic mail it soon becomes painfully clear that many literate people still have trouble with spelling and grammar. Some observers characterize the material exchanged in online discussions and newsgroups as crude, silly, uninformed, and self-serving. This criticism implies that instead of helping writers, computers have somehow lowered literary standards.

Perhaps much of this criticism is misplaced. Pulp fiction lined bookstore shelves long before computers graced the drawing boards of IBM and Apple. In any case, people—not computers—create documents. Those spelling errors, grammatical blunders, incoherent arguments, and unverified assertions are probably attributable to human fallibility, rather than to some computer-sponsored plot to subvert literature as we know it.

InfoWeb

Improve
Your
Writing
3

When used skillfully, computerized document production tools can help you improve the quality of your writing. With such tools, it is easy to edit the first draft of your document to refine its overall structure, then zero in to make detailed improvements to your sentence structure and word usage.

Figure 3-4

The late Isaac Asimov was one of this century's most prolific writers. When describing the writing process, he said, "My routine was (and still is) to write a story in its first draft as fast as I can. Then go over it, and correct errors in spelling, grammar, and word order."

Using document production tools, you can easily insert text, cut sections of text, and move entire paragraphs or pages to improve the structure and logical flow of a document. In document production terminology, sections of your document are referred to as **blocks**. Deleting or moving blocks are sometimes referred to as **block operations**.

Although document production software simplifies block operations, you first need to decide how to rearrange your document for a more effective progression of ideas. Some writers find that the limited amount of text displayed on the screen prevents them from getting a good look at the overall flow of ideas throughout the document. One solution is to use the outline feature of your software.

An **outliner** helps you develop a document as a hierarchy of headings and subheadings. This textbook, for example, is structured into chapters, sections, and subsections. When you create a hierarchical document you "tag" each heading to identify whether it starts a chapter, section, or subsection. To get an overall view of the document your software can show only the chapter headings. Or, to view the structure in more detail, the outliner can display the chapter headings and the section headings. When you move a heading in outline view, the outliner automatically moves all its subheadings and paragraphs.

As an alternative to outlining, you might try a time-tested, low-tech technique that works for creative writing as well as hierarchically structured documents. Print out your first draft, then cut it into pieces, paragraph by paragraph. Spread these paragraphs out on the floor and rearrange them until you're satisfied that you have the most logical, effective, and compelling organization. Finally, you can use the block move feature of your software to duplicate your new organization.

Once you have taken care of the overall structure of your document, you can turn to the details of word usage, spelling, and grammar. For example, you might use your software's **thesaurus** to help you find more descriptive words to clarify and enliven your writing.

Some writers know that they tend to overuse certain words or use them incorrectly. For instance, you might tend to overuse the word "however." If you have specific writing problems such as this, you might use the **search feature** to hunt for all the occurrences of your problem word. For each occurrence, you can decide to leave it or revise it. Another feature, **search and replace**, is handy if you want to substitute one word or phrase for another. For example, after you finish the first draft of a short story, you might change its location by using search and replace to change every occurrence of "Texas" to "New Mexico."

Now, what about spelling? A document with spelling errors reflects poorly on the writer. Most document production tools, including newer e-mail editors, have some type of spell check feature. An **in-line spell checker** shows you errors as you type. A less sophisticated, but equally useful, spell checker looks through your entire document any time you activate it. You would generally use this type of spell checker when you have completed your first draft, then again just before you print (Figure 3-5).

Figure 3-5

Using a full-document spell checker

The spell checker finds a misspelled word and highlights it.

The speller checker offers some correctly spelled options.

You can select one of the options to replace the misspelling using the Change button. To leave the word as is, you would click the Ignore button.

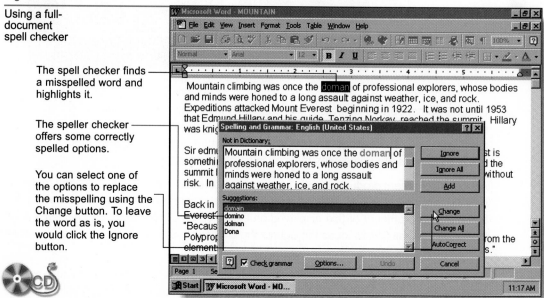

Don't depend on a spell checker to proofread your document. A spell checker works by looking for each word from your document in a list called a **dictionary**. If the word from your document is in the dictionary, the spell checker considers the word correctly spelled. If the word is not in the dictionary, the word is counted as misspelled. Sounds OK, right? Well, suppose your document contains a reference to the city of "Negaunee." This word is not in the dictionary, so the spell checker considers it misspelled. It might even suggest that you change the word to "negate"—a word that does appear in the dictionary. Because they are not in the dictionary, proper nouns and scientific, medical, and technical words are likely to be flagged as misspelled, even if you have spelled them correctly. If you plan to use such words often, you can add them to the dictionary.

Now suppose that your document contains the phrase "a pear of shoes." Although you meant to use "pair," not "pear," the spell checker will not catch your mistake because "pear" is a valid word in the dictionary. Your spell checker won't help if you have trouble deciding whether to use "there" or "their," "its" or "it's," "too" or "to." Remember, then, that a spell check will not substitute for a thorough proofread.

InfoWeb

Grammar
4

All languages are complex. English, for example, is characterized by many linguists as having an exception to every rule. You can clear up many grammatical questions by using a **grammar checker**, a feature of most word processors that coaches you on correct sentence structure and word usage. Think of a grammar checker as an assistant that will proofread your document, point out potential trouble spots, and suggest alternatives. If English is your second language, a grammar checker might be especially helpful.

A grammar checker will not change your document for you. Instead it points out possible problems, suggests alternate words or phrases, and gives you the option of making changes. For example, if a document contains the sentence, "Did the plot turn out like you expected?" a grammar checker might point out that you should consider using "as" instead of "like." Refer to Figure 3-6.

Figure 3-6

A grammar checker suggests a change, but you decide whether to accept the suggestion.

The grammar checker highlights the sentence it is currently checking.

The problem is indicated in green.

A suggestion for improvement.

If requested, the grammar checker explains the basis for its suggestion.

Formatting a Document

How does document production software help create documents that look great?

Before the printing press, documents were hand copied. In the Middle Ages, artists and monks huddled in cavernous rooms called "scriptoria" to painstakingly hand copy religious documents. Many of these hand-copied documents, called "illuminated manuscripts," were works of art in addition to a means of communicating information. These manuscripts often contained illustrations, elaborately detailed initial letters on each page, and decorative borders. Most of these manuscripts were commissioned by wealthy aristocrats. Figure 3-7 shows an example of an illuminated manuscript.

Figure 3-7

Vatican library illuminated manuscript

Beautifully crafted documents are no longer a special perk of wealth. Modern printing techniques make it cost-effective to produce beautiful documents that are available to everyone in libraries, bookstores, and newsstands. In addition, today's document production software provides individuals with the tools necessary to produce professionally formatted and illustrated documents. When you create documents, you'll want to take advantage of formatting tools such as document templates, wizards, fonts, styles, borders, and clip art.

A **document template** is a preformatted document into which you type your text. Most document production software encourages you to select a template before you type the text for your first draft. If you don't select a template, the software will select one for you—usually a plain template suitable for letters and reports. Format settings such as margins, line spacing, heading fonts, and type size have all been set up for you. Figure 3-8 shows some of the document templates typically available with today's word-processing software.

Figure 3-8

Document templates

Template categories include letters, memos, reports, and publications.

Within each category you can choose from several different templates.

The preview shows you an example of a document created using the selected template.

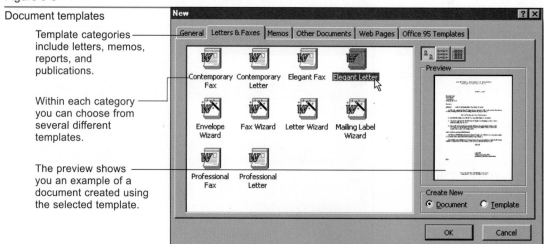

You might wonder if selecting a template before you begin to type contradicts the convention-al advice to ignore formatting issues for your first draft. In practice, you'll want to select a template and perhaps format your headings as you type. You can postpone the rest of your formatting activities until you're satisfied with the content.

Some software goes a step further than templates by furnishing you with **document wizards** that not only provide you with a document format, but take you step by step through the process of entering the text for a wide variety of documents. You'll want to check out the templates and wizards provided by your software before you struggle with creating your own formats. For example, to create an entry-level resume, you might find it easy to use a resume wizard like the one shown in Figure 3-9.

Figure 3-9

Entry-level resume wizard

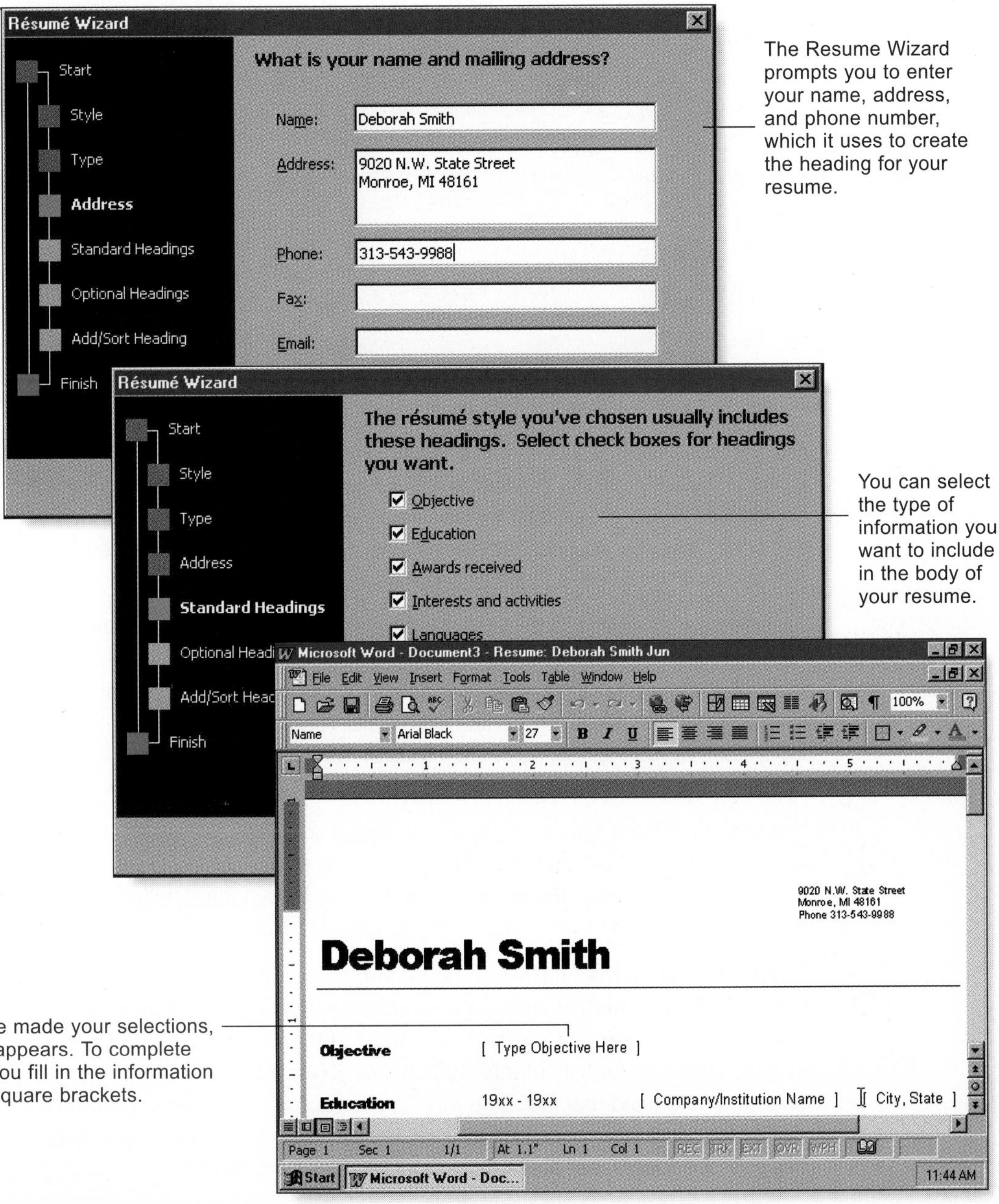

The Resume Wizard prompts you to enter your name, address, and phone number, which it uses to create the heading for your resume.

You can select the type of information you want to include in the body of your resume.

After you have made your selections, your resume appears. To complete the resume, you fill in the information indicated by square brackets.

InfoWeb

Fonts
5

The **font** you select has a major impact on the look of your document. Fonts are designed by typesetters and artists. Your document production software generally supplies you with many fonts. If you want even more variety, you can purchase and install additional font collections.

Typeset fonts such as Times New Roman and Arial make your document look formal and professionally produced. Research studies show that serif fonts are easier to read on the printed page, whereas sans serif fonts are easier to read on the computer screen. In addition, a kerned font is easier to read than a monospaced font. Figure 3-10 shows you the difference between a serif and a sans serif font, and the difference between a kerned font and a monospaced font.

Figure 3-10

Serifs and kerning

Each character of a monospaced font takes up the same amount of space.	Wow, look at this!
A kerned font provides a wider space for wide letters such as "w," but reduces the amount of space allotted to narrow letters such as "t."	Wow, look at this!
A serif font has small embellishments called "serifs" on the ends of the lines that form the characters.	**Wow, look at this!**
A sans serif font lacks serifs.	Wow, look at this!

You can also use simulated **handwriting fonts** to give your document a more personal appeal. Why not just write the document by hand? You can spell check your work—something you can't do if you just scribble a note—and you can mix the handwriting fonts with more conventional, typeset fonts. Some companies will scan in your handwriting and convert it into your own personal handwritten font for use on your computer.

In addition to selecting fonts, you can manipulate the look of your document by adjusting the line spacing, margins, indents, tabs, borders, and frames. Additional space makes a document easier to read. Larger margins and double-spacing generate white space, make your document appear less dense, and make reading seem easier. The margins for most papers and reports should be set at 1 inch or 1.5 inches. Unless double spacing is required, most word processors set the line spacing at an appropriate distance for the font size.

Justification defines how the letters and words are spaced across each line. Typeset documents are often fully justified so the text on the right margin as well as on the left margin is aligned evenly. Your document will look more formal if it is fully justified than if it has a ragged right margin.

Columns enhance readability and tables organize data. In document production terminology, **columns** generally mean newspaper-style layout of paragraphs of text. **Tables** arrange data in a grid of rows and columns. Tables are more appropriate than columns for numeric data and for lists of information. For example, if you are creating a "two-column" resume, you should use the table function in your word-processing software. Don't waste your time trying to arrange columns or tables using the tab key and space bar. Instead, use your software's automatic table feature or column format.

When you summarize or list information, or even when you type your answers to homework questions, your points will stand out if you use hanging indents, bulleted lists, or numbered lists as shown in Figure 3-11.

Figure 3-11

Hanging indent

The number is positioned at the left margin.

The hanging indent text is aligned under the tab stop, not at the left margin.

1. Before assembling your X-wing fighter model, compare the parts in your kit to the parts list on page 6.
2. Attach the left wing mount in the left wing slot A. The wing mount will snap into place and does not require glue.

To add visual interest to your documents, incorporate borders, rules, and graphics. A **border** is a box around text or graphics—usually around a title, heading, or table. A **rule** is a line, usually positioned under text. Rules can be horizontal, vertical or diagonal. The thinnest rule is one pixel thick and called a **hairline rule**.

Graphics are pictures and illustrations. Clip-art collections provide hundreds of images that you have permission to use in non-commercial works. You can also find graphics on the Internet. With the right equipment, you can scan pictures from books and magazines. Just be sure you check for permission before you use any graphic in your documents.

Most document production software uses frames as containers for graphics. A **frame** is an invisible box that you can position anywhere on the page. Generally you can flow text around the frame and layer frames one on top of another to achieve complex layout effects as shown in Figure 3-12.

Figure 3-12

Frames

Frames can contain graphics or text.

A frame can be positioned anywhere on the page—even in the top margin.

Text runs around this frame set in the middle of the page.

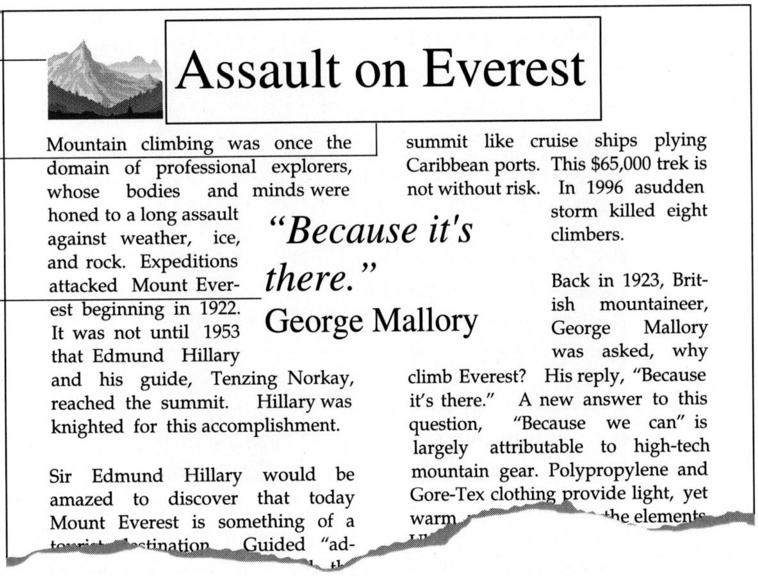

Assault on Everest

Mountain climbing was once the domain of professional explorers, whose bodies and minds were honed to a long assault against weather, ice, and rock. Expeditions attacked Mount Everest beginning in 1922. It was not until 1953 that Edmund Hillary and his guide, Tenzing Norkay, reached the summit. Hillary was knighted for this accomplishment.

Sir Edmund Hillary would be amazed to discover that today Mount Everest is something of a tourist destination. Guided "ad-

"Because it's there."
George Mallory

summit like cruise ships plying Caribbean ports. This $65,000 trek is not without risk. In 1996 a sudden storm killed eight climbers.

Back in 1923, British mountaineer, George Mallory was asked, why climb Everest? His reply, "Because it's there." A new answer to this question, "Because we can" is largely attributable to high-tech mountain gear. Polypropylene and Gore-Tex clothing provide light, yet warm the elements.

The Power of the Printed Word

What are the options for printing and publishing documents? Printing with moveable type existed in Asia as early as 1000 A.D. However, until Johann Gutenberg demonstrated his moveable type printing press in 1448, this technology did not exist in Europe. Printing eventually replaced hand copying as a means of producing documents, but as with many technological innovations, the printing press had to overcome initial resistance from some segments of society. Apparently, people in Europe were initially suspicious that the new printing techniques were black magic. How, they wondered, could copies of documents be produced so quickly and look exactly alike? To alleviate such fears, Gutenberg and other early printers produced Bibles and other religious documents.

InfoWeb

Publishing
6

The change from hand copying to machine printing had a massive effect on Western culture and civilization by making information available to all who could read. Thomas Paine harnessed the power of the printed word in 1776 when he sold 500,000 copies of a 50-page pamphlet, *Common Sense*. This document asserted that it was just common sense for the American colonies to become independent from Great Britain. Six months later, the Declaration of Independence was signed. Thomas Paine and his compatriot, Thomas Jefferson, envisioned a free press as the cornerstone of a free society. They hoped that publishing would spread ideas, foster dialogs between diverse interest groups, and help to establish a common social agenda (Figure 3-13).

Figure 3-13

When Thomas Paine sold 500,000 copies of *Common Sense*, the colonies had a population of only four million.

Early expectations were that computerized document production would make it easy for individuals, not just publishing companies, to produce professional-quality books and pamphlets. Word processors have made it possible for individuals to create more documents, such as newsletters and manuscripts. However, computerized document production has had only a moderate effect on traditional paper-based publishing. If you assumed that document production technology would produce a huge glut of new books, think again. Between 1993 and 1995 American book production actually declined by 5,000 titles. Although computers help produce documents faster, the cost of paper and the economics of distribution still limit the number of books published.

One of the most significant effects of computerized document production came as a somewhat unexpected surprise. The expedient development of a worldwide data communications network has opened up amazing opportunities for **electronic publishing**. Today, it is old fashioned to think of a computer as just a place to store information before it is committed to paper. Once a document is in electronic format, why not keep it there? Electronic documents are easy to send, store, and manipulate. They might even bring us closer to the global democracy that Thomas Paine envisioned. Today virtually anyone can post a document on the World Wide

Web, send an e-mail message, or participate in online discussion groups. The power of the printed word seems to be evolving into the power of the electronically published word (Figure 3-14).

Figure 3-14

Many activists believed that certain provisions of the U.S. Telecommunications Act of 1996 would limit freedom of speech on the Internet. Massive protests on electronic forums and a well-engineered lawsuit prompted the Supreme Court to declare that many parts of the Act were unconstitutional.

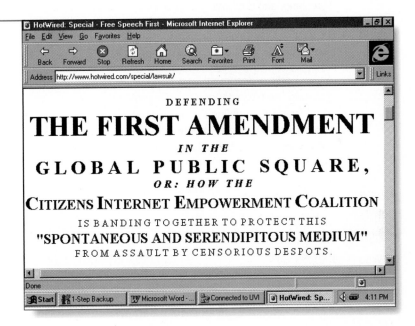

To create Web pages, many word processors and desktop publishers automatically generate an HTML formatted document from any document you have entered and stored. When you create a Web page, your goal should be to effectively combine and format basic Web elements to create a visual display that enhances the content of your page. The basic elements of a Web page are shown in Figure 3-15.

Figure 3-15

Web page elements

Web page title

URL

Two separately scrolling frames

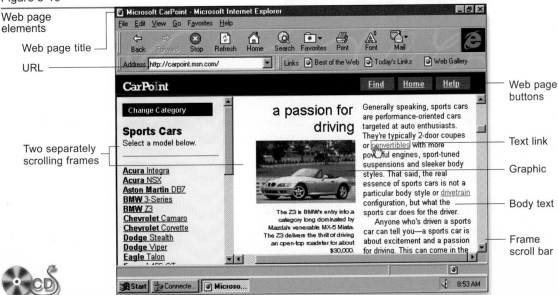

Web page buttons

Text link

Graphic

Body text

Frame scroll bar

Automating Document Production

How can I harness the power of a computer to automate document production tasks?

Computers are pretty talented when it comes to repetitive tasks such as counting, numbering, searching, and duplicating. Document production software makes clever use of the computer's talents in these areas to automate many of the repetitive tasks associated with document production. Automating such tasks saves time and increases productivity. Let's look briefly at a few of the more useful tasks in this category.

As you edit a document and change its format, you might remove large sections of text, reducing the page count. Or, your professor or publisher might insist that you double space the document, doubling the page count. It makes sense then to let the software take care of numbering your pages. **Automatic page numbering**, sometimes called **pagination**, means the computer automatically numbers and renumbers the pages as you edit and format your document.

Who Wrote It? 7

You usually tell your software to include page numbers in a header or footer. A **header** is text that automatically appears in the top margin of every page. A **footer** is text that appears in the bottom margin of every page. Headers and footers help identify the document and make your documents look more like published works. Look at a page in this book. It has a header. Published books will often have either a header, a footer, or both on each page. Your documents can easily have these professional elements. A simple footer might be the word "Page," followed by the current page number. For identification purposes, you might put your name in the header of your documents.

Figure 3-16

Joe Klein, the "anonymous" author of *Primary Colors*

Does your English professor want a 1,000-word essay? Your computer can count the words in a document with the **automatic word count** feature of your document production software. Another use for a computer's ability to count words is for literary analysis. A **concordance** is an alphabetized list of words in a document and the frequency with which each word appears. Concordance has been used to determine authorship of historical and contemporary documents by comparing the frequencies of words used in a document by an unknown author to the frequencies of words used in a document of known authorship. The anonymously authored novel, *Primary Colors*, was widely speculated to be based on behind-the-scenes wheeling and dealing during Bill Clinton's first presidential campaign. Vassar professor Donald Foster used concordance techniques to compare the text of *Primary Colors* to a series of columns written by journalist Joe Klein. Mr. Klein later admitted his authorship.

Most grammar checkers have built in **readability formulas** that count the number of words in each sentence and the number of syllables per word. As you write, you can use readability formulas to target your writing to your audience. The longer your sentences and words, the higher the reading level required to understand your writing. Most writers aim for a seventh- or eighth-grade reading level on documents for the general public.

Scholarly documents often require **footnotes** that contain citations for works mentioned in the text. As you revise your text, the footnotes need to stay associated with their source in the text and must be numbered sequentially. Your document production software includes footnoting facilities that correctly position and number the footnotes even if you move blocks of text. Need end notes instead of footnotes? Your software can gather your citations at the end of your document and print them in order of their appearance in the document or in alphabetical order. Some word processors even have wizards that help you enter your citations in the correct format depending on whether they are books or magazine articles.

Longer documents benefit from a **table of contents** and an **index**. Because of document production technology, many people have come to expect that all documents, not just those created by professional publishers, have indexes and tables of contents. Most document production software will automatically generate an index and table of contents, then automatically update them as you edit your document.

Boilerplating refers to the process of merging standard paragraphs to create a new document. Law offices frequently use boilerplating to draw up legal documents for wills, divorces, trusts, and so on.

Mail merge automates the process of producing customized documents such as letters and advertising flyers. You might use mail merge to send out application letters when you're searching for a job. Figure 3-17 explains how it works.

Figure 3-17

To set up a mail merge, you create a document containing specially marked "blanks." You also create a file of information that goes in the blanks each time the document is printed. Your document production software will merge the document and the information.

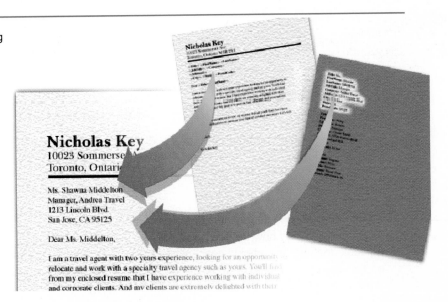

Document Production Technology

Now I'm convinced that I need a word processor—what are my options? In a consumer society, the name of the game is "variety." Consumers who shop for document production technology have a dazzling variety of hardware and software options. To get the right product and stay within your budget, you should be aware of the major product categories.

Word-processing technology includes inexpensive electronic typewriters, personal word processors, and personal computers. In Figure 3-18 you can compare the price and features of today's word-processing technologies.

Figure 3-18

Word-processing technology

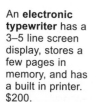

An **electronic typewriter** has a 3–5 line screen display, stores a few pages in memory, and has a built in printer. $200.

A **personal computer** set up for word-processing includes hard and floppy disk drives, and a screen. Word-processing software and a printer might need to be purchased separately. $1,500 to $2,000 including printer and software.

A **personal word processor** includes a larger screen, floppy disk drive, and printer, but does not run a large variety of other software. $400.

QuickCheck Ⓐ

1. The spread of literacy went hand-in-hand with technology developments, culminating in today's use of computers and _____ software.

2. When you type a document, it is best not to get distracted by how the final product will look. Instead, you should concentrate on expressing your ideas.
True or false? _____

3. A feature of word-processing software called _____ takes care of where to break lines of text.

4. The spell check feature of word-processing software would alert you if you accidentally used the word "see" instead of "sea" when referring to a large body of water. True or false? _____

5. A(n) _____ provides preset formats for a document, whereas a(n) _____ is a feature that coaches you step-by-step through the process of entering text into a document.

6. One of the most significant effects of computerized document production has been to encourage _____ publishing.

7. _____ has been used to establish the authorship of historical and contemporary documents.

8. Documents that are posted on the World Wide Web must be in _____ format.

B Spreadsheets and Worksheets

Mathephobia /maθ(ə) ˈfəʊbiə/ mathe after Fr *mathematiques* the abstract deductive science of number and quantity + phobia L f. Gk,f. `*phobos* denoting fear, dislike, antipathy as in hope to never take another math class again.

LAB

Spreadsheets

The United States is one of the most technological societies on earth. Therefore, the population's resistance to math, as evidenced by standardized test scores, is somewhat surprising. People with mathephobia hate to balance their checkbooks, calculate their tax returns, work out expense budgets, or decide what to do about financing their retirement.

Sensing financial opportunity, entrepreneurs have devised a number of tools to ease the burden of making calculations. To date, the most ambitious of these tools is the computerized spreadsheet. A **spreadsheet** is a numerical model or representation of a real situation. For example, your checkbook register is a sort of spreadsheet because it is a numerical representation of the cash flowing in and out of your bank account. One expert describes spreadsheets as "intuitive, natural, usable tools for financial analysis, business and mathematical modeling, decision making, simulation, and problem solving."

Using a spreadsheet is fairly straightforward. You enter the numbers you want to calculate and then indicate how you want the computer to manipulate those numbers. For example, suppose you're planning a one-week trip to Mexico to see the Mayan ruins at Chichen Itza (Figure 3-19).

Figure 3-19

Caracol at Chichen Itza

You're interested in the total cost of the trip. Using spreadsheet software, you can enter the cost of transportation, food, and lodging. Then, you can tell the computer to add these numbers together to give you a total. Does this sound like a job you can do with your trusty handheld calculator? You can, but spreadsheet software has advantages your calculator just can't provide.

A handheld calculator might be useful for simple calculations, but it becomes less convenient as you deal with more numbers and as your calculations get more complex. For example, the food and lodging calculation for the Mexico trip requires several steps as shown in Figure 3-20.

Figure 3-20

Calculations for
the Mexico Trip

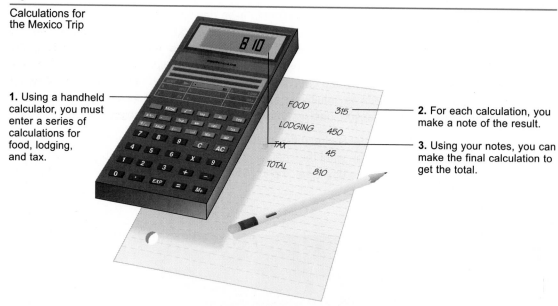

1. Using a handheld calculator, you must enter a series of calculations for food, lodging, and tax.

2. For each calculation, you make a note of the result.

3. Using your notes, you can make the final calculation to get the total.

FOOD   315
LODGING   450
TAX   45
TOTAL   810

The biggest disadvantage of most calculators is that the numbers you entered are stored, but you can't see them. You can't verify if they're accurate. Also, it is difficult to change the numbers you have entered without starting the whole calculation over again. By contrast, if you use spreadsheet software, all your numbers are visible on the screen, and they are easy to change. You can print your results as a nicely formatted report, you can convert your numbers into a graph, and you can save your work and revise it later. You can easily incorporate your calculations and results into other electronic documents, post them as Web pages, and e-mail them to your colleagues.

Spreadsheet Basics

What does a spreadsheet look like? A company that publishes spreadsheet software estimates that today there are more than 20 million people in the world busily using spreadsheets. Certainly this software has had a major effect on the way people work with numbers. What's the big attraction? To answer this question, it's important to understand how spreadsheets work.

You use spreadsheet software to create an on-screen spreadsheet called a **worksheet**. A worksheet is based on a grid of **columns** and **rows.** Each column is lettered and each row is numbered. The intersection of a column and row is called a **cell**. Each cell has a unique **address** derived from its column and row location. For example, the upper-left cell in a worksheet is cell A1 because it is in column A of row 1.

A cell can contain a number, text, or a formula. A **number** is a value that you want to use in a calculation. **Text** is used for the worksheet title and for labels that identify the numbers. For example, suppose your worksheet contains the number $2,559.81. You could use text to identify this number as "Income." A **formula** tells the computer how to use the contents of cells in calculations. You can use formulas to add, subtract, multiply, and divide numbers. Figure 3-21 illustrates a simple spreadsheet that performs subtraction to calculate savings.

Figure 3-21

A typical worksheet displays numbers and text in a grid of rows and columns. Cell B6 contains the result of a calculation performed by the spreadsheet software.

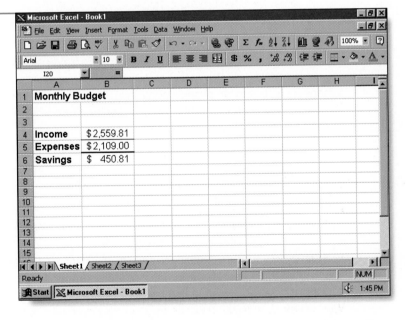

Calculations

How does spreadsheet software work? The value of spreadsheet software is the way it handles the numbers and formulas in a worksheet. Think of the worksheet as having two layers—the layer you see and a hidden layer underneath. The hidden layer can hold formulas, but the result of these formulas appears on the visible layer. Figure 3-22 shows how this works.

Figure 3-22

The formula =B4-B5 works behind the scenes to tell the computer to subtract the number in cell B5 from the number in cell B4. The formula is located in cell B6, but what appears in cell B6 is not the formula but its results.

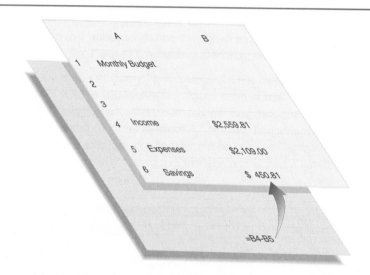

Whenever you add or change something in a cell, the spreadsheet calculates all the formulas. This means that the results displayed on your worksheet always reflect the current figures contained in the cells.

Formulas can include numbers and references to other cells. This is what gives a spreadsheet such flexibility. If you have a formula that says "subtract the contents of cell B5 from the contents of B4" it doesn't matter what those cells contain. The result will be accurate even if you later change the contents of these cells. Using **cell references** such as B5 and B4, you can create generic formulas such as =B4-B5 that work no matter how many times you change the data in these cells.

You can enter your own formulas to specify how to carry out calculations. As another option, you can select a predefined formula called a **function**. Suppose you've got a research assignment and you need to find the standard deviation of test scores for a school district. You can't find your old statistics textbook. No problem. Your spreadsheet software has a built-in function to calculate standard deviations. You just enter the test scores in a series of cells and tell the computer to use the standard deviation function for the calculation. Most spreadsheet software includes hundreds of functions for mathematical, financial, and statistical calculations.

Creating a Simple Worksheet

How do I create a simple worksheet? Building a worksheet from scratch requires thought and planning so that you end up with an accurate and well-organized worksheet. When you create your own worksheets, use these seven steps as guidelines:

InfoWeb

Spreadsheet
Tips
8

1. **Determine the main purpose of the worksheet.** Write down the purpose to make sure it is clear. For example, if you were going to make a worksheet for the Mexico trip, you might write, "The purpose of this worksheet is to calculate the total cost of a trip to Chichen Itza for one person next October."

2. **List the information available to solve the problem**. In the case of the Mexico trip, your list might include cost of airfare, number of days for the trip, daily lodging cost, the lodging tax percent, and daily food costs. Consider which of your numbers might be variable. For example, if you're planning a trip to Mexico, the number of days you'll stay might be variable—depending on what you can afford.

3. **Make a list of the calculations you'll need**. For example, your Mexico trip calculations include adding up the cost of food, lodging, and tax.

4. **Enter numbers and labels in the cells.** When you enter the numbers, make sure you put a descriptive label in an adjoining cell, usually to the left of the data. It's also a good idea to include a title at the top of the worksheet.

5. **Enter the formulas**.

6. **Test the worksheet.** There are various ways to do this that you'll learn about later, but the first question to ask yourself is "Do these results make sense?" If the results shown on the worksheet don't seem to be "in the ballpark" of what you expected, maybe you've made a typo when entering a formula. You'll need to check your numbers and formulas and make revisions until the worksheet produces correct results.

7. **Save and print the worksheet.** Figure 3-23 shows the Mexico worksheet before printing.

Figure 3-23

Mexico trip
worksheet

Every worksheet should have a title.

Documentation helps you keep track of revisions and explains how the sheet was created in case someone else needs to revise it.

Labels identify data.

These numbers are used in the formulas in column C.

In the cells that contain formulas, only the results appear.

	A	B	C	D
1	Worksheet to calculate the total			
2	cost of a trip to Mexico			
3	Created by:	Pat Graulich		
4	Latest revision:	March 12, 1997		
5				
6	Days	7		
7	Nights	6		
8				
9	Item	Cost	Total	
10	Airfare		$649.00	
11	Lodging	$75.00	$450.00	
12	Lodging tax	0.1	$45.00	
13	Food	$45.00	$315.00	
14	Total		$1,459.00	
15				

Worksheet Templates

What if I'm not sure how to set up a worksheet? If you have trouble creating a worksheet from scratch, you might find a predefined template that meets your needs. A template is essentially a worksheet form created by professionals who have done all the formatting and formulas for you. If you decide to use a template, you simply select the template you want and then fill it in with your numbers. One popular spreadsheet program offers templates for the following tasks:

- Tracking a household budget
- Deciding on the best car lease option
- Creating a business plan
- Invoicing customers
- Providing customers with a sales quote

- Creating purchase orders
- Calculating monthly loan payments
- Recording business expenses while you travel
- Tracking the time you work on various projects

Who's Responsible?

How do I know if my spreadsheet is producing correct results? The United States has more lawyers per capita than any other country in the world. In a society where lawsuits seem as common as weddings, it might be prudent to consider who is responsible for the accuracy of a spreadsheet. For example, who's fault is it when a project runs over budget because the formula to total up all the costs was not accurate?

InfoWeb

Errors
9

In a well-publicized case, a company discovered that an incomplete worksheet formula resulted in a loss of several hundreds of thousands of dollars. The company sued the spreadsheet publisher, claiming that the software was faulty. The lawsuit was dropped. Responsibility for the accuracy of a worksheet lies with the person who creates it.

In a business situation, an error in a worksheet formula can cost a company hundreds of thousands of dollars. But even if the stakes are not that high for the worksheets you create, you should make an effort to verify the accuracy of your data and formulas. The prime directive of worksheet design is "Don't rely on your worksheet until you test it." Testing, called **auditing** in spreadsheet jargon, is important.

To test a worksheet, you can enter some test data for which you already know the result. For example, if you are designing a worksheet to calculate monthly payments for a car loan, you can use a loan table to find the actual payment for a $12,000 car at 8.5% interest on a three-year loan. Then you can enter this data into your worksheet and see if the result matches the actual payment.

Another test strategy is to enter simple data that you can figure out "in your head." For example, you might enter "1" for all the numbers on the Mexico worksheet and see if the total appears accurate.

More sophisticated tests are required for more complex worksheets. Most spreadsheet software includes **auditing features** to help you find references to empty cells, cells not referenced, and formulas that reference themselves, causing a never-ending calculating loop.

Modifying Worksheets

Can I modify my spreadsheets? Modifying the text, numbers, and formulas on a worksheet is as easy as using a word processor's insert and delete features. As soon as you enter new numbers in a worksheet, the computer recalculates all the formulas, keeping the results up-to-date.

You can also modify the structure of a worksheet by inserting rows and columns, deleting rows and columns, or moving the contents of cells to other cells. Many inexperienced spreadsheet users might hesitate to make such structural changes. Why? Suppose you've created a spreadsheet and have tested all its formulas. You decide to delete row 3, which is currently blank. All the labels, numbers, and formulas move up one row. But what's happened to that formula that used to reference cells B4 and B5? Now those numbers have moved up to cells B3 and B4. Do you have to revise all the formulas on your worksheet? Happily, the answer is no.

When you insert, delete, or move cells, the spreadsheet software attempts to adjust your formulas so the cell references they contain are still accurate, as shown in Figure 3-24.

Figure 3-24

Spreadsheet software adjusts formulas when you insert or delete cells.

1. A formula in cell B6 calculates savings based on numbers in cells B4 and B5.

2. The spreadsheet software automatically changes the formula to reflect the new location of the Income and Expenses numbers.

What if you don't want the formula to change? You can define any reference in a formula as an absolute reference. An **absolute reference** never changes when you insert rows or copy or move formulas. Understanding when to use absolute references is one of the key aspects to developing spreadsheet design expertise.

Spreadsheet "Intelligence"

In what sense is spreadsheet software intelligent? When mainframe computers first made the headlines in the 1950s, they had an unsettling effect on the American public. And no wonder. Headlines dubbed these computers "Giant Brains," and journalists speculated how long it might be until computers "took over." The public was pacified when word spread that computers could only follow the instructions of their human programmers.

Fifty years have passed since the Giant Brain headlines appeared. Computer technology has improved to the point where it sometimes seems that computers do have some sort of intelligence—or at least they seem to anticipate what you want them to do. You'll run into some examples of this when you use spreadsheet software.

An example that you'll recognize as soon as you begin to use spreadsheet software is its ability to distinguish between the data you're using for text and the data you're using for numbers. At first this might seem easy—text is letters and numbers are, well, numbers. But suppose that you want to enter a social security number in a cell. When you enter 375-80-9876 should the spreadsheet regard this as the subtraction formula—375 minus 80 minus 9876? Should the spreadsheet regard this as a single number 375809876 that can be used for mathematical operations? Or should the spreadsheet regard this as text that can not be mathematically manipulated? The answer is that your spreadsheet software will regard 375-80-9876 as text. If you think about this, you'll see that is correct. Even though we call these social security numbers, we don't add, subtract, multiply, or divide them. We treat them as text.

Shortcuts are another example of spreadsheet "intelligence." Spreadsheet software contains many handy shortcuts to help simplify the process of creating, editing, and formatting a worksheet. For example, fill operations continue a series you have started. Type "January" in one cell and "February" in the next, then use a fill operation and the spreadsheet will automatically enter the rest of the months in the next 10 cells. Fill operations also complete numerical sequences such as "1, 2, 3, 4.." or "1990, 1995, 2000…". Figure 3-25 shows how a fill operation works.

Figure 3-25

Filling cells with data

1. Type the first few numbers in a series.

2. The spreadsheet software will fill in the rest of the series.

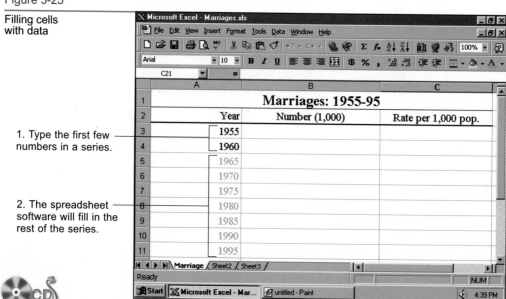

Formatting Worksheets

Does spreadsheet software provide formatting options similar to those provided by word-processing software? As the business world embraced spreadsheets, sharing them with colleagues, employees, and customers became important. Today, business meetings have an element of theater as computer projection devices display full-screen, full-color, beautifully formatted worksheets.

Spreadsheet software provides you with formatting options to improve the appearance of your worksheet. The formatting you use for a spreadsheet depends on your output plan. Worksheets that you intend to print might be formatted differently from worksheets that you intend to view only on the screen. Worksheets that you want to project for presentations often require a format different from printed worksheets.

Worksheets for routine calculations are much handier to use if you can see all the information without scrolling, so try to place all the labels, numbers, and formulas on one screen. If necessary, you can make the columns narrow so that more of them fit on the screen. If you're creating a worksheet for your own use, there's probably no need to spend time making it look attractive.

If you are going to print your spreadsheet, you'll want to spend some time creating an attractive format. Use a larger font for the title, and consider italicizing or boldfacing important numbers and their labels. Your worksheet will look more polished if you omit the grid lines between rows and columns. As when you format documents with a word processor, maintain a liberal amount of white space on the page. However, don't try to skip every other row to give the appearance of double spacing. If you do this, you'll have trouble graphing this data. Figure 3-26 provides some tips for improving the Mexico worksheet.

Figure 3-26

Formatting for a printed worksheet

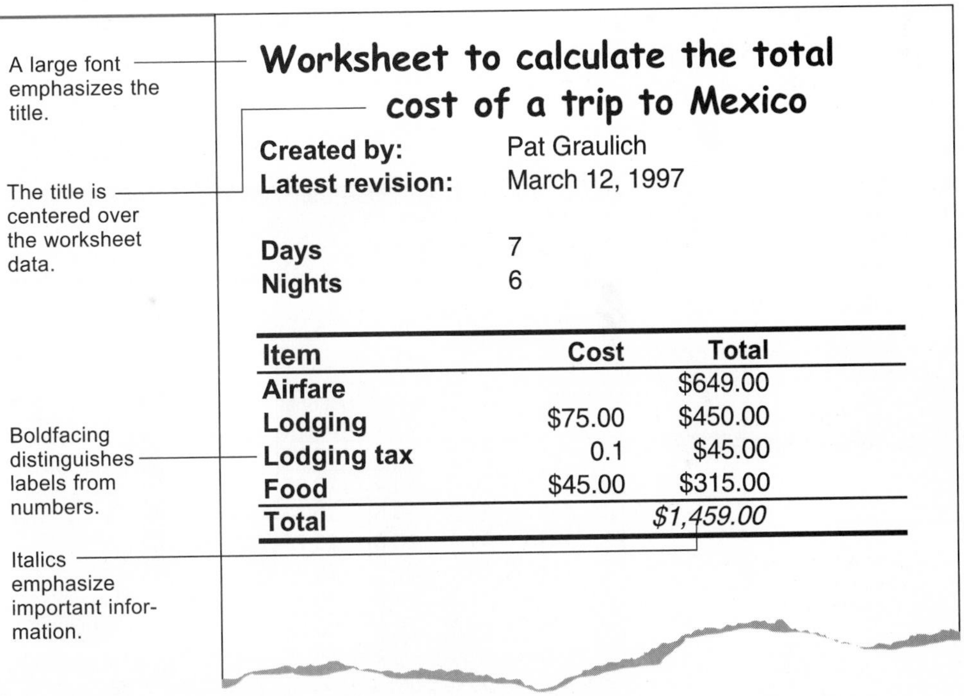

A large font emphasizes the title.

The title is centered over the worksheet data.

Boldfacing distinguishes labels from numbers.

Italics emphasize important information.

Worksheet to calculate the total cost of a trip to Mexico

Created by: Pat Graulich
Latest revision: March 12, 1997

Days   7
Nights   6

Item	Cost	Total
Airfare		$649.00
Lodging	$75.00	$450.00
Lodging tax	0.1	$45.00
Food	$45.00	$315.00
Total		*$1,459.00*

Spreadsheets for presentations must be legible when displayed by a projection device. You might consider a larger type size—one that can be easily viewed from the back of the room in which your worksheet will be projected. Scrolling is usually not desirable in a presentation situation, so try to fit the worksheet on one screen. You might have to move the documentation to another worksheet of the workbook to make room for the data and results that are important to your audience. Place your graphs on other pages of your workbook so you don't have to scroll to display them.

The use of color will make your presentation more interesting and help to highlight important data on the worksheet. However, if you are also planning to print your worksheet in black and white, select your colors carefully. Colors appear in shades of gray on a black-and-white printout. Some colors produce a dark shade of gray that obscures labels and numbers. Figure 3-27 provides some tips for formatting worksheets for presentations.

Figure 3-27

Spreadsheets for presentations should use large fonts and colors.

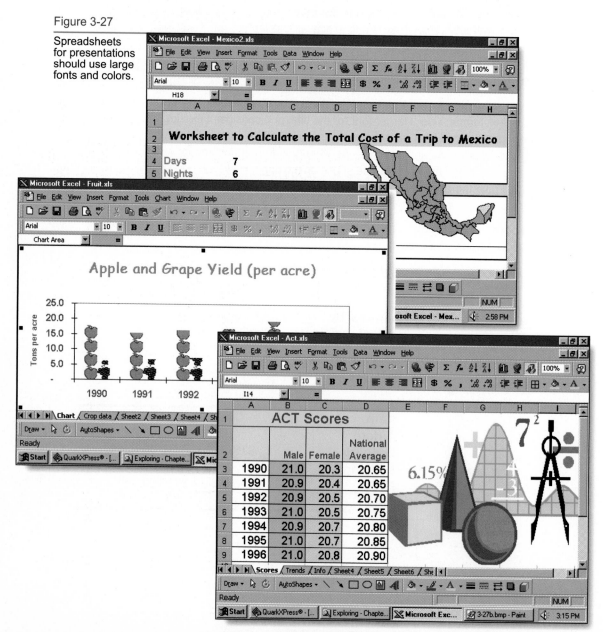

The Monkey's Paw

What about graphs and charts? During the 1992 Presidential election, the candidates jumped on the "one picture is worth a thousand words" bandwagon. This precipitated a parade of media events in which candidates spoke with great solemnity about trend lines, investments, and deficits against a backdrop of colorful charts and graphs. Especially noteworthy was Ross Perot brandishing a mummified monkey's paw to explain his opponent's policy of "voodoo economics" on a series of graphs (Figure 3-28).

Figure 3-28

Ross Perot used graphs during campaign '92.

Spreadsheet software is characterized by its ability to easily create professional-looking graphs and charts. Remember the unsatisfactory results you got by using graph paper and colored pencils? With spreadsheet software it is simple to create an attractive pie graph that illustrates opinion poll data, a line graph that drives home the alarming increase in the national debt, or a bar graph that compares market share for U.S. and foreign automobile manufacturers.

InfoWeb

Lie
11

Graphs, as you know, provide a quick summary or overview of a set of data. Trends that might be difficult to detect in columns of figures come into focus when skillfully graphed. Graphs are an effective presentation tool because they are simple to understand and visually interesting. However, when you design graphs, you have a responsibility to your audience to create a visual representation of the truth. Although you might not intentionally design a graph to "lie" it is all too easy to design a graph that implies something other than the truth. For example, which of the two graphs from Figure 3-29 do you think a sales manager would prefer to show?

The sales figures represented by the graph on the right certainly look better than those on the left. Look closely. The sales figures on both graphs are the same, but by changing the shape of the graph, the trend in sales can look either pretty tame or very dramatic. When you design a graph, try to consider how the average person would interpret it, then make sure that interpretation coincides with reality.

Figure 3-29

Graphs can "stretch the truth."

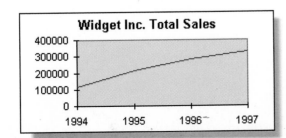

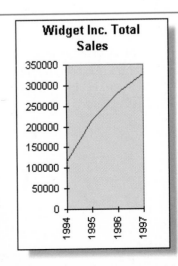

Claw Your Way to the Top with Spreadsheet Software

In what situations can I use spreadsheet software? Computerized spreadsheet software was invented in 1978 by a Harvard Business School student, Dan Bricklin. Many computer historians believe that his software, called VisiCalc, not only launched a new genre of computer software, but also put a rocket under the fledgling microcomputer industry and launched the Digital Age. Before the availability of VisiCalc, consumers couldn't think of much use for a personal computer. VisiCalc provided business people with a handy tool for making calculations without visiting a statistician or accountant. It contained all the basic elements of today's electronic spreadsheets—a screen-based grid of rows and columns, predefined functions, automatic calculations, formatting options, and rudimentary "intelligence" for copying and replicating formulas.

A spreadsheet works well for recording and graphing data, for making calculations, and for constructing numerical models of the real world. The main advantage of spreadsheet software is the time it saves—once you create a worksheet, you can change your data without redoing all your calculations. In addition, worksheet data is stored in electronic format so it can be merged with word-processing documents, posted on the Internet, or transmitted as part of an e-mail message.

Figure 3-30

Claw Your Way to the Top

In his tongue-in-cheek book, *Claw Your Way to the Top* (Figure 3-30), Dave Barry defines a spreadsheet as "a kind of program that lets you sit at your desk and ask all kinds of neat 'what if?' questions and generate thousands of numbers instead of actually working." The what-if questions are part of a process called spreadsheet modeling.

Spreadsheet modeling means setting up numbers in a worksheet to describe a real-world situation. For example, spreadsheets are often used for business modeling. The worksheet data represents or describes the financial activities in a business—products sold, expenses for employees, rent, inventory and so forth. By looking at the numbers in such a business model, you can get an idea of its current profitability. You can also experiment with changing some of the numbers in the model to see how changes in business activities might affect profitability. The process of setting up a model and experimenting with different numbers is often referred to as **what-if analysis**.

What-if analysis is certainly a useful tool. Imagine having answers to questions such as "What if I get an A on my next two economics exams? But what if I get Bs?"; "What if I invest $100 a month in my retirement plan? But what if I invest $200 a month?"; "What if our sales reps increase sales by 10%? But what if sales decline by 5%?"; "What if I take out a 30-year mortgage at 8.5%? But what if I take out a 15-year mortgage at 7.75%?". Spreadsheets make these questions easy to answer.

Spreadsheet software is applicable in just about every profession. Educators use spreadsheets for grade books and analyzing test scores. Farmers use spreadsheets to keep track of crop yield, to calculate the amount of seed to purchase, and to estimate expenses and profits for the coming year. At home, spreadsheets help you balance your checkbook, keep track of household expenses, track your savings and investments, and calculate your taxes.

Entrepreneurs use spreadsheets to define business plans. Corporate executives use spreadsheets to keep tabs on finances. Athletes use spreadsheets to track training programs and sports statistics. Contractors use spreadsheets to make bids on construction projects. Scientists use spreadsheets to analyze data from experiments. The list goes on and on. You'll want to consider how spreadsheets can help you in your career field.

QuickCheck B

1. In a spreadsheet grid, each _____ is lettered, each _____ is numbered.

2. B3 and B4 are called cell _____ .

3. Most spreadsheet software includes hundreds of predefined formulas called _____ for mathematical, financial, and statistical calculations.

4. A worksheet that will be viewed on the screen would generally be formatted differently than a worksheet that will be printed in black and white. True or false? _____

5. When you move or copy a cell, a spreadsheet typically adjusts any formulas in that cell relative to their original position. You must use an absolute reference if you don't want the formula to change. True or false? _____

6. The spreadsheet software publisher is responsible for the validity of the figures and formulas in your worksheets. True or false? _____

7. The process of setting up a model and experimenting with different numbers is often referred to as _____ analysis.

Databases

LAB

Databases

Sometime in the middle of this century our industrial society began to evolve into an information society. The way we live has changed in many ways. We more frequently interact with information, we enter careers connected to information management, we increasingly attach a cash value to information, we tend to depend on information, and we are becoming aware of the potential problems that can occur when information is misused.

The Information Age is fueled by an explosion of data that is collected and generated by individuals, corporations, and government agencies. Some experts estimate that the amount of information doubles every year. This information is stored in an uncountable number of databases, most of them computerized. In the course of an ordinary day, you're likely to interact with more than one of these databases. It's pretty clear, then, that understanding and using databases is an important skill for living in the Information Age (Figure 3-31).

Figure 3-31

The rock group Police sings "Too much information running through my brain. Too much information, driving me insane."

The term "database" is a slippery thing. There is a technical definition of the term, but it is largely ignored in popular usage. In this section, we'll focus on the popular rendition of databases, using a broad, non-technical definition. We'll define a **database** as a collection of information stored on one or more computers.

In this section, we'll also focus on software that's designed to search for information in databases, rather than on database management software that's designed to create and manipulate databases. You might like this approach because it's so practical. Of 100 times that you encounter a database, 95 of those times you'll be looking for information, not creating or adding information.

Structured and Free-Form Databases

What kind of databases am I likely to use? In a typical day, you're likely to encounter many types of databases such as a library card catalog, your bank's database of checking and savings account balances, CD-ROM encyclopedias, the computer's directory of files, and your e-mail address book. You might also have experience interacting with collections of information accessed via the Internet such as Web sites devoted to hip-hop music, the stock market, the job market, or travel.

Databases come in two flavors: structured databases and free-form databases. A **structured database** (also called a **structured data file**) is a file of information organized in a uniform format of records and fields. Figure 3-32 shows an example of a record from a structured database for a library card catalog.

Figure 3-32

A structured database

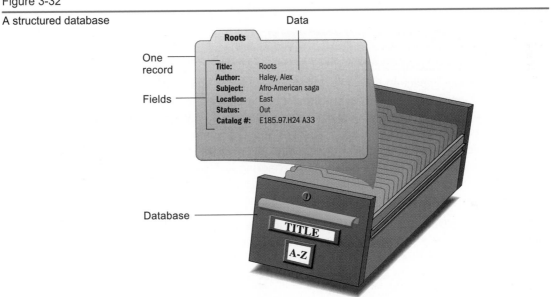

Structured databases typically store data that describes a collection of similar entities. A medical database stores data for a collection of patients. An inventory database stores data for a collection of items stocked on store and warehouse shelves.

A **free-form database** is a loosely structured collection of information, usually stored as documents, rather than as records. You might consider the collection of word-processing documents stored on your computer to be a free-form database of your own writing. A CD-ROM containing documents and videos of the Civil War would be another example. The World Wide Web, with its millions of documents stored worldwide, is another example of a free-form database. Whether stored on your hard disk, a CD-ROM, or the Internet, free-form databases have the potential to contain varied and useful information for you as a student or as a career professional.

Searching for Information

How do I find the information I'm looking for in a database? When you're searching for information, as opposed to creating and maintaining a database, you typically don't need to know whether you're accessing a structured database or a free-form database because your data access software hides the details of the database structure. **Data access software** is the interface you use to search for information in a database. You tell the data access software what you're looking for, and it will attempt to find it. The data access software understands the structure and details of the database, so you don't need to.

Different databases inevitably use different data access software. Therefore, becoming an effective information gatherer in the Information Age requires you to be flexible and willing to learn different searching procedures for different data access software. Depending on your data access software, you might enter your search specifications using a menu, a hypertext index, a keyword search engine, a query by example, a query language, or a natural language.

Menus and Hypertext Indexes

What's the easiest way to access database information? The Information Age has had a major impact on our lives. Consider how it has changed the way we do our banking. Information is now the basic product of the banking industry. As one expert points out, "Money is today only a special case of information." You've probably used your bank's phone-in automated account information system that asks you to "press 1 for account information, press 2 for help with your PIN number" and so on. Such a system is your interface to the bank's database of checking and savings account information. With so many people using this type of database, access must be simple. Therefore, most access software for bank customers is based on menus.

The collection of choices you're given to interact with a database is referred to as a **menu**. Database menus are similar to those you use in most other software. Menus that access database information can be screen-based or audio. Menus are typically arranged as a hierarchy, so that after you make a choice at the first level of the menu, a second series of choices appears.

The trick to using telephone menus is to put your finger over the best choice as you hear it. Leave your finger there until you hear a better choice. Then when the voice is through explaining the menu options, you don't have to recall the number of the one you want. Screen-based menus are easier to use because you always have all the options in view. For this reason, they can also be more complex, displaying many options on multiple levels. If you frequently use the same menu-based data access software, you'll become more proficient at gathering information if you try to envision the hierarchy of menus.

Screen-based menus have become a popular format for providing access to information via the Internet. Yahoo!, one of the most popular indexes to the Internet World Wide Web, features what is sometimes called a **hypertext index** that links you to information in categories such as education, entertainment, and business. To use a hypertext index such as Yahoo!, you select a general category such as News. Yahoo! then presents you with a list of news topics. You might select Politics from this list. Yahoo! will then show you another list from which to choose. Eventually, after you have navigated enough lists, you'll see a document containing the information you were seeking. Figure 3-33 shows Yahoo!'s hypertext index.

Figure 3-33

Yahoo!'s hypertext index

1. Select News and Media.

2. From the News and Media list, select Politics.

3. From the list of political information, select Today's White House Press Release.

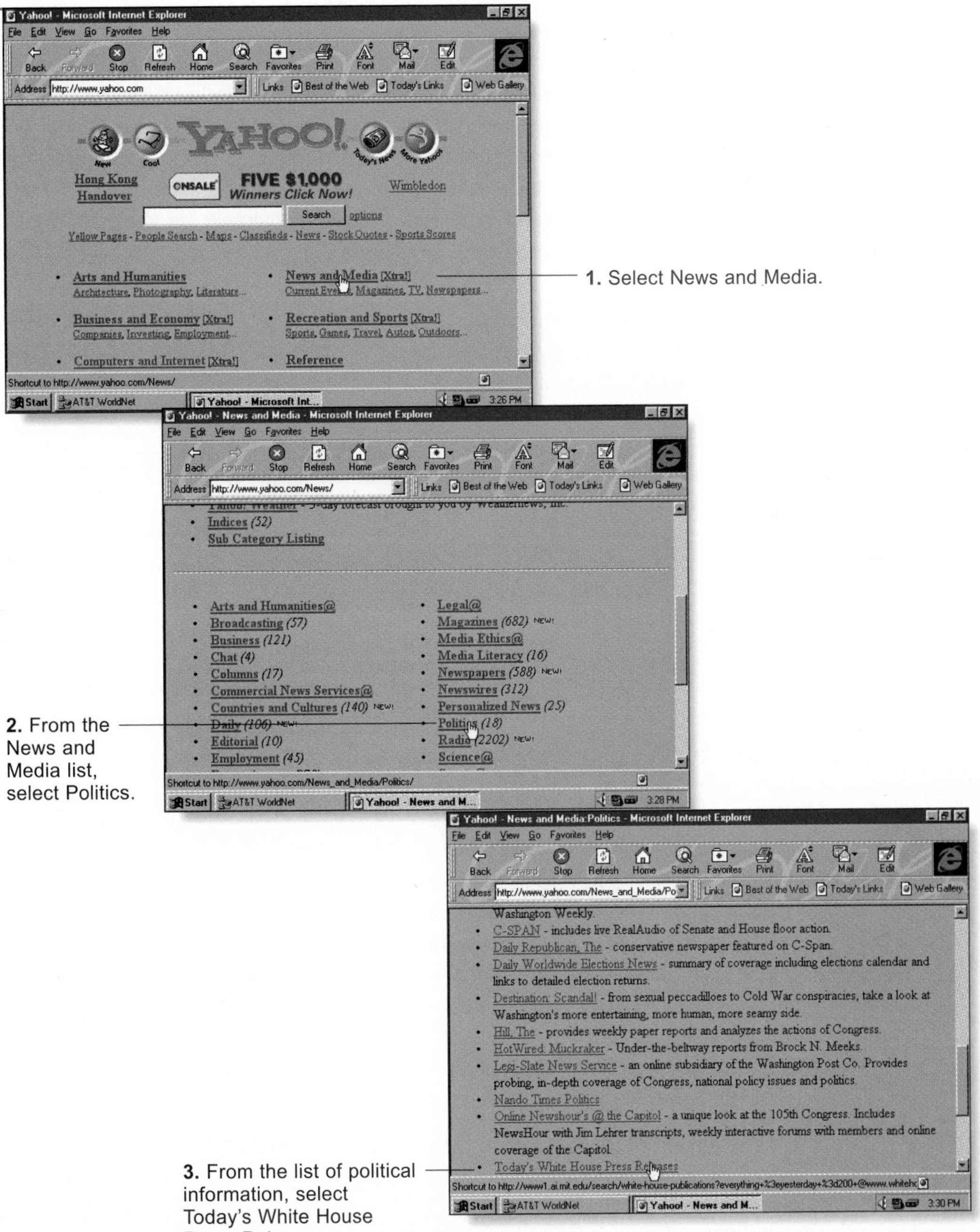

Keyword Searches

What if I don't want to wander through all the levels of a menu to find information?

InfoWeb

Information
Science
11

Libraries have influenced the way we organize information. Traditionally, we have found it handy to place information into categories, for example, following John Dewey's classifications or those of the Library of Congress. Therefore, it seems natural to use similar classifications to organize electronic information, such as World Wide Web documents. Yahoo!'s menu structure, for example, reflects such a classification scheme. However, not everything can be neatly classified. Now, using the power and speed of computers, you can search for information by keyword, instead of by topic.

A **keyword search engine** lets you access data without slogging through a menu of subject categories. Keyword search engines are especially popular for searching through the many documents stored in a free-form database such as the World Wide Web. To use a keyword search engine, you simply type in a word such as "parties" and the search engine locates related information. Usually, it shows you short summaries of the documents that contain the word you typed. You can then select those documents you think are most useful. The user interface for a keyword search engine is usually very simple, as shown in Figure 3-34.

Figure 3-34

A keyword search engine has a simple user interface.

Enter your search topic here, then click the Go Get It button to begin the search.

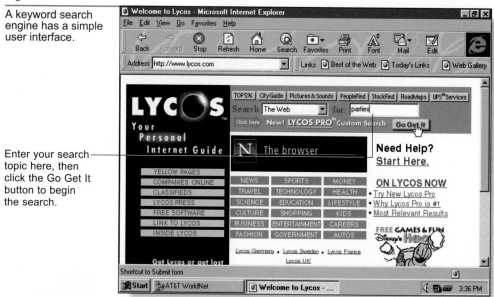

InfoWeb

Search
Engines
12

A search for a broad topic such as "parties" generally provides too much information. Therefore, search engines allow you to compose "expert" searches using more specific search criteria. For example, you could search for the *phrase* "political parties" to limit your search to the political arena. You could use *operators* such as "and" and "or" to look for more than one specific item as in the search for "democratic party *and* political conventions." You can also specify whether you want an exact match or an "in the ballpark" match. If you ask for an exact match to "political parties" you won't get articles on party politics.

Although different keyword search engines have similar features, their user interfaces are likely to be somewhat different. Happily, these differences are mostly cosmetic. Almost every search engine lets you enter topics, define expert searches, and specify the strength of the match. Therefore, many of the general skills you learn using one search engine apply when you use other search engines.

Query by Example (QBE)

What about finding data in structured databases? Remember the scene at the end of the film *Raiders of the Lost Ark*? Indiana Jones' valuable archeological discovery is unloaded from a forklift in a cavernous government warehouse full of crates and boxes. How long would it take to find it again?

Today, we expect to have information instantly. We want to know our bank balance right away. We want our Social Security checks on time. We want our tax refunds sooner, rather than later. We don't want to wait for a clerk to run back to the dairy aisle to check the price of a carton of yogurt.

When the information in a database needs to be accessed quickly, it is usually stored as a structured database. Because of its structure, a computer can generally locate data in a structured database faster than it can locate information in a free-form database. For example, in a warehouse database, the description of an item is stored in a particular field. Suppose you tell the computer to find the records for any item described as "Lost Ark." The computer will look at the description field of each record until it finds a record containing the words "Lost Ark."

Although computers can more easily find information in structured databases, the structure can cause a problem for humans. The problem is that users might not know the format for the records in a database. For example, how would you know whether an online library card catalog stores book titles in a field called Title, BookTitle, or T? Is the title the first field? Or does the first field contain the name of the author? One way to help users search structured databases is by providing a **query by example** (QBE for short) user interface like the one shown in Figure 3-35.

Figure 3-35

When you use a QBE interface, you see a blank record on the screen. Into this record you enter examples of what you want the computer to find. In this case, the user is looking for a book published in 1993 or later that includes "Economics" in the title.

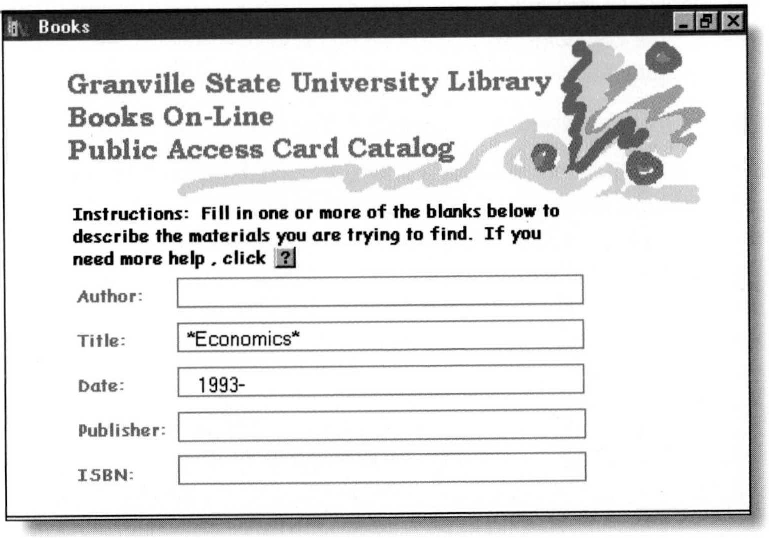

Books

Granville State University Library
Books On-Line
Public Access Card Catalog

Instructions: Fill in one or more of the blanks below to describe the materials you are trying to find. If you need more help , click [?]

Author:

Title: *Economics*

Date: 1993-

Publisher:

ISBN:

In Figure 3-35 the user has entered *Economics* in the title field to indicate the word economics should appear somewhere in the title of the book. "Economics" (without the asterisks) would tell the computer to find books titled only "Economics." As you might guess from this example, using QBE requires you to learn a few "tricks" such as the use of the asterisk and dash. Different QBE software might use different symbols. Your best bet when using a new QBE is to read the help instructions carefully before you set up your query.

Query Languages and Natural Language

Can I just type in a question to find information? Many science fiction writers and film-makers have speculated about the impact on society of intelligent computers and robots. Of course, one aspect of such intelligence would be the ability to understand human speech. It would be handy if we could access databases in the same way we describe the type of data we wanted to find to a research librarian (Figure 3-36). The first step in this direction is the use of query languages.

Figure 3-36

Robots with intelligence are a common theme in science fiction and films. When will computers respond to our database queries with the insight of a skilled reference librarian?

A **query language** is a set of command words that you can use to direct the computer to create databases, locate information, sort records, and change the data in those records. In situations where fairly sophisticated users want to access a structured database, a query language provides good flexibility for pin-pointing information.

To use a query language, you need to know the command words and the grammar or syntax that will let you construct valid query "sentences." For example, the SQL query language command word to find records is "select." When you type the command "select *" the computer will look for all records. To locate all the Byzantine statues in an art museum database you would enter an SQL query something like this:

Select * from artworks where style = 'Byzantine' and media = 'statue'

Before you can compose such a query, you must have a fairly extensive knowledge of the database and its structure. You must know that the name of the database is "artworks." You must also know that the artistic style of each work is stored in a field called "Style" and that works are categorized as painting, statue, pottery, and so on, in a field called "Media." You can see that this interface is not suitable for casual users. Imagine if you had to compose SQL queries to use your library card catalog! Many people would find it easier to just wander around the stacks.

Advances in artificial intelligence have made some progress in the ability of computers to understand queries formulated in a **natural language** such as English, French, or Japanese. To make such natural language queries you don't need to learn an esoteric query language. Instead, you just enter questions such as:

What Byzantine statues are in our museum collection?

Computers still have some interpretation difficulties arising from ambiguities in human languages, so the use of natural language query software is not yet widespread.

Using Search Results

What can I do with the information I find? The power of information comes not only from finding it, but from using it. In an information-rich society, finding information that is astonishing, amusing, and informative is not difficult. Finding information that is bizarre, offensive, destructive, and confidential is not difficult either. Keep in mind that the information you seek, collect, and disperse is a reflection of your values and ethics. It seems that laws and regulations on the publication and use of information in electronic form have not kept up with the technology. Therefore, it is up to you to "use it, but don't abuse it." Once you find information in a database, you can use it in a number of ways.

Print it. When you find information in a structured database, you can generally print out a single record or a list of selected records. You might want to print a particular record, for example, if you're looking through a real estate database and find your dream house. In another scenario, suppose you were looking in the ERIC database to find some academic articles for a paper you're writing about male role models in elementary schools. You could print out a list of article titles and the journals in which they appeared. If call numbers for the journals are available, including that information on the printout would make it much easier to locate the articles in your library.

Copy and Paste. Most of today's graphical user interfaces provide a way to highlight database information you see on the screen and copy it to a worksheet or document. This technique is especially useful with the information you find in free-form databases because often you want just the information from one section of one document. For example, suppose you've been cruising the Internet for information on forest canopies for your botany seminar. You locate a Green Peace document that contains relevant information. Figure 3-37 shows you how to copy this information from the Web to one of your own word-processing documents.

Figure 3-37

Copy and paste

1. Highlight the text you want to copy.

2. Then, click the Edit menu, then select Copy. The text is copied to a special area of computer memory called the Clipboard. You can now switch to your word-processing software and paste the text into a document.

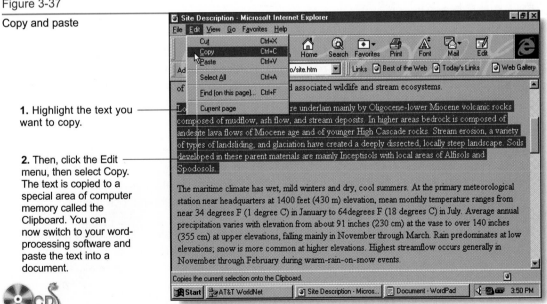

Export it. You might find some data that you want to analyze or graph using spreadsheet software. Many databases automatically **export data** by transforming it into a format that's acceptable to your spreadsheet software. If your database does not have this capability, your spreadsheet software might be able to **import data** by reading the database data and translating it into a worksheet. As another option, your spreadsheet software might include a wizard to help you transport data between databases and worksheets.

Save it. When you find a group of records in a structured database that you want to work with later, your database software might provide you with an option to save the records as a file on a hard or floppy disk. If you opt for this route, you should be aware that to manipulate the records later you are likely to need the same database software that was originally used to enter and create the records. This is not always practical, so you might have to use export or copy options instead. If you find data on the Web, the software you're using to access the information usually provides you with a way to save it on your own computer. This is particularly useful if you find a long document that you want to read at your leisure.

Transmit it. Today, we're plugged into a "global village" where e-mail arrives just minutes after it was sent and where you can "chat" online with people from countries all over the world. You can electronically distribute the information you collect; an easy way is to insert information into e-mail messages. A more ambitious project would be to develop your own World Wide Web site from which people could view Web pages and download databases.

Whether you print, import, copy, save, or transmit the data you find in databases, it is your responsibility to use it appropriately. Respect copyrights by giving credit to the original author in a footnote or end note. The information in corporate and government databases is often confidential. When you have access to such data, respect the privacy of the individuals who are the subject of the data. Don't divulge the information you find or introduce inaccuracies into the database.

QuickCheck C

1. In popular terminology, a(n) _____ is a collection of information stored on one or more computers.

2. A(n) _____ database is a file of information organized in a uniform format of records and fields, whereas a(n) _____ database is a loosely structured collection of information.

3. Menus, keyword searches, query by example, a query language, and natural language are all methods used to _____ information in a database.

4. To use a keyword search engine, you simply type in a word such as "music" and the search engine locates all related information in the database. True or false? _____

5. When using a(n) _____ user interface to search a database, you use a blank record to enter examples of the data you want the computer to find.

6. A(n) _____ such as SQL consists of a set of command words that you can use to direct the computer to create databases, locate information, sort records, and change the data in those records.

7. Once you locate information in a database, you can print it, export it to other software packages, copy and paste it into other software, save it for future reference, or transmit it. True or false? _____

User Focus

D Putting It All Together

You shouldn't finish this chapter with the impression that you use only one software tool per project. It is true that word-processing, spreadsheet, and database software tools each have their own strengths. But you often can be more productive if you use the tools together. Suppose you are writing a report. How can you use the tools you've learned about to gather information, organize it, analyze it, and report your results?

Researching a Topic

Where do I start? Got to write a paper, but you find yourself staring at a blank sheet of paper or a blank computer screen? Just take one step at a time. Use your technology tools. You'll be surprised at how fast your paper materializes.

InfoWeb

Online
Card
Catalogs
13

First, choose your topic. Then browse around your library and the Internet to find sources of information. Whereas most research once took place in library buildings, the trend today is to use a computer to search online. From your home or office you can look through millions of Web documents and search through the card catalogs of many libraries, including the Library of Congress.

You might want to make photocopies of interesting articles, check out relevant books, and save any information you find on the Web. If you seem to be finding bits and pieces of information on the Web, copy and paste these bits into a document you create with word-processing software. Don't worry about the organization of the document for now. Just think of it as notes that you can use later.

Make sure you keep track of where you obtain your information. Make a note of the magazine name and issue date on any photocopies you make. For information you gather from the Internet, make note of its source. Every document on the World Wide Web has a unique address called a URL. Most Web browser software has a setting to include the URL on any Web pages you send to your printer. If you note the URL for every bit of information you gather, you will be able to give credit to the authors in your final report. Figure 3-38 illustrates a Web page URL.

Figure 3-38

A Web page
URL

Make sure that as part of your information-gathering activities, you have a way to distinguish which information you copy verbatim and which information you have paraphrased using your own words. You might simply put quotes around the material that you copied verbatim, as you would in your final draft. This will help keep you honest about which parts of the report are your own work.

Organizing and Analyzing Information

How do I add my own viewpoint and analysis to the report? After you collect information, you need to read through it and think about what it means. What are the trends? What are the controversies? What stands out as interesting? With this background, you can determine what you want to say.

Begin a new document using your word-processing software and type in your main point. You should be able to write this as a single, clear sentence. Use the editing features of your software to work on this sentence until it is perfect.

The next step is to create an outline of items that will support your main point. Use the outlining feature of your word processor to type in the headings and subheadings for your report. Refer back to the information you have gathered when you need to. You can have two or more documents open at the same time when you use word-processing software, so it's easy to flip back and forth between the document that contains your outline and the one that contains your research notes.

With your outline in place you can begin to move your research notes into the appropriate places in your outline. Use the copy and paste feature while both documents are open to make this process a breeze.

Figure 3-39

Don't forget to proofread your work!

Of course, you don't want your paper to simply be a collage of other people's work. As a rule of thumb, in your final paper at least 8 of every 10 paragraphs should be your own words. Now is your chance to add your viewpoint and skillfully weave together the facts. Don't be misled into thinking that paraphrasing just means rearranging a few words in each of the sentences you copied from someone else's work. If you're tempted to do this, read your research note, then delete it and rewrite it completely using your own words.

Work on your document until you're satisfied, then run a spell check and a grammar check if one is available. Don't forget to proofread it (Figure 3-39)!

Before you finalize the content of your paper, you might consider if some sections would be clearer if you included a graph or other illustration. You can use spreadsheet software to create graphs for data you have gathered. You can use your copy and paste commands to insert the graphs into your document.

When you're happy with the content of your document save it on disk. Make an extra copy of your work on a different disk, just to be safe. You might also want to print your paper, even though you have not formatted it yet. If you lose your electronic copies, you can then still reconstruct it from the printout.

Following a Style Guide

How do I know how to format my paper? If you have not been provided with style guide-lines from your instructor or boss, you should follow a standard style manual such as the *Publication Manual of the American Psychological Association*, *The Chicago Manual of Style*, or Turabian's *Guide to Style*. These manuals tell you how large to make your margins, what to include in headers and footers, how to label graphs and illustrations, how to format your footnotes or end notes correctly, and so forth. You'll use the formatting features of your word-processing software to follow the style guidelines.

InfoWeb

Internet
Citations
14

A style guide devotes many pages to the correct format for the book and magazine citations you include at the end of a paper or in footnotes. But what is the correct citation format for materials you use from Web pages or other Internet sources? Most style guides are now including this information. If your style guide does not, you can access one of several Web sites that provide formats for electronic citations.

Presentations

What if I have to give a speech? If you're going to present your report, you need some speaking notes and some visual aides. Create your speaking notes using your word-processing software. Use a large boldface font and double or triple spacing. After you print these notes, use different color highlighters to mark the first word in each para-graph. This will help you keep your place as you speak.

Visual aids could mean handouts or computer-generated "slides." Consider whether an out-line, graph, list of important points, or graphics would be most useful for your audience. Your word-processing software can help you produce printed handouts. Your spreadsheet soft-ware might help you put together a few graphs to support your main point. You could also consider using **presentation software** to create a computer-generated slide presentation (Figure 3-40). You could include an opening graphic, a list of important points, and a graph. Don't forget to practice before you're "on stage!"

As you continue to work with electronic documents, you'll discover even more "tricks" for harnessing their features to increase your productivity and the quality of your work. Watch for tips in magazines and newspapers, on computer TV shows, and on the Web.

Figure 3-40

Use presentation software to create effective visual aids.

EndNote

In today's computing environment, you can hardly avoid using computer-based documents, worksheets, and databases. The software you use to manipulate these documents provides you with tools that can improve the quality of your work. It also can provide considerable savings for previously tedious tasks such as typing the final draft of a document—and getting it perfect!

But don't expect to pare down the time you spend on projects such as a written report or essay. It seems that because your tools allow you to do more, you *will* do more. You'll spend more time gathering information because now with the Internet much more information is available. You'll do more editing because it's so easy. You'll grammar check your documents because you end up with clearer writing. And you'll spend a little time creating a graph because it adds a professional touch to your final package.

With today's software tools, you'll work smarter and produce better work, but your time commitment will remain about the same. Get yourself a scheduler if you don't have one already. Procrastination doesn't work today—any more than it worked before you used word-processing, spreadsheet, and database tools.

InfoWeb

InfoWeb

Chapter
Links

The InfoWeb is your guide to print, film, television, and electronic resources. Use it to obtain updates on quickly changing technical information and to locate information for research papers. If you're using the New Perspectives CD-ROM, click the InfoWeb icon on the left side of this paragraph to access the online InfoWeb links. Otherwise, use your Web browser and type in the address of the New Perspectives site: www.cciw.com/np3. At the New Perspectives site you'll find up-to-date links to the topics covered in this chapter.

1 Literacy

We assume that everyone can read and write, but that is not true in either North America or around the world. According to the UN, almost 97% of adult populations in Western developed countries are literate. But the media in the U.S. often claims that 20 to 30% of Americans are functionally illiterate—they cannot read well enough to understand a newspaper, understand a paycheck stub, or complete a simple form. What is the cause of this discrepancy? It all depends on how you measure literacy and illiteracy, and there are many ways to do so. "Measuring the Nation's Literacy: Important Considerations" by Terrence Wiley from the ERIC Digest at **www.ed.gov/databases/ERIC_Digests/ed334870.html** will fill you in on the problems of defining and measuring illiteracy. Literacy is important because how well you read and write influences your ability to participate in economic, social, and political life. Although nearly 10 years old, the classic book **Illiterate America** by Jonathan Kozol (New American Library Trade, 1988) will give you a good start in understanding the problems of illiteracy, why literacy is critical to success in life, and what you can do about illiteracy. On the World Wide Web, connect to Summer Institute of Linguistics at **www.sil.org** where you can find information about literacy around the world and the connection between economic development and literacy. At the Laubach Literacy Web site, **www.laubach.org**, you can find information about volunteer-based literacy programs around the world.

2 Typing

Gregory Arakelian holds the record as the world's fastest typist at 158 words per minute. A "good" typist's speed is around 60 words per minute. If you are still hunting and pecking, you might want to try working with a typing tutor, such as **Typing Tutor VII** or **Typing Instructor Deluxe CD**. To learn more about typing tutorial software and some tidbits about typewriters and typing, read the article "Time to Start Typing?" at **www.zdnet.com/familypc/content/960819/columns/parental/960819.html**. Some researchers claim that the arrangement of keys on the QWERTY keyboard limits typing speed. Read the article "Typing Errors" at the Reason Online site, **www.reasonmag.com/9606/Fe.QWERTY.html**, for a different discussion of the facts. At the Mavis Beacon Teaches Typing Web site, **www.mavisbeacon.com**, you can find information about the history of typing, links to information on repetitive stress injuries, and more.

3 Improve your Writing

The World Wide Web has many, many resources for writers of all experience and talents. A number of universities have online writing labs that offer writing tips, style guidelines, and advice about conducting research for and writing term papers. An excellent example is The Writing Place at Northwestern University which offers the Working Writers Project at **www.writing.nwu.edu/wwriters/heller.html**. This project is a collection of talks given by professional writers at Northwestern University on the art and craft of writing. For non-fiction writing, the book **The Complete Guide to Writing Nonfiction** by the American Society of

Journalists and Authors (Harper & Row, 1988) provides a broad and candid look at the writing business from the research process to writing for specific markets. You might also want to read the classic book on writing fiction, **The Art of Fiction**, by John Gardner (Alfred A. Knopf, 1984). And if you need inspiration, connect to the Isaac Asimov Home Page at **www.clark.net/pub/edseiler/WWW/ asimov_home_page.html** where you'll find advice from one of the world's most prolific and broad-based writers.

4 Grammar

How's your grammar? You can take a grammar quiz (more interesting than it sounds) at **w3.one.net/ ~sparks25/quizcht.html**. If you want to avoid the 11 most commonly violated rules of writing, check them out at **www.concentric.net/~rag/writing.shtml**. For an entertaining viewpoint on grammar, read the Grammar Lady's column at **www.grammarlady.com**. At this site you can also submit questions to the grammar hotline. A good desk reference is **Webster's New World Guide to Current American Usage** by Bernice Randall (Prentice Hall, 1988).

5 Fonts

Fonts or typefaces are the clothes that your words wear. The book **Typographic Design: Form and Communication** by Rob Carter, Ben Day, and Philip Meggs (Van Nostrand Reinhold, 1985) provides a good introduction to typeforms, their organization, and their relationship to content. At the Graphion's Online Type

Serif

Serif

Museum Web site, **www.slip.net/~graphion/museum.html**, you can learn about the history and practice of typesetting. At the typoGRAPHIC Web site, **www.subnetwork.com/typo**, you can learn about the evolution and development of letterforms, view a timeline of the recent history of typography, find a glossary of typographic terms, and browse a gallery of typographic imagery. Microsoft Typography at **www.microsoft.com/ truetype** contains free TrueType fonts and a discussion of the future of typography on the Web. At the Shareware and Freeware Fonts Web page, **desktoppublishing.com/fonts-free.html**, you can find links to many Web sites that provide electronic fonts either for free or for a small fee. Brendan's Font Collection at **www.geocities.com/Athens/8368** claims to be one of the Web's largest sources of free fonts for downloading.

6 Publishing: Electronic New Frontiers

Some inventions and discoveries have not only changed the trajectory of human endeavor, but have also changed the way we see the world around us. Printing and, as many suspect, electronic publishing are inventions with such impact. At The Media History Project Web site, **www.mediahistory.com/ histhome.html**, you can contemplate these types of questions. You can also find at that site a timeline of media from 5,000 B.C.E. to the present, reviews of books, archives of the Dead Media Project, and links to Internet resources on various media from oral history to the printing press to digital media. You can find a discussion of Thomas Paine as the moral father of the Internet at "The Age of Paine," by Jon Katz at **wwww.wired.com/wired/3.05/features/paine.html/**. For some speculation about the future of books and electronic publishing, read "The Future of the Book" by Nicholas Negroponte at **www.wired.com/wired/ 4.02/negroponte.html**.

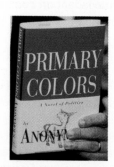

7 Who Wrote It?

A concordance was the key tool used to unmask the anonymous author of *Primary Colors*. To learn more about concordances, connect to the Web Concordances and Workbook Web site at **www.dundee.ac.uk/english/wics/wics.htm**, a site in Dundee, Scotland, which includes concordances of selected poems of Shelley, Coleridge, Keats, Blake, and other poets. Concordances and Corpora at **www.georgetown.edu/cball/ corpora/tutorial3.html** discusses how computerized concordances work and presents information on several programs. You might also want to read **"End of the Game"** by L. Reilbstein (*Newsweek*, July 29, 1996), which summarizes the controversy over the authorship of *Primary Colors*.

8 **Spreadsheet Tips**

For tips on how to get the most out of spreadsheet software, connect to *PC World's* Spreadsheet site at **www.pcworld.com/software/spreadsheet**. The Spreadsheet Page at **www.j-walk.com/ss** contains information, files, and FAQs, about Excel, Lotus 1-2-3, and Quattro Pro. At the Unofficial Microsoft Excel Page, **www.vex.net/~negandhi/excel**, you can find tips, reports on bugs, and files to download. You can link to tutorials, tips, free software and templates at both the Microsoft Excel site, **www.microsoft.com/excel/**, and the Lotus 1-2-3 site, **www2.lotus.com/123.nsf**. For some tips and guidance on how to create a well-designed spreadsheet, connect to Spreadsheet Etiquette at **www.melbpc.org.au/pcupdate/9409/409sset.htm**.

9 **Errors**

In 1986, Joseph A. Cummings, Inc. a construction firm, unsuccessfully tried to sue Lotus Development Corporation because a spreadsheet they used generated a $250,000 contract error. Research on spreadsheet errors has been carried out by Raymond R. Panko at the University of Hawaii. You can find out more about the alarming rate of spreadsheet errors at **www.cba.hawaii.edu/panko**.

10 **Lie: Don't Do it With Statistics or Graphs**

You should avoid the temptation to tell tall tales with statistics. Find out how with the video **How Numbers Lie: Self-Defense Against Misleading Statistics** (1996). If you need to brush up on statistics, head for **nilesonline.com/stats** where you'll find an entertaining tutorial. The updated 1954 classic, **How to Lie With Statistics** by Darrell Huff, (W W Norton & Co, 1993) is still a "must read." For information on creating effective and truthful graphs, read **The Visual Display of Quantitative Information** by Edward R. Tufte (Graphics Press, 1992).

11 **Information Science**

A career in information science is not new in the '90s, but this career has new challenges in the Information Age. What is information science? Is it the career for you? To learn more about information science, read Careers in Research Libraries and Information Science: The Dynamic Role of the Research Librarian at **arl.cni.org/careers/CareersPaper.html**. At the Education and Careers for the 21st Century Web site, **www-slis.lib.indiana.edu/21stCentury/**, you can learn more about careers for information professionals, in areas such as social informatics or content management. The American Society for Information Science (ASIS) was founded in 1937 and brings together information professionals from fields as diverse as computer science, linguistics, librarianship, engineering, and medicine. These professionals all share an interest in "improving the ways society stores, retrieves, analyzes, manages, archives and disseminates information." To learn more about ASIS, visit their Web site at **www.asis.org/**.

12 **Search Engines**

Search engines such as Yahoo! and Excite can help you locate information, and there are many search engines you can use. But how do you use them most effectively? For a basic introduction to searching for information, read "Secrets of the Super Searchers: Introduction," by Reva Basch at **www.onlineinc.com/pempress/secrets/intro.html**. "The Spider's Apprentice: How to Use Web Search Engines" at **www.monash.com/spidap4.html** provides helpful guidance about some of the Internet's main search engines, AltaVista, InfoSeek, Excite, WebCrawler, Lycos, Hotbot, OpenText, and Yahoo!. If you've ever asked yourself how these search engines work read the online article, "Seek and Ye Shall Find (Maybe)" by Steve G. Steinberg at **wwww.wired.com/wired/4.05/features/indexweb.html**. The Search Engine Watch Web site at **searchenginewatch.com/** includes reviews and tutorials, an overview of the major search engines and their history, and a search engine game. For a more in depth discussion of searching the Web, connect to "Beyond Surfing: Tools and Techniques for Searching the Web" by Kathleen Webster and Kathryn Paul at **magi.com/~mmelick/it96jan.htm**.

13 Online Card Catalogs

From your computer you can search through the four-million book card catalog of the Library of Congress. Just connect to **lcweb2.loc.gov/catalog**. Another great card catalog is at the U.S. National Archives and Records Administration at **www.nara.gov** where you'll find, among other things, the Kennedy Assassination Records Collection. The British Library also has an online card catalog that you can access at **opac97.bl.uk**.

14 Internet Citations

As you become an expert at locating information on the Web and Internet, you will want to start using that information in your term papers and reports. The **MLA Handbook for Writers of Research Papers** and the **APA Manual**, two books you can find in your library's reference department, present discussions and examples of how to cite source material from the Internet. "Beyond the MLA Handbook: Documenting Electronic Sources on the Internet" by Andrew Harnack and Gene Kleppinger of Eastern Kentucky University at **falcon.eku.edu/honors/beyond-mla/** provides a thorough discussion of citation style for Internet sources.

Review

1 Make a list of the boldface terms that appear in each section of this chapter. Make sure you understand the definition of each word. Select five words from each section. Write one sentence for each word (15 sentences total) to show that you know how to use the word in context.

2 Answer the questions below each heading in this chapter *using your own words*.

3 List the features of word-processing software that make it easy for you to enter the text of your documents.

4 Make a list of editing tasks that word-processing software can help you accomplish.

5 Explain the difference between a document template, a font, a style, and document wizard.

6 Explain the difference between the terms "kerning" and "serif" as they apply to fonts.

7 In document production terminology what is the difference between a column and a table?

8 Make a list of popular document automation features included with most word processors. Then describe a real-life situation in which each feature would be used effectively.

9 Write one or two paragraphs describing how a spreadsheet works to someone who has never seen one or used one.

10 Explain the difference between the following spreadsheet characteristics: a number, a formula, a function, and a cell reference.

11 Make a list of 10 careers, then write a brief description of a spreadsheet application that would be useful in each.

12 Make a list of tips for formatting worksheets. Divide your tips into three categories: on-screen, printed, and projected.

13 Explain what happens to the cell references in a formula when you copy that formula to a different column. How does this relate to absolute references?

14 Describe three techniques for auditing a worksheet.

15 Explain the difference between a structured database and a free-form database.

16 List and describe at least six search procedures that you might use to locate information in a database.

17 Describe five different ways you can use search results.

18 Outline the steps from the *User Focus* section of this chapter for using computer tools to create a research report.

19 Use the New Perspectives CD-ROM to take a practice test or to review the new terms presented in this chapter.

Projects

1 **Font Master** Do fonts make your document look formal or casual, simple or difficult, important or trivial? Look in magazines for samples of five different font treatments, including italics, serif, sans serif, mono-spaced, and kerned fonts. It is not necessary to find all five in a single article. Photocopy the best examples you find. After you study the documents that contain these fonts, write a one-page summary of how these different font treatments appear to be used to enhance readability, accentuate information, or add a certain personality to a document. Turn in your photocopies and your one-page summary.

2  **INTERNET Optional**

The March of Progress

The progress of document production, literacy, and civilization are closely linked. Create a timeline showing key developments in the history of document production. You should be able to find an abundance of information on this topic in your library and on the Internet. You can discuss the format for your timeline with your instructor. Depending on the time you have allocated for the project, you might simply use a word processor to list dates and events, you might incorporate graphics, or you might create a Web page.

3 Who's pear of shoes our over their?

Most word-processing software includes a grammar checker that helps you locate potential problems with sentence structure, punctuation, and word usage. When you use a grammar checker it is important to remember that you must evaluate its suggestions and decide whether to implement them. In this project you'll use a grammar checker to revise some of your own writing.

Begin with a first draft of at least one page of your writing. You can use something you have previously composed, or you can write something new. You'll need to type your document using word-processing software with grammar checking capabilities. Print out your first draft.

After you've printed your first draft, activate the grammar checker. Consider each of its suggestions and implement those you think will improve your writing. Make sure you proofread your document after you've completed the changes to make sure it still flows well.

Print out your revised document, then use a highlighter to indicate the changes you made. Turn in both drafts of your document.

4 See Dick Run. See Jane. See Spot Play.

Although close to 80% of the population for most industrialized countries has completed high school, journalists supposedly write for an audience with only an eighth-grade reading level. Is this true? To find out, you can use your word-processing software to discover the reading level of typical articles in popular magazines and newspapers.

To complete this project, locate two articles you think are typical of the writing style for the magazines or newspapers you read. Using your word processor, enter at least 10 sentences from the first article. Use your word processor's reading-level feature to find the reading level for the passage you typed. Print out the passage and on it note the reading-level statistics you obtained from your word processor. Do the same with the second article. Turn in both of your printouts. Be sure to include full bibliographical data on both articles.

5 True Lies Arnold Schwarzenegger and Jamie Lee Curtis starred in an action-thriller spoof about a secret agent who pretended to be a nerdy computer technician. Another character in the film was actually a used car salesman, but pretended to be a secret agent. The theme of *True Lies*—that things are not always what they seem—applies to spreadsheet graphs as well. What graphs appear to show is not always what the data actually means.

For this project look through magazines, books, and newspapers to find an example of a misleading graph. You might find that the dimensions of the graph distort the true picture. Perhaps a line graph was used when a pie graph would have been more meaningful. Maybe some of the data was omitted.

Photocopy the graph, then write a paragraph describing how the graph is misleading and what you would suggest to make it better depict the real data.

6 **INTERNET Required**

Searching for Godot

Knowing how to use a search engine is becoming a pivotal skill for the Information Age. Most key word search engines include instructions or short tutorials on their use. For this project, you'll connect to one of the Web search engines and learn how to use it.

To do this project, you must have access to the Internet and you must have a Web browser such as Netscape or Microsoft Internet Explorer. Start your browser and connect to one of the following sites:

www.lycos.com   www.altavista.com

www.excite.com   www.hotbot.com

Read through the instructions carefully, paying close attention (and maybe taking notes) on the options available for advanced searches, exact matches, and Boolean operators (AND, OR, NOT). Next try a few searches to make sure you've got the hang of it.

Finally, write a mini-manual about how to use your keyword search engine, providing examples of different types of searches.

7 **Information Science Careers** Writing for *Wired* magazine, Steve Steinberg says, "The hard problems of knowledge classification and indexing are suddenly of commercial importance." Much has happened since Melvil Dewey set up the first formal training program for librarians in 1887. The field of library science has broadened to become information science and encompass the vast pool of electronic documents.

INTERNET Optional

For this project, you will find information about training and careers in information science. You should use a variety of resources to gather information—you can interview librarians, check the Web sites for universities that offer information science degrees, and look in general reference books for background and historical information.

Summarize your findings by writing a pamphlet called "A Career Guide to Information Science." Anticipate that the audience will be high school seniors and college freshmen making career decisions.

8 **With Two You Get Egg Roll** Time was when the word "menu" evoked images of elegant restaurants—or at least Chinese take-out. Today, menus just as often mean electronic choices on automated phone systems and computer screens. Many times we use menus without really thinking about how they're organized or presented. But as a consumer in the Information Age you should take a more critical look at this ubiquitous tool.

For this project, pick an electronic menu that you use to access a database. It might be an ATM machine, a phone system at work, or an information kiosk. Draw a hierarchy diagram of the options available on the menus. To do this, you'll need to play around with the menus to examine all the options offered.

9 **Brave New World** Because computerized databases have become such an integral part of our society, we don't often consider what life would be like without them. However, without computerized databases, banking, shopping, communications, entertainment, education, and health care would probably be far different from what they are today. For this project, you should first make a list of assumptions about how your life would be different if there were no computerized databases. For example, one of your assumptions might be, "Without computerized databases, we would have to pay for everything in cash because banks couldn't process enough checks by hand, nor could credit card companies verify charges."

After you have a list of assumptions, write a short story about one day in the life of a person who lives in a society where there are no computerized databases. In your story, try to depict how this person's life is different from what we think of as "normal."

Turn in your list of assumptions and your short story.

10 **Edit Yourself** After reading the *User Focus* section of this chapter, you might have some ideas about how you can use software tools to collect facts, improve your writing, analyze numeric data, and give presentations. Select a report, paper, or presentation that you recently created. Think about specific ways in which you could improve it.

Make a list of improvements you could make, indicating the tools you would use. Be specific. For example, you might say "Gather additional facts about per capita coffee consumption using a Web search engine" or "Check the reading level using a word processor and make adjustments to bring it to the eighth- to tenth-grade level.

Turn in a photocopy of your original project as well as your list of improvements.

Lab Assignments

Word Processing

Word-processing software is the most popular computerized productivity tool. In this Lab you will learn how word-processing software works. When you have completed this Lab, you should be able to apply the general concepts you learned to any word-processing package you use at home, at work, or in your school lab.

1 Click the Steps button to learn how word-processing software works. As you proceed through the Steps, answer all of the Quick Check questions that appear. After you complete the Steps, you will see a Quick Check Summary Report. Follow the instructions on the screen to print this report.

2 Click the Explore button to begin. Click File, then click Open to display the Open dialog box. Click the file **Timber.tex**, then press the Enter key to open the letter to Northern Timber Company. Make the following modifications to the letter, then print it out. You do not need to save the letter.

　a. In the first and last lines of the letter, change "Jason Kidder" to your name.

　b. Change the date to today's date.

　c. The second paragraph begins "Your proposal did not include…" Move this paragraph so it is the last paragraph in the text of the letter.

　d. Change the cost of a permanent bridge to $20,000.

　e. Spell check the letter.

3 In Explore, open the file **Stars.tex**. Make the following modifications to the document, then print it out. You do not need to save the document.

　a. Center and boldface the title.

　b. Change the title font to size 16 Arial.

　c. Boldface the DATE, SHOWER, and LOCATION.

　d. Move the January 2-3 line to the top of the list.

　e. Double-space the entire document.

4 In Explore, compose a one-page double-spaced letter to your parents or to a friend. Make sure you date the letter and check your spelling. Print the letter and sign it. You do not need to save your letter.

Spreadsheets

Spreadsheet software is used extensively in business, education, science, and humanities to simplify tasks that involve calculations. In this Lab you will learn how spreadsheet software works. You will use spreadsheet software to examine and modify worksheets, as well as to create your own worksheets.

1 Click the Steps button to learn how spreadsheet software works. As you proceed through the Steps, answer all of the Quick Check questions that appear. After you complete the Steps, you will see a Quick Check Summary Report. Follow the instructions on the screen to print this report.

2 Click the Explore button to begin this assignment. Click OK to display a new worksheet. Click File, then click Open to display the Open dialog box. Click the file **Income.xls**, then press the Enter key to open the **Income and Expense Summary** worksheet. Notice that the worksheet contains labels and values for income from consulting and training. It also contains labels and values for expenses such as rent and salaries. The worksheet does not, however, contain formulas to calculate Total Income, Total Expenses, or Profit. Do the following:

a. Calculate the Total Income by entering the formula =sum(C4:C5) in cell C6.

b. Calculate the Total Expenses by entering the formula =sum(C9:C12) in C13.

c. Calculate Profit by entering the formula =C6-C13 in cell C15.

d. Manually check the results to make sure you entered the formulas correctly.

e. Print your completed worksheet showing your results.

3 You can use a spreadsheet to keep track of your grade in a class. In Explore, click File, then click Open to display the Open dialog box. Click the file **Grades.xls** to open the Grades worksheet. This worksheet contains all the labels and formulas necessary to calculate your grade based on four test scores.

Suppose you receive a score of 88 out of 100 on the first test. On the second test, you score 42 out of 48. On the third test, you score 92 out of 100. You have not taken the fourth test yet. Enter the appropriate data in the **Grades.xls** worksheet to determine your grade after taking three tests. Print out your worksheet.

4 Worksheets are handy for answering "what if" questions. Suppose you decide to open a lemonade stand. You're interested in how much profit you can make each day. What if you sell 20 cups of lemonade? What if you sell 100? What if the cost of lemons increases?

In Explore, open the file **Lemons.xls** and use the worksheet to answer questions a through d, then print the worksheet for question e:

a. What is your profit if you sell 20 cups a day?

b. What is your profit if you sell 100 cups a day?

c. What is your profit if the price of lemons increases to $.07 and you sell 100 cups?

d. What is your profit if you raise the price of a cup of lemonade to $.30? (Lemons still cost $.07 and assume you sell 100 cups.)

e. Suppose your competitor boasts that she sold 50 cups of lemonade in one day and made exactly $12.00. On your worksheet adjust the cost of cups, water, lemons, and sugar, and the price per cup to show a profit of exactly $12.00 for 50 cups sold. Print this worksheet.

5 It is important to make sure the formulas in your worksheet are accurate. An easy way to test this is to enter 1's for all the values on your worksheet, then check the calculations manually. In Explore, open the worksheet **Receipt.xls**, which calculates sales receipts. Enter 1 as the value for Item 1, Item 2, Item 3, and Sales Tax %. Now, manually calculate what you would pay for three items that cost $1.00 each in a state where sales tax is 1% (.01). Do your manual calculations match those of the worksheet? If not, correct the formulas in the worksheet and print out a *formula report* of your revised worksheet.

6 In Explore, create your own worksheet showing your household budget for one month. You may use real or made up numbers. Make sure you put a title on the worksheet. Use formulas to calculate your total income and your total expenses for the month. Add another formula to calculate how much money you were able to save. Print a formula report of your worksheet. Also, print your worksheet showing realistic values for one month.

Databases

The Database Lab demonstrates the essential concepts of file and database management systems. You will use the Lab to search, sort, and report the data contained in a file of classic books.

X ①Click the Steps button to review basic database terminology and to learn how to manipulate the classic books database. As you proceed through the Steps, answer the Quick Check questions that appear. After you complete the Steps, you will see a Quick Check Summary Report. Follow the instructions on the screen to print this report.

② Click the Explore button. Make sure you can apply basic database terminology to describe the classic books database by answering the following questions:

a. How many records does the file contain?

b. How many fields does each record contain?

c. What are the contents of the Catalog # field for the book written by Margaret Mitchell?

d. What are the contents of the Title field for the record with Thoreau in the Author field?

e. Which field has been used to sort the records?

③ In Explore, manipulate the database as necessary to answer the following questions:

a. When the books are sorted by title, what is the first record in the file?

b. Use the Search button to search for all books in the West location. How many do you find?

c. Use the Search button to search for all books in the Main location that are checked in. What do you find?

④ In Explore, use the Report button to print out a report that groups the books by Status and sorted by title. On your report, circle the four field names. Put a box around the summary statistics showing which books are currently checked in and which books are currently checked out.

COMPUTERFILES
ANDDATASTORAGE

4

InfoWeb

World
Records
1

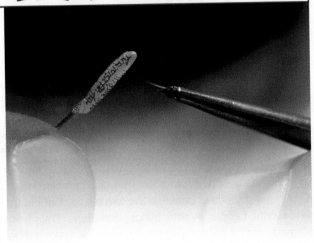

How much data can you pack into a small area? In 1968, Frederick Watts hand-printed 9,452 characters on a piece of paper the size of a postage stamp. In 1983, Tsutomu Ishii of Tokyo, Japan wrote the Japanese characters for *Tokyo, Japan* on a human hair. A few years later, Surendra Apharya of Jaipur, India managed to squeeze 241 characters on a single grain of rice. That seems like a lot of data packed into a small area, but a computer can store hundreds of times as much data in the same area. For example, an entire encyclopedia can fit on a single 4.75-inch CD-ROM disk.

How can computers store so much data in such a small area? How can you search through all that data to find what you want? Can you change data once it is stored? What happens if you run out of space?

In this chapter you will learn the answers to these and many more questions. After learning the definitions of the terms *file*, *data*, and *information*, you will learn that there are different types of files, and you will find out how to use each type. You will see how the operating system provides a metaphor to help visualize and manipulate files and how this metaphor is quite different from the way the computer actually stores and keeps track of files. Finally you will learn about the speed, cost, and storage capacity of popular microcomputer storage media. With this information, you can make decisions about the storage devices that are right for your computing needs.

CHAPTERPREVIEW

This chapter provides a practical foundation for using a computer to manage your data. You will find out which disk drive to use when you store data and how to create a valid filename that the computer will accept. You will learn how to use DOS or Windows to organize the files on your disk so they are easy to locate. You will also learn what happens in the computer when you save, retrieve, or modify a file, so you will know what to do when the computer asks if you want to "Replace file?" After you have completed this chapter you should be able to:

- Correctly use the terms data and information
- Determine if a file is an executable file, data file, or source file
- Create valid filenames under DOS and Windows
- Explain how file extensions and wildcards simplify file access
- Describe the difference between logical and physical file storage

- Discuss how the directory and the FAT help you access files
- Select a storage device based on characteristics such as its capacity and access speed
- Describe the process of saving, retrieving, revising, deleting, and copying files

LABS

DOS Directories
and File
Management

Windows
Directories,
Folders, and Files

Defragmentation
and Disk
Operations

Using Files

A Data, Information, and Files

Computer professionals have special definitions for the terms *data*, *information*, and *file*. Although we might refer to these as technical definitions, they are not difficult to understand. Knowing these technical definitions will help you communicate with computer professionals and understand phrases such as "data in, information out."

Data and Information: Technically Speaking

Aren't data and information the same thing? In everyday conversation, people use the terms *data* and *information* interchangeably. However, some computer professionals make a distinction between the two terms. **Data** is the words, numbers, and graphics that describe people, events, things, and ideas. Data becomes information when you use it as the basis for initiating some action or for making a decision. **Information**, then, is defined as the words, numbers, and graphics used as the basis for human actions and decisions.

To understand the distinction between data and information, consider the following: AA 4199 ORD 9:59 CID 11:09. These letters, numbers, and symbols, which describe an event—a flight schedule—are typical of the *data* stored in a computer system. Now, suppose that you decide to take a trip from Chicago (ORD) to Cedar Rapids, Iowa (CID). Your travel agent sees the following on the computer screen:

Carrier	Flight Number	From	Departs	To	Arrives
AA	4199	ORD	9:59	CID	11:09

Here, the letters, numbers, and symbols displayed on the screen are considered *information* because your travel agent is using them to make your reservation.

The distinction between data and information might seem somewhat elusive, because "AA 4199 ORD 9:59 CID 11:09" can be both data and information. Remember that the distinction is based on usage. Usually, if letters, numbers, and symbols are stored in a computer, they are referred to as data. If letters, numbers, and symbols are being used by a person to complete an action or make a decision, they are referred to as information. Remember this: Data is used by computers; information is used by humans.

Incidentally, in Latin, the word *data* is the plural for *datum*. According to this usage, it would be correct to say "The January and February rainfall *data* are stored on the disk," and "The March *datum* is not yet available." Most English dictionaries accept the use of *data* as either singular or plural. In this text *data* is used with the singular verb, as in "The *data is* stored on the disk."

Computer Files

What kinds of files will I have on my computer? A **file** is a named collection of program instructions or data that exists on a storage medium such as a hard disk, a floppy disk, or a CD-ROM. Suppose you use a computer to write a memo to your employer. The words contained in the memo are stored on a disk in a file. The file has a name to distinguish it from other files on your disk. Although there are several kinds of files, a typical computer user deals mainly with executable files and data files. Understanding the difference between these two kinds of files is important because you use them in different ways.

Executable Files

How do I use executable files? An **executable file** contains the instructions that tell a computer how to perform a specific task. For example, the word-processing program that tells your computer how to display and print text is stored on disk as an executable file. Other executable files on your computer system include the operating system, utilities, and application software programs.

To use an executable file, you *run* it. In Chapter 1 you learned how to run programs. In DOS you type the name of the program, in Windows 3.1 you double-click a program icon, and in Windows 95 and Windows 98 you select the program from a menu. The programs you run are one type of executable file.

Your computer also has executable files that you cannot run. These files are executed at the request of a computer program, not the user. For example, a word-processing program may request that the computer use an executable file to check the grammar in a document.

Most operating systems help you identify the executable files you can run. DOS uses part of the filename to indicate an executable file. You will learn more about this later in the section "Filenaming Conventions." Windows uses icons to indicate which files you can run, as shown in Figure 4-1.

Figure 4-1

Program icons

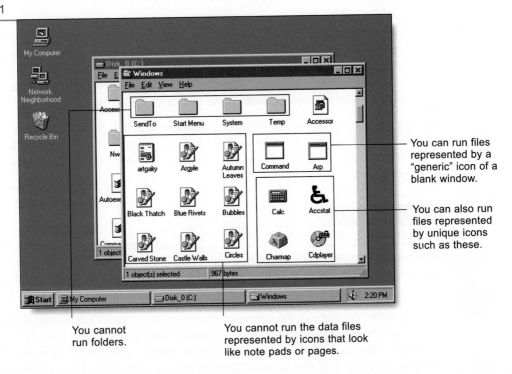

You can run files represented by a "generic" icon of a blank window.

You can also run files represented by unique icons such as these.

You cannot run folders.

You cannot run the data files represented by icons that look like note pads or pages.

The instructions in an executable file are directly executed by the computer. The instructions are stored in a format that the computer can interpret, but this format is not designed to be readable to humans. If you try to look at the contents of an executable file, the file will appear to contain meaningless symbols such as ☺□¬%■ý.

Data Files

How do I use data files? A **data file** contains words, numbers, and pictures that you can view, edit, save, send, and print. Typically, you create data files when you use application software. For example, you create a data file when you store a document you have written using word-processing software or a picture you have drawn using graphics software. You also create a data file when you store a spreadsheet, a graph, a sound clip, or a video.

You probably won't create all the data files you use. You might receive data files as part of a software package you purchase. For example, word-processing software often includes a dictionary data file that contains a list of words the software uses to check spelling.

You can also purchase specific data files that contain information you need. Suppose you own a business and want to mail product information to prospective customers. You could purchase a data file that contains the names and addresses of people in your geographical area who fit the age and income profile of consumers who are likely to buy your product.

Whether you create or purchase a data file, you typically use it in conjunction with application software. The application software helps you manipulate the data in the file. You usually view, revise, and print a data file using the same software you used to create it. For example, if you create a data file using word-processing software such as Microsoft Word, you would usually use Microsoft Word to edit the file.

If you purchase a data file, how do you know what application software to use it with? Usually, a software product that contains data files will also contain the program you need to manipulate the data. If the program that manipulates the data is not included, the user manual indicates which program you can use. For example, if you purchase a collection of data files that contain graphical images, the user manual might indicate that you need a program such as Microsoft Paintbrush to view and modify the images.

So how can you remember the difference between data files and executable files? Think of data files as passive—the data does not instruct or direct the computer to do anything. Think of executable files as active—the instructions stored in the file cause the computer to do something.

Source Files

Is Autoexec.bat an executable file or a data file? If you look at the files on most DOS or Windows computers, you will see a file named **Autoexec.bat**. This is an example of a batch file. A **batch file** is a series of operating system commands that you use to automate tasks you want the operating system to perform.

InfoWeb

Autoexec
2

When you turn on your PC, the operating system looks for a batch file called **Autoexec.bat** and executes any instructions the file contains. Usually the **Autoexec.bat** file contains instructions that customize your computer configuration. For example, **Autoexec.bat** might tell your computer that you have a CD-ROM drive or that the computer should establish connection with a network.

Because batch files contain instructions, you might assume that they are executable files. However, unlike most executable files, a batch file does not contain instructions in a format that the computer can directly carry out. Instead, a batch file contains instructions that computer users can read and modify. The commands in a batch file must go through a translation process before they can be executed. Batch files belong to a third category of files called **source files**, which contain instructions that the computer must translate before executing.

The Document-centric Approach to Files

How important is it for me to distinguish between executable files, data files, and source files? Understanding the difference between executable, data, and source files helps you understand how a computer works. Once you understand the characteristics of these file types, you understand that the computer performs the instructions in executable files to help you create data files. It follows, then, that the way you use a computer is to run an application program and use it to create data files. For example, first you run a word-processing program, then you use it to create a report.

The problem with this model is that to revise a document, you must remember what software you used to create it. Suppose you create a list of people who contributed to your organization's 1998 fund-raising campaign. The next year, you want to use this list again. You remember you called the file Contributors 98, but what program did you use to create it? Did you use Microsoft's Excel spreadsheet or Access database? Or did you use a word-processing program such as Microsoft Word?

An alternative approach to using files is referred to as the document-centric approach. The term is derived from two words: document and centric. **Document-centric** means that the *document* is *central* to the way you use a computer. Under the document-centric model, once you indicate the document you want to revise, the computer automatically starts the appropriate application program. For example, if you are using Windows, when you click the Contributors 98 document, the computer starts the Microsoft Word application, then retrieves the data file Contributors 98, as shown in Figure 4-2.

Figure 4-2

Windows supports a document-centric approach, as well as the traditional approach to using files. With the document-centric approach, you select the data file you want to revise. The operating system automatically starts the appropriate application software and opens the data file you selected.

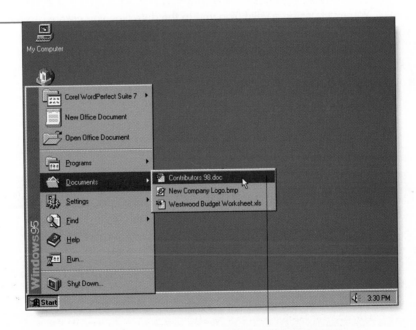

Clicking the document starts the appropriate program.

The operating system on your computer determines whether you can use the document-centric or traditional approach to files. To summarize the difference, under the document-centric approach, you select the data file you want to revise and the computer automatically runs the appropriate application program. Under the traditional approach, you run an application program first, then select the file you want to revise.

Filenaming Conventions

May I use any name I want when I create my own files? A **filename** is a unique set of letters and numbers that identifies a file and usually describes the file contents. For example, **Excel** is the name of one of the main files for the Microsoft Excel spreadsheet software.

The filename might be followed by a **filename extension** that further describes the file contents. Filename extensions are also referred to as *file extensions* or *extensions*. The filename **Excel.exe**, with the **.exe** extension, indicates it is an executable file. The extension is separated from the filename with a period, called a *dot*. So, if you were to tell someone the name of this file, you would say "Excel dot e-x-e."

As a computer user, you are not usually responsible for naming executable files. These files are included with the application software you purchase, and the files are named by the programmers who write them. When you look through a list of files on a disk, you can quickly identify executable files by their file extensions. See Figure 4-3.

Figure 4-3

The executable files you can run generally have either a **.com** (for *command*) extension or **.exe** (for *executable*) extension.

File Type	File Extension
Files you can run	.exe .com
Files you cannot run	.sys .dll .drv .vbx .ocx

InfoWeb

Filename Extensions 3

You must assign a valid filename to the data files you create. A **valid filename** adheres to specific rules, referred to as **filenaming conventions**. Each operating system has a unique set of filenaming conventions. You can use Figure 4-4 to determine whether **Aux**, **My File.doc**, and **Bud93/94.txt** are valid filenames under the operating system you use.

Figure 4-4

Filenaming conventions

	DOS and Windows 3.1	Windows 95	MacOS	UNIX
Maximum length of filename	eight character filename plus three character extension	255 character filename including the three character extension	31 characters No extensions used	14–256 characters (depends on the version of UNIX), including an extension of any length
Character to separate filename from extension	. (period)	. (period)	No extensions	. (period)
Spaces allowed	No	Yes	Yes	No
Numbers allowed	Yes	Yes	Yes	Yes
Characters not allowed	/[];="\:.|*?	\?:"<>|	None	!@#$%^&*()[]{}'"\\|;<>
Reserved words	AUX, COM1, COM2, COM3, COM4, CON, LPT1, LPT2, LPT3, PRN, or NUL	AUX, COM1, COM2, COM3, COM4, CON, LPT1, LPT2, LPT3, PRN, or NUL	None	Depends on version of UNIX
Case sensitive	No	No	Yes	Yes—use lowercase

Using DOS or Windows filenaming conventions, **Aux** is not a valid filename because it is a reserved word. **My File.doc** is not valid under DOS, Windows 3.1, or UNIX because it contains a space between My and File. The filename **Bud93/94.txt** would be valid only under Mac OS because it contains a slash. Filenames such as **Session**, **Report.doc**, **Budget1.wks**, and **Form.1** are valid under all the operating systems listed in Figure 4-4.

Filename extensions for data files fall into two categories: generic and application-specific. A **generic filename extension** indicates the type of data a file contains, but it does not tell you exactly which software application was used to create the file. For example, a **.bmp** extension tells you that the file contains graphical data, but the file might have been created by any of several graphics packages such as Microsoft Paint or MicroGraphx PicturePublisher. Figure 4-5 lists some generic filename extensions.

Figure 4-5

Generic filename extensions

File Type	File Extension
Text	.txt
Sound	.wav .mid
Graphics	.bmp .pcx .tif .wmf .jpg .gif
Animation/Video	.flc .fli .avi .mpg
Web documents	.html .htm

Figure 4-6

Application Software	File Extension
WordPerfect	.wpd
Microsoft Word and WordPad	.doc
Microsoft Works	.wps
Lotus Word Pro	.sam
Lotus 1-2-3	.wk4
Microsoft Excel	.xls
Corel Quattro Pro	.wb1
Lotus Approach	.apr
Microsoft Access	.mdb
Claris FileMaker Pro	.fm

An **application-specific filename extension** is associated with a particular application and indicates which software was used to create the file. For example, when you create a file with Microsoft Word for Windows, the software assigns a **.doc** extension to your filename. By automatically assigning an extension, the application helps you identify the files you created using that application.

Suppose that you had many files on a disk—some created using Word and others created using a spreadsheet program and a graphics program. Now you want to view or edit one of the files you created using Microsoft Word. The Word software searches through all the files on your disk and shows you a list of only those filenames that have a **.doc** extension. Because you see only the files you created using Word, you do not have to wade through a long list of files that include your spreadsheets and graphics. Figure 4-6 lists some application-specific filename extensions that you are likely to encounter.

Wildcards

What's *.* ? Files have unique names, but sometimes you want to refer to more than one file. For example, suppose you want to list all the files on your disk with an .exe extension. You can specify *.exe (pronounced "star dot e-x-e"). The asterisk is a **wildcard character** used to represent a group of characters. *.exe means all the files with an .exe extension. Suppose your disk contains the files: **Excel.exe**, **Spell.exe**, **Excel.cfg**, and **Budget.dat**. You could use Excel.* to represent **Excel.exe** and **Excel.cfg**.

. (pronounced "star dot star") means all files. When you use DOS, the command DEL *.* will delete all the files in a directory. Be careful if you use this command!

Most operating systems use wildcards to make it easier to manipulate a collection of files. For example, using wildcards, you can delete all the files on a disk in one operation, instead of deleting each file individually. You will use wildcards even with a graphical user interface, as shown in Figure 4-7.

Figure 4-7

Wildcards help you locate files in Microsoft Word for Windows.

The list includes only those files that begin with the letter R and have a .doc extension.

R* uses a wildcard to mean all files that begin with the letter R.

*.doc uses a wildcard to mean all files that have a .doc extension.

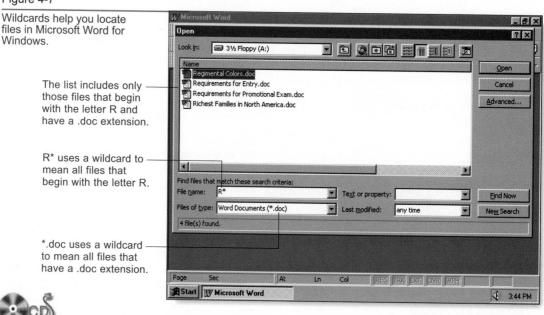

Logical File Storage

How do I keep track of all the files on my disks? Your computer system might contain hundreds, even thousands of files stored on disks and other storage devices. To keep track of all these files, the computer has a filing system that is maintained by the operating system. Once you know how the operating system manages your computer's filing system, you can use it effectively to store and retrieve files.

Most computers have more than one storage device that the operating system uses to store files. Each storage device is identified by a letter. Floppy disk drives are usually identified as A and B. The hard disk drive is usually identified as C. Additional storage devices can be assigned letters from D through Z. The drive letter is usually followed by a colon as in C:. Figure 4-8 shows some microcomputer configurations and the letters typically assigned to their storage devices. Does one of these match the configuration for the computer you use?

Figure 4-8

Storage device letter assignments

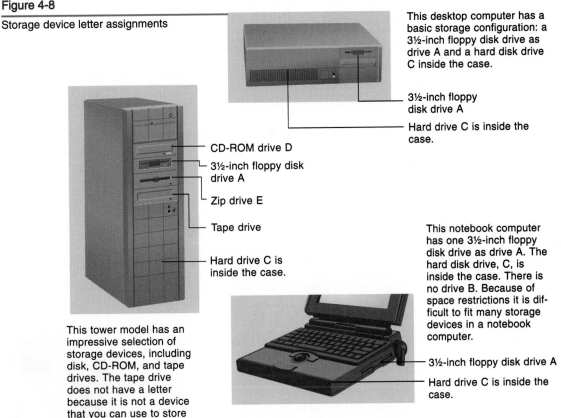

This desktop computer has a basic storage configuration: a 3½-inch floppy disk drive as drive A and a hard disk drive C inside the case.

3½-inch floppy disk drive A

Hard drive C is inside the case.

CD-ROM drive D

3½-inch floppy disk drive A

Zip drive E

Tape drive

Hard drive C is inside the case.

This tower model has an impressive selection of storage devices, including disk, CD-ROM, and tape drives. The tape drive does not have a letter because it is not a device that you can use to store individual files from your applicatons.

This notebook computer has one 3½-inch floppy disk drive as drive A. The hard disk drive, C, is inside the case. There is no drive B. Because of space restrictions it is difficult to fit many storage devices in a notebook computer.

3½-inch floppy disk drive A

Hard drive C is inside the case.

The operating system maintains a list of files called a **directory** for each disk or CD-ROM. The directory contains information about every file on a storage device such as the filename, the file extension, the date and time the file was created, and the file size. You can use the operating system to view the directory of a disk. Study the figures on this and the next page to compare different directory styles for DOS and Windows.

Figure 4-9

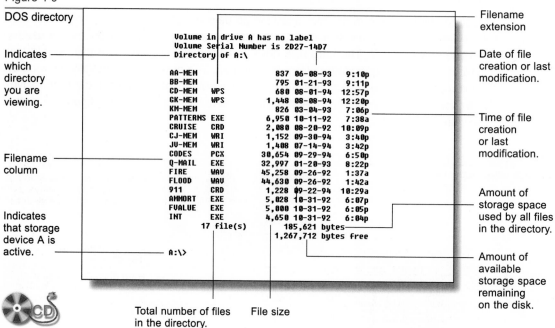

DOS directory

Indicates which directory you are viewing.

Filename column

Indicates that storage device A is active.

Filename extension

Date of file creation or last modification.

Time of file creation or last modification.

Amount of storage space used by all files in the directory.

Amount of available storage space remaining on the disk.

Total number of files in the directory.

File size

Figure 4-10

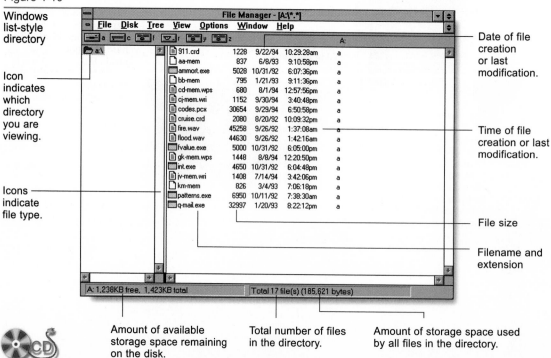

Windows list-style directory

Icon indicates which directory you are viewing.

Icons indicate file type.

Date of file creation or last modification.

Time of file creation or last modification.

File size

Filename and extension

Amount of available storage space remaining on the disk.

Total number of files in the directory.

Amount of storage space used by all files in the directory.

Figure 4-11

Windows icon-style
directory

Indicates that
directory is for
drive A.

Filenames,
extensions, and
icons

Amount of
storage space
used by all files
in the directory.

Total number of
files in the
directory.

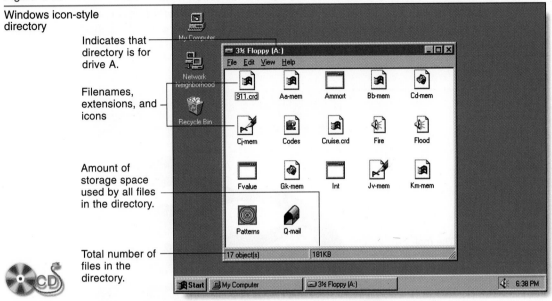

Windows Directories, Folders, and Files

The main directory of a disk, sometimes referred to as the **root directory**, provides a useful list of files. It could be difficult, however, to find a particular file if your directory contains several hundred files. To help you organize a large number of files, most operating systems allow you to divide your directory into smaller lists called **subdirectories** or **folders**. For example, you can create one subdirectory to hold all your files that contain documents and another subdirectory to hold all your files that contain graphical images.

A subdirectory name is separated from a drive letter and a filename by a special symbol. In DOS and Microsoft Windows, this symbol is the backslash \. For example, the root directory of drive C might have a subdirectory called **Graphics**, written as **C:\Graphics**.

A **file specification** is the drive letter, subdirectory, filename, and extension that identifies a file. Suppose you create a subdirectory on drive A named Word for your word-processing documents. Now suppose you want to create a list of things to do called **To-do.doc** and store it on drive A in the Word subdirectory. The file specification is:

A:\Word\To-do.doc

Drive letter | Extension
Subdirectory |
Filename

InfoWeb

Subdirectories can be further divided into what you might think of as *sub-subdirectories*. As you create more and more subdirectories on a disk, it becomes important to pay attention to the structure of the directories.

Directories
4

Metaphors of directory structures are sometimes called *logical models* because they represent the way you logically conceive of them. **Logical storage** is a conceptual model of the way data is stored on your disk. Figure 4-12 illustrates some metaphors for computer storage systems.

Figure 4-12

Metaphors of directory structures

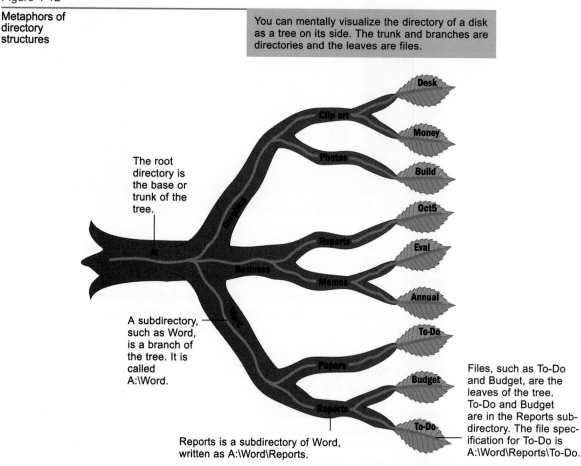

You can mentally visualize the directory of a disk as a tree on its side. The trunk and branches are directories and the leaves are files.

The root directory is the base or trunk of the tree.

A subdirectory, such as Word, is a branch of the tree. It is called A:\Word.

Reports is a subdirectory of Word, written as A:\Word\Reports.

Files, such as To-Do and Budget, are the leaves of the tree. To-Do and Budget are in the Reports subdirectory. The file specification for To-Do is A:\Word\Reports\To-Do.

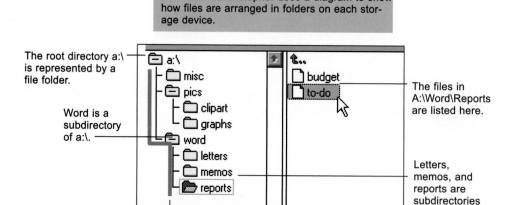

A hierarchical metaphor uses a diagram to show how files are arranged in folders on each storage device.

The root directory a:\ is represented by a file folder.

Word is a subdirectory of a:\.

The red line shows the path for files in A:\Word\Reports.

The files in A:\Word\Reports are listed here.

Letters, memos, and reports are subdirectories of Word.

Figure 4-12

Metaphors of directory structures (continued)

A boxes-within-boxes metaphor uses nested windows to represent the contents of folders.

The window for the root directory of 3½ Floppy (A:) holds the file folders Pics, Word, and Misc.

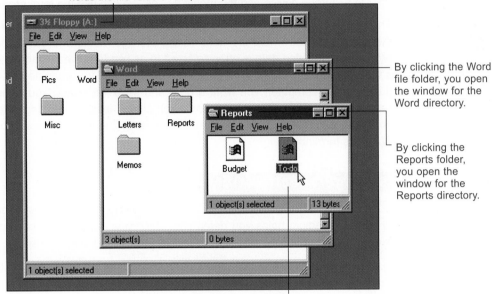

By clicking the Word file folder, you open the window for the Word directory.

By clicking the Reports folder, you open the window for the Reports directory.

The files in A:\Word\Reports are shown in the Reports window.

A logical view of storage is a convenient mental model that helps you understand the computer's filing system; however, it is not how the data is actually stored. **Physical storage** refers to how data is actually stored on the physical disk. To find out more about how computers physically store data, it is useful to understand a bit about storage media and storage devices. That is the topic of Section B.

QuickCheck A

1 To differentiate between data and information, use the rule: _____ is used by computers; _____ is used by humans.

2 What is the filename extension in the path: A:\Research\Primates\Jan5.Dat. _____

3 Files that you can run have _____ or .com extensions.

4 Nested file folders and directory trees are ways of representing _____ storage.

5 The main directory for a disk is called the _____ directory.

6 **Autoexec.bat** is an example of a(n) _____ file that needs to be translated by the computer before its instructions are executed.

⬛ Storage Technologies

When it comes to computer storage, users have two questions: How much data can I store? How fast can I access it? The answers to these questions depend on the storage medium and the storage device. A **storage medium** (storage *media* is the plural) is the disk, tape, paper, or other substance that contains data. A **storage device** is the mechanical apparatus that records and retrieves the data from the storage medium. When we want to refer to a storage device and the media it uses, we can use the term **storage technology**.

The process of storing data is often referred to as **writing data** or **saving a file** because the storage device *writes* the data on the storage medium to *save* it for later use. The process of retrieving data is often referred to as **reading data**, **loading data**, or **opening a file**. The terms "reading" and "writing" make sense if you imagine that you are the computer. As the computer, you *write* a note and save it for later. You retrieve the note and *read* it when you need the information it contains. The terms *reading data* and *writing data* are often associated with mainframe applications. The terms *save* and *open* are standard Windows terminology.

Storage Specifications

How do I compare storage technologies? Knowing the characteristics of a storage device or storage medium helps you determine which one is best for a particular task. Storage technology comparisons are often based on storage capacity and speed.

Data is stored as bytes. Each **byte** usually represents one character—a letter, punctuation mark, space, or numeral. The phrase "profit margin" requires 13 bytes of storage space because the phrase contains 12 characters and the space between the two words requires an additional byte of storage space. **Storage capacity** is the maximum amount of data that can be stored on a storage medium and is usually measured in kilobytes, megabytes, or gigabytes. A **kilobyte** (KB) is 1,024 bytes, but this is often rounded to one thousand bytes. A **megabyte** (MB) is 1,048,576 bytes, approximately one million bytes. A **gigabyte** (GB) is 1,073,741,824 bytes, approximately one billion bytes. When you read that the storage capacity of a computer is 5.1 gigabytes, it means the hard disk on that computer can store up to 5.1 billion bytes of information. This is equivalent to approximately 1,350,000 single-spaced pages of text—that would be a stack of paper 450 feet high!

In addition to storage capacity, users are concerned with access time. **Access time** is the average time it takes a computer to locate data on the storage medium and read it. Access time for a microcomputer storage device, such as a disk drive, is measured in milliseconds. One **millisecond** (ms) is a thousandth of a second. When you read, for example, that disk access time is 11 ms, it means that on average, it takes the computer eleven thousandths of a second to locate and read data from the disk.

It is fairly easy to compare two storage technologies based on storage capacity and access time; these specifications are usually included in advertisements and product descriptions. However, additional characteristics of storage technologies must be considered. The durability and access methods of a storage technology are also important characteristics to compare.

Magnetic or Optical Storage?

Will the metal detector in an airport erase the data on my disks? Magnetic and optical storage technologies are used for the majority of today's micro, mini, and mainframe computers. Each of these technologies has advantages and disadvantages.

With **magnetic storage** the computer stores data on disks and tape by magnetizing selected particles of an oxide-based surface coating. The particles retain their magnetic orientation until that orientation is changed, thereby making disks and tape fairly permanent but modifiable storage media. Figure 4-13 shows how a computer stores data on magnetic media.

Figure 4-13

Storing data on magnetic media

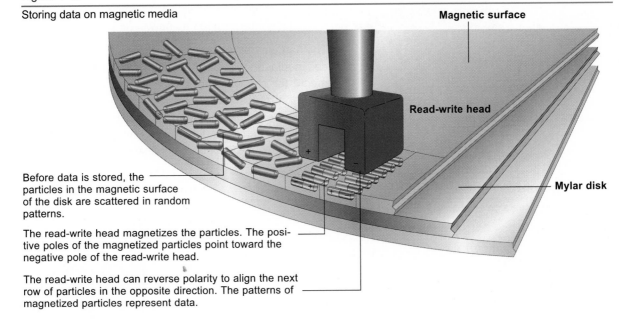

Magnetic surface

Read-write head

Mylar disk

Before data is stored, the particles in the magnetic surface of the disk are scattered in random patterns.

The read-write head magnetizes the particles. The positive poles of the magnetized particles point toward the negative pole of the read-write head.

The read-write head can reverse polarity to align the next row of particles in the opposite direction. The patterns of magnetized particles represent data.

You can intentionally change or erase files stored on magnetic media. If you run out of disk space, you can make more space available by erasing files you no longer need.

Data stored on magnetic media such as floppy disks can also be unintentionally altered by the environment and by device or media failure. In the environment, magnetic fields, dust, mold, smoke particles, and heat are the primary culprits causing data loss. Placing a magnet on your disk is a sure way of losing data. The metal detectors in an airport use a magnetic field, but the field is not strong enough to disrupt the data on your floppy or hard disks. You are more likely to damage your disks by leaving them on the dashboard of your car in the sun or carrying them around in your backpack where they will pick up dust and dirt. At many mainframe installations, magnetic media are stored in climate-controlled vaults to protect against environmental hazards such as dust, extreme temperatures, smoke, and mold.

Media failure is a problem with storage media that results in data loss. Magnetic media gradually lose their magnetic charge, resulting in lost data. Some experts estimate that the reliable life span of data stored on magnetic media is about three years, and they recommend that you refresh your data every two years by recopying it.

A device failure can damage a disk and result in data loss. A **device failure** is a problem with a mechanical device such as a disk drive. Storage devices fail as a result of power or circuitry problems.

With **optical storage**, data is burned into the storage medium using beams of laser light. The burns form patterns of small pits in the disk surface to represent data, as shown in Figure 4-14.

Figure 4-14

The pits on an optical storage disk as seen through an electron microscope. Each pit is 1 micron in diameter—1,500 pits lined up side by side would be about as wide as the head of a pin.

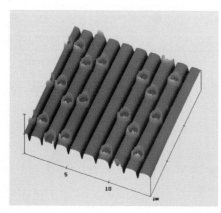

After creating a master, optical disks can be mass produced. During the manufacturing process copies of the disk are stamped out on a plastic disk. A thin layer of reflective aluminium is added, then a laquer coating for protection.

Optical media are very durable—the useful life of a CD-ROM is estimated to exceed 500 years. They are not susceptible to humidity, fingerprints, dust, or magnets. If you spill coffee on a CD-ROM disk, you can just rinse it off and it will be as good as new.

The data on optical media is permanent. Therefore, optical media do not give you the flexibility of magnetic media for changing data once it is stored. An optical drive that reads the data on an optical disk uses laser light, but less powerful than the laser that burns the pits in the original master. Figure 4-15 illustrates how light is used to read the data on an optical disk.

Figure 4-15

Reading data on an optical disk

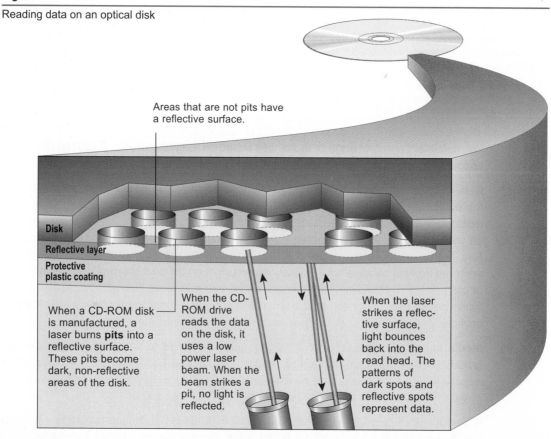

Areas that are not pits have a reflective surface.

Disk

Reflective layer

Protective plastic coating

When a CD-ROM disk is manufactured, a laser burns **pits** into a reflective surface. These pits become dark, non-reflective areas of the disk.

When the CD-ROM drive reads the data on the disk, it uses a low power laser beam. When the beam strikes a pit, no light is reflected.

When the laser strikes a reflective surface, light bounces back into the read head. The patterns of dark spots and reflective spots represent data.

Floppy Disk Storage

Why is it called a floppy disk? A **floppy disk** is a round piece of flexible mylar plastic covered with a thin layer of magnetic oxide. The disk is sealed inside a protective casing. Those brightly colored computer disks that fit conveniently in your pocket or backpack are sometimes mistakenly called "hard disks" because of their rigid plastic casing. If you break open the disk casing (something you should never do unless you want to ruin the disk), you would see that the mylar disk inside is thin and, well, floppy. Floppy disks are also called **floppies** or **diskettes**. A special high capacity floppy disk manufactured by iomega, Corp. is called a **Zip disk**.

Floppy disks come in several sizes: 3½ inch, 5¼ inch, and 8 inch. The disk size most commonly used on today's microcomputers is 3½ inch. A 3½-inch circular disk made of flexible mylar is housed inside a protective case of rigid plastic. When the disk is inserted in the disk drive, the spring-loaded access cover slides to the side to expose the disk surface for reading and writing data. Figure 4-16 shows the construction of a 3½-inch disk.

Figure 4-16

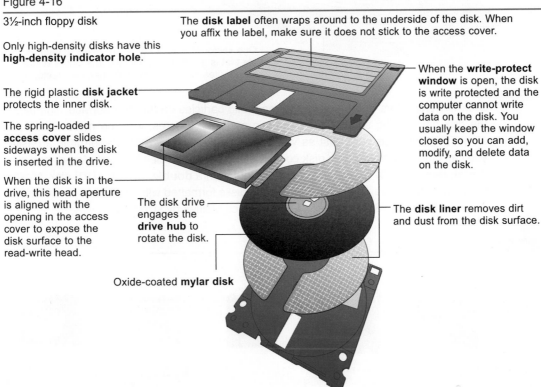

3½-inch floppy disk

Only high-density disks have this **high-density indicator hole**.

The rigid plastic **disk jacket** protects the inner disk.

The spring-loaded **access cover** slides sideways when the disk is inserted in the drive.

When the disk is in the drive, this head aperture is aligned with the opening in the access cover to expose the disk surface to the read-write head.

The disk drive engages the **drive hub** to rotate the disk.

Oxide-coated **mylar disk**

The **disk label** often wraps around to the underside of the disk. When you affix the label, make sure it does not stick to the access cover.

When the **write-protect window** is open, the disk is write protected and the computer cannot write data on the disk. You usually keep the window closed so you can add, modify, and delete data on the disk.

The **disk liner** removes dirt and dust from the disk surface.

In the past, floppy disks stored data only on one side; but today most store data on both sides. As you might guess, a **double-sided disk**, sometimes abbreviated as DS, stores twice as much data as a single-sided disk.

The amount of data a computer can store on each side of a disk depends on the way the disk is formatted. In Chapter 2 you learned that a disk must be formatted before you can store data on it. The formatting process creates a series of concentric **tracks** on the disk, and each track is divided into smaller segments called **sectors**, as shown in Figure 4-17.

Figure 4-17

Tracks and sectors of a formatted disk

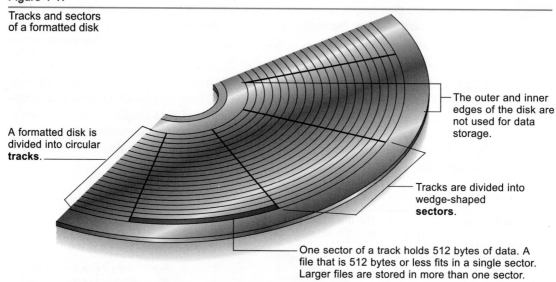

A formatted disk is divided into circular **tracks**.

The outer and inner edges of the disk are not used for data storage.

Tracks are divided into wedge-shaped **sectors**.

One sector of a track holds 512 bytes of data. A file that is 512 bytes or less fits in a single sector. Larger files are stored in more than one sector.

Disk density refers to the size of the magnetic particles on the disk surface. The higher the disk density, the smaller the magnetic particles it stores, and the more data it can store. Think of it this way: Just as you can put more lemons than grapefruit in a basket, you can store more data on a disk coated with smaller particles than with larger particles. A **high-density (HD) disk** can store more data than a **double-density (DD) disk**. Most of today's computers use high-density 3½-inch disks formatted with 18 sectors and 80 tracks per side. Figure 4-18 summarizes floppy disk capacities by size and density.

Figure 4-18

Floppy and Zip disk capacities

Size	5¼ inch	5¼ inch	3½ inch	3½ inch	3½ inch
Density	Double-density	High-density	Double-density	High-density	N/A
Capacity	360 KB	1.2 MB	720 KB	1.44 MB	100 MB
Sectors per side	9	15	9	18	32
Tracks per side	40	80	80	80	3065

The storage device that records and retrieves data on a floppy disk is a **floppy disk drive**. Figure 4-19 shows you a 3½-inch floppy disk drive and a Zip drive, along with the disks that they use.

Figure 4-19

Two popular disk drives

A 3½-inch disk drive has an eject button to release the disk and a drive light to indicate when the drive is in use. You insert the disk so the label goes in last. Virtually every computer has a 3½-inch disk drive.

A Zip drive uses special Zip disks that are slightly larger than a 3½-inch floppy disk. The green light indicates that the drive is ready. A yellow light indicates that the drive is in use. Insert the Zip disk so the label enters last. Zip disks are increasing in popularity and use.

In both a floppy disk drive and a Zip drive, the read-write head can read or write data from any sector of the disk, in any order. This ability to move to any sector is referred to as **random access** or **direct access**. Random access is a handy feature of disk-based storage that provides quick access to files anywhere on a disk. Even with random access, however, a floppy disk drive is not a particularly speedy device. It takes about 0.5 seconds for a 3½-inch drive to spin the disk up to speed and then move the read-write head to a particular sector. A Zip drive is about 20 times faster.

You don't usually run programs from floppy or Zip disks, so a 3½-inch or Zip drive would not be the main storage device in a computer system. Instead, floppies and Zip disks are typically used for transporting or shipping data files.

Newer technologies are decreasing the use of floppy disks. In the past, software was distributed on floppy disks. Now, most software vendors use CD-ROMs instead. Local computer networks and the Internet have made it easy to share data files, so floppy disks are shipped less frequently. Floppy disks have also been used to make duplicate copies of data files in case something happens to the originals, a process known as **backup**. The role of floppy disk storage for backup is being taken over, to some extent, by tape storage. Floppies are still used in many college computer labs so students can transport their data to different lab machines or to their home computers.

Hard Disk Storage

How can a hard disk be the same size as a floppy, but store so much more data? Hard disk storage is the preferred type of main storage for most computer systems because it provides faster access to files than floppy or Zip disk drives. A **hard disk platter** is a flat, rigid disk made of aluminum or glass and coated with a magnetic oxide. A **hard disk** is one or more platters and their associated read-write heads. You will frequently see the terms *hard disk* and *hard disk drive* used interchangeably. You might also hear the term *fixed disk* used to refer to hard disks.

InfoWeb

Speed Update 6

Microcomputer hard disk platters are typically 3½ inches in diameter—the same size as the circular mylar disk in a floppy. However, the storage capacity of a hard disk far exceeds that of a floppy disk. Also, the access time of a hard disk is significantly faster than a floppy disk's. Hard disk storage capacities of 5 GB and access times of 10 ms (.001 seconds) are not uncommon. Figure 4-20 explains how is it possible to pack so much data on a hard disk and access it so quickly.

Figure 4-20

How a hard disk drive works

Each data storage surface has its own **read-write head**. Read-write heads move in and out from the center of the disk to locate a specific track. The head hovers only five micro inches above the disk surface so the magnetic field is much more compact than on a floppy disk. As a result, more data is packed into a smaller area on a hard disk platter.

The **drive spindle** supports one or more **hard disk platters**. Both sides of the platter are used for data storage. More platters mean more data storage capacity. Hard disk platters rotate as a unit on the drive spindle to position a specific sector under the read-write heads. The platters spin continuously making thousands of revolutions per minute.

The platter surfaces are formatted into cylinders and sectors. A **cylinder** is a vertical stack of tracks. A hard disk could have between 312 and 2,048 cylinders. To find a file, the computer must know the cylinder, sector, and platter in which the file is stored.

Like floppy disks, hard disks provide random access to files. Unlike floppy disks, which begin to rotate only when you request data, hard disks are continually in motion, so there is no delay as the disk spins up to speed. As a result, hard disk access is faster than floppy disk access.

It is important to keep track of how much space is available on your disk, so you don't inadvertently fill it up. You can ask your computer operating system to tell you the capacity of your hard disk and how much of the capacity is currently used for data. The screens in Figures 4-21, 4-22, and 4-23 show you how to find out your disk capacity and utilization under DOS, Windows 3.1, Windows 95 and Windows 98.

Figure 4-21

Hard disk capacity and utilization in DOS

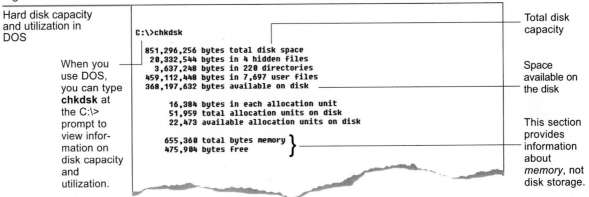

Total disk capacity

Space available on the disk

This section provides information about *memory*, not disk storage.

When you use DOS, you can type **chkdsk** at the C:\> prompt to view information on disk capacity and utilization.

Figure 4-22

Hard disk capacity and utilization in Windows 3.1

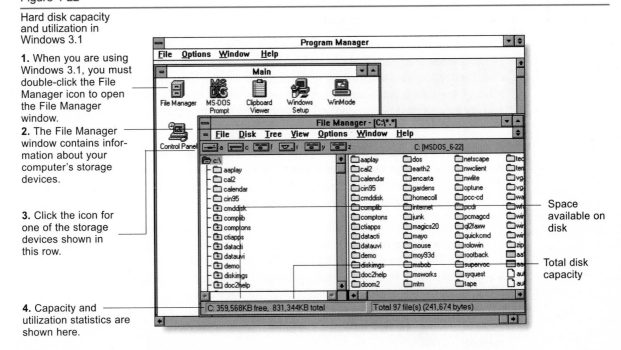

1. When you are using Windows 3.1, you must double-click the File Manager icon to open the File Manager window.

2. The File Manager window contains information about your computer's storage devices.

3. Click the icon for one of the storage devices shown in this row.

4. Capacity and utilization statistics are shown here.

Space available on disk

Total disk capacity

Figure 4-23

Hard disk capacity and utilization
in Windows 95 and Windows 98

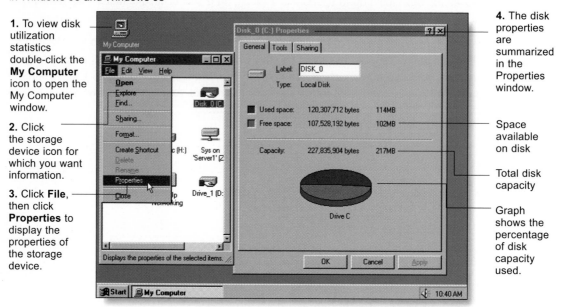

1. To view disk utilization statistics double-click the **My Computer** icon to open the My Computer window.

2. Click the storage device icon for which you want information.

3. Click **File**, then click **Properties** to display the properties of the storage device.

4. The disk properties are summarized in the Properties window.

Space available on disk

Total disk capacity

Graph shows the percentage of disk capacity used.

The read-write heads in a hard disk hover a microscopic distance above the disk surface. If a read-write head runs into a dust particle or some other contaminant on the disk, it might cause what is called a **head crash**. A head crash damages some of the data on the disk. To help eliminate contaminants from contacting the platters and causing head crashes, a hard disk is sealed in its case. A head crash can also be triggered by jarring the hard disk while it is in use. Although hard disks have become considerably more rugged in recent years, you should still handle and transport them with care.

Some hard disks are removable. **Removable hard disks** or hard disk cartridges contain platters and read-write heads that can be inserted and removed from the drive much like a floppy disk. Removable hard disks increase the potential storage capacity of your computer system, although the data is available on only one disk at a time. Removable hard disks also provide security for your data by allowing you to remove the hard disk cartridge and store it separately from the computer.

Mainframe users refer to disk storage as DASD (pronounced "daz-dee"). **DASD** stands for direct access storage device. As a direct, or random, access device, DASD can directly access data, much like a microcomputer hard disk drive. The DASD at most mainframe installations is either disk packs, high-capacity fixed disks, or RAID.

Many mainframe installations still use removable disk packs, although they are a fairly old technology. A **disk pack** contains from 6 to 20 hard disks. Each disk is a little larger than 10 inches. The entire pack can be removed and replaced with another pack. Disk packs are gradually being replaced by high-capacity fixed disk drives. **High-capacity fixed disk drive** technology is similar to a microcomputer hard disk with its platters and read-write heads, but with higher storage capacity. Each high-capacity fixed disk drive is housed in a cabinet. A mainframe computer system might include as many as 100 fixed disk drive cabinets.

RAID, another type of hard disk storage, is found in an increasing number of mainframe and microcomputer installations. RAID stands for redundant array of independent disks. A **RAID** storage device contains many disk platters, provides redundancy, and achieves faster data access than conventional hard disks. The **redundancy** feature of RAID technology protects data from media failures by recording data on more than one disk platter.

To further increase the speed of data access, your computer might use a disk cache. A **disk cache** (pronounced "cash") is a special area of computer memory into which the computer transfers the data you are likely to need from disk storage. Figure 4-24 shows how a disk cache works.

Figure 4-24

How disk caching works

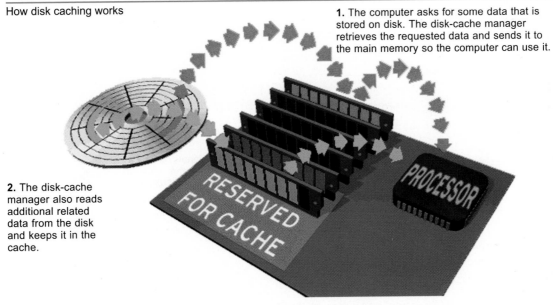

1. The computer asks for some data that is stored on disk. The disk-cache manager retrieves the requested data and sends it to the main memory so the computer can use it.

2. The disk-cache manager also reads additional related data from the disk and keeps it in the cache.

3. When the computer asks for more data, the disk-cache manager first checks the cache to see if the data is there. If the requested data is in the cache, it is immediately sent for processing. If the requested data is not in the cache, the disk-cache manager must take the time to locate the data on the disk, retrieve the data, then send it on to the main memory.

How does a disk cache help speed things up? Suppose your computer retrieves the data from a particular sector of your disk. There is a high probability that the next data you need will be from an adjacent sector—the remainder of a program file, for example, or the next section of a data file. The computer reads the data from nearby sectors and stores it in the cache. If the data you'll use next is already in the cache, the computer doesn't need to wait while the mechanical parts of the drive locate and read the data from the disk.

Tape Storage

| Do they still use those big tape drives on computers that you see in old movies? | In the
1960s, magnetic tape was the most popular form of mainframe computer storage. When
IBM introduced its first microcomputer in 1981, the legacy of tape storage continued in the
form of a cassette tape drive, similar to those used for audio recording and playback.

Using tape as a primary storage device instead of a hard disk would be slow and inconvenient because tape requires sequential, rather than random, access. With **sequential access**, data is stored and read as a sequence of bytes along the length of the tape. Study the diagram in Figure 4-25 to learn how computers store data on tape.

Figure 4-25

Sequential file access on
magnetic tape

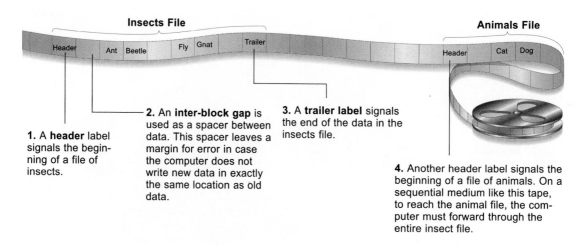

1. A **header** label signals the beginning of a file of insects.

2. An **inter-block gap** is used as a spacer between data. This spacer leaves a margin for error in case the computer does not write new data in exactly the same location as old data.

3. A **trailer label** signals the end of the data in the insects file.

4. Another header label signals the beginning of a file of animals. On a sequential medium like this tape, to reach the animal file, the computer must forward through the entire insect file.

Microcomputer users quickly abandoned tape storage for the convenience and speed of random access disk drives. Recently, however, tape storage for microcomputers has experienced a revival—not as a principal storage device, but for backing up data stored on hard disks. As you have learned in this chapter, the data on disks can be easily destroyed, erased, or otherwise lost. Protecting the data on the hard disk is of particular concern to users because it contains so much data—data that would be difficult and time-consuming to reconstruct. A **tape backup** is a copy of the data on a hard disk, stored on magnetic tape, and used to restore lost data. A tape backup is relatively inexpensive and can rescue you from the overwhelming task of trying to reconstruct lost data. If you lose the data on your hard disk, you can copy the data from the tape backup back to the hard disk. Typically, you do not use the data directly from the tape backup because the sequential access is too slow to be practical.

The large reels of computer tapes you might have seen in old movies are called **open reel tapes** and resemble spools of 16 mm film. Access speeds for open reel tapes are measured in seconds, not miliseconds. Open reel tapes are still used as a distribution medium for mainframe and microcomputer systems. Newer tape storage devices for these computers typically use half-inch tape cartriges. A **tape cartridge** is a removable magnetic tape module similar to a cassette tape.

InfoWeb

Tape
7

The most popular types of tape drives for microcomputers also use tape cartridges, but there are several tape specifications and cartridge sizes. **QIC** (quarter-inch cartridge) is a tape cartrige that contains quarter-inch wide tape. Depending on tape length, QIC tape capacities range from 340 MB to 2 GB. **DAT** (digital audio tape) was originally an audio recording format, but is now also used for data storage. The 4 mm wide DAT tape format storage capacity ranges from 2 GB to 12 GB. When you purchase tapes, check the tape drive manual to make sure the tapes you purchase are the correct type for your tape drive.

For a backup device, access time is less important than the time it takes to copy data from your hard disk to tape. Drive manufacturers do not usually supply such performance specifications, but most users can expect a tape drive to back up 100 MB in 15–20 minutes. Figure 4-26 shows a tape backup device that you might typically find in a microcomputer system.

Figure 4-26

Cartridge tape storage

Tape drives are typically incorporated in microcomputer systems to backup the contents of the hard drive. An external tape drive such as this one is a standalone unit that can be easily moved from one computer to another. Internal tape drives are installed in the system unit, similar to a floppy or CD-ROM drive.

The tape cartridge sequentially stores a backup of the data on the computer's hard disk drive

CD-ROM Storage

If CD-ROMs are read only, doesn't that limit their use? **CD-ROMs** are based on the same technology as the audio CDs you buy at your favorite music store. CD-ROM (pronounced "cee dee rom") stands for Compact Disc Read Only Memory. A computer CD-ROM disc, like its audio counterpart, contains data that has been stamped on the disk surface as a series of pits. To read the data on a CD-ROM, an optical read head distinguishes the patterns of pits that represent bytes. Figure 4-27 shows how you load a CD into the CD-ROM drive.

InfoWeb

CD-ROM Update 8

Figure 4-27

CD-ROM storage

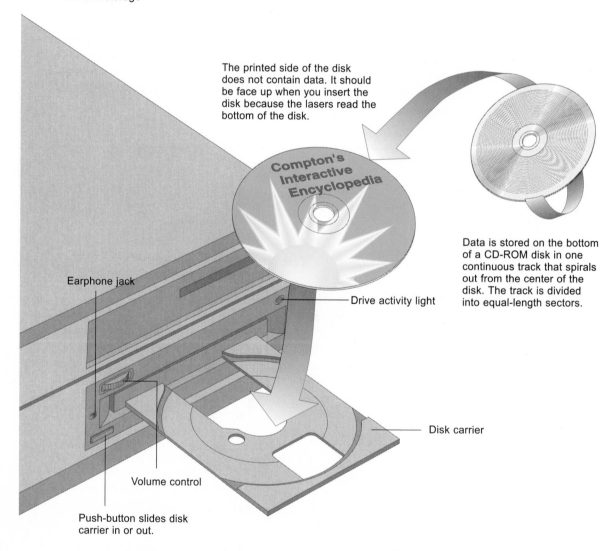

The printed side of the disk does not contain data. It should be face up when you insert the disk because the lasers read the bottom of the disk.

Compton's Interactive Encyclopedia

Earphone jack

Drive activity light

Data is stored on the bottom of a CD-ROM disk in one continuous track that spirals out from the center of the disk. The track is divided into equal-length sectors.

Disk carrier

Volume control

Push-button slides disk carrier in or out.

CD-ROMs provide tremendous storage capacity. A single CD-ROM disk holds up to 680 MB, equivalent to more than 300,000 pages of text, and is quite durable. The surface of the disk is coated with a clear plastic, making the data permanent and unalterable.

A CD-ROM drive supplements, rather than replaces, a hard disk drive because a CD-ROM is a read-only storage medium. **Read only** means that the computer can retrieve data from a CD-ROM but cannot save any new data on it. In this respect, CD-ROM technology differs from hard disk storage, on which you can write, erase, and read data.

A CD-ROM disk is relatively inexpensive to manufacture, making it an ideal way for software publishers to distribute large programs and data files. CD-ROM is the media of choice for delivery of multimedia applications because it provides the large storage capacity necessary for sound, video, and graphics files.

InfoWeb

CD-R
9

A recent technological development is the creation of CDs on which you can write data. **CD-R** (compact disc-recordable) technology allows the computer to record data on a CD-R disk using a special CD-R recording device. Disks that have been produced with the CD-R device can be used on a regular CD-ROM drive, like the one you might have on your computer. As with regular CD-ROMs the data on the disk cannot be erased or modified.

CD-R is a useful technology for archiving data. **Archiving** refers to the process of moving data off a primary storage device when that data is not frequently accessed. For example, a business might archive its accounting data for previous years or a hospital might archive billing records once the accounts are paid. What's the difference between an archive and a backup? Archived data does not generally change, but the data you back up might change frequently.

Physical File Storage

What's the difference between physical and logical storage? Whether you store a file on a disk, CD-ROM, or tape, you have to know the filename and the letter of the device on which it was stored. That is the *logical* view of data storage, and it includes whatever desktop metaphor that makes it easy for you to view and select files. The *physical* view of data storage is how the computer keeps track of the location of your files on the physical disk, CD-ROM, or tape. To understand how the computer keeps track of your data, we'll look at how the computer manages data stored on a floppy disk.

Although a disk is formatted into tracks and sectors that provide physical storage locations for data, files are actually stored in clusters. A **cluster** is a group of sectors; it is the smallest storage unit the computer can access. The number of sectors that form a cluster depends on the type of computer and the capacity of the disk. For example, IBM-compatible microcomputers form a cluster from two sectors on a 360 K disk or 32 sectors on a 1 GB disk. Each cluster is numbered and the operating system maintains a list of which sectors correspond to each cluster.

InfoWeb

FAT
10

When the computer stores a file on a disk, the operating system records the cluster number that contains the beginning of the file in a file allocation table (FAT). The **FAT** is an operating system file that maintains a list of files and their physical location on the disk. The FAT is such a crucial file that if it is damaged by a head crash or other disaster, you generally lose access to all the data stored on your disk. This is yet another reason to have a backup of the data on your hard drive.

When you want to store a file, the operating system looks at the FAT to see which clusters are empty. The operating system then puts the data for the file in empty clusters. The cluster numbers are recorded in the FAT. The name of the new file and the number of the first cluster that contains the file data are recorded in the directory.

A file that does not fit into a single cluster will spill over into the next adjacent or *contiguous* cluster unless that cluster already contains data. If the next cluster is full, the operating system stores the file in a noncontiguous (non-adjacent) cluster and sets up instructions called *pointers*. These "point" to each piece of the file, as shown in Figure 4-28.

Figure 4-28

How the FAT works

1. The directory is a file maintained by the operating system that contains a list of files on the disk and the number of the cluster that contains the start of the file. The directory and FAT work together to keep track of the files on a disk.

2. Here the directory shows that a file called **Jordan.wks** begins in cluster 7.

Directory	
Filename	**Starting Cluster**
Bio.txt	3
Jordan.wks	7
Pick.wps	9

3. The file allocation table (FAT) is a file maintained by the operating system to keep track of the physical location of files on a disk.

4. Each cluster is listed in the FAT, along with a number that indicates the status of the cluster. If status is "1," the cluster is reserved for technical files. If status is "0," the cluster is empty, so new data can be stored there. If the status is "999," the cluster contains the end of a file. Other status numbers indicate the sector that holds more data for a file.

5. Looking at the FAT entry for cluster 7, you see that the **Jordan.wks** file continues in cluster 8.

6. The FAT entry for cluster 8, shows that the **Jordan.wks** file continues in cluster 10. The file is stored in **non-contiguous** clusters 7, 8, and 10.

7. The FAT entry for cluster 10 shows that this is the end of the **Jordan.wks** file.

FAT		
Cluster	**Status**	*Comment*
1	1	*Reserved for operating system*
2	1	*Reserved for operating system*
3	4	*First cluster of Bio.txt. Points to cluster 4 which holds more data for Bio.txt.*
4	999	*Last cluster of Bio.txt*
5	0	*Empty*
6	0	*Empty*
7	8	*First cluster for Jordan.wks. Points to cluster 8 which holds more data for the Jordan.wks file.*
8	10	*Points to cluster 10 which holds more data for the Jordan.wks file.*
9	999	*First and last cluster containing Pick.wps*
10	999	*Last cluster of Jordan.wks*

When you want to retrieve a file, the operating system looks through the directory for the filename and the number of the first cluster that contains the file data. The FAT tells the computer which clusters contain the remaining data for the file. The operating system moves the read-write head to the cluster that contains the beginning of the file and reads it. If the file is stored in more than one cluster, the read-write head must move to the next cluster to read more of the file. It takes longer to access a file stored in noncontiguous clusters than one stored in contiguous clusters because the disk or head must move farther to find the next section of the file.

When you erase a file, the operating system changes the status of the appropriate clusters in the FAT. For example, if a file is stored in clusters 1, 2, 5, and 7 and you erase it, the operating system changes the status for those four clusters to "empty." The data is not physically removed or erased from those clusters. Instead, the old data remains in the clusters until a new file is stored there. This rather interesting situation means that if you inadvertently erase a file, you might be able to get it back using the operating system's **undelete utility**. Of course, you can only undelete a file if you haven't recorded something new over it, so undelete works only if you discover and correct mistakes immediately.

InfoWeb

Storage
Basics
11

As you use random-access storage, files tend to become **fragmented**, that is, each file is stored in many noncontiguous clusters. Drive performance generally declines as the drive works harder to locate the clusters that contain the parts of a file. To regain peak performance, you can use a **defragmentation utility** to rearrange the files on a disk so that they are stored in contiguous clusters. Study Figure 4-29, which explains more about fragmentation and defragmentation.

Figure 4-29

Defragmenting a disk

LAB

Defragmentation
and Disk
Operators

Fragmented disk

On this fragmented disk the purple, yellow, and blue files are stored in noncontiguous clusters. Accessing the clusters for these files is not efficient because of the time required to move the read-write head over the data.

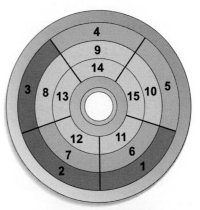

Defragmented disk

When the disk is defragmented, the clusters of data for each file are moved to contiguous clusters. Data access becomes more efficient because drive head and disk movement are minimized.

QuickCheck B

1. Storage capacity is measured in _____, and access time is measured in _____.

2. A magnet can disrupt data on _____ storage, but _____ storage technology is more durable.

3. The formatting process creates a series of concentric _____ and triangle-shaped _____ on the disk.

4. The computer can move directly to any file on a(n) _____ access device, but must start at the beginning and read through all the data on a(n) _____ access device.

5. Two popular formats for microcomputer tape cartridges are _____ and DAT.

6. The primary storage device on a microcomputer is the _____.

7. The _____ keeps track of the physical location of files on a disk.

8. Data files that are entered by the user, changed often, or shared with other users are generally stored on optical media. True or false? _____

UserFocus

C Using Files

LAB

Now that you have learned about logical and physical file storage, let's apply what you've learned to how you typically use files when you work with application software. Using word-processing software to produce a document illustrates the way you use files on a computer, so look at the file operations for a typical word-processing session illustrated in Figure 4-30.

Using Files

Figure 4-30

File operations for a typical word-processing session

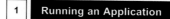

1   Running an Application

Suppose you want to create a document about the summer vacation packages your company offers. You decide to create the document using the word-processing software, Microsoft Word. Your first step is to start the Microsoft Word program. When you run Microsoft Word, the program file is copied from the hard drive to the memory of the computer.

2   Creating a File

You begin to type the text of the document. As you type, your data is stored in the memory of the computer. Your data will not be stored on disk until you initiate the Save command.

Word.exe is loaded into memory from hard disk

Your data is stored in memory while you type

3   Saving a Data File

When you create a file and save it on disk for the first time, the application or the operating system prompts you to name the file so you can later retrieve it by name. You know from earlier in this chapter that the name you give to a file must follow the naming convention for the operating system. You name the file A:Vacation.doc. By typing A: you direct the computer to save the file on the floppy disk in drive A. The computer looks for empty clusters on the disk where it can store the file. The computer then adds the filename to the directory, along with the number of the cluster that contains the beginning of the file. Once you have saved your file, you can exit the Word program or work on another document.

A:Vacation.doc is copied from memory to the floppy disk

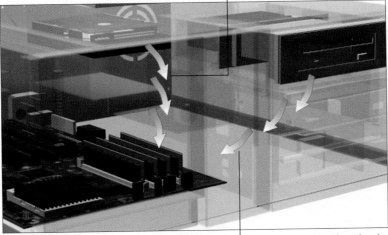

Word.exe is loaded
into memory

A:Vacation.doc is
copied from disk into
memory

The changes you make
to the document are
stored in memory.
When you save your
revisions, they over-
write the previous ver-
sion of **Vacation.doc**.

| 4 | **Retrieving a Data File** |

Now suppose that a few days later,
you decide that you want to re-read
Vacation.doc. You need to start
Microsoft Word. Once the Word
program is running, you can retrieve
the Vacation.doc file from the disk on
which it is stored.

When you want to use a data file
that already exists on disk storage,
you must tell the application to open
the file. In Microsoft Word you either
type the name of the file,
A:Vacation.doc, or select the filename from a list of files stored on
the disk. The application communi-
cates the filename to the operating
system.

The operating system looks at the
directory and FAT to find which clusters contain the file, then moves the
read-write head to the appropriate
disk location to read the file. The
electronics on the disk drive transfer
the file data into the main memory of
the computer where your application
software can manipulate it. Once the
operating system has retrieved the
file, the word-processing software
displays it on the screen.

| 5 | **Revising a Data File** |

When you see the Vacation.doc file on the screen, you
can make modifications to it. Each character that you
type and each change that you make is stored temporarily in the main memory of the computer, but not on
the disk.

The Vacation.doc file is already on the disk, so when
you are done with the modifications you have two
options. Option one is to store the revised version in
place of the old version. Option two is to create a new
file for your revision and give it a different name, such
as Holiday.

If you decide to go with option one—store the revised
version in place of the old version—the operating system copies your revised data from the computer memory to the same clusters that contained the old file. You
do not have to take a separate step to delete the old
file—the operating system automatically records the
new file over it.

If you decide to go with option two—create a new file for
the revision—the application prompts you for a filename. Your revisions will be stored under the new filename. The original file, **Vacation.doc**, will still remain
on the disk in its unrevised form.

Copying Files

Can I copy a file from the hard disk to my floppy disk and vice versa? You can copy a file from one storage medium to another. When you copy a file, the original file remains intact. You'll find that copying files is a task you will do frequently. Making copies of important files as backup, copying files from your hard disk to a floppy disk to share with a friend, or transferring files you receive on a floppy disk to your hard disk are only a few of the tasks that require you to know how to copy files.

DOS Directories and File Management

Suppose you want to copy the **Vacation.doc** file from a floppy disk to your hard disk. The operating system is responsible for maintaining the list of files on your disk, so you usually use the operating system to copy files. With a graphical operating system such as Microsoft Windows, you can drag the icon that represents **Vacation.doc** from its place in the directory of drive A to the icon that represents drive C, as shown in Figure 4-31.

Figure 4-31

To copy the file **Vacation.doc** to drive C, drag the file icon to the drive C icon.

Drive C icon

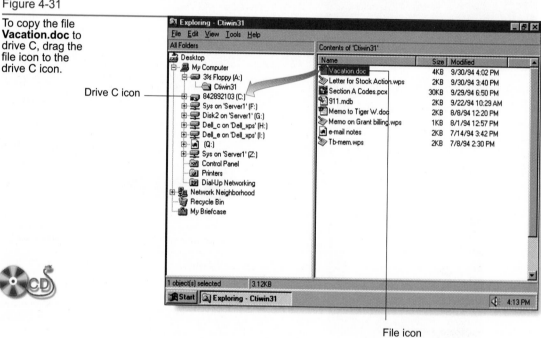

File icon

With the DOS operating system, you use the Copy command to copy a file. Let's assume that the disk containing **Vacation.doc** is in drive A and your hard disk drive is drive C. The DOS command to copy **Vacation.doc** from drive A to a subdirectory called Plans on drive C is:

COPY A:Vacation.doc C:\ Plans\Vacation.doc

Deleting Files

What if I run out of hard disk space? Eliminating files that you no longer need opens space for new files. If you want to eliminate a file that you have saved on disk, you **delete** or **erase** the file. As you know, when you delete a file, the operating system does not physically erase the cluster that contains the data belonging to that file. Instead, it changes the entries in the FAT to indicate that the clusters are available for storing other files. As additional files are stored on the disk, the sectors that formerly contained the deleted file are gradually overwritten.

To delete the file **Vacation.doc** from the disk in drive A using DOS, you type: DEL A:Vacation.doc. To delete a file using Windows 3.1, you highlight the file in the File Manager window, then press the Delete key. Using Windows 95 you delete a file by pressing the Delete key to delete the icon that represents the file.

EndNote

InfoWeb

Past & Future
12

Storage technology has dramatically advanced over the last 40 years. In 1956 IBM researchers introduced the world's first computer disk storage system. It stored 5 MB of data on fifty 24-inch disks. The disk drive's major advantage over tape storage was its ability to directly access any data on any of the disks, without sequentially reading all the data in between. Suddenly, computers could be used for interactive computing applications such as airline reservations and automated banking. In 1995 IBM researchers achieved a world record by storing 3 GB of data per square inch.

Such advances in storage technology did not eliminate tape storage. Quite to the contrary— tape drives have become faster and more efficient. By 1973, tapes were whizzing along at 200 inches per second, accelerating to that speed in less than 750 millionths of a second. Is that fast? You bet. At that rate of acceleration, tape speed would reach 12,000 mph in one second.

CD-ROMs, once thought to be the ultimate for multimedia storage are not large enough to store an entire two-hour feature film. Enter DVD (digital video disk). By increasing storage density, a DVD stores 4.7 GB of data on a disk the same size as a CD-ROM. Used in both the computing and entertainment industries DVD is designed to hold the data for a feature-length movie with theater-quality Dolby Surround Sound. DVD drives could be the next hot PC storage technology.

And what does the next 40 years hold for storage technology? How about holographic storage? Thinking in three-dimensions, instead of two-dimensional flat storage on disks and tapes, holographic storage is essentially a three-dimensional snapshot of data stored in a crystal medium. In the laboratory, researchers have achieved storage densities of 48 MB per cubic centimeter, but expected storage density is 10 GB per cubic centimeter. To put this in perspective, think about a couple of holographic storage cubes like a pair of dice that hold the contents of a half-mile high stack of books.

Researchers at the IBM Research Division's Zurich laboratory are working on another technology with the potential to revolutionize computer storage. They discovered that it is possible to manipulate individual molecules at room temperature. The researchers created a nano-abacus using microscopic soccerball-like carbon 60 molecules as the beads. A scanning tunneling microscope moves the beads along steps just one atom high. The process is similar to the earliest form of abacus in which the beads moved in groves instead of rods. These atoms could represent bits of stored data and eventually replace the much larger magnetic particles we use today on floppy and hard disks.

Figure 4-32

IBM's nano-abacus demonstrates that it might be possible in the future to use individual molecules to represent data bits for computer storage.

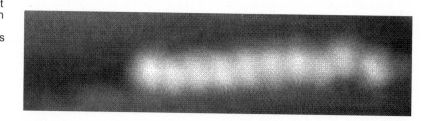

InfoWeb

InfoWeb

Chapter Links

The InfoWeb is your guide to print, film, television, and electronic resources. Use it to obtain updates on quickly changing technical information and to locate information for research papers. If you're using the New Perspectives CD-ROM, click the InfoWeb icon on the left side of this paragraph to access the online InfoWeb links. Otherwise, use your Web browser and type in the address of the New Perspectives site: www.cciw.com/np3. At the New Perspectives site you'll find up-to-date links to the topics covered in this chapter.

1 World Records

In 1951 a hunting party in Ireland shot at, but missed, some golden plovers. The hunters discussed at length whether the golden plover was Europe's fastest game bird. The managing director of Guinness breweries, Sir Hugh Beaver was a member of the hunting party. With sudden inspiration he realized that what the world needed was a book of records to settle such debates, and the *Guinness Book of World Records* was born. Now published annually, you can find it in your library or bookstore. There's even a *Guinness Disk of Records* published on CD-ROM by Grolier Electronic Publishing. For world record sites on the Web, connect to the Saxonia page **www.imn.htwk-leipzig.de/~saxonia/links.html**. You won't find records, but you will find lots of fun facts about computers in **The Official Computer Bowl Trivia Book** by Christopher Morgan (The Computer Museum, 1996).

2 Autoexec

To understand what the Autoexec.bat file is all about, you need to see an example. You can start the Sysedit program on your Windows computer to see what the Autoexec.bat file looks like, or you can look at an example online with explanations of what each line does at **www.ids.net/~jimwy/ autoexec.html**.

3 Filename Extensions

You learned that much of today's software adds an application-specific filename extension to the files you save. Suppose you receive a file that has an unfamiliar extension. What software should you use to view the file? On the Web you'll find a list of filename extensions in alphabetical order at **stekt.oulu.fi/~jon/jouninfo/extension.html**.

4 Directories

To become more familiar with the terms associated with file management—such as directory, folder, root directory, and path—log on to the *Webopaedia* at **www.pcwebopaedia.com** and enter the term "directory." Follow the links for similar words, and check out the links to magazine articles.

5 Floppies & Zips

What if your floppy disk stops working? Get some hints on fixing it at **www.louisville.edu/~ajsmit01/floppy.html**. You'll learn more about the Zip drive at Iomega's site, **www.iomega.com**.

6 Speed Update

To find the latest information on disk drive storage capacities and access speeds, check out these manufacturer sites: Seagate at **www.seagate.com** and Western Digital Corporation at **www.wdc.com**. For RAID and mainframe storage solutions try **www.storage.ibm.com** and **www.storage.digital.com**.

7 Tape

What's new with tape drive capacity and tape technology? Check these manufacturers' sites: Hewlett Packard at **www.hp.com/storage/cms/index.html**, Exabyte at **www.exabyte.com**, and Seagate at **www.seagate. com/ tape/tapetop.shtml**.

8 CD-ROM Update

For the latest on CD-ROM access times and transfer rates, connect to manufacturer sites such as Mitsumi at **www.mitsumi.com** or NEC at **www.nec.com**.

9 CD-R Technology

Thinking of buying a CD-R drive and making your own CDs? There are pitfalls when you burn your own pits! See the advice from *PC Magazine* columnist Jim Seymour at **www8.zdnet.com/pcmag/ issues/1507/pcmg0043.htm**. For general information about CD-ROM drives, check out the CD Information Center at **www.cd-info.com/index.shtml**, sponsored by the CD-Info Company. Look for the CD-R FAQs and check out the latest on new packet writing software. Hewlett Packard manufactures one of the most popular CD-R drives. Connect to **www.hp.com** and search for CD-R. At HP's site you'll find a page "CDTechnology Introduction" that includes information on CD standards, data access, data formats, access speed, and more.

10 FAT

Learn about the FAT File System at **www.hptech.com/education.html**. FAT 32 allows your computer to use larger storage devices and provides more efficient storage with less wasted space. You can read about FAT 32 at **www.microsoft.com/windows/pr/fat32.htm**. You'll find additional information about the FAT, microcomputer storage, and a wide variety of other computer topics in Peter Norton's best-selling book, **Inside the PC** (Sams, 1995).

11 Storage Basics

Disk drive manufacturer Quantum maintains a Web site with an excellent overview of computer storage at **www.quantum.com/ssrc/storage_basics**. If you're looking for more information on mainframe and RAID storage, try the RAID Advisory Board Web site at **www.raid-advisory.com**. Another good source of basic information about disks and defragmentation is the complete online book *Fragmentation: the Condition, the Cause, the Cure* by Craig Jensen at **www.execsoft.com/fragbook/frame2.htm**.

12 Past & Future of Storage Technology

IBM maintains a visually stunning site about the history of computer storage at **www.almaden.ibm.com/ storage/firsts/n1956t.htm**. You'll find "believe it or not" factoids about how engineers pushed storage technology to its limits and beyond. What does the future have in store? You'll find an excellent introduction to DVD at **www.c-cube.com/technology/dvd.html#ES**. At the Creative Labs Web site, **www.creativelabs.com** you can follow the multimedia links to find the latest on DVD products. Learn about holographic storage by taking the easy-to-read tutorial at the Optitek Web site, **www.optitek.com/hdss_tutorial.htm**.

Review

1. Answer the questions below each heading in this chapter, *using your own words*.

2. List the three most *practical* things you learned from this chapter. Why do you think they are the most practical?

3. List each of the boldface terms used in this chapter, then *use your own words* to write a short definition of each term. If you would like clarification of one or more terms, refer to a computer dictionary or a computer science encyclopedia such as those listed in the InfoWeb section of Chapter 1. You can also refer to the Glossary/Index for this textbook.

4. Copy the following chart on paper. Place an X in the Data Files column if the feature applies to data files. Place an X in the Executable Files column if the feature applies to executable files. If a feature applies to both, put an X in both columns.

Feature	Data Files	Executable Files
Created by you, the user		
Created by programmers		
Use an application to view it		
Supplied with software		
Has an .exe or .com extension		
Referred to as a program or application		

5. Indicate which filenames in the following list are not valid under the operating system used in your school's computer lab. Which filenaming convention does each nonvalid filename violate?

Wp.exe	Ppr	Win.exe
Autoexec.bat	Results*.wks	Monthly.wk1
Report#1.txt	Smith&Smith.doc	Sep/94.wri
Asia map.doc	Ocean.tif	Mn43-44.dbf

6. Examine the directory listing below and answer the following questions:

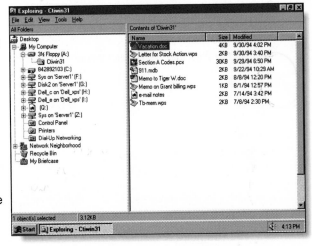

a. What is the size of the file **Emergency.doc**?

b. On what date was **911.mdb** last modified?

c. How many program files are listed?

d. What is the name of the folder that contains these files?

e. What application was used to create **Memo to Tiger W.**?

f. How many of these files are data files?

g. What is the largest file on the disk?

h. Does **Section A Codes.pcx** contain text or graphics?

i. What type of data does the file **Fire.wav** contain?

j. How many of the files appear to be memos?

k. How would you use a wildcard to get a directory of all the files with .xls extensions?

l. How many files match the specification S*.*?

m. How many files match the specification *.*?

7 Suppose you have a disk with the following files:

Minutes.doc	Report.doc	Budget.xls
Jacsmemo.doc	Report1.doc	Shipjan.xls
Shipfeb.xls	Shipmar.xlx	Shipapr.xls
Minutes.txt	Roger.txt	Roadmap.bmp

If you could specify all the files with a .doc extension by *.doc. How would you specify the following files?

a. All the files with .txt extensions

b. All the files that contain "minutes"

c. All the files that begin with "Ship"

d. All the files on the disk

e. All the files that begin with the letter "R"

8 Suppose you need to retrieve a file from Sarah's computer. She tells you that the file is stored as D:\Data\Payables.xls.

a. What is the filename? *peyables*

b. What is the file extension? *.xls*

c. On which drive is the file stored? *D*

d. In which directory is the file stored? *Data*

e. What type of file is it likely to be? *excel*

f. Will you need a specific software program to retrieve and view the file? *yes*

9 Suppose you need to defragment the files manually on the disk shown below. Using the disk on the right, show how the files are arranged after you complete the defragmentation. Use colored pencils or different patterns to show each file clearly.

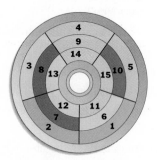 

10 Use the New Perspectives CD-ROM to take a chapter quiz or to review the new terms presented in this chapter.

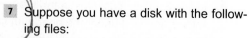

Projects

1 **File Extensions** Many software applications use a specific file extension for data files created with that application. Determine the extensions used by five applications on your own computer or a lab computer. Run each software application and attempt to retrieve a file. If the software application uses a specific file extension, you will usually see the extension indicated in a box on the screen. For example, you might see *.doc if you are using Microsoft Word for Windows.

For each of the five programs you select:

a. Specify the program name.

b. Sketch a picture of the program icon (if you are using Windows) or indicate the executable filename (if you are using DOS).

c. Indicate the filename extension the program uses. If the program does not use a specific filename extension, indicate that this is the case.

2 **Storage Devices You Use** You should be aware of the storage devices on your computer so that you use the best device for each task. You will need to take a hands-on look at your computer at home or a computer in your school lab to answer the following questions:

a. Where is this computer located?

b. What is the hard disk capacity? (Hint: Refer to Figure 4-18.)

c. What is the hard disk drive letter?

d. What is the floppy disk size?

e. What is the floppy disk capacity?

f. What is the floppy disk drive letter?

g. Is there a tape storage device?

h. Is there a CD-ROM drive?

i. Which storage device do you usually use for the data files you create?

j. Which storage device holds most of the applications software that you use?

k. Which storage device would you use for backups?

3 **Calculating Storage Requirements** How much storage space would be needed to store this textbook? To calculate approximately how many bytes of storage space this text (not including pictures) requires:

a. Count the number of lines on a typical page.

b. Count the number of characters (including blanks) in the longest line of text on the page.

c. Multiply the number of lines by the number of characters in the longest line to calculate the number of characters (bytes) per page.

d. Multiply this figure by the number of pages in the book.

e. What do you estimate is the computer storage space required for this text?

4 **Calculating Hard Disk Capacity** Most manufacturers list the storage capacity of their hard disk drives on the drive itself or in the user manual. The manufacturer calculates storage capacity in bytes using the formula:

capacity = cylinders X surfaces X sectors X 512

The 512 in the formula is the number of bytes stored in each sector of each cylinder. Suppose you have a hard disk with 615 cylinders, 4 surfaces (two platters), and 17 sectors. What is the capacity in bytes of this disk?

5  INTERNET Optional

Shopping for Storage Use a recent computer magazine or a Web site such as Computer Express at **www.cexpress.com** to fill in the following "shopping list:"

Item	Brand	Merchant	Price
Package of 10 3½-inch floppy disks			
High-density 3½-inch floppy disk drive			
850 MB, 10 ms hard disk drive			
Tape drive			
Quad-speed CD-ROM			

6 **What's in That File?** Earlier, you learned to distinguish between executable, data, and source files. In this project, you will look at the contents of each file type. When you view an executable file, you should see meaningless symbols. When you view a data file, you should be able to read the data. When you view a source file, you should be able to read the commands it contains. The Type command lets you view the contents of a file without changing it. You can use the Type command to look at the **Autoexec.bat** source file, the **Command.com** executable file, and the **Country.txt** data file.

If you are using DOS, make sure you are at the C:\> prompt. If you are using Windows 3.1, double-click the MS-DOS prompt icon in the Main window. If you are using Windows 95, click the Start button, select Programs, then select MS-DOS prompt. Do each of the following steps, and write down the first line you see on the screen:

a. Type the following command (including "type"), then press the Enter key:
   type c:\autoexec.bat|more

b. Type the following command, then press the Enter key:
   type c:\command.com

c. Type the following command, then press the Enter key:
   type c:\dos\country.txt|more

7 **Troubleshooting a Storage Problem**
Read the following scenario and determine what went wrong, then write a paragraph describing what you would do to correct the problem. Your instructor will indicate if you should do this project individually or discuss it in a small group.

Toni's 1 GB hard disk contained about 75 MB of files on February 18. On that day, she made a tape backup of the entire disk. On February 19, Toni moved to a company office one block away. The company maintenance staff moved the computer, along with Toni's paper files, in the late afternoon. The people on the maintenance crew left the computer on the desk in the new office.

On February 20, Toni set up the computer and tried to open a data file containing the names and addresses of her clients. The computer displayed a message—something about an error on drive C. Toni turned off her computer and then turned it back on, hoping the error would go away, but the computer wouldn't let her access any data on the hard disk.

8 **CD-Mania** What's the difference between the CDs that contain your favorite music album and the CD-ROMs you use in a computer? You might be surprised to learn that some computer

INTERNET Optional

CD-ROM drives can play your music CDs. In fact, there are several CD formats, including CD-DA, CD-I, CD-ROM, PhotoCD, and CD-R. For this project, use your library and Internet resources to write a paper describing these CD formats. The length of your paper will depend on the scope of the project: a three-page paper is suitable for a short project, a term paper might require 10–15 pages. Be sure you include a bibliography.

Your paper can deal with CDs from the technical perspective or from the applied perspective. If you take the technical perspective, you should look for answers to questions such as, but not limited to:

a. What are the capacity and storage formats for each type of CD?

b. Why did these specifications originate?

c. What are the advantages and disadvantages of each?

If you take the applied perspective, you should try to find the answers to questions such as, but not limited to:

a. What are the primary uses for each type of CD?

b. What are the advantages and disadvantages of each?

c. How do the costs of each format compare?

9 **Data Storage in Organizations**
Organizations take different approaches to data storage, depending on the volume of their data, the value of their data, and the need for data security. The purpose of this project is to interview the person responsible for maintaining the data for an organization and discover the answers to the following questions:

a. What is the position title of the person responsible for this organization's data storage?

b. What preparation did this individual have to qualify for this position?

c. What are this individual's job responsibilities?

d. How does this individual keep up with trends that affect data storage?

e. What type of data does the organization store?

f. What percent of this data is stored on a computer system?

g. What types of storage devices are used in this organization?

h. What is the capacity of each storage device?

i. What happens when the storage devices are full?

j. What problems are associated with maintaining the data for this organization?

This project works well if the class is divided into teams and each team interviews a person from a different organization. Each team can then present a 15-minute report to the rest of the class, along with a two- to three-page written report of its findings.

10 **The Future of Computer Storage** Ten years ago, the idea of 4 GB of storage on a personal computer seemed incredible. But technology turned that dream into reality. What storage technologies might we use in the future? Will optical storage cubes the size of a nine-volt battery hold gigabytes of data? Will smart credit cards hold all our financial data? Will magneto-optical devices combine the flexibility of magnetic media with the permanence of optical media? Will data be stored as holograms?

INTERNET Optional

Use recent computer magazines and journals to research trends and projections for computer storage technology. You might want to do a survey and write a paragraph or two on each new technology, or you might want to take an in-depth look at a technology that you find interesting.

The paper you write as the result of your research can be as short as three pages or as long as 25 pages, depending on the scope of the project specified by your instructor.

11 **Organizing Files and File Folders** How are you going to organize the information you plan to store on your hard drive? As you'll recall from reading the section on logical file storage, your hard disk storage is like a filing cabinet. You can create file folders in which to store your files. There is no one right way to organize your files, but it is important that your filing system work for you. Take time to think about the filing system you plan to create.

Read the following possibilities. Then comment on the advantages and disadvantages of each. Finally write a description and draw a picture to show how you plan to organize your folders.

a. Create a folder for each file that you make.

b. Create a folder for each application you plan to use and store only documents you generate with that application in that folder.

c. Create folders for broad topics such as Memos, Letters, BudgetItems, and Personal, and store documents that match those headings in the appropriate folder regardless of the application used to create these documents.

d. Create folders around specific topics such as Applications, Personal, Taxes, etc. and store all files related to that specific topic in the appropriate folder regardless of the application used to create these documents.

e. Basically the same as d. but create additional subfolders in each folder to help group similar files.

12 **Downsizing: Sizing up Future Storage Technologies** Storage always seems to be an issue with PCs. Just when you thought you couldn't possibly fill up that 1 GB hard drive, you find yourself scrambling to make disk space available. As you will recall from the *End Notes* section, there are several

INTERNET Optional

breakthroughs in storage technologies. Choose one of the following to research using the Internet and other available resources. Then create a presentation for the class.

a. Research how the size and capacity of storage technologies have changed over time. In your presentation, be sure to answer the following questions:

- What has the trend been? Why?
- How does the saying "Good things come in small packages" apply to storage technology?
- Is smaller better? Why? Is smaller more expensive? Why?
- What happens to the cost of new storage technologies when they are first introduced to the market and then over time? Why? Give examples.

b. Create a timeline to show past storage technologies including tape, floppies, Zip drives, and CD-ROMs. Then research and include in your timeline future storage technologies. You might use those mentioned in the *End Notes* section as a starting point.

c. Compare and contrast future storage technologies including holographic storage, molecule storage, and quantum-logic gate storage.

d. Suppose you are the head of a research and development department for a major computer company. The president of the company has come to your office to tell you that funds are running low and it is your responsibility to acquire more funds. Determine which future technology your company is pursuing and create a presentation for investors to convince them about why they should invest in the R & D project.

Lab Assignments

DOS Directories and File Management

DOS is an operating system used on millions of computers. Even if your computer has a graphical user interface, such as Microsoft Windows, understanding DOS commands helps you grasp the basic concepts of computer file management. In this Lab, you learn how to use basic DOS commands.

1 Click the Steps button to learn basic DOS commands. As you proceed through the Steps, answer all of the Quick Check questions that appear. After you complete the Steps, you will see a Quick Check Summary Report. Follow the instructions on the screen to print this report.

2 Go through the Steps for this Lab once again. This time, create a mini DOS manual by listing each DOS command and its function. For each command, you should also provide a sample of a valid command, for example:

DIR   Provides a listing of all the files on a disk

Example: DIR A:

3 Click the Explore button and make a new disk. (You can copy over the disk you used for the Steps.) Do each of the following tasks and record the command you used:

a. Display the directory for drive A.

b. Display only those files on drive A that begin with the letter "T."

c. Erase all the files that have names beginning with "New."

d. Create a directory called PAPERS.

e. Move all the files with .DOC extensions into the PAPERS directory.

f. Rename OPUS27.MID to SONG.MID.

g. Delete all the files with names that start with "Budget."

4 In Explore, make a new disk. (You can copy over the disk you used for earlier Lab activities.) Do each of the following tasks, then give your disk to your instructor. Don't forget to put your name on the disk label.

a. Make two subdirectories on your disk: PICS and BUDGETS.

b. Move all the files with .BMP extensions into the PICS directory.

c. Move all the files with .WKS extensions into the BUDGETS directory.

d. Delete all the files except README.TXT from the root directory. (Do not delete the files from PICS or BUDGETS.)

e. Rename the file README.TXT to READ.ME.

5 Use the TYPE command to view the contents of the START.BAT file. Describe the file contents. Use the TYPE command to view the contents of OPUS27.MID. Describe what you see. Explain the different results you obtained when you used the TYPE command with START.BAT and OPUS27.MID.

Windows Directories, Folders, and Files

Graphical user interfaces such as Mac OS, Windows 3.1, Windows 95, and Windows 98 use a filing system metaphor for file management. In this Lab, you will learn the basic concepts of these file system metaphors. With this background, you will find it easy to understand how to manage files with graphical user interfaces.

1 Click the Steps button to learn how to manipulate directories, folders, and files. As you proceed through the Steps, answer all of the Quick Check questions that appear. After you complete the Steps, you will see a Quick Check Summary Report. Follow the instructions on the screen to print this report.

2 Make sure you are in Explore. Change to drive C as the default drive. Double-click the c:\ folder to display its contents, then answer the following questions:

a. How many data files are in the root directory of drive C?

b. How many program files are in the root directory of drive C?

c. Does the root directory of drive C contain any subdirectories? How can you tell?

d. How many files are in the DOS folder?

e. Complete the diagram to show the arrangement of folders on drive C. Do not include files.

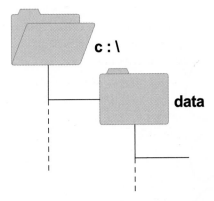

3 Click the Explore button. Make sure drive A is the default drive. Double-click the a:\ folder to display the folder contents, then answer the following questions:

a. How many files are in the root directory of drive A?

b. Are the files on drive a: data files or program files? How can you tell?

c. Does the root directory of drive A contain any subdirectories? How can you tell?

4 Open and close folders, and change drives as necessary to locate the following files. After you find the file, write out its file specification:

a. config.sys

b. win.ini

c. toolkit.wks

d. meeting.doc

e. newlogo3.bmp

f. todo.doc

Defragmentation and Disk Operations

In this Lab you will format a simulated disk, save files, delete files, undelete files to see how the computer updates the FAT. You will also find out how the files on your disk become fragmented and what a defragmentation utility does to reorganize the clusters on your disk.

1. Click the Steps button to learn how the computer updates the FAT when you format a disk and save, delete, and undelete files. As you proceed through the Steps, answer all of the Quick Check questions that appear. After you complete the Steps, you will see a Quick Check Summary Report. Follow the instructions on the screen to print this report.

2. Click the Explore button. Click the Format button to format the simulated disk. Try to save files 1, 2, 3, 4, and 6. Do they all fit on the disk?

3. In Explore, format the simulated disk. Try to save all the files on the disk. What happens?

4. In Explore, format the simulated disk. Save FILE-3, FILE-4, and FILE-6. Next, delete FILE-6. Now, save FILE-5. Try to undelete FILE-6. What happens and why?

5. In Explore, format the simulated disk. Save and erase files until the files become fragmented. Draw a picture of the disk to show the fragmented files. Indicate which files are in each cluster by using color, crosshatching, or labels. List which files in your drawing are fragmented. Finally, defragment the disk and draw a new picture showing the unfragmented files.

Using Files

In this Lab you manipulate a simulated computer to view what happens in memory and on disk when you create, save, open, revise, and delete files. Understanding what goes on "inside the box" will help you quickly grasp how to perform basic file operations with most application software.

1. Click the Steps button to learn how to use the simulated computer to view the contents of memory and disk when you perform basic file operations. As you proceed through the Steps, answer all of the Quick Check questions that appear. After you complete the Steps, you will see a Quick Check Summary Report. Follow the instructions on the screen to print this report.

2. Click the Explore button and use the simulated computer to perform the following tasks.

   a. Create a document containing your name and the city in which you were born. Save this document as NAME.

   b. Create another document containing two of your favorite foods. Save this document as FOODS.

   c. Create another file containing your two favorite classes. Call this file CLASSES.

   d. Open the FOOD file and add another one of your favorite foods. Save this file without changing its name.

   e. Open the NAME file. Change this document so it contains your name and the name of your school. Save this as a new document called SCHOOL.

   f. Write down how many files are on the simulated disk and the exact contents of each file.

   g. Delete all the files.

3. In Explore, use the simulated computer to perform the following tasks.

   a. Create a file called MUSIC that contains the name of your favorite CD.

   b. Create another document that contains eight numbers and call this file LOTTERY.

   c. You didn't win the lottery this week. Revise the contents of the LOTTERY file, but save the revision as LOTTERY2.

   d. Revise the MUSIC file so it also contains the name of your favorite musician or composer, and save this file as MUSIC2.

   e. Delete the MUSIC file.

   f. Write down how many files are on the simulated disk and the exact contents of each file.

InfoWeb
WWW

April
Fools
1

An article in the April 1988 issue of *Scientific American* announced that "archaeologists had discovered the rotting remnants of an ingenious arrangement of ropes and pulleys thought to be the first working digital computer ever constructed." The article described in detail how the people of an ancient culture, known as the Apraphulians, built complex devices of ropes and pulleys, housed these devices in huge black wooden boxes, and used them to perform complex mathematical computations. Some of the devices were so colossal that elephants were harnessed to pull the enormous ropes through the pulley system.

A computer constructed of ropes and pulleys? As you might have guessed, this was an April Fools' article. And yet, such a device, if it were constructed, could accurately be called a digital computer. That you could build a computer out of ropes and pulleys reinforces the notion that a computer is, in many respects, a very simple device.

How does a computer work? This chapter, takes you on a tour inside the case of a modern computer system. The basic concepts you learn in this chapter apply to micro, mini, and mainframe computers.

CHAPTER**PREVIEW**

In this chapter you'll learn how a computer works, so you can troubleshoot problems you encounter in the lab, at work, or at home. You'll learn how, when, and why you should expand your computer system. You'll also learn terminology that will help you understand much of the jargon you read in computer ads and hear in conversations with computer professionals. When you have completed this chapter you should be able to:

- Identify the components that are on the main circuit board of a microcomputer
- Explain how RAM, virtual memory, CMOS, and ROM differ
- Explain how the CPU performs the instructions contained in a computer program
- List the factors that affect CPU performance
- Describe how the data bus and expansion bus work
- List the components necessary to connect a peripheral device to a computer and describe each component's role
- Trace the boot process of your computer system

LABS

Binary Numbers

CPU Simulator

Troubleshooting

Ⓐ Digital Electronics

Computer architecture refers to the design and construction of a computer system. The architecture of any computer can be broadly classified by considering two characteristics: what the computer uses for power and how the computer physically represents, processes, stores, and moves data. Most modern computers are electronic devices, that is, they are powered by electricity. Also, a modern computer uses electrical signals and circuits to represent, process, and move data.

InfoWeb

Inside the Case 2

Inside the System Unit

What does the inside of a computer look like? If you have never looked inside a computer, you might stop reading for a moment and try to visualize the inside of a computer's system unit. Did you picture a maze of wires and other electronic gizmos? Many people do. But you might be surprised to find that the inside of a computer looks pretty simple. We took the cover off a microcomputer in Figure 5-1 to show you what's inside.

Figure 5-1

Inside the system unit

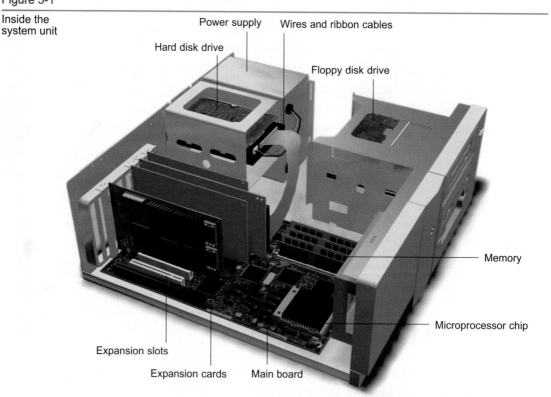

The arrangement of elements inside the case of a desktop computer differs somewhat from that inside a tower or notebook case. For example, the limited space inside of a notebook computer means that circuit boards and other components are more tightly packed together. Keep in mind, however, that the general componets of today's micro, mini, mainframe, and supercomputers are remarkably similar.

InfoWeb

Integrated Circuits 3

Integrated Circuits

Why isn't the system unit filled with a lot of wires? Most of the components inside a computer are integrated circuits, commonly called **chips** or **microchips**. An **integrated circuit** (IC) is a thin slice of crystal packed with microscopic circuit elements such as wires, transistors, capacitors, and resistors.

Figure 5-2

A single integrated circuit less than a quarter-inch square could contain more than one million microscopic circuit elements.

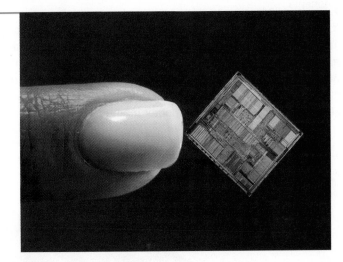

A chip is packaged in a ceramic carrier that provides connectors to other computer components. Inside of a computer you are likely to find several kinds of chip packages, including DIP, SIMM, SEC, and PGA, as shown in Figure 5-3.

Figure 5-3

Computer chip packages

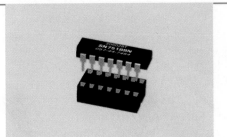

A DIP (dual in-line pin) has two rows of connecting pins. Once used for memory, DIPs now contain specialized support circuitry.

A SIMM (single in-line memory module) is a small circuit board containing several chips typically used for memory.

A PGA (pin-grid array) is a square chip with pins arranged in concentric squares. Most of today's powerful microprocessors are housed in PGA packages.

An SEC (single edge contact) cartridge is a new IC package designed for the Pentium II processor created by Intel Corporation.

The Motherboard

How do the chips fit together to make a computer? Inside the system unit, chips are housed on a circuit board called the **main board** or **motherboard**. If you look carefully at a computer circuit board you'll see that some chips are soldered, that is fused, to the board, but other chips are plugged into the board and can be removed. Soldered chips are permanent and aren't likely to work loose. Removable chips allow you to upgrade your computer components.

In a microcomputer, the motherboard contains the processor chip, the chips for computer memory, and chips that handle basic input and output. Circuits etched into the motherboard act like wires, providing a path so the computer can transport data from one chip to another as needed for processing. In addition, the motherboard contains expansion slots that allow you to connect peripheral devices to the computer. Figure 5-4 illustrates the major components of a microcomputer motherboard.

InfoWeb

Motherboards
4

Figure 5-4

Microcomputer motherboard

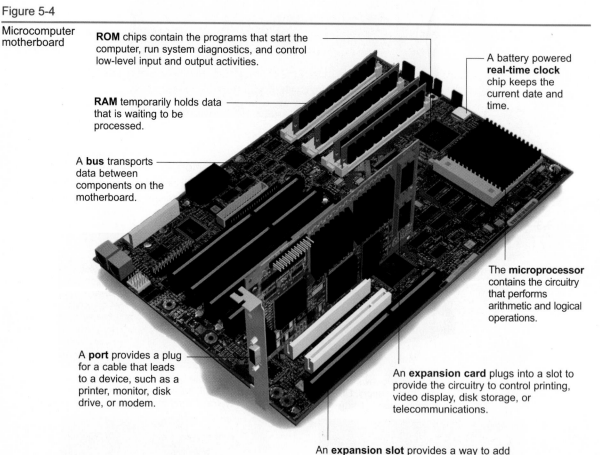

ROM chips contain the programs that start the computer, run system diagnostics, and control low-level input and output activities.

RAM temporarily holds data that is waiting to be processed.

A **bus** transports data between components on the motherboard.

A **port** provides a plug for a cable that leads to a device, such as a printer, monitor, disk drive, or modem.

A battery powered **real-time clock** chip keeps the current date and time.

The **microprocessor** contains the circuitry that performs arithmetic and logical operations.

An **expansion card** plugs into a slot to provide the circuitry to control printing, video display, disk storage, or telecommunications.

An **expansion slot** provides a way to add devices to a computer system.

Digital Data Representation

But if a computer is just a bunch of electrical circuits, how can it manipulate numbers and letters? **Data representation** refers to the form in which information is conceived, manipulated, and recorded. When people add a column of numbers or sort a list of names, they represent numbers and names by writing symbols such as 2, G, and 8. A computer is an electronic device, so it doesn't write down the data it works with. A computer somehow needs to use electrical signals to represent data.

The way a computer represents data depends on whether the computer is a digital or an analog device. A **digital device** works with discrete, that is, distinct or separate numbers or digits, such as 0 and 1. An **analog device** operates on continuously varying data. For example, a traditional light switch has two discrete states: off and on. The light switch is a digital device. A dimmer switch, on the other hand, has a rotating dial that increases or decreases brightness smoothly over a range from bright to dark. A dimmer switch is an analog device.

The circuits in a digital computer have only two possible states. For convenience let's say that one of those states is "on" and the other state is "off." If you equate the on state with 1 and the off state with 0, you can grasp the basic principle of how a digital computer works.

In a digital computer, each number or letter is represented by a series of electrical signals. Think about the way Morse code uses dashes and dots to represent letters. In a similar way, digital computers represent numbers, letters, and symbols with a code that uses a series of 0s (zeros) and 1s. Data that is represented digitally can be easily moved or stored electronically as a series of "ons" and "offs."

Each 1 or 0 that represents data is referred to as a **bit**. Most computer coding schemes use eight bits to represent each number, letter, or symbol. A series of eight bits is called a **byte**. Study Figure 5-5 to make sure you understand how the term *byte* is related to the terms *bits* and *characters*.

Figure 5-5

Bits, bytes, and characters

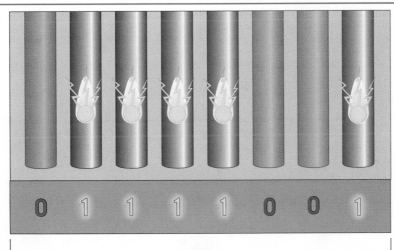

The smallest unit of information in a computer is a **bit**. A bit can be a 0 or a 1. The electronic circuits in a computer carry a 1 bit as a pulse of electricity.

A collection of eight bits is called a **byte**. This byte is composed of eight bits: 01111001.

A byte represents one **character**—a letter, numeral, or punctuation symbol. This byte, 01111001, represents a lowercase y.

Data Representation Codes

LAB

Binary
Numbers

| Do all digital computers use the same code to represent data? | Digital computers use many different coding schemes to represent data. The coding scheme the computer uses depends on whether the data is numeric data or character data.

Numeric data consists of numbers that represent quantities and that might be used in arithmetic operations. For example, your annual income is numeric data. You use it in arithmetic operations every April when you calculate your income taxes.

Digital computers represent numeric data using the **binary number system**, or base two. In the binary number system, there are only two digits: 0 and 1. The numeral 2 cannot be used in the binary number system, so instead of writing "2," you would write "10." The first eight numbers in the binary number system are 1, 10, 11, 100, 101, 110, 111, 1000. If you need to review binary numbers, study Figure 5-6.

Figure 5-6

Binary numbers

Decimal		Binary			
Place	Place	Place	Place	Place	Place
10	1	8	4	2	1
	0				0
	1				1
	2			1	0
	3			1	1
	4		1	0	0
	5		1	0	1
	6		1	1	0
	7		1	1	1
	8	1	0	0	0
	9	1	0	0	1
1	0	1	0	1	0

1. In the decimal number system, there are ten digits: 0, 1, 2, 3, 4, 5, 6, 7, 8, 9. When we put one of these digits in the column for the 1's place, it represents a different number than when we put it in the column for the 10's place. For example, the digit 1 in the 1's column is worth 1, but the digit 1 in the 10's column is worth 10. As you know, after you use the digit 9, you must "carry" a one to the next column and use a zero as a placeholder to represent the number 10.

2. The columns or "places" for the binary number system are 1s, 2s, 4s, 8s, and so on. To find out the value of the next place, you double the value of the previous place. The next place to the left would be 16s.

3. In the binary number system there are only two digits: 0 and 1. When you are counting in binary, you run out of digits when you get to the number 2. To represent "2" in binary, you must move the digit 1 left into the next column and use a zero for a place holder. In binary, the number 10 (pronounced "one zero") means "2".

4. Suppose you want to convert the binary number 11001 into its decimal equivalent.

$$? \quad 11001 \quad ?$$

5. You can set up a conversion table like this one, using the the place values for the binary number system. Because the binary number 11001 has five places, our conversion table also needs five places: 16, 8, 4, 2, and 1.

16	8	4	2	1
1	1	0	0	1

$$16 + 8 \qquad + 1 = 25$$

6. Next, add the place values for any column that contains the digit 1. The sum is the decimal equivalent of the binary number. Here you see that binary 11001 is equivalent to the decimal number 25.

Character data is composed of letters, symbols, and numerals that will not be used in arithmetic operations. Examples of character data include your name, hair color, and Social Security number. Are you surprised that your Social Security *number* is considered character data? Because you are not going to use your Social Security number in arithmetic operations it is considered character data.

Digital computers typically represent character data using either the ASCII or EBCDIC codes. ASCII is the seven-bit data representation code used on most microcomputers, on many minicomputers, and on some mainframe computers. **ASCII** stands for American Standard Code for Information Interchange and is pronounced "ASK ee." The ASCII code for an uppercase "A" is 1000001.

IBM computers often use the EBCDIC code. **EBCDIC** stands for extended binary-coded decimal interchange code (pronounced "EB seh dick"). Figure 5-7 shows the EBCDIC codes in addition to the ASCII codes. See if you can spot some of the differences between the ASCII and EBCDIC coding schemes.

Figure 5-7

ASCII and EBCDIC codes

SYMBOL	ASCII	EBCDIC	SYMBOL	ASCII	EBCDIC	SYMBOL	ASCII	EBCDIC
(space)	0100000	01000000	?	0111111	01101111	^	1011110	
!	0100001	01011010	@	1000000	01111100	_	1011111	
"	0100010	01111111	A	1000001	11000001	a	1100001	10000001
#	0100011	01111011	B	1000010	11000010	b	1100010	10000010
$	0100100	01011011	C	1000011	11000011	c	1100011	10000011
%	0100101	01101100	D	1000100	11000100	d	1100000	10000100
&	0100110	01010000	E	1000101	11000101	e	1100101	10000101
'	0100111	01111101	F	1000110	11000110	f	1100110	10000110
(	0101000	01001101	G	1000111	11000111	g	1100111	10000111
)	0101001	01011101	H	1001000	11001000	h	1101100	10001000
*	0101010	01011100	I	1001001	11001001	i	1101001	10001001
+	0101011	01001110	J	1001010	11010001	j	1101010	10010001
,	0101100	01101011	K	1001011	11010010	k	1101011	10010010
−	0101101	01100000	L	1001100	11010011	l	1101000	10010011
.	0101110	01001011	M	1001101	11010100	m	1101101	10010100
/	0101111	01100001	N	1001110	11010101	n	1101110	10010101
0	0110000	11110000	O	1001111	11010110	o	1111111	10010110
1	0110001	11110001	P	1010000	11010111	p	1110100	10010111
2	0110010	11110010	Q	1010001	11011000	q	1110001	10011000
3	0110011	11110011	R	1010010	11011001	r	1110010	10011001
4	0110100	11110100	S	1010011	11100010	s	1110011	10100010
5	0110101	11110101	T	1010100	11100011	t	1110100	10100011
6	0110110	11110110	U	1010101	11100100	u	1110101	10100100
7	0110111	11110111	V	1010110	11100101	v	1110110	10100101
8	0111000	11111000	W	1010111	11100110	w	1110111	10100110
9	0111001	11111001	X	1011000	11100111	x	1111000	10100111
:	0111010	01111010	Y	1011001	11101000	y	1111001	10101000
;	0111011	01011110	Z	1011010	11101001	z	1111010	10101001
<	0111100	01001100	[	1011011	01001010	{	1111011	
=	0111101	01111110	\	1011100		}	1111101	
>	0111110	01101110	]	1011101	01011010			

Data Transport

What happens to the data in a computer? Typically, data travels from one location to another within the computer on an electronic pathway or circuit called a **data bus**. The data bus is a series of electronic circuits that connect the various electrical elements on the motherboard. The bus contains data lines and address lines. **Data lines** carry the signals that represent data. **Address lines** carry the location of data to help the computer find the data that it needs to process.

A computer data bus "picks up" a load of bits from one of the components on the motherboard, then transfers these bits to another motherboard component. After dropping off this load of bits, the bus collects another load, as shown in Figure 5-8.

Figure 5-8

How a data bus works

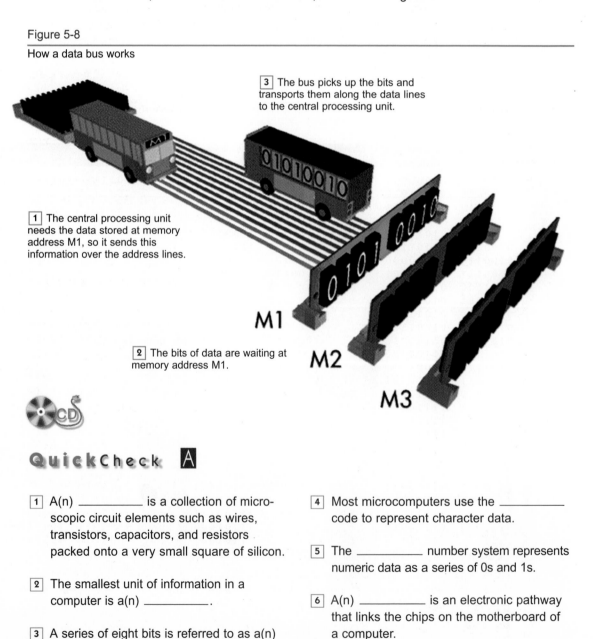

3 The bus picks up the bits and transports them along the data lines to the central processing unit.

1 The central processing unit needs the data stored at memory address M1, so it sends this information over the address lines.

2 The bits of data are waiting at memory address M1.

M1

M2

M3

QuickCheck A

1 A(n) _____ is a collection of microscopic circuit elements such as wires, transistors, capacitors, and resistors packed onto a very small square of silicon.

2 The smallest unit of information in a computer is a(n) _____.

3 A series of eight bits is referred to as a(n) _____.

4 Most microcomputers use the _____ code to represent character data.

5 The _____ number system represents numeric data as a series of 0s and 1s.

6 A(n) _____ is an electronic pathway that links the chips on the motherboard of a computer.

B Memory

InfoWeb

Memory
Technology
5

So far in this chapter you have learned that digital computers represent data using electronic signals. You know that the data bus transports these electronic signals from one place to another inside the computer. Now you will find out where the computer puts data when it is not in transit.

Memory is electronic circuitry that holds data and program instructions. Memory is sometimes called *primary storage*, but this term is easily confused with disk storage. It is preferable to use the term *memory* to refer to the circuitry that has a direct link to the processor and to use the term *storage* to refer to media, such as disks, that are not directly linked to the processor.

There are four major types of memory: random access memory, virtual memory, CMOS memory, and read-only memory. Each type of memory is characterized by the kind of data it contains and the technology it uses to hold the data.

Random Access Memory

How does RAM work? **Random access memory**, or **RAM**, is an area in the computer system unit that temporarily holds data before and after it is processed. For example, when you enter a document, the characters you type usually are not processed right away. They are held in RAM until you tell your software to carry out a process such as printing.

Figure 5-9

RAM addresses and data

Each RAM location has an address. A RAM location holds one byte of data by using eight capacitors to represent the eight bits in a byte.

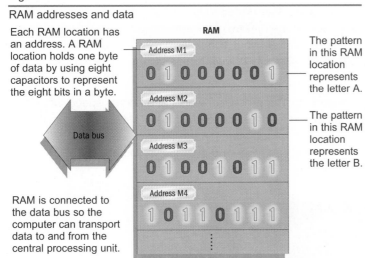

The pattern in this RAM location represents the letter A.

The pattern in this RAM location represents the letter B.

RAM is connected to the data bus so the computer can transport data to and from the central processing unit.

In RAM, microscopic electronic parts called **capacitors** hold the electronic signals for the ASCII, EBCDIC, or binary code that represents data. A charged capacitor represents an "on" bit. A discharged capacitor represents an "off" bit.

You can visualize the capacitors arranged in banks of eight. Each bank of capacitors holds eight bits, or one byte of data. A **RAM address** on each bank helps the computer locate the data contained in the bank, as shown in Figure 5-9.

In some respects, RAM is like a chalkboard. You can use a chalkboard to write mathematical formulas, erase them, and then write an outline for a report. In a similar way, RAM can hold numbers and formulas when you use a spreadsheet, then hold the text of your English essay when you use a word processor. The contents of RAM can change just by changing the charge of the capacitors. Because its contents can be changed, RAM is a reusable resource.

Unlike hard disk or floppy disk storage, most RAM is *volatile*. In other words, if the computer is turned off or the power goes out, all data stored in RAM instantly and permanently disappears. When someone unhappily says, "I have lost all my data!" it often means that the person was entering data for a document or worksheet, and the power went out before the data was saved on disk.

RAM Functions

Why is RAM so important? RAM is the "waiting room" for the computer's processor. RAM holds raw data that is waiting to be processed. RAM holds the instructions that will process the raw data. RAM also holds processed data before it is stored more permanently on disk or tape. For example, when you use personal finance software to balance your checkbook, you enter raw data for check amounts, which is held in RAM. The personal finance software sends the instructions to process this data to RAM. The processor uses the instructions to process the data, then sends the results back to RAM. From RAM, the results can be stored on disk, displayed, or printed.

In addition to data and software instructions, RAM holds operating system instructions that control the basic functions of the computer system. These instructions are loaded into RAM every time you start your computer and remain there until you turn the computer off.

RAM Capacity and Speed

How much RAM does my computer need? The storage capacity of RAM is measured in megabytes. Today's microcomputers typically have between 16 and 64 megabytes of RAM, which means they can hold between 16 and 64 million characters of data or instructions.

InfoWeb

Grace
Hopper
6

The amount of RAM your computer needs depends on the software you use. RAM requirements are usually specified on the outside of the software box. What if the software you want to use requires more RAM than your computer has? You can purchase additional RAM to expand the memory capacity of your computer up to the limit set by the computer manufacturer.

The speed of RAM is also important. The processor works at a certain speed, but would be forced to slow down if it had to wait for data from RAM. Most RAM today has an access speed of 60 nanoseconds. Slower, older memory has access speeds of 70 or 80 nanoseconds. How long is a nanosecond? Figure 5-10 will give you an idea.

Figure 5-10

Grace Hopper, a pioneer in the early computer industry used a 12-inch piece of wire to illustrate the distance electricity could travel in a nanosecond—one billionth of a second. By contrast a microsecond would be a coil of wire nearly a thousand feet long.

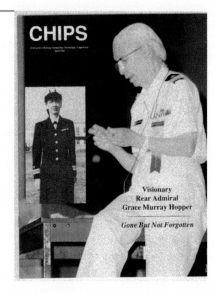

CHIPS

Visionary
Rear Admiral
Grace Murray Hopper

Gone But Not Forgotten

Virtual Memory

What if I run out of RAM? Suppose you use a word-processing program that requires 4 MB of RAM and a spreadsheet program that requires 2 MB of RAM. You might suspect that you would run out of RAM if you tried to run both programs at the same time. However, you need only 4 MB to run both programs. How can this be so?

With today's operating systems, you won't run out of RAM because the computer uses space on your computer's hard disk as an extension of RAM. A computer's ability to use disk storage to simulate RAM is called **virtual memory**. Figure 5-11 explains how virtual memory works.

Figure 5-11

How virtual memory works

3. The spreadsheet program can now be loaded into the RAM vacated by the least-used segment of the word-processing program.

1. Your computer is running a word-processing program that takes up most of the program area in RAM, but you want to run a spread-sheet program at the same time.

2. The operating system moves the least-used segment of the word-processing program into virtual memory on disk.

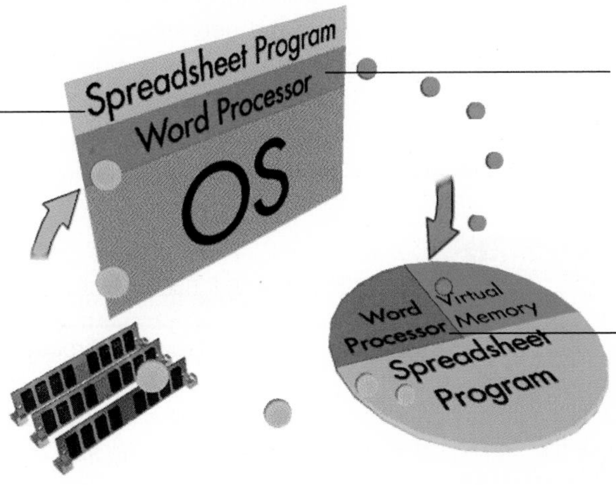

Virtual memory allows computers without enough real memory to run large programs, manipulate large data files, and run more than one program at a time. Unfortunately, virtual memory is not as fast as RAM. It takes longer to retrieve data from virtual memory because the disk is a mechanical device. Disk access time of 10 milliseconds is quite a bit slower than RAM access speeds of 60 nanoseconds.

Like RAM, data in virtual memory becomes inaccessible if the power goes off. You might wonder why—normally disks do not lose data when the power goes off. Data in virtual memory is not erased from the disk if the power fails, but the computer cannot access it even after power is restored. The instructions that direct the computer to the location of virtual memory are stored in RAM and are lost when power fails.

Read-only Memory

If a computer has RAM, why does it need ROM? **Read-only memory**, or **ROM**, is a set of chips containing instructions that help a computer prepare for processing tasks. The instructions in ROM are permanent, and the only way to change them is to remove the ROM chips from the main board and replace them with another set. You might wonder why the computer includes chips with programs permanently stored in them. Why not use the more adaptable RAM?

The answer to this question is that when you turn on your computer, the central processing unit receives electrical power and is ready to begin executing instructions. But because the computer was just turned on, RAM is empty—it doesn't contain any instructions for the central processing unit to execute. This is when ROM plays its part. ROM contains a small set of instructions called the **ROM BIOS** (basic input output system). The BIOS is a small, but critical part of the operating system that tells the computer how to access the disk drives. When you turn on your computer, the central processing unit performs the instructions in the ROM BIOS to search the disk drive for the main operating system files. The computer can then load these files into RAM and use them for the remainder of the computing session.

CMOS Memory

If the boot instructions are permanent, does that mean I can't change any hardware on my computer system? The computer is not ready to process data until it has copied certain operating system files from the hard disk into RAM. But, the computer can only find data on the hard disk if it has some information about how the hard disk is formatted. The computer must know the number of tracks and sectors and the size of each sector, or it cannot know where to look for the operating system files.

If information about the hard disk was permanently stored in ROM, you would never be able to replace your hard disk drive with a larger one. The computer could not access the new hard disk using information about the old disk. Therefore, a computer must have some semipermanent way of keeping boot data, such as the number of hard disk drive cylinders and sectors. For this, a computer needs a type of memory more permanent than RAM, but less permanent than ROM.

CMOS memory (complementary metal oxide semiconductor, pronounced "SEE moss") holds data, but requires very little power to retain its contents. Because of its low power requirements, a CMOS chip can be powered by battery. The battery trickles power to the CMOS chip so that it can retain vital data about your computer system configuration, even when your computer is turned off.

When your system configuration changes, the data in the CMOS memory must be updated. Some operating systems have special utilities that help you update the CMOS settings. For example, most of today's computers have a **plug-and-play** feature that helps you update CMOS if you install a new hard drive. You can manually change the CMOS data, by running the CMOS configuration, or setup, program as shown in Figure 5-12.

Figure 5-12

CMOS holds computer configuration settings, such as date and time, hard disk capacity, number of floppy disks, and RAM capacity.

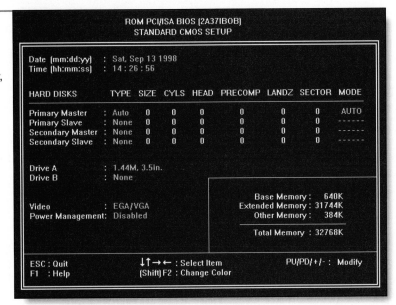

QuickCheck B

1. _____ is electronic circuitry that holds data and programs.

2. Having a steady power source is important for a computer because RAM is _____.

3. RAM capacity is measured in _____.

4. In RAM, microscopic electronic parts called _____ hold the electrical signals that represent data.

5. RAM speed is measured in _____.

6. If your computer does not have enough RAM to run several programs at once, your computer operating system might simulate RAM with disk-based _____ memory.

7. The series of instructions that a computer performs when it is first turned on are permanently stored in _____.

8. System configuration information, such as the number of the hard disk cylinders and sectors, is stored in battery-backed _____ memory.

C Central Processing Unit

So far in this chapter you have learned that digital computers represent data using a series of electrical signals. You know that data can be transported over the data bus or held in memory. But a computer does more than transport and store data. A computer is supposed to process data—perform arithmetic, sort lists, format documents, and so on.

The **central processing unit** is the circuitry in a computer that executes instructions to process data. The central processing unit retrieves instructions and data from RAM, processes those instructions, then places the results back into RAM so they can be displayed or stored. Figure 5-13 will help you visualize the flow of data and instructions through the processor.

Figure 5-13

The data bus transports data and instructions between RAM and the CPU.

The data bus transports data and instructions from RAM to the CPU for processing.

RAM contains data and instructions about how to process the data.

The CPU processes data.

RAM

Data

Central Processing Unit

Processed Data

The data bus transports the processed data to RAM so it can be displayed, output, or stored on disk.

InfoWeb

CPUs
7

Central Processing Unit Architecture

What does the CPU look like? At one time, computer CPUs were huge, unreliable expensive devices that guzzled a tremendous amount of electrical power. In 1945, the size of a CPU was measured in feet (Figure 5-14), whereas today it is measured in **mils** (.001 inch).

Figure 5-14

The ENIAC, built in 1944 had 20 processing units, each about two feet wide and eight feet high. Today, this circuitry fits on an integrated circuit less than 560 mils (.56 inches) square.

The central processing unit of a mainframe computer usually contains several integrated circuits and circuit boards. In a microcomputer the central processing unit is a single integrated circuit called a **microprocessor**. Figure 5-15 shows a microprocessor similar to the one that is probably in the computer you use.

Figure 5-15

A microprocessor

The central processing unit has two main parts: the arithmetic logic unit and the control unit. Each of these units perform specific tasks to process data. The **arithmetic logic unit (ALU)** performs arithmetic operations such as addition and subtraction. It also performs logical operations such as comparing two numbers to see if they are the same. The ALU uses **registers** to hold data that is being processed. In the ALU the result of an arithmetic or logical operation is held temporarily in the **accumulator**, as shown in Figure 5-16.

Figure 5-16

How the ALU works

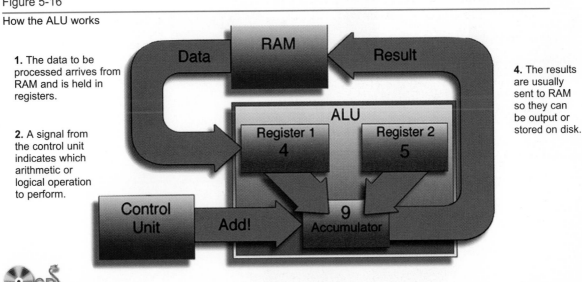

1. The data to be processed arrives from RAM and is held in registers.

2. A signal from the control unit indicates which arithmetic or logical operation to perform.

4. The results are usually sent to RAM so they can be output or stored on disk.

3. The ALU performs the operation and places the result in the accumulator.

How does the ALU get its data, and how does it know which arithmetic or logical operation it must perform? The **control unit** directs and coordinates processing.

The control unit retrieves each instruction in sequence from RAM and places it in a special **instruction register**. The control unit then interprets the instruction to find out what needs to be done. According to its interpretation, the control unit sends signals to the data bus to fetch data from RAM, and to the arithmetic logic unit to perform a process.

The control unit makes a significant contribution to processing efficiency. It is analogous to the director on a movie set, because it executes a series of instructions just as a director follows a script. The control unit directs the movement of data just as a director positions actors and props on the set. A movie director schedules production to make sure that the camera operators, actors, sound technicians, and lighting crew are ready to film each scene. The control unit schedules processing by making sure that the data and instructions arrive in the ALU where they are processed. Figure 5-17 diagrams the role of the control unit.

Figure 5-17

How the control unit works

2. The RAM address of the instruction is kept in the **instruction pointer**. When the instruction has been executed, the address in the instruction pointer changes to indicate the RAM address of the next instruction to be executed.

1. The control unit retrieves an instruction from RAM and puts it in the **instruction register**.

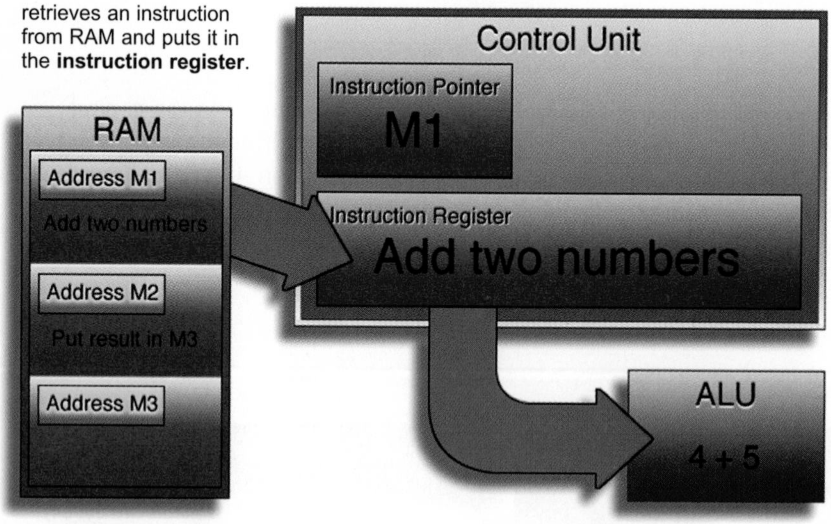

RAM

Address M1
Add two numbers
Address M2
Put result in M3
Address M3

Control Unit

Instruction Pointer
M1

Instruction Register
Add two numbers

3. The control unit interprets the instruction in its instruction register.

ALU
4 + 5

4. Depending on the instruction, the control unit will get data from RAM, tell the ALU to perform an operation, or change the memory address in the instruction pointer.

Instructions

InfoWeb

Instruction
Sets
8

What specifies the steps that the CPU must perform to accomplish a task? A computer accomplishes a complex task by performing a series of very simple steps, referred to as instructions. An **instruction** tells the computer to perform a specific arithmetic, logical, or control operation.

An instruction has two parts: the op code and the operands. An **op code**, which is short for operation code, is a command word for an operation such as add, compare, or jump. The **operands** for an instruction specify the data or the address of the data for the operation. Let's look at an example of an instruction:

op code ⟶ **JMP M1** ⟵ operand

In the instruction JMP M1, the op code is JMP and the operand is M1. The op code JMP means *jump* or go to a different instruction. The operand M1 is the RAM address of the instruction to which the computer is supposed to go. The instruction JMP M1 has only one operand, but some other instructions have more than one operand. For example, the instruction to add the contents of register 1 and register 2 has two operands:

op code ⟶ **ADD REG1 REG2** ⟵ second operand
first operand

LAB

CPU
Simulator

The list of instructions that a central processing unit performs is known as its **instruction set**. Every task a computer performs must be described in terms of the limited list of instructions in the instruction set. As you look at the list of instructions in Figure 5-18, consider that the computer must use a set of instructions such as this for all the tasks it helps you perform—from word-processing to database management.

Figure 5-18

A simple microcomputer instruction set

Op Code	Operation	Example
INP	Input the given value into the specified memory address	INP 7 M1
CLA	Clear the accumulator to 0	CLA
MAM	Move the value from the accumulator to the specified memory location	MAM M1
MMR	Move the value from the specified memory location to the specified register	MMR M1 REG1
MRA	Move the value from the specified register to the accumulator	MRA REG1
MAR	Move the value from the accumulator to the specified register	MAR REG1
ADD	Add the values in two registers, place result in accumulator	ADD REG1 REG2
SUB	Subtract the value in the second register from the value in the first register, place the result in the accumulator	SUB REG1 REG2
MUL	Multiply the values in two registers, place the result in the accumulator	MUL REG1 REG2
DIV	Divide the value in the first register by the value in the second register, place the result in the accumulator	DIV REG1 REG2
INC	Increment the value in the register by 1	INC REG1
DEC	Decrement the value in the register by 1	DEC REG1
CMP	Compare the values in two registers; if values are equal, put 1 in the accumulator, otherwise put 0 in the accumulator	CMP REG1 REG2
JMP	Jump to the instruction at the specified memory address	JMP P2
JPZ	Jump to the instruction at the specified address if the accumulator holds a 0	JPZ P3
JPN	Jump to the instruction at the specified address if the accumulator does not hold a 0	JPN P2
HLT	Halt program execution	HLT

Figure 5-19

Instruction cycle

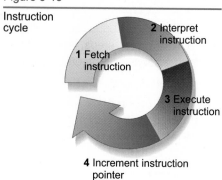

Instruction Cycle

How does a computer process instructions? The term **instruction cycle** refers to the process in which a computer executes a single instruction. The instruction cycle is repeated each time the computer executes an instruction. The steps in this cycle are summarized in Figure 5-19.

You have all the pieces you need to understand the details of the instruction cycle. You know how the ALU performs arithmetic and logical operations and how the control unit retrieves data from RAM and tells the ALU which operation to perform. Figure 5-20 shows how the ALU, control unit, and RAM work together to process instructions.

Figure 5-20

Processing an instruction

1. The instruction pointer indicates the memory location that holds the first instruction (M1).

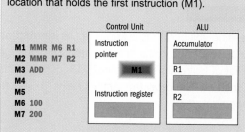

2. The computer fetches the instruction and puts it into the instruction register.

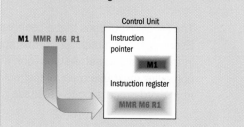

3. The computer executes the instruction that is in the instruction register; it moves the contents of M6 into register 1 of the ALU.

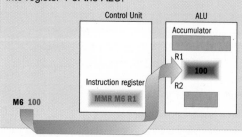

4. The instruction pointer changes to point to the memory location that holds the next instruction.

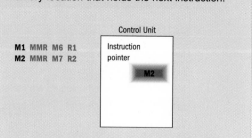

5. The computer fetches the instruction and puts it into the instruction register.

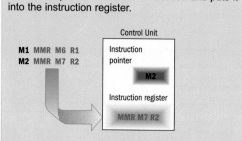

6. The computer executes the instruction; it moves the contents of M7 into register 2 of the ALU.

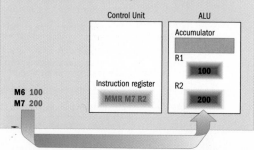

Figure 5-20

Processing an instruction (continued)

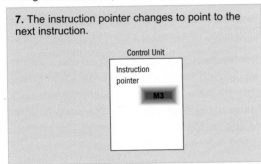

7. The instruction pointer changes to point to the next instruction.

Control Unit

Instruction pointer

M3

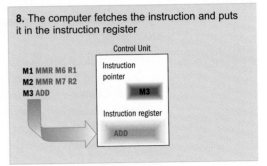

8. The computer fetches the instruction and puts it in the instruction register

M1 MMR M6 R1
M2 MMR M7 R2
M3 ADD

Control Unit

Instruction pointer

M3

Instruction register

ADD

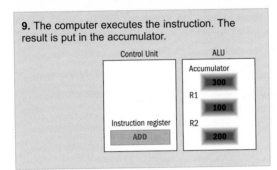

9. The computer executes the instruction. The result is put in the accumulator.

Control Unit

ALU

Accumulator

300

R1

100

Instruction register

ADD

R2

200

CPU Performance

How does the architecture of a computer contribute to its performance? Integrated circuit technology is the basic building block of CPUs in today's micro, mini, mainframe, and supercomputers. Remarkable advances in this technology have produced exponential increases in computer speed and power. In 1965, Gordon Moore, co-founder of chip-production giant, Intel Corporation, predicted that the number of transistors on a chip would double every 18 to 24 months. Much to the surprise of engineers and Moore himself, "Moore's Law," accurately predicted 30 years of chip development. In 1958, the first integrated circuit contained two transistors. The Pentium II processor, introduced in 1997, has 7.5 million transistors.

More transistors mean more processing power, so on the whole, today's CPU chips are faster than those of the past. However, all CPUs are not created equal; some process data faster than others. CPU speed is influenced by several factors including clock rate, word size, cache, and instruction set size. Specifications for these factors allow you to compare different CPUs.

Before you learn more about the factors that affect CPU performance, you should understand that a computer system with a high-performance CPU might not necessarily provide great overall performance. You know the old saying that a chain is only as strong as its weakest link. A computer system might also have weak links. Even with a high-performance processor, a computer system with a slow hard disk, no disk cache, and a small amount of RAM is likely to be slow at tasks such as starting programs, loading data files, printing, and scrolling through long documents.

Clock Rate

What does the date and time have to do with CPU performance? A computer contains a **system clock** that emits pulses to establish the timing for all system operations. The system clock is not the same as a "real-time clock" that keeps track of the time of day.

The system clock sets the speed or "frequency" for data transport and instruction execution. To understand how this works, visualize a team of oarsmen on a Viking ship. The ship's coxswain beats on a drum to coordinate the rowers. A computer's system clock and a ship's coxswain accomplish essentially the same task—they set the pace of activity. Boom! A stream of bits takes off from RAM and heads to the CPU. Boom! The control unit reads an instruction. Boom! The ALU adds two numbers together.

The clock rate set by the system clock determines the speed at which the computer can execute an instruction and, therefore, limits the number of instructions the computer can complete within a specific amount of time. The time to complete an instruction cycle is measured in **megahertz** (MHz), or millions of cycles per second.

The microprocessor in the original IBM PC performed at 4.77 MHz. Today's processors perform at speeds exceeding 300 MHz. If all other specifications are identical, higher megahertz ratings mean faster processing.

Word Size

Which is faster, an 8-bit processor or a 64-bit processor? **Word size** refers to the number of bits the central processing unit can manipulate at one time. Word size is based on the size of the registers in the CPU and the number of data lines in the bus. For example, a CPU with an 8-bit word size is referred to as an 8-bit processor; it has 8-bit registers and manipulates 8 bits at a time.

Computers with a large word size can process more data in each instruction cycle than computers with a small word size. Processing more data in each cycle contributes to increased performance. For example, the first microcomputers used 8-bit microprocessors, but today's faster computers use 32-bit or 64-bit microprocessors.

Cache

Disk cache speeds up access to data on disk; is there a similar process that speeds access to data from RAM? Another factor that affects CPU performance is cache. **Cache**, sometimes called **RAM cache** or **cache memory**, is special high-speed memory that gives the CPU more rapid access to data. A high-speed CPU can execute an instruction so quickly that it often waits for data to be delivered from RAM; this slows processing. The cache ensures that data is immediately available whenever the central processing unit requests it.

As you begin a task, the computer anticipates what data the central processing unit is likely to need and loads this data into the cache area. When an instruction calls for data, the central processing unit first checks to see if the required data is in the cache. If so, the central processing unit takes the data from the cache instead of fetching it from RAM, which takes longer. All other factors being equal, more cache means faster processing.

RISC
9

Instruction Set Complexity

What's the difference between CISC and RISC? As programmers developed various instruction sets for computers, they tended to add more and more complex instructions that took up many bytes in memory and required several clock cycles for execution. A computer based on a central processing unit with a complex instruction set came to be known as a **complex instruction set computer**, or **CISC**.

In 1975 John Cocke, an IBM research scientist, discovered that most of the work done by a microprocessor requires only a small subset of the available instruction set. Further research showed that only 20 percent of the instructions of a CISC machine do about 80 percent of the work. Cocke's research resulted in the development of microprocessors with streamlined instruction sets, called RISC machines.

The microprocessor of a **reduced instruction set computer**, or **RISC**, has a limited set of instructions that it can perform very quickly. In theory, therefore, a RISC machine should be faster than a CISC machine for most processing tasks. Some computer scientists believe, however, that a balance or hybrid of CISC and RISC technologies produce the most efficient and flexible computers.

Parallel
&
Pipelining
10

Pipelining and Parallel Processing

Can a CPU increase its performance by executing more than one instruction at a time?

Computers with a single processor execute instructions "serially," that is, one instruction at a time. Usually, the processor must complete all four steps in the instruction cycle before it begins to execute the next instruction. However, with a technology called **pipelining**, the processor begins executing an instruction before it completes the previous instruction. Pipelining speeds up processing, as shown in Figure 5-21.

Figure 5-21

How pipelining works

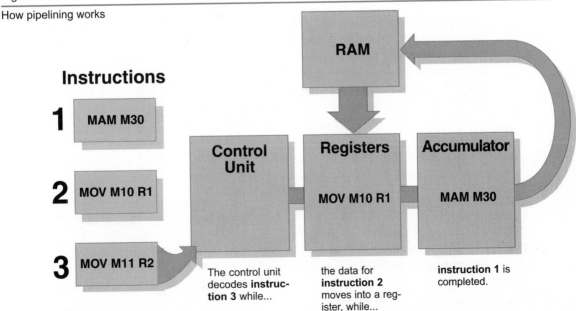

A computer that has more than one processor can execute multiple instructions at the same time. **Parallel processing** increases the amount of processing a computer can accomplish in a specific amount of time. Computers that are capable of parallel processing are called **parallel computers** or **non-von Neumann machines**. Figure 5-22 explains the concept of parallel processing.

Figure 5-22

How parallel processing works

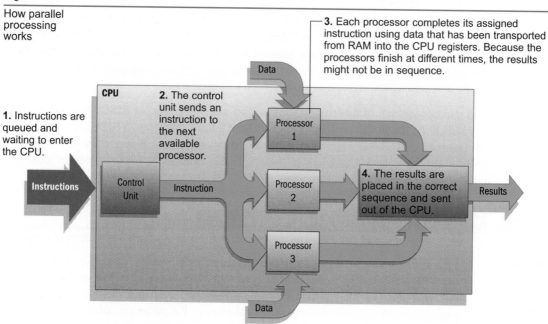

1. Instructions are queued and waiting to enter the CPU.

2. The control unit sends an instruction to the next available processor.

3. Each processor completes its assigned instruction using data that has been transported from RAM into the CPU registers. Because the processors finish at different times, the results might not be in sequence.

4. The results are placed in the correct sequence and sent out of the CPU.

To get a clearer picture of serial, pipelining, and parallel processing techniques, consider an analogy in which computer instructions are pizzas. Serial processing executes only one instruction at a time, just like a pizzeria with only one oven that can bake only one pizza (instruction) at a time. Pipelining is similar to a pizza conveyor belt. A pizza starts moving along the conveyor belt, but before it reaches the end of the belt, another pizza starts moving along the belt. Likewise, a pipelining computer starts processing an instruction; but before it completes the instruction, it begins processing another instruction. Finally, parallel processing is similar to a pizzeria with many ovens. Just as these ovens can bake more than one pizza at a time, a parallel processor can execute more than one instruction at a time.

QuickCheck C

1 A microcomputer uses a(n) _____ chip as its CPU.

2 The _____ in the CPU performs arithmetic and logical operations.

3 The _____ in the CPU directs and coordinates the operation of the entire computer system.

4 A computer instruction has two parts: the op code and the _____.

5 CPU speed is measured in _____.

6 The timing in a computer system is established by the _____.

Ⅾ Input/Output

When you purchase a computer, you can be fairly certain that before its useful life is over, you will want to add equipment to expand its capabilities. If you understand computer input/output, you will see how it is possible to expand a computer system. **I/O**, pronounced "eye-oh," is computer jargon for input/output. I/O refers to collecting data for the microprocessor to manipulate, and transporting results to display, print, and storage devices.

You already learned that a data bus transports data between RAM and the CPU. The data bus also extends to other parts of the computer. The segment of the data bus that transports data between RAM and peripheral devices is called the **expansion bus**. I/O between the central processing unit and peripheral devices often involves a long path that moves data over the expansion bus, slots, cards, ports, and cables. Figure 5-23 is an overview of the I/O architecture described in the rest of this section.

Figure 5-23

I/O architecture

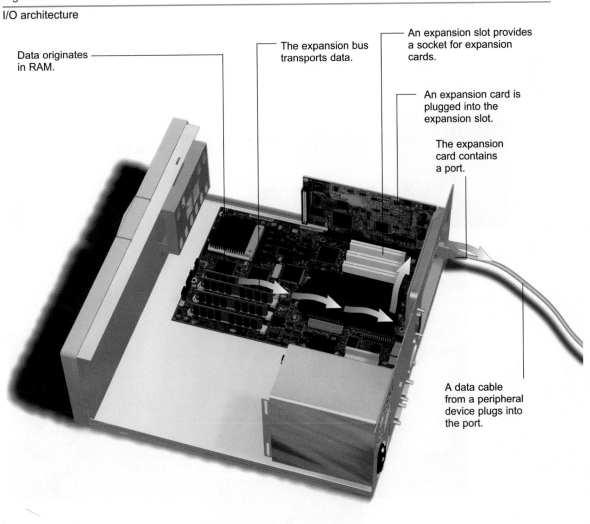

Data originates
in RAM.

The expansion bus
transports data.

An expansion slot provides
a socket for expansion
cards.

An expansion card is
plugged into the
expansion slot.

The expansion
card contains
a port.

A data cable
from a peripheral
device plugs into
the port.

Expansion Slots

How do I use expansion slots? On the main board, the expansion bus terminates at an expansion slot. An **expansion slot** is a socket into which you can plug a small circuit board called an expansion card. The expansion slots on mainframes, minicomputers, and microcomputers provide a way to connect a large variety of peripheral devices.

Most microcomputers have four to eight expansion slots, but some of these slots usually contain expansion cards when you purchase the computer. The number of empty slots in your computer dictates its expandability.

Suppose that a few months after you purchase your computer, you decide you want to add sound capability. To find out if you have adequate expansion capability, turn your computer off, unplug it, then open the system unit case. Some computers contain more than one type of expansion slot, so the slots in your computer might appear to be different sizes. If you have an empty expansion slot, you can insert an expansion card, as shown in Figure 5-24.

Figure 5-24

Inserting an expansion card into a slot

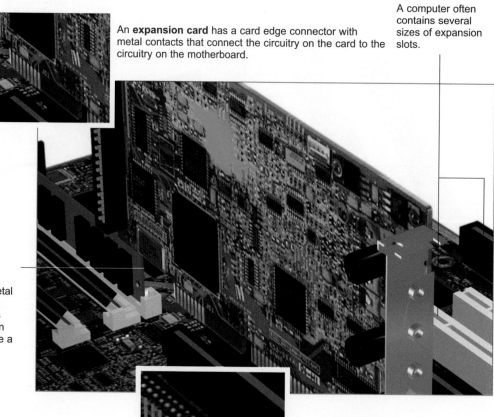

An **expansion card** has a card edge connector with metal contacts that connect the circuitry on the card to the circuitry on the motherboard.

A computer often contains several sizes of expansion slots.

When the card is inserted into the slot, the metal card edge connector contacts the connector in the slot to make a circuit for data transport.

An **expansion slot** contains metallic contacts that connect to the expansion bus.

Expansion Cards

What kinds of expansion cards are available? An **expansion card**, also referred to as an **expansion board** or a **controller card**, is a circuit board that plugs into an expansion slot. An expansion card provides the I/O circuitry for peripheral devices and sometimes contains an expansion device. For example, if you want to add sound capability, you would purchase and install an expansion card called a sound card. The sound card contains the circuitry to convert digital signals from your computer to sounds that play through speakers. Once you have inserted the sound card into an expansion slot, you can connect speakers or headphones. Microcomputer users can select from a wide variety of expansion cards, such as those shown in Figure 5-25.

Figure 5-25

Expansion cards

A **graphics card** connects your monitor and computer.

A **network card** connects your computer to the other computers on a local area network.

A **modem card** connects your computer to the telephone system so you can transport data from one computer to another over phone lines.

Expansion Ports

How do I connect a peripheral device to an expansion card? To connect a peripheral device to an expansion card, you plug a cable from the peripheral device into the expansion port on the expansion card. An **expansion port** is a location that passes data in and out of a computer or peripheral device. An expansion port is often housed on an expansion card so that it is accessible through a hole in the back of the computer system unit. A port might also be connected directly to the main board, instead of to an expansion card.

To many computer users, the back of a computer is a confusing array of unlabeled ports, connectors, and cables. Study Figure 5-26 to become familiar with the shapes of the most frequently used expansion ports.

Figure 5-26

Microcomputer expansion ports

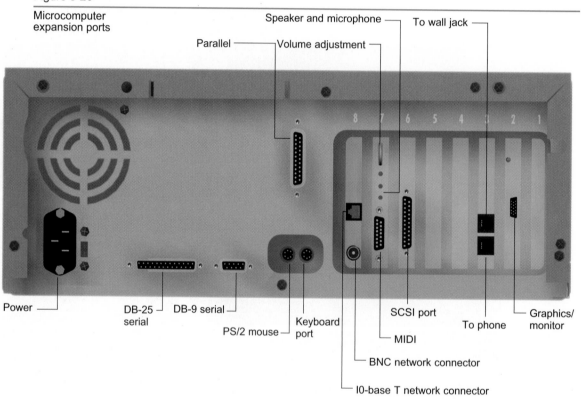

Speaker and microphone — To wall jack
Parallel — Volume adjustment
Power — DB-25 serial — DB-9 serial — PS/2 mouse — Keyboard port — SCSI port — To phone — Graphics/ monitor — MIDI — BNC network connector — I0-base T network connector

InfoWeb

Connectors 11

The cable that you plug into the computer port will contain a corresponding **connector**. Each type of connector has a designation such as DB-9 or C-50. The first part of the designation indicates the shape of the connector. For example, DB and C connectors are trapezoidal, whereas DIN connectors are round. The second part of the designation indicates the number of pins. A DB-9 connector has nine pins. In general, larger size connectors have more pins than smaller connectors. Most types of connectors have male and female versions. The male version has pins that stick out, whereas the female version has holes.

Connectors are designed so you can't plug them in upside down. Before you plug a cable into a port, make sure you have the correct connector and it is aligned with the pins. Figure 5-27 describes the cable connectors you'll typically find on a PC.

Figure 5-27

Cables and connectors

Cable/Connector		Description	Devices
	DB9F or DB25F	Serial port sends data over a single data line one bit at a time at speeds of .005 MB/second	Mouse or modem
	USB A	Universal serial bus (USB) port sends data over a single data line at speeds of 1.5 MB/second; connects up to 127 devices	Modem, keyboards, joystick, scanner, mouse
	DB-25M	Standard parallel port sends data simultaneously over eight data lines at speeds of 1.5 MB/second	Printer
	IEEE 1284 A-B cable (DB25M)	Enhanced parallel port sends data simultaneously over eight data lines, bi-directional, .5 MB/second	Printer, external CD-ROM drive, Zip drive, external hard disk drive, or tape backup
	C50F	SCSI ("scuzzy") port sends data simultaneously over eight or 16 data lines at speeds from 5 MB/ seconds to 40 MB/second. May daisychain eight or 16 peripheral devices, depending on SCSI type.	Hard disk drive, scanner, CD-ROM drive, tape drive
	HDB15	VGA port transfers data from the computer to the monitor	Monitor

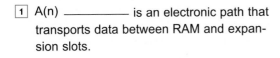

QuickCheck D

1. A(n) _____ is an electronic path that transports data between RAM and expansion slots.

2. A(n) _____ is a small circuit board that plugs into an expansion slot.

3. An expansion _____ is located inside the system, whereas an expansion _____ is located on the exterior of the system unit.

4. A(n) _____ port allows you to connect up to 127 peripheral devices to a single port.

E The Boot Process

LAB

Trouble-shooting

Now that you have an understanding about how I/O, RAM, ROM, and the CPU operate, you're ready to learn how they all work together to prepare a computer for accepting commands each time you turn it on.

The sequence of events that occurs between the time you turn on a computer and the time it is ready for you to issue commands is referred to as the **boot process**. Micro, mini, and mainframe computers all require a boot process. In this section of the chapter you'll learn about the microcomputer boot process because that is the type of computer you are most likely to use.

You'll find out what happens during each step of the boot process for a typical PC and what you should do when the boot process doesn't proceed smoothly. Of course, even when you know how to troubleshoot computer problems, you should always follow the guidelines provided by your school or employer when you encounter equipment problems.

An Overview

If the computer memory is blank when I turn it on, how does it know how to start up?

As you learned earlier, one of the most important components of a computer—RAM—is volatile, so it cannot hold any data when the power is off. It also cannot hold the operating system instructions when the power is off. Therefore, the computer cannot use RAM to "remember" any basic functions, such as how to deal with input and communicate output to the external world. A computer needs some way to get operating system files into RAM. That's one of the main objectives of the boot process. In general, the boot process follows these six steps:

1. **Power Up**—When you turn on the power switch, the power light is illuminated, and power is distributed to the internal fan and main board.

2. **Start Boot Program**—The microprocessor begins to execute the instructions stored in ROM.

3. **Power-On Self-Test**—The computer performs diagnostic tests of crucial system components.

4. **Load Operating System**—The operating system is copied from a disk to RAM.

5. **Check Configuration and Customization**—The microprocessor reads configuration data and executes any customized start-up routines specified by the user.

6. **Ready for Commands and Data**—The computer is ready for you to enter commands and data.

Power Up

What's the first thing that happens when I turn the power on? The first stage in the boot process is the power-up stage. The fan in the power supply begins to spin, and the power light on the case of the computer comes on, as shown in Figure 5-28.

Figure 5-28

Power up

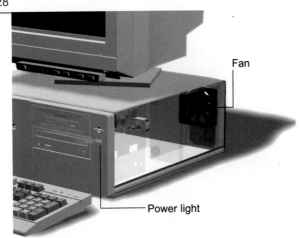

Fan

Power light

If you turn on the computer and the power light does not come on, the system is not getting power. You should check the power cord at the back of the computer to make sure it is firmly plugged into the wall and into the system unit. Also, make sure that the wall outlet is supplying power. If the power light still does not come on, then the computer's power supply might have failed. If you encounter this problem, you need to contact a technical support person for assistance.

Start Boot Program

What happens if the ROM is malfunctioning? When you turn on the computer, the microprocessor begins to execute the boot program stored in ROM, as shown in Figure 5-29.

If the ROM chips, RAM modules, or microprocessor are malfunctioning, the microprocessor is unable to run the boot program and the computer stops or "hangs." You know you have a problem at this stage of the boot process if the power light is on and you can hear the fan, but there is no message on the screen and nothing else happens. This problem requires the assistance of a technical support person.

Figure 5-29

ROM boot program activated

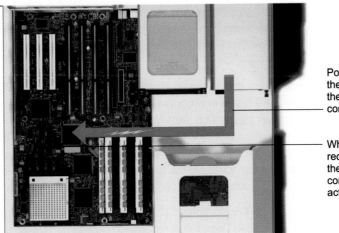

Power flows through the power supply to the main board components.

When ROM receives power, the programs it contains are activated.

Power-On Self-Test

Can the computer check to determine if all its components are functioning correctly?

The next step in the boot process is the **power-on self-test (POST)**, which diagnoses problems in the computer, as shown in Figure 5-30.

Figure 5-30

Power-on self-test

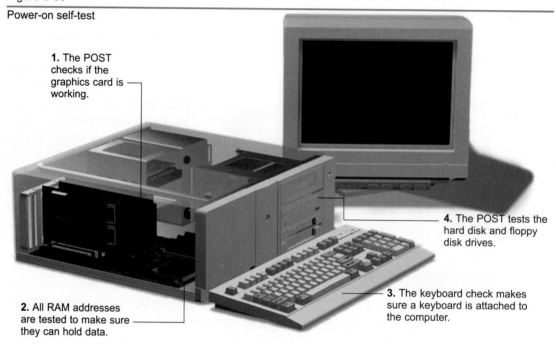

1. The POST checks if the graphics card is working.

4. The POST tests the hard disk and floppy disk drives.

3. The keyboard check makes sure a keyboard is attached to the computer.

2. All RAM addresses are tested to make sure they can hold data.

The POST first checks the graphics card that connects your monitor to the computer. If the graphics card is working, you'll see a message such as "Video BIOS ver 2.1 1997." If your computer beeps and does not display the video BIOS message, the graphics card is probably malfunctioning. You should contact a technical support person to have the graphics card checked.

The computer next tests RAM by placing data in each memory location, then retrieving that data to see if it is correct. The computer displays the amount of memory tested. If any errors are encountered during the RAM test, the POST stops and displays a message that indicates a RAM problem.

The POST then checks the keyboard. On most computers you can see the keyboard indicator lights flash when the keyboard test is in progress. If the keyboard is not correctly attached or if a key is stuck, the computer beeps and displays a keyboard error message. If a keyboard error occurs, you should turn the computer off and make sure that nothing is holding down a key on the keyboard. Next, unplug the keyboard and carefully plug it back into the computer. Finally, turn on the computer again to repeat the boot process. If the problem recurs, you might need to have your keyboard repaired or replaced.

The final step in the POST is the drive test. If you watch the hard disk drive and floppy disk drives during this test, you will see the drive activity lights flash on for a moment, and you will hear the drives spin. The drive test should only take a second or two to complete. If the computer pauses on this test, there might be a problem with one of the drives, and you should consult a technical support person.

Load Operating System

How does the computer load the operating system into RAM? After successfully completing the POST, the computer continues to follow the instructions in ROM to load the operating system, as shown in Figure 5-31.

Figure 5-31

Loading the operating system

1. If the computer finds a disk in drive A, that drive becomes the default drive.

2. If the computer cannot find a disk in drive A, it uses drive C as the default drive.

3. The computer loads the operating system from the default drive into RAM.

The computer first checks drive A to see if it contains a disk. If there is a disk in this drive, drive A becomes the **default drive**. The computer uses the default drive for the rest of the computing session unless you specify a different one.

If there is no disk in drive A but the computer has a drive C, the computer uses drive C as the default drive. If your computer has a hard disk, you generally want drive C to be the default drive, so it is best not to put disks in any of the floppy disk drives until the boot process is complete. Otherwise, the computer recognizes the floppy disk drive as the default.

Next, the computer tries to locate and load operating system files from the default drive. First, the computer looks for two operating system files: **Io.sys** and **Msdos.sys**. If these files do not exist on the disk, the boot process stops and displays a message such as "Non-system disk or disk error" or "Cannot load a file." If you see one of these messages, there is probably a disk in drive A that should not be there. Remove the disk from drive A so your computer looks on the hard drive for the operating system files.

The microprocessor next attempts to load another operating system file, **Command.com**. Two problems could occur at this stage of the boot process, and both problems have the same error message—"Bad or missing command interpreter." First problem: the file **Command.com** might be missing because someone inadvertently erased it. Second problem: your disk might contain the wrong version of **Command.com** because someone inadvertently copied a different version onto the computer.

If you encounter either problem, you should turn the computer off, then find a bootable floppy disk. A **bootable floppy disk**, such as the one that came with the computer, contains operating system files. Put this floppy disk in drive A and turn on the computer again. Even if you are successful using a floppy disk to boot your system, you need to correct the **Command.com** problem on your hard disk. A technical support person or experienced user can help you do this.

Check Configuration and Customization

Does the computer get all its configuration data from CMOS? Early in the boot process, the computer checks CMOS to determine the amount of installed RAM and the types of available disk drives. Often, however, more configuration data is needed for the computer to properly access all available devices and set up your screen-based desktop. In the next stage of the boot process, the computer searches the root directory of the boot disk for configuration and setup files, as shown in Figure 5-32.

On some computers these instructions are stored in a file called **Autoexec.bat** or a Windows startup group, which you can modify to customize your computing environment. For example, you might customize the startup instructions so your To-do list document appears every time you start your computer.

Figure 5-32

Load configuration data

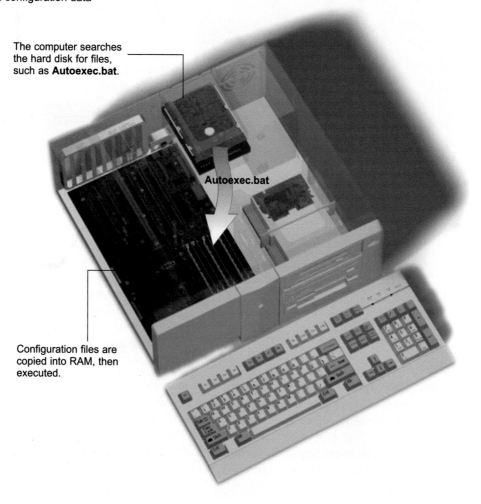

The computer searches the hard disk for files, such as **Autoexec.bat**.

Autoexec.bat

Configuration files are copied into RAM, then executed.

Ready for Commands and Data

How do I know when the computer has finished booting? The boot process is complete when the computer is ready to accept your commands. Usually the computer displays the operating system main screen or prompt at the end of the boot process. If you are using Windows, you will see the Windows desktop or, if you are using DOS, you will see the operating system prompt (Figure 5-33).

Figure 5-33

You can enter commands and launch programs when the computer displays the DOS operating system prompt C:\>, or the Windows desktop.

c:\>

EndNote

Today's computers are digital electronic devices that accomplish complex tasks by performing a fairly limited set of instructions at breakneck speed. Understanding how a computer manipulates data coded as 1s and 0s should help dispel some of the mystery about what goes on "under the hood" of a microcomputer. Also, you can apply this understanding to troubleshooting your way past computer equipment problems.

Trouble-
shooting
12

Troubleshooting is not difficult if you follow a logical procedure and think creatively. When you have a problem with a computer, first try to make a specific statement that describes the problem. Saying "It's broken!" is not very useful. A more specific description might be something like, "I turned my computer on, but the screen is blank."

Try to make some hypotheses, or guesses, about the cause of the problem. Be creative—try to think of at least three potential causes. If your screen is blank, you might hypothesize that the monitor isn't getting power, that it is not getting a video signal, or that it has somehow "burned out."

Ask yourself which of these potential causes would have the simplest solution. Start with the simple solution first—the monitor might not be getting power because it's not turned on or because the power cable isn't plugged in. These are the things you check first. Of course, you should follow the repair policies of your school or place of employment by not trying to fix equipment that must be repaired by a qualified service agent. And remember the golden rule of troubleshooting: Don't panic.

InfoWeb

InfoWeb

**Chapter
Links**

The InfoWeb is your guide to print, film, television, and electronic resources. Use it to obtain updates on quickly changing technical information and to locate information for research papers. If you're using the New Perspectives CD-ROM, click the InfoWeb icon on the left side of this paragraph to access the online InfoWeb links. Otherwise, use your Web browser and type in the address of the New Perspectives site: www.cciw.com/np3. At the New Perspectives site you'll find up-to-date links to the topics covered in this chapter.

1 April Fools

The Apraphulian computer was the subject of A. K. Dewdney's article, **Computer Recreations: An ancient rope-and-pully computer is unearthed in the jungle of Apraphul** published in *Scientific American*, April 19, 1988. What begins as an April Fools' joke turns out to be an excellent explanation on the basic circuitry in a digital computer. Although this article is not online, you'll find more recent editions of *Scientific American* at **www.sciam.com**. Each issue contains at least one article about computers and don't miss "Ask the Experts" where you'll find authoritative answers to questions such as "Can computers be made from strands of DNA?"

2 Inside the Case

If you have a chance to visit the Computer Museum in Boston, make sure you tour the Walk-through Computer 2000 exhibit where you'll walk inside the system unit of a gigantic PC to get an up-close view of the computer components discussed in this chapter. The Computer Museum Web site at **www.tcm.org** contains a text-based description of the exhibit; select Resources, then click "The Walk-through Computer 2000."

3 Integrated Circuits

Without the invention of the integrated circuit, computers would still be room-sized devices affordable to only the largest and most powerful governments and organizations. You can see a picture of the first IC and read the inventor's original notes at the Texas Instruments site at **www.ti.com/corp/docs/history/firstic.htm**. For information on Ted Hoff and other inventors, visit the Invention Dimension site at **web.mit.edu/invent** and go to the Inventor of the Week archives. To get an idea of how many ICs have been manufacturered and to see what kinds of products they're in, check out the QuestLink Technology site **www.questlink.com**.

4 Motherboards

For an update on what's new in motherboard technology look for the Mainboard Guide site at **sysdoc.pair.com/mainboard.html** where you'll find FAQs and recommendations for selecting a motherboard. A more technical site with links to motherboard manufacturers and other motherboard sites is the Motherboard Homeworld at **web2.superb.net/motherboard**. Intel recently introduced a new motherboard "form factor" design called NLX. You'll find a picture and description at **www.intel.com/design/motherbd/nlx.htm**.

5 Memory Technology

Bob Campbell has kindly posted the first chapter of his excellent book, *Beyond the Limits: Secrets of PC Memory Management* (Sybex, 1993) on the Web at **www.well.com/user/memory/memtypes.htm**. Another Web site worth browsing is the Memory Manual at **pdsys.com/mem_man.htm**. Here you can search an acronym dictionary to discover the meaning of memory terms such as EDO and FPM. In addition you will find up-to-date information on memory speed and capacity.

6 Grace Hopper

Never one to follow gender stereotypes, Grace Hopper graduated with a Ph. D. in mathematics, joined the United States Naval Reserves, and in 1944 became one of the first computer programmers. Until her death in 1992, Dr. Hopper presented fascinating lectures peppered with her particular brand of wit and wisdom. Read about her at **www.cs.yale.edu/HTML/YALE/CS/HyPlans/tap/Files/hopper-wit.html**. In 1997 the U.S. Navy commissioned a destroyer in her honor, the U.S.S. Hopper. It is the first time a destroyer has been named after a woman. The navy maintains a site with information on the woman and the ship at **www.navysea.mil/hopper**. You'll find additional information at **www.sdsc.edu/Hopper/hopper_links.html**.

7 CPUs

A microprocessor is a fascinating microworld of nearly invisible circuitry. To get a glimpse into this world, visit **micro.magnet.fsu.edu/chipshot.html.cards**, where you'll see excellent pictures of microprocessors taken through an electron microscope. There are more pictures at **infopad.eecs.berkeley.edu/CIC/die_photos**. Don't leave without looking at some of the photos with overlays—they show you the location of the microscopic ALU, registers, and control unit. For updates on current microprocessor technology, follow the site links for microprocessor manufacturers, such as **www.intel.com**, **www.amd.com**, **www.cyrix.com**, **www.motorola.com**, and **www.ibm.com**.

8 Instruction Sets

For a more in-depth look at what happens in a microprocessor, read *How Microprocessors Work* by Wyant and Hammerstrom (Ziff-Davis Press, 1994). This book has many excellent illustrations that help you visualize what happens within the microprocessor circuitry. Microprocessor instruction sets are a pretty esoteric subject. The instruction set you saw in Figure 5-18 is very small, compared to those of most CISC processors. To get a taste of a real instruction set, take a quick browse through the instruction set cards at **ftp.comlab.ox.ac.uk/archive/cards**.

9 RISC

Read an interview with the founder of RISC technology, John Cocke, at **www.rs6000.ibm.com/resource/interviews**. A good comparison table of CISC vs. RISC architectures is available at the Seoul National University Architecture Courseware Home page, **archi.snu.ac.kr/course**, where you need to scroll down and select "Instruction Set Architecture."

10 Parallel and Pipelining

Parallel processing technology is a key to today's supercomputer architecture. In a test run, an Intel computer using 9,200 Pentium Pro microprocessors running in parallel clocked a new record by performing 1.34 trillion operations per second. Read more about it at **www.intel.com/pressroom/archive/releases/CN0611B.HTM**.

Spend a few minutes with an easy-to-understand basic tutorial on pipelining by Tony Wesley at **www.acs.oakland.edu/~awesley/pipetop.htm**. To get an idea of how parallel architecture is applied in the real world, visit the Lawrence Livermore National Laboratory Web site on parallel computing at **www.llnl.gov/liv_comp/parcomp**.

11 **Connectors**

You'll find everything you wanted to know about ports, cables, and connectors in the *Hardware Book*, and its online site at **www.blackdown.org/~hwb/hwb.html**. Also check out the pictures of PC cables and connectors at ConnectPro's online catalog at **www.connectpro.com/pccable.htm**. For a tour of USB technology, link to Intel's USB page at **www.intel.com/design/usb/index.htm**.

12 **Troubleshooting**

The PC Mechanic site at **www.geocities.com/SiliconValley/Lakes/3553** is where to go if you want to learn more about the parts of a PC. You'll find all sorts of handy information, such as the meaning of those beeps you hear when your computer doesn't boot up. If you really get into computer hardware, you might want to build your own computer. Before you get started, visit the Build Your Own PC site at **www.verinet.com/pc**. You'll love the graphics here and the casual easy-to-understand style. If you're having trouble with a computer, try A:1 Computer's site at **aloha-mall.com/a-1/START.HTM** where you can click the links to Preventive Maintenance Tips or Troubleshooting Tips. The Troubleshooting Flowchart is particularly useful. Successful troubleshooting begins with an organized approach to problem solving. Read tips from an expert at the Troubleshooters.Com site, **www.troubleshooters.com**. Another source of good troubleshooting information might be a users group near you. Search for "users groups" on Yahoo! for a group you might visit or join.

Review

1 Below each heading in this chapter, there is a question. Look back through this chapter and answer each of these questions using your own words.

2 Make a list of the boldface terms in this chapter, and use your own words to define each term.

3 Place an X in the following table to indicate which characteristics apply to each type of memory.

	RAM	Irtual Memory	ROM	CMOS
Holds user data such as documents				
Holds program instructions such as word processor				
Holds boot program				
Holds configuration data for hard disk type				
Temporary				
Permanent				
Battery powered				
Disk-based				

4 Use Figure 5-7 to write out the ASCII code for the following phrase: **Way Cool!**

5 Create a conceptual diagram like the one in Figure 5-9 to show how the phrase **Way Cool!** is stored in RAM.

6 Label the microcomputer components shown in a through g.

a.
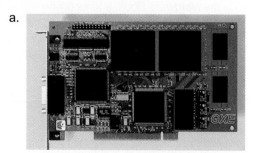

b.

c.

d.

e.
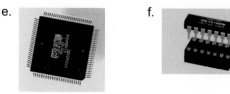

f.

g.

7 Imagine you are a teacher. Write a one- or two-page script explaining the instruction cycle to your class, and design at least three visual aids you would use as illustrations.

8 Compare the ASCII and EBCDIC coding schemes in Figure 5-7 and describe some of the differences between them.

9 After the processor executes the three instructions in RAM, what are the final values in Register 1, Register 2, and the accumulator? (Hint: Refer to Figure 5-18.)

Program			
P1	MMR	M1	REG1
P2	MMR	M2	REG2
P3	ADD	REG1	REG2
P4	MAM	M3	
P5	HLT		
Data			
M1	5		
M2	3		
M3	0		

CONTROL UNIT	
INSTRUCTION POINTER	P1
INSTRUCTION REGISTER	

ALU	
ACCUMULATOR	
REG1	
REG2	

10 What are the values in Register 1, Register 2, and the accumulator when the computer has completed the instructions in the RAM shown below?

Program			
P1	MMR	M1	REG1
P2	MMR	M2	REG2
P3	INC	REG1	
P4	DEC	REG2	
P5	MUL	REG1	REG2
P6	MAM	M3	
P7	HLT		
Data			
M1	7		
M2	4		
M3	0		

CONTROL UNIT	
INSTRUCTION POINTER	P1
INSTRUCTION REGISTER	

ALU	
ACCUMULATOR	
REG1	
REG2	

11 Use your own words to write a one-paragraph description of pipelining.

12 Compare the specifications for Computer 1 and Computer 2 below. Circle the best performance rating in each category.

Performance Factor	Computer 1	Computer 2
Clock Rate	266 MHz	200 MHz
Word Size	32 bit	64 bit
Cache	256 K	32 K
Instruction Set	CISC	RISC
Pipelining	Yes	No
Parallel Processing	No	Yes

13 Label each of the components illustrated below:

14 Think about the concepts in the first four sections of this chapter: Digital Electronics, Memory, Central Processing Unit, and I/O. Using these concepts, put together your own description of how a computer processes data. You can use a narrative description and/or sketches.

15 Use the New Perspectives CD-ROM to take a practice test or to review the new terms presented in this chapter.

Projects

1 **The Apraphulians' Computer** Read the article about the Apraphulian computer in the April 19, 1988 issue of *Scientific American*, entitled "An Ancient Rope-and-Pulley Computer is Unearthed in the Jungle of Apraphulia," then answer the following questions:

a. The Apraphulians did not use electricity. How then did they represent 0s and 1s?

b. What did the Apraphulian's *inverter box* accomplish?

c. The archaeologists excavating the Apraphulian site found a large overgrown field where several thousand rotting flip-flop boxes were buried. What part of the computer was at this site?

d. Redraw the flip-flop diagram from the article and label it to show how it worked.

2 **Looking From the Inside Out** After disconnecting the power cable, carefully open the case of a computer system unit. Draw a sketch and label each of the components you see inside. Try to locate and label all the components shown in Figure 5-1.

3  **The History of the IC** Computers would not be available to individuals today if not for the invention of the integrated circuit. Just four months apart in 1959, Jack Kilby and Robert Noyce independently created working models of the circuit that was to transform the computer industry. Jack Kilby worked at Texas Instruments, and you can find reproductions of his original research notes on the Web site, **www.ti.com/corp/docs/history/firstic.htm.** Robert Noyce developed the integrated circuit while CEO of Fairchild Semiconductor, but he left Fairchild to form Intel.

Use your library and Internet resources to research the impact of the integrated circuit on the computer industry, then do one of the following:

a. Write a two- to three-page paper summarizing how the integrated circuit was used in the first five years after it was invented.

b. Write two one-page biographical sketches; one of Jack Kilby and one of Robert Noyce.

c. Create a diagram of the "family tree" of computer technologies that resulted from the development of the integrated circuit.

d. Based on the facts you have gathered about the development of the computer industry, write a two- to three-page paper describing the computer industry today if the integrated circuit had not been invented.

4 **Scanning a Computer Ad for Key Terms** Photocopy a full-page computer ad from a current issue of a computer magazine, such as *Computer Shopper*. On the copy of the ad use a colored pen and circle any of the key terms that were presented in this chapter. Make sure you watch for abbreviations; they are frequently used in computer ads. On a separate sheet of paper, or using a word processor, make a list of each term you circled and write a definition of each.

5  **Researching and Writing about RAM** Suppose you are a computer industry analyst preparing an article on computer memory for a popular computer magazine. Gather as much information as you can about RAM, including current pricing, the amount of RAM that comes installed in a typical computer, tips for adding RAM to computers, and so forth. Use a word processor to write a one- to two-page article that would help your magazine's readers understand all about RAM.

6

INTERNET Optional

Researching and Writing about RISC Write a one- to two-page paper about RISC technology. You might want to explore the history of the concept beginning with John Cocke's research. You can also look at the use of RISC processors for the type of powerful workstations typically used for engineering and CAD applications. You might also research Apple's PowerPC computer that uses the PowerPC RISC chip. If you have Internet access, start your research with the resources listed in InfoWeb 9.

7 **Expansion Ports** Look in computer magazines to find advertisements for three peripheral devices that connect to a computer using different ports or buses. For example, you might find a modem that connects to the serial port. Photocopy each of these three ads. For each device circle on the photocopy the device's brand name, model name and/or number, and the port or bus it uses. Also make sure you provide your instructor with the name and publication date of the magazine and the page number on which you found the information.

8 **Interview with a Computer User** Complete the following steps to interview one of your friends who has a computer, and write a report that describes how your friend could expand his or her computer system.

a. Find out as many technical details as you can about your friend's computer, including the type of computer, the type and speed of the microprocessor, the amount of memory, the configuration of disk drives, the capacity of the disk drives, the resolution of the monitor, and so on.

b. Find out how your friend might want to expand his or her computer system either now or sometime in the future. For example, your friend might want to add a printer, a sound card, CD-ROM drive, memory, or a monitor.

c. Look through computer magazines to find a solution for at least one of your friend's expansion plans. What would you recommend as a solution? If money was no object would your recommendation change? Why or why not?

d. Write a two-page report describing your friend's computer and his or her expansion needs. Then describe the solution(s) you found.

9 **Observing the Boot Process** Using the *User Focus* section of this chapter as your guide, make a detailed list of each step in the boot process. Take your list into the computer lab and boot one of the computers. As the computer boots, read your list to make sure it is correct. For which steps in the boot process can you see or hear something actually happening?

10

INTERNET Optional

Can a Computer Make Errors? In 1994 Intel released the Pentium microprocessor. Within a matter of weeks, rumors began to circulate that the Pentium chip had a bug that caused errors in some calculations. As the rumors spread, corporate computer users became nervous about the numbers that appeared on spreadsheets calculated on computers with the Pentium processor. How can a computer make such mistakes? Are computers with Pentium processors destined for the dumpster? Is there any way users can save the money they have invested in their Pentium computers?

Suppose you own a computer store that sold many computers with the flawed Pentium microprocessor. Your customers are calling you to get the straight facts. Use your library and Internet resources to gather as much reliable information as you can about the Pentium flaw. Use this information to write a one-page information sheet for your customers. You might find the following resources useful:

- Intel's Internet site: **www.intel.com**
- "The Truth Behind the Pentium Bug" *Byte*, March 1995.

11 Troubleshooting Scenarios—What Would You Do? Your instructor might want you to do this project individually or in a small group. For each of the following scenarios, indicate what might be wrong.

a. You turn on the computer's power switch and nothing happens—no lights, no beep, nothing. What's the most likely problem?

b. You turn on your computer and the computer completes the POST test. You see the light on drive A and you hear the drive power up, but you get a message on the screen that says "Cannot load file." Explain what caused this message to appear and explain exactly what you should do to complete the boot process.

c. You are using a word processor to write an essay for your English composition course. You have completed eight pages, and you have periodically saved the document. Suddenly, you notice that when you press a key nothing happens. You try the mouse, but it no longer moves the pointer on the screen. What should you do next?

d. You turn on your computer, see the power light, and hear the fan. Then, the computer begins to beep repeatedly. What would you suspect is the problem?

Lab Assignments

Binary Numbers

Computers process and store numbers using the binary number system. Understanding binary numbers helps you recognize how digital computers work by simply turning electricity on and off. In this Lab, you learn about the binary number system and you learn how to convert numbers from binary to decimal and from decimal to binary.

1 Click the Steps button to learn about the binary number system. As you proceed through the Steps, answer all of the Quick Check questions that appear. After you complete the Steps, you will see a Quick Check Summary Report. Follow the instructions on the screen to print this report.

2 Click the Explore button, then click the Conversions button. Practice converting binary numbers into decimal numbers. For example, what is the decimal equivalent of 00010011? Calculate the decimal value on paper. To check your answer, enter the decimal number in the decimal box, and then click the binary boxes to show the 1s and 0s for the number you are converting. Click the Check It button to see if your conversion is correct.

Convert the following binary numbers into decimals:

a. 00000101

b. 00010111

c. 01010101

d. 10010010

e. 11111110

3 In Explore, click the Conversions button. Practice converting decimal numbers into binary numbers. For example, what is the binary equivalent of 82? Do the conversion on paper. To check your answer, enter the decimal number in the decimal box, and then click the binary boxes to show the 1s and 0s of its binary equivalent. Click the Check It button to see if your conversion is correct.

Convert the following decimal numbers to binary numbers:

a. 77

b. 25

c. 92

d. 117

e. 214

4 In Explore, click the Binary Number Quiz button. The quiz provides you with ten numbers to convert. Make each conversion and type your answer in the box. Click the Check Answer button to see if you are correct. When you have completed all ten quiz questions, follow the instructions on the screen to print your quiz results.

CPU Simulator

In a computer central processing unit (CPU), the arithmetic logic unit (ALU) performs instructions orchestrated by the control unit. Processing proceeds at a lightning pace, but each instruction accomplishes only a small step in the entire process. In this Lab you work with an animated CPU simulation to learn how computers execute assembly language programs. In the Explore section of the Lab, you have an opportunity to interpret programs, find program errors, and write your own short assembly language programs.

1 Click the Steps button to learn how to work the simulated CPU. As you proceed through the Steps, answer all of the Quick Check questions that appear. After you complete the Steps, you will see a Quick Check Summary Report. Follow the instructions on the screen to print this report.

2 Click the Explore button. Use the File menu to open a program called **Add.cpu**. Use the Fetch Instruction and Execute Instruction buttons to step through the program. Then answer the following questions:

a. How many instructions does this program contain?

b. Where is the instruction pointer after the program is loaded but before it executes?

c. What does the INP 3 M1 instruction accomplish?

d. What does the MMR M1 REG1 instruction accomplish?

e. Which memory location holds the instruction that adds the two numbers in REG1 and REG2?

f. What is in the accumulator when the program execution is complete?

g. Which memory address holds the sum of the two numbers when program execution is completed?

3 In Explore, use the File menu to open a program called **Count5.cpu**. Use the Fetch Instruction and Execute Instruction buttons to step through the program. Then answer the following questions:

a. What are the two input values for this program?

b. What happens to the value in REG1 as the program executes?

c. What happens when the program executes the JPZ P5 instruction?

d. What are the final values in the accumulator and registers when program execution is complete?

4 In Explore, click File, then click New to make sure the CPU is empty. Write a program that follows these steps to add 8 and 6:

a. Input 8 into memory address M3.

b. Input 6 into memory address M5.

c. Move the number in M3 to Register 1.

d. Move the number in M5 to Register 2.

e. Add the numbers in the registers.

f. Move the value in the accumulator to memory address M1.

g. Tell the program to halt.

Test your program to make sure it produces the answer 14 in address M1. When you are sure your program works, use the File menu to print your program.

5 In Explore, use the File menu to open a program called **Bad1.cpu**. This program is supposed to multiply two numbers together and put the result in memory location M3. However, the program contains an error.

a. Which memory location holds the incorrect instruction?

b. What instruction will make this program produce the correct result?

6 In Explore, use the CPU simulator to write a program to calculate the volume, in cubic feet, of the inside of a refrigerator. The answer should appear in the accumulator at the end of the program. The inside dimensions of the refrigerator are 5 feet, by 3 feet, by 2 feet. Make sure you test your program, then print it.

Troubleshooting

Computers sometimes malfunction, so it is useful to have some skill at diagnosing, if not fixing, some of the hardware problems you might encounter. In this Lab, you use a simulated computer that has trouble booting. You learn to make and test hypotheses that help you diagnose the cause of boot problems.

1 Click the Steps button to learn how to make and test hypotheses about hardware malfunctions during the boot process. As you proceed through the Steps, answer all of the Quick Check questions that appear. After you complete the Steps, you will see a Quick Check Summary Report. Follow the instructions on the screen to print this report.

2 Click the Explore button. Use the File menu to load **System11.trb**. Click the Boot Computer button and watch what happens on the simulated computer (in this case, actually, what does not happen!). Make your hypothesis about why this computer does not boot. Use the Check menu to check the state of various cables and switches. When you think you know the cause of the problem, select it from the Diagnosis list. If you correctly diagnosed the problem, write it down. If your diagnosis was not correct, form another hypothesis and check it, until you have correctly diagnosed the problem.

3 Sometimes problems that appear very similar, result from different causes. In Explore, use the File menu to load **System03.trb**, then diagnose the problem. Do the same for **System06.trb**. Describe the problems with these two systems. Then describe the similarities and differences in their symptoms.

4 In Explore, use the File menu to load System02 and System08. Both systems produce keyboard errors, but these errors have different causes. Describe what caused the problem in System02, and what caused the problem in System08. Once you have diagnosed these problems, what can you do about them?

5 In Explore, use the File menu to load Systems 04, 05, 07, 09, and 14. These systems produce similar symptoms on boot up. However, these systems have different problems. Diagnose the problem with each of these systems and indicate the key factor (the symptom or what you checked) that led to your diagnosis.

THE COMPUTER MARKETPLACE

CHAPTER PREVIEW

When you have completed this chapter, you should be able to:

- Read a computer ad and understand how the technical specifications affect price and performance
- Explain why there are so many models of computers at so many different prices
- Research reliable information about computer products
- Determine which products are of good quality and value
- Take a systematic approach to shopping for a computer
- Use technology resources to research career options and create an effective resume

It is one of those dreary afternoons when the rain fogs up the windows. Your friend Matt is sprawled on the floor amidst a small mountain of computer magazines. Now and then he tags a page with a Post-it note or jots down the price of a computer system. You munch on a sandwich while browsing employment sites on the Web.

"Hey, what's up?" you ask.

"See all these magazines! See all these ads! How's a person supposed to know what to buy? The more I look, the more confused I get!" He opens the latest issue of *Computer Shopper*—all 800 pages of it—and you see that he has marked at least 30 ads with Post-it notes!

"Look," he says, "here's a computer with a Pentium processor...$1,995. Here's another one from a different company...$2,195."

"There's got to be some difference between them." You try to help.

Matt frowns. "Yeah. That's the trouble. One has more RAM, but the other one has a better monitor. I could spend $2,295 and get Surround Sound plus a larger hard drive, but that would wreck my budget. What am I going to do!"

Whether you're shopping for a computer or considering a career, the computer industry offers a huge variety of choices. As a consumer, understanding the computer industry is just as important as understanding world events. In fact, much of the news about the computer-industry has global significance for today's information age. You'll see increasing coverage of computers and the computer industry on the evening news, in magazines, on the Internet, and on TV.

The purpose of this chapter is to help you learn about the computer industry. You'll discover what you need to know to be a smart computer shopper. You'll discover who does what in the computer industry, and maybe you'll even identify a computer career that appeals to you.

LABS

Buying a Computer

A Consumer's Guide to Computer Systems

Sometime in the not-too-distant future you are likely to participate in a computer purchase decision—if not for your own computer, then one for your friend, your parents' small business, your employer, or your children. Buying the right computer and keeping within your budget are challenges.

Suppose you decide to buy a computer. You'll probably look at computer ads to get an idea of features and prices. Most computer ads list technical specifications describing the computer's components, capabilities, and special features. Do you need to understand the technical specifications to make an intelligent purchase decision? The answer is definitely "yes!" Suppose that you see a computer ad such as the one in Figure 6-1. This computer system costs $2,295. Would it be a good "deal"?

Figure 6-1

MicroPlus computer ad

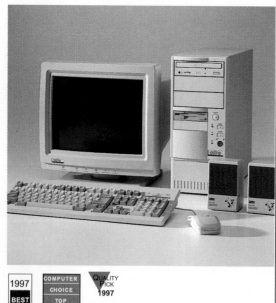

MicroPlus HomePC

MicroPlus award-winning computers offer strong performance at a reasonable price. Simply the fastest Windows machines you can buy. MicroPlus computers feature superior engineering, starting with a genuine Intel processor and a motherboard designed specifically to take advantage of the latest technological advancements. Of course, you are covered by our one-year on-site parts and labor warranty.*

*ON-SITE SERVICE AVAILABLE FOR HARDWARE ONLY AND MAY NOT BE AVAILABLE IN CERTAIN REMOTE AREAS. SHIPPING AND HANDLING EXTRA. ALL RETURNS WILL BE EXCHANGED FOR LIKE PRODUCT ONLY. ALL RETURNS MUST BE IN ORIGINAL BOX WITH ALL MATERIALS. CALL FOR AN RMA NUMBER. DEFECTIVE PRODUCTS WILL BE REPAIRED AT MICROPLUS DISCRETION. THE COST FOR RETURNED MERCHANDISE IS NOT INCLUDED WITH ANY MONEY-BACK GUARANTEE. PRICES AND AVAILABILITY SUBJECT TO CHANGE WITHOUT NOTICE.

- Intel Pentium II 266 MHz, 512 KB cache
- 32 MB EDO RAM expandable to 128 MB
- 6.4 GB 10 ms EIDE hard drive with 512 K cache
- 16X variable CD-ROM drive
- 3.5" 1.44 MB floppy drive
- Creative Labs stereo sound card and speakers
- 64-bit video card with 4 MB RAM
- 17" 1600 x 1200 .26 dp color monitor (15.7" vis)
- Six-bay tower case
- Mouse
- Microsoft Windows 98
- Three PCI and four ISA slots
- RS-232, USB, and parallel ports
- 33.6 bps fax/modem

1997 BEST TECH !

COMPUTER CHOICE TOP AWARD

QUALITY PICK 1997

All Credit Cards Welcome Call Toll Free 1-800-555-0000 and order today!

You can't tell if the MicroPlus computer is a good deal unless you can compare its specifications to those of computers from other vendors. Let's take a closer look at what the specifications mean in terms of price and performance.

Selecting a Microprocessor

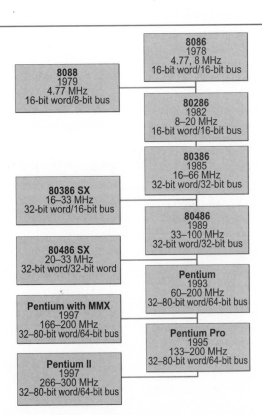

InfoWeb

Which Chip?
1

Does the processor affect the price of a computer? The microprocessor is the core component in a computer and is featured prominently in product descriptions. Computer ads typically indicate the type of microprocessor and its speed. Most of today's microcomputers are designed around a microprocessor from one of two product families: x86, or PowerPC.

The original IBM PC used the Intel 8088 microprocessor, one of the first models in the **x86 family** of microprocessors. Today's PCs still contain x86 processors such as the **Pentium**. Most of these processors are manufactured by Intel, but companies such as Cyrix and AMD have produced what are called "work-alike" processors. Computers with work-alike processors are generally less expensive than an equivalent computer with an Intel processor. Most computer ads specify which company manufactured the microprocessor. If you want to run Windows software, choose a computer with an x86 processor.

If you would rather run Macintosh software, select a computer with a 68000-series or PowerPC microprocessor. Until 1994, Macintosh computers contained a **68000-series microprocessor** manufactured by Motorola. More recent models, called "Power Macs" contain a **PowerPC microprocessor** that implements RISC architecture to provide relatively fast performance at a low cost.

Computers that contain recent-model microprocessors are more expensive than computers that contain older microprocessor technology. The geneology tree in Figure 6-2 will help you determine if the microprocessor technology in a PC is new or old.

Figure 6-2

PC processor geneology

8086
1978
4.77, 8 MHz
16-bit word/16-bit bus

8088
1979
4.77 MHz
16-bit word/8-bit bus

80286
1982
8–20 MHz
16-bit word/16-bit bus

80386
1985
16–66 MHz
32-bit word/32-bit bus

80386 SX
16–33 MHz
32-bit word/16-bit bus

80486
1989
33–100 MHz
32-bit word/32-bit bus

80486 SX
20–33 MHz
32-bit word/32-bit word

Pentium
1993
60–200 MHz
32–80-bit word/64-bit bus

Pentium with MMX
1997
166–200 MHz
32–80-bit word/64-bit bus

Pentium Pro
1995
133–200 MHz
32–80-bit word/64-bit bus

Pentium II
1997
266–300 MHz
32–80-bit word/64-bit bus

Comparing Pentiums

Which Pentium is right for me? The x86 chip family descended from Intel's 8086 microprocessor. The 80286, 80386, and 80486 models that followed were usually referred to by the last three digits, 286, 386, and 486. For the next generation, however, Intel broke with tradition. Initially, the 80586 chip was dubbed the P5, until it was officially christened the **Pentium**. Intel introduced the Pentium processor in 1993. This processor packed an impressive 3.3 million transistors on a chip .36-inch square. Using **dual-pipeline architecture**, the chip could execute two instructions at a time.

In 1995, Intel produced the P6 generation of processors called the **Pentium Pro**. With five execution pipelines and 5.5 million transistors, the Pentium Pro was optimized for the 32-bit instruction set that Microsoft had used to develop the Windows NT operating system. A Level 2 cache contributes to the speed of this chip and is often referred to in computer ads. A **Level 2 cache** (L2 cache) is memory circuitry housed off the processor on a separate chip. The cache chip connects to the main processor by a dedicated high-speed bus. Level 2 cache is much faster than RAM and almost as fast as cache built into the processor chip.

In 1997, Intel launched two new processors. The **Pentium with MMX technology** was a jazzed-up version of the original Pentium chip and contained circuitry to speed the execution of multimedia applications. A second chip, the **Pentium II**, added MMX technology to the Pentium Pro chip.

InfoWeb

Benchmarks
2

Most experts agree that the Pentium with MMX technology provides the most processing power for your dollar. The Pentium with MMX technology is less expensive than the Pentium Pro but has similar performance levels on tests such as SYSmark32. **SYSmark32** is a standard benchmark test that measures computer speed for word-processing, graphics, spreadsheet, and database tasks. If cost is not a factor, the Pentium II is a more expensive chip but will provide you with the highest level of performance. The chart in Figure 6-3 summarizes features and performance factors for each of the Pentium processors.

Figure 6-3

Pentium feature summary

	Pentium	Pentium Pro	Pentium with MMX technology	Pentium II
Speed	75–200 MHz	166–200 MHz	166–233 MHz	233–300 MHz
SySmark 32	175	214	203	249
MMX	No	No	Yes	Yes
On-chip cache	16 K	16 K	32 K	32 K
L2 cache	No	Yes	No	Yes
Transistors	3.3 million	5.5 million	4.5 million	7.5 million
Execution pipelines	2	5	2	5
Chip package	PGA single chip	PGA dual chip	PGA single chip	SEC cartridge
Introduced	1993	1995	1997	1997

RAM: Requirements and Cost

How much RAM is enough? The amount of RAM a computer needs depends on the operating system and applications software you plan to use. RAM costs have dropped in recent years. Today, RAM costs about $10 per megabyte, so it doesn't have a major impact on the price of a computer system. To run Windows software effectively, your computer should have at least 32 MB of RAM.

If a computer features **EDO** (Extended Data Out) RAM technology, you can expect better perfomance from it than from computers with standard memory technology.

It is possible to add RAM after you purchase a computer system. For example, the MicroPlus computer includes 32 MB of RAM, but additional memory modules can be added up to a maximum of 128 MB. Most consumer advocates recommend that you get as much RAM as you can afford with your initial purchase.

Floppy Disk Drives: How Many?

Do I need more than one floppy disk drive? Most microcomputers today are configured with a single 3½-inch high-density floppy disk drive. Older computers often included an additional 5¼ inch drive. These two disk drive sizes were useful during the transition from the earlier 5¼-inch disks to the newer 3½-inch disks. Today, most software is shipped on 3½-inch disks or on CD-ROMs, so a 5¼-inch drive is unnecessary.

A popular misconception is that a computer needs two disk drives to copy the contents of one disk to another, but this is not the case. Both Windows and DOS allow you to make a copy of an entire disk by reading data from the original disk into memory, then inserting the destination disk and copying the data from memory to the destination disk. One 3½-inch floppy disk drive should be sufficient for your computing needs.

Hard Drive Specifications

What's the difference between SCSI and EIDE? The factors that influence hard drive performance and price include storage capacity, access time, and controller type. The more storage space you have, the better. So when comparing computer systems, the hard drive capacity is a significant factor. Most computers today are shipped with at least 5 GB of hard disk capacity.

Computer ads usually specify hard disk access time as an indication of drive performance. Access times of 9, 10, or 11 ms are typical for today's microcomputer hard drives.

The two most popular types of hard drives are EIDE and SCSI. A hard drive mechanism includes a circuit board called a **controller** that positions the disk and read-write heads to locate data. Disk drives are categorized according to the type of controller they have. An **EIDE** (Enhanced Integrated Device Electronics) drive features high storage capacity and fast data transfer. **SCSI** (Small Computer System Interface) drives provide a slight performance advantage over EIDE drives and are recommended for high-performance microcomputer systems and minicomputers.

CD-ROM Drive: Worth the Cost?

Do I need a CD-ROM drive? A CD-ROM drive is a worthwhile investment that lets you use multimedia, game, educational, and reference applications that are available only on CD-ROM disks.

Today, most microcomputers are configured with a CD-ROM drive. Compared to a floppy disk drive, a CD-ROM drive delivers data at a faster rate and provides better performance, especially with multimedia applications. You should purchase the fastest CD-ROM drive that you can afford.

The access time of today's CD-ROM drives is 100 to 200 ms, ten times slower than a hard disk drive. In ads, however, the speed of a CD-ROM drive is measured by comparing its data transfer rate to the rate of the original CD-ROM drive technology. For example, the original CD-ROM drives had a data transfer rate of 150 KB per second. Dual speed or 2X CD-ROM drives have a data transfer rate of 300 KB per second.

Today's 12X CD-ROM drives have a data transfer rate of 1.8 MB per second. As a point of reference, the data transfer rate of a hard drive is about 3 MB per second. The computer ad in Figure 6-1 describes the CD-ROM drive as "16X variable." This means that the data transfer rate of the CD-ROM drive varies between a minimum transfer rate of 1.8 MB per second (12X) and a maximum speed of 2.4 MB per second (16X). Alternative terminology for 16X variable includes 12–16X and 16X max. The table in Figure 6-4 will help you compare the actual data transfer rates and access times of CD-ROM drives.

Figure 6-4

CD-ROM drive data-transfer rates

Speed	Seek Time (ms)	Data Transfer Rate
Single-speed	600	150 KB per second
2X	320	300 KB per second
3X	250	450 KB per second
4X	135–180	600 KB per second
6X	135–180	900 KB per second
8X	135–180	1.2 MB per second
10X	135–180	1.6 MB per second
12X	100–180	1.8 MB per second
16X	100–180	2.4 MB per second

Selecting a Sound System

What's wave table synthesis, and do I need it? With the proliferation of multimedia applications, a sound system has become an essential part of a computer system. A basic computer sound system includes a sound card and a set of small speakers; but if you want your computer-generated tunes to blow you away, you will want to invest in a more sophisticated sound system.

InfoWeb

Sound
Systems
3

A sound card converts the digital data in a sound file into analog signals for instrumental, vocal, and spoken sounds. In addition, a sound card lets you make your own recordings by converting analog sounds into **digitized sound files** that you can store on disk. To record your own sounds, you'll need to add a good quality microphone to your sound system. Digitized sound files require lots of storage space. Ten seconds of digitized stereo sound can consume up to 1.8 MB of disk space.

A more compact alternative to digitized sound is to store music as **MIDI sound**. A sound card generally supports one of two MIDI standards. **FM synthesis** provides instructions for the computer to synthesize sounds by simulating the sounds of real musical instruments. **Wave table synthesis** creates music by playing digitized sound samples of actual instruments. Wave table synthesis provides better quality sound, but at a higher price than FM synthesis.

Most multimedia software specifies the type of sound required. A basic sound card with FM synthesis is usually sufficient for most reference software and educational software. Some games require Sound Blaster compatible sound. If you own such software, make sure your sound card is described as "Sound Blaster compatible."

A sound card outputs sound to speakers or earphones. As with any audio system, higher quality speakers provide richer sound and enhanced volume. If you're really serious about sound, consider a subwoofer for big bass sound. An Altec Lansing sound system with Dolby Surround Sound such as the one in Figure 6-5 uses only two speakers but envelops you in a 3-D soundscape for a price of about $300.

Figure 6-5

Altec Lansing's ACS500 produces a Dolby Surround Sound environment.

Computer Display Systems

What is the relationship between the graphics card and the monitor? A computer display system consists of a monitor and a **graphics card**, also called a **video display adapter** or **video card**. A graphics card is an expansion card that controls the signals that the computer sends to the monitor. The clarity of a computer display depends on the quality of the monitor and the capability of the graphics card. As a consumer, your goal is to buy the best display system that fits your budget.

InfoWeb

Display System 4

Factors that influence the quality of the monitor include screen size, maximum resolution, and dot pitch. **Screen size** is the measurement in inches from one corner of the screen diagonally across to the opposite corner. Most computer systems are packaged with a 14-inch or 15-inch screen. You might want to consider paying an additional $300 to $500 for a 17-inch monitor if you have a vision problem or if you often work with more than one program at the same time. With a 17-inch monitor you can switch to a high resolution to fit more windows on the screen, and the text will still be reasonably large.

Figure 6-6

As with a TV, the monitor's viewable image size is less than the screen size.

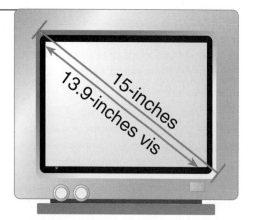

15-inches

13.9-inches vis

On most monitors, the viewable image does not stretch to the edge of the screen. Instead a black border makes the image smaller than, for example, the 15-inch size specified. Many computer vendors now include a measurement for the **viewable image size (vis)**. A 15-inch monitor has approximately a 13.9-inch vis as shown in Figure 6-6.

Dot pitch is a measure of image clarity; a smaller dot pitch means a crisper image. Technically, dot pitch is the distance in millimeters between like-colored pixels. A .28 or .26 dot pitch is typical for today's monitors.

The specifications for a monitor include its **maximum resolution**—the maximum number of pixels it can display. Standard resolutions include 640 x 480, 800 x 600, 1024 x 768, 1280 x 1024, and 1600 x 1200. Today's monitors typically have a maximum resolution of 1280 x 1024; but most people continue to use 640 x 480 resolution because it provides large, easy to read text. At higher resolutions the text appears smaller; but you can display a larger work area—for example, an entire page of a document.

It is important to realize that the maximum resolution you can use is determined by both the graphics card and the monitor. If your graphics card supports 1600 x 1200 resolution, but your monitor supports only 1280 x 1024, the maximum resolution you can use will be 1280 x 1024.

Most graphics cards use special graphics chips to boost performance. These **accelerated graphics cards** can greatly increase the speed at which images are displayed. An accelerated graphics card connected to a fast **PCI bus** can move data between the microprocessor and the graphics card as fast as the microprocessor can process it.

You can set your computer to display either 16, 256, 65,000, or 16 million colors. More colors provide more realistic images, but also require more computer resources. For higher resolutions and more colors, your graphics card needs more memory. To display photographic-quality images at 640 x 480 resolution, a graphics card should have at least 1 MB of memory. If you plan to display such images at 800 x 600 or 1024 x 768 resolutions, the graphics card should have 2 MB to 4 MB of memory. Figure 6-7 shows you how to change your display settings.

Figure 6-7

Change your display settings using Windows Control Panel.

Open the Display Properties dialog box.

Number of colors

Monitor resolution

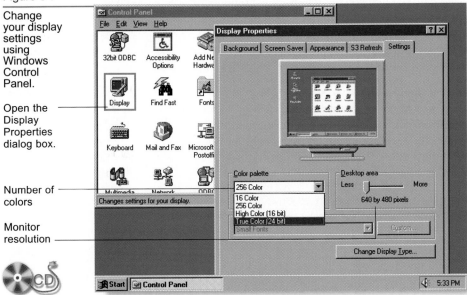

Comparing Notebook Displays

Is it true that the screen image on a notebook computer is not as good as the image on a desktop computer? Notebook computers do not use monitors, which are big, heavy, and require too much electrical power to run on batteries. Instead, notebooks have a flat panel liquid crystal display. A **liquid crystal display** (LCD) uses a technically sophisticated method of passing light through a thin layer of liquid crystal cells to produce an image. The resulting flat panel screen is lightweight and compact.

InfoWeb

Notebooks
5

Many older notebooks have a passive matrix screen, sometimes referred to as *dual-scan*. A **passive matrix screen** relies on timing to make sure the liquid crystal cells are illuminated. As a result, the process of updating the screen image does not always keep up with moving images, and the display can appear blurred. Passive matrix technology is not suitable for multimedia applications that include animations and videos.

An **active matrix screen**, referred to as **TFT** (thin film transistor), updates more rapidly and provides image quality similar to that of a monitor. Active matrix screens are essential for a crisp display of animations and video. However, active matrix screens are difficult to manufacture—approximately 50 percent are rejected due to defects—and add significantly to the price of a notebook computer.

Most notebook computers have a port to connect an external monitor. The advantage of an external monitor is the high-quality display. The disadvantage is that you need to disconnect the external monitor when you transport the computer.

Planning for Expansion

How can I make sure that I can expand my computer system? No matter how many bells and whistles your new computer system includes, you'll want to add to it in the future. Before you purchase a computer, make sure it has empty bays and unused expansion slots for additional storage devices and expansion cards.

The system unit case holds the main board and provides openings, called **bays**, for mounting disk, CD-ROM, and tape drives. An **external bay** provides an opening for installing a device that you need to access from the outside of the case. For example, you would install a floppy disk drive in an external bay because you need to insert and remove the floppy disks. An **internal bay** provides a mounting bracket for devices that do not need to be accessible from outside the system unit case. Hard disk drives typically use internal bays because they don't require you to insert and remove disks.

A system unit with many bays provides greater expansion capability. Notice in Figure 6-1 that the MicroPlus computer tower case has six bays. From the picture in the ad, it appears that there are five external bays, so one of the bays must be internal. The hard disk drive occupies one internal bay, while the floppy disk drive and CD-ROM each occupy one external bay. That leaves three external bays for expansion—probably enough for most home and business uses.

To add peripheral devices such as a printer, scanner, or graphics tablet, your computer needs an open port or expansion slot. In Chapter 5 you learned that you can plug an expansion card for a peripheral device into an expansion slot on the motherboard, or you can plug it into a serial, parallel, USB, or SCSI port. When you purchase a new computer, some ports and slots will already be connected to peripheral devices. Be sure to ask how many slots are free for later expansion.

Expanding a Notebook Computer

There doesn't seem to be much room in a notebook computer case—how do I add expansion cards? A **PCMCIA slot** (Personal Computer Memory Card International Association) is a special type of expansion slot developed for notebook computers, which do not have space in the case for full-size expansion slots and cards. A PCMCIA slot is a small, external slot into which you can insert a PCMCIA card, as shown in Figure 6-8.

Figure 6-8

 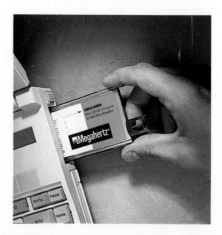

To add a modem, sound card, or a hard disk to a notebook computer, plug in a PCMCIA card.

PCMCIA cards, also called **PC cards**, are credit-card-sized circuit boards that incorporate an expansion card and device. So, for example, some PCMCIA cards contain a modem, others contain memory expansion, and others contain a hard disk drive. You can plug in and remove PCMCIA devices without turning the computer off, unlike desktop computer expansion cards. In this way you can switch from one PCMCIA device to another without disrupting your work.

PCMCIA slots are categorized by size. Type I slots accept only the thinnest PCMCIA cards such as memory expansion cards. Type II slots accept most of the popular PCMCIA cards—those that contain modems, sound cards, and network cards. Type III slots accept the thickest PCMCIA cards, which contain devices such as hard disk drives. Many notebooks provide a multipurpose PCMCIA slot that will accept two Type I cards, two Type II cards, or one Type III card.

Notebook computer expansion devices tend to be more expensive than those for desktop computers, but it is possible to use desktop peripherals with notebook computers if you have a docking station or a port replicatior.

A **docking station** is essentially an additional expansion bus into which you plug your notebook computer. The notebook provides the processor and RAM. The docking station provides expansion slots for cards that would not fit into the notebook case. It allows you to purchase inexpensive expansion cards and peripherals designed for desktops, instead of the more expensive devices designed specifically for notebooks. You sacrifice portability—you probably won't carry your docking station and external CD-ROM drive with you—but you gain the use of low-cost, powerful desktop peripherals. Figure 6-9 illustrates how a docking station works.

Figure 6-9

Notebook docking station

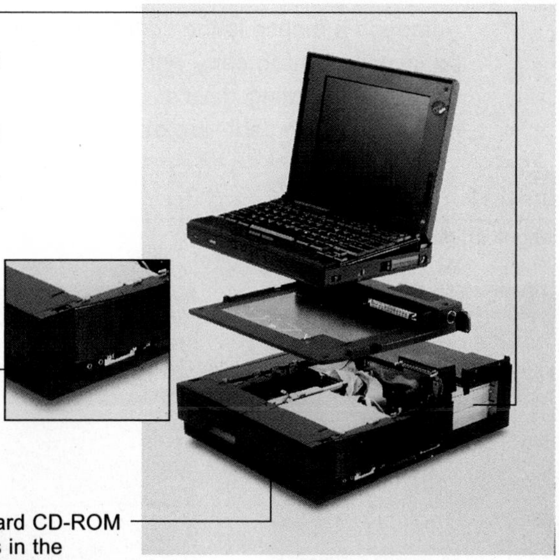

A docking station rests under or behind the notebook computer, and has room for speakers as well as other devices designed for full size desktop computers.

The docking station's external keyboard connector lets you use the keyboard from your desktop computer.

A standard CD-ROM drive fits in the docking station.

A **port replicator** is an inexpensive device that connects to a notebook computer by a bus connector plug; it contains a duplicate of the notebook computer's ports and makes it more convenient to connect and disconnect your notebook computer from devices such as an external monitor, mouse, and keyboard. Port replicators do not include expansion slots and typically cannot be used to add a sound card or CD-ROM drive to your notebook computer.

Selecting Input Devices

Should I settle for a standard keyboard and mouse?   Most desktop computers include a standard keyboard and a mouse, but you might want to consider alternative input devices. Cases of carpal tunnel syndrome, a stress-related wrist injury, are on the rise. Intensive keyboard and mouse use are the suspected culprits. Ergonomically designed keyboards, such as the one in Figure 6-10 may prevent computer-related injuries.

Figure 6-10

Microsoft claims that its Natural Keyboard was based on ergonomic and usability research.

Although a mouse is the standard pointing device used with desktop computers, it can be inconvenient to carry and use while traveling. Most notebook computers include an alternative pointing device. The three most popular options—built-in track ball, track point, and touch pad—are explained in Figure 6-11.

Figure 6-11

Notebook pointing devices

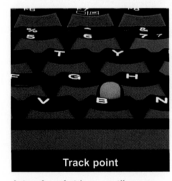

Track point

A **track point** is a small eraser-like device embedded among the typing keys. To control the on-screen pointer, you push the track point up, left, right, or down. Buttons for clicking and double-clicking are located in front of the spacebar.

Track ball

A **track ball** is like an upside-down mouse. By rolling the ball with your fingers, you control the on-screen pointer. Buttons for clicking are often located above or to the side of the track ball.

Touch pad

A **touch pad** is a touch-sensitive device. By dragging your finger over the surface, you control the on-screen pointer. Two buttons equivalent to mouse buttons are located in front of the touch pad.

Considerations for Notebook Power Sources

How long will a notebook computer run on batteries? Most notebook computers operate on power from either rechargeable batteries or a wall outlet. Because notebooks are designed for portability, the computing time provided by batteries is important. For example, an executive who frequently travels to Asia might want at least six hours of computing time during the 14-hour flight.

The length of time a notebook computer can operate from battery power depends on many factors. Fast processors, active matrix LCDs, and additional peripheral devices demand significant power from notebook computer batteries. Notebook manufacturers attempt to reduce power consumption by building power-saving features into their computers. These features automatically switch off the hard disk drive, LCD display, or even the processor if you do not interact with the computer after a short period of time. These devices are reactivated when you press a key or move the mouse.

On battery power, notebook computers typically provide two to four hours of operating time before the batteries need to be recharged. Most notebook computers use one of three types of batteries: Nicad (nickel cadmium), NiMH (nickel-metal hydride), or Lithium ion. Nicad batteries typically store less power than NiMH or Lithium ion batteries of equivalent size and weight. Therefore, Nicad batteries provide the shortest operating times. Most ads for notebook computers indicate the battery type and estimated computing times. Consumers need to be aware that many ads indicate maximum operating times. An ad that proclaims "Runs *up to* four hours!" might mean that the battery can supply four hours of operating time with no additional devices attached and with minimal use of the hard disk drive. Under typical working conditions the computer with fully charged batteries may run for significantly less than four hours.

The easiest way to extend the operating time of your notebook computer is to purchase extra batteries. When the first battery wears down, you can swap in a new battery and get back to work. Some notebook computers allow you to insert several batteries at the same time; as soon as one is discharged, the notebook switches to the next. Switching batteries while the computer is on is called a **hot swap** (Figure 6-12).

Figure 6-12

Notebook batteries are specially designed modules, made to slip into the notebook battery port.

Most notebook computers require an external AC adapter to plug into a wall outlet or to recharge the batteries. This adapter—about the size and weight of a small brick—can add significantly to the traveling weight of the notebook. Some notebook computers have eliminated the external adapter and require only a power cable to plug into a wall outlet. It is a good idea to use AC power whenever possible, such as when you use your notebook at home. Using AC power saves your batteries for when AC power is not available.

Choosing the Right Printer

What kind of printer should I buy?

InfoWeb

Printers
7

Occasionally a computer vendor offers a *hardware bundle* that includes a computer, printer, and software. More often, however, printers are sold separately so consumers can choose the quality, features, and price they want. Ink–jet and personal laser printers are most popular with today's consumers because they provide high-quality print on plain paper. Figure 6-13 is a guide to the features of laser and ink-jet printers. A dot-matrix printer is an older technology that creates letters and graphics by striking an inked ribbon with wires called pins. Athough these printers are inexpensive, their print-quality is not as crisp as an ink-jet or a laser printer. Today, dot-matrix printers are used mainly for applications that require multi-part forms.

Figure 6-13

Laser printers use the same technology as duplicating machines. A laser charges a pattern of particles on a drum which picks up a powdery black substance called toner. The toner is transferred onto paper that rolls past the drum. In the past, the price of laser printers limited their use to businesses and large organizations. Laser printer prices have decreased, however, making them affordable for individuals.

Color laser printers work by reprinting each page for each primary color. For each reprint, the paper must be precisely positioned so each color is printed in exactly the right spot. This dramatically increases the complexity of the print mechanism and the amount of time required to print each page.

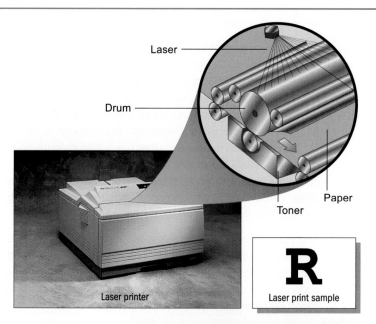

Laser printer

Laser print sample

Operating costs of laser printers include replacement toner cartridges and print drums. The estimated cost of laser printing is about $.05 per page.

Characteristics	
✓	Moderate to high price
✓	High-quality output
✓	More expensive to operate
✓	Cannot print multipart forms
✓	Fast
✓	Quiet
✓	Expensive, high-quality color
✓	Durable

Ink-jet printers produce characters and graphics by spraying ink onto paper. The print head is a matrix of fine spray nozzles. Patterns are formed by activating selected nozzles. An ink-jet printer typically forms a character in a 20 x 20 matrix, producing a high-quality printout.

Color ink-jet printers cost a little more, but produce much higher-quality output than color dot matrix printers. Using special paper, some color ink-jet printers can produce vivid, high-quality, color printouts. Ink-jet printers are inexpensive to operate, requiring only a new ink cartridge or ink refill. Estimated cost per page is about $.01.

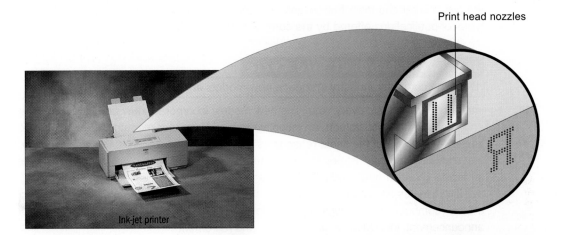

Print head nozzles

Ink-jet printer

Ink-jet print sample

Characteristics	
✓	Moderate price
✓	High-quality output
✓	Inexpensive to operate
✓	Cannot print multipart forms
✓	Slow
✓	Quiet
✓	Low-cost, low-quality color
✓	Durable

QuickCheck A

1. Most of today's PCs contain an Intel _____ model microprocessor.

2. If a computer features EDO RAM, you can expect better performance than from standard RAM. True or false? _____.

3. A SCSI hard drive has a slight performance advantage over a(n) _____ hard drive.

4. If you purchase a high-resolution monitor, the resolution of the graphics card is not important. True or false? _____.

5. Most notebook computers have either an active or passive matrix _____ display.

6. If you want to display photographic-quality images at 640 x 480 resolution, you need a graphics card with at least _____ of video memory.

7. A(n) _____ slot is important for adding peripheral devices to a notebook computer.

8. The best value for color printing is a(n) _____ printer.

B The Computer Industry

The **computer industry** consists of corporations and individuals that supply goods and services to people and organizations that use computers. The computer industry is in a continual state of change as new products appear and old products are discontinued; as corporations form, merge, and die; as corporate leadership shifts; as consumers' buying habits evolve; and as prices steadily continue to decrease. You will be a better informed consumer if you understand product life cycles, the tiered structure of computer vendors, the five market channels from which you can purchase hardware and software, and the types of publications offered by the computer press.

Hardware Product Life Cycle

Does the computer industry introduce new models annually? Automobile manufacturers introduce new models every year. The new models incorporate new and improved features and, therefore, give customers an incentive to buy. Computer manufacturers also introduce new models—and for the same reasons as their counterparts in the automotive industry. But the computer industry is not on an annual cycle so the computer marketplace seems rather chaotic with new product announcements and pre-announcements, ship dates, and availability dates all occurring at irregular intervals. In the computer industry, the life cycle of a new computer model typically includes five phases: product development, product announcement, introduction, maintenance, and retirement.

A **product announcement** declares a company's intention of introducing a new product. Products are announced at trade shows and press conferences. As a consumer, you should be wary of making purchasing decisions based on product announcements. A product announcement can precede the actual product by several years. Sometimes, products are announced but are never produced. These products are referred to as **vaporware**.

When a hardware product is first introduced, initial supplies of the product are generally low while manufacturing capacity increases to meet demand; consumers who want the scarce product must pay a relatively high price. As supply and demand for the product reach an equilibrium, the price of the product decreases slightly. Usually the price decrease is due to discounting by dealers, rather than a change in the manufacturer's list price. In Figure 6-14, you can see that the price of computers using the Pentium 133 MHz processor dropped significantly during the first year after their introduction.

Figure 6-14

The street price of the Compaq133 MHz Pentium computer shows a dramatic drop between April 1996 and June 1997.

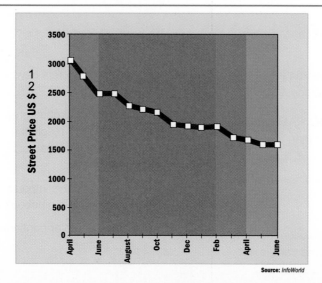

Source: *InfoWorld*

When a new product becomes available, it is usually added to the vendor's product line. The prices of products with older technology, such as Pentium 133 MHz processors, are reduced to keep them attractive to buyers. Gradually, the oldest products are discontinued as demand for them declines. As you can see from the ad in Figure 6-15 the less expensive products tend to have slower processors, less RAM, and lower-capacity hard disk drives. If your budget is not severely limited, a computer in the middle of a vendor's product line usually gives you the most computing power per dollar.

Figure 6-15

Microcomputer
product line

Software Product Life Cycle

What's the difference between a version and a revision? Companies that produce computer software are referred to as **software publishers**. Software, like hardware, begins with an idea that is then shaped by a design team and marketing experts. For some software products, such as Windows 95, the software publisher orchestrates a glitzy rollout as described in Figure 6-16.

Figure 6-16

The glitzy roll-out of Microsoft Windows 95 included full-page ads in national newspapers, television ads, and product rallies.

Microsoft released Windows 95 on August 24, 1995. The Rolling Stones blast out their version of *Start me up!* during the product rollout. The Start button, a prominent new feature of Windows 95, is supposed to make the software easier to use.

The release of Windows 95 was a major event for investors as well as for consumers. It made front-page news in the *New York Times* (July 31, 1995).

James Dawson for The New York Times

Software Hype and Hopes

It is not a lunar landing or the cure for a disease. It is simply an improved version of a computer's operating system — like a more efficient transmission for a car. But 100 million personal computers use the Microsoft Corporation's software. And on Aug. 24, when Microsoft begins selling a new version of Windows, a multibillion-dollar economy will be set in motion. Besides deciding whether to buy the $100 Windows 95 software itself, consumers and corporations will need to consider whether to spend hundreds of dollars more on hardware and software that takes advantage of it — or thousands more to buy whole new machines. Meanwhile, the Justice Department is still considering whether to try to prevent Microsoft from including access to its new on-line service in Windows 95.

Coverage begins on page D1.

A new software product can be an entirely new product, a new **version** (also called a **release**) with significant enhancements, or a **revision** designed to add minor enhancements and eliminate bugs found in the current version. Before you buy software, you should be familiar with the difference between versions and revisions.

The original version of a software product is typically called version 1.0. Software publishers release a revision to fix bugs or make small changes to product features. The revision number is separated from the version number with a period. The first revision of a product will be 1.1. A major improvement to a software product would be indicated by a new version number, such as 2.0. You can usually find the revision and version numbers in a Windows program by clicking Help, then selecting About.

Software products undergo extensive testing before they are released. But even after testing, bugs inevitably remain. If you discover a software bug that effects usability, check with the software vendor to see if a revision of the product exists that includes with a "bug fix." The publisher will often supply a revision for free or nominal shipping costs.

"No one pays list price for software!" say industry analysts. A variety of discounts and special offers make it worth while to shop around. You can purchase a $495 software package for less than $100 if you're a smart shopper.

When a new software product first becomes available, the publisher often offers a special **introductory price** to entice customers. Several software products that now carry a list price of $495 were introduced at a special $99 price. Even after the introductory price expires, most vendors offer sizable discounts. The average dicounted price is referred to as the **street price**. Expect software with a list price of $495 to be offered for a street price of $299.

If you own an earlier version of a software package, you are probably eligible for the **version upgrade price**. By supplying the vendor with proof that you own the earlier version, you can get the new version at a discount. For example, if your word-processing software is version 7 and you want to upgrade to version 8, you can upgrade for $75 instead of paying the $299 street price.

A **competitive upgrade** is a special price offered to consumers who switch from one company's software product to the new version of a competitor's product. For example, suppose you've been using ClarisDraw, but you decide to switch to GRAFIX 7. You would pay $149 for a competitive upgrade, instead of paying the $399 street price as shown in Figure 6-17.

Figure 6-17

Competitive software upgrades provide an incentive for switching to a competitor's product.

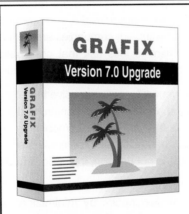

GRAFIX
Version 7.0 Upgrade

GRAFIX 7
Competitive Upgrade
for only
$149.95

• Windows qualifying products: Illustrator, Deneba Canvas, CorelDraw, ClarisDraw, or Freehand. Mail or fax a photocopy of either the user manual or the original program disk

(full price is $399)

Wholesale Computers 800-123-4567

Unlike computer hardware products, older versions of software do not remain in the vendor's product line. Soon after a new version of a software product is released, the software publisher usually stops selling earlier versions. When a publisher offers a new version of the software you are using, it is a good idea to upgrade; but you can wait for several months until the initial rush for technical support on the new product decreases. If you don't upgrade, you might find that the software publisher offers minimal technical support for older versions of the program. Also, if you let several versions go by without upgrading, you might have to purchase the software at full price when you eventually decide to upgrade.

Market Tiers

What accounts for price differences for computers with the same specifications from different vendors? Since 1981, hundreds of companies have produced personal computers. Industry analysts often refer to three tiers or categories of microcomputer companies, although not all analysts agree on which companies belong in each tier.

The top tier consists of large companies that have been in the computer business for more than ten years and have an identifiable percentage of total computer sales—companies such as IBM, Apple, Compaq, and Hewlett-Packard. The second tier includes newer companies with high sales volume, but with somewhat less financial resources than companies in the first tier. Most analysts place companies such as Gateway, Dell, and Packard Bell in the second tier. The third tier consists of smaller startup companies that sell primarily through mail order.

Computer prices vary by tier. Computers from the top-tier vendors generally are more expensive than computers offered by second-tier or third-tier vendors. For example, a computer with specifications similar to the MicroPlus computer featured in the ad at the beginning of this chapter might cost $2,699 from a first-tier vendor, $2,199 from a second-tier vendor, and $1,999 from a third-tier vendor.

Why do these prices vary by tier? Because first-tier companies often have higher overhead costs, management is often paid higher salaries, and substantial financial resources are devoted to research and development. The first-tier companies are responsible for many of the innovations that have made computers faster, more powerful, and more convenient. Also, many consumers believe that computers sold by first-tier companies are better quality and are a safe purchasing decision. They believe there is less risk that computers from first-tier companies will quickly become obsolete or that the vendor will go out of business.

Computers from second-tier companies are generally less expensive than those from the first tier, although the quality can be just as good. Most PCs are constructed from off-the-shelf circuit boards, cables, cases, and chips. This means that the components in the computers sold by second-tier companies are often the same as those in computers sold by the first tier. The quality of the off-the-shelf parts, however, is not uniform; it is difficult for the consumer to determine the quality of parts.

Second-tier companies often maintain their low prices by minimizing operating costs. These companies have a limited research and development budget. Also, they try to maintain a relatively small work force by contracting with another company to provide repair and warranty work.

Computers from third-tier companies often appear to be much less expensive than those in other tiers. Sometimes this reflects the low overhead costs of a small company, but other times it reflects poor-quality components. A consumer who is knowledgeable about the market and has technical expertise can often get a bargain on a good-quality computer from a third-tier company. But some consumers think it's risky to purchase computers from third-tier companies. Third-tier companies are smaller and perhaps more likely to go out of business, leaving their customers without technical support.

Marketing Channels

Is it safe to buy a computer by mail? Computer hardware and software are sold by marketing outlets or "channels," as shown in Figure 6-18.

Figure 6-18

Marketing channels

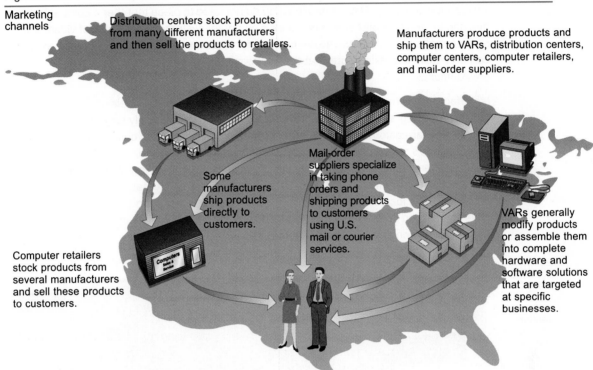

Distribution centers stock products from many different manufacturers and then sell the products to retailers.

Manufacturers produce products and ship them to VARs, distribution centers, computer centers, computer retailers, and mail-order suppliers.

Some manufacturers ship products directly to customers.

Mail-order suppliers specialize in taking phone orders and shipping products to customers using U.S. mail or courier services.

Computer retailers stock products from several manufacturers and sell these products to customers.

VARs generally modify products or assemble them into complete hardware and software solutions that are targeted at specific businesses.

A **computer retail store** purchases computer products from a manufacturer or distribution center and then sells the products to consumers. Computer retail stores are either small local shops or nationwide chains that specialize in the sale of microcomputer software and hardware. The employees at computer retail stores are often knowledgeable about a variety of computer products and can help you select a hardware or software product to fit your needs. Many computer retail stores also offer classes and training sessions, answer questions, provide technical support, and repair hardware products. A computer retail store is often the best source of supply for buyers who are likely to need assistance after the sale, such as beginning computer users or those with complex computer systems such as networks. But computer retail stores can be a fairly expensive channel for hardware and software. Their prices reflect the cost of purchasing merchandise from a distributor, maintaining a retail storefront, and hiring technically qualified staff.

Mail-order suppliers take orders by mail or telephone and ship the product directly to consumers. Mail-order suppliers generally offer low prices but provide limited service and support. A mail-order supplier is often the best source of products for buyers who are unlikely to need support or who can troubleshoot problems with the help of a technical support person on the telephone. Experienced computer users who can install components, set up their software, and do their own troubleshooting are often happy with mail-order suppliers. Inexperienced computer users might not be satisfied with the support and assistance they receive from mail-order suppliers.

Value-added resellers (VARs) combine commercially available products with specialty hardware or software to create a computer system designed to meet the needs of a specific industry. Although VARs charge for their expertise, they are often the only source for a system that really meets the needs of a specific industry. For example, if you own a video rental store and want to automate your store, the best type of vendor might be a VAR. The VAR can offer you a complete hardware and software package that is tailored to the video rental business. This means that you do not need to piece together a computer, scanner, printer, and software components for a computer system to keep track of video rentals. VARs are often the most expensive channel for hardware and software, but their expertise can be crucial in making sure that the hardware and software work correctly in a specific environment.

Manufacturer direct refers to hardware manufacturers that sell their products directly to consumers using a sales force or mail order. The sales force usually targets large corporate or educational customers where large volume sales can cover costs and commissions. Manufacturers also use mail order to distribute directly to individual consumers. Manufacturers can sell their products directly to consumers for a lower price than when they sell them through retailers, but they cannot generally offer the same level of support and assistance as a local retailer. In an effort to improve customer support, some manufacturers have established customer support lines and provide repair services at the customer's home or place of business as shown in Figure 6-19.

Figure 6-19

Many reputable mail-order vendors offer on-site service in the continental U.S., Alaska, Hawaii, and Canada. Make sure you ask about service policies. Some computer components are not covered by the on-site service plan.

The Computer Press

Where can I get reliable information about computers to help me make informed purchases? Computer publications provide information on computers, computing, and the computer industry. The type of computer publication you need depends on the kind of information you want.

InfoWeb

Publications 8

Computer magazines contain articles and advertisements for the latest computer products. One of the earliest computer magazines, *Byte*, began publication in August 1975 and still remains one of the most widely read sources of computer information. The success of *Byte* might be attributed to its wide coverage of computers and computing topics. Many magazines that featured only a single type of computer, such as the Apple II, had staying power only as long as the computer maintained good sales. There are exceptions, however, magazines for specific computers, such as *MacWorld*, have a healthy subscription list.

Computer magazines generally target users of both personal and business computers. Articles focus on product evaluations, product comparisons, and practical tips for installing hardware and using software. These magazines are full of product advertisements, which are useful if you want to keep informed about the latest products available for your computer. You can find computer magazines such as those in Figure 6-20 on virtually any newsstand and at the library.

Figure 6-20

Popular computer magazines

Computer industry trade journals have a different focus than computer magazines because they target computer professionals, rather than consumers. Computer trade journals, such as *InfoWorld* and *Computer Reseller News*, focus on company profiles, product announcements, and sales techniques. Often free subscriptions to trade journals are given to corporate decision makers because advertisers want them to be aware of their products. Trade journals are not always available on newsstands, and subscriptions are not always available to the general public.

Computing journals offer an academic perspective on computers and computing issues. Such journals focus on research in computing, with articles on such topics as the most efficient sorting technique to use in a database management system, the implication of copyright law for educational institutions, or the prevalence of spreadsheet use by executives in Fortune 500 companies. Academic journals rarely advertise hardware and software products because it might appear that advertisers could influence the content of articles.

An article in a computing journal is usually "refereed," which means that it is evaluated by a committee of experts who determine if the article is original and based on sound research techniques. The best place to find computing journals is in a university library. Some of the most respected journals in the computing field include *Communications of the ACM* (Association for Computing Machinery), *Communications of the IEEE* (Institute of Electrical and Electronics Engineers), *SIAM* (Society of Industrial and Applied Mathematics) *Journal on Computing*, and *Journal of Information Science*.

Web Resources 9

Internet sites are an excellent source of information about the computer industry and computer products. Several computer magazines and trade journals maintain Internet sites with articles from back issues. Current issues are also available from some sites for a fee. Many computer companies have Internet sites where consumers can access up-to-date information about products and services. Here you can usually find product specifications, product announcements, sales literature, technical support forums, and pricing information.

Computer TV 10

Television shows about computers provide hardware and software reviews, tips, and computer industry news for new and experienced users. The PCTV network produces shows such as *The Internet Cafe*, *Computer Chronicles* (Figure 6-21), *@Home*, and *User Group*. CNET produces *The Web*, *The New Edge*, and *CNET Central*. Jones Cable Network and Mind Extension University offer *Using the Computer in Business*, *The Home Computing Show*, and *New Media News*. CNN Financial Network includes a high tech overview called *Digital Jam*, also available in video format on the Internet. ZDTV, operated by Ziff-Davis, has teamed up with Microsoft to broadcast technology news on MSNBC. Most of these networks are carried on cable TV. Check your cable listings for airtimes.

Figure 6-21

For over 12 years, viewers have tuned into *Computer Chronicles* on the Public Broadcasting System. Hosted by Steward Chiefet, the show features demonstrations of new hardware and software products.

The computer industry has many **industry analysts** who monitor industry trends, evaluate industry events, and make predictions about what the trends seem to indicate. Computer industry analysts range from professional financial analysts, who report on the computer industry for the *Wall Street Journal* and *Forbes* magazine, to the "rumor-central" analysts, who spark up the back pages of trade journals and computer magazines with the latest gossip about new products.

If you want to invest in a computer corporation's stock, the financial analysts might offer some good insights. If you want to invest in a personal computer, rumor-central columns, such as the one in Figure 6-22 are the place to get the scoop about product shortages, hardware glitches, software bugs, and impending customer service problems.

Figure 6-22

Robert X. Cringely is one of the best known computer columnists. Look for his column, *Notes From the Field*, on the back pages of *InfoWorld* magazine.

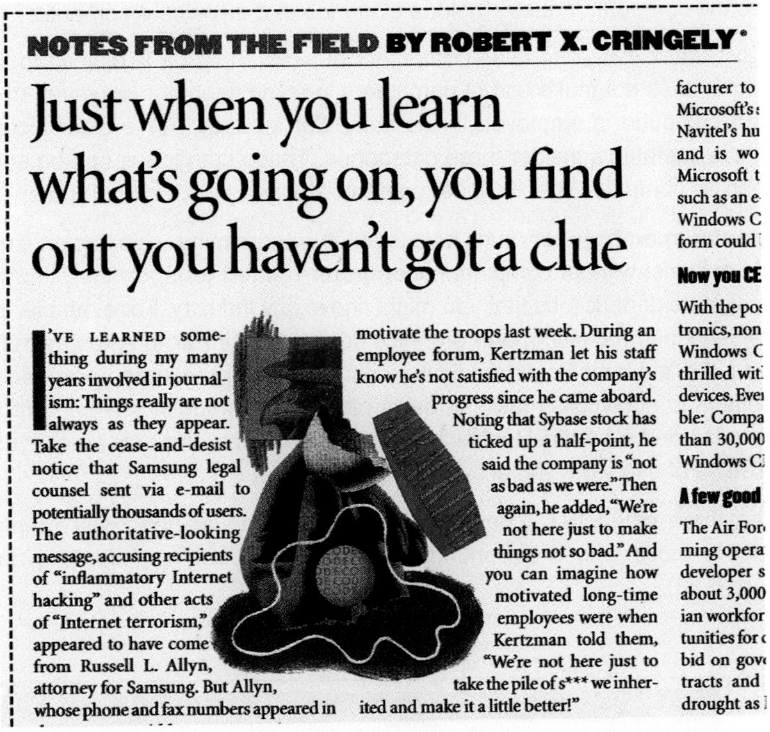

NOTES FROM THE FIELD BY ROBERT X. CRINGELY

Just when you learn what's going on, you find out you haven't got a clue

I'VE LEARNED something during my many years involved in journalism: Things really are not always as they appear. Take the cease-and-desist notice that Samsung legal counsel sent via e-mail to potentially thousands of users. The authoritative-looking message, accusing recipients of "inflammatory Internet hacking" and other acts of "Internet terrorism," appeared to have come from Russell L. Allyn, attorney for Samsung. But Allyn, whose phone and fax numbers appeared in

motivate the troops last week. During an employee forum, Kertzman let his staff know he's not satisfied with the company's progress since he came aboard. Noting that Sybase stock has ticked up a half-point, he said the company is "not as bad as we were." Then again, he added, "We're not here just to make things not so bad." And you can imagine how motivated long-time employees were when Kertzman told them, "We're not here just to take the pile of s*** we inherited and make it a little better!"

QuickCheck B

1. Products that are announced, but never shipped are called _____.

2. If your budget is not severely limited, a computer in the middle of a vendor's product line usually gives you the most computing power per dollar. True or false? _____

3. A(n) _____ upgrade is a special price offered to consumers who switch from one company's software product to a new version of a competitor's product.

4. Computer vendors are often categorized into three _____ based on market share and financial resources.

5. Computer books offer the most up-to-date information about computer products. True or false? _____

6. A(n) _____ sells complete computer solutions for a specific industry such as video stores or medical offices.

C Computer Industry Careers

InfoWeb

BLS
11

The $290 billion computer industry employs more than 1.5 million people. Over the past 50 years, it has created jobs that never before existed and financial opportunities for those with motivation, creative ideas, and technical skills. Since 1970, high-tech business has produced more than 7,000 millionaires and more than a dozen billionaires. According to the U.S. Bureau of Labor Statistics, computer and data processing services are projected to be third fastest growing industry; systems analysts, computer engineers, and data processing equipment repairers are expected to be among the 30 fastest growing occupations between now and 2005.

Computer Industry Job Categories

Does the computer industry include every job that involves a computer? It seems today that just about everyone uses computers at work. In fact it is difficult to find a job nowadays that does not make use of computers in some capacity. However, not everyone who uses a computer is employed in the computer industry. For a clear picture of computer jobs, it is useful to consider three categories. These categories can be somewhat loosely defined as computer-specific jobs, computer-related jobs, and computer-use jobs.

Computer-specific jobs—such as computer programming, chip design, and Webmaster—would not exist without computers. **Computer-related jobs**, on the other hand, are variations of more generic jobs that you might find in any industry. For example, jobs in computer sales, high-tech recruiting, and graphics design are similar to sales, recruiting and design jobs in the automobile or medical industries. **Computer-use jobs** require the use of computers to accomplish tasks in fields other than computing. Writers, reporters, accountants, retail clerks, medical technicians, auto mechanics, and many others use computers in the course of every day job activities.

Of the three categories, computer-specific jobs require the most preparation and will appeal to those who like working with, learning about, and thinking about computers (Figure 6-23).

Figure 6-23

Jay Nunamaker, a computer science professor and chairman of a computer consulting firm explores how computers can facilitate group interaction.

Computer-Specific Jobs

What are the qualifications for computer jobs? Jobs for people who design and develop computer hardware and software require a high degree of training and skill. A college degree is required for virtually any of these jobs, and many require a master's degree or doctorate.

InfoWeb

College Connection 12

Most colleges offer degrees in computer engineering, computer science, and information systems that provide good qualifications for computer-specific jobs. There is some overlap between these fields of study, but the emphasis for each is different.

Computer engineering degrees require a good aptitude for engineering, math, and electronics. Career opportunities for computer engineering graduates focus on the design of computer hardware and peripheral devices, often at the chip level (Figure 6-24).

Figure 6-24

Technicians in a chip fabrication plant wear "Bunny Suits" to maintain a sterile environment.

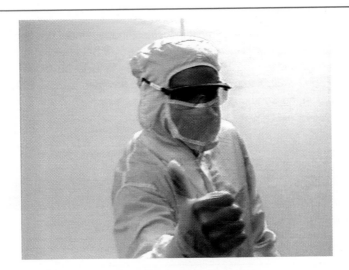

Computer science degrees require a good aptitude for math and computer programming. The main object of study in a computer science program is the digital computer, and the main objective is to make the computer work effectively and efficiently. Computer science graduates generally find entry-level jobs as programmers and Webmasters with good possibilities for advancement as software engineers, object-oriented/GUI developers, and project-leaders in technical applications development.

Information systems degree programs focus on the application of computers in a business or organizational environment. Coursework in business, accounting, computer programming, communications, systems analysis, and human psychology are usually required. For students who want to become computer professionals but lack strong math aptitude, most academic advisors recommend the information systems degree. An information systems degree usually leads to an entry-level programming or PC support job with good possibilities for advancement to systems analyst, project manager, database administrator, network manager, or other management positions.

Working Conditions

What are the advantages of working in the computer industry? Graduates with computer engineering, computer science, and information systems degrees generally work in a comfortable office or laboratory environment. Many high-tech companies offer employee-friendly working conditions that include childcare, flexible hours, and the opportunity to telecommute. As in any industry, the exact nature of a job depends on the company and the particular projects that are in the works. Some jobs and some projects are more interesting than others.

Many computer professionals like to pick and choose projects, which might account for the recent trend toward contract work and consulting. Contract programmers, consultants, and technical writers are self-employed, seek out short-term projects, and negotiate a per-project compensation rate. They set their own schedule, but often work 60-hour weeks. It takes motivation and discipline to be successful, but the rewards include control over your working environment.

In the computer industry, as in most industries, management positions command the highest salaries and salary levels increase with experience. Salaries vary by geographic location. In the Northeast and on the West Coast salaries tend to be higher than in the Southeast, Midwest, Southwest, and Canada. Figure 6-25 provides sample 1997 salaries for computer-related jobs in the Southeastern United States.

Figure 6-25

1997 computer industry salaries

Job Title	Salary (1997)	Job Title	Salary (1997)
Chief information officer	$122,000	Software engineer	$54,500
Information systems director	91,000	Senior database analyst	61,200
Manager of analysts and programmers	74,100	Object-orientated/GUI developer	58,100
Manager of systems programmers and technical support personnel	73,100	Web/Internet developer	51,700
Network manager	72,000	Network administrator	49,550
Project leader	62,000	Systems analyst/programmer	52,400
Database administration manager	69,800	PC applications specialist	41,900
Telecommunications manager	66,500	Technical writer	31,400
Data center manager	63,600	Consultant	58,100
PC workstation manager	48,500	Computer sales representative	74,100
Senior software engineer	64,000	Computer assembly worker	25,000

Preparing for a Computer Career

How do I prepare for a career in the computer industry? Education and experience are the keys to a challenging computer job with good potential for advancement. In addition to a degree in computer science, computer engineering, or information systems, think about how you can get on-the-job experience through internships, military service, government-sponsored training programs, or work-study programs. However, these experiences are only supplements to formal education. Most computer industry employers will not consider an applicant without a bachelor's degree in an appropriate field.

Figure 6-26

Not all computer science majors wear their computers around campus, but Computer Science and Information Systems degrees provide excellent credentials for a career in computing.

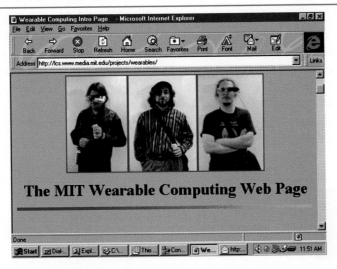

The MIT Wearable Computing Web Page

Organizations
13

Owning your own computer, installing software, and troubleshooting provide good basic experience and familiarity with mass-market computing standards. You might pick up additional experience from projects sponsored by clubs and organizations. The three largest computer organizations in North America are the Association for Computing Machinery (ACM), the Association of Information Technology Professionals (AITP), and Institute of Electrical and Electronic Engineers - Computer Society (IEEE-CS).

Certification
14

To beef up your credentials, you might also consider certification. The Institute for Certification of Computing Professionals (ICCP) has a regular schedule of comprehensive exams for computer jobs such as computer programming, systems analysis, and network management. If you are considering a career in computer network management, it might be worthwhile to complete the test for Novell NetWare or Microsoft NT certification. Certification for application software such as Microsoft Word, Excel, PowerPoint, and Access are also available.

Keep track of the job market in your area of specialty. You'll want to develop a good mix of generalized knowledge and specialized skills. Generalized knowledge, and your ability to apply it, will help you generate creative and feasible solutions to problems. Specialized skills such as experience with Visual Basic programming will give you marketable tools to match specific jobs. The trick is to anticipate which computer skills will be in demand when you next search for a job. By obtaining those skills, you put yourself in a good competitive position against other applicants.

Use Technology to Find a Job

How do I find a computer industry job? The first step in a job search is to realistically assess your qualifications and needs. Your qualifications include your computer skills, educational background, previous work experience, communications skills, and personality. By comparing your qualifications to the requirements for a job, you can assess your chances of being hired. Your needs include your preferred geographical location, working conditions, corporate lifestyle, and salary. By comparing your needs to the information you discover about a prospective employer, you can assess your chances of enjoying a job once you've been hired. Several excellent books and Web sites provide information to help you assess your qualifications and needs. It is an important step. Your goal is not to "get a job," but to get a job you like, that provides opportunity for advancement, and rewards you with a good salary.

InfoWeb

Career Resources 15

Today, researching the job market has become much easier, thanks to the Internet. In 1997, an estimated one out of every five employers in North America used the Internet for recruiting. Popular Web-based "want ads" post descriptions of job openings. Usually the employers pay for these postings, so access is free to prospective employees. Web sites, such as the one in Figure 6-27, include general information about jobs, employment outlook, and salaries in computer-industry jobs.

Figure 6-27

One of the most popular career Web sites

Because the salaries for most jobs are vaguely stated as "commensurate with experience," it is useful to discover what you're worth by studying Web-based salary reports. If you're asked to name a figure during a job interview, you will then be able to provide your prospective employer with your salary requirements, based on occupation, experience, and geographic area. The Web is not the only source of job listings. You can and should consult newspaper want ads, attend job fairs, and consider using the services of a professional recruiter.

You will need to prepare a resume with your career goal, experience, skills, and education. Some career counselors suggest that high-tech candidates should not follow many of the rules delineated in traditional resume guidebooks. For example, if you have a substantial list of technical skills, you might not be able to limit your resume to a single page. Your resume should demonstrate technical savvy without appearing overly "packaged." For example, dot-matrix printing is hard to read and old fashioned, but would not automatically qualify for the wastebasket in a stack of engineering resumes. By contrast, unless you're applying for a job as a Web site or graphical designer, you don't want your resume to look like a page from *Wired* magazine. Such advice is interesting, but remember that corporate cultures differ. What might get your foot in the door at a shirt-and-tie corporation such as IBM could be different than at a jeans-and-sandals start-up such as Yahoo! Don't despair. You can use your word processor to tailor your resume to the corporate culture of each prospective employer.

Contact Prospective Employers

How do I get my information out? The standard procedure for mailing letters of application and resumes remains valid even in this age of high technology. However, alternatives some-times prove even more effective. Many companies will accept resumes by fax to reduce the time it takes to process applicants. E-mail is another route that speeds up the process. Use it if you can, and make sure you include your e-mail address on your application materials. In addition to speeding communication, using e-mail demonstrates your familiarity with one of the most pervasive technology tools in the world today.

You can post your resume on a placement Web site where it can be viewed by corporate recruiters. Some of these Web sites charge a small fee for posting resumes; others are free. You can also post your resume along with your personal Web page, if you have one. This is particularly effective if you design these pages to showcase technical skills that are applicable to the job you're seeking. College students beware. Some employers have discovered much more than they bargained for by visiting the Web pages created by job applicants. If you are searching for employment, take a moment to look at your Web page through the eyes of a middle-aged, conservative, corporate recruiter. Remember that this page is public. Even if you don't include its Web address in your application materials, it is not difficult to find.

QuickCheck C

1. The U.S. Bureau of Labor Statistics estimates that computer and data processing services will be the fastest growing industry between now and 2001. True or false? _____

2. A(n) _____ degree program focuses on the application of computers in a business or organizational environment.

3. High-tech salaries tend to be highest on the West Coast and in the _____ section of the United States.

4. Education and _____ are the keys to a challenging computer job with good potential for advancement.

5. The AITP, ACM, and IEEE-CS are professional _____.

6. In addition to using Web-based job listings, you can consult newspaper want ads, attend _____, and use the services of a professional recruiter.

User Focus

D Computer Shopping Strategies

If you are like most consumers in pursuit of a good computer value, you will talk to salespeople, read computer magazines, look through computer catalogs, and chat with your friends who own computers. Here are some shopping strategies that should help you purchase a computer that meets your needs within a budget you can afford.

LAB

Buying a Computer

Determine Your Needs and Budget

Where do I start? Start by setting a budget and stick to it! Computer vendors have very carefully priced the computers in their model line so that you will be tempted to spend "just a few hundred dollars more" to get a model with more features. The trouble is that if you decide to spend that few hundred dollars, you will be tempted to spend just a little more to get even more features.

Once you have established a budget, consider how you plan to use the computer. A computer can be a valuable tool for completing your college degree, it can be a useful educational tool for your children, and it can increase your competitive edge in your career. Consider these factors before you begin shopping for a computer:

Notebook or desktop? If you plan to carry your computer with you, a notebook computer is the optimal choice. However, a notebook costs more than a similarly configured desktop, so you will pay for portability or give up features.

InfoWeb

Consumer Info 16

Multimedia? If you want to use multimedia applications, you should buy a system with a CD-ROM drive and sound card. Multimedia notebooks can be pricey, but a docking bay might allow you to add multimedia capabilities and still stay within your budget.

Compatibility? Most computers sold today are IBM compatible PCs. However, you should consider a Macintosh computer if most of the computers in your school are Macintoshes, if the computer is for your children who are using Macintosh computers in school, or if Macintosh is the major computer used in your career field.

Printer? Remember that you must include the cost of a printer in your budget. Unless you need to print multipart forms, you should not buy a dot matrix printer. A black-and-white ink jet printer is in the same price range, but it uses single-sheet paper and produces better print quality. Inexpensive laser printers, referred to as "personal laser printers," cost $100 to $300 more than a black-and-white ink-jet printer. Also consider a printer's operational cost. If you are on a very limited budget, it is easier to replace a $15 ink cartridge than a $100 toner cartridge.

Collect the Facts

| What information do I need? | Before you make a decision, shop around to collect information on pricing, features, and support. Although you might be tempted to buy the computer with the lowest price and best features, don't forget to consider the warranty and the quality of the support you are likely to get from the vendor. The checklist in Figure 6-28 will help you gather facts about pricing, features, and support.

Figure 6-28

Comparison data sheet

Computer Purchase Data Sheet
Specifications

Computer brand, model and manufacturer: _____

Processor type: _____

Processor speed: _____ MHz

MMX technology? ❑ Yes ❑ No

RAM capacity: _____ MB

Number and size of floppy disk drives: _____

Capacity of hard disk drive: _____ GB

Speed of CD-ROM drive: _____

Capacity of tape drive: _____

Amount of cache memory: _____ KB

Monitor screen size: _____ vis or inches

Maximum monitor resolution: _____

Amount of memory on graphics card: _____ MB

Modem speed: _____ bps

Number of expansion slots: _____

Upgrade path for new processor? ❑ Yes ❑ No

Operating system: _____

Mouse included? ❑ Yes ❑ No

Sound card and speakers included? ❑ Yes ❑ No

Value of bundled software: $_____

Service and Support

What is the warranty period? _____ years

Does the warranty cover parts and labor? ❑ Yes ❑ No

Does the vendor have a good reputation for service? ❑ Yes ❑ No

Are technical support hours adequate? ❑ Yes ❑ No

Free 800 number for technical support? ❑ Yes ❑ No

Can I contact technical support without waiting on hold for a long time? ❑ Yes ❑ No

Are technical support people knowledgeable? ❑ Yes ❑ No

Can I get my computer fixed in an acceptable time period? ❑ Yes ❑ No

Are the costs and procedures for fixing the computer acceptable? ❑ Yes ❑ No

Are other users satisfied with this brand and model of computer? ❑ Yes ❑ No

Is the vendor likely to stay in business? ❑ Yes ❑ No

Are the computer parts and components standard? ❑ Yes ❑ No

Price: $_____

Evaluate the Facts

How do I make the decision? After you have collected the facts, your decision might be obvious. In an ideal situation, a local vendor with a reputation for excellent support is selling a computer with features and price comparable to those sold by many reputable mail-order vendors. In the real world, however, your local vendor's price might be higher, and then your decision is not so clear. You might want to make a decision support worksheet like the one shown in Figure 6-29.

Figure 6-29

Decision support worksheet

1. List at least two possible options. This worksheet is designed to help you choose between Computer #1 and Computer #2.

2. List the factors that are important criteria for making your selection.

3. Assign a weight to each factor using a scale of 1 to 10.

4. After you research the options, assign a raw score for each factor.

5. Add a formula in the spreadsheet to multiply the raw score by the weighting factor to produce a weighted score.

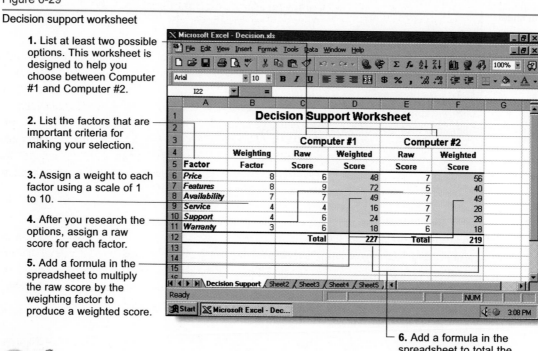

6. Add a formula in the spreadsheet to total the weighted scores for each option. The option that has the highest total is the best system for you to purchase.

EndNote One strategy for buying a computer is to decide how much you want to spend and then buy whatever computer a major manufacturer offers at that price. You probably won't get a great deal. You might not even get a computer that really meets your needs. But you will have a computer. If you want to be a more effective consumer in today's computer marketplace, you must understand the terminology in computer ads and use magazines, journals, and the Internet to keep up-to-date on the latest computer models. If you are planning a career in computing, it is essential to keep track of current events in the computer industry so you can develop marketable skills and select an employer that produces state-of-the-art products and has an employee-friendly working environment.

InfoWeb

InfoWeb

Chapter
Links

The InfoWeb is your guide to print, film, television, and electronic resources. Use it to obtain updates on quickly changing technical information and to locate information for research papers. If you're using the New Perspectives CD-ROM, click the InfoWeb icon on the left side of this paragraph to access the online InfoWeb links. Otherwise, use your Web browser and type in the address of the New Perspectives site: www.cciw.com/np3. At the New Perspectives site you'll find up-to-date links to the topics covered in this chapter.

1 Which Chip?

Since 1993, Intel has introduced four versions of the Pentium processor. Competitors AMD and Cyrix have introduced additional work-alike chips. Which chip is best for your computing needs? Articles such as "Picking Your Processor" by Michael Slater (*Computer Shopper* May 1997; **www5.zdnet.com/cshopper/content/9705/cshp0083.html**) and "What's the Best CPU?" by Bill Howard (*PC Magazine*, June 10, 1997; **www8.zdnet.com/pcmag/issues/1611/bhoward.htm**) can help you answer that question. More information on the Web is in *The Link* newsletter article "The Silicon Shuffle" by Dinos Lambropoulos at the Earthlink Network site **www.earthlink.net/daily/tuesday/microprocessors**. You can get the offical party line about these chips at the Web sites for Intel at **www.intel.com**, AMD at **www.amd.com**, and Cyrix at **www.cyrix.com**.

2 Benchmarks

Want to test your own PC to see how it performs on standard benchmark tests? You can download benchmark tests and test your own PC using *PC Magazine's* Winstone 97 and WinBench 97 benchmark test files at **www8.zdnet.com/pcmag/pclabs/bench/bench.htm**. You'll find links to results of various benchmark tests at Scott Wainner's System Optimization site, **www.sysopt.com/bench.html**, and the Ideas International site at **www.ideasinternational.com/benchmark/bench.html**.

3 Sound Systems

You can purchase $10 speakers for your computer or you can purchase $500 speakers. What's the difference? The quality of sound you hear depends on the quality of your speakers, the capabilities of your sound card, and the quality of the sound file you're playing. To compare the quality of sound produced by expensive wave table synthesis, download the files at **pubweb.nwu.edu/~jll544/sndsmpl.html** and take the wavetable sound card test drive. Interested in Dolby Surround sound? CNET reports on the Altec's ACS500 speaker system at **www.cnet.com/Content/Reviews/Compare/Speakers/ss02b.html**. For an update on the latest speaker technology, check out Altec Lansing's Web site at **www.altecmm.com** and click the Product Selector icon. Then

check out the site of other popular speaker vendors: Creative Labs at **www.creativelabs.com**, Labtec at **www.labtec.com**, and Koss at **www.koss.com**.

4 Display System: Two to Tango

It takes two to tango and your display system is only as good as your monitor and graphics card. For advice on choosing a monitor, read page 123 of the October 7, 1996 issue of *Computerworld* magazine and search for "How to Select a PC Display System" at **www.techweb.com/encyclopedia**. At the TechWeb site you'll also find an article on "How to Buy a Video Card". Look for comparative reviews such as "Big Screens for Big Jobs" (*Byte* January 1997; **www.byte.com/art/9701/sec8/art1.htm**) and "13 Graphics Cards for Business" (*Byte* February 1997; **www.byte.com/art/9702/sec8/sec8.htm**) For an update on current monitor models, connect to vendor sites: NEC Technologies, Inc at **www.nec.com**, Sony Electronics Inc. at **www.sony.com**, Samsung Electronics America, Inc. at **www.samsung.com**, and Philips Electronics at **www.philips.com**. You can check out graphics card manufacturer's sites: Diamond Multimedia Systems Inc. at **www.diamondmm.com**, ATI Technologies Inc. at **www.atitech.com**, Matrox Electronic Systems Ltd. at **www.matrox.com**, and STB Systems, Inc. at **www.stb.com**.

5 Notebooks

Thinking of buying a notebook computer? *PC World* magazine has an excellent Web site just for you at **www.pcworld.com/hardware/t2010/noplus_nb.html**. If you're interested in the latest information of flat panel LCD displays, connect to the O'mara & Associates Web site at **www.omara-assoc.com**. An illustrated tutorial, *Introduction to Liquid Crystal Displays* at **abalone.phys.cwru.edu/tutorial/enhanced/files/lcd/Intro.htm** provides a good solid background in LCD technology. You might want to visit AT&T Bell Labs gallery of exquisite liquid crystal photos at **www.bell-labs.com/new/gallery/thumbnails.html**.

6 PCMCIA

The definitive site about PCMCIA is the PCMCIA Home Page at **www.pc-card.com**. Here you'll find links to PCMCIA FAQs, products, and press releases. You'll find a good primer on PCMCIA technology and markets at the Accurite Technologies site **www.accurite.com/PCMCIAprimer.html**.

7 Printers

Most computer users have heard of Epson, the printer manufacturer that set the standard for dot matrix printing. What many people don't know is that Epson's history spans over 100 years and includes the invention of the world's first quartz watch. In 1964, Epson created printing timers for the Tokyo Olympics. Epson (**www.epson.com**) competes for the lion's share of the computer printer market with Hewlett-Packard (**www.hp.com**). You can visit either Web site for an update on current printer technology. For buyer's guidelines look in recent editions of computer magazines, such as the April 1997 issue of *Windows* magazine (**www.winmag.com/library/1997/0401/featu153.htm**) or the April 1997 issue of *Byte* (**www.byte.com/art/9704/sec11/sec11.htm**).

8 Publications: Computer Industry Magazines and Journals

The number of computer publications reflects our interest in computing. On the Web, you can find listings of currently published computer magazines and journals at **www.amarillo.isd.tenet.edu/Computer_Journals.html** and **www.netvalley.com/netvalley/top100mag.html**. For PC users, the most popular hardware and software magazines are probably *Byte* (**www.byte.com**), *Computer Shopper* (**www.cshopper.com**), *InfoWorld* (**www.infoworld.com**), *PC Magazine* (**www.pcmag.com**), *PC Computing* (**www.pccomputing.com**), and *Windows* (**www.winmag.com**). The most readable academic journal is *Communications of the ACM*. For general commentary about the computer industry, check your newsstand or the Web for *Forbes* (**www.forbes.com**), *Upside* (**www.upside.com**), and the *Wall Street Journal* (**www.wsj.com**).

9 Web Resources: News and Views

For the latest breaking news about the computer industry, check out Yahoo! Technology Headlines at **www.yahoo.com/headlines/tech**, Infoseek's computer page at **www.infoseek.com/Computers**, or WebCrawler's computer page at **www.webcrawler.com/select/comput.new.html**. You can see live video of the CNN Financial Network Digital Jam show at **cnnfn.com/fnonair**. News at **www.computernewsdaily.com** includes articles from the *New York Times Syndicate*, a collection of excellent newspapers from North America, Europe, and Asia. Another great source of news and views on computing is Jeffrey Harrows' The Rapidly Changing Face of Computing at **www.digital.com/info/rcfoc**.

10 Computer TV

You'll have to check your local listings for the broadcast schedule for computer TV shows such as *Computer Chronicles* and *@Home*. To find out the topics on this week's shows, you can use the Web. Check the CNET site at **www.cnet.com** for information about The Web, The New Edge, and CNET Central. The PCTV Web site **www.pctv.com** provides information on *The Internet Cafe*, *Computer Chronicles*, *@Home*, and *UserGroup*. Jones Cable Network at **www.jec.com** gives you the run down on several high-tech shows, including *Computer Kids*, *Cyber City Diner*, *Digital Gurus*, *Home Computing*, and *Smart Alex*. Also, check out schedules for MSNBC at **www.msnbc.com**.

11 BLS: Bureau of Labor Statistics

The U.S. Bureau of Labor Statistics provides projections for computer industry employment at **stats.bls.gov/news.release/ecopro.table6.htm** and **stats.bls.gov/news.release/ecopro.table14.htm**. The BLS *Occupational Outlook Handbook* describes computer industry jobs, typical working conditions and salary levels at **stats.bls.gov.oco/oco10023.htm**.

Bureau of Labor Statistics

12 College Connection

An excellent site that lets you interactively search for a college by major, location, size and tuition is CollegeNET at **www.collegenet.com**.

13 Organizations

What's up with computer professional organizations? Check out their Web sites or call for information. Your campus might have a student chapter of one or more of these organizations.
Association for Computing Machinery (**www.acm.org**) 212-626-0500
IEEE Computer Society (**www.computer.org**) 714-821-8380
Association for Women in Computing (**www.awc-hq.org/awc**) 415-905-4663
Association of Information Technology Professionals (**www.aitp.org**) 800-224-9371

14 Certification

The ICCP claims that "the CCP designation...Certified Computing Professional...from ICCP is recognized worldwide by employers and peers as validation of its holders' computing knowledge and experience." Find out more about the ICCP certification program for students and professionals at **www.iccp.org**. Information about preparing for and taking the Novell certification exams for computer networking is at **education.novell.com**. Connect to the Microsoft site **www.microsoft.com/train_cert/** to discover the benefits of becoming a Microsoft Certified Professional (MCP). To find out how to get certification for your expertise with Microsoft Office software, check out **www.microsoft.com/office/train_cert/ default.htm**.

15 Career Resources

At the Resumix site **www.resumix.com/resume/resumeindex.html** you can fill in a form that will become an electronic resume. When you register for the High-Tech Career Alert at the HiTechCareers site **www.hitechcareer.com**, you will receive weekly e-mail of jobs in your career field. The comprehensive CareerBuilder site at **www.careerbuilder.com** contains tips for creating your resume, job listings, an interactive page that helps you compare the cost of living for different cities, and tips on successful job interviews. Another comprehensive site, *CareerMagazine's* **www.careermag.com**, includes job listings, a resume bank, employer profiles, and products and services to help you manage your career. One of the first and largest sources of career resources is the Monster Board at **www.monster.com**. Newer, but very active career sites include **www.headhunter.net** and **www.tcm.org**. A must-read for college students preparing for computing careers is *The No-Nonsense Guide to Computing Careers* published by the ACM in 1993. If you want inspiration, rent the video *Triumph of the Nerds*. Information and script for this video are available at **www.pbs.org/nerds**.

16 Consumer Information: Buying a Computer

The online *U-Geek* magazine includes a buyer's guide that features recommendations for selecting a processor, case, storage devices, sound system, and display system. *BusinessWeek* runs a great site at **www.maven.businessweek.com** where you can enter specifications for a computer system or printer to get information on its features, price, and performance. For comparison pricing connect to ComputerESP at **www.computeresp.com**, a site that claims to update over 100,000 prices daily on computers, peripherals, and components. Pick the product you want to buy and Computer ESP shows you a list of vendors and current prices. Price Watch at **www.pricewatch.com** is a similar site for price comparisons. *PC Magazine* sponsors an annual survey that evaluates the service and reliability of PC vendors. You can find the results of the 1997 survey in the August issue or at **www8.zdnet.com/pcmag/features/perfectpc/surveypc/_open.htm**.

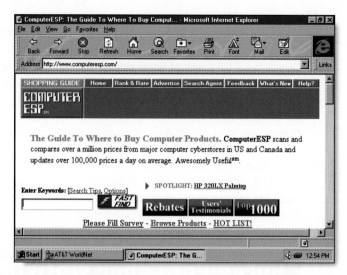

You can buy computers and components online at CompUSA's site **www.compusa.com**. In addition, computer vendors such as Dell and IBM offer online sales. Before you purchase anything by mail or online, read "Ten Tips for Direct Success" on page 80 of the July 1997 *Computer Shopper*. Connect to Consumer World at **www.consumerworld.org** for links to consumer information, the Better Business Bureau, and product reviews.

Review

1. Make a list of the key points you need to remember about buying a desktop computer.

2. Make a list of the additional factors you must consider when buying a notebook computer.

3. Demonstrate your understanding of the terminology and issues involved in purchasing a computer by answering the following questions about the computer ad in Figure 6-1.

   a. The microprocessor in the MicroPlus computer would be categorized in which microprocessor family?

   b. The software that you could run with the MicroPlus computer would not generally be compatible with which other types of computers?

   c. Does the processor for the MicroPlus computer include MMX technology?

   d. Does the MicroPlus computer have enough RAM to run Windows 95?

   e. About how much would it cost to upgrade the MicroPlus computer to 64 MB of memory?

   f. Why does the MicroPlus computer come with only one floppy disk drive?

   g. How fast is the CD-ROM drive?

   h. Can you add a second internal hard disk drive to the MicroPlus computer? Why or why not?

   i. Would you be able to display photographic-quality images at 1024 x 768 resolution? Why or why not?

j. Would you be able to run multimedia software on the MicroPlus computer? Why or why not?

k. What bundled software, if any, is included with the MicroPlus computer?

l. If you purchase the MicroPlus computer and a week after you receive it, the monitor stops working, what is the MicroPlus company policy on repairs?

4 For each of the following computer components, indicate the unit of measurement used to describe the component's capacity:

a. microprocessor speed

b. microprocessor word size

c. hard disk capacity

d. disk drive access time

e. floppy disk capacity

f. CD-ROM drive speed

g. RAM capacity

h. video memory

i. disk cache capacity

j. screen resolution

k. image clarity

5 Draw a diagram to illustrate the life cycle of a computer hardware product.

6 Describe the difference between a version upgrade and a competitive upgrade.

7 Describe the characteristics of each of the three market tiers in the computer industry.

8 List the advantages and disadvantages of purchasing a computer from each computer industry market channel.

9 In your own words, describe the difference between computer-specific jobs, computer-related jobs, and computer-use jobs.

10 List the ways in which you can use technology to find a job.

11 Your parents are thinking of buying a computer. Because you are taking a computer course, they turn to you for advice. The first thing you tell them is to decide how much they want to spend. Think about everything you have learned in this chapter—especially the tips in the *User Focus* section. Based on what you have learned, compose a letter to your parents giving them advice about buying a computer.

12 Use the New Perspectives CD-ROM to take a practice test or to review the new terms presented in this chapter.

Projects

1 **The *Computer Shopper* Experience** The story about Matt at the beginning of this chapter is fairly realistic. Many people purchase mail-order computers, and *Computer Shopper* is the most popular source of information for mail-order prices. Suppose you decide to buy a computer, and you decide your budget is $2,000. You don't need to buy a printer because your friend is giving you a useable, but older printer. Look through the ads in a recent issue of *Computer Shopper* to find the best computer that fits your computing needs and your budget. Write the list of features, the price, and the vendor for the computer, as well as the month and page of the issue. Then explain why you think this computer is the best one for the money.

2 **Product Announcements** Find a product announcement in a computer magazine. How would you classify this announcement? Is it a trial balloon, an anticipated ship date, or a product release? How can you tell? Was it written by a vendor or by a reporter?

3 **Today's Microprocessors** Microprocessor technology changes rapidly. New models arrive every couple of years, and the clock speed for a particular model seems to increase every few months. As you learned in this chapter, computers that contain state-of-the-art microprocessors are usually priced at a premium. Because the latest microprocessors are so expensive, the most popular computers—those that are purchased by the most people—tend to contain a previous model microprocessor. When you are in the market for a computer, it is useful to be able to differentiate between the state-of-the-art microprocessors and previous models.

Browse through several computer magazines to determine which microprocessor is most popular and which microprocessor is currently state-of-the-art. Write a brief description of your findings. Include the following information:

a. The clock speed, processor model name or number, and word size for the most popular microprocessor.

b. The clock speed, processor model name or number, and word size for the state-of-the-art microprocessor.

c. A brief explanation of what factors helped you determine that these particular microprocessors are the most popular and the most state-of-the-art.

d. A bibliography of your sources.

4 **Comparison Shopping** Comparison shopping is a good strategy for finding the best deal in a computer system. Use the hardware checklist in Figure 6-29 to gather comparative information about two computer systems. You can gather the information from a computer magazine, the Internet, or from a local computer retail store. Be sure you exercise courtesy, especially if you visit a small retail store. Let the salesperson know that you are working on a class project, and recognize that the sales person's priority is shoppers who intend to actually buy a computer. Your instructor might assign this as a group project.

5 **Computer Industry** Although the computer industry is less than half a century old, it has more than its share of good luck and hard luck stories. The history of each computer company has contributed in some way to the current state of the computer industry. Select a well-known company in the computer industry such as IBM, Digital, Microsoft, Apple, Compaq, Hewlett-Packard, Cray Research, or Toshiba. Use library and/or Internet resources to research the history of the company and trace the events that led to the company's current status in the computer industry. Write a report that summarizes your research. Follow your instructor's requirements for the length of your report.

6 **The Latest "Scoop"** Different industry analysts tend to give their readers the scoop on many of the same "hot topics." It's fascinating to see how the rumors spread and how analysts see events from different perspectives. Read at least 10 industry analysts' columns from several computer magazines published in the same month and year. Although 10 columns might sound like a lot, they are not long and many are fairly entertaining. Summarize what you read by indicating the topics that were "hot" that month and how the analysts agreed or disagreed.

7 **Your Dollar Buys a Lot More Today** You have probably heard that computer technology changes at an amazing speed. Today, your money buys much more computing power than it did in 1990. How much more? Look through the computer ads in back issues of computer magazines for June 1990, June 1993, and June 1995. Create a chart that shows the changes in the specifications for computers for a price of $2,000. Be sure you compare the processor type, processor speed, RAM capacity, hard disk drive capacity, screen resolution, and bus type.

8 **Product Comparison Reviews** Many computer magazines feature extensive product comparison reviews in which several hardware or software products are evaluated and compared. Suppose you are working for an organization and your job is to select hardware and software products.

a. Describe the organization for which you work, then specify which type of product (notebook computers, word-processing software, group scheduler, and so on) you are looking for and why.

b. Explain the important factors that will influence your decision, such as budget or special features that your organization requires from the product.

c. Find and read an appropriate comparative review in a recent computer magazine.

d. Based on the comparative review, which product would you recommend? Why?

9 Career Research Books, magazines, and the Web supply plenty of resources to help you choose a career. Or, if you're considering a career change, these resources can help you decide if it is the right thing to do. Use the resources in your library and on the Web to gather information about a career in which you are interested. Unless your instructor requires it, you do not need to limit yourself to computing careers. Answer the following questions:

a. In one paragraph, how would you describe the nature of the work you would perform in this career?

b. What types of businesses and organizations typically hire people in your chosen career field?

c. What are the working conditions?

d. What specific qualifications would you need to successfully compete in this career?

e. What is the employment outlook for this career?

f. What is a typical starting salary? What is the salary range?

g. What sources did you use to locate information about this career?

10

INTERNET Required

Web Resume The Web provides a way to publish your resume where it might be seen by prospective employers. But like a stack of resumes on a recruiter's desk, your Web resume can get quickly rejected for spelling and grammar errors, if it is difficult to read, or if your credentials are not presented in a logical format. It takes several drafts to produce a good resume.

Begin by creating your resume using a word-processing program. Use a reference book or Web site about resumes to help organize your content. Spell check this first draft and print it.

Next show the first draft to at least three friends, colleges, or instructors. Make revisions based on their comments. When you are satisfied with your resume, generate a Web page. Store the page on a floppy disk and hand it in.

11 Your Compatibility Needs When you purchase a computer, it is likely you will want to maintain compatibility with the type of computers used in your field. For example, if most elementary schools use Apple computers and your field is elementary education, you might have a strong reason for purchasing an Apple computer instead of an IBM compatible. For this project, research the type of computers most typically used in your field or major. Keep a lookout for hard data, such as the number of Apple II computers still in use in schools. Write a one- to two-page report describing your findings; conclude with the computer you would purchase today to prepare for your career of the future. Your instructor might suggest that you do this project in a small group with other students who have similar career goals.

12 Using a Decision Support Spreadsheet for Buying a Computer A decision support spreadsheet like the one in Figure 6-30 helps you prioritize your computing needs and compare the value of several computers based on these priorities. For this Project, do the following:

a. Create a spreadsheet like the one shown in Figure 6-30.

b. Modify the factors listed in column A to reflect your computing needs.

c. Modify the weighting factors in column B to reflect their importance to you.

d. Gather information about two different computer systems that you might consider purchasing.

e. Give each computer a raw score for each factor. For example, if Computer #1 has all the features you seek, enter a 10 in cell B7. If Computer #2 only has half the features you want, enter a 5 in cell E7.

f. Notice which computer has the highest total score. This should be the best computer for your needs.

g. Somewhere on the spreadsheet include a short description of each computer, including its brand name, price, and model.

h. Print out your spreadsheet. Be sure to include your name.

13 **Computer Companies on the Internet** Many hardware and software companies maintain Internet sites. A major purpose of these sites is to distribute information to potential and existing customers. Access the Web page for one of the following companies, then answer questions a through d:

http://www.microsoft.com
http://www.ibm.com
http://www.intel.com
http://www.apple.com

a. How would you characterize the information at this site? Is it primarily sales, technical, and/or company background?

b. Give an example of information at this site that would help you decide whether you wanted to buy a particular product.

c. Would you be able to use this site to contact a company representative? If so, how would you do this?

d. Even if you weren't thinking of purchasing a product from this company, describe in detail something at the site you found to be interesting.

Lab Assignments

Buying a Computer

When buying from a mail-order or Internet computer vendor, consumers don't have an opportunity to take various computer models for a "test drive." They make a computer purchase decision based solely on a list of specifications. Thus, it is essential to understand the specifications in

computer ads. In this Lab, you will find out how to use a Shopping Glossary to interpret the specifications.

1 Click the Steps button to learn how to use the Shopping Glossary. As you proceed through the Steps, answer all of the Quick Check questions that appear. After you complete the Steps, you will see a Quick Check Summary Report. Follow the instructions on the screen to print this report.

2 Click the Explore button and read the ad for the VectorMicro Computer system. Use the Shopping Glossary to define the following terms:

a. Write-back cache   d. Burst cache
b. EIDE   e. Wavetable
c. NI   f. EDO RAM

3 In Explore, read the ads for the ZeePlus Multimedia Value Pak and the ZeePlus Multimedia Pro computers. The two systems differ substantially in price. If you purchase the more expensive system, what additional features do you get?

4 In Explore, read the ad for the ZeePlus Multimedia Pro Computer (233 MHz and the NP2 Super Systems Computer. What is the price difference between these two systems? What factors might account for this price difference?

5 In Explore, read the ads to find a notebook computer that's priced within $100 of the Nevada Tech Systems desktop computer. Make a list of the features the desktop computer has, that the notebook computer does not have. Which one would you buy? Why?

6 Photocopy a computer ad from a recent issue of a computer magazine. On a separate sheet of paper, write each specification (for example, Intel Pentium processor). For each specification, define each term (for example, Intel is a microprocessor manufacturer, Pentium is a type of microprocessor in the x86 family). Write out all acronyms (for example, RAM means random access memory). If you have difficulty with some of the terms and acronyms, click the Explore button and use the Shopping Glossary.

Local Area Networks and E-mail

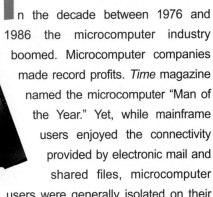

CHAPTER**PREVIEW**

In this chapter you will learn how to use microcomputer networks, such as those in your school labs or in a business where you work. You'll learn how to select a secure password and how to log into a network. You'll also learn how to share files with other users, and you'll pick up some tips for using electronic mail. When you have completed this chapter you should be able to:

- Describe the resources you would find on a typical local area network
- Explain how using a computer on a network is different from using a standalone computer
- List the advantages of using a local area network
- Explain the difference between sharing files on a network and using groupware
- Describe how processing differs on networks that use dedicated file servers, peer-to-peer capability, client/server architecture, and host-based time-sharing
- Describe the types of software you can use on a local area network
- Explain how software licenses for networks differ from those for stand-alone computers
- Explain how a network uses store-and-forward technology for e-mail

In the decade between 1976 and 1986 the microcomputer industry boomed. Microcomputer companies made record profits. *Time* magazine named the microcomputer "Man of the Year." Yet, while mainframe users enjoyed the connectivity provided by electronic mail and shared files, microcomputer users were generally isolated on their standalone computers. Communication between microcomputers was jokingly referred to as "the sneaker net"—meaning that to transfer a file from one computer to another, you put the file on a floppy disk, then walked with the disk to another computer. White Reeboks were popular corporate footwear at the time.

The idea that microcomputer users could benefit by connecting their computers into a network became feasible about 10 years ago with the introduction of reliable, reasonably priced software and hardware designed for microcomputer networks. The availability of this hardware and software ushered in a new era of computing, which increasingly provides ways for people to collaborate, communicate, and interact.

The purpose of this chapter is to help you understand the type of local area computer networks you would typically find in a college, university, or business. This chapter emphasizes the user perspective, beginning with a tour of network resources, then presenting practical information on network hardware and software including network applications such as groupware and electronic mail.

LABS

E-mail

Ⓐ Local Area Networks

A **computer network** is a collection of computers and other devices that communicate to share data, hardware, and software. A network that is located within a relatively limited area such as a building or campus is referred to as a **local area network** or **LAN**. A network that covers a large geographical area is referred to as a **wide area network** or **WAN**. In this chapter you will learn about local area networks.

Local area networks are found in most medium-sized and large businesses, government offices, and educational institutions. Worldwide an estimated 25 million computers are connected to local area networks.

InfoWeb

LANs
1

Not all LANs are the same. Different types of networks provide different services, use different technology, and require users to follow different procedures. The information in this section describes how a majority of microcomputer networks work. However, any specific network you use might work differently and require different user procedures. Don't hesitate to ask questions when you use an unfamiliar network.

Network Resources

What's the advantage of a computer network? A computer that is not connected to a network is referred to as a **standalone computer**. When you physically connect your computer to a local area network, using a cable or other communications channel, your computer becomes a **workstation** on the network and you become a "network user."

Your workstation has all its usual resources, referred to as **local resources**, such as your hard drive, software, data, and printer. You also have access to **network resources**, which typically include application software, storage space for data files, and printers other than those with your local workstation.

On a network, application software and storage space for data files are typically provided by a network server. A **network server** is a computer connected to the network that "serves," or distributes, resources to network users. A **network printer** provides output capabilities to all the network users. Each device on a network, including workstations, servers, and printers, is referred to as a **node** as shown in Figure 7-1.

Figure 7-1

Network nodes include workstations, printers, and servers.

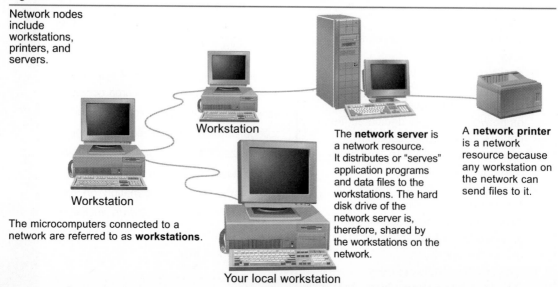

Workstation

The microcomputers connected to a network are referred to as **workstations**.

Workstation

Your local workstation

The **network server** is a network resource. It distributes or "serves" application programs and data files to the workstations. The hard disk drive of the network server is, therefore, shared by the workstations on the network.

A **network printer** is a network resource because any workstation on the network can send files to it.

The Login Process

Do I have to do anything special to access network resources? | Even if your computer is physically connected to a network, you cannot use network resources until you log into the network. When you log in, you formally identify yourself to the network as a user.

During the login process you are prompted to enter your user ID and password. Your **user ID**, sometimes referred to as your **user name**, is a unique set of letters and numbers. Your **password**, a special set of symbols known only to you and the network administrator, gives you security clearance to use network resources. Your user ID and password are the basis for your user account. A **user account** provides access to network resources and accumulates information about your network use by tracking when you log in and log out. A **network administrator**, also called a **network supervisor**, is the person responsible for setting up user accounts and maintaining a network. The network administrator provides each new user with a user ID and a "starter" password.

On most networks, you can change your starter password to one of your own choosing. If you have this option, you should select a secure password so other people cannot log in as you and access your files. Your password should be unique, yet something you can remember. How do you select a secure password? Refer to the chart in Figure 7-2 for some password do's and don'ts.

Figure 7-2

Password do's and don'ts

Do	**Don't**
• Select a password that is at least five characters long.	• Select a password that is a word that can be found in the dictionary.
• Try to use numbers as well as letters in your password.	• Use your name, nickname, Social Security number, birth date, or name of a close relative.
• Select a password you can remember.	
• Consider making a password by combining two or more words.	• Write your password where it is easy to find—under the keyboard is the first place a password thief will look.
• Consider making a password by using the first letters of the words in a poem or phrase.	
• Change your password periodically.	

Entering a valid user ID and password is the beginning of the login process. As the login process continues, your workstation is connected to network drives, allowing you to use programs and data files stored on a server. The login process also connects your workstation to network resources such as a network printer. The next two sections explain how this works.

Drive Mapping

How does my computer access data files and application software from a network server?

Your workstation gains access to the file server and its hard drive when the server hard drive is *mapped* to a drive letter. **Mapping** is network terminology for assigning a drive letter to a network server disk drive. For example, on a typical workstation with a floppy drive A and a hard drive C, the login process maps the server hard drive as drive F.

Once a drive letter has been mapped, you can access data files and application software from that drive just as you would from your local hard disk drive. Essentially, you can then use the hard drive on the server just as if it was part of your workstation computer.

Drive mappings vary from one network to another, depending on the needs of the organization and its users. One organization might map the server drive as F, while another organization might map the server drive as J. In other organizations, multiple drives on more than one server might be mapped as F, I, J, and Z. As a network user, you will find it useful to know the drive mapping so you can more easily find programs and files. Figure 7-3 shows a typical drive mapping available to a workstation in a network with a single server.

Figure 7-3

A typical workstation drive map

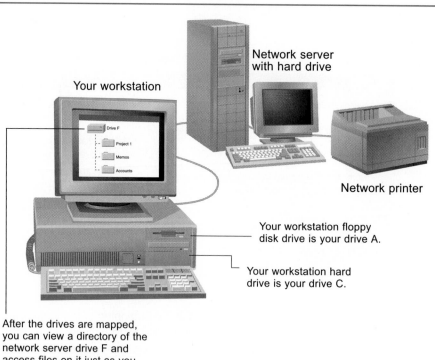

Network server with hard drive

Your workstation

Network printer

Your workstation floppy disk drive is your drive A.

Your workstation hard drive is your drive C.

After the drives are mapped, you can view a directory of the network server drive F and access files on it just as you access files on drives A or C.

Using Programs on a Network

When I start a program supplied by a network server, is it the same as starting a program on a standalone computer? Remember from Chapter 5 that when you launch a program on a standalone computer, it is copied from your hard disk into RAM. Suppose you want to use a word-processing program that is stored on the hard disk of a network server. Will the program be loaded into the memory of the server or into the memory of your workstation?

When you start a program that is stored on a server, the program is copied to the RAM of your workstation. Once the program is in memory, it runs just as if you had started it from your workstation hard disk drive. Figure 7-4 shows how this works.

Figure 7-4

Starting a program that is stored on the file server

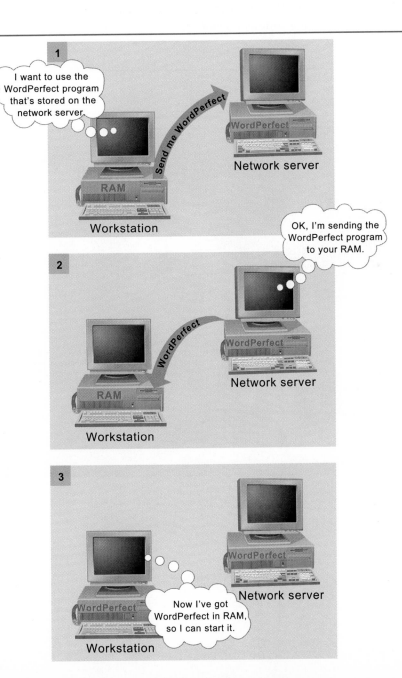

You might wonder if more than one user on a network can simultaneously use the same program. One advantage of a network is that with proper licensing many users can access a program at the same time. This is called **sharing** a program. For example, while CorelDraw is running on your workstation, other users can start the same program. The network server sends a copy of CorelDraw to the RAM of each user's workstation.

Sharing programs is effective for several reasons. First, less disk storage space is required because the program is stored only once on the server, instead of being stored on the hard disks of multiple standalone computers. Second, when a new version of the software is released, it is easier to update one copy of the program on the server than to update many copies stored on standalone computers. Third, purchasing a software license for a network can be less expensive than purchasing single-user licenses for each workstation on the network (Figure 7-5).

Figure 7-5

Sharing programs on a network saves disk space, reduces maintenance, and reduces licensing costs.

Using Data Files on a Network

Is there any advantage to storing data files on the server instead of my local hard disk?

Suppose that while connected to a network, you create a document using a word-processing program. You can store the document either on your local hard disk or on the server hard disk. If you store the file on your local hard disk, you can access the file only from your workstation. However, if you store the file on the hard disk of the server, you, or any other user, can access the file from any workstation on the network, as shown in Figure 7-6.

Figure 7-6

Network file access

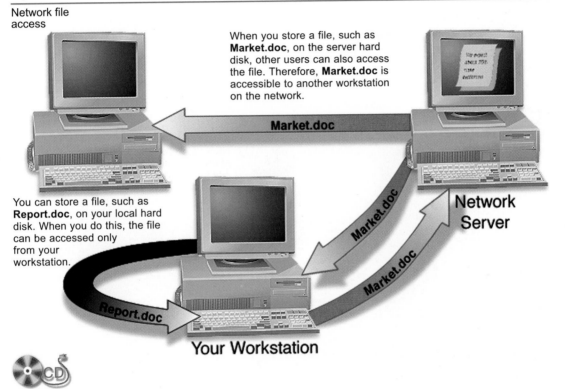

When you store a file, such as **Market.doc**, on the server hard disk, other users can also access the file. Therefore, **Market.doc** is accessible to another workstation on the network.

You can store a file, such as **Report.doc**, on your local hard disk. When you do this, the file can be accessed only from your workstation.

Market.doc

Market.doc

Market.doc

Report.doc

Network Server

Your Workstation

Although a *program file* from the file server can be used on more than one workstation at the same time, most of the *data files* on a network server can be opened by only one user at a time. When one user has a file open, it is **locked** to other users. File locking is a sensible precaution against losing valuable data. If the network allowed two users to open and edit the same data file, both users could make changes to the file; but one user's changes might contradict the other user's changes. Whose changes would be incorporated in the final version of the file?

Suppose two users were allowed to make changes to the same file at the same time. Each user would open a copy of the original file and make changes to it. The first user to finish making changes would save the file on the server. So far so good—the first user has replaced the original version of the file with an edited version. Remember, however, that the second user has been making revisions to the *original* file, but she has no idea of the first user's revisions. When the second user saves her revised version of the file, the changes made by the first user are overwritten by the second user's version, as shown in Figure 7-7.

Figure 7-7

Why networks lock files

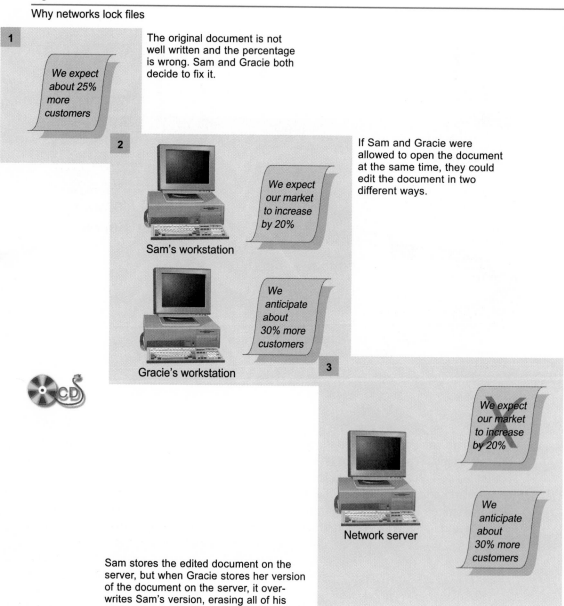

1 The original document is not well written and the percentage is wrong. Sam and Gracie both decide to fix it.

We expect about 25% more customers

2 If Sam and Gracie were allowed to open the document at the same time, they could edit the document in two different ways.

Sam's workstation — We expect our market to increase by 20%

Gracie's workstation — We anticipate about 30% more customers

3 Network server — We expect our market to increase by 20% / We anticipate about 30% more customers

Sam stores the edited document on the server, but when Gracie stores her version of the document on the server, it overwrites Sam's version, erasing all of his work.

Using a Network Printer

How does my word-processing software know it is supposed to send documents to the network printer instead of to my local printer? Most application software sends files you want to print to the printer that is connected to your computer's parallel port. But network workstations often do not have local printers. Instead, they need to access a network printer. Figure 7-8 shows how data sent to your workstation's parallel port is **captured** and **redirected** to the network printer.

Figure 7-8

Capturing your workstation printer port

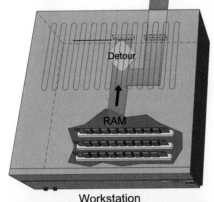

Network printer

To network printer ⟶

1. When your workstation is not attached to the network, the file you want to print is sent to the parallel port and out to your printer.

2. The process of logging into a network captures your parallel port and diverts data headed for your printer to the network instead.

3. The data travels over the network to the network printer, where it is printed.

Detour

RAM

Workstation

What happens if a network printer receives more than one file to print? Most networks would not allow two files to travel simultaneously over the network. However, it is possible that before the printer has completed one printout, other files arrive to be printed. Files sent to a network printer are placed in a **print queue**. A print queue is a special holding area on a network server where files are stored until they are printed. When more than one user sends a file to the print queue, the files are added to the print queue and printed in the order in which they are received.

Figure 7-9 shows what happens when one user sends a document to the printer before another user's printout is completed.

Figure 7-9

The network print queue

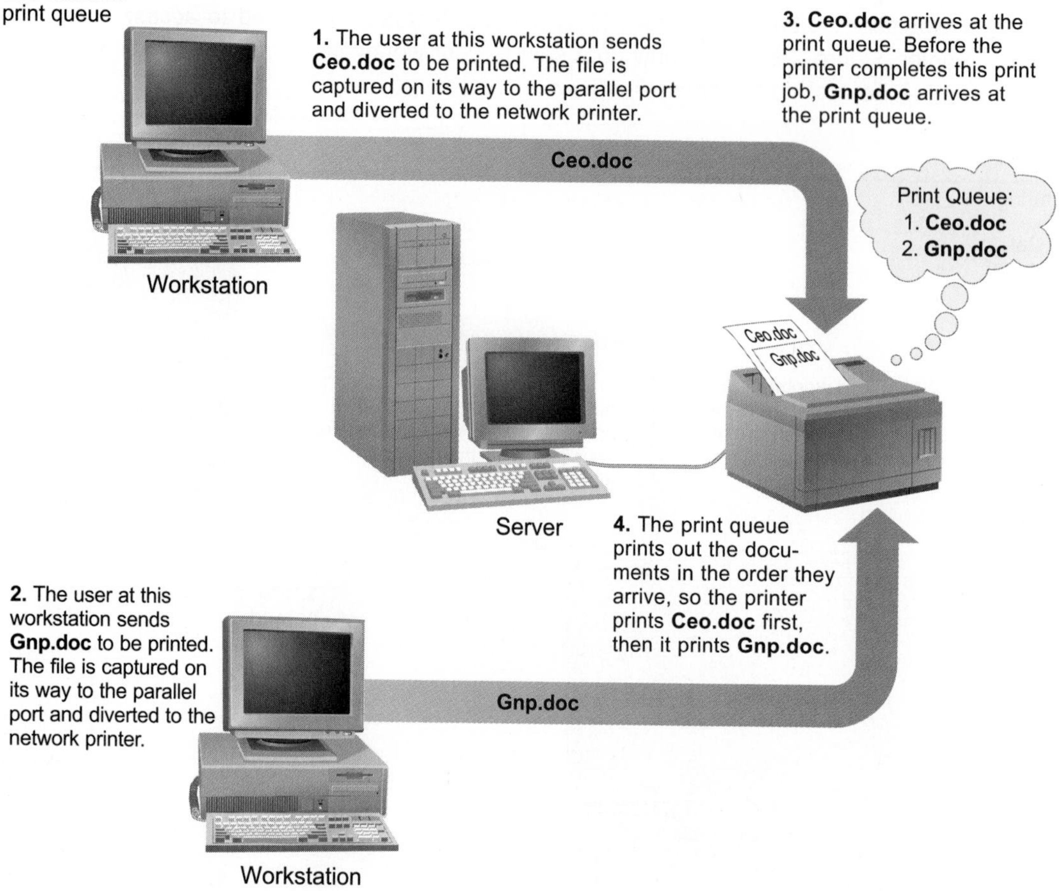

1. The user at this workstation sends **Ceo.doc** to be printed. The file is captured on its way to the parallel port and diverted to the network printer.

3. Ceo.doc arrives at the print queue. Before the printer completes this print job, **Gnp.doc** arrives at the print queue.

Ceo.doc

Print Queue:
1. **Ceo.doc**
2. **Gnp.doc**

Workstation

Server

4. The print queue prints out the documents in the order they arrive, so the printer prints **Ceo.doc** first, then it prints **Gnp.doc**.

2. The user at this workstation sends **Gnp.doc** to be printed. The file is captured on its way to the parallel port and diverted to the network printer.

Gnp.doc

Workstation

QuickCheck A

1. A network _____ is a computer connected to a network that distributes files to network users.

2. A(n) _____ provides access to network resources and accumulates information about your use of the network.

3. In many networks, the server hard drive is _____ as drive F.

4. Assuming proper licensing, while Jenny uses a spreadsheet program from the network server, Atkin can use this spreadsheet program at the same time. True or false?

5. While Joan is editing a word-processing document called Budget.doc, Karl can also edit this document at the same time. True or false? _____

6. When a network printer is assigned to your workstation, any data sent to the workstation's parallel port is _____ and redirected to the network printer.

B Network Hardware

In the previous section, you looked at local area network resources and learned about the advantages of computer networks. Now let's look at the hardware components of a network.

Network Interface Cards

What establishes the physical connection for the computers in a network? A network interface card is the key hardware component for connecting a computer to a local area network. A **network interface card** or **NIC** (pronounced "nick") is a small circuit board that sends data from your workstation out over the network and collects incoming data for your workstation. A desktop computer NIC plugs into an expansion slot on the computer motherboard. A notebook computer NIC is usually a PCMCIA card. Figure 7-10 shows you NICs for desktop and notebook computers.

Figure 7-10

Desktop and notebook
network interface cards

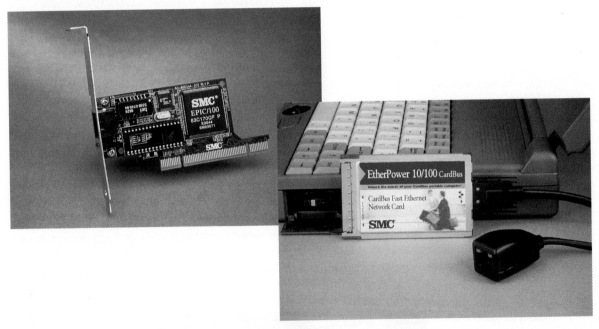

InfoWeb

Ethernet
2

Each server, workstation, printer, or other device on a network must have an NIC. Different types of networks use different types of network interface cards. If you want to add a computer to a network, you need to know the network type so you can purchase the appropriate NIC. Popular network types include **Ethernet**, **Token Ring**, **ARCnet**, **FDDI**, and **ATM**.

Cable and Wireless Networks

The NICs have to be connected by a cable, right? Most networks use cables to connect servers, workstations, and printers. On a typical network, you would find one of the two cable types shown in Figure 7-11.

Figure 7-11

Network cables

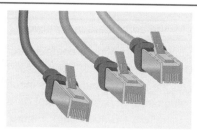

A **twisted pair cable**, sometimes referred to as **UTP**, looks similar to a telephone cable with a square plastic **RJ-45 connector** on either end.

A **coaxial cable** resembles a cable-TV cable with a round, silver **BNC connector** on either end.

InfoWeb

Wireless Networks 3

Instead of using cables, **wireless networks** use radio or infrared signals to transmit data from one network device to another. Wireless networks are handy in environments where wiring is difficult to install, such as in historical buildings. In addition, wireless networks provide mobility. For example, a wireless network would make it possible to carry a notebook or hand-held computer throughout a large warehouse to take inventory. A third application for wireless networks is for temporary installations, when drilling holes to install wiring is not practical or economical.

The network interface cards for a wireless network contain the transmitting devices necessary to send data to other devices on the local area network. Signals can be sent by radio waves, microwave, or infrared. Figure 7-12 describes T.G.I. Fridays' wireless network.

Figure 7-12

Using a wireless network, the hostess at T.G.I. Fridays adds names to the waiting list for dinner. Note the antenna used to transmit data to the main dining room management database.

Network Servers

When I use a network, is my data processed locally or on the network server? You have already learned the general functions of a network server. However, there are different kinds of network servers. They are explained in this section. When you use a standalone computer, all your data is processed by your computer's microprocessor. The device that processes your data when you are connected to a network depends on the type of servers included on your network.

A **dedicated file server** is devoted only to the task of delivering programs and data files to workstations. As you can see in Figure 7-13, a dedicated file server does not process data or run programs for the workstations. Instead, programs run using the memory and processor of the workstation.

Figure 7-13

A dedicated file server

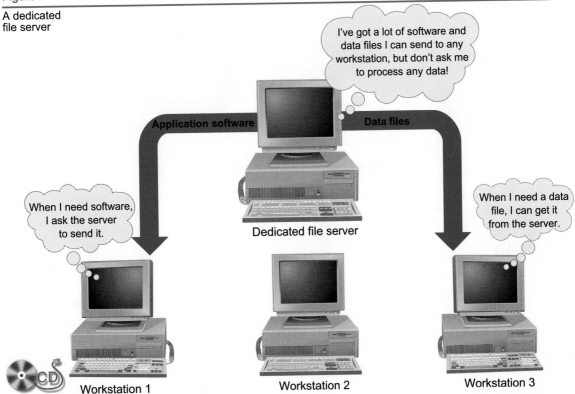

A typical local area network uses a microcomputer as a file server; but, a minicomputer or a mainframe computer can also be a file server. Many businesses with older minicomputer and mainframe systems have essentially recycled this equipment by adding microcomputer networking capabilities.

In some cases, a network computer performs a dual role as both file server and workstation. This is referred to as a **non-dedicated server** or **peer-to-peer** capability. When you use a non-dedicated server, your computer functions like a normal workstation, but other workstations can access programs and data files from the hard disk of your computer, as shown in Figure 7-14.

Figure 7-14

A non-dedicated file server

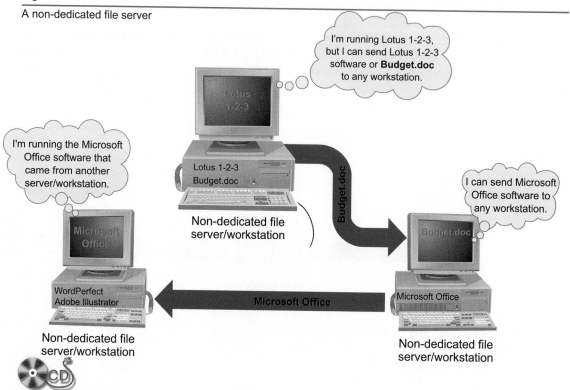

A **print server** stores files in a print queue and sends each queued file to the network printer. A **print job** is a file that has been sent to the printer. Print jobs are processed locally on workstations that have a local printer, but a print server controls the print jobs on a network server. A print server can be the same computer as the file server, or it can be another micro, mini, or mainframe computer connected to the network.

InfoWeb

Client/
Server
4

An **application server** is a computer that runs application software and forwards the results of processing to workstations as requested. An application server makes it possible to use the processing power of both the server and the workstation. Also referred to as **client/server architecture**, use of an application server splits processing between the workstation *client* and the network *server*. Suppose you want to search for a particular record in a 50,000-record database stored on a network server. Study Figure 7-15 to see how client/server architecture makes use of the processing capacity of both the workstation and server.

Figure 7-15

Client/server
architecture

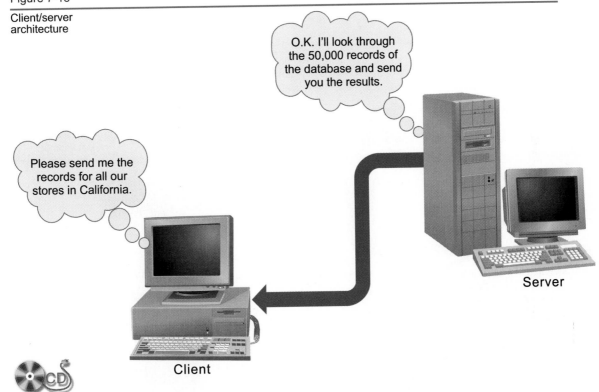

Some networks include a **host computer**, usually a minicomputer or a mainframe with attached terminals. When you use a host computer from a terminal, all the processing takes place on the host. Your **terminal** has a keyboard and a screen, but it does not have a local storage device, and it does little or no processing on its own. The host accepts commands from terminals and sends back a display of results. Because the terminals do not have processing power of their own, they cannot further process the results they receive. For example, if your terminal receives a list of 50 people sorted by address, you could not sort the list by last name on your terminal. You would have to ask the host to sort the list and send you the new results.

Although a system containing a host computer and terminals fits our general definition of a *network*, it is more customary to call it a **time-sharing system**. Because terminals can do little or no processing of their own, every terminal must wait for the host to process its request. The terminals essentially *share* the host's processor by being allocated a fraction of a second of processing time.

Before powerful microcomputer networks became available, connecting terminals to a host computer provided relatively low-cost computer access. For economic reasons, many organizations have not yet moved important data and programs from mainframe hosts to microcomputer networks.

It is possible to connect a microcomputer to a host using **terminal emulation software**, but your microcomputer will behave just like a terminal and will receive only a display of results, not data that you can process (Figure 7-16). If you want to process data you receive from a host, instead of using terminal emulation software you must use communications software to transfer the data to your computer.

Figure 7-16

Mainframe host

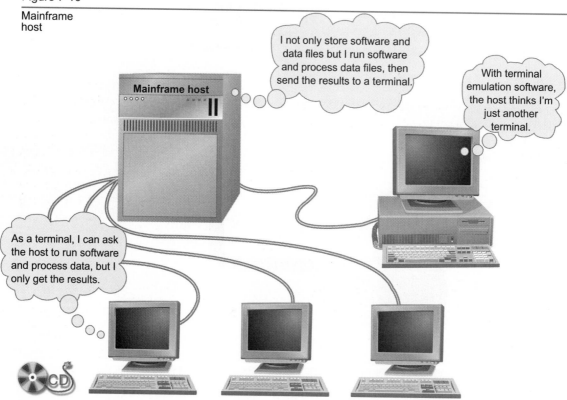

QuickCheck B

1 The circuit board that connects a computer to a local area network is called a(n) _____ .

2 If a network computer functions both as a file server and as a workstation, it is referred to as a(n) _____ server.

3 A(n) _____ is devoted to the task of delivering programs and data files to workstations.

4 Client/server architecture takes advantage of the processing capabilities of both the workstation and the server. True or false? _____

5 On some networks, a(n) _____ computer processes data, then outputs the results on the screen of a terminal.

C Software for Networks

The software on a local area network typically includes specialized network software as well as many of the same applications you might use on a standalone computer.

Network Operating System

Does a network require any special software? A network requires a **network operating system** (NOS) to control the flow of data, maintain security, and keep track of user accounts.

InfoWeb

NOS
5

Network operating systems such as **Novell NetWare**, **Banyan Vines**, and **LANtastic** are software packages designed exclusively to control network data flow. Also, popular computer operating systems such as Windows 95, Windows 98, Windows NT, and UNIX include networking capability. What about Windows 3.1? This early version of Windows does not include networking capability. Therefore, if you want to network computers that use Windows 3.1 you must also install a network operating system such as Novell NetWare, shown in Figure 7-17.

Figure 7-17

A popular network operating system

A network operating system usually has two components: server software and client software. **Network server software** is installed on a file server and controls file access from the server hard drive, manages the print queue, and tracks user data such as IDs and passwords. **Network client software** is installed on the local hard drive of each workstation and is essentially a device driver for the network interface card. When your computer boots up, the network client software is activated and establishes the connection between your workstation and other devices on the network.

Standalone Applications

Do I need to buy a special version of my favorite application software to use it on a network? Most applications designed for standalone computers can be installed on a network server, which sends them to individual workstations as requested. Typically, your favorite word-processing, spreadsheet, graphics, and presentation software will work on a network just as they do on a standalone computer.

Some applications that you use on a standalone computer have built-in features for networking that appear only when the software is installed on a network. For example, when your word-processing software is installed on a network, it might show you a dialog box that lets you send files to another person on the network.

As you learned in the first section of this chapter, a network can supply an application to more than one person at a time by copying the program into the memory of the workstations. This capability applies to most standalone software. Therefore, software designed for standalone computers can usually be used on a network by more than one user at a time. However, most applications designed for standalone computers do not allow more than one person at a time to work on the same *data file*.

Installing Windows Software on a Network

How does my Windows menu know what's on the file server? Suppose the office is buzzing about a great new graphics package that has just been installed on the network server. You check out your Windows menu of programs, but can't find the new software. What's the problem? Before you can access a program on the file server, your local version of Windows needs to know that the software's been installed.

After a new Windows program has been installed on a network server, you or your network manager needs to also complete a workstation installation of the software. A **workstation installation** usually copies some, but not all, of the program files to your local hard disk, then it updates your Windows menu to include a listing for the new program. On some networks, the workstation installation can be done from a remote location such as the network manager's office. Sound complicated? Just remember that if you don't have a listing for a program that's on the network server, you probably need to complete a workstation installation.

Software Licenses for Networks

Can an organization buy just one copy of a software package and put it on the network for every one to use? It would be very inexpensive for an organization to purchase a single copy of a software package, then place it on the network for everyone to use. In an organization with 100 users, for example, word-processing capability might cost $295 for a single copy, instead of $29,500 for 100 copies. However, using a single-user license for multiple users violates copyright law.

Most single-user software licenses allow only one person to use the software at a time. However, many software publishers also offer a **network license** that permits use by multiple people on a network. Typically, such a network license will cost more than a single-user license, but less than purchasing single-user licenses for all of the users. For example, a word-processing software package that costs $295 for a single-user license might have a $5,000 network license that allows up to 100 people to use the software. Network licenses are available for most software packages by contacting the software publisher.

Workflow Software and Groupware

Is there a way for two or more people to work together on the same data file? When local area networks were first introduced, the concept of sharing files was limited because only one user at a time could work on a document. This concept of sharing does not, however, support many of the organizational activities that require collaboration and communication among employees. For example, in most organizations, people exchange information using memos, phone conversations, and face-to-face meetings. Employees collect, organize, and share information, which must be stored in a centralized repository. Documents and forms flow through organizations, picking up required signatures and approvals. Employees contribute sections of text that are compiled into a single report.

As the use of networks increased, organizations and businesses began to demand software that would facilitate the flow and sharing of documents. Software publishers responded to this demand by producing groupware and workflow software.

InfoWeb

Groupware
6

Groupware is application software that supports collaborative work by managing schedules, shared documents, and intra-group communications. Essentially, groupware manages a pool of documents and allows users to access those documents simultaneously as shown in Figure 7-18.

Figure 7-18

Groupware provides simultaneous access to a pool of documents.

A key feature of groupware is *document version management*. When more than one group member revises a document, whose revisions should be accepted for the final version? The solution frequently implemented by groupware is to maintain all revisions within the document so the workgroup can accept or reject each revision as shown in Figure 7-19.

Figure 7-19

In this shared document, one user's revisions are shown in red, the other user's revisions are shown in blue.

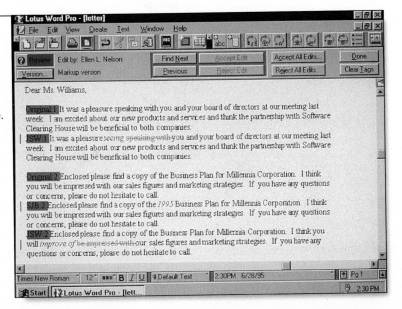

InfoWeb

Workflow
Software
7

Workflow software, also referred to as **document routing software**, automates the process of electronically routing documents from one person to another in a specified sequence and time. Workflow software facilitates a process or a series of steps. For example, suppose you apply for a loan. The bank has a specific procedure for processing the loan application. First, a credit officer checks your credit rating and makes a recommendation whether to accept or reject your application. Next, the bank loan committee must approve the application. Finally, the approved application is processed by your loan officer. To facilitate this process, workflow software would route the loan application to the first bank officer, specify the due date for action, collect the necessary approval, then route the application to the next officer, and so on.

Workflow software is based on a "process-centered model" as opposed to groupware's "information-centered model." With workflow software the focus is on a series of steps. With groupware the documents are the focus. You can compare Figures 7-18 and 7-20 to see the difference between workflow software and groupware.

Figure 7-20

Workflow
software
facilitates a
process.

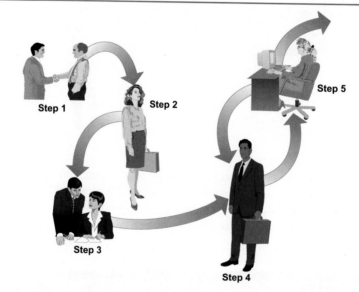

Step 1   Step 2   Step 5

Step 3   Step 4

QuickCheck C

1 Novell Netware would be classified as a(n) _____ system.

2 If your computer is connected to a network, you must install a special network version of your favorite application software. True or false? _____

3 If an organization is planning to use software on a network, it should purchase a(n) _____ so multiple users can legally use the software.

4 If you are a team leader and you want your team members to collaborate on a project using the network, you might try to find a(n) _____ product.

5 If you were the manager of a loan department in a bank, you might use _____ software to automatically send loan applications to each member of your department for processing and approval.

U s e r F o c u s

[D] Electronic Mail

Electronic mail, or **e-mail**, is correspondence conducted between one or more users on a network. E-mail is a more efficient means of communication than ground or air mail. Rather than waiting for a piece of paper to be physically transported by office mail or U.S. mail, you can send an electronic version of a message directly to someone's electronic "mail box." E-mail also helps you avoid frustrating "telephone tag."

LAB

E-mail

How E-mail Works

When I send an e-mail message does it go directly to the recipient's workstation? What if the recipient's workstation is not turned on? An **e-mail message** is essentially a letter or memo sent electronically from one user to another. An **electronic mail system** is the hardware and software that collects and delivers e-mail messages. Typically, a local area network provides electronic mail services to its users. The software on the network server that controls the flow of e-mail is called **mail server software**. The software on a workstation that helps each user read, compose, send, and delete messages is called **mail client software**. Electronic mail systems are often classified as groupware because they facilitate communication among members of a workgroup.

InfoWeb

E-mail
8

E-mail messages are *stored* on a server. When you want to read this mail, the server *forwards* the messages to your workstation. Hence e-mail is called a **store-and-forward** technology. Because the server stores the messages, your workstation does not need to be on when someone sends you e-mail (Figure 7-21).

Figure 7-21

E-mail uses store and forward technology so your mail remains stored on a server until you are ready to read it.

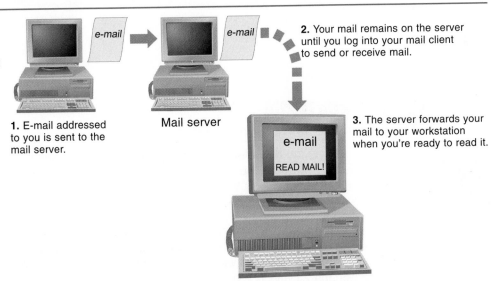

1. E-mail addressed to you is sent to the mail server.

Mail server

2. Your mail remains on the server until you log into your mail client to send or receive mail.

3. The server forwards your mail to your workstation when you're ready to read it.

e-mail

READ MAIL!

Your workstation

What if you want to send e-mail to someone who is not connected to your computer network or host? Many e-mail systems are connected to other e-mail systems through electronic links called **gateways**. When you send an e-mail message to a user on another computer network, the message is transferred through the gateway to a larger e-mail system, which delivers the message to the recipient's network or host computer system.

Reading E-mail

How do I use e-mail? Your e-mail is transmitted through an electronic mail system and stored on a host or network server in an area you can think of as your **mailbox**. When you log into the electronic mail system and check your mail, unread messages are listed as new mail. You can choose to display and read the mail on your computer screen, print it, delete it, reply to it, forward it, or save it on disk, as shown in Figure 7-22.

Figure 7-22

Your e-mailbox lists new messages.

Buttons at the top of the mail window help you reply to, forward, send, and delete messages.

Your Inbox lists all the messages in your mailbox. An icon that looks like an unopened envelope indicates unread mail.

The text of the new message is displayed in the lower section of the window.

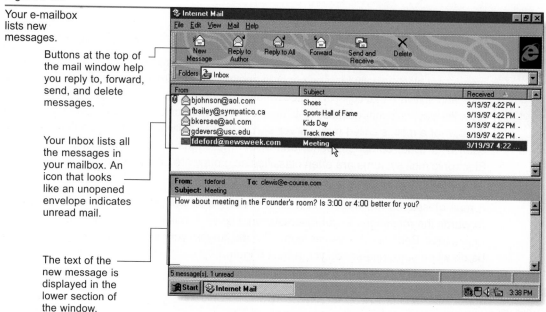

Replying to E-Mail

Smileys
9

What are all those > symbols in my e-mail? Suppose you receive e-mail from your supervisor containing the dates for the next sales meeting. The sales meeting conflicts with your scheduled vacation. You decide to reply to the supervisor's e-mail to see if you need to reschedule your vacation. You click the Reply button on your e-mail software. The screen changes and now you see the supervisor's message, but each line has a > symbol in front of it. What's happened?

As part of your reply, most e-mail software includes the text of the message to which you are replying. This text is preceded with > symbols. Type the text of your reply before the text marked with the > symbols. When you send your reply, it will include your message and the message to which you are replying. In that way, your reply contains the text of the original e-mail to help remind the recipient.

Composing New Messages

How does my e-mail software help me compose and send messages? Your e-mail software has a button or menu option for New Mail that displays a message form. The first item for the form is the recipient's mail address. You can type this address or select it from an address book that contains a list of e-mail addresses for the people you correspond with frequently. You can even set up groups in your address book. For example, you could have a "CarPool" group containing the e-mail addresses of the people in your car pool. Then, you can easily e-mail everyone in the car pool by sending one e-mail addressed to "Car Pool."

The e-mail form usually contains a **cc: option** so that you can send a copy of an e-mail to someone other than the main recipient. The e-mail form also includes a **subject option** so you can specify the topic of the e-mail.

The e-mail form includes a space for you to type the text of your message. Like most word processors, the e-mail software takes care of word wrap. But, don't expect your e-mail to provide you with many formatting options. Standard e-mail is plain text—no bold, no underlines, no fancy fonts. If you want to send a formatted document, you'll have to use an attachment.

Most e-mail systems allow you to send an **attachment**, which is a file such as a word-processing document, worksheet, or graphic that travels through the e-mail system along with an electronic mail message. For example, suppose you've created a poster for a community beach cleanup day. You've stored the file on your disk as "Beach Cleanup.bmp". You want to send it to the head of the cleanup committee so she can have it printed. Figure 7-23 shows you how to attach this file to an e-mail message.

Figure 7-23

Sending
an e-mail
attachment

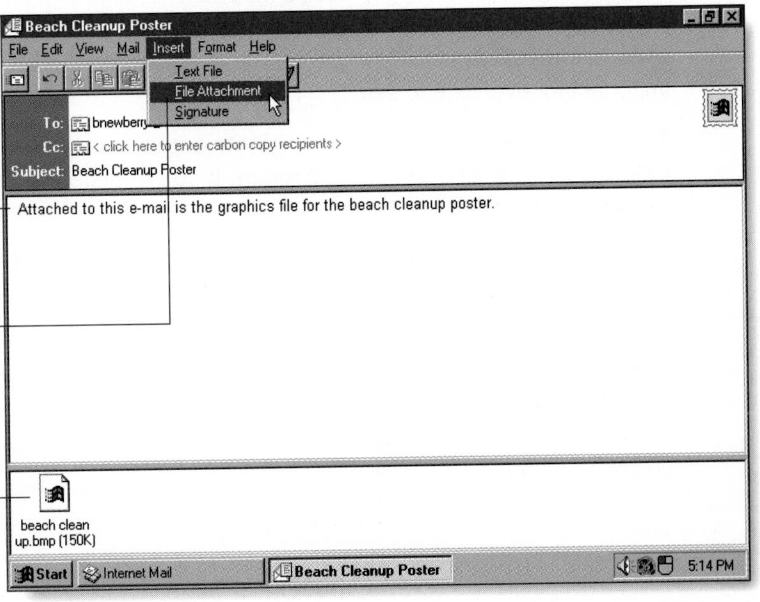

1. Create a new message and address it to the person to whom you are sending the attachment.

2. Use the menus provided by your e-mail software to attach the file containing the attachment.

3. An icon indicates the name of the file you attached. Send the mail following your usual procedures. The recipient of the message can click the icon to see the attachment.

Managing Your E-mail

I know how to write letters and memos—is there anything special I need to know about writing e-mail messages? E-mail is not exactly the same as using the post office. With e-mail you can send messages right away—your letters don't sit around waiting for you to take them to the post office. You can send the same message to multiple people as easily as to a single person. It is easy to send replies automatically to messages you receive as well.

The advantages of e-mail can also create potential problems—for example, you might regret the contents of a message sent off in haste. Also, it's easy to accumulate an overwhelming number of messages in your mail box. Here are some tips to help you avoid e-mail problems:

Read your mail regularly. When you use electronic mail, your correspondents expect a quick response. You lose much of the advantage of e-mail if you check your mailbox only once every two weeks!

Delete messages after you read them. Your e-mail is stored, along with everyone else's, on a file server where storage space is valuable. Leaving old messages in your mailbox takes up space that could be used more productively.

You don't have to reply to every e-mail message. The purpose of some e-mail messages is to give you information. Don't reply unless you have a reason to respond, such as to answer a question. Sending a message to say "I got your message" just creates unnecessary mail traffic.

If you receive mail addressed to a group, it might be better to reply only to one person in the group. You might receive mail as a member of a mailing list; the same message will be sent to everyone on the list. If you use the automatic reply feature of your e-mail system, your message is likely to be sent to everyone on the list. Do this only if your reply is important for everyone to see.

Think before you send. It is easy to write a message in haste or in anger and send it off before you have time to think it through. If you're upset, write your message, but wait a day before you send it.

Don't write anything you want to remain confidential. Electronic mail is easily forwarded to other people. Suppose you write something unflattering about Rob in an e-mail message to Julie. Julie can easily forward your message to Rob.

Don't get sloppy. Your e-mail is a reflection of you, your school, and your employer. Use a spell checker if one is available; if not, proofread your message before you send it. Use standard grammar, punctuation, and capitalization. A message in all uppercase means you're shouting.

EndNote

Local area networks have come a long way since the days of the sneaker net; they now provide connectivity for workgroups using groupware and for individuals exchanging e-mail. New technologies create opportunities, but they also create issues. Privacy is an important issue relevant to networks and e-mail.

E-mail
Privacy
10

Be aware that your e-mail might be read by someone other than the recipient. Although the U.S. justice system has not yet made a clear ruling, current legal interpretations indicate that e-mail is not legally protected from snooping. You cannot assume that the e-mail you send is private. Therefore, you should not use e-mail to send any message that you want to keep confidential.

Why would an employer want to know the contents of employee e-mail? You might immediately jump to the conclusion that employers who read employee e-mail are snooping. This might be the case with some employers who, for example, want to discover what a union is planning. However, some employers read employee e-mail to discover if any illegal activities are taking place on the computer system. Many employers are genuinely concerned about such activities because they could, in some cases, be held responsible for the actions of their employees.

Also, the network administrator sometimes sees the contents of e-mail messages while performing system maintenance or when trying to recover from a system failure. Even if an employer does not intentionally read e-mail exchanges, technical difficulties might still expose the contents of e-mail messages to people other than the intended recipient.

Many businesses are now implementing policies and procedures to address e-mail privacy. Before you use a network at school or at work, make sure that you ask about network policies relating to privacy and security.

InfoWeb

InfoWeb

Chapter
Links

The InfoWeb is your guide to print, film, television, and electronic resources. Use it to obtain updates on quickly changing technical information and to locate information for research papers. If you're using the New Perspectives CD-ROM, click the InfoWeb icon on the left side of this paragraph to access the online InfoWeb links. Otherwise, use your Web browser and type in the address of the New Perspectives site: www.cciw.com/np3. At the New Perspectives site you'll find up-to-date links to the topics covered in this chapter.

1 LANs

For a more in-depth look at LANs, browse through the fine illustrations in **How Networks Work** by Derfler and Freed (Ziff-Davis Press, 1993). For answers to your technical questions about networks, refer to Novell's complete **Encyclopedia of Networking** by Werner Feibel (Novell Press, 1995). On the Web, connect to *LAN Times Online* at **www.wcmh.com** for updates on the latest LAN technologies. The British magazine *Network World* at **www.network-world.com** has excellent articles and links to a buyer's guide.

2 Ethernet

Today, most networks use the Ethernet standard, which was invented in 1976 by Robert Metcalfe. You can see Metcalfe's original sketch of an Ethernet at **wwwhost.ots.utexas.edu/ethernet**. For information on other network standards, connect to **www.webopaedia.com** and look up Token Ring, ARCnet, ATM, and FDDI.

3 Wireless Networks

Wireless networks are popping up everywhere. You'll find an excellent tutorial about wireless LANs at **www.wlana.com**. Lucent Technologies produces a popular wireless system called WaveLAN that you can check out at **www.wavelan.com**. To get a look at some wireless data collection devices, connect to IBM's Networking site at **www.networking.ibm.com**.

4 Client/Server

Client/server is now a somewhat tired buzzword in the computer industry, but it is still mentioned frequently in the press. You'll find a wealth of information on client/server computing at the Client Server Group Web site at **www.isa.co.uk/csg**.

5 NOS: Network Operating Systems

In the world of PCs, Novell NetWare is the best-selling network operating system. Visit Novell's Web site at **www.novell.com** for information about local area networks and Novell products. Is NetWare better than Windows NT? A *LAN Times* article sums up this debate at **www.wcmh.com/lantimes/usetech/compare/pcNWvsNT.html**. Why fight two giants like Microsoft and Novell? Ask Artisoft, the publisher of the LANTastic network operating system. You'll find the Artisoft site at **www.artisoft.com**. A fourth NOS vendor, Banyan, maintains a Web site at **www.Banyan.com**.

6 Groupware

The July 1996 issue of *LAN Times*—on the Web at **www.lantimes.com/97/97jul/707a051a.html**—contains an excellent report on groupware, including case studies. Lotus Notes is one of the most popular groupware packages. Connect to the Lotus Notes site at **www2.lotus.com** to find out how the product works. For an insightful look at groupware from the perspective of management, look for the book **Groupware: Collaborative Strategies for Corporate LANs and Intranets** by David Coleman (Prentice Hall, 1997).

7 Workflow Software

On the Web, you can take a short tutorial on workflow systems at **cne.gmu.edu/modules/workflow**. For more information, check your library for **The Workflow Imperative** by Thomas Koulopolous (Van Nostrand Reinhold, 1995).

8 E-mail

For basic instruction on using e-mail, connect to the U-Wanna-What site at **www.uwannawhat.com/NetCourse/Internet/NetCH3PG2.html**. Unlike five years ago, today it is rare to receive e-mail THAT'S TYPED IN ALL CAPS TO FIT A 40 CHARACTER SCREEN. Instead, most people realize that e-mail messages should follow basic rules of grammar and basic guidelines for business letter format. For a discussion of e-mail context and contents, read *A Beginner's Guide to Effective Email* at **http://www.webfoot.com/advice/email.top.html**. At the Albion Cybercasting site, **www.albion.com/netiquette**, you'll find links to a Netiquette Quiz and excerpts from Virginia Shea's book, *The Core Rules of Netiquette*.

9 Smileys

Those > symbols aren't the only ones you'll find in e-mail messages. "Smileys" such as :-) (happy face) and =|:-] (Abraham Lincoln) add a little feeling and a little bit of whimsey into the otherwise stark world of electronic messaging. The book **Smileys** by D. Sanderson (O'Reilly, 1993) contains a collection of more

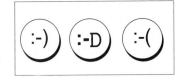

than 650 smileys and answers to your deepest questions such as "Why are smileys sideways?" You can find loads of information about smileys on the Web at sites such as the Geocities' Smiley House at **www.geocities.com/Heartland/6959/smiley.html**. To find other smiley sites, just enter the word "smiley" in any search engine.

10 E-mail Privacy

Concerned about the privacy of your e-mail? Many of your questions are answered at the E-Mail Privacy FAQ Web page at **www.well.com/user/abacard/email.html**. You can read an excellent article on e-mail privacy at the American Civil Liberties Union site, **www.aclu.org/issues/cyber/priv/privpap.html**.

An Amazon Book Store ad reads, "Reagan tried to destroy them, Bush tried to steal them, and Clinton tried to hide them—but the White House e-mail messages survived. Here are the highest-level communications on the most secret national security affairs of the US during the 1980s—shockingly candid electronic exchanges you were never meant to see!" It's all in the book, **White House E-Mail: The Top-Secret Messages the Reagan/Bush White House Tried to Destroy** by Thomas S. Blanton (New Press, 1995).

Review

1 Use your own words to answer the questions below each heading in this chapter.

2 List three reasons why sharing programs is effective for an organization.

3 Suppose Latisha Simms needs to select a password for herself. Rank the following, listing the most secure password first: BZ39A (a totally random selection of letters and numbers), LASIMMS (for Latisha Alexandra Simms), SSOSAPFOR (the first letters of "sing a song of sixpence, a pocket full of rye"), SMMIS (Latisha's last name spelled backwards), and Thomas (Latisha's husband's name).

4 Create a sentence outline of Section A that highlights the main concepts network users need to know.

5 Fill in the following table to summarize the characteristics of different network servers:

	File Server	Print Server	Non-dedicated Server	Client/server	Host
Are shared files stored locally?					
Are shared programs stored locally?					
Does some, all, or none of the processing take place on the server?					
Does some, all, or none of the processing take place on the terminals or workstations?					

6 Explain the difference between sharing files on a network and using a groupware product on a network.

7 Diagram the difference between groupware and workflow software.

8 Explain the purpose of network server software and network client software.

9 Explain the purpose of a workstation installion of Windows software.

10 Summarize the software licensing issues that pertain to local area networks.

11 Explain how store-and-forward technology applies to electronic mail systems.

12 Explain when you would use an e-mail attachment.

13 What is the purpose of the > symbol in the body of an e-mail reply?

14 Use the New Perspectives CD-ROM to take a practice test or to review the new terms presented in this chapter.

Projects

1 **Your School Network** Research your school network to answer the following questions:

    a. What is the network operating system?

    b. What drives are mapped to a student workstation?

    c. Is the file server a micro, mini, or mainframe computer?

    d. Is the print server a different device than the file server?

2 **Network Operating System Efficiency** Network operating systems are designed to optimize the process of sending program and data files to workstations. This means that the amount of time it takes multiple users to open the same file should not be much longer than it takes a single user to open the file. How efficient is the file server in your lab? To find out, form a team of three to five class members and do the following:

a. Using a stopwatch or the second hand of your watch, record the number of seconds it takes a word-processing software application to start on a workstation in your lab. For example, if your lab has Microsoft Word, click the Word icon to highlight it, then start timing when you press the Enter key to launch the program. Stop timing when the word processor is ready for you to start typing.

b. Exit the word-processing application to get ready for the second part of the test.

c. Position each member of your team at other workstations on the network. Each team member should click the word-processing icon so it is highlighted. One of the team members should give a signal so all the team members press the Enter key at the same time. Each team member should record how long it takes before the word-processing application is ready for typing.

d. Record each team member's results. Prepare a one-page document in which you summarize your experiment and results. Be sure you explain exactly how you carried out the experiment— how many members were on your team, which lab you used, and which software you used. Also, present your conclusions about the efficiency of your network server.

3 **Client/Server Architecture in Corporations**
Client/server architecture is becoming more and more popular in corporations. To find out more about client/server computing, use library and Internet resources to look for case studies and articles about corporations using client/server applications. Write a one- or two-page description of an effective use of client/server computing. Be sure to include a list of references.

4 **Networks in Action** Make an appointment to interview the network supervisor in an organization or business related to your career field. To prepare for the interview, make a list of questions you will ask about how the network works and how it is used. Use the topics in this chapter to help organize your questions about network hardware, network software, application software, and groupware. After the interview, write a two- to three-page summary of your findings. Include the name of the person you interviewed, the business or organization, and the date of the interview. In addition to the report summarizing your findings, submit a list of your questions.

5 **Network Careers** The companies that produce network operating systems encourage computer professionals to obtain professional certification to demonstrate their knowledge of networking. Such certification is often one of the qualifications listed in ads for network supervisor jobs. Novell offers certification as a CNE (Certified NetWare Engineer) or a CNA (Certified NetWare Administrator). Microsoft also offers a certification program for its Windows NT operating system. Write a one- to two-page paper that describes Microsoft's or Novell's certification process. Include the answers to the following questions: What is the process for certification? What is the cost? How would you prepare for the certification exam? What sort of jobs would you qualify for once you are certified?

6 **E-mail Smileys** E-mail has spawned a language of *emoticons*, or *smileys*, that are composed of keyboard characters. For example, the smiley ;-) looks like a person winking. You could use this smiley in an e-mail message to indicate that you are joking. Lists of smileys have been published on the Internet and in books, computer magazines, and newspapers. Find a list of smileys and select five that you would like to use. Make a list of your five smileys and describe what each means. Submit your list and indicate the source of your selection.

7 **Anonymous E-mail?** When you send e-mail, your user ID is automatically attached to your message. This return address indicates who sent the message (in case you forgot to include your name), lets your correspondents easily send you replies, and helps the mail system return messages that have incorrect addresses. Recently, some networks have offered a way to send anonymous e-mail. What are the pros and cons of anonymous mail? Under what circumstances would you want to send anonymous mail? Would you expect people to abuse this capability? Discuss this issue in a small group or research the issue individually. Write a one-page summary of your position on whether people should be allowed to send anonymous e-mail.

8 **E-mail Ethics** Assume that you are the network administrator at a small manufacturing company. While doing some maintenance work on the electronic mail system, you happen to view the contents of a mail message between two employees. The employees seem to be discussing a plan to steal equipment from the company. What would you do? Write a one-page essay explaining what you would do and describing the factors that affected your decision.

9 **E-mail Practice** Learn how to use the e-mail system available on your school network. Briefly describe how you do each of the following:

a. Compose and send a message.

b. Reply to a message you received.

c. Delete a message you received.

d. Forward a message you received to someone other than the person who sent the message.

e. Send a carbon copy of the message.

f. Send a message to a mailing list.

Lab Assignments

E-mail

E-mail that originates on a local area network with a mail gateway can travel all over the world. That's why it is so important to learn how to use it. In this Lab you use an e-mail simulator, so even if your school computers don't provide you with e-mail service, you will know the basics of reading, sending, and replying to electronic mail.

1 Click the Steps button to learn how to work with e-mail. As you proceed through the Steps, answer all of the Quick Check questions that appear. After you complete the Steps, you will see a Quick Check Summary Report. Follow the instructions on the screen to print this report.

2 Click the Explore button. Write a message to re@films.org. The subject of the message is "Picks and Pans." In the body of your message, describe a movie you have recently seen. Include the name of the movie, briefly summarize the plot, and give it a thumbs up or a thumbs down. Print the message before you send it.

3 In Explore, look in your In Box for a message from jb@music.org. Read the message, then compose a reply indicating that you will attend. Carbon copy mciccone@music.org. Print your reply, including the text of JB's original message before you send it.

4 In Explore, look in your In Box for a message from leo@sports.org. Reply to the message by adding your rating to the text of the original message as follows:

Equipment:	Your Rating:
Rollerblades	2
Skis	3
Bicycle	1
Scuba gear	4
Snowmobile	5

Print your reply before you send it.

THE INTERNET

The data jack slipped smoothly into the socket just behind Kyle's ear. He flipped the switch on his computer. The power light blinked green, and the universe shifted. A moment ago, Kyle was sitting at his desk in his apartment. Now, he seems to be standing in a landscape of sur-realistic terrain and fantastic buildings. Messages swirl and pulse down massive conduits, cre-ating data links between heavily guarded corporate computing centers. The World Health Organization cube spins lazily, tipped on one of its corners. In the distance—the towers of the Library of Congress. The golden pyramid of the Information Cartel dominates the landscape; its glowing forcefield a reminder that access requires security clearance.

InfoWeb

Cyberspace
1

This is a vision of **cyberspace**—a computer-generated mental image of a computer world. The term *cyberspace* was coined in 1984 by science-fiction writer William Gibson. Today, "cyberspace" has been popularized by journalists writing about worldwide information networks. No, you cannot plug your brain into a computer to prowl around in cyberspace. But your computer can provide you access to a digital "information highway" called the Internet that winds through a landscape of useful and fascinating information, on topics as diverse as hip hop music and military academies. In this chapter you will discover the astonishing potential of the Internet.

CHAPTER**PREVIEW**

In this chapter you will learn how the Internet works and you'll discover how your Web browser provides access to many different Internet services. You'll also find out how to publish your own Web pages. The *User Focus* section explains how to connect your own computer to the Internet. When you have completed this chapter, you should be able to:

- Describe how you can use a dial-up connection to access an ISP that in turn connects to an NSP on the Internet backbone
- Explain the difference between an IP address, domain name, URL, and e-mail address
- List the Internet services that you can access using a Web browser
- Explain the difference between downloading a file, viewing a Web page, and playing multimedia elements on a Web page
- Compare and contrast push and pull technologies
- Explain how synchronous and asynchronous interactions apply to chat groups, discussion groups, and interactive gaming
- Explain the purpose of HTML tags
- Evaluate the effectiveness of the design used for a Web page

LABS

The Internet:
World Wide Web

Web Pages
&
HTML

ⒶHow It Works

The **Internet** is a collection of local, regional, and national computer networks that are linked together to exchange data and distribute processing tasks. The Internet evolved over the past 30 years from a fledgling experiment with four computers into a vast information network that connects millions of microcomputers, minicomputers, mainframes, and supercomputers. Why was the Internet created and how does it work? The answers to these questions will help you navigate cyberspace.

The Internet Then and Now

How did the Internet get started? The history of the Internet begins in 1957 when the Soviet Union launched Sputnik, the first artificial satellite. In response to this display of Soviet superiority, the U.S. government resolved to improve its science and technical infrastructure. One of the resulting initiatives was the Advanced Research Projects Agency (ARPA).

InfoWeb

Internet History 2

ARPA swung into action with a project to help scientists communicate and share valuable computer resources. The **ARPANET**, created in 1969, connected computers at four universities. Using ARPANET technology, the National Science Foundation (NSF) created a similar, but larger network, linking not just a few large computers, but entire local area networks at each site. Connecting two or more networks creates an **internetwork** or **internet**. The NSF network was an internet (with a lowercase i). As this network grew, it became known as "The Internet" (with an uppercase I) as described in Figure 8-1.

Figure 8-1

The simple NSF network expanded to become today's Internet, providing access to information on every continent.

Early Internet pioneers—mostly educators and scientists—used primitive command-line user interfaces to send e-mail, transfer files, and run scientific calculations on Internet supercomputers. Finding information was not easy. Without search engines, Internet users relied on word of mouth and e-mail to tell colleagues "the data you need is on the Stanford computer in a file called Chrome.txt." In the early 1990s, software developers created new user-friendly Internet access tools, and Internet accounts became available to anyone willing to pay a moderate monthly fee. Today, the Internet connects computers all over the globe and supplies information to people of all ages and interests.

Internet Growth

How big is the Internet? To measure the size of the Internet, you can consider how many computers are connected, how many people use it, or how much data flows through it. Whatever measurement you use, the Internet is huge and continues to grow.

Internet Statistics 3

In 1969, the ARPANET consisted of four computers. In 1980, the Internet included 200 computers. By the beginning of 1997, the Internet had mushroomed to include 1.7 million computers worldwide, not counting computers making temporary connections. The graph in Figure 8-2 shows the incredible increase in the number of computers on the Internet over just the past 5 years.

Today, the Internet is the largest and most widely used network in the world, serving an estimated 57 million people in 194 countries. Over 15 million households in the U.S., 700,000 households in Canada, 700,000 households in the U.K., and 600,000 households in Australia have an Internet connection. Worldwide, more than 33,000 new users sign up for Internet accounts each day. About one third of all Internet users are females.

Figure 8-2

Internet growth

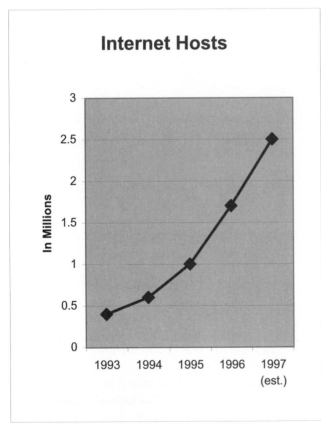

Although millions of people access the Internet, there is plenty of room for growth. The number of Internet users is less than two percent of the world population and less than 16 percent of the U.S. population age 15 and older.

Internet traffic is the number of bytes transmitted from one Internet host computer to another. By 1997, Internet traffic exceeded 100 terabytes a week. A **terabyte** is 1,000,000,000,000 bytes. One hundred terabytes is roughly equivalent to the amount of information printed on the paper made from 500,000 trees or the amount of information stored in books in the U.S. Library of Congress. Vast quantities of data are transmitted over the Internet, but how much data is actually stored on Internet computers? No one really knows. It is not currently possible to poll each computer to find out how many bytes of data are accessible.

Michael Dertouzos, director of the MIT Laboratory of Computer Science, estimates that the world has an exabyte of data to store. An **exabyte** is a quintillion (10^{18}) bytes. The Internet, as large as it is, probably has a long way to go before it contains an exabyte of data.

Internet Technology

How does data travel over the Internet? To understand how you can use the Internet to access information from a computer that is thousands of miles away, it is useful to have a little background on the Internet communications network. The cables, wires, and satellites that carry Internet data form an interlinked communications network. Data traveling from one Internet computer to another is transmitted from one link in the network to another, along the best possible route. If some links are overloaded or temporarily out of service, the data can be routed through different links. The major Internet communications links are called the **Internet backbone**. Figure 8-3 illustrates the Internet backbone in the continental United States and shows, for example, that data traveling from Seattle to Dallas could be routed through Chicago, Denver, or Los Angeles.

Figure 8-3

The Internet backbone in the continental U.S. provides many alternative pathways for data traveling from one computer to another.

DS3=
T3=
OC3=

In the U.S. nine **network service providers** (NSPs) each maintain a series of nationwide links. IBM, MCI, PSINet, and UUnet are the largest NSPs. The Internet backbone communications links are analogous to "pipes." Data flows through the pipes and large pipes can carry more data than smaller pipes. In Figure 8-3 the colors indicate the size of the data pipes. Blue OC3 links are the largest, with a capacity of about 155 million bits per second. If you had exclusive use of this line, you could transfer the contents of an entire 680 megabyte CD-ROM in 34.9 seconds. Green T3 and orange DS3 links have a capacity of about 44 million bits per second. Transferring the contents of a CD-ROM using one of these pipes would take about two hours. When Internet traffic is high, data takes longer to arrive at its destination. NSPs are continually adding new communications links to the backbone to accommodate increased Internet use.

Where does your computer fit into the scheme of things? When you connect your computer to the Internet, you do not connect directly to the backbone. Instead, you connect to an ISP that in turn connects to the backbone. An **Internet service provider** (ISP) is a company that provides Internet access to businesses, organizations, and individuals.

An ISP works in much the same way as your local phone company. You arrange for service, in this case for Internet access, and the ISP charges you a monthly fee. The ISP provides you with communications software and a user account. You supply a modem that connects your computer to your phone line. Your computer dials the ISP's computer and establishes a connection over the phone line. Once you are connected, the ISP routes data between your computer and the Internet backbone.

A connection that uses a phone line to establish a temporary Internet connection is referred to as a **dial-up connection**. Your dial-up connection is only temporary. When your computer hangs up, the connection is broken. A phone line provides a very narrow pipe for transmitting data. Its typical capacity is only 28.8 thousand bits per second. Using a phone line, the time to transfer the contents of a 680 megabyte CD-ROM would be over 53 hours. Figure 8-4 illustrates the layers of communication that make it possible for your home computer to access the Internet.

Figure 8-4

Your computer establishes a dial-up connection to an ISP. The ISP connects to the Internet backbone.

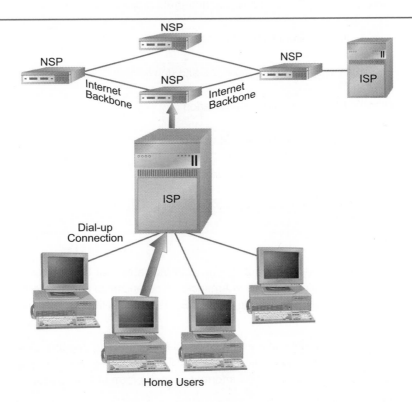

The efficient flow of data over all the communications links on the Internet requires a standard mechanism for routing data to its destination. **TCP/IP** is the acronym for **Transport Control Protocol/Internet Protocol**, a standard set of communications rules used by every computer that connects to the Internet. By following the rules of TCP/IP, Internet computers can efficiently control and route data between your computer and the Internet computers maintained by ISPs and NSPs.

Hosts, Domains, and Sites

How does the Internet know where to send data? The Internet includes computers that perform different functions. Some computers on the Internet handle communications and route e-mail, but most publicity about the Internet focuses on computers that provide information such as stock quotes, movie reviews, and sports scores. Regardless of function, every computer connected to the Internet is referred to as a **host**. Each host has a unique identifying number called an **IP address**. An IP address is a set of four numbers between 0 and 255 that are separated by periods. For example, 204.146.144.253 is the IP address of the Coca Cola Company. When data travels over the Internet, it carries the IP address of its destination. At each intersection on the backbone, the data's IP address is examined by a device called a **router**, which forwards the data towards its destination.

InfoWeb

Domain Names 4

Although an IP address works for inter-computer communications, humans find it difficult to remember long strings of numbers. Therefore, many host computers also have an easy-to-remember name such as cocacola.com. The official term for this name is **Fully Qualified Domain Name** (FQDN), but most people just refer to it as a **domain name**. By convention, you should type domain names using all lowercase letters. A domain name ends with a three-letter extension that indicates its top-level domain. A **top-level domain** groups the computers on the Internet into the categories shown in Figure 8-5.

Figure 8-5

Top-level domains

ORG	Professional and non-profit organization
COM	Commercial businesses
EDU	Four-year colleges and universities
NET	Internet administration
GOV	U.S. government agencies
MIL	U.S. military organizations
INT	Organizations established by international treaties

In the domain name cocacola.com, *com* indicates that the computer is maintained by a commercial business. In North America, an organization called **InterNIC** handles requests for IP addresses and domain names. By 1997, InterNIC had assigned over 16 million IP addresses.

Computers with domain names are popularly referred to as **sites**. A site is a metaphor for a virtual place that exists in cyberspace. For example, a Web site provides a virtual location that you can visit to view information in the form of Web pages.

URLs

What's the difference between a domain name and a URL? To access Web pages on the Internet, you use a **Uniform Resource Locator** (URL). A URL, like a domain name, is an Internet address. A URL is the address of a *document* on a computer, whereas a domain name represents the IP address of a *computer*. It is handy to understand how a URL is formed, in case you want to make an educated guess about the address to use to access a Web page.

Each Web page has a unique URL that begins with http://. The acronym HTTP stands for **HyperText Transfer Protocol**. Many of today's Web browsers assume that any address you type begins with http://. If you are using such a browser, you can omit http:// from the URL.

The next part of the URL is the server name. A **server** is a computer and software that make data available. A **Web server**, for example, is a computer that uses Web server software to transmit Web pages over the Internet. Most Web server names are domain names prefixed with www. The Web server name for your favorite Chinese restaurant might be something like www.fooyong.com.

Suppose you indicate to your Web browser that you want to access www.fooyong.com. By entering the Web server name, you'll access the site's home page. A **home page** is similar to the title page in a book. It identifies the site and contains links to other pages at the site.

A Web site usually contains more than one page. Each page is stored as a separate file and referred to by a unique URL. The URL of a Web page reflects the name of any folder or folders in which it is stored. For example, suppose the Chinese restaurant has a page listing its daily specials. The specials are stored in a file called specials.html in a folder called "information." The URL for this page would be www.fooyong.com/information/specials.html.

Some Internet computers are case sensitive. So although the domain name is always lower-case, parts of a URL might be uppercase. When you type URLs, you should be sure to use the correct case. Information/Specials.html is not the same as information/specials.html. Figure 8-6 illustrates the parts of a URL.

Figure 8-6

Components of a URL

http://www.fooyong.com/information/specials.html

Protocol   Web server name   Folder name   Document name and filename extension

Internet Mail

| How does Internet e-mail reach its destination? | As you learned in Chapter 7, sending e-mail on a local area network is simple. Each network user has a user ID such as wgibson. When you send an e-mail message to wgibson, the network stores it on the network mail server until Gibson logs in and checks his mail.

InfoWeb

Find It
5

Suppose that you want to send mail to wgibson; but you're in Baltimore and he is in Vancouver, British Columbia. You cannot simply address your e-mail to wgibson. How would it find its way over the Internet to Vancouver?

E-mail that travels over the Internet requires an **Internet mail address** that consists of a user ID and the user's mail server domain name. When Internet e-mail reaches an intersection on the Internet backbone, a router sends the e-mail on toward the mail server specified by the domain name. When the e-mail arrives at the mail server, it is held in a mailbox until the user next logs on to read mail. Figure 8-7 illustrates the parts of an Internet mail address.

Figure 8-7

Components
of an Internet
mail address

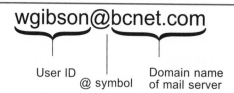

User ID   @ symbol   Domain name
                         of mail server

QuickCheck A

1. The term _____ was originally coined by science-fiction writer William Gibson to refer to a computer-generated reality that people could experience by connecting their brain to a computer network.

2. An internetwork, also referred to as a(n) _____ is created by connecting two or more networks.

3. Internet traffic is measured in _____.

4. Typically, you would connect your home computer directly to the Internet backbone using a T3 link. True or false? _____

5. All the computers on the Internet use a standard set of communications rules called _____.

6. The address **http://www.cyberspace.com** is a(n) _____.

Ⓑ The Versatile Web Browser

The Internet:
World Wide
Web

InfoWeb

WWW
6

Internet host computers function as servers that locate information, transfer data from one computer to another, and handle electronic mail. If you want access to the services provided by a server, you need corresponding client software. For example, as you learned in Chapter 7, the purpose of an e-mail server is to store and forward electronic mail messages. To access e-mail services, you must have e-mail client software.

On the Internet, **FTP servers** maintain a collection of data that you can transfer to your own computer. **Web servers** maintain a collection of Web pages that you can view on your computer screen. A **Usenet server** handles the exchange of comments among members of Internet discussion groups.

In the past, you needed a separate client software program to access each type of server. For e-mail, you needed an e-mail client. For FTP, you needed an FTP client. Archie, WAIS, TelNet, Gopher, and Newsreader clients were all part of the Internet user's software toolbox. Today, a single tool has replaced this awkward collection of client software. A **Web browser** provides Internet users with all-purpose client software for accessing many types of servers. You can use your Web browser to view Web pages, transfer files between computers, access commercial information services, send e-mail, and interact with other Internet users.

Web Pages

Sometimes my browser can't seem to get to a Web page. What's wrong? Back when disco music was popular, Ted Nelson was trying to devise a computer system that could store virtually every literary document, link them according to logical relationships, and allow readers to comment and annotate what they read (Figure 8-8). The establishment turned up its nose. Where would so much information come from and what computer would be powerful enough to handle it? Who would be interested in following hypertext links to find information? Who, except for scholars and scientists, would be interested in communicating online? Nelson's project Xanadu never became a reality, but his ideas resurfaced twenty-five years later as the World Wide Web.

The World Wide Web, created in 1990, is partially responsible for the explosion of interest in the Internet. As an easy-to-use, graphical source of information, the Web opened the Internet to millions of people interested in finding information rather than learning complex computer commands. Today, Web surfers (as Web users are sometimes called) can visit an estimated 80 million Web pages on over 1 million Web sites.

Figure 8-8

An early sketch of project Xanadu, a distant relative of the World Wide Web

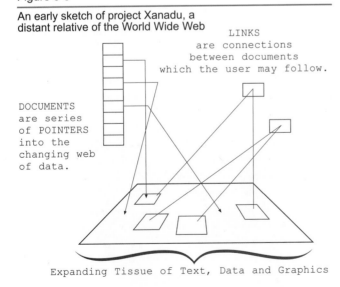

The official description of the World Wide Web is a "wide-area hypermedia information retrieval initiative aiming to give universal access to a large universe of documents." The World Wide Web consists of documents, called Web pages, that contain information on a particular topic. A Web page might also include one or more **links** that point to other Web pages. Links make it easy to follow a thread of related information, even if the pages are stored on computers located in different countries. Figure 8-9 shows a conceptual model of linked Web pages.

Figure 8-9

How the World Wide Web works

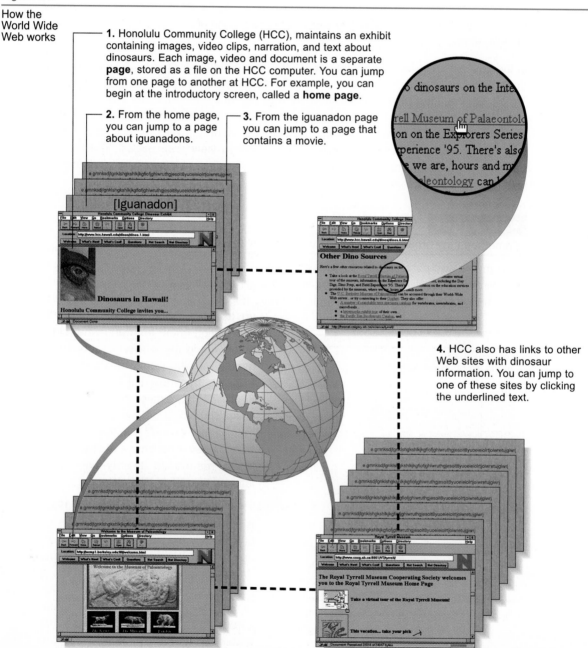

1. Honolulu Community College (HCC), maintains an exhibit containing images, video clips, narration, and text about dinosaurs. Each image, video and document is a separate **page**, stored as a file on the HCC computer. You can jump from one page to another at HCC. For example, you can begin at the introductory screen, called a **home page**.

2. From the home page, you can jump to a page about iguanadons.

3. From the iguanadon page you can jump to a page that contains a movie.

4. HCC also has links to other Web sites with dinosaur information. You can jump to one of these sites by clicking the underlined text.

6. Another jump and you are in California at the University of California Museum of Paleontology where more Web pages on dinosaurs are stored.

5. A quick jump from Hawaii and you are at the Royal Tyrrell Museum of Palaeontology in Alberta, Canada where additional Web pages on dinosaurs are stored.

You use a Web browser to request a Web page from a Web server. To request a page, you either type a URL or click a Web page link. The server sends the data for the Web page over the Internet to your computer. This data includes two things: the information you want to view and a set of instructions that tells your browser how to display it. The instructions include specifications for the color of the background, the size of the text, and the placement of graphics. Additional instructions tell your browser what to do when you click a link.

The Web is a constantly changing environment as new Web sites come online and old sites close. As a result, links are not always valid. Sometimes when you click a link nothing happens or you get an error message. If a Web server is off-line for maintenance or busy from heavy traffic, you won't be able to get the Web pages you requested, or you might get them slowly. If a Web page doesn't appear after fifteen to twenty seconds, you can click your browser's Stop button and try to access the page later. If you receive a message that the site no longer exists, you'll need to look for information elsewhere as shown in Figure 8-10.

Figure 8-10

If you have trouble connecting to a Web site, a message might indicate the site has closed or moved.

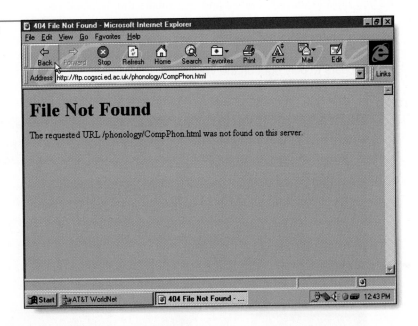

Your browser's **home page** is the first page you see displayed when your browser starts. You can always return to this page by clicking the browser's Home button. Most browsers let you pick any Web page as the home page, so select one that you use often, such as your favorite search engine.

Your browser's menu and tool bars help you navigate the Web as you follow links and then retrace your steps. You'll make frequent use of the Back and Forward buttons to retrace your path through the links you've followed from one Web page to another. Your browser stores a History list of the pages you visit during each session. It can display this list if you want to take big jumps to previously visited Web sites, instead of using the Back and Forward buttons. Your browser can also store a list of your favorite sites, often called **bookmarks**, so you can jump directly to them instead of entering a URL.

Internet Multimedia

Can I listen to music and play videos on the Web? It's hard to imagine that less than five years ago, Web pages contained only text. Now, Web pages include multimedia elements such as sound, animation, and video.

A media element is stored on the Web server in a file. When you click a Web page to play a media element, the Web server sends a copy of the media file to your computer. This can happen in one of two ways, depending on how the Web server has been set up. In one case, the Web server sends you the entire media file before starting to play it. For large video files, you might wait five minutes or more before the video begins to play.

A newer technology, sometimes referred to as **streaming media**, sends a small segment of the media file to your computer and begins to play it. While this first segment plays, the Web server sends the next part of the file to your computer, and so on until the media segment ends. With streaming media technology, your computer essentially plays a media file while receiving it.

As you browse the Web, you'll find multimedia that is displayed in place and multimedia that runs in a separate window. Of the two, in-place is technologically more sophisticated. **In-place multimedia technology** plays a media element as a seamless part of a Web page. For example, an animated GIF like the one in Figure 8-11, uses in-place technology so it appears to play right on the Web page.

Figure 8-11

An animated GIF runs in place as part of a Web page.

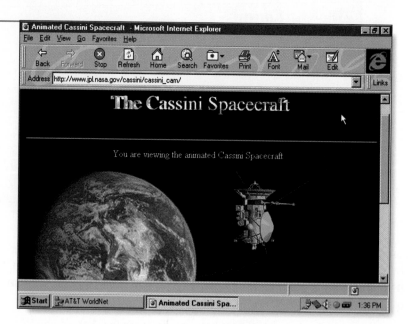

Multimedia overlay technology adds a separate window to your screen in which multimedia elements appear. With some overlay technologies, you must manually close the window when the multimedia segment is finished. Figure 8-12 illustrates a media window that overlays a Web page.

Figure 8-12

Some multimedia plays in a window that overlays the Web page.

InfoWeb

Plug-ins
7

A software program called a **media player**, provides you with controls to start, stop, and rewind media segments. Many media players play only one type of media file. For example, a media player might play only sound files with .wav extensions. Another media player might play only videos with .avi extensions. Before you can use a media element on the Web, your computer must have a corresponding media player. How does this work?

Your browser maintains a list of media players that have been installed on your computer. Suppose you're on the Financial News Network (FNN) site and you want to run a movie segment. FNN videos require a media player called Web Theater. You click the movie window. The Web server checks your browser to see if the Web Theater player has been installed on your computer. If not, the Web server usually gives you an opportunity to download and install it.

A software module that adds a specific feature to a system is called a **plug-in** or **viewer**. In the context of the Web, a plug-in adds a feature to your browser, such as the capability to play Web Theater videos. Popular plug-ins include Acrobat Reader, Shockwave, Real Audio, Real Video, VoxChat, and Cool Talk.

Push and Pull

InfoWeb

Push
8

With all this multimedia, isn't the Web becoming a lot like TV? The way most people use the Web is shaped by pull technology. With **pull technology** you use your browser to request Web pages and "pull" them into view on your computer screen. You only get those pages that you request and a Web server will not send you information unless you request it.

An alternative, called **push technology** sends you information that you didn't directly request. To receive pushed information from a Web site, you first register and then download the push plug-in software. There are several variations of push technology, and each requires its own plug-in. At most sites, the registration and the plug-in are free. Once you've registered, you receive pushed information whenever your computer is connected to the Internet. For example, suppose you register at a site that pushes stock information. Every time you connect to the Internet, your computer receives and displays current stock prices.

A growing number of Web sites provide "pushed" information. For example, many popular news sites, such as CNN and *The New York Times* allow you to set up a **personalized newspaper** by selecting the topics that interest you. You might, for example, request information about your local weather, stocks you own, your favorite sports team, or technology news. Whenever you visit the news site, you'll receive a personalized newspaper containing the latest information on the topics you selected when you first registered at the site. Figure 8-13 shows an example.

Figure 8-13

A personalized newspaper includes a pushed ticker-tape of headlines, temperatures, and sports scores.

Scrolling news and temperature ticker

A **webcast** uses push technology to broadcast a stream of continually changing information over the Web. Sometimes used for special event coverage, a webcast continues only as long as you remain connected to the Internet. If you are using a dial-up connection, you might not want to tie up your phone line for lengthy webcasts. Webcasts will be much more practical when everyone has a permanent high-speed connection to the Internet.

File Transfers

Can I get a copy of a picture, sound, or video that I find on the Web? When you're viewing a Web page, it is held temporarily in the RAM of your computer, but it is not stored as a file on disk. Suppose that a Web page contains a graphic, sound, or video that you would like to store on disk for later use. The process of transferring a copy of a file from a remote computer to your computer's disk drive is called **downloading**. Most Web browsers allow you to easily download Web page elements such as pictures, sounds, animations, and videos. Figure 8-14 explains how to do this.

Figure 8-14

Downloading a graphic from a Web page

1. To download a Web page element, point to it and click the right mouse button.

2. From the shortcut menu, select "Save Picture as..." to save a graphic. To save a sound or other media element, use the "Save Target As..." option.

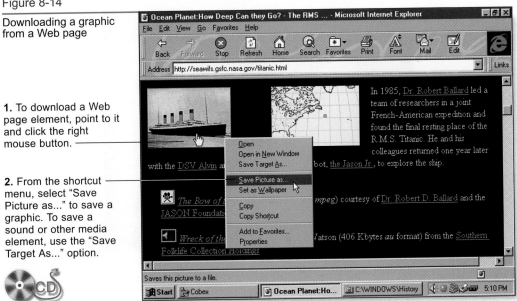

Uploading is the process of sending a copy of a file from your computer to a remote computer. Suppose, for example, that a writer living in British Columbia wants to send an 8 MB file containing the manuscript for a new novel to an editor in New York. What is the best way to deliver the manuscript to the editor? The writer could copy the file containing the manuscript to a Zip disk and send it via FedEx, but that would take at least 12 hours. Another possibility would be to attach the file to an e-mail, but some e-mail systems do not accept large attachments. A third option would be to upload the file to an Internet FTP server. The editor could then download the file from the server.

Although most browsers allow you to download files, not all browsers allow you to upload. If your browser does not have upload capabilities, you can accomplish the task using **FTP client software**, such as WinFTP, published by Ipswitch, Inc.

InfoWeb

FTP
Software
9

Many FTP servers allow people to log in and obtain downloads using "anonymous" as the user ID and their e-mail address as the password. For security reasons, however, most FTP servers provide upload capabilities only to people who have valid user accounts. To upload a file using your browser or FTP client software, you'll need to know the domain name for an FTP server on which you have an account. You must log in using your user ID and password before you can initiate the upload.

Commercial Information Services

Why would I want to subscribe to a commercial information service? Your versatile browser is the gateway to commercial information services as well as the free sites on the Internet. A **commercial information service** provides access to computer-based information for a fee. In 1997, approximately 17 million people subscribed to the top four commercial information services—America Online, CompuServe, Microsoft Network, and Prodigy. Most commercial information services are ISPs, offering dial-up Internet connections and e-mail, along with additional proprietary services described in Figure 8-15.

InfoWeb

Commercial
Services
10

Figure 8-15

Microsoft
Network
offers its
own chat
groups,
games, and
news
services that
are
accessible
only to
subscribers.

Commercial information services typically charge a $20 per month fee to access basic services, but the number of hours you can spend on the Internet might be limited. You might be charged additional fees, called **surcharges**, for additional Internet access or premium services. A **premium service** is information that has been designated as more valuable by the commercial information service. For example, many business-related services such as airline reservations, up-to-the-minute stock reports, and legal searches are often premium services.

If you have free access to the Internet provided by your school, you might not want to pay for a subscription to a commercial information service. However, many people do not have free Internet access, and would still like to send and receive e-mail, participate in online discussions, shop online, and have access to online information. For these people, a commercial information service might be the right choice.

Interactions

Chats &
Discussions
11

Can I interact directly with other people who are online? By far the most popular way to interact with other people on the Internet is with e-mail. It accounts for about one-third of all Internet activities. You can use your browser to send e-mail over the Internet. As an alternative, you can use standalone mail software such as Eudora or Pegasus.

Another way of interacting with people on the Internet is to join a **discussion group** in which participants share views on a specific issue or topic. On the Internet you'll find thousands of discussion groups on such diverse topics as snowboarding, urban policy, rave music, and William Gibson's cyberspace novels. Discussion groups take place **asynchronously**, meaning that the discussion participants are not online at the same time. For example, an English teacher might ask a question such as "Who has had the most impact on the development of cyberpunk novels?" Over the next few days other participants will post responses. When the English teacher next logs into the discussion group, he can read these responses, comment on them, or ask another question.

If you would rather interact synchronously with people who are online at the same time, you can join a **chat group**. To participate in a chat, you generally choose a nickname, then enter a chat room. As chat participants type, their messages appear on your screen. You'll see the messages from everyone in the chat room. Chat groups are often less focused than discussion groups as participants banter about the weather and themselves. That is not to say that serious chats never occur. On the contrary, chats can be an effective forum for professional interaction such as when physicians in different locations use the Internet to collaborate on a diagnosis.

Recently chat groups have come under fire because of potential dangers to personal safety and privacy. Use common sense in your chat room interactions. Don't represent yourself as something you're not. Don't provide personal information such as your name or address. Internet society, like society as a whole, has its share of deviants and rip-off experts. Most chats, however, are fairly civilized as shown in Figure 8-16.

Figure 8-16

A sample
chat session

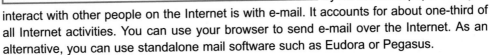

Games
12

Another aspect of Internet interaction is online **multi-player gaming**. From simple competitive word games to massive adventure games, the world of Internet gaming has it all. Imagine creating a cyber personna with the strength of a giant and the cunning of an elf. Arm yourself with your favorite weapon and venture into an imaginary world where you can defeat evil and accumulate treasure. Your fellow adventurers are people from all over the world (Figure 8-17).

Figure 8-17

Multi-player games give you an opportunity to play with, or play against, other players from all over the Internet.

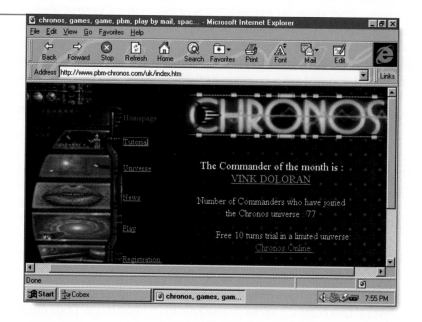

Some multi-player games are synchronous and others are asynchronous. As with chat groups, to participate in a synchronous game, you and the other players must be online at the same time. To participate in asynchronous games, you post each move to the game's referee, then you can pick up the results and submit new moves the next time you are online. Many multi-player games require a small fee to participate.

QuickCheck B

1. Your browser's _____ page is the first one you see when your browser starts.

2. A technology called _____ essentially plays a media file while your computer receives it.

3. A(n) _____ is a software module that adds a specific feature to your browser, such as the capability to play Web Theater videos.

4. Webcasting is pull technology that broadcasts information over the Web. True or false? _____

5. Most commercial information services are ISPs. True or false? _____

6. To participate in a chat group you must be online at the same time as other participants. True or false? _____

C Web Authoring and Site Management

LAB

Web Pages HTML

Using the Web as a source for information and interaction is great, but at some time you might want to become a Web author and publish your own pages. You might become even more ambitious and decide to create and manage your own Web site. Using today's software tools, Web authoring and publishing is not much more difficult than word processing or desktop publishing.

Why would you want to publish on the Web? You might have information that you want to make available to the public, such as your resume or a calendar of events for your club. You might have services or products to offer that you would like people to easily obtain from any geographic location. You might want to collect information from people by using surveys or questionnaires. Web publishing will help you get your message out and collect data.

Web Publishing

What can I publish? The Web provides opportunities for publishing tasks ranging from a single page to an entire Web site.

A single Web page is simple to create and can publish useful information such as your resume or a publicity flyer for a small business. Another use for a single Web page is to provide a list of links to sites with information on a particular topic.

A series of interlinked Web pages is like a mini site, except that it does not have its own domain name. You might publish a series of Web pages as part of a corporate site to describe the products and services of your department. Freelance artists or programmers could use a series of Web pages to publish examples of their work. A university instructor might publish a series of Web pages containing the syllabus, study guide, and assignments for a course.

A Web site includes a series of Web pages and has its own domain name. Businesses and organizations of all sizes create Web sites to provide information to customers and to sell products. With the availability of security software to protect customers' credit card numbers, e-commerce is becoming popular. Having a recognizable domain name such as www.hilfinger.com is an asset that helps customers arrive at a site without a lengthy search.

Basic Web pages contain text, graphics, and links. More sophisticated Web pages include animation, sound, and video. Your pages can also include interactive elements such as questionnaires or surveys. To incorporate these sophisticated features in your Web pages, your Web server might require special server software, but you need only a few tools to publish basic pages that feature text, graphics, and links.

HTML

| What's an HTML tag? | Every Web page is stored as an HTML document. An **HTML document** contains special instructions that tell a Web browser how to display the text, graphics, and background of a Web page. These instructions, called **HTML tags**, are inserted into the text of the document. If you look at the text of a Web page before it is displayed by a browser, you'll see the HTML tags set off in angle brackets. For example, the HTML tag <B> means to begin boldfaced text. A companion tag </B> means to end the boldface. In Figure 8-18 you can examine an HTML document as it looks before and after it is displayed by a browser. See if you can figure out the purpose of the HTML tags <BR> and <IMG SRC>.

InfoWeb

HTML
13

Figure 8-18

An HTML document and
corresponding Web page

```
<HTML>
<HEAD><TITLE>Nichole F. Kase Home Page</TITLE></HEAD>
<BODY>a
<BODY BGCOLOR = "#ffffff">
<TR><IMG SRC="canyon.gif" ALIGN="LEFT">
<CENTER>
<FONT SIZE=+3><B>Nichole F. Kase</B><BR>
<B>Canyon Web Design</B></FONT><BR><BR>
<B>Email: </B>
<A HREF="MAILTO:Nichole.Kase@mail.state.edu">Nichole.Kase@state.edu</A>
<BR><BR><BR>
<IMG SRC="bluebar.gif">
</CENTER>
</BODY>
</HTML>
```

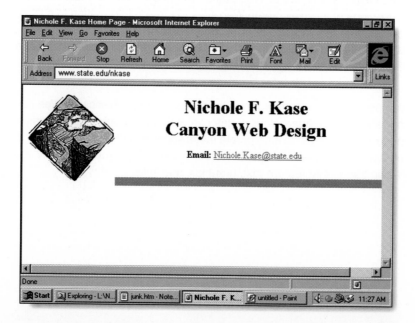

A basic HTML document has two parts. The **head** of the document specifies a title that appears on the title bar of the Web browser when the Web page is displayed. The **body** of the document contains informational text, graphics, and links.

Every HTML document should begin with the tag <HTML> and end with the tag </HTML>. This illustrates that some HTML tags work in pairs. The tag without the slash (/) is the opening tag. The tag with the slash is the ending tag. Some tags do not have a corresponding end tag. For example, you only need a single <BR> tag to create a line break. The table in Figure 8-19 contains a basic set of HTML tags that you can use to create HTML documents for Web pages.

The traditional way to create an HTML document is with a basic text editor such as the Notepad program included with Microsoft Windows. Simply type the HTML tags and the text for your Web page, then save the file with an .htm extension. You can also use a full-featured word processor such as Word, but saving the document is tricky because you don't want the word processor to insert its own non-HTML tags that confuse Web browsers. You'll learn more about using word-processing software to create Web pages in the next section.

Figure 8-19

Basic HTML tags

HTML Tags	Meaning and location
<HTML></HTML>	States that the file is an HTML document. Opening tag begins the page; closing tag ends the page (required).
<HEAD></HEAD>	States that the enclosed text is the header of the page. Appears immediately after the opening HTML tag (required).
<TITLE></TITLE>	States that the enclosed text is the title of the page. Must appear within the opening and closing HEAD tags (required).
<BODY></BODY>	States that the enclosed material (all the text, images, and tags in the rest of the document) is the body of the document (required).
<H1></H1>,	States that the enclosed text is a heading.
 	Inserts a line break. Can be used to control line spacing and breaks in lines.
<UL></UL>, <OL></OL>	Indicates an unordered list (list items are preceded by bullets) or an ordered list (list items are preceded by numbers or letters).
<LI>	Indicates a list item. Precedes all items in unordered or ordered lists.
<CENTER></CENTER>	Indicates that the enclosed text should be centered on the width of the page.
<B></B>	Indicates that the enclosed text should appear bold face.
<I></I>	Indicates that the enclosed text should appear italic.
<A HREF=""></A>	Indicates that the enclosed text is a hypertext link; the URL of the linked material must appear within the quote marks after the equal sign.
<IMG SCR=""	Inserts an in-line image into the document. The URL of the image appears within the quote marks following the SRC="" attribute.
<HR>	Inserts a horizontal rule.

HTML Authoring Tools

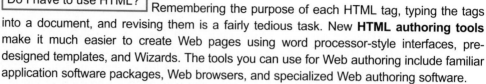

Do I have to use HTML? Remembering the purpose of each HTML tag, typing the tags into a document, and revising them is a fairly tedious task. New **HTML authoring tools** make it much easier to create Web pages using word processor-style interfaces, pre-designed templates, and Wizards. The tools you can use for Web authoring include familiar application software packages, Web browsers, and specialized Web authoring software.

InfoWeb
Authoring Tools
14

If you have recent-generation word-processing software, it is likely to include Web authoring capabilities. You enter text and insert graphics just as you would for a standard document, then the software outputs that document in HTML format (Figure 8-20). Some spreadsheet, desktop publishing, and presentation software packages offer similar capabilities.

Figure 8-20

Your word-processing software might have a feature that converts your documents into HTML format.

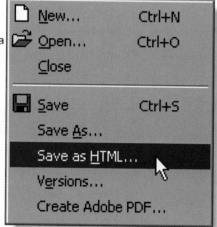

These familiar software tools create your Web page with a minimum of fuss, but they do not provide a high level of control over the final appearance of your Web page. For example, word-processing software is designed to create printed documents and includes features that are not available in HTML. Your word processor will do its best to translate your word-processing document into an HTML document. However, the exact formats and arrangement of elements that you see on your word processor's screen are not necessarily what will appear on the Web page.

Your browser might provide tools to create Web pages. For example, Netscape Communicator Professional Edition includes a module called Netscape Composer designed to make it easy to construct Web pages by selecting components from menus. The software automatically inserts HTML tags for each of the elements you've selected.

Web authoring software is designed specifically to create HTML documents that will be displayed as Web pages. Some of the top Web-authoring software titles include Microsoft FrontPage, Claris Home Page, Adobe Page Mill, and Corel Web Designer. Most of these packages provide a word processor-style interface, but allow you to implement only those features that are available in HTML. As you enter text, select type styles, and insert graphics, the Web authoring software automatically inserts appropriate HTML tags. Using this software, what you see is pretty much what you get, although slight format and placement variations might result depending on the browser used to view the page.

Many Web authoring software packages also provide tools to manage an entire Web site. In addition to helping you create individual Web pages, this software maintains a map of page links and automatically tests links to pages at other sites to make sure the links are still valid. Your Web authoring software might also include Web server software so you can turn any Internet host into a Web site accessible to Web surfers.

Compared to your familiar word-processing software, it takes a little longer to get up and running with Web authoring software because you are learning a new package. However, if you are planning to create more than an occasional Web page, you'll have more flexibility in Web page design, and you'll save time testing and maintaining your pages.

Page Design Tips

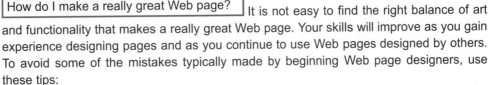

How do I make a really great Web page? It is not easy to find the right balance of art and functionality that makes a really great Web page. Your skills will improve as you gain experience designing pages and as you continue to use Web pages designed by others. To avoid some of the mistakes typically made by beginning Web page designers, use these tips:

InfoWeb

Authoring
Tips
15

Plan your Web page so it fulfills its purpose. Determine the function of your Web page. Is its purpose to entertain, to persuade, to inform, or to instruct? A clear idea of your page's goals and functions will guide all of your design decisions. In this way, the function of your Web page will determine the form that it takes. Designs are more effective when form follows function rather than when form is used for form's sake.

Design a template to unify your pages. A design template is a set of specifications for the location and format of all the elements that you want to include on your Web pages. The purpose of a design template is to visually tie together a series of Web pages and provide a consistent interface. Your template design might include any of the following elements: background, graphics, title, text, lists, headings, subheadings, video clips, music, animations, and navigation buttons. Get design ideas and develop a sense of style by looking at Web pages that are similar to those you plan to create.

Follow basic rules for good Web page design. Viewers will loose patience and move on to other Web sites if it takes too long for your pages to appear or if the text is illegible. Figure 8-21 summarizes basic design rules for the text, backgrounds, and graphics on your Web pages.

Figure 8-21

Basic Web design rules

Text:	■ For readability, use black type for large sections of text.
	■ Maintain narrow line widths. Text that stretches across the entire width of the screen is more difficult to read than text in columns.
	■ Make sure you proofread your document for spelling errors.
Background:	■ White or a very pale color makes a good background.
	■ Avoid drab gray and don't let your background color or graphic make it difficult to read the text.
Graphics:	■ Try not to use graphics files that exceed 30 KB because larger files take too long to transfer, load, and appear on a Web page.
	■ Use graphics with .gif, not .bmp extensions.
	■ To include a large graphic, present it as a small "thumbnail" with a link to the larger version of the graphic.

If your Web site will have multiple pages, sketch a hierarchy chart that shows how the pages will link to each other. Avoid a link plan that looks like a spider web. Although it is acceptable to have many exit links going to other pages, if possible, each page on your site should have only one entry link as shown in Figure 8-22.

Figure 8-22

Sketch a plan that shows the structure of your Web site. Each box that represents a page has only one arrow pointing into the box, indicating a single entry point.

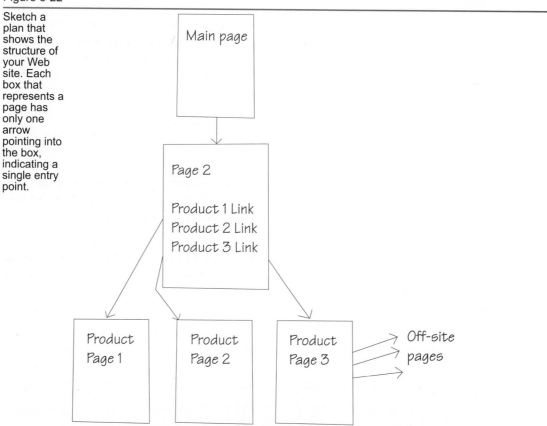

Include navigation elements. A carefully selected set of navigational buttons or links make it easy for people to jump from page to page in a logical order. Navigation elements should be clearly visible and easy to understand. If you have multiple pages, always include a navigation element that takes the viewer back to your home page. Use the same navigation system on every page of your site.

Respect copyright and intellectual property rights of other Web sites. If you use images and backgrounds that you have downloaded from the Web, make sure that you understand any copyright laws that apply to their reuse. Obtain permission before you use material from other Web sites and include a credit line on your page. For example, you could place a statement such as "Images courtesy of Paramount Pictures" at the bottom of your page.

Identify your pages. Make sure to use the <TITLE> tag on every page so it has a title. Also, include a way for people to contact you by including a link to your e-mail address. Place a copyright statement at the bottom of your page. The general format is the word "copyright," followed by the year or a range of years, followed by your name: Copyright 1998 Bobby Quine.

Publishing Your Pages

How do I get my pages on the Internet? Creating a Web page is not the end of the publishing process. You also need to test your pages, transfer them to a Web server, and test all your links. Figure 8-23 summarizes the process.

Figure 8-23

Four steps to publishing Web pages

1. Create each page

2. Test each page locally

3. Transfer the page to a Web server

4. Test all links

When you've completed the first draft of a Web page, you must test it to make sure every element is displayed correctly by a browser. You can do this without connecting to the Web by using your browser or Web authoring software. One caution: Your hard drive is much faster than a dial-up connection, so the text and graphics for your Web page appear more quickly during your test than they will for someone viewing your page over the Internet.

Whether you're publishing a single page, a series of pages, or an entire Web site, you must put your pages on a Web server. Although Web server software is available for your home computer, you'll probably not want to leave your computer on all the time with a live phone line link to the Internet. Instead, you should look for a site that will host your pages.

Many universities allocate space for student home pages and resumes. ISPs such as America Online and AT&T also offer space for individual home pages. If you are setting up a site for your business, consider a **Web hosting service** such as www.highway.com that provides space on its Internet servers for a monthly fee.

After you post your pages on a Web server, make sure you test the links between your pages and your links to pages on other sites. Then, sit back and watch as visitors flock to your site!

QuickCheck C

1 To create basic Web pages that contain only text, graphics, and _____, your Web server will not require additional software.

2 When HTML tags come in pairs, the first tag begins with a slash (/). True or false? _____

3 A basic HTML document has two parts—the head and the _____.

4 The traditional way to create HTML documents is with word-processing software. True or false? _____

5 _____ software is specifically designed to create HTML documents that will be displayed as Web pages.

6 A basic Web design rule is to avoid using graphic files larger than 30 KB on your Web pages. True or false? _____.

7 A careful selection of _____ buttons or links makes it easy for people to jump from page to page in a logical order.

8 When you test your pages locally, your Web pages appear more quickly than when viewed by a user with a dial-up Web connection. True or false? _____

Ⅾ Connecting to the Internet

If your school has Internet access, your Academic Computing department has installed the hardware and software you need to access the Internet from your school lab, and possibly from your dorm room. But what if you want to access the Internet from your computer at home? To access the Internet from your home computer, you must set up the necessary computer equipment, locate an Internet service provider, install the appropriate software on your computer, then dial in.

Set Up Equipment

What special equipment do I need to access the Internet?   The basic equipment for setting up online communications is a computer, a modem, and a telephone line. The equipment you use does not change the activities you can do online, but it can affect the speed at which you can accomplish these activities.

PCs and Macintosh computers can both connect to online services. A fast computer such as a 200 MHz Pentium speeds up some activities such as viewing graphics online. However, the overall speed of online activities is limited by the speed of the server, the speed of your modem, and the speed of your communications link.

InfoWeb

Modems
16

A **modem** converts the data from your computer into signals that can travel over telephone lines. It also translates arriving signals into data that your computer can store, manipulate, and display. A fast modem speeds the process of sending and receiving data. For example, a 33.6 Kbps (33,600 bits per second) modem provides you with faster online response than a 28.8 Kbps (28,800 bits per second) modem. Be careful when choosing a modem. Some require special phone lines. Follow the instructions included with your modem to set it up (Figure 8-24).

Figure 8-24

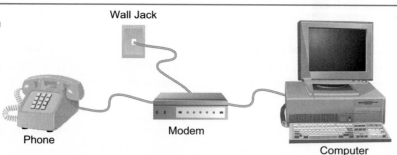

Connect your modem to your computer, then connect it to your phone line.

Wall Jack

Modem

Phone

Computer

The telephone line that you use for voice communications is suitable for most online activities. Corporations sometimes use faster communications links such as ISDN or T1. Your telephone line, though not the speediest communications link, is certainly the least expensive. When you are using your telephone line for online activities, you can't simultaneously use it for voice calls; while you are online, people who call you will get a busy signal. If you pick up the telephone receiver to make an outgoing call while you are online, your online connection will terminate.

Locate an Internet Service Provider

Who will provide me with an Internet connection, and how much will it cost? An Internet

InfoWeb

ISPs
17

service provider supplies you with a user account on a host computer that has access to the Internet. When you connect your personal computer to the host computer using a modem and the appropriate software, you gain access to the Internet. Your school might provide Internet access for students and faculty who want to use the Internet from off campus. An Internet connection provided by an educational institution is typically free.

Many commercial information services such as CompuServe, Prodigy, Microsoft Network, and America Online provide Internet access. Internet connections are also offered by some telephone companies, cable TV companies, and independent telecommunications firms. These firms charge between $20 and $30 per month for Internet access. Unlike commercial information services, they usually do not maintain their own online information, discussion groups, or downloadable software (Figure 8-25).

Figure 8-25

Internet service providers advertise in local newspapers and the Yellow Pages.

Internet Service Provider

SMALLTOWN TELEPHONE/INTERNET SERVICE

- FAST, RELIABLE SERVICE
- PROFESSIONAL TECHNICAL ASSISTANCE
- LOCAL ACCESS
- ENTER THE INTERNET THROUGH A FAMILIAR SOURCE

SMALLTOWN TELEPHONE

SMALLTOWN TELEPHONE
297 Main St S   Wood 222-3201

Install Software

Where do I get the software I need? Many ISPs provide subscibers with a complete software package that includes a browser and Internet communications software. **Internet communications software** allows your computer to transmit and receive data using the Internet TCP/IP communications protocol. Standard TCP/IP software handles Internet communication between computers that are directly cabled to a network. **SLIP (Serial Line Internet Protocol)** and **PPP (Point to Point Protocol)** are versions of TCP/IP designed to handle Internet communications over dial-up connections. When you want to access the Internet from a computer using a modem, you must use PPP, SLIP, or other similar communications software.

In the past, luck played an important role in establishing successful computer communications. Today, the software supplied by most Internet service providers is self-configuring; in other words, the first time you run the software, it examines your computer system and automatically selects the appropriate software settings. You have to deal with technical specifications only if your computer equipment, modem, or telephone line are not standard.

Dial In

After my hardware is set up and my software is installed, how do I dial in to the Internet?

Most Internet communications software is represented by an icon on your computer's desktop or Start menu. You start the software by clicking this icon, and it automatically establishes a connection to the Internet. Figure 8-26 shows what happens when you dial in.

Figure 8-26

Dialing into the Internet

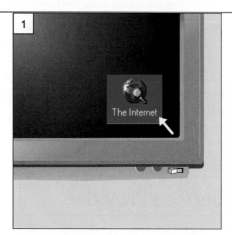

Click the Internet icon supplied by your Internet service provider.

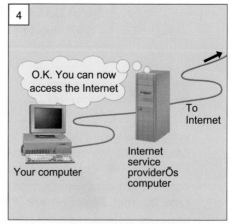

By clicking the Internet icon, you tell the computer to load your Internet communications client software. Your communications client will probably use SLIP or PPP to handle the TCP/IP protocols as your computer transmits and receives data through your modem.

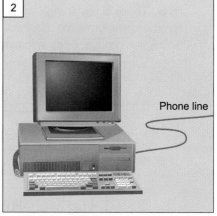

Your communications client dials the Internet service provider. Usually, your communications client has stored the telephone number, so you do not need to enter it each time you want to connect.

If your communications client has stored your user ID and password, it will automatically log you in. Some people prefer to enter their password manually for better security.

EndNote

The Internet has received much publicity. Many people agree that such a vast information network has potential to improve the quality of our lives. It provides us with an opportunity to interact with people of diverse backgrounds, engage in life-long education, and enrich our knowledge of the global community.

InfoWeb

Information
Quality
18

Fifty years ago a new technology called television promised similar advantages. Today, many people believe that television has failed. They point to inane soap operas, an over-abundance of graphic violence, the commercialization of gratuitous sex, and popularity of talk shows featuring bizarre human experiences.

Will the information highway also fail to fulfill its potential? The answer to this question is difficult to predict. The amount of information available online is growing. Much of this data is useful, but other information is of questionable value. Online computer technical support helps thousands of people keep their computers operational, but who is helped by online instructions for manufacturing homemade bombs? Satellite photographs from NASA's online database contribute to our knowledge of the universe, but what is the contribution of graphical images of sexual exploitation?

Smart consumers know that they can't believe everything they read or hear. This holds true for information on the Internet as well as television, radio, newspapers, tabloids, and books. Don't be deceived by conspiracy theories, disinformation, pseudo-science, and wacky medicine. Check for the facts. The Internet has many reliable resources that make their best effort to validate the information they publish (Figure 8-27).

In many ways, the Internet is a reflection of the interests as well as the problems of our society. Its development is worth watching throughout your lifetime.

Figure 8-27

It is easy to spread conspiracy theories on the Internet, but several "watchdog" sites try to present the "facts" that dispute or confirm the theories.

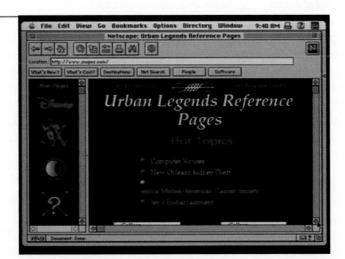

InfoWeb

Chapter
Links

The InfoWeb is your guide to print, film, television, and electronic resources. Use it to obtain updates on quickly changing technical information and to locate information for research papers. If you're using the New Perspectives CD-ROM, click the InfoWeb icon on the left side of this paragraph to access the online InfoWeb links. Otherwise, use your Web browser and type in the address of the New Perspectives site: www.cciw.com/np3. At the New Perspectives site you'll find up-to-date links to the topics covered in this chapter.

1 Cyberspace

According to *Forbes Magazine* (July 7, 1997 p. 348), "Science fiction is more than an inelegant prose for pencil-necked teenagers. Businesspeople and investors looking to discover where technology is taking us would do well to pay attention to it." The article describes how science fiction can sometimes become reality. For a serious analysis of the potential impact of cyberspace on society, check your library for the book **Cyberspace: First Steps**, edited by Michael Benedikt (MIT Press, 1993). William Gibson is generally recognized as the person who coined the term "cyberspace." His novel, **Neuromancer**, was the first of a literary genre now called cyberpunk. Visit William Gibson's Yardshow at **www.idoru.com/yardshow.html**. At The Electronic Freedom Foundation page, **www.eff.org/pub/Publications/William_Gibson**, you'll find some links to essays and interviews. You can scope out additional links by using the Yahoo! search engine and entering "William Gibson." On the lighter side of cyberspace literature, pick up the book **Dave Barry in Cyberspace** (Crown Publishers, 1996).

2 Internet History

Many reliable sources have reported that the Internet was built because the U.S. military wanted a computer network that would survive nuclear attack. Bob Taylor, father of the ARPANET refutes this myth in the book **Where Wizards Stay Up Late** by Hafner and Lyon (Simon & Schuster, 1996). A good video introduction to the Internet is **Understanding and Using the Internet** (PBS Home Video, 1996). Several of the people involved in the initial development and evolution of the Internet have written "A Brief History of the Internet" at **www.isoc.org/internet-history**. "The Roads and Crossroads of Internet's History" at **www.internetvalley.com/ intval.html** is an annotated timeline of events that contributed to cur-

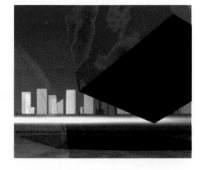

rent Internet technology such as: the laying of transoceanic cable connecting the U.S. and Europe in 1866, the founding of the Advanced Research Projects Agency (ARPA) in 1957, and the invention of the Web at CERN in 1989. Also check out "NetHistory: The Discovery Channel: A History of the Internet: How Did We Get Here Anyway?" at **www.discovery.com/area/history/internet/inet1.html** for a timeline of the Internet illustrated with drawings and photographs and interspersed with other technological events of the time. For an on-going discussion of the history and evolution of the Internet, check out the Computer Professionals For Social Responsibility's Community Memory: Discussion List on the History of Cyberspace at **memex.org/community-memory.html**.

3 Internet Statistics: Amazing Growth

It's difficult to keep track of the wild growth of the Internet. Measuring the number of computers and users on the Internet seems to produce sometimes conflicting statistics. For a roundup of statistics from various sources, connect to the CyberAtlas site at **www.cyberatlas.com**. Twice a year, a company called Network Wizards counts the number of hosts on the Internet. You'll find a summary of their research at Matthew Gray's site. Find the site by searching for "mkgray" at **www.mit.edu**. Hop over to **www.genmagic.com/Internet/Trends** to see Tony Rutkowski's collection of slides about the Internet. You can have some fun and produce your own wild projections about the Internet using the Internet Statistic Generator at **www.anamorph.com/docs/stats/stats.html**.

4 Domain Names

If you set up your own Internet site, you'll want your own domain name. How will you know if the name you want is available? At the site **www.checkdomain.com** you can enter a domain name such as neuromancer.com to see if it has already been reserved. Could you select a generic domain name such as www.government.com? For information on restricted domain names, tips on creating a valid domain name, and instruction on how to register a domain name, connect to the InterNIC server at **www.internic.net**.

5 Find It: Where to Find Internet Addresses

Have you lost track of your high school friends and wonder if they're online? You don't have to wonder for long. Search services on the Internet can help you locate people's telephone numbers, addresses, and e-mail addresses. Yahoo! People Search at **www.yahoo.com/search/people** allows you to look up a telephone number if you know the person's first name, last name, city and state. This service also allows you to look up an e-mail address if you know the person's first name, last name, and Internet domain. An alternative source is C/NET Search.com at **www.search.com**, then select the link for Yellow Pages, Phone Numbers, or e-mail Addresses.

6 WWW

CERN (the European Particle Physical Laboratory) is the birthplace of the World Wide Web. You can visit its site at **www.cern.ch** and follow the link for World Wide Web to read a bit about its history. Official information about the Web is maintained by the World Wide Web Consortium (W3C) at **www.w3.org/History.html**. The same site contains a page of great links about everything Web at **www.w3.org/TheProject**.

7 Plug-ins

Plug-ins provide access to audio, video, graphics, and 3-D file formats. Netscape's Plug Ins page (access it from **home.netscape.com**) lists 154 Netscape plug-ins currently available. How do you know which plug-ins you really need? How do you know which plug-ins are worth trying? You can read reviews and download plug-ins from the Internet Plug-ins page at **www.download.com** (enter plug-in in the search box). BrowserWatch - Plug-In Plaza at **browserwatch.internet.com/plug-in.html** provides links to all of the plug-ins available on the Internet. Plug-ins are one of the most quickly changing aspects of the Web industry, and most computer magazines run one or two articles about plug-ins and browsers every six months. "Plunging into Plug-Ins" at **www.pcworld.com/software/internet_www/articles/apr97/ 1504p110m.html** from the April 1997 issue of *PC World*, gives a list of indispensable plug-ins with brief descriptions of each and a link to a Web page for downloading. This article also includes a good discussion of how to remove plug-ins that you no longer want to use—something that is not as easy to do as you would hope.

8 Push

A pioneer in push technology, PointCast hosts a site at **www.pointcast.com/tour** where you can take a quick tour of push technology. For an excellent article on push technology that includes links to some of the more popular push sites, connect to the Push Publishing page at the National Library of Canada at **www.nlc-bnc.ca/pubs/netnotes/notes41.htm**. Some experts would argue that there is no such thing as push technology, only variations of pull. Edmund DeJesus explains this viewpoint in **The Pull of Push** (*Byte*, August 1997). What do you use to wrap up a fish? A newspaper. That's the point of MIT's experimental personalized newspaper project, fishWrap at **fishwrap.mit.edu**. Where else can you sign up for a personalized newspaper? Head for the Newspage site at **pnp.individual.com** or CNN at **www.cnn.com** and follow the Custom News link.

9 **FTP Software**

FTP (file transfer protocol) software is probably one of the oldest, most useful, and easy to use Internet applications of them all. It allows you to upload and download files from computers throughout the world. Windows 95 includes a basic FTP utility, but it uses a command-line interface, so most users prefer other GUI-based FTP software such as WS_FTP Professional. You can download the shareware version from **www.ipswitch.com/Products/WS_FTP/index.html**. File Dog at **www.edgepub.com/fd** is a shareware FTP software for Windows that has been highly rated by *PC Magazine*. File Dog makes a free evaluation copy available to potential users. Fetch at **www.dartmouth.edu/pages/softdev/fetch.html** is FTP software for the Macintosh that is free for users affiliated with an educational institution or charitable non-profit organization. WinFTP at **www.winsite.com/info/pc/win3/programr/winftp.zip** is a popular Windows FTP program that also has Web functions.

10 **Commercial Information Services**

Commercial information services are generally considered to provide a good entry-level Internet experience for the novice. There are four major online services operating today. Each service offers some unique content and has a different personality. CompuServe at **www.compuserve.com** is one of the oldest online services and is often perceived as being strongest in technical content and its discussion forums are highly regarded. America Online at **www.aol.com** is the largest of the four online services in terms of members. It pioneered online interactive sessions with famous writers, politicians, sports figures, and rock stars. Prodigy Internet at **www.prodigy.com**, is often viewed as a family-friendly online service, and it has file libraries, chat rooms, and proprietary content, such as a Consumer Reports library. In February 1997, Prodigy re-launched itself as a full service Internet provider, while keeping its online service as a smaller part of its business. Finally, Microsoft Network at **www.msn.com** is the newest of the online services. It is generally regarded as having the coolest, most extravagant proprietary content. You can learn more about commercial information services through computer industry magazines. For example, *PC World's* **Best Routes to the Net**, in the February 1997, issue reviewed 12 Internet service providers, including the commercial information services. In addition, check out the Online Connection at **www.barkers.org/online/index.html**. This Web site provides news, comparisons of commercial information services and national ISPs, discusses pricing and features, and provides service profiles.

11 **Chats and Discussion Groups**

To participate in discussion groups using your browser, connect to **www.dejanews.com**. Make sure you read the rules before you begin posting comments. For interactive chats, the options seem limitless. If you log into Yahoo! chats at **www.yahoo.com** (and follow the Chat links) you'll see that typically over 5,000 "chatters" are logged on at any time. Chatweb at **www.chatweb.com** has an easy-to-use interface, making it a good place to get started. If you're a member of AOL, CompuServe, MSN, or Prodigy their members-only chat groups are also a good place to try out Internet Chat. At The WebChat Broadcasting System site, **wbs.net**, you can "just visit" or you can register (free) and participate. *Salon Magazine* sponsors chats that have a reputation for being more substantive than chats at other sites. Connect to the Salon site at **www.salonmagazine.com** and follow the Table Talk links.

12 **Games**

MOOs (MUD Object Oriented), MUDs (Multi User Dimension or Dungeon), and MUSHEs began as text-based role playing games. With the advent of graphical Web browsers and VRML, these games are evolving into graphical, 3-D interactive worlds. You can visit some of these interactive sites with a standard Web browser. To participate in other sites, you need to download their VRML browser. If you have a vivid imagination, text-based MOOs, MUDs, and MUSHEs still exist, and you can connect to them on the Web. The Sprawl at **sensemedia.net/sprawl** is one of the oldest running MOOs existing on the Internet. Two sites where you can find people to play traditional board games online are Gamer's Zone at **www.worldvillage.com/wv/gamezone/html/games.htm** and Microsoft's Internet Gaming Zone at **www.zone.com**. The Realm at **www.realmserver.com** is an interactive adventure game from Sierra online. You can carry out quests in a world of monsters, magic, and medieval society in the companionship of thousands of players from across the world. The Realm costs $49.95 a year for unlimited play. The Games Domain Games Information Pages at **www.gamesdomain.com/gdmain.html** is a good source of information about both off-line and online games, including hints, walk throughs, and reviews. Hot links to the Virtual World Industry at **www.ccon.org/hotlinks/hotlinks.html** has information about and links to most of the major virtual reality game sites and browsers. It is a good launching point if you want to explore the world of virtual reality on the Web.

13 HTML

According to Nicholas Negroponte of the Media Lab at MIT, the Web is doubling in size every 50 days, and people are publishing home pages at a rate of one every four seconds. How can you join the rush to the Web and publish your own home page? The key is HTML-hypertext markup language. For a basic introduction on how to use HTML to create a Web page, connect to NCSA's A Beginner's Guide to HTML at **www.ncsa.uiuc.edu/General/Internet/WWW/HTMLPrimer.html**. You can find additional instruction at Learning HTML by the Tags Tutorial at **wally.rit.edu/depts/via/HTML/Tutorial/tutorial.html**, which provides links to information about graphics for the Web and how to publicize your Web site, in addition to basic instruction. If you prefer to use a book, **Teach Yourself Web Publishing with HTML 3.2 in a Week**, Third Edition by Laura Lemay (Sams.net, 1996) will be a helpful reference. For clip art, connect to the Image Finder at **wuecon.wustl.edu/other_www/wuarchimage.html**. For more clip art and animations connect to Andy's Art Attack at **www.andyart.com/**.

14 Authoring Tools

Web authoring tools allow you to create and work on Web pages from within a graphical interface. They help you generate HTML documents and view the result in a browser window or page viewer. Three popular Web authoring applications are Microsoft's FrontPage (**www.microsoft.com/frontpage**), Claris's Home Page (**www.claris.com/smallbiz/products/claris/clarispage**), and Adobe's PageMill (**www.adobe.com/prodindex/pagemill/main.html**). For a comparative review of HTML authoring tools, check out "HTML Editors: find the right tool," at **www.cnet.com/Content/Reviews/Compare/Htmleditors/index.html**.

15 Authoring Tips

The Web contains many resources that provide suggestions, tips, and information on Web page design. Written in a highly entertaining style, Crafting A Nifty Personal Web Site at **www2.hawaii.edu/jay/styleguide** provides lots of great tips with illustrated examples. For a more serious presentation, connect to Yale's C/AIM Web Style Guide at **info.med.yale.edu/caim/manual**. You'll enjoy the Web page makeovers in the Ziff-Davis *Internet MegaSite Magazine*. Pick up a copy from your newsstand or visit online at **www.zdimag.com** and follow the Makeovers links. *Internet Magazine*, published by emap Business Communications in the U.K. contains excellent information for Web designers. As you gain experience in Web page design, you'll find critiques of real sites at the award-winning site, HTML Style Guide: Common Problems in Web Design at **www.cire.com/patrick/design**.

16 Modems

Modem technology is changing as fast as any other segment of the computer industry. In 1994, most people had 9.6 Kbps modems. Today, most computers come equipped with 28.8 Kbps or 33.6 Kbps voice/fax modems, but on the Internet faster is better. What's the next step up in modem speed? A 56 Kbps modem? ISDN connection? Cable modem? Your questions about modems and Internet connections are answered at Modem FAQ–Curt's High Speed Modem Page at **www.teleport.com/~curt/modems.html**. Modems, Modems, Modems at **www.rosenet.net/~costmo** has a section of links to the home pages of modem makers, tips and troubleshooting tips, and sources of FAQs and drivers. According to *PC World* in the summer of 1997, the top five modem makers were U.S. Robotics (**www.usr.com**), Diamond MultiMedia (**www.diamondmm.com**), Practical Peripherals (**www.practinet.com**), Zoom Telephonics (**www.zoomtel.com**), and Motorola Modems (**www.mot.com/modems**).

17 ISPs

To avoid long-distance charges when you connect to the Internet, you'll want an ISP with a dial-in number within your local calling area. How can you find a local ISP? CNET ISP Review at **www.cnet.com/Content/Reviews/Compare/ISP/highest.html** provides comparative reviews of ISPs and information about how to select an ISP. CNET conducts a national survey of ISPs in which national and local ISPs are rated by their subscribers. The List at **thelist.internet.com** includes over 3,006 Internet Service Providers from the U.S., Canada, and around the world. You can search for an ISP by area code or by country code. Finally, PC World ISP Finder at **www.pcworld.com/interactive/ isps/isps.html** is a database that you can search by area code.

18 Information Quality

Some conspiracies are now classics—the JFK assassination, Elvis sightings, and the Roswell UFO Incident. And new conspiracies keep popping up—the missile that shot down TWA flight 800, the spaceship hidden behind the Hale-Bopp comet. The Disinformation Web site at **www.disinfo.com** provides a database of information about the origins and credibility (or lack of it) of many conspiracy theories. The site includes 'dossiers,' which cover many sides of a given issue or topic, both pro and con. Worth reading is Lucian Floridi's thought-provoking article about the future direction of the Internet and disinformation. You'll find the article, "Brave.Net.World: The Internet as a Disinformation Superhighway?" at **www.well.com/user/hlr/texts/disinfo.html**. The National Fraud Information Center at **www.fraud.org** helps consumers report fraud and offers helpful advice on how to avoid becoming a victim.

Review

1 Below each heading in this chapter, there is a question. Look back through the chapter and answer each of these questions using your own words.

2 Draw a conceptual diagram that shows how the Internet connects computers. Include and label the following elements: backbone, dial-up connection, host computers, router, NSP computer, ISP computer, home computer.

3 Provide an example of an IP address, a domain name, a URL, and an e-mail address. Then in your own words, describe the elements each contains.

4 Make a list of the Internet services you can access using a Web browser.

5 Indicate the type of software you can use to do each of the following:

a. Download a file

b. View a Web page

c. Play a multimedia element

6 Describe what happens when you view a Web page and how it differs from downloading a file.

7 Describe the difference between a Web server and a Web site.

8 Use your own words to define the difference between push and pull technology.

9 On the Internet, you can interact with people in discussion groups, chat groups, and interactive games. Describe the difference between synchronous and asynchronous interactions and explain how each relates to chats, discussion groups, and games.

10 List four categories of tools that you can use to create HTML documents.

11 Make a list of the steps you would take to connect your computer at home to the Internet.

12 Use the New Perspectives CD-ROM to take a practice test or to review the new terms presented in this chapter.

Projects

The Great Internet Hunt For several years Rick Gates hosted a monthly Internet scavenger hunt. The object of his hunt was to find information on the Internet. The hunt in this project is a little different from Gates' hunt. For this hunt, there are 10 questions. The questions are located at the CTI Web site, **www.cciw.com/np3/project8-1.html**. Go to this site and print out the questions. Each question carries a point value between 1 and 5. Use the Web to answer as many questions as you can. For each question, you must supply the answer, the URL of the site where you found the answer, and a one-page printout to verify that you actually visited the site.

2 **Censored!** Prodigy, which bills itself as a family information service, monitors the content of its services to remove X-rated and R-rated text and graphics. However, no such policing occurs at most other Internet services.

The Internet and commercial information services provide a growing forum for discussions on a wide range of topics. Recently, some online observers have begun to question the advisability of information exchanged over the Internet. Megabytes of Internet storage space are devoted to X-rated images. Several Usenet groups regularly discuss the details of making bombs and hollow point bullets. Other groups discuss methods of torture. In a well-publicized incident, a discussion group participant described in gory detail how he was going to murder a female college student.

Free speech laws protect the rights of Americans to express themselves, but should the Internet, which is supported with public taxes, provide a medium for transmitting pornographic or terrorist information?

For this project, research the issue of online censorship. Write a position paper arguing for or against censorship. Support your position with facts and examples. Be sure to include a bibliography. After you complete your research, your instructor might suggest that you discuss your ideas in a small group session.

Personalized News It's a good idea to keep informed of current events and keep up with issues and activities that interest you. Connect to one of the Personalized News Web sites described in the *InfoWeb* section and create a personalized newspaper of your own. As verification that you completed the assignment, indicate which site you used, describe the options you selected, and write a short summary of your opinions about the usefulness of your personalized newspaper.

4 **No One Knows You're a Dog** In a novel called *Ender's War*, two children are catapulted to national prominence because they have innovative ideas about how to solve critical social and economic issues. No one knows they are children, however, because they communicate their ideas on a public information service, which is the central political forum in their society. This brings up an interesting issue, humorously alluded to in the P. Steiner cartoon.

"On the Internet, nobody knows you're a dog."

Discuss this issue in a small group. In your discussion address questions a through e.

a. Does a communications medium that depends on the written word, rather than on videos, reduce cultural, class, ethnic, and gender bias?

b. According to pollsters, in 1980 many Americans voted for Ronald Reagan because they didn't like his opponent's southern accent. Do you think the election would have been different if campaigning was carried out over the Internet?

c. There is evidence that the younger generation does not like to read and write. Do you think this generation needs a communications medium that is more like television?

d. Do you believe that online communications have the potential to reduce biases in our society?

e. Can anyone in your group relate an experience when online communications would have been preferable to face-to-face communication?

5 **Compare ISPs** When you use a dial-up line to connect to the Internet, it is preferable to dial a local call, rather than long distance. Therefore, you should pick an ISP that offers a dial-up number in your local calling area. Use the Internet, your library, and other resources to find a list of ISPs in your area. Don't forget to check commercial information services such as CompuServe, Prodigy, MSN, and America Online. Discover all the information you can about rates, reliability, quality of technical support, and services. Now, suppose that you are a reporter for your local newspaper. Write an article (about two pages, double-spaced) for the paper that compares the ISPs that offer local dial-up connections to the Internet.

6 **Web Site Makeover** To some extent, good design is a matter of taste and when it comes to Web page design, there are usually many possible solutions that provide a pleasing look and efficient navigational tools. On the other hand, there are some designs that just don't seem to work because they make the text difficult to read or navigate.

For this project, select a Web page that you think could use improvement. You may find the page by browsing on the Web or by looking in magazines for screen shots of Web pages. Use colored pencils or markers to sketch your plan for the improved page. Annotate your sketch by pointing out the features you have changed and why you think your makeover will be more effective than the original Web page.

7 **Design Your Own Home Page** For this project, you'll design your own home page. Depending on the tools you have available, you might be able to create a real page and publish it on the Web. If these tools are not available, you will still be able to complete the initial design work. Your instructor will provide you with guidelines on which of the following steps to complete.

a. Write a brief description of the purpose of your home page and your expected audience. For example, you might plan to use your home page to showcase your resume to prospective employers.

b. Make a list of the elements you plan to include on your home page. Briefly describe any graphics or media elements you want to include.

c. Create a document that contains the information you want to include for your home page. If you have the tools, create this document in HTML format.

d. Make a sketch of your home page showing the colors you plan to use and the navigation elements you plan to include. Annotate this sketch to describe how these elements follow effective Web page design guidelines.

e. If you have the tools to create the entire HTML document for your home page, do so. Make sure that you test the page locally using your browser. Use the Print option on the File menu of your browser to print your page.

f. If you have permission to publish your Web page on a Web server, do so. Provide your instructor with the URL for your page.

Virtual Reality: Writer William Gibson envisioned a time when people would connect their brains directly to a computer to experience a virtual world in cyberspace. Technology and medical science have not found a way to make a direct connection between our brains and a computer, but today virtual reality takes other forms. On the Internet, interactive technologies provide virtual environments for games, meetings, and socializing. On microcomputers, the multi-player game Doom provides hours of virtual reality adventure. Using equipment, such as the stereo-optic goggles and sensor gloves, you can see and manipulate objects that do not exist.

Use your library and Internet resources to learn more about virtual reality. You might also try some virtual reality experiences. If you have Internet access, participate in an interactive 3-D game. Play a virtual reality computer game such as Doom or Myst. If available, try out virtual reality goggles.

Now suppose you are asked to produce a three-minute TV news segment on virtual reality. Based on the information you gathered from your library, the Internet, and your personal experiences, write the narrative and describe the images and video clips you would show.

Good Netiquette The Internet, like most societies has certain standards for behavior. What's generally acceptable online behavior in cyberspace culture? Use the Internet or your library resources to research this topic, then design a poster of netiquette rules. You can decide what audience your poster targets: children, high school students, college students, business people—you could even select a specific business. Try to use words and images that will appeal to your target audience.

Lab Assignments

The Internet: World Wide Web

One of the most popular services on the Internet is the World Wide Web. This Lab is a Web simulator that teaches you how to use Web browser software to find information. You can use this Lab whether or not your school provides you with Internet access.

1. Click the Steps button to learn how to use Web browser software. As you proceed through the Steps, answer all of the Quick Check questions that appear. After you complete the Steps, you will see a Quick Check Summary Report. Follow the instructions on the screen to print this report.

2. Click the Explore button on the Welcome screen. Use the Web browser to locate a weather map of the Caribbean Virgin Islands. What is its URL?

3. A SCUBA diver named Wadson Lachouffe has been searching for the fabled treasure of Greybeard the pirate. A link from the Adventure Travel Web site **www.atour.com** leads to Wadson's Web page called

"Hidden Treasure." In Explore, locate the Hidden Treasure page and answer the following questions:

  a. What was the name of Greybeard's ship?
  b. What was Greybeard's favorite food?
  c. What does Wadson think happened to Greybeard's ship?

4 In the Steps, you found a graphic of Jupiter from the photo archives of the Jet Propulsion Laboratory. In the Explore section of the Lab, you can also find a graphic of Saturn. Suppose one of your friends wanted a picture of Saturn for an astronomy report. Make a list of the blue, underlined links your friend must click in the correct order to find the Saturn graphic. Assume that your friend will begin at the Web Trainer home page.

5 Enter the URL **http://www.atour.com** to jump to the Adventure Travel Web site. Write a one-page description of this site. In your paper include a description of the information at the site, the number of pages the site contains, and a diagram of the links it contains.

6 Chris Thomson is a student at UVI and has his own Web pages. In Explore, look at the information Chris has included on his pages. Suppose you could create your own Web page. What would you include? Use word-processing software to design your own Web pages. Make sure you indicate the graphics and links you would use.

Web Pages & HTML

It's easy to create your own Web pages. As you learned in this chapter, there are many software tools to help you become a Web author. In this Lab you'll experiment with a Web authoring wizard that automates the process of creating a Web page. You'll also try your hand at working directly with HTML code.

1 Click the Steps button to activate the Web authoring wizard and learn how to create a basic Web page. As you proceed through the Steps, answer all of the Quick Check questions. After you complete the Steps, you will see a Quick Check summary Report. Follow the instructions on the screen to print this report.

2 In Explore, click the File menu, then click New to start working on a new Web page. Use the wizard to create a Home page for a veterinarian who offers dog day-care and boarding services. After you create the page, save it on drive A or C, and print the HTML code. Your site must have the following characteristics:

  a. Title: Dr. Dave's Dog Domain
  b. Background color: Gold
  c. Graphic: Dog.jpg
  d. Body text: Your dog will have the best care day and night at Dr. Dave's Dog Domain. Fine accommodations, good food, play time, and snacks are all provided. You can board your pet by the day or week. Grooming services also available.
  e. Text link: "Reasonable rates" links to www.cciw.com/np3/rates.htm
  f. E-mail link: "For more information:" links to **daveassist@drdave.com**

3 In Explore, use the File menu to open the HTML document called Politics.htm. After you use the HTML window (not the wizard) to make the following changes, save the revised page on Drive A or C, and print the HTML code. Refer to Figure 8-19 of your textbook for a list of HTML tags you can use.

  a. Change the title to Politics 2000
  b. Center the page heading
  c. Change the background color to FFE7C6 and the text color to 000000
  d. Add a line break before the sentence "What's next?"
  e. Add a bold tag to "Additional links on this topic:"
  f. Add one more link to the "Additional links" list. The link should go to the site **http://www.elections.ca** and the clickable link should read "Elections Canada".
  g. Change the last graphic to display the image "next.gif"

4 In Explore use the Web authoring wizard and the HTML window to create a Home page about yourself. You should include at least a screenful of text, a graphic, an external link, and an e-mail link. Save the page on drive A, then print the HTML code. Turn in your disk and printout.

DATASECURITY andCONTROL

According to legend, the war between the Trojans and the Greeks continued for more than nine years, until one of the Greek leaders conceived a brilliant plan. He ordered his men to create a huge wooden horse. When it was completed, a few soldiers hid inside and the Greek army pretended to sail away. The Trojans believed that the horse was a gift, pulled it into the city, and spent the day celebrating what they thought was a great victory. Late that night, the soldiers hidden inside the horse crept out and opened the city gates for the waiting Greek army.

What does the Trojan War have to do with computers? Like the city of Troy, modern computer users are under siege. They are battling computer criminals, pranksters, viruses, equipment failures, and human errors. There is even a modern software version of the Trojan horse that might erase your data after you unknowingly bring it into your computer system.

This chapter begins by describing mistakes and equipment failures that inadvertently cause lost or inaccurate data. Next, the focus moves to intentional acts of vandalism and computer crime in which data is tampered with or stolen. The section on risk management explains the steps you can take to protect your data. This chapter concludes with an in-depth look at a most important computing activity—data backup.

CHAPTERPREVIEW

In this chapter you learn about threats to the data stored on computer systems. You will find out why data backup is one of the most effective security measures for protecting your data. On a practical level, you will learn how to disinfect disks that contain viruses, make backups, and design an effective backup plan for your data. After you have completed this chapter you should be able to:

- List some of the causes for lost or inaccurate data
- Describe how you can protect your computer data from damage caused by power problems and hardware failures
- List at least five symptoms that might indicate your computer is infected by a virus
- Differentiate between the terms virus, Trojan horse, worm, logic bomb, and time bomb
- Describe techniques for avoiding, detecting, and eradicating a computer virus
- Explain why special computer crime laws are necessary
- Describe the process of risk management
- List the advantages and disadvantages of the most popular data security techniques

LABS

Data Backup

A What Can Go Wrong

Today's computer users battle to avoid lost, stolen, and inaccurate data. **Lost data**, also referred to as **missing data**, is data that is inaccessible, usually because it was accidentally removed. **Stolen data** is not necessarily missing, but it has been accessed or copied without authorization. **Inaccurate data** is data that is not accurate because it was entered incorrectly, was deliberately or accidentally altered, or was not edited to reflect current facts.

Despite all the sensational press coverage of computer criminals and viruses, the cause of many data problems is simply operator error, power abnormalities, or hardware failure.

Operator Error

What's the most likely cause of lost or inaccurate data? **Operator error** refers to a mistake made by a computer user. At one time or another, everyone who has used a computer has made a mistake. A few examples will illustrate that it is not an exclusive club.

- Working late at night the President's press secretary finished the final revisions for the next day's speech. Intending to make a copy of the speech as a backup, he mistakenly copied the old version of the speech over the new version.

- The head of personnel grabbed a disk without a label and thinking it was unformatted, shoved it in the disk drive and started the formatting process. Unfortunately, the disk contained her only copy of a report that had been mailed from the Houston office.

- A hospital clerk makes a typing error and bills a patient for 555 aspirins instead of 5.

It might seem that nothing can prevent operator error. After all, mistakes do happen. However, the number of operator errors can be reduced if users pay attention to what they're doing and establish habits that help them avoid mistakes.

Computer software designers can help prevent mistakes by designing products that anticipate mistakes that users are likely to make. For example, Microsoft Windows users can activate a feature that requests confirmation before the computer carries out any activity that might destroy data. Figure 9-1 shows a Windows dialog box that asks for confirmation before a file is deleted.

Figure 9-1

A confirmation dialog box helps reduce operator error

1. The user selects the file Sales Summary. Pressing the Delete key initiates an operation that will, in effect, destroy the data in the selected file.

2. The Microsoft Windows operating system displays a prompt asking the user to confirm the delete. The file is deleted only if the user clicks the Yes button.

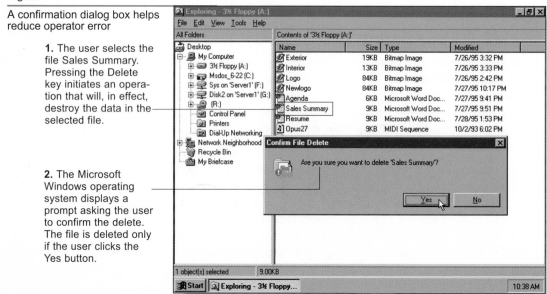

Power Failures, Spikes, and Surges

| If the power goes out, will I lose all my data? | A **power failure** is a complete loss of power to the computer system. Although you can lose power by accidentally bumping the computer on/off switch, a power failure is usually caused by something over which you have no control, such as a downed power line or a malfunction at the local power plant.

Data stored in RAM is lost if power is not continuously supplied to the computer system. Even a brief power interruption, noticeable only as a flicker of the room lights, can force your computer to reboot and lose all the data in RAM.

InfoWeb

UPS
1

An uninterruptible power supply is the best protection against power problems. An **uninterruptible power supply**, or **UPS**, is a device containing a battery and other circuitry that provides a continuous supply of power. A UPS is designed to provide enough power to keep your computer working through momentary power interruptions and to give you time to save your files and exit your programs in the event of a longer power outage. A UPS for a microcomputer costs from $100 to $600, depending on the power requirements of the computer and the features of the UPS. Most computer dealers can help you determine your computer's power requirements and recommend the appropriate size and features for a UPS that meets your needs. Figure 9-2 shows a typical UPS.

Figure 9-2

A UPS contains a battery that keeps your computer going for several minutes during a power failure. The battery does not supply indefinite power, so in the event of a power failure that lasts more than two or three minutes you should save your work and turn off your computer.

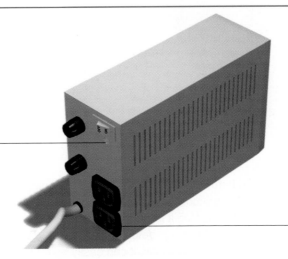

A light on the case lets you know that the UPS is charged and ready.

To connect a UPS, plug it into a wall outlet, then plug your computer and monitor cables into the outlets on the UPS.

Lightning and malfunctions at the electric company can cause spikes and surges that can damage sensitive computer components. A **power spike** is an increase in power that lasts only a short time—less than a millionth of a second. A **power surge** lasts a little longer—a few millionths of a second. Power surges and spikes are potentially more damaging than power failures. A surge or spike can damage your computer's motherboard and the circuit boards on your disk drives, putting your computer out of action until the boards are replaced.

Many experts recommend that you unplug your computer equipment, including your modem, during electrical storms. Unfortunately, there is not much you can do to increase the reliability of the local power system. However, the same UPS you use to provide a few minutes of power in the event of a power loss will also filter out power surges and spikes. As a low-cost alternative, you can plug your computer into an inexpensive device called a **surge strip** (also called a **surge suppressor** or **surge protector**) shown in Figure 9-3.

Figure 9-3

A surge strip is a small device that contains electrical outlets, so you can plug in your computer, monitor, and printer. It protects your equipment from electrical spikes and surges. It does not have a battery and cannot keep your computer running if the power goes off.

Hardware Failure

How reliable are the components of my computer system? The reliability of computer components is measured as **mean time between failures**, or **MTBF**. This measurement is somewhat misleading to most consumers. For example, you might read that your hard disk drive has an MTBF of 125,000 hours, which is about 14 years. Does this mean your hard drive will work for 125,000 hours before it fails? Unfortunately, the answer is no.

A 125,000 hour MTBF means that, *on average*, a hard disk drive like yours is likely to function for 125,000 hours without failing. The fact remains, however, that your hard disk drive might work for only 10 hours before it fails. With this in mind, you should plan for hardware failures, rather than hope they won't happen.

The effect of a hardware failure depends on the component that fails. Most hardware failures are simply an inconvenience. For example, if your monitor fails, you can obtain a replacement monitor, plug it in, and get back to work. If a RAM chip fails, you must obtain and install a replacement chip before you can boot your computer again. Even if your computer's microprocessor chip fails, it can easily be replaced. Unless you were in the middle of a long project that you had not saved, problems with the monitor, RAM chips, or processor would not cause any data loss.

On the other hand, a hard disk drive failure can be a disaster because you might lose all the data stored on the hard disk. The impact of a hard disk drive failure is considerably reduced if you have complete, up-to-date backup copies of the programs and data files on your hard disk.

Fires, Floods, and Other Disasters

Should I buy insurance for my computer? Computers are not immune to unexpected damage from smoke, fire, water, and breakage. However, it is not practical to barricade your computer from every potential disaster. Many insurance policies provide coverage for computers. Under the terms of many standard household and business policies, a computer is treated like any other appliance. You should make sure, however, that your insurance policy covers the full cost of purchasing a new computer at current market prices.

InfoWeb

Computer
Insurance
2

Replacing your damaged computer equipment will not replace your data. Some insurance companies provide extra coverage for the data on your computer. This coverage would provide you a sum of money to cover the time it takes to reload your data on a replacement computer. However, being able to reload your data assumes that you have a computer-readable backup copy of your data. Without a backup, much of your data cannot be reconstructed. For a business, the situation is even more critical. Customer accounts, inventory, daily transactions, and financial information are difficult, if not impossible, to reconstruct.

To summarize, a good insurance policy provides funds to replace computer equipment, but the only insurance for your data is an up-to-date backup copy on tape or disk.

QuickCheck A

1. Inadvertently deleting a file is an example of _____ error.

2. As a result of a power failure your computer will lose all the data stored in RAM and the hard disk. True or false? _____

3. A(n) _____ contains a battery that provides a continuous supply of power to your computer during a brief power failure.

4. A(n) _____ protects your computer from electrical spikes and surges, but it does not keep your computer operating if the power fails.

5. The circuitry on your computer circuit boards can be damaged by accidentally turning off your computer. True or false? _____

6. MTBF tells you how often an electronic device needs to be serviced. True or false? _____

7. The best insurance for your data is _____.

B Viruses, Vandalism, and Computer Crime

Computer data can be damaged, destroyed, or altered by vandals called **hackers**, **crackers**, or **cyberpunks**. The programs these hackers create are colorfully referred to by various sources as *malware*, *pest programs*, *vandalware*, or *punkware*. More typically, these programs are referred to as *viruses*. What would you do if you saw the message in Figure 9-4 on your computer screen?

Figure 9-4

A virus alert:
real or fake?

It is possible for a virus to migrate to a file other than the one to which it was originally attached.

Viruses can replicate themselves and spread to other programs on hard or floppy disks.

Viruses can destroy the contents of your hard disk.

The first hint that the message is a fake: Experts have not been able to confirm the existence of any viruses that damage hardware.

The prank becomes obvious: Printing out all your files, then erasing them from computer storage is *definitely not* the way to deal with a virus attack! If you see a message like this, ignore it.

```
Warning! A serious virus is on the loose. It is
disguised as a program called AVBKGD2, however, the
virus will remain on your system even after you have
erased this file. The virus does the following:
1.Copies itself to other programs on hard and floppy
  disks.
2.Randomly scrambles the contents of your data files.
3.Sends an electrical signal to your printer that
  causes it to short circuit.
This virus is not detectable using any anti-virus
software. The only safe way to protect yourself
against this virus is to print all your files, erase
all the disks on your system, and type in all your
data again.
```

Virus
Alert
3

The term *virus* technically refers to only one category of troublesome program. Additional categories include Trojan horses, time bombs, logic bombs, and worms. As you'll learn in this chapter, the programs in each of these categories behave differently when attacking a computer system.

Viruses, Trojan horses, time bombs, logic bombs, and worms lurk on disks and on the Internet waiting to destroy data and cause mischief to your computer system. Understanding how these programs work is the first line of defense against attacks.

Computer Viruses

Exactly what is a computer virus? A **computer virus** is a program that attaches itself to a file, reproduces, and spreads from one file to another. A virus can destroy data, display an irritating message, or otherwise disrupt computer operations. The jargon that describes a computer virus sounds similar to medical jargon. Your computer is a "host," and it can become "infected" with a virus. A virus can spread from one computer to another. You can "inoculate" your computer against many viruses. If your computer has not been inoculated and becomes infected, you can use anti-viral software to "disinfect" it.

A computer virus generally infects the executable files on your computer system, not the data files. When you run an infected program, your computer also runs the attached virus instructions to replicate or deliver its payload. The term **payload** refers to the ultimate mission of a virus. For example, the payload of the "Stoned" virus is the message, "Your PC is now stoned." Figure 9-5 illustrates how a computer virus spreads and delivers its payload.

Figure 9-5

How a computer
virus works

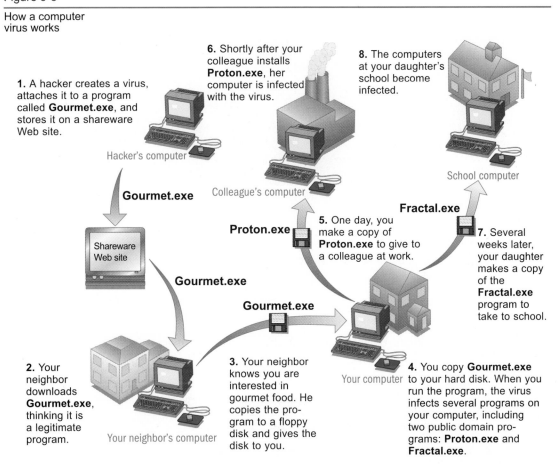

1. A hacker creates a virus, attaches it to a program called **Gourmet.exe**, and stores it on a shareware Web site.

Hacker's computer

6. Shortly after your colleague installs **Proton.exe**, her computer is infected with the virus.

8. The computers at your daughter's school become infected.

School computer

Gourmet.exe

Shareware Web site

Gourmet.exe

Colleague's computer

Proton.exe

5. One day, you make a copy of **Proton.exe** to give to a colleague at work.

Fractal.exe

7. Several weeks later, your daughter makes a copy of the **Fractal.exe** program to take to school.

Gourmet.exe

2. Your neighbor downloads **Gourmet.exe**, thinking it is a legitimate program.

Your neighbor's computer

3. Your neighbor knows you are interested in gourmet food. He copies the program to a floppy disk and gives the disk to you.

Your computer

4. You copy **Gourmet.exe** to your hard disk. When you run the program, the virus infects several programs on your computer, including two public domain programs: **Proton.exe** and **Fractal.exe**.

Most viruses attach themselves to executable files because these are the files that your computer runs. If a virus attaches to an executable file that you rarely use, it might not have an opportunity to spread and do much damage. On the other hand, **boot sector viruses**, which infect the system files your computer uses every time you turn it on, can cause widespread damage and persistent problems.

InfoWeb

Macro
Viruses
4

A **macro virus** infects documents such as those created with a word processor. Infected documents are stored with a list of instructions called a macro. A **macro** is essentially a miniature program that usually contains legitimate instructions to automate document production. However, a hacker can create a destructive macro, attach it to a document, and then distribute it over the Internet or on disk. When anyone views the document, the macro virus duplicates itself into the general macro pool where it is picked up by other documents. The two most common macro viruses are the Concept virus that attaches to Microsoft Word documents, and Laroux that attaches to Microsoft Excel spreadsheets.

Experts say there are over 2,000 viruses. However, 90 percent of virus damage is caused by fewer than 10 viruses. Of the top ten viruses, macro viruses account for about 75 percent of the virus attacks as shown in Figure 9-6.

Figure 9-6

Of the top ten viruses, macro viruses are the most prolific.

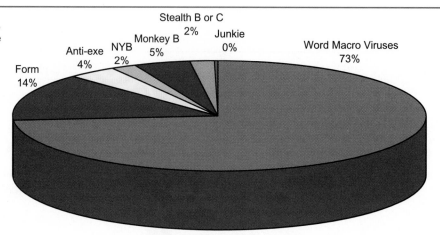

Data source: NCSA 1997 Virus Prevalence Survey

The symptoms of a virus infection depend on the virus. The following symptoms *might* indicate that your computer has contracted a virus. However, some of these symptoms can have other causes.

- Your computer displays annoying messages such as "Gotcha! Arf Arf," "You're stoned!," or "I want a cookie."

- Your computer develops unusual visual or sound effects. For example, characters begin to disappear from your screen or the sound of a flushing toilet comes from your computer's speaker.

- You have difficulty saving files or files mysteriously disappear.

- Your computer suddenly seems to work very slowly.

- Your computer reboots unexpectedly.

- Your executable files unaccountably increase in size.

Viruses are just one category of software designed by hackers to disrupt or damage the data on computers. After looking at other categories, you'll find out how to avoid and minimize the damage they cause.

A Modern Trojan Horse

How can I avoid being fooled by a Trojan horse? At the beginning of this chapter, you learned about the legendary Trojan horse. A modern **Trojan horse** is a computer program that appears to perform one function while actually doing something else. A Trojan horse might carry a virus that replicates itself once it reaches your computer system. Hackers also design Trojan horses that don't carry replicating viruses, but that do other damage. For example, suppose a hacker writes a program to format hard disks and embeds this program in a file called **Sched.exe.** The hacker then distributes disks containing this Trojan horse and posts it on the Internet where other users are likely to assume it is a free scheduling program. Users who download and run **Sched.exe** will discover that the program has erased all the files on their hard disk. This Trojan horse does not harbor a virus because it does not replicate itself. Figure 9-7 shows how this type of Trojan horse program works.

Figure 9-7

How a Trojan horse works

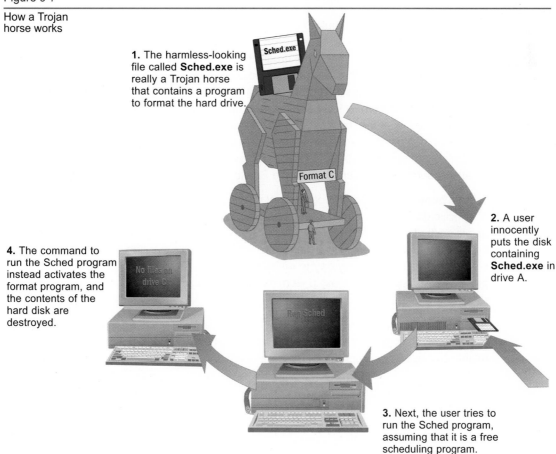

1. The harmless-looking file called **Sched.exe** is really a Trojan horse that contains a program to format the hard drive.

2. A user innocently puts the disk containing **Sched.exe** in drive A.

3. Next, the user tries to run the Sched program, assuming that it is a free scheduling program.

4. The command to run the Sched program instead activates the format program, and the contents of the hard disk are destroyed.

Another popular Trojan horse looks just like the login screen on a network. However, as a user logs in, the Trojan horse collects the user's ID and password. These are stored in a file that a hacker can access later. Armed with a valid user ID and password, the hacker can access the data stored on the network. As with the earlier example, this Trojan horse does not harbor a virus. The hacker's program, designed to defeat network security measures, does not replicate itself.

Time Bombs and Logic Bombs

Can a virus lurk in my computer system without my knowledge? Although a virus usually begins to replicate itself immediately when it enters your computer system, it will not necessarily deliver its payload right away. A virus or other unwelcome surprise can lurk in your computer system for days or months without discovery. A **time bomb** is a computer program that stays in your system undetected until it is triggered by a certain event in time, such as when the computer system clock reaches a certain date. A time bomb is usually carried by a virus or Trojan horse. For example, the Michelangelo virus contains a time bomb designed to damage files on your hard disk on March 6, the birthday of artist Michelangelo. The Olivia virus activates on April 10th and December 23rd, automatically opens the CD-ROM drive, and displays a message instructing the user to insert a music CD. After the CD begins, the virus overwrites the FAT on the hard disk and displays a message in Taiwanese. Many other time bomb attacks are keyed to dates such as Halloween, Friday the 13th, and April Fool's day.

InfoWeb

Year 2000
5

A surprising number of computers contain a time bomb that was unintentionally designed into software. The **year 2000 time bomb** refers to a problem with software that does not require a four-digit date field. The programmers who wrote this software decided that dates entered as 89 instead of 1989 would save disk space and processing time. As it turns out, this decision has the potential to cause havoc when the year 2000 arrives. Why? Suppose a person born in 1984 applies for a driver's license in 1999. The computer uses the last two digits of the dates, subtracts 84 from 99, and determines that the applicant is 15 years old. Now suppose the same person applies for a license in the year 2000. The computer subtracts 84 from 00 and gets -84 years old! Many banks and government organizations, such as the Internal Revenue Service are currently wrestling with this problem.

A **logic bomb** is a computer program that is triggered by the appearance or disappearance of specific data. For example, suppose a programmer in a large corporation believes that she is on the list of employees to be terminated during the next cost-cutting campaign. Her hostility overcomes her ethical judgment, and she creates a logic bomb program that checks the payroll file every day to make sure her employment status is still active. If the programmer's status changes to "terminated," her logic bomb activates a program that destroys data on the computer.

A time bomb or logic bomb might do mischief in your computer long before the timer goes off. If the bomb contains a virus, it could replicate and spread to other files. Meanwhile, you might send files from your computer to other computers, not knowing that they are infected.

Worms

Is a worm some type of virus?

InfoWeb

Internet
Worm
6

"At 2:28 a.m. a besieged Berkeley scientist—like a front-line soldier engulfed by the enemy—sent a bulletin around the nation: *We are currently under attack...* Thus began one of the most harrowing days of the computer age." This lead story in *The Wall Street Journal* reported the now famous Internet worm that spread to more than 6,000 Internet host computers. A software **worm** is a program designed to enter a computer system—usually a network—through security "holes." Like a virus, a worm reproduces itself. Unlike a virus, a worm does not need to be attached to a document or executable program to reproduce.

The software worm that attacked the Internet entered each computer through security holes in the electronic mail system, then used data stored on the computer to, in effect, mail itself to other computers. The worm spread rapidly, as shown in Figure 9-8.

The Internet worm was not designed to destroy data. Instead, it filled up storage space and dramatically slowed computer performance. The only way to eradicate the Internet worm was to shut down the electronic mail system on the Internet hosts, then comb through hundreds of programs to find and destroy the worm, a process that took up to eight hours for each host.

Figure 9-8

A worm attacks
the Internet.

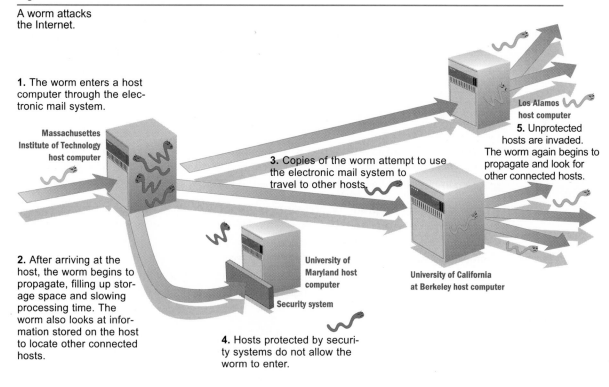

1. The worm enters a host computer through the electronic mail system.

Massachusettes
Institute of Technology
host computer

2. After arriving at the host, the worm begins to propagate, filling up storage space and slowing processing time. The worm also looks at information stored on the host to locate other connected hosts.

3. Copies of the worm attempt to use the electronic mail system to travel to other hosts.

University of
Maryland host
computer

Security system

4. Hosts protected by security systems do not allow the worm to enter.

University of California
at Berkeley host computer

Los Alamos
host computer

5. Unprotected hosts are invaded. The worm again begins to propagate and look for other connected hosts.

Avoidance and Detection

Can I protect my computer from viruses and other types of attacks? Computer viruses and other types of malicious software typically lurk on disks containing shareware or pirated software, in files downloaded from the Internet, and in e-mail attachments. A virus cannot, however, hitch a ride in a plain e-mail message. The graph in Figure 9-9 illustrates the sources of most infected files.

Figure 9-9

Sources of infected files

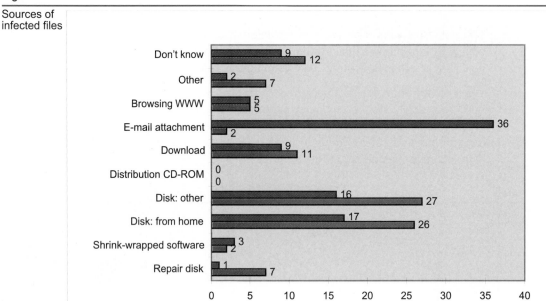

Data source: NCSA 1997 Virus Prevalence Survey

You can generally avoid a computer virus if you do not use files from high-risk sources. If you need to use a disk that you suspect might be infected, you can use a virus detection program to check for infection before you use the files.

A **virus detection program**, or **anti-virus program**, examines the files stored on a disk to determine if they are infected with a virus, then disinfects the disk, if necessary. Virus detection programs use several techniques to find viruses. As you know, a virus attaches itself to an existing program. This often increases the length of the original program. The earliest virus detection software simply examined the programs on a computer and recorded their length. A change in the length of a program from one computing session to the next indicated the possible presence of a virus.

In response to early virus detection programs, hackers became more cunning. They created viruses that insert themselves into unused portions of a program file but do not change its length. Of course, the people who designed virus detection programs fought back. They designed programs that examine the bytes in an uninfected application program and calculate a checksum. A **checksum** is a value that is calculated by combining all the bytes in a file. Each time you run the application program, the virus detection program recalculates the checksum and compares it to the original. If any byte in the application program has been changed, the checksum will be different, and the virus detection program assumes that a virus is present. The checksum approach requires that you start with a copy of the program that is not infected with a virus. If you start with an infected copy, the virus is included in the original checksum, and the virus detection program never detects it.

Another technique used by virus detection programs is to search for a signature. A **virus signature** is a unique series of bytes that can be used to identify a known virus, much as a fingerprint is used to identify an individual. A signature is usually a section of the virus program, such as a unique series of instructions. Most of today's virus detection software scans for virus signatures; for this reason, virus detection software is sometimes referred to as a "scanner."

The signature search technique is fairly quick, but it can identify only those viruses with a known signature. To detect new viruses—and new viruses seem to appear every week—you must obtain regular updates for your virus detection program that include new virus signatures.

Some viruses are specifically designed to avoid detection by one or more of these virus detection methods. For this reason, the most sophisticated virus protection schemes combine elements from each of these methods.

A common misconception is that write protecting your disks prevents virus infection. Although a virus cannot jump onto your disk when it is write protected, you have to remove the write protection each time you save a file on the disk. With the write protection removed, your disk is open to virus attack.

What to Do If You Detect a Computer Virus

What should I do if my computer gets a virus? If you detect a virus on your computer system, you should immediately take steps to stop the virus from spreading. If you are connected to a network, alert the network administrator that you found a virus on your workstation. The network administrator can then take action to prevent the virus from spreading throughout the network.

If you are using your own computer system and you detect a virus, you should remove it to prevent any further damage. There are two methods for removing a virus. First, you can attempt to restore the infected program to its original condition by deleting the virus with the disinfect function of virus detection software. However, depending on how the virus attached itself to the program, it might not be possible to remove the virus without destroying the program. If the virus cannot be removed successfully, you must use the second method: erase the infected program, test the system again to make sure the virus has been eliminated, then reinstall the program from the original disks. In cases where the virus has infected most of the programs on the system, it's often best to make a backup of your data files (which are unlikely to have been infected), reformat the hard disk, and install all the programs again from the original disks or CD-ROM.

If your computer is attacked by a macro virus, you might have to manually extract the macros from each infected document. You'll find information on combating macro viruses at Microsoft's Web site and in recent editions of computer magazines.

When your computer contracts a virus, you must check and, if necessary, remove the virus from every floppy disk and backup used on your computer system. If you don't remove every copy of the virus, your system will become infected again the next time you use an infected disk or restore data from an infected backup. You should also alert your colleagues, and anyone with whom you shared disks, that a virus might have traveled on those disks and infected their computer systems.

Computer Crime

Is it a crime to spread a computer virus?   The accounting firm Ernst & Young estimates that computer crime costs individuals and organizations in the United States between $3 billion and $5 billion a year. "Old-fashioned" crimes that take a high-tech twist because they involve a computer are often prosecuted using traditional laws. For example, a person who attempts to destroy computer data by setting fire to a computer might be prosecuted under traditional arson laws.

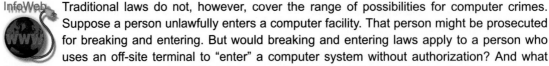
InfoWeb

Computer
Crime
7

Traditional laws do not, however, cover the range of possibilities for computer crimes. Suppose a person unlawfully enters a computer facility. That person might be prosecuted for breaking and entering. But would breaking and entering laws apply to a person who uses an off-site terminal to "enter" a computer system without authorization? And what about the situation in which a person steals a file by copying it without authorization? Is the file really "stolen" if the original remains on the computer?

Most U.S. states have computer crime laws that specifically define computer data and software as personal property. These laws also define as a crime the unauthorized access, use, modification, or disabling of a computer system or data.

In early 1995, cybersleuth Tsutomu Shimomura tracked down a hacker who broke into dozens of corporate, university, government, and personal computers. Before his arrest, the hacker stole thousands of data files and more than 20,000 credit card numbers. "He was clearly the most wanted computer hacker in the world," commented assistant U.S. attorney Kent Walker. The hacker's unauthorized access and use of computer data are explicitly defined as criminal acts by computer crime laws.

Under most U.S. state laws, intentionally circulating a destructive virus is a crime. Study the excerpt from a typical computer crime law in Figure 9-10 to see what is specifically defined as illegal.

Figure 9-10

Excerpt
from a state
computer
crime law

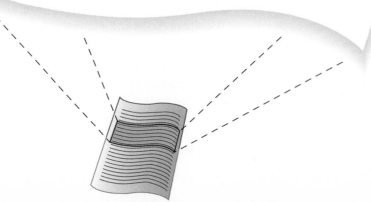

No person shall intentionally access any computer system or computer network for the purpose of devising or executing any scheme or artifice; to defraud, or extort, or obtain money, property, or services with false or fraudulent intent, representations, or promises; or to maliciously access, alter, delete, damage, or destroy any computer system, computer network, computer program, or computer data.

In the U.S., State authorities have jurisdiction over computer crimes committed in one state, but crimes that occur in more than one state or across state boundaries are under federal jurisdiction. The Computer Fraud and Abuse Act of 1986 makes it a federal crime to access a computer across state lines for fraudulent purposes. This act also specifically outlaws the sale of entry pass codes, passwords, and access codes that belong to others.

In a well-publicized espionage case, dramatized in a documentary called *Computers, the KGB, and Me*, hackers used an unclassified military network and the Internet to piece together details on current military research in the United States, which they then sold to the KGB. The hackers, based in Germany, used stolen passwords and telephone access codes to set up communications links from Europe to Virginia, and on to California. The communications crossed state lines, so under the Computer Fraud and Abuse Act the case was placed under federal jurisdiction. With FBI assistance, the case was ultimately cracked by Cliff Stoll, a computer operator of an Internet host computer at the Lawrence Berkeley Laboratory in California.

Laws are made to deter criminals, bring them to trial if they are caught, and punish them if they are convicted. But laws don't actually protect your data. That is something you need to do by making frequent backup copies and taking steps to prevent unauthorized access to data.

QuickCheck B

1. A(n) _____ is a program that reproduces itself when the computer executes the file to which it is attached.

2. A(n) _____ virus attaches itself to documents, rather than to an executable file.

3. A(n) _____ is a software container that might contain a virus or time bomb.

4. A(n) _____ is a program that reproduces itself without being attached to an executable file.

5. Suppose that your computer displays a weird message every time you type in the word "digital." You might suspect that your computer has contracted a(n) _____.

6. Three sources of files that should be considered a high risk virus infection are , disks brought from home, downloads, and _____.

7. Many virus detection programs identify viruses by looking for a unique series of bytes called a(n) _____.

8. Computer crime laws define computer software and _____ as personal property.

C Data Security and Risk Management

Data security is the collection of techniques that provide protection for data. Sometimes computer users cite Jeff Richards' Laws of Data Security as tongue-in-cheek advice on how to attain foolproof security:

1. Don't buy a computer.
2. If you buy a computer, don't turn it on.

InfoWeb

Risks
8

Richards' Laws emphasize the point that it is not practical to totally protect computer data from theft, viruses, and natural disasters. In most situations, providing total security is too time-consuming, too expensive, or too complex. For example, if you are using your computer primarily for word processing, it is too time-consuming to make daily backups, too expensive to keep your data in a fire-proof vault, and too complex to implement password security. On the other hand, if you take no precautions, one day you will be sorry.

In the context of computers, **risk management** is the process of weighing threats to computer data against the amount of data that is expendable and the cost of protecting crucial data. The steps in risk management are listed in Figure 9-11.

Figure 9-11

Planning a risk
management strategy

1. Determine the likely threats to computer data. In the case of individual computer users, the major threats are hardware failure, operator error, and data vandalism.

2. Assess the amount of data that is expendable. For this assessment you must ask yourself how much data you would *have* to re-enter if your hard drive was erased and how much of your data would be forever lost because it could not be reconstructed.

3. Determine the cost of protecting all of your data versus protecting some of your data. Costs include time as well as money.

4. Select the protective measures that are affordable, effective against the identified threats, and easy to implement.

Data security techniques evolve quickly to meet the challenges offered by new technology and by clever hackers. You'll notice that many of these techniques apply to organizations. This information is also important for you as an individual for three reasons. First, it is likely that you will work with computers within an organization as part of your career, so you will share the responsibility with your coworkers for that organization's data. Second, many organizations maintain data about you such as your credit rating, educational record, and health records. You have a vested interest in the accuracy and the confidentiality of this data. Finally, you currently have data stored on disks that might be time-consuming to reconstruct. You should consider using two of the techniques discussed in this section—backup and virus detection—to secure your own data.

Establish Policies and Procedures

How can an organization educate its employees on the rules for acceptable computer use?

In a computing environment, **policies** are the rules and regulations that specify how a computer system should be used. Policies are most often determined by management and used by large organizations to stipulate who can access computer data. Policies also help an organization define appropriate uses for its computers and data.

InfoWeb

Acceptable
Use
9

For example, an organization might have a policy that provides e-mail accounts, but does not guarantee the privacy of e-mail messages, especially if there is reason to believe that those messages might be used for illegal or unethical transmission of data. Many employers have specific policies prohibiting software piracy and limiting the use of company computers to company business.

The advantages of policies are that they define how a computer system should be used, make users aware of limits and penalties, and provide a framework for legal or job action for individuals who do not follow policies. Policies are an inexpensive building block in the overall structure of data security. Policies do not require any special hardware or software. The cost of policies is the time it takes to compose, update, and publicize them. The disadvantage of policies for data security is that some users disregard policies.

Policies do not typically prevent operator errors that lead to lost or corrupted data. However, many mistakes can be prevented. Successful computer users develop habits that significantly reduce their chances of making mistakes. These habits, when formalized and adopted by an organization, are referred to as **procedures**. Procedures, such as those listed in Figure 9-12 can help you avoid lost or corrupted data.

Figure 9-12

Following procedures can help you avoid lost or corrupted data.	Save your files frequently as you work so you don't lose too much data if the power fails.
	When you format a disk, always view a directory of its contents first to make sure the disk in the drive is the one you want to format.
	Use virus detection software immediately to scan any files that you have downloaded from a commercial information service or the Internet.
	When entering long columns of data, check off each number as it is entered.

By now you might have already figured out how policies and procedures differ. Policies are rules and regulations that apply to computer use in a general way. Procedures describe steps or activities that are performed in conjunction with a specific task. Because procedures are more specific, they generally take longer to write than policies, making them somewhat more costly for an organization to create and document.

The major advantage of procedures is reducing operator error. However, procedures have two disadvantages. First, they must be kept up to date as equipment and software change. Second, there is no way to make sure that people follow them.

Restrict Physical Access to the Computer System

If it is so easy for hackers to access data from networked computers or terminals, or over phone lines, is there any point to keeping computers locked up? In 1970, during the Vietnam War, anti-war activists bombed the Army Mathematics Research Center at the University of Wisconsin. A graduate student was killed, the building was damaged, and the computer, along with 20 years of accumulated research data, was destroyed (Figure 9-13).

One of the best ways to prevent people from damaging equipment is to restrict physical access to the computer system. If potential criminals cannot get to a computer or a terminal, stealing or damaging data becomes more difficult. Here are some ways to physically protect computer equipment and data:

- Restrict access to the area surrounding the computer to prevent physical damage to the equipment.

- Keep floppy disks and data backups in a locked vault to prevent theft and to protect against fire or water damage.

- Keep offices containing computers locked to prevent theft and to deter unauthorized users.

- Lock the computer case to prevent theft of components such as RAM and processors.

Figure 9-13

In 1970, anti-war activists bombed the Army Mathematics Research Center at the University of Wisconsin.

Restricting physical access to computers has disadvantages. Locks and other screening measures can make it more difficult for authorized users to access the computer system. Also, restricting physical access will not prevent a determined criminal from stealing data. Access from a remote location is more difficult, but it might not be impossible. Finally, although restricting access might deter intentional acts of destruction, it will not prevent accidents.

Restrict Online Access to Data

Can people be prevented from accessing data so they can't steal it or tamper with it?

Obviously everyone should not have access to the data stored in military computers, banks, or businesses. And yet, the communications infrastructure makes it technically possible for anyone with an Internet connection to interact with these systems. In today's web of interlaced computer technologies, it has become critical to restrict data access to authorized users. The question is, how do you identify authorized users, especially those who are logging in from remote sites thousands of miles away?

There are three methods of personal identification: something a person carries, something a person knows, or some unique physical trait. Any one of these methods has the potential to positively identify a person, and each has a unique set of advantages and disadvantages.

An identity badge featuring a photo and, perhaps a fingerprint or bar code, is still a popular form of personal identification in hospitals and government agencies. Designers have created high-tech identity card readers, like the one in Figure 9-14, that can be used from any off-site PC.

Figure 9-14

A disk-shaped carrier allows a floppy disk drive to read an identity card.

Because an identity badge can be easily lost, stolen, or duplicated, it works best on-site where a security guard checks the face on the badge with the face of the person wearing the badge. Without visual verification, the use of identity badges from a remote site is not secure, unless combined with a password or PIN (personal identification number).

The most common way to restrict access to a computer system is with user IDs and passwords. These fall into the "something you know" category of personal identification. When you work on a multiuser system or network, you generally must have a user ID and password. Data security on a computer system that is guarded by user IDs and passwords depends on password secrecy. If users give out their passwords, choose obvious passwords, or write them down in obvious places, hackers can break in.

How easy is it, really, to discover someone's password? It is easier to find a password written on the bottom of a keyboard than to try to guess it from nicknames and birthdates as they always do in the movies. There is also the brute force method of trying every word in an electronic dictionary, but the success of the method decreases if a password is based on two words, a word and number, or a nonsense word that does not appear in a dictionary. Figure 9-15 shows how the composition of passwords affects the chance of unauthorized access.

Figure 9-15

How password length and composition affect the chances of unauthorized access

Password Strategy	Example	Number of Possibilities	Average Time to Discover
Any short or long name	Ed, Christine	2,000 (a name dictionary)	5 hours
Any short or long word	It, electrocardiogram	60,000 (in a spell checker)	7 days
Two words together	Whiteknight	3,600,000,000	1,140 years
Mix of initials and numbers	JP2C2TP307	3,700,000,000,000,000	1,200,000,000 years
First line of a poem	Onceuponamidnightdreary	10,000,000,000,000,000, 000,000,000,000	3,000,000,000,000,000, 000,000 years

InfoWeb

Biometrics 10

A third method of personal identification called **biometrics** bases identification on some unique physical characteristic, such as a fingerprint or the pattern of blood vessels in the retina of the eye. Unlike passwords, biometric data can't be forgotten, lost, or borrowed. Once the technological fiction of spy thrillers such as *Goldfinger* and *Man from U.N.C.L.E*, biometric devices are today becoming affordable technologies that could be built into personal computer systems. Biometric technologies include hand-geometry scanners, voice recognition, face recognition, and fingerprint scanners (Figure 9-16).

Figure 9-16

Fingerprint scanners cost less than $500 and can confirm your identity in less than two seconds, even from a pool of thousands of employees.

User Rights: A Second Line of Defense

What if a hacker slips past the security screening? One way to limit the amount of damage from a break-in is to assign user rights. **User rights** are rules that limit the directories and files that each user can access. When you receive an account on a computer system, the system administrator gives you rights that allow you to access only particular directories and files. For example, in your computer lab, you might have only read rights to the directories that contain software. This would prevent you from deleting or changing the programs on lab computers. Most networks and host computers allow the system administrator to assign user rights such as those in Figure 9-17.

Figure 9-17

User rights

Rights	Description
Erase rights	Allow you to erase files
Create rights	Allow you to create new files
Write rights	Allow you to save information in existing files
Read rights	Allow you to open files and read information
File find rights	Allow you to list files with a directory command

Granting users only the rights they need helps prevent both accidental and deliberate damage to data. If users are granted limited rights, a hacker who steals someone's password has only those rights granted to the person from whom the password was stolen.

Hackers occasionally gain unauthorized access to computer systems through something called a trap door. A **trap door** is a special set of instructions that allows a user to bypass the normal security precautions and enter the system. Trap doors are often created during development and testing; they should be removed before the system becomes operational.

InfoWeb

War Games 11

In the 1983 film *WarGames*, a trap door was the key to preventing widespread nuclear destruction. A young hacker breaks into a secret military computer that has been programmed to deal with enemy nuclear attacks. The hacker begins to play what he thinks is a detailed computer game. The computer, however, thinks it is an actual attack. Soon the computer passes the stage at which it can be stopped from launching nuclear missiles, except by a trap door designed by the reclusive programmer who created the original program. The trap door provides a way for the programmer to bypass official military channels and access the computer's fail-safe program. A special password is required to enter the trap door, and in the exciting climax of the film, the hacker races against time to get the password and gain access to the computer deep within the military installation in Cheyenne Mountain. In this fictional example, a trap door helped save the world. In general, however, if a trap door is not removed, it becomes a possible means of entry for any hacker who discovers it.

Encrypt Data

Is there any way to prevent criminals from using stolen data? When an unauthorized person reads data, the data is no longer confidential. Although password protection and physical security measures are taken to limit access to computer data, hackers and criminals still manage to access data.

Encryption is the process of scrambling or hiding information so it cannot be understood until it is decrypted, or deciphered, to change it back to its original form. Encryption provides a last line of defense against the unauthorized use of data. If data is encrypted, unauthorized users obtain only scrambled gibberish instead of meaningful information. Edgar Allan Poe, the American writer famous for his tales of horror, was quite interested in secret codes. He was convinced that it was impossible to design an unbreakable method of encryption. You might be familiar with simple encryption and decryption techniques, such as the one shown in Figure 9-18.

InfoWeb

Encryption
12

Figure 9-18

Encryption
by simple
substitution

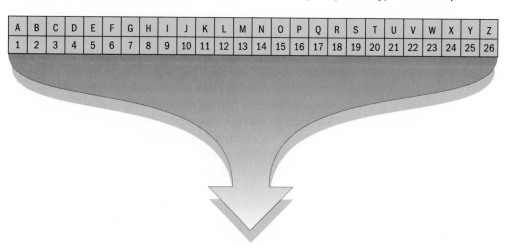

17 21 15 20 8 20 8 5 18 1 22 5 14 14 5 22 5 18 13 15 18 5

1. This is a message encrypted using a simple substitution technique in which the number of each letter's position in the alphabet represents the letter.

2. The key to this encryption looks like this. The 17 in the encrypted message is the "Q," the 21 is the letter "U," and so forth. This is a very simple encryption technique.

A	B	C	D	E	F	G	H	I	J	K	L	M	N	O	P	Q	R	S	T	U	V	W	X	Y	Z
1	2	3	4	5	6	7	8	9	10	11	12	13	14	15	16	17	18	19	20	21	22	23	24	25	26

Quoth the Raven "Nevermore"

3. Once you know the key, you can then decipher the message to see that it is the famous quote from Edgar Allan Poe's poem "The Raven."

Important data such as credit card accounts, bank records, and medical information should be stored in encrypted format to foil hackers who break into computers. In addition, when this sort of data is transmitted over the Internet, it should also be encrypted.

When a computer encrypts data for storage, the program that encrypts the data also decrypts it. The encryption method or key needs only to be known by the encrypting computer. Encrypting transmitted data presents a different problem because the sender's computer that encrypts the data is not the same computer that decrypts the data on the recipients end of the transmission. Somehow, transmitted data must use an encryption key that is shared by everyone, but that cannot be decrypted by everyone. Impossible as it might seem, such an encryption method exists.

Public key encryption (PKE) is an encryption method that uses a pair of keys, a public key known to everyone and a private key known only to the message recipient. The public key encrypts a message. The private key decrypts a message. Suppose you want to send an encrypted message to CitiBank. You would use the CitiBank public key to encrypt the message. Once a message is encrypted, no one can use the public key to decrypt it. To decrypt the message, Citibank uses its private key. Because CitiBank does not publish its private key, no one else can decrypt it. Figure 9-19 explains more about public key encryption.

Figure 9-19

Public key encryption

Software is available to encrypt data on micro, mini, and mainframe computers. The cost of this software varies with its sophistication. Regardless of its cost, encryption software is virtually a necessity for some businesses—such as financial institutions that transmit and store funds electronically. Several public key encryption systems are currently available, including the popular and easy-to-use **Pretty Good Privacy** (PGP).

Install and Use Virus Detection Software

How effective is virus detection software? Virus detection software is an important weapon in your security arsenal, but it is not 100 percent reliable. It might fail to detect viruses without a known signature, **polymorphic viruses** that change after they infect your computer, and viruses that use **stealth technology** to hide from virus detection programs. Virus detection software generally does not detect Trojan horses unless they carry a virus. When virus detection software does not detect a virus in an infected computer, it is called a "false negative report." Sometimes virus detection software tells you that your computer is infected, but a virus is *not* actually present. This is a "false positive report." False negative and false positive reports are infrequent. Virus detection software generally succeeds in detecting and eradicating most widespread viruses, so you should include it in your software collection.

InfoWeb

Antivirus
Software
13

There are many virus detection programs, produced by different software publishers. You can purchase these programs from your local computer dealer, by mail order, or you can download a trial version from the Web. The cost of a virus detection program for microcomputers is generally less than $100.

Virus detection software can both detect viruses and eradicate them. But this software works only if you use it. You should run your virus detection program periodically to check if any viruses have found their way into your computer system. If viruses are a recurring problem in your computing environment, you might want to configure your virus detection software to continually monitor the behavior of your computer files and alert you if it spots signs of virus-like activity.

There is no "magic pill" that will protect your computer from hackers, crackers, and cyberpunks. However, you can reduce the risk of infection if you follow the checklist in Figure 9-20.

Figure 9-20

Reduce the risk of infection

Install and use virus detection software.
Keep your virus detection software up to date.
Make frequent backups *after* you use virus detection software to scan your files for viruses.
Download software only from virus free sources. Use a virus detection program to scan downloaded software before you use it.
Exercise care with disks that contain shareware or pirated software. Scan them before you run or copy any of the files they contain.

Internet Security

Should I have special security concerns when I'm using the Internet? When you download a file from the Internet, you can use virus detection software to make sure the file is virus free before you run it. But some Web sites automatically send a program to your computer and run it before you have a chance to check it for viruses. Can you just trust that this program is harmless? Unfortunately, the answer to this question is "no." While you're connected to the Internet, you could be unaware of a program that is reformatting your hard drive, getting ready to shut down your computer, making your browser hang, or scanning your hard disk for your IP address, user ID, and password. Many security problems on the Internet are the result of two technologies: Java applets and ActiveX controls.

Internet
Security
14

Java applets are small programs that are intended to add processing and interactive capabilities to Web pages. For example, a Java applet might total the cost of the merchandise you are purchasing online. When you access a Web page containing a Java applet, it is downloaded automatically to your computer, and executed in a supposedly secure area of your computer known as a **sandbox**. In theory, the sandbox limits Java applets from running amok and damaging files in your computer's regular RAM and disk areas. However, some hackers have been able to breach sandbox security and create hostile Java applets that damage or steal data.

ActiveX controls provide another way to add processing capabilities and interaction to Web pages. Programs that use ActiveX controls are downloaded automatically to your computer. Unlike Java applets, ActiveX controls are not limited by a sandbox, so they have full access to your entire computer system. It is possible for hackers to use ActiveX controls to cause havoc. A partial solution to this problem is the use of a **digital certificate** that identifies the author of an ActiveX control. A programmer in effect "signs" a program by attaching his or her digital certificate. Theoretically, a programmer would not sign a hostile program, so all programs with a digital certificate should be "safe." Your browser will warn you about programs that do not have a digital certificate so you can decide whether or not to accept them, as shown in Figure 9-21.

Figure 9-21

Your browser will warn you before it accepts an unsigned Java applet or ActiveX control.

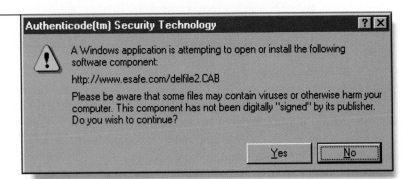

The only way to entirely avoid dangerous Java applets and ActiveX controls is to tell your browser not to accept any of them. However, many Web pages include legitimate applets and controls. If your browser doesn't accept them, you might miss some valuable features and interactions. As an alternative, you could consider installing **personal firewall software** that protects your computer from hostile Java applets and ActiveX controls.

Secure e-Commerce

Is it safe to use the Internet for shopping and banking? The increasing popularity of on-line shopping has created some nervousness about the security of on-line transactions. Publicity about intercepted credit card numbers and high-tech crimes make most consumers think twice before providing credit card numbers or other personal information over the Internet. The security of an Internet transaction is about the same as when you purchase merchandise by mail or by phone. However, as with mail and phone transactions, current Internet security technology does not guarantee a secure transaction. Therefore, caution is justified.

Want to purchase sunglasses from www.niemanmarcus.com? Before you send your credit card number over the Internet, make sure the Neiman Marcus Web server encrypts your transmission with a security protocol such as SSL or S-HTTP. **SSL**, short for **Secure Sockets Layer**, uses encryption to establish a secure connection between your computer and a Web server. When you use an SSL page, the URL will begin with https: instead of http:, and you will generally receive a message that transactions are secured. **S-HTTP** (**Secure HTTP**) also encrypts data sent between your computer and a Web server, but does so one message at a time rather than by setting up an entire secure connection.

Encrypted transactions ensure that your credit card number cannot be intercepted as it travels from your computer, through Internet routers, and to a Web server. As shown in Figure 9-22 your browser shows you if you are using a secure transaction.

Figure 9-22

During secure transactions, Internet Explorer displays a lock icon and Netscape Navigator displays a key icon.

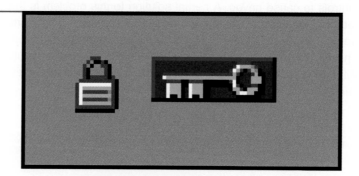

Some Web sites keep track of your visits. These sites use a "cookie" to remember the date of your last visit, your e-mail address, your last purchase, and the links you followed at the site. A **cookie** is a message sent from a Web server to your browser and stored on your hard disk. When you use a Web site that distributes cookies, it collects information such as your name, e-mail address, and the pages you visit. This information is incorporated into the cookie that the Web server stores on to your computer. The next time you connect to that Web site, your browser sends the cookie to the Web server.

Cookies are usually harmless, but some Web sites might ask for information that you would not want to make public. Try to use good sense when responding to requests for personal information. Supply information about your address, credit cards, bank accounts, and social security number only to sources that you're certain are reputable and that use adequate security measures to protect personal data—that includes encrypting the data stored in cookies. Even though the cookies are on your computer, they can be accessed by other cookie-like programs from disreputable sources.

Provide Redundancy

Can anything be done to minimize the damage from accidents? Accidents can destroy data and equipment. The result is **downtime**, computer jargon for the time a computer system is not functioning. The most dependable way to minimize downtime is to duplicate data and equipment. You will learn about duplicating data in the *User Focus* section of this chapter. Duplicating equipment simply means maintaining equipment that duplicates the functions critical to computing activities. This is sometimes referred to as **hardware redundancy**.

Hardware redundancy reduces an organization's dependency on outside repair technicians. If it maintains a stock of duplicate parts, an organization can swap parts and be up and running before the manufacturer's repair technician arrives. Duplicate parts are expensive, however, and these costs must be weighed against lost revenue or productivity while repairs are underway. Figure 9-23 shows some of the equipment that can be used to provide hardware redundancy.

Figure 9-23

Hardware redundancy

 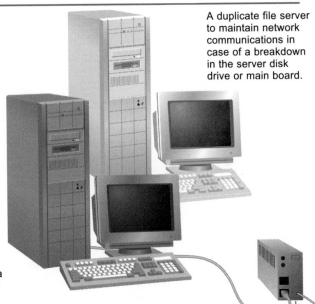

An extra printer in case the main printer breaks down.

A duplicate file server to maintain network communications in case of a breakdown in the server disk drive or main board.

RAID storage to keep copies of data on several platters in case one platter is damaged.

A UPS or generator to provide electricity in case of a power failure.

Make Backups

If I implement only one security measure, should it be a backup? A **backup** is a duplicate copy of a file or the contents of a disk drive. If the original file is lost or damaged, you can use the backup copy to restore the data to its original working condition. Back-up probably provides the best all-round security for your data. It protects your data from hardware failures, vandalism, operator error, and natural disasters, as long as you do the following:

- Make frequent backups. You can't restore data that you haven't backed up; so if you wait a month between backups, you could lose a month's worth of data.

- Scan for viruses before you backup. If your computer is infected with a virus when you back up, your backup will also be infected.

- Store your backup away from your computer. If your backup is next to your computer, a fire or flood could also damage your backup.

- Test your backup. Before you depend on your backups, make sure that you can restore data from your backup to your hard disk. You would not want to discover that your back-up files were blank because you didn't correctly carry out the backup procedure.

The major disadvantage of backups is user forgetfulness and procrastination. You will learn more about backups in the next section of this chapter.

QuickCheck C

1. _____ is the process of weighing threats to computer data against the amount of data that is expendable and the cost of protecting crucial data.

2. A(n) _____ is a rule designed to prohibit employees from installing software that has not been pre-approved by the information systems department.

3. Procedures help reduce human errors that can erase or damage data.
True or false? _____

4. If a network administrator assigns _____, users can access only certain programs and files.

5. Hackers sometimes gain unauthorized entry to computer systems through a(n) _____ that is not removed when development and testing are complete.

6. A(n) _____ is a digital message that a Web server uses to store information about your visits to its Web site.

7. _____ is computer jargon that refers to the time a computer system is not functioning.

8. If your virus detection software tells you that your computer is infected when it really is not, the software has given you a false _____ report.

D Backup

LAB

Data
Backup

Losing all your data is one of the most distressing computing experiences. It might be the result of a hardware failure or a virus. Whatever the cause, most users experience only a moment of surprise and disbelief before reaching the depressing realization that they might have to recreate all their data and reinstall all their programs (Figure 9-24). A backup can pull you through such trying times, making the data loss a minor inconvenience, rather than a major disaster.

Figure 9-24

A hard drive failure might happen at any time.

Industry experts recommend that all computer users make backups. Sounds simple, right? Unfortunately, this advice tells you what to do, not how to do it. It fails to address some key questions: How often should I make a backup?, What should I back up?, and What should I do with the backups? To keep your data safe, you need a data backup plan, one tailored to your computing needs. To devise your data backup plan, you should consider factors such as the value of your data, the amount of data stored on your computer, the frequency with which your data changes, and the type of backup equipment you have. As these factors change, you need to revise your plan. For example, the backup plan you use while in college is likely to change as you pursue your career. In this section of the chapter you will learn about the advantages and disadvantages of various backup tools and techniques, so you can select those appropriate for your own data backup plan.

Backup Equipment

Does my computer need a tape drive so I can make backups? Tape backups are the most popular microcomputer backup solution for small businesses, and they are gaining popularity with individuals as the price of tape drives decreases. When you make a tape backup, data from the hard disk is copied to a magnetic tape. If the data on the hard disk is lost, the backup data is restored by copying it from the tape to a functional hard disk drive. Tape backup requires tapes and a tape drive, costing less than $300. However, you can back up your data without a tape drive.

Many microcomputer users back up their data onto floppy disks. This method is unrealistic for backing up the entire contents of today's high-capacity disk drives—a drive with a 4 GB capacity would require at least 2,800 floppy disks for a complete backup! However, backing up every file is not necessary. Many users back up only those directories that contain data files. In the event of a hard disk failure, these users would need to reinstall all their software from original disks or CD-ROMs, then copy their data files from the backups (Figure 9-25).

Figure 9-25

You can backup selected files, instead of backing up an entire disk.

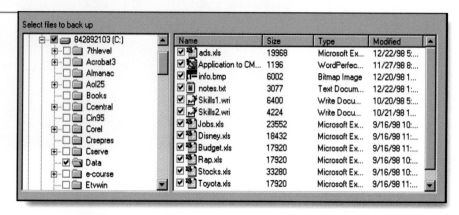

If you use the computers in a college computer lab, your situation is somewhat unique because you might store your data on a floppy disk instead of the hard disk. An effective way to back up if you're in this situation is to make a copy of your disk using the Copy Disk utility, described in the next subsection, "Backup Software."

Usually, backups are stored on magnetic media such as disk or tape. However, you can also use a printout of your data for backup purposes. To restore the data from a printout, you can use a scanner or you can retype it. With either restoration method, you can easily introduce errors, so paper backups should be considered only as a last resort.

Backup Software

Do I need special software to make backups? A backup is essentially a copy of data. You must use software to tell the computer what to copy. There are three types of software you might use: backup software, a copy utility, or a disk copy program.

Backup software is designed to manage hard disk backup to tapes or disks. When you use backup software you can select the files you want to back up. Most operating systems include backup software. However, if your tape drive requires special proprietary backup software, you should use it. Most backup software offers automated features that allow you to schedule automatic backups and back up only those files that have changed since the last backup.

A **copy utility** is a program that copies one or more files. You can use a copy utility to copy files between a hard disk and a floppy disk, between two floppy disks of any size, from a CD-ROM to a hard disk, or from a CD-ROM to a floppy disk. A copy utility is usually included with a computer operating system.

The **Copy Disk** utility is a program that duplicates the contents of an entire floppy disk. You can use a Copy Disk utility only to copy all the files from one floppy disk to another floppy disk of the same size. You cannot use the Copy Disk utility for files on a hard disk drive. Figure 9-26 shows how to duplicate a floppy disk.

Figure 9-26

Using Copy Disk to back up a floppy

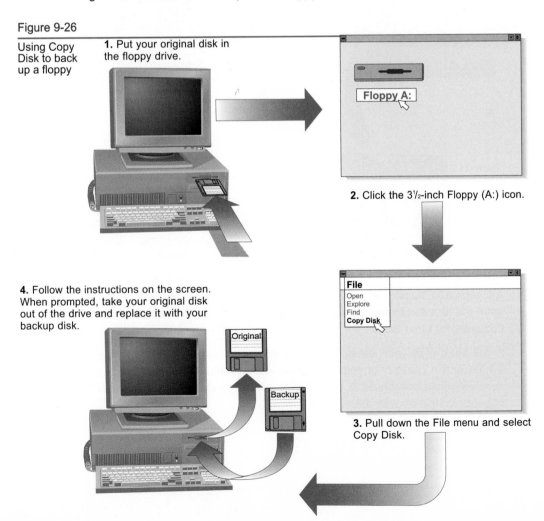

1. Put your original disk in the floppy drive.

2. Click the 3½-inch Floppy (A:) icon.

3. Pull down the File menu and select Copy Disk.

4. Follow the instructions on the screen. When prompted, take your original disk out of the drive and replace it with your backup disk.

Types of Backups

Should I back up everything on my disk? A **full backup** is a copy of all the files on a disk. A full backup is very safe because it ensures that you have a copy of every file on the disk—every program and every data file. Because a full backup includes a copy of every file on a disk, it can take a long time to complete. While the backup is in progress, the computer cannot generally be used for other tasks. Some users consider it worth the time because this type of backup is easy to restore. You simply have the computer copy the files from your backup to the hard disk, as shown in Figure 9-27.

Figure 9-27

Full backup

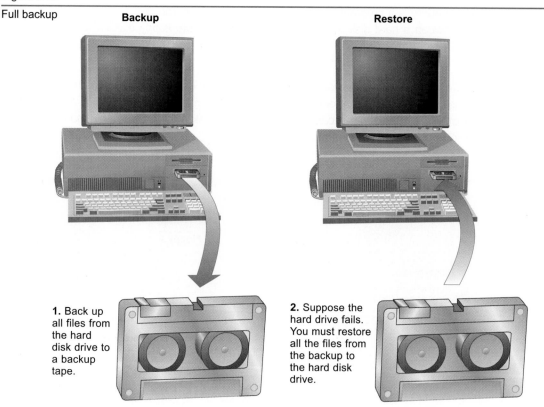

Backup

Restore

1. Back up all files from the hard disk drive to a backup tape.

2. Suppose the hard drive fails. You must restore all the files from the backup to the hard disk drive.

Although a full backup takes a long time to complete, many backup programs let you automate the process so the backup takes place overnight when you don't want to use your computer for other tasks.

A full backup of your computer's hard disk is likely to be many megabytes of data. Whatever the capacity of your hard disk, you'll eventually fill it almost to capacity. Make sure you have purchased a tape backup device and backup tapes that have enough capacity to hold all your data.

A **differential backup** is a copy of all the files that have changed since the last full backup. You'll use a differential backup in conjunction with a full back up. First, you'll make a full backup of all the files on your system. Then, at regular intervals you will make a differential backup. It takes less time to make a differential backup than to make a full backup; however, restoring data from a differential backup is a little more complex. To restore your data after a differential backup, you first restore data from the last full backup, then restore the data from the latest differential backup, as shown in Figure 9-28.

Figure 9-28

Differential backup

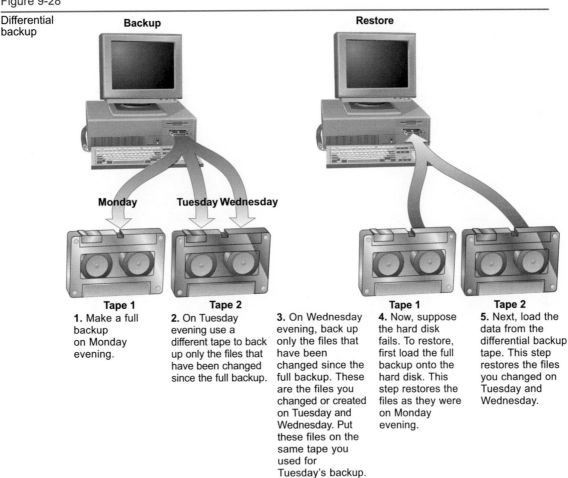

Backup

Restore

Monday

Tuesday Wednesday

Tape 1

Tape 2

Tape 1

Tape 2

1. Make a full backup on Monday evening.

2. On Tuesday evening use a different tape to back up only the files that have been changed since the full backup.

3. On Wednesday evening, back up only the files that have been changed since the full backup. These are the files you changed or created on Tuesday and Wednesday. Put these files on the same tape you used for Tuesday's backup.

4. Now, suppose the hard disk fails. To restore, first load the full backup onto the hard disk. This step restores the files as they were on Monday evening.

5. Next, load the data from the differential backup tape. This step restores the files you changed on Tuesday and Wednesday.

Differential backups are probably the most popular type of backups because they are easy to create. If you are using tapes for your backup, you need only two tapes, one for the full backup and one for the differential. Take care to label your tapes so you know which one contains the full backup and which one contains the differential files.

An **incremental backup** is a copy of the files that have changed since the last backup. When you use incremental backups, you must have a full backup and you must maintain a series of incremental backups. The incremental backup procedure is similar to the differential backup procedure, but there's a subtle difference. With a differential backup, you maintain one full backup and one differential backup. The differential backup contains any files that were changed since the last full backup. With an incremental backup procedure, you maintain a full backup and a series of incremental backups. Each incremental backup contains only those files that changed since the last incremental backup.

To restore the data from a series of incremental backups, you restore the last full backup, then sequentially restore each incremental backup. Figure 9-29 illustrates the backup and restore process for an incremental backup.

Figure 9-29

Incremental backup

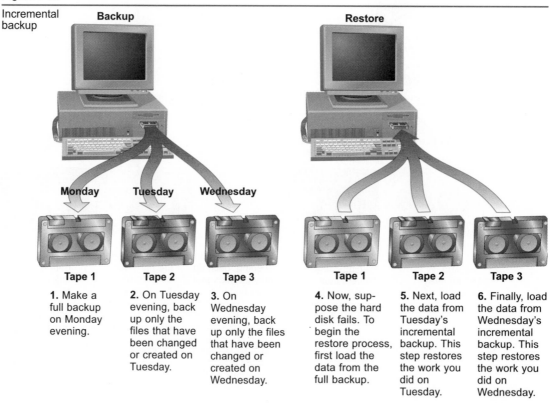

Backup   **Restore**

Monday   Tuesday   Wednesday

Tape 1   **Tape 2**   **Tape 3**   **Tape 1**   **Tape 2**   **Tape 3**

1. Make a full backup on Monday evening.

2. On Tuesday evening, back up only the files that have been changed or created on Tuesday.

3. On Wednesday evening, back up only the files that have been changed or created on Wednesday.

4. Now, suppose the hard disk fails. To begin the restore process, first load the data from the full backup.

5. Next, load the data from Tuesday's incremental backup. This step restores the work you did on Tuesday.

6. Finally, load the data from Wednesday's incremental backup. This step restores the work you did on Wednesday.

Incremental backups take the least time to make and provide a little better protection from viruses than other backup methods because your backup contains a series of copies of your files. However, incremental backups are the most complex type of backup and require good record keeping. You must make sure you accurately label the tape you use for each incremental backup. Otherwise, you might not be able to restore the tapes in the correct order.

Backup Schedule

How frequently should I make a backup? Any data backup plan is a compromise between the level of protection and the amount of time devoted to backup. To be absolutely safe, you would need to back up your data every time you change the contents of a file, which would seriously reduce the amount of work you could complete in a day. Realistically, however, you should make backups at regular intervals. The interval between backups will depend on the value of your data—what that data is worth to you or your employer in terms of time and money.

An individual using a personal computer might not be particularly worried about the consequences of data loss. Data backup for such an individual should be quick and easy to complete and should reduce some of the inconvenience of data loss. However, it would not necessarily restore all data or programs. A backup schedule that offers this minimal amount of protection would require a once-a-week backup of those data files that have changed since the last backup, as shown in Figure 9-30.

Figure 9-30

A basic
backup plan

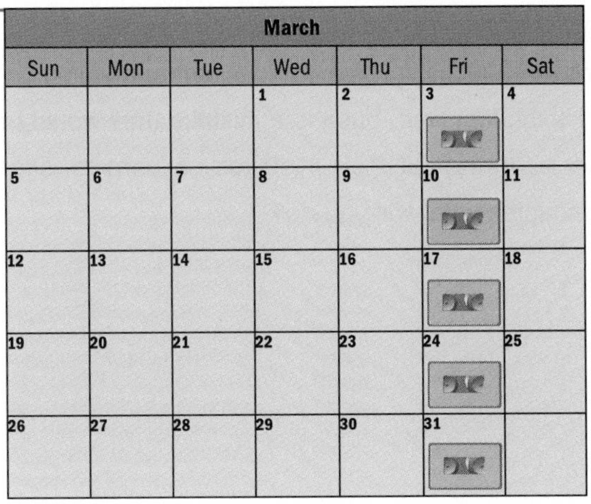

March						
Sun	Mon	Tue	Wed	Thu	Fri	Sat
			1	2	3	4
5	6	7	8	9	10	11
12	13	14	15	16	17	18
19	20	21	22	23	24	25
26	27	28	29	30	31	

In the event of a hard disk drive failure, an individual who uses this backup plan would have to reinstall all software from original disks and restore all the data from the backup disks. The data entered or changed since the last backup would be lost. If the last backup was made at the end of the day on Monday and the hard disk failed on Thursday, the data from Tuesday, Wednesday, and Thursday would be lost.

A more rigorous backup plan would be required for more valuable data, particularly if the data was produced by an application, such as an accounting system or payroll program, that operates on a weekly or monthly cycle. Every time you use an accounting system, for example, you do not use all the files that contain your data. Therefore, a file could be damaged by a virus or disk error, but you might not know it for several days or weeks until you try to access the file. In the meantime you might have made backups that contain the damaged file. A more sophisticated backup procedure—one that you might use with an accounting system—would typically combine daily, weekly, and monthly backups to allow you to reconstruct data at any point before file damage occurred.

End Note

The amount of data stored on computer systems, combined with the vulnerability of those systems, creates a potentially risky situation. A surprising amount of personal data about you is stored on computers. All of it might not be accurate. It can be accessed and altered by criminals. It can be destroyed by hardware failure, human sabotage, or natural disaster. The same can be said for national security data or the data that keeps the world financial market running smoothly. One of the main issues of the computer age concerns the security and ethical use of computer data. Risk management has, therefore, become a necessity in most organizations.

In the story of the Trojan War, the Trojans seem so naive. Who would be so foolish as to pull such a suspicious horse into the city? But you have learned that today's computer users are often just as naive about modern technology. They install programs on their computers without checking for viruses, they store massive amounts of data without back-ups, and they transmit sensitive data without first encrypting it. The Trojans fell for the wooden horse trick the first time, but it is a mistake they would be unlikely to repeat. Will modern computer users repeat their mistakes or learn to take precautions? Now that you've read this chapter, what will you do?

InfoWeb

Chapter
Links

The InfoWeb is your guide to print, film, television, and electronic resources. Use it to obtain updates on quickly changing technical information and to locate information for research papers. If you're using the New Perspectives CD-ROM, click the InfoWeb icon on the left side of this paragraph to access the online InfoWeb links. Otherwise, use your Web browser and type in the address of the New Perspectives site: www.cciw.com/np3. At the New Perspectives site you'll find up-to-date links to the topics covered in this chapter.

1 UPS: Uninterruptible Power Supplies

Buying and using an uninterruptible power supply (UPS) is the best way to avoid the problems that power outages cause. Periodically, computer magazines feature articles about the latest UPS technology. For example, *PC Computing*, "Usability Test: Call for Backup" by David Gerding at **www4.zdnet.com/pccomp/features/excl0897/zap/zap.html** is where you can read about several of the latest UPS devices and the companies that make them. *Information Week's* "Keep The Power On" by Logan Harbaugh at **www.techweb.com/se/directlink.cgi?IWK19970414S0050** will fill you in on why you need a UPS and how to evaluate various models. The major UPS vendors are American Power Conversion (**www.apcc.com**), Best Power Technology, Inc. (**www.bestpower.com**), Deltec Electronics Corp. (**www.deltecpower.com**), MGE UPS Systems (**www.mgeups.com**), and Tripp Lite (**www.tripplite.com**).

2 Computer Insurance

Does your homeowner's insurance policy cover your desktop computer? Your notebook computer? You might want to check with your insurance agent. Before you do, learn more about computer insurance in an article from *Computer Shopper*, "Sure, My PC's Insured: you may think so, but check your policy carefully" by Tami D. Peterson at **www5.zdnet.com/cshopper/filters/9610/buyper.html**. You can learn about laptop theft and insurance in another *Computer Shopper* article, "Laptop Theft Largely Overestimated" by Erik Sherman at **www5.zdnet.com/cshopper/content/9705/cshp0077.html**. A few insurance companies offer special insurance on computer equipment, and Safeware at **www.safeware-ins.com/** is one of them. Safeware publishes an annual report on computer theft losses, "Theft Losses 95-96: $2.3 Billion in Computers Lost During 1996," that you can read at their Web site, **www.safeware-ins.com/losses96.html**. You can also learn about techniques for preventing computer theft from Business Protection Products at **www.pc-security.com/**. "Crime Statistics That Will Surprise You" at the PC Guardian site, **www.pcguardian.com/facts-crst.html**, is interesting reading about hardware and information theft.

3 Viruses Alert!

To learn more about viruses, what they are, and how they work, read "Frequently Asked Questions" on Virus-L/comp.virus at **www.bocklabs.wisc.edu/~janda/virl_faq.html**. You can also find information about the latest viruses including descriptions of what specific viruses do at Symantec's AntiVirus Research Center at **www.symantec.com/avcenter/index.html** and at McAfee's Virus Info & Technical Documentation Library at **www.mcafee.com/support/techdocs/vinfo/index.html**. Would you like to see the screens of some computers with viruses? Connect to Data Fellows at **www.datafellows.com/usa.htm**. Some virus reports are hoaxes. Before you panic and spread information about a fake virus, check it out at the site, "Don't spread that hoax!" at **www.nonprofit.net/hoax/hoax.html**.

4 **Macro Viruses**

Macro viruses are some of the most prolific. By attaching themselves to macros in documents or spreadsheets, these viruses are transmitted over networks and with e-mail attachments by users who are not aware that their documents are infected. For up-to-date information on combatting macro viruses, your first stop should be Microsoft's site. Use the Search button to locate their list of articles for "macro virus." A good explanation of the Word Concept virus is at **www.microsoft.com/ msword/freestuff/mvtool/mvtool2.htm**. TechWeb at **www.techweb.com** is another good source of information if you search for "macro virus." Look for information on the ShareFun virus that automatically creates and mails infected e-mail attachments. While at the TechWeb site, you might want to read about how macro viruses work in the April 1, 1997 article, "Anatomy of a Macro Virus".

5 **Year 2000**

Can we really expect a rash of computer glitches when the year 2000 arrives? The "year 2000 problem," sometimes called the "year 2000 time bomb" or "Y2K" is real and programmers are feverishly working to correct hardware and software. An excellent site with links to articles, press releases, user groups, vendors, and FAQs is **www.year2000.com**. At that site you should find a link to Peter de Jager's chatty, but informative article "You've got to be Kidding!" at **www.year2000.com/y2kkidding.html**. An older, but still relevant article at **http://www.cnn.com/TECH/9601/2000/index.html** explains why "The year 2000 does not compute." Is your PC Year 2000 compliant? You'll find instructions for testing your PC at **www.tyler.net/tyr7020/y2kinput.htm**.

6 **The Internet Worm**

In November 2, 1988 Robert Morris, a computer science graduate student at Cornell and the son of the chief scientist at the National Computer Security Center, launched a worm that invaded thousands of Internet computers. A *Tour of the Worm* at **www.mmt.bme.hu/~kiss/docs/opsys/worm.html**, written by Donn Seeley of the Department of Computer Science at the University of Utah, presents a chronology and a detailed description of the internal workings of the Internet Worm. The Internet Worm at **www2.ncsu.edu/eos/info/computer_ethics/www/worm/index.html** is part of an instructional site on computer ethics at North Carolina State University. The site includes links to various articles that analyze the worm attack, the ethics of computer hacking, chronological reports on the worm and its aftermath, and the ethics of computer hacking.

7 **Computer Crime**

Computer crime law is a double edged sword. We need laws that protect us from computer crimes, yet we also need to make sure that computer crime laws are not so broad and sweeping that they infringe on our civil liberties and constitutional rights. In "Civil Liberties in Cyberspace: When does hacking turn from an exercise of civil liberties into crime" at **www.eff.org/pub/Legal/cyberliberties_kapor.article** Mitchell Kapor discusses government's response to computer crimes. The Electronic Frontier Foundation at **www.eff.org** was founded by Kapor and others to protect civil liberties as technology changes the way we work and do business. At the EFF Web site you can find of articles about computer crime, civil liberties,  computer searches and seizures, and other topics related to computers and the law. At the Laws and Crime site, **www.blkbox.com/~guillory/comp4.html**, you can find a directory that includes links to U.S. state and federal computer crime laws, computer crime sentencing guidelines, and computer crime categories. At the National Security Institute (**nsi.org/**), you can read "Computer Security and the Law" (**nsi.org/Library/Compsec/cslaw.txt**), an article that provides information for lawyers on the legal aspects of computer security. For an international perspective, read *International Security: Issues involving Computers* at **stuweb.ee.mtu.edu/~jdhansen/320.html**. **Computer Crime: A Crime Fighter's Handbook** by David Icove, Karl Seger, and William VonStorch (O'Reilley, 1995) is a highly regarded book about computer crime. You can read a synopsis and review of this book at **www.ora.com/catalog/crime/desc.html**.

8 Risk Management

To learn more about data security and the dangers to which your data can be exposed, read "RIMS Report; Risk Management; Don't Overlook Data Security: Technology A Powerful Tool, But Exposure to Hackers Can Prove Costly" *Business Insurance*, May 6, 1996 at **rmisweb.com/rmisartc/ 050696a.htm**. One of the best ways to protect yourself from data loss is to always keep a backup of important data. The Internet offers new ways to provide data backup and data warehousing. Panorama Software Corporation at **www.pansoft.com/index.html** is one of many companies that offer products that allow corporations to back up their large computer systems over the Internet. To learn more about risk management analysis, services, and products, check out IBM's Risk Management Web pages at **www.brs.ibm.com/rmdescr.html**. If you would like to read about some of the latest computer incidents, connect to the *Risks Digest* at **http://www.csl.sri.com/~risko/risks.txt**.

9 Acceptable Use Policy

Have you ever thought about starting a word-processing business using the computers in one of your school's computer labs? Could you operate such a business from your dorm room using your own computer? Can you use your company's e-mail for personal business? You can find the answers to these questions in your school's or company's acceptable use policy. For an example of an acceptable use policy, check out "Acceptable Use Policy for Computer Facilities at Nassau Community College" at **www.sunynassau.edu/policies/labpol.htm**. Nassau's policy specifies who can use the college's computer equipment, what that computer equipment consists of, and who is responsible for activity on an assigned computer account. It also specifies what activities are unethical, unacceptable, and in violation of state or federal law. Mountainview Computer Technology, Inc. (MCT)—Acceptable Use Policy at **www.new-hampshire.net/aup.htm** list rules for MCT's Internet customers. "Developing a School or District 'Acceptable Use Policy' for Student and Staff Access to the Internet," **www.etdc.wednet.edu/aup/index.html**, discusses guidelines and a philosophy for developing an acceptable use policy for K-12 school districts. This Web site also includes links to a PowerPoint slide presentation; samples of policies, consent forms, and letters to parents; an article that reviews Internet case law; and other resources on legal aspects of acceptable use and the Internet.

10 Biometrics

The New York Times article, "Use of Recognition Technology Grows in Everyday Transactions" at **www.nytimes.com/library/cyber/week/082097biometrics.html** gives you a good introduction to new computer technology that is making computer use more secure. To learn about the latest biometric technology, check out Automatic Data Collection at Purdue University at **www.tech.purdue.edu/it/adc/**. Another great basic article is **"The Body as a Password"** by Ann Davis (*Wired* magazine, July 1997).

What about commercial products? Mr. Payroll Corporation, at **www.mrpayroll.com/** makes an automatic check cashing machine that compares a picture of your face with a picture it has on file. The Mr. Payroll automated check cashing system uses face recognition software developed by Miros, Incorporated at **www.miros.com**. International Automated Systems at **www.iaus.com/** has developed equipment for grocery stores that allows customers to check out their own groceries without waiting in long lines. You can check out their new grocery stores at **www.iaus.com/ucheck.htm**. Biometrics Identification Inc. is one of several companies that make fingerprint verification equipment. You can learn more about Biometrics' products at **www.biometricid.com**.

11 WarGames

In the 1983 film *WarGames* a young boy with an amazing grasp of computers accidentally engages a secret government supercomputer in what he thinks is a game. Unfortunately, the supercomputer, which controls the U.S. nuclear armaments, believes it is engaged in a real World War 3-type engagement with Russia. To learn more about this film, check out its page at the Internet Movie Database at **us.imdb.com/M/title-exact?WarGames+(1983)** where you can find a plot summary, cast list, trivia information, and more. For a Web-based Java-enabled taste of what the film is like, check out WarGames Logon at **www-public.rz.uni-duesseldorf.de/~ritterd/wargames/logon.htm**. At this Web site, you can view pictures from the film, listen to sound clips, play some games, take a tour of a decommissioned missile silo, and engage in some nostalgia for the 1980s.

12 Encryption Methods

You can learn about encryption at Netsurfer Focus on Cryptography and Privacy at **www.netsurf.com/nsf/v01/03/nsf.01.03.html**. This Web site presents an introduction to cryptography, information about key certification, a discussion of e-mail issues, information on the current status of the Clipper Chip, and other resources. One of the most popular and well-publicized encryption methods is Pretty Good Privacy (PGP). You can learn all about PGP at "Getting Started with encryption: An Introduction to PGP" at **www.cs.uchicago.edu/~cbarnard/pgptalk/index.html**. This Web site is an online PGP tutorial that was presented at the Computer Professionals for Social Responsibility conference in October 1995. The MIT distribution site for PGP at **web.mit.edu/network/pgp.html** includes information on how to integrate PGP with mail programs, a link to frequently asked questions, and links to Internet information on PGP, in addition to a link through which you can download a copy of the program. There are also several recent books on encryption, including **Building in Big Brother: The Cryptographic Policy Debate** by Lance J. Hoffman (Springer Verlag, 1995), **The Computer Privacy Handbook: A Practical Guide to E-Mail Encryption, Data Protection, and PGP Privacy Software** by Andre Bacard (Peachpit Press, 1995), and **Internet Cryptography** by Richard E. Smith (Addison-Wesley, 1997).

The Spartans of ancient Greece might have been the first to use military cryptography perhaps as early as the fifth century B.C. Since then cryptography has been used to keep secrets, provide mental exercise, and amuse those who appreciate mathematics and analysis, as well as to preserve and protect military secrets. Are there coded messages in the works of Francis Bacon and Shakespeare? Find out at "Setting.Forth." at **fly.hiwaay.net/~paul/cc.html**. Was Edgar Allan Poe also a dabbler in cryptography? You can learn the answer at "The Legend of Poe the Cryptographer" by Daniel W. Dukes at **www.nadn.navy.mil/EnglishDept/poeperplex/cryptop.htm**. If you're interested in trying your hand at cryptograms, check out Today's Cryptogram and Contest at **www.mindspring.com/~fmnshare/today.html**, and the Magic Decoder Game at **raphael.math.uic.edu/~jeremy/crypt/cgi-bin/magic-gateway.cgi**.

13 **Anti-virus software**

Many anti-virus software packages are available—some commercial, some shareware, and some even freeware. The two most highly rated companies that make antivirus software are Symantec (**www.symantec.com**) and McAfee (**www.mcafee.com**). Their products will protect your computer from virus attacks of all sorts. If you purchase and use their software, make sure you download the updates regularly so that new viruses don't slip by.

14 **Internet Security**

A great introduction to Web security issues is the Web Security Primer at **http://www.entrust.com/ primer.htm**. You might also check **www.techweb.com** for the August 1, 1996 article "Safety on the Net" by David Methvin. A good set of FAQs and links to a variety of security issues is **http://www.consensus.com/security/ssl-talk-sec02.html**. Many of the digital certificates you'll see on the Web have been registered with VeriSign. You can read more about the certification process at **www.verisign.com**. Cylink, a network security firm, provides an excellent summary of digital certificates at **http://www.cylink.com/products/security/x509.htm**. Find out if your browser maintains the security of your Internet mail address at **http://www.helie.com/BrowserCheck/**. Want to find out more about cookies? Marc Slayton's HotWired Geek Talk column at **www.hotwired.com/webmonkey/ webmonkey/geektalk/96/45/index3a.html** explains how cookies work and how to read the cookie file on your computer. A new Internet security standard called SET is currently in the testing phase. For updates, check VISA's Website at **www.VISA.com**.

Personal firewall software provides some protection against Web-borne vandalism. Cybermedia's firewall named Guard Dog is designed to protect your computer from Internet intruders that can damage your hard drive or steal private files, such as viruses, cookies and Trojan Horses. Read all about Guard Dog at **www.cybermedia.com**. eSafe Protect creates a secure SandBox for Internet files that you can download. The eSafe Web site at **www.esafe.com** is really great. You can take a quick tour of the eSafe Protect software, then download it. You can view simulations of vandal software that might be transmitted over the Internet and you can take a "test" to find out how your computer security rates. A third product, SurfinShield is published by Finjan Software. You can download a product demo at **www.finjan.com** and link to some excellent articles on the dangers of the Internet at **www.finjan.com/educate/news.html**.

R e v i e w

1 Use your own words to answer the questions that appear under each section heading in this chapter.

2 List each of the boldface terms used in this chapter, then use your own words to write a short definition of each term.

3 Complete the following chart to review the factors that cause data loss or misuse. List the factors you learned about in this chapter in the first column. Then place an

X in the appropriate column to indicate if the factor causes data loss, inaccurate data, stolen data, or intentionally damaged data. Some factors might have more than one X.

Factor	Unintentional data loss	Inaccurate data	Stolen or misused data	Intentional data loss or damage
Operator error				
[You fill in the rest of the factors]				

4 Complete the following chart to summarize what you have learned about viruses, macro viruses, Trojan horses, time bombs, logic bombs, and software worms.

Type	Spreads by	Triggered by
Virus		
Trojan horse		
Worm		
Time bomb		
Logic bomb		
Macro virus		

5 Make a check list of steps to take if you suspect that your computer is infected with a virus.

6 List the four steps in the risk management process.

7 Make a list of the data security techniques discussed in the *Data Security and Risk Management* section. Then indicate the advantages and disadvantages of each technique.

8 Use your own words to write descriptions of full, incremental, and differential backup procedures. Make sure your descriptions clearly explain the difference between incremental and differential backups.

9 Thinking back over the entire chapter, what was the most useful concept you learned? What questions do you have about data security that still remain unanswered?

10 On a sheet of paper, list all the reasons you can think of for making a backup of computer data.

11 Use the New Perspectives CD-ROM to take a practice test or to review the new terms presented in this chapter.

Projects

1 **Lost Data: What's Your Experience?** Describe a situation in which you or someone you know lost data stored on a computer. What caused the data loss? What steps could have been taken to prevent the loss? What steps could you or the other person have taken to recover the lost data?

2 **Risk Management: A Personal Perspective** Assess the risk to the programs and data files stored on the hard disk of your computer by answering the following questions:

a. What threats are likely to cause your data to be lost, stolen, or damaged?

b. How many files of data do you have?

c. If you add up the size of all your files, how many megabytes of data do you have?

d. How many of these files are critical and would need to be replaced if you lost all your data?

e. What would you need to do to reconstruct the critical files if the hard disk drive failed and you did not have any backups?

f. What measures could you use to protect your data from the threats you identified in the first question? What is the cost of each of these measures?

g. Balancing the threats to your data, the importance of your data, and the cost of protective measures, what do you think is the best plan for the security of your data?

3 **Lost Weekend: Full, Incremental, and Differential Backups** Assume that your hard disk drive fails on a Friday afternoon. Explain how you would restore your data over the weekend if you had been using each of the following backup systems:

a. A full backup every Friday evening

b. A full backup every Friday evening with a differential backup on Wednesday evening

c. A full backup every Friday evening with an incremental backup Monday through Thursday evenings

4 **Word Macro Viruses** In this chapter you learned that Word documents can harbor a macro virus. Using library or Internet resources, find a list of symptoms for the Word macro viruses that are currently circulating. Check your disks to see if you have the virus.

Write a one-page report describing what you learned about the Word macro virus and its presence on, or absence from, the documents you have on your disks.

5 **The Internet Worm** The Internet worm created concern about the security of data on military and research computer systems, and it raised ethical questions about the rights and responsibilities of computer users. Select one of the following statements and write a two-page paper that argues for or against the statement. You might want to use the Internet or library resources to learn more about each viewpoint. Be sure you include the resources you used in a bibliography.

a. People have the "right" to hone their computing skills by breaking into computers. As a computer scientist once said, "The right to hack is held higher than the right of someone to tell you not to. It's an inalienable right."

b. If problems exist, it is acceptable to use any means to point them out. The computer science student who created the Internet virus was perfectly justified in claiming that he should not be convicted because he was just trying to point out that security holes exist in large computer networks.

c. Computer crimes are no different from other crimes, and computer criminals should be held responsible for the damage they cause by paying for the time and cost of replacing or restoring data.

6 **Understanding an Acceptable Use Policy** Obtain a copy of your school's student code or computer use policy, then answer the following questions. If your school does not have such a policy, create one that addresses these questions.

a. To whom does the policy apply— students, faculty, staff, community members, others?

b. What types of activities does the policy specifically prohibit?

c. If a computer crime is committed, would the crime be dealt with by campus authorities or by state law enforcement agents?

d. Does the policy state the penalties for computer crimes? If so, what are they?

7  **Hoax!** Most Internet users have received panicked e-mail about the GoodTimes virus. It turns out that this virus does not exist—it is a hoax. How can you tell the difference between a real virus alert and a hoax? The best policy is to check a reliable site. You can easily locate sites that list hoaxes by entering "hoax" in any Internet search engine such as Yahoo! Sites with reliable reports include **www.nonprofit.net/ hoax/hoax.html**, **www.goodfellows.com**, **www.urbanlegends.com**, and **ciac.llnl.gov/ciac/CIACHoaxes.html**.

Visit at least one of these sites and find the descriptions of five hoaxes. Write a one-page summary that includes the name and description of each hoax, how the hoax is spread, and why you think people believe the hoax.

8 **Virus Detection Software** If you suspect your computer has become infected, it is prudent to immediately activate virus detection software to scan your files for a virus. With the continued spread of viruses, virus detection software has become an essential utility in today's computing environment. Many virus detection software packages are available in computer stores, on computer bulletin boards, and on the Internet. Find information about three virus detection software packages and fill out the following comparison chart.

	Software 1	Software 2	Software 3
Product name			
Publisher			
Price			
Current version			
Update frequency			
Special features			

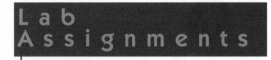

Lab Assignments

Data Backup

The Data Backup Lab gives you an opportunity to make tape backups on a simulated computer system. Periodically, the hard disk on the simulated computer will fail, which gives you a chance to assess the convenience and efficiency of different backup procedures.

1 Click the Steps button to learn how to use the simulation. As you work through the Steps, answer all of the Quick Check questions that appear. After you complete the Steps, you will see a Summary Report of your Quick Check answers. Follow the directions on the screen to print this report.

2 Click the Explore button. Create a full backup every Friday using only Tape 1. At some point in the simulation, an event will cause data loss on the simulated computer system. Use the simulation to restore as much data as you can. After you restore the data, print the Backup Audit Report.

3 In Explore, create a full backup every Friday on Tape 1 and a differential backup every Wednesday on Tape 2. At some point in the simulation, an event will cause data loss on the simulated computer system. Use the simulation to restore as much data as you can. Print the Backup Audit Report.

4 In Explore, create a full backup on Tape 1 every Monday. Make incremental backups on Tapes 2, 3, 4, and 5 each day for the rest of the week. Continue this cycle, reusing the same tapes each week. At some point in the simulation an event will cause data loss on the simulated computer system. Use the simulation to restore as much data as you can. Print the Backup Audit Report.

5 Photocopy a calendar for next month. On the calendar indicate your best plan for backing up data. In Explore, implement your plan. Print out the Backup Audit Report. Write a paragraph or two discussing the effectiveness of your plan.

THE IMPACT OF COMPUTERS
ON YOUR LIFE

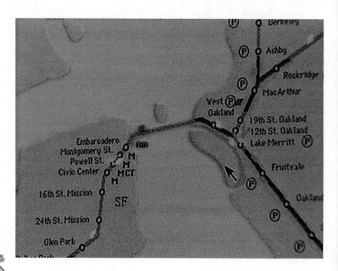

Sitting in her home office with a panoramic view of San Francisco Bay, Erica checks her hand held data retriever for the current status of the subway lines. She sees the subway is running on time and she knows her client will be arriving soon. Next, Erica watches the NASDAQ stock ticker on PCQuote's Web site as the price of her company's stock soars on the first day of its initial public offering. It is hard for Erica to believe that only a year ago she formed a virtual corporation with three partners; one in the Netherlands, another in the U. S., and a third in Japan. Their company, VirtualDesigns, develops three-dimensional Web pages for online virtual communities around the world. When they start a new project, Erica and her partners meet online and brainstorm ideas using video conferencing technologies. As the project takes shape, they electronically circulate proposals, ideas, strategies, and designs through e-mail, video conferencing, and the World Wide Web.

Erica's thoughts are interrupted by the sound of an incoming e-mail message. She opens the message to discover it is not from a coworker, but contains a request from her daughter, Michele, who attends college in Florida, for money to take a weekend trip. Erica logs on to her bank's Web page to transfer funds to her daughter's account.

How will you use technology in your career and life outside of work? This chapter examines the impact of technology on the workplace, education, politics, and interpersonal relationships. You will learn what new technologies are currently available, get a glimpse of future technologies, and examine how experts predict they will affect you.

CHAPTER PREVIEW

In this chapter you will explore the impact of technology on the way we live, learn, and work. Computers and technology help us to become more productive workers, lifelong learners, and informed and involved citizens. Through computers, we can even form new relationships. You will also explore cutting-edge technologies and the impact they have on society as a whole. After you have completed this chapter, you should be able to:

- Discuss the impact of computers and technology on job market trends
- Describe the importance of intranets and virtual corporations
- Describe how to hunt for a job online
- Explain the value of technology in education including computer-assisted instruction, distance learning, and virtual colleges
- Discuss how you can use the Web to become an informed citizen
- Describe the pros and cons of electronic town hall meetings and electronic voting
- Describe how to develop online relationships, interact with others online, and participate in online interest groups or virtual communities

A Technology in a Changing Workplace

Since the introduction of the first IBM PC in 1981, microcomputers have become indispensable tools in the business world. Although businesses continue to rely on supercomputers, mainframe computers, and minicomputers to track massive amounts of data and handle sophisticated processing tasks, microcomputers have revolutionized our business practices. By providing employees with powerful desktop tools, they increase the productivity of businesses. For example, the rapid shift to microcomputers freed up valuable processing time on corporate mainframe and minicomputers and gave employees greater control over their work. In terms of simple computing power, today's microcomputers combined into networks can outperform mainframe and minicomputers at considerably less cost and complexity.

InfoWeb

Technology in the News 1

The story is not a completely positive one, however. Too often we depend on computers to perform tasks that still need to be overseen by a person. For example, as reported by the *New York Times*, a small programming bug—an error in one line of code—caused an explosion that destroyed the European Space Agency's $7 billion Ariane 5 rocket and its payload of scientific satellites. The four satellites were expensive—and uninsured.

Microcomputers provide employees with access to the information they need for their jobs, allowing them to work more efficiently, effectively, and rapidly. As a consequence, people are more productive and creative, thereby contributing to a sense of greater control over their jobs and to greater self-esteem.

With the increasing importance of the Internet and World Wide Web to businesses, plus the rapidly evolving technology for microcomputers, the challenge for today's employee is to keep pace with continued accelerated change in computer technologies. Software companies introduce new or major upgrades to operating systems and software applications yearly. Every company that is a major player in the software industry—Microsoft, IBM, Adobe, Intuit, Lotus—is releasing minor updates, interim releases, and new versions every 6 to 18 months. Internet technologies are changing at an even faster pace. In 1997, new technologies for connecting to the Internet—ISDN, cable modems, and digital satellite connections—were announced almost monthly. How can you keep pace with this ever-changing landscape of new technology?

Job Market Trends

What skills will I need to get a good job? Computer skills are an important component of the basic skills that you need to ensure your future success. No matter what career you choose or which type of work you do, your ability to perform your job will depend directly or indirectly on computers. Some jobs, such as telecommunications specialists, network support personnel, software developers, and Web masters, require a broad spectrum of advanced computer skills. Traditional clerical jobs require familiarity with productivity software, such as suites that include word processors, spreadsheets, presentation, data management, and scheduling. Now clerical workers must also know how to use groupware, Web browsers, and Web authoring tools. Individuals in service sector jobs that once required little or no computer skills, such as freelance editors or organizational consultants, use applications to write correspondence, track cash flow and business expenditures, file tax statements, schedule projects and appointments, and organize contacts and clients.

Workers in fast food restaurants use computers to take orders as shown in Figure 1. Manual laborers working in the home construction or home remodeling industry might use electronic stud finders or electronic tape measures.

Figure 1

Computers are used to place orders, generate receipts for customers, and help with inventory control in many restaurants.

Communication skills have always been critical to developing a successful career—knowing how to work with your colleagues and superiors, and crafting effective memos and letters. Technology such as e-mail and voice mail make communication skills an even larger part of work life. For many jobs, experience and proficiency in sending and receiving e-mail and accessing and using voice-mail systems are essential. For example, some people receive as many as 1,200 e-mail messages a week. Knowing how to use all of the features of your e-mail system is a critical skill when you are inundated with this volume of information. Some of the tasks you might carry out are attaching files to e-mail messages, saving attached files, responding to or forwarding messages, creating folders in which to save messages so that your Inbox isn't overflowing, and deleting messages.

In some jobs, such as marketing and sales, voice-mail messages can have a comparably high volume. Knowing how to access, listen to, save, and delete messages are basic skills. More advanced users will know how to send voice-mail messages marked as high priority and how to send messages to groups, such as members of a sales force.

Furthermore, many jobs require the use of communications software or Web browsers to access information on company networks. Individuals who travel or work at home depend on dial-up networking. **Dial-up networking** is the use of a phone connection to access a network server. Often the server is part of the Internet, but it is also possible to use a phone connection to access a local area network. When traveling, employees use dial-up networking to connect their laptop computers to their company's networks to access information critical to their job and to communicate with other staff members. Once connected to the company network, whether you are working from home, a hotel, or an airport lobby, you can access e-mail and other parts of the corporate network. Laptop computers also offer flexibility to the employee who must fly often. While the employee cannot connect to the company's networks while flying, he or she can work on word-processing documents, spreadsheets, databases, or graphics presentations.

In this information-rich environment, knowing how to prioritize information becomes even more important. Knowing what messages to keep and which to discard has become a required productivity skill. As more and more employers monitor e-mail and voice-mail usage, knowing when not to use technology for personal business becomes a basic survival skill.

In addition to the need for new skills, there are new job opportunities. The exponential growth of the World Wide Web means increased opportunities in the future for Web-based jobs, such as designing, developing, and enhancing Web sites; managing Web sites; and traditional jobs such as advertising, customer service, and sales. The popularity of online services will also increase the demand for skilled and talented individuals familiar with communications software and Internet technologies.

InfoWeb

Labor Statistics 2

According to the U.S. Department of Labor, three of the fastest growing occupations through the year 2006 will be computer scientists, computer engineers, and systems analysts. By the year 2006, the number of people employed in computer and data processing services will grow by 108 percent. Look at Figure 2. The occupations with the fastest employment growth are predicted to be database administrators, computer support specialists, and all other computer scientists, computer engineers, and systems analysts.

Figure 2

Predicted occupational growth 1996–2006

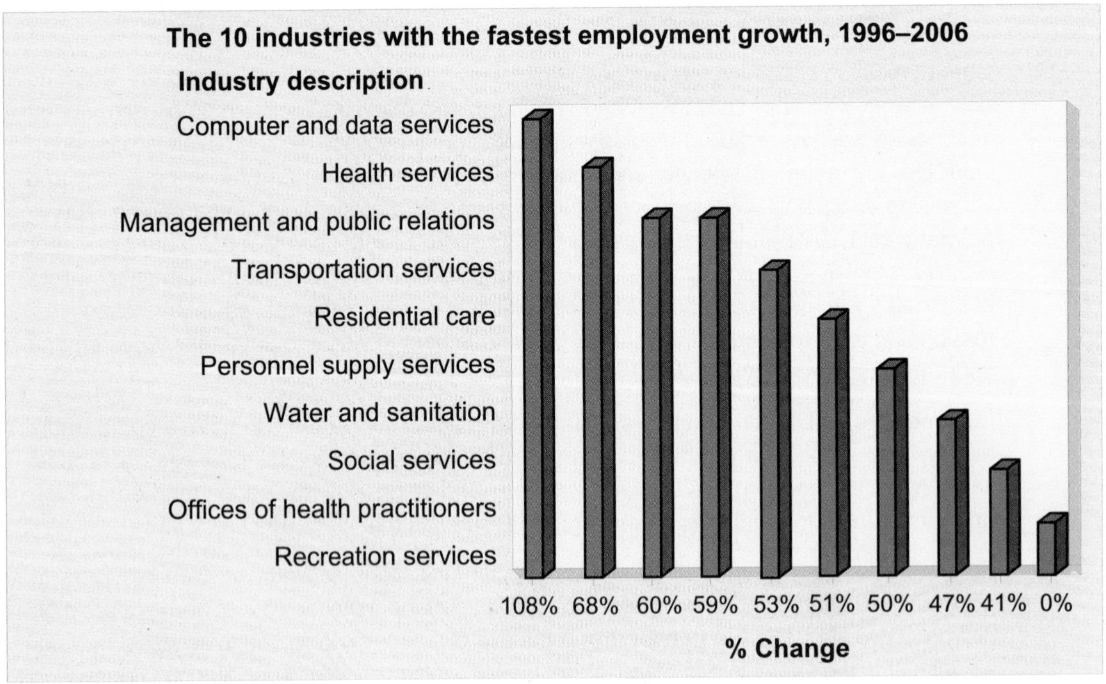

The 10 industries with the fastest employment growth, 1996–2006

Industry description

Industry description	% Change
Computer and data services	108%
Health services	68%
Management and public relations	60%
Transportation services	59%
Residential care	53%
Personnel supply services	51%
Water and sanitation	50%
Social services	47%
Offices of health practitioners	41%
Recreation services	0%

% Change

Olsten Staffing is a leading supplier of temporary workers. In its 1998 Managing Workforce Technology Survey, Olsten reported network management as the top skill in demand, cited by 51 percent of the 294 businesses who participated in the survey. Also significant is the demand for employees with groupware skills (32 percent), Web/Internet skills (32 percent), and database management skills (47 percent).

Olsten's findings indicate the continued interest of American businesses to use alternative employment options. The 1998 study also reported that almost one out of four professionals in computer-related fields were either working part-time or as consultants or as other types of temporary workers.

American companies are **outsourcing**—relying on external resources—many functions that were once performed by internal employees. Companies outsource to reduce costs and to focus more resources on core business functions. Individuals looking for jobs in support areas might find more opportunities with firms that provide these services on a contract basis than with the organizations ultimately served. It is technology such as e-mail, voice mail, and dial-up networking that allows corporations to outsource these types of functions and still operate smoothly and seamlessly.

An interesting new trend is the increasing number of companies which are willing to allow workers to telecommute. **Telecommuting** refers to employees who work away from a formal office, usually at home, using a telephone, fax machine, and computer with a modem. See Figure 3.

Figure 3

Telecommuting has increased employment options for many workers.

As reported in the 1998 Managing Workforce Technology Survey, the number of companies that have telecommuting arrangements increased from 44 percent in 1996 to 51 percent in 1997. Telecommuters utilize e-mail and file-sharing techniques to transmit their work to and from the office rather than driving back and forth. The employer saves the cost of maintaining a physical office for those employees, and the telecommuter maintains a more flexible lifestyle.

Several other technologies are making telecommuting even easier. **Audiographic teleconferencing**, commonly known as **whiteboarding**, uses Internet technologies to transfer audio and textual data in the same way. Participants use an electronic whiteboard to look at the same computer display controlled by one or more persons, and they comment on what they see. **Video conferencing** allows two or more groups of people to see and hear each other from separate locations. As personal computers and modems become capable of transmitting large amounts of data more quickly, video conferencing becomes more possible.

Intranets

How will networking and communications technology change the way I work? You already know that the Internet is an organization of networks that communicate among themselves using Internet Protocol (IP), and that the World Wide Web is a structure of data that is accessible through the Internet. An **intranet** is an infrastructure that businesses use for internal communication using Web technology. The availability of data is confined to a network within a business or organization, and not accessible from outside. An **extranet** is similar to an intranet, except its data is shared by businesses within a particular industry. How do they change the way you work? You no longer use applications specific to your desktop PC, Macintosh, or UNIX-based computer to access information stored on a network server. See Figure 4.

Figure 4

An intranet allows employees to communicate through Web technology.

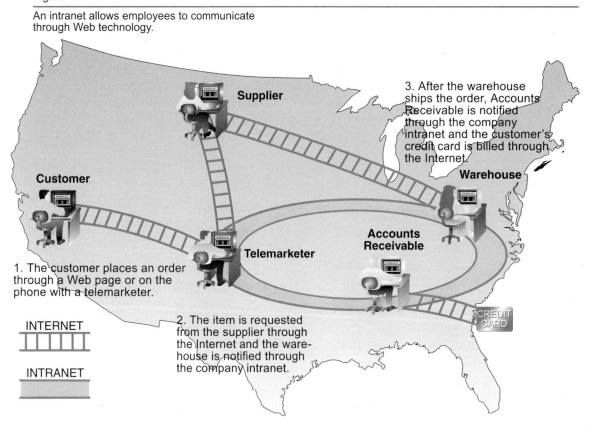

Supplier

3. After the warehouse ships the order, Accounts Receivable is notified through the company intranet and the customer's credit card is billed through the Internet.

Customer

Warehouse

Accounts Receivable

Telemarketer

1. The customer places an order through a Web page or on the phone with a telemarketer.

2. The item is requested from the supplier through the Internet and the warehouse is notified through the company intranet.

INTERNET

INTRANET

CREDIT CARD

The intranet allows access to all the company's information, applications, data, knowledge, and processes using the same software and communications tools that it would use to communicate with the broader Internet community. The intranet facilitates collaboration among employees through shared documents, video conferencing, e-mail, discussion forums, and electronic whiteboards. The end result is an organization that is better able to respond to competitive market forces and better able to communicate with its customers and clients.

Virtual Corporations

How can I use these online technologies to develop my own business? If you are an entrepreneur, you can maximize your business potential by creating a virtual corporation. A **virtual corporation** is a company that consists of a group of individuals who use online technologies as the medium for developing, promoting, and conducting a business. The business venture might focus on a commercial product, such as health foods or sporting goods, or it might develop and sell information, one of the most important and lucrative businesses in the United States today.

First Virtual Corporation (see Figure 5) develops desktop interactive multimedia technology, such as video conferencing, that virtual corporations need to conduct their business. Like other traditional businesses, First Virtual forms business alliances with companies like IBM that are leaders in the development of technology. Because it focuses on developing and implementing new technologies in conjunction with other companies, First Virtual contracts out all other business functions.

Figure 5

First Virtual Corporation describes its company's goal at its Web site.

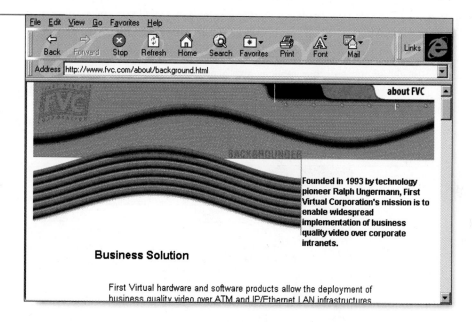

A virtual corporation can operate without buildings, manufacturing facilities, or a broad range of support staff positions. This saves money and resources while providing greater flexibility in adapting to changing economic conditions. Virtual corporations offer entrepreneurs the opportunity to develop new business markets that capitalize on the availability of online and communications technologies, the Internet and World Wide Web, and global markets. In fact, with the increased emphasis on doing business on the Web, the owners and chief executives of traditional corporations can transform their businesses into virtual corporations.

InfoWeb

Virtual Corporations 3

Traditional organizations in some industries are now beginning to see serious competition from virtual corporations. For example, in 1996 the Virtual Shipbuilding Consortium won a two-year, $19 million contract from the Defense Advanced Research Projects Agency (DARPA) to design and build the next generation of ships for the U.S. Navy. The diverse components that make up the virtual organization use an electronic information framework to carry out each phase from preliminary design to construction of a ship.

Online Job Hunting

| How can I use online technologies to find a job? | When you are looking for just the right job, it is in your best interest to take advantage of all the resources available to you. In addition to using traditional job-hunting approaches, you can use job-search services on the Internet. Using the World Wide Web can make your job search and related activities more effective and efficient.

InfoWeb

Online Job
Hunting
4

If you are searching for an out-of-state job, an electronic job search can place a variety of resources virtually at your fingertips. Job banks such as Careerpath (**www.careerpath.com**) and America's Job Bank (**www.ajb.dni.us**) contain position openings in many fields—from education to journalism to high tech to management to government—from all across the country. For example, Careerpath includes job listings from six major U.S. newspapers. Other resources such as CareerNet (**www.careers.org**) can help you formulate career plans and research potential employers. Some sites focus on jobs in a particular industry. For instance, Job Engine (**www.jobengine.com**) covers only jobs available in the computer industry.

You can use search engines to locate information about the city or region that surrounds your potential employer. Career forums can provide you with help and advice from other job searchers and career development professionals. You can even find Web sites that will help you practice answering common interview questions.

Other online career services also allow you to take a career planning test to determine which types of jobs match your personality. See Figure 6. In addition, you can use online services to prepare and post an electronic resume. Online resume banks make your resume accessible to companies and recruiters so that they can look for you while you are searching for them.

Figure 6

A career planning site

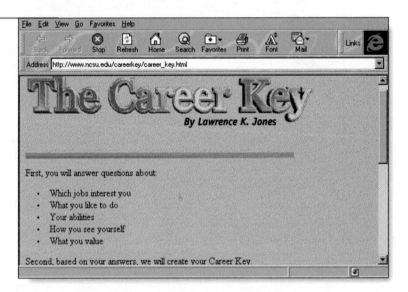

Even if you are using more traditional sources to turn up job leads—such as classified ads in local newspapers, networking, and jobs posted through your campus career counseling center—online resources can improve your chances of landing the right job. For example, Internet search engines can streamline the process of researching a company. Armed with detailed information about a company's goals, products, and clients, you can make a strong impression during an interview.

JobWeb, which is administered by the National Association of Colleges and Employers, is one of the largest job search services on the World Wide Web. See Figure 7. You can use JobWeb to search for jobs by keyword or employer and access information on career planning, salaries, resume preparation, interviewing techniques, employment statistics, job fairs, and job counseling.

Figure 7

JobWeb's Web site offers a variety of job-hunting services at **www.jobweb.org.**

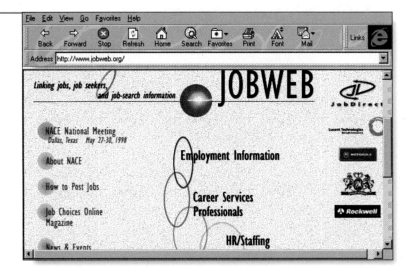

Besides online job services, many companies post current job openings on their Web sites and welcome e-mail versions of cover letters and resumes in response to these postings. In fact, some companies only accept resumes submitted through e-mail or forms that you fill out through a Web browser. Therefore it pays to have an electronic version of your resume as well as a printed version. The 1998 Managing Workforce Technology Survey, reported that 38 percent of its responding companies use Internet-based recruiting. That number represented a 100 percent increase over the number of companies who used such recruiting techniques the year before.

One important development in the job search arena is the move toward scannable, searchable resume requirements. Some companies find employees through employment service bureaus, and these companies use resume databases as well. As a consequence, you need to make sure that your resume is scannable. Follow the tips in Figure 8 on the next page. In addition, make sure that your resume includes keywords and industry jargon that will enhance the chances that your resume will be retrieved from an automated resume tracking system or database during a search.

Figure 8

Tips to help you make
your resume scannable

- Send originals.

- Use white 8½" x 11" paper.

- Print your resume on one side of each page.

- Use standard resume sections like "Work Experience" and "Education" because these are the key words the employer's computer will use to categorize your employment record and skills inventory.

- Use keywords and industry jargon.

- Use popular sans serif fonts (Helvetica or Arial) in point sizes 10–14.

- Avoid graphics, shading, script fonts, italics, underlining, and boldfaced text.

- Avoid horizontal and vertical lines.

- Use wide margins around the text.

- Don't fold the resume.

- Use laser or inkjet printers; don't use dot matrix printers.

- Avoid stapling the resume.

QuickCheck A

1. Employees who travel or work at home can use _____ to connect their computers to their company's networks so that they can access information critical to their job and communicate with other staff members.

2. More and more companies are _____ by relying on external resources to perform many functions that were once performed by internal employees.

3. Businesses are using Internet and Web technologies to create _____ over which they can conduct their business.

4. A group of individuals can create a _____ and use online technologies as the medium for developing, promoting, and conducting a business.

5. Online _____ offers individuals the opportunity to search for job openings, prepare and post resumes, and develop job-search strategies using the World Wide Web.

B Technology in Education

Culture and society shape the structure and content of educational systems. Elementary and secondary (K-12) education in the United States is designed to prepare children for adult life by helping them develop the skills they need to become successful members of society. The current structure of K-12 schooling is a product of the factory-model of education that was designed to meet the needs of nineteenth century industrial society. In this model, a teacher imparts information to passive learners through lectures and drill-type exercises and uses tests to assess how well students have absorbed the information. In the nineteenth century, most K-12 students did not go on to college; many of them did not even complete high school. Instead, they entered a variety of jobs—mostly jobs in factories. At that time it did not make sense to teach students more than the basic skills, such as reading, writing, arithmetic, and citizenship.

As the United States changes to a post-industrial, technology-based society, our educational system must also change to keep pace. Today, the majority of jobs are information-based; they involve analyzing existing information, generating new information, storing and retrieving information, and they rely heavily on computers and other technology. The key to success in the information society will be learning and applying computer skills in a variety of jobs.

Technology itself holds out the promise of transforming the educational system from one that is largely passive and lecture-based to one that requires active engagement from students. If this promise is realized, technology in education will foster an environment that will help students at all levels—whether K-12 or college—develop the thinking skills they need to become successful, lifelong learners as adults.

Computers in K-12 Education

How can computers help change the educational process in K-12 education? In the late 1970s microcomputers and educational computing began to enter the school system. There was some focus on using the computer to solve problems in high school mathematics classes, but more often the focus was on teaching about computers. **Computer literacy** is the basic understanding of what a computer is, what it does, and why computers are important to your society.

By the end of 1982, Apple Computer had begun offering schools special prices on its Apple II+ computers. See Figure 9. However, teachers were not given adequate training or support to learn to use them for more than a decade. At that time, computers were used largely for skill-and-drill exercises.

Figure 9

In 1982, Apple Computer offered schools a 64K RAM Apple II+ computer with a 128K floppy disk drive and a color monitor at a low price.

In contrast to the late 1970s and early 1980s, today there is a strong push toward student-centered learning, and computers are facilitating this transformation. In this new environment, teachers become mentors, guides, and facilitators, rather than lecturers and testers. See Figure 10.

Figure 10

Students use computers and online resources for student-centered learning.

The goals of education are to help students develop problem-solving, critical thinking, and discussion and negotiation skills. Other goals include fostering the capacity for self-directed learning and the capacity to work cooperatively in groups. Knowledge and understanding are assessed through student portfolios, notebooks, and projects that are an outgrowth of the learning process, rather than through paper-and-pencil tests.

In this new educational environment, computers are being used in many different ways:

InfoWeb

Technology and Education 5

- Presentation software allows teachers and students to create interactive learning sessions.

- Course management software reduces teachers' administrative tasks and gives them more time for teaching and interacting with students.

- Productivity software—such as word processors, spreadsheets, and databases—are used by students and teachers as tools to prepare reports, analyze data, and organize facts.

- Computer-aided instruction allows students to interact with learning materials at their own pace, supports a variety of learning styles, and fosters an exploratory style of learning.

- Multimedia encyclopedias and other reference materials are available for students to use as resources when working on projects and reports.

- Simulation programs allow students to interact with and learn from experiences and phenomena that would not normally be accessible to them.

- Internet and the World Wide Web link public schools to libraries, universities, research centers, private companies, and homes both in the United States and around the world.

Computers and other technology are instrumental parts of changing today's educational system. Just about everyone agrees that change is necessary, but this change is coming slowly. Although most public schools have computers, many of those computers are old, cannot be networked, and cannot run the latest software. Often, student access to any computer in the school is severely limited; nationally, the student to computer ratio is very high.

Despite these obstacles, the federal government and states, in conjunction with businesses and citizens who understand the importance of computer technology to the learning process, are joining forces to make sure that public schools have the equipment they need to implement new educational goals. For example, Bill Gates of Microsoft Corporation and Mayor Rudolph Giuliani of New York City worked on a cooperative venture whereby Microsoft donated PCs and Internet access technology to all of New York City's public libraries. Over the last several years, government and citizens have participated in many similar programs to wire schools to the Internet.

For example, on NetDay (March 9, 1996), more than 20,000 volunteers, including President Bill Clinton and Vice President Al Gore, laid six million feet of cable which had been donated by businesses to California high schools. See Figure 11. These efforts benefit both the students and the businesses donating the equipment.

Figure 11

President Clinton and
Vice President Gore ran
cable to help hook up
classrooms on NetDay

In an effort to ensure that technology is adequately provided to schools and that it is used effectively, many states require school districts to develop and implement technology use plans. The school district works with community members, businesses, parents, students, and staff to identify goals, gaps, and strategies that provide a systematic approach to integrating technology into each school.

Technology in the University Classroom

How do my instructors use technology in the classroom? The very best instructors have always found ways to enrich lecture-format instruction and make it more interactive. Even Socrates used question-and-answer instruction with small groups of students to create an active learning experience. More recently, teachers have used overhead display projectors and transparencies, which provide a medium for using concept art, graphics, and bulleted points, to present information to classes. Today, however, new computer-based technologies make it possible to create an even richer learning environment.

Using presentation graphics software, instructors can create and present attention-getting, computer-based slide shows on specific topics. See Figure 12. In an astronomy class, a teacher might present a multimedia slide show on planets in the solar system. This presentation might include pictures of a planet and its satellites transmitted to earth from orbiting spacecraft, video that depicts the rotational properties of a planet, animation that shows the rotation of this planet around the sun, and a sound track that heightens the feeling of traveling around or landing on the planet.

Figure 12

Instructors use computer technology in classrooms to deliver presentations.

Instructors are using **computer-assisted instruction (CAI)** to teach concepts, reinforce lecture presentations, deliver information, and test mastery of the material. For example, students might use computer-based tutorials (CBTs) and simulations to explore a topic such as the structure and properties of atoms. The CBT might include questions to test the student. If the student misses the answer to a question, the CBT reinforces the learning process by reviewing the concepts missed before continuing. In a classroom setting, the instructor has more opportunity to assist individual students. The most important advantage of CAI over lecture presentations is that the computer prompts the student to interact and become an active participant in the learning process.

By combining multimedia technology with overhead display panels, instructors can effectively demonstrate concepts and features. In a biology lab for instance, an instructor and students can use software to simulate a dissection, which can be more informative and less costly than hands-on dissection. For example, the software might zoom in and magnify arteries so that students can examine the different types of white and red blood cells and view the flow of blood. Figure 13 illustrates an example of an anatomy simulation called A.D.A.M. which stands for Animated Dissection of Anatomy for Medicine.

Figure 13

Using A.D.A.M.,
The Inside
Story, students
can explore the
human body
using
animations,
including
simulated 3D
graphics of
different
systems, such
as muscle, skin,
circulation and
the skeleton.

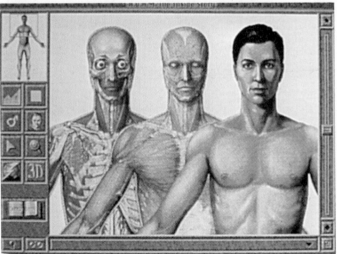

Students also have access to encyclopedias, dictionaries, and other important reference tools on CD-ROMs. Perhaps the ideal learning environment is one in which students have a computer on their desktops. As the instructor demonstrates on a computer in front of the class, students can perform the same steps on their computer. In an organic chemistry or physics class students might view the three-dimensional effects of van der Wahl forces between molecules, change the atomic structure of a molecule, and view how the change affects the bonding properties of the molecule. Technology in the classroom means students no longer have to visualize complex, three-dimensional structures and properties from hand-rendered, two-dimensional drawings on a whiteboard or blackboard.

These various approaches to **interactive education** stimulate students' interest and engage them in the educational process. In a passive learning environment, such as straight lecture, a student might retain 10 percent of what she or he learns. However, in an interactive learning environment, a student's retention can easily approach 80 to 90 percent. To improve the quality of education and make education worthwhile to the student, colleges must invest in interactive computer technology and educators must learn how to use these interactive training techniques effectively.

Distance Learning

How can I take classes without moving or changing my job? Traditionally and historically, universities and colleges are built on the foundation of a faculty, student body, and a library all bound by time and place. With the exception of correspondence degrees, if you want to get a college degree, at minimum you need to enroll in a college and attend classes at a particular time and place. In this setting, the faculty and students form a small community in which they directly interact with one another throughout the learning process. See Figure 14.

Figure 14

A traditional campus is defined by buildings, landmarks, and people interacting as they pass from class to class.

With the advent of telecommunications technologies, universities and colleges can now use distance learning to offer classes at locations other than local campuses. In **distance learning**, the instructor and the student do not have to be in the same room, so it opens up the university to individuals who are in remote locations. For example, the Massachusetts Institute of Technology (MIT) is well known for the quality of its engineering education. Students who live in regions with colleges that do not offer engineering programs could enroll in any distance learning programs that MIT offers. Furthermore, an increasing number of businesses are looking for individuals with multidisciplinary degrees and international experience. Using distance learning, students can pursue several degrees by registering in different programs of study at traditional colleges and universities around the world without physically attending.

Distance learning employs a variety of strategies and technologies for delivering education: correspondence courses, videotape, broadcast TV, microwave and satellite broadcast programs, voice mail, e-mail, fax, audiographic teleconferencing, text chat, and video conferencing. The World Wide Web is becoming one of the most cost-effective mediums for delivering distance education because more Americans are purchasing home computer systems, becoming members of online services, and using the World Wide Web to seek out services and information. Figure 15 shows how a Web-based course offers students the opportunity to communicate with each other and the instructor, as well as take tests and turn in assignments online.

Figure 15

Web-based distance learning offers efficient delivery of instruction to students all over the world.

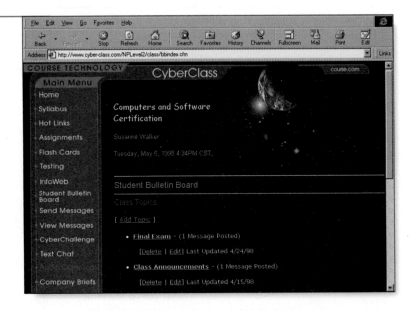

InfoWeb

Distance Learning 6

Even though distance learning opens doors to educational opportunities that a person might not otherwise have, it does have disadvantages. For example, interaction among faculty and students might be delayed or limited. Students learn by interacting, not only with the instructor, but also with other students. Instructors cannot judge the effectiveness of their presentations from students' expressions. Likewise, students cannot pick up information as easily from the instructor's gestures and nuances.

To some extent, the Web's capability to send and receive multimedia—video, real-time audio, text chat—can help overcome some disadvantages of distance learning. The logistics of submitting assignments for feedback has been overcome by the capability to attach files to e-mail messages or to transfer files via the Internet. Students can still obtain timely assistance with questions on lab assignments or other types of course work, whether or not they ever meet the instructor face-to-face. **Text chat**, made possible by **Internet Relay Chat** (**IRC**) technology, allows the class to interact by typing questions and responses to one another. The participants can see everything that is typed with the sender's identity, so it becomes an effective replacement for class discussions.

Ultimately, distance learning requires more preparation and effort by the instructor and the staff responsible for managing the transmission. In addition, it requires that students learn independently and manage their own educational program. This dramatically changes the way instructors teach and students learn. The ideal learning environment occurs when Web-based distance learning courses are supplemented with traditional learning resources. This combination of new technology and traditional teaching methods provides a total learning environment for a diverse student population.

Virtual Colleges

Do all colleges and universities have to have buildings and campuses? Professionals, college students, and anyone with the time and technology can take advantage of virtual colleges and virtual universities to further their education. Virtual Online University Services International, a nonprofit corporation, offers various levels of courses and programs. See Figure 16. This university exists only online and students attend through the use of communications software and Web browsers.

Figure 16

Virtual Online University Services International only exists as an electronic campus at **www.vousi.com**.

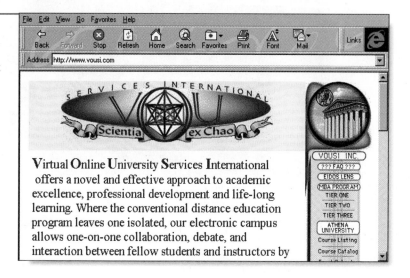

Online Universities 7

Virtual colleges and universities do not have the requirements or expenses of traditional colleges and universities. These educational institutions do not need to construct, heat, cool, clean, or maintain buildings, and they do not need to landscape campus grounds. They do not need cafeterias and dormitories for feeding and housing students and staff. Like traditional colleges and universities, they do need to purchase, maintain, and upgrade technology for use in their business. They also need to hire and pay instructors as well as a small technical, administrative, and support staff. Virtual colleges and universities can remain open 24 hours a day, 7 days a week. Learning is freed from the constraints of time and place.

As mentioned above, some virtual colleges exist only in cyberspace, such as the International University College, Western Governors University, The Graduate School of America, and the Open University of the United Kingdom, which has more than 250,000 students. Other virtual colleges or universities are associated with one or more existing traditional educational institutions. For example, Compass in CyberSpace is associated with the University of Maryland.

Some online services have their own online learning institutes. Microsoft Online Learning Institute Information Center maintains a list of its Online Learning Partners (as shown in Figure 17) and a searchable course catalog, from which you can select courses on operating systems, applications, software, programming, networking, and Internet technologies. The Web site offers step-by-step assistance to businesses that need to build and run effective online learning for employees.

Figure 17

The Online
Learning
Information
Center at
www.microsoft.com

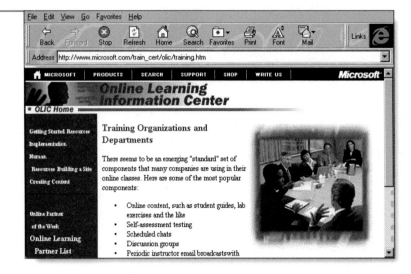

Although computers and the Internet clearly offer benefits to education, there is an inherent danger in valuing the contribution of computers too highly. Technology can influence the way we act, think, and view the world. Computers, like any other tool, can amplify some values and diminish others. Think about how computers function: Logic is the key element. In working with a computer you use logic skills, but not necessarily intuition, physical contact, emotional experience, and spiritual experience. When you use a computer, even if you are interacting with a lifelike simulation or with other people through the Internet, you do not use all of your intellectual resources.

Computers are best at accessing and manipulating information. They do not lend themselves well to reflection, contemplation, and understanding—activities essential to the development of new ideas. Even though it would be impossible to generate new ideas without information, information itself cannot take the place of ideas as the foundation of knowledge.

QuickCheck B

1 In contrast to the late 1970s and early 1980s, today there is a push toward _____ learning.

2 Educators use _____ software to prepare and present computer slide shows that organize information in an effective and easily understandable format.

3 In _____ a computer is used to teach concepts, deliver information, and test assimilation of the material.

4 Universities and colleges use _____ to offer instruction to students who cannot get to the classroom.

5 _____ is a college that offers courses and degree programs to students and professionals only through online technologies and the World Wide Web.

6 By using _____ technology, educators and students can communicate with each other directly in a distance learning environment.

C The Changing Face of Citizenship

"A popular government without popular information, or the means of acquiring it, is but a Prologue to a Farce or Tragedy; or perhaps both. Knowledge will forever govern ignorance; and a people who mean to be their own Governors must arm themselves with the power that knowledge gives."—James Madison

James Madison and the other framers of the Constitution clearly recognized that democracy is strongest when the people are well informed. They also recognized that the ability to become informed, in turn, rests on the free flow of information. Modern technology—from cellular telephones to the Internet—offers opportunities for information to flow more freely and rapidly than ever before. Technology also offers one more way that you can be better informed and make your voice heard in the affairs of the nation.

An Informed Citizenry

How do I become a better informed citizen? It might come as a surprise to you that the largest publisher in the United States is the federal government. From the laws of the nation and deliberations of Congress to pamphlets on pest control and stain removal, our tax dollars subsidize the publication of a vast array of information compiled by all federal agencies. And to protect the public's access to information for which they have paid, the Government Printing Office has long distributed these materials to libraries across the nation that participate in the Federal Depository Library Program.

For most of the hundred-year history of the Depository Library Program, this information was provided absolutely free. However, in the 1980s, in an attempt to prune what it perceived as a bloated federal budget, the Reagan Administration discontinued publication of some of this material and instituted charges for other portions of it. The effect was to reduce citizen access to knowledge of the workings of their government. An outcry from the academic and library community did little to reverse these policies.

InfoWeb

Public Information Resources 8

It took the rapid growth of the Internet in the 1990s to begin to turn things around. First Gopher, and now the World Wide Web, provide an economical way for government agencies to publish and distribute information. The Library of Congress now provides access to the Congressional Record and Federal statutes through a Web site called Thomas (named for Thomas Jefferson). See Figure 18. The Census Bureau also publishes facts and figures about all aspects of American life on its Web site. Even the Internal Revenue Service has a Web site, allowing citizens to download tax forms and publications and get answers to their tax questions.

Figure 18

Thomas is
one of many
Web sites
from which
you can
access public
information.

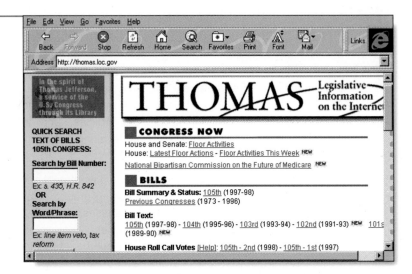

Access to much of this information is free to citizens. However, many fear that the replacement of government information on paper with the electronic form might reduce access to it. At the end of 1996, only about 10 percent of American homes had Internet access. Although that number continues to grow, access is mostly available from middle-income or high-income households. Proposed changes in the laws governing the Depository Loan Program might, however, address these concerns by making free access to all governmentally produced electronic databases available at participating public libraries.

Private groups provide many additional sources of information on important issues and politics. Most print and broadcast news organizations, including the networks, major newspapers, and magazines have established and maintain Web sites. Educom, a nonprofit consortium of American colleges and universities, sends its EduPage newsletter to subscribers via e-mail. Each issue of EduPage contains a news synopsis on the implementation of technology in education.

Your computer can help you link to nonprofit public interest and special-interest groups to stay up to date on current issues and to better understand the views of social and political groups at all points of the political spectrum. The Public Agenda Foundation, a nonpartisan, nonprofit opinion research organization, conducts and tallies the results of opinion polls, prepares voters' guides and citizen guides to major policy issues, and distributes material to journalists so that they can more effectively explain complex issues.

You can also learn more about the positions, voting records, and campaign contributors of candidates running for public office. The Federal Election Commission's Web site provides campaign spending information on presidential and congressional candidates as well as on the Democratic and Republican parties. You can also view the names of the top 50 Political Action Committees (PACs) that contributed the most money to each of the candidates in the last presidential election. Armed with this information, you are a better informed citizen as you select, work for, and vote for candidates and referenda.

Improving the Political Process

How can I have a greater voice in government and the political process? The United States government is a representative democracy in which citizens elect people to public office to carry out the business of government. Essentially, we delegate the job of governing at all levels—national, state, and local—to specialists. In our country's early years, relatively few voters and elected officials communicated with each other through public forums and debates, pamphlets, newspaper articles, and letters. Communication between elected officials and informed citizens, resulting in a high degree of participation, is what makes democracy work.

Today, you might feel that you have little voice in the government and little influence on electoral outcomes. Special-interest groups and lobbying groups seem to have captured the government's ear. Fax machines, marketing databases, computer-generated letters, and mailing lists have all made the job of lobbying easier. Ads, opinion polls, talk-radio spots, mass mailings, mass telephone calls, and toll-free numbers have increased the output and impact of professional lobbyists. For example, a lobbyist listening to a congressional hearing can use a cellular telephone to alert his or her main office to an upcoming vote. Then a broadcast fax can be sent to hundreds of sympathizers, and the process of blitzing politicians can start.

InfoWeb

Politics and Media
9

Radio, television, and print media—one-way broadcast media—are all vehicles for politicians to communicate with voters, but until the late 1990s there didn't seem to be an effective way for voters to communicate with politicians. Now, well-informed citizens are using technology to lobby their government representatives directly, to influence their elected officials' decisions on many issues.

New, less traditional lobbying groups are utilizing technology and Internet access to inform their members and to suggest strategies for communicating with elected public officials. One example of a political activist group is the American Association of Retired Persons (AARP). Their Web site, shown in Figure 19, offers information about which issues matter and recommends what and how to lobby. As a result, senior citizens and retired persons have a larger influence on how Congress votes on legislation with economic and social impact.

Figure 19

The AARP Web site

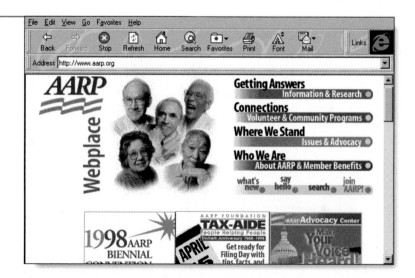

In contrast to the potential negative impact of lobbying, futurists and technology enthusiasts see technology, and particularly the Internet, as a way to improve the quality and quantity of political information, participation, and communication. E-mail, electronic town halls, and other uses of technology, such as cellular telephones and fax machines, are seen as tools to increase participation and possibly to give voters the ability to make policy decisions themselves—a trend toward direct democracy.

Public Interest and Special Interest Groups 10

On the other hand, if you consider the percentage and demographics of Americans who own computers, many critics will argue that the concept of a representative democracy through computers and the Internet might not be representative of the full population. Fortunately, the availability of computers in such places as public libraries and community centers is narrowing the gap between those who have access and those who do not have access to new technology.

For the increasing number of people who have access, the Internet offers a new way for politicians to talk with voters and voters with politicians. For example, information on voting records of members of Congress appears periodically in newspapers and newsletters, but this information is hard to come by unless you know exactly where to look for it. Knowing how your candidates voted in the past or would vote on key legislation is very influential in decision making on election day. For example, the National Taxpayers Union (NTU) Web site offers frequent online updates on the spending votes of each member of congress. The NTU claims that, as a result of its Web site, the number of Congress members who cosponsor expensive bills has declined. See Figure 20.

Figure 20

The National Taxpayers Union Web site

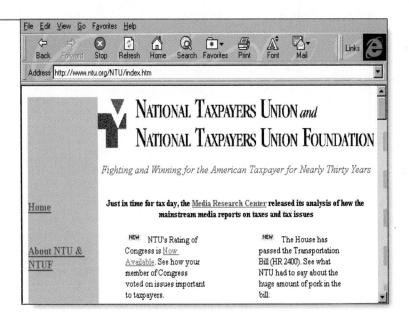

The Democratic and Republican parties, as well as third parties, have their own Web sites with information on their candidates and the full text of their party platforms. During an election year, you can participate online in the presidential debates between the major party candidates. In the 1996 presidential campaign, President Clinton and former Senator Bob Dole had their first presidential debate in Hartford, Connecticut. Using a Web browser and RealAudio™, people connected to the debate site, asked questions of commentators in an online chat as the debate occurred, and listened to the debate on their computer's speakers.

Another venue that allows for more direct participation in political discourse is the **electronic town hall meeting**, where you meet elected officials, candidates, and political analysts; discuss issues in depth; and perhaps even vote on issues. In 1995 the Indiana University School of Continuing Studies sponsored an electronic town hall meeting on health care. The school collected questions and comments from citizens using voice mail, e-mail, fax, and the World Wide Web. Since then, many political interest groups have sponsored electronic town hall meetings with a variety of officials. The Web site shown in Figure 21, nicknamed "Government Without Walls," is a service of the group called democracy.net.

Figure 21

"Government Without Walls" conducts regular electronic town hall meetings.

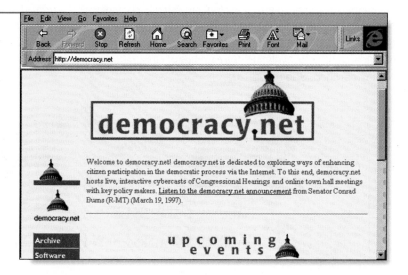

If a representative democracy is going to function well, voters need to participate in elections. But over the past several decades, voter turnout in national, state, and local elections has been decreasing or holding steady at less than 50 percent of registered voters. As a result, government officials are evaluating new strategies and technologies, such as voting by telephone or computer, that will make it easier for people to vote and thereby increase participation in elections. New approaches to voting also hold the hope of improving access to individuals with disabilities.

New computer technologies, such as optical scanners, touch-screen ballot systems, and perhaps voice-activated systems, allow on-the-spot tallying of results by computers. These new technologies improve access and are expected to replace traditional methods that rely on mechanical levers, paper ballots, and punch cards. Optical scanners use a laser beam to check for the presence of a mark on a ballot, touch-screens use a technology similar to touch-screen ATMs, and voice-activated systems recognize specific words within a spoken sentence or phrase.

InfoWeb

Internet
Enabled
Political
Activity
11

Televoting, or voting with a touch-tone telephone, allows the convenience of voting over a certain time span, such as a week. You do not have to take time off from work to vote on a specific day or readjust your schedule so that you can race to the polls hoping that you will make it before they close. You can vote in the privacy of your home at a time that is convenient for you. To televote, you call a special telephone number, provide a digital code to verify that you have the right to cast a vote, then enter a code that indicates your vote on a specific issue. That response is converted to digital information and transmitted to a computer system that tallies the information.

Although access to the World Wide Web is still limited, some experts speculate that the Internet will become a viable medium for voting sometime in the future. Like voting by telephone, Internet voting would have you provide a special access code that permits you to cast a vote. Then you would select your choices from a Web page, and a computer would tally the results. In addition to voting for candidates in national elections, citizens might also vote on national referenda. Even though these new technologies automate the voting process and result in faster compiling and analysis of election results, their real benefit will be realized if they are able to increase voter participation.

The potential benefits that the new technologies can bring to voting and the political process are innumerable. But whether those potential benefits become realities depends on how our society implements the technology. Some experts, politicians, and futurists would like to see these technologies lead us to a more direct form of democracy in which citizens make many of the policy decisions. But not everyone thinks that direct democracy is a good idea.

There are two key questions:

- First, can we trust ourselves to make sensible decisions that take into account the needs of *all* members of society and can we balance short-term gratification against long-term needs? While the founding fathers had a certain amount of faith in human nature, they weren't willing to trust it completely in the realm of good governance. Our current government is purposely structured to avoid quick decisions made by the majority.

- Second, who will benefit most from new technologies: voters in general, special interest groups, or only those who have the money and technological know-how?

We won't begin to reap the benefits of technology in politics until we can develop satisfactory answers to these questions.

QuickCheck C

1. The Library of Congress now provides access to the Congressional Record and federal statutes through a Web site called _____.

2. You can participate in electronic _____ meetings where you meet candidates and political analysts, discuss issues in depth, and perhaps even vote on issues.

3. _____ allows you the convenience of voting by telephone.

4. _____ opens the possibility of developing a virtual democracy where individuals cast votes online for candidates and national referenda.

5. When you vote by telephone or over the Internet, you provide a(n) _____ to verify that you have the right to cast a vote.

UserFocus

D Community and Relationships

Throughout this chapter, you've seen that the computer and new telecommunications technologies are very useful tools in many arenas—business and work, education, home life, and government and politics. Implementation of these tools has dramatically changed the way our society works, learns, plays, and governs. As a tool, the computer and its related technologies can help open doors for you, just as books and literacy open doors. Some of these doors include exposure to new knowledge; some include new job opportunities. Some of these doors, you will see, open into virtual worlds where you can shop, meet new people, and "live" in what are called virtual communities. However, it is equally important to realize that these doors are not open to everyone and to understand the implications this virtual world can have on our society.

Virtual Communities

Why would I want to participate in a virtual community? Traditionally, people think of community as a geographical area that includes their immediate neighborhoods as well as local schools, mosques, churches, temples, civic and political organizations, clubs, social groups, and businesses. See Figure 22. With technology we can reach beyond our local geographical region to all corners of the world, and we can interact personally and professionally with individuals and businesses from around the globe.

Figure 22

Communities are integral to our society.

InfoWeb

Virtual
Communities
and
Relationships
12

By developing relationships based on common interests instead of geographical proximity, we can enrich our lives by participating in virtual communities. A **virtual community** is a group of people who meet through their computers via the Internet and whose members share a common goal or interest, such as education or grassroots politics, or a common relationship, such as residing in a specific neighborhood, city, or geographical region.

When you connect to the World Wide Web, you become part of a larger community of individuals who share an interest in the Internet. When you access a commercial online service, such as America Online, Microsoft Network, Prodigy, or CompuServe, you become part of that online community. You share its resources, interact with other individuals participating in that same service, and contribute to the growth of that community by your participation in its various services. When you participate in online chats, you open up the possibility of building new friendships.

The Berkeley Interactive Virtual Community, shown in Figure 23, is a virtual community that electronically ties together individuals who live in the real city of Berkeley, CA. The structure and layout of this virtual community mirrors the structure and layout of the real community, and it expands opportunities for social interaction and commerce. The Web pages for individuals within the same physical neighborhood form a virtual neighborhood. Individuals who do not own a computer use free public computer workstations in strategic locations, such as libraries, to connect to this virtual community.

Figure 23

A virtual community
for the city of
Berkeley, CA

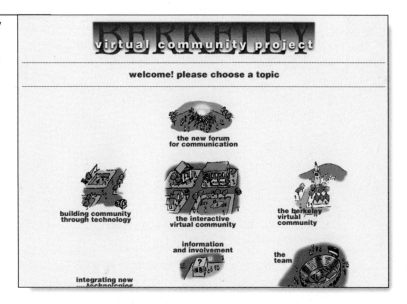

The developers of virtual communities hope that this new way of interaction will ultimately create a greater sense of community among citizens. The goal is to provide access to community resources and to break down societal barriers that separate people.

However, these virtual relationships can lead to disappointment. When you meet someone new online, how do you know that person is representing himself or herself honestly? It has become too easy to create a whole virtual personality that is meant to deceive others. Unfortunately, the news media report regularly on individuals who have been tricked into doing everything from sending money to being physically harmed by people they meet online. On the other hand, you could meet someone interesting that you might not have met otherwise. The best advice is to use caution if you travel into the virtual world of relationships.

Universal Access

Will everyone have the same access to computer technology that I have? Businesses depend on breakthroughs in computer technologies to improve the efficiency, productivity, and morale of their work force, as well as to automate production, track business transactions, cut their operating costs, and improve communication among employees. Without computer skills, you might very well be consigned to a low-paying or minimum-wage job. See Figure 24. The Department of Labor forecasts the greatest job growth in industries and professions that require strong, not minimal or average, computer skills. Indeed, an ongoing WWW user survey, first conducted in 1994 by Jim Pitkow through Georgia Tech in Atlanta, indicates a new division of haves and have-nots between those who have computer skills and those who do not. The Graphics, Visualization, & Usability (GVU) Center's WWW User Survey continues to be conducted every six months and has become a valuable tool in analyzing the demographics of the WWW.

Figure 24

Computer haves and have-nots

In spite of potential benefits, there is a real danger that the expansion of telecommunications technology and computers could create a new class—the information elite. Some people predict that a new class of knowledgeable and technologically savvy people will result in a **technocracy**—a society in which the decisions will be made by those who have technological competence.

The *New York Times* reported in 1996 that personal computers can be found only in about 33 percent of U.S. households. The majority of these households are affluent: more than 60 percent of the households purchasing computers have incomes of at least $40,000. In 1997, the *Huntsville Times* reported 38.5 percent of households owned computers, with the largest increase in homes that reported $10,000 to $30,000 annual incomes. These statistics indicate that the growth of computer ownership might have peaked, especially in homes with higher incomes who already own computers.

InfoWeb

Technorealism
13

The idea that computers will be used everywhere and at any time might be a reality only for those who can afford them. More important, combined with labor market trends that point to a need for strong computer skills, we could inadvertently end up being a society of technology and information haves versus have-nots. People without access to personal computers and computer skills are in danger of becoming disenfranchised from the rest of a technologically savvy society.

In response to the very real danger of a technological schism in U.S. society, the government and public policy advocates are promoting the idea of universal access to computers and the Internet. For example, the 1996 Telecommunications Act includes provisions that encourage telephone and cable television companies to make access to the Internet possible for everyone. In response, federal and state regulators are mandating access and service at lower-than-market rates for schools and public libraries. Another initiative is to provide inexpensive Internet access for residents of low-income areas. Public policy activists want to ensure that low-income families have equal access to the benefits that computers and telecommunications technology can deliver through the Internet.

EndNote The computer and new telecommunications technologies are powerful tools, but it is what you do with them that counts the most. To optimize your chances for success in this world and to enjoy life fully, you must invest in lifelong learning, explore the right types of resources, and apply these resources effectively. Easy access to information on the Internet and World Wide Web will give you some of the resources you need to develop informed opinions and to learn about the global community. Computer-mediated communication with other individuals around the world can broaden your perspective, open the potential for new friendships and relationships, and involve you in a community that knows no boundaries. It is our challenge to learn how to synthesize the benefits that new tools bring with our fundamentally human ways of thinking and knowing.

InfoWeb

InfoWeb

Chapter Links

The InfoWeb is your guide to print, film, television, and electronic resources. Use it to obtain updates on quickly changing technical information and to locate information for research papers. If you're using the New Perspectives CD-ROM, click the InfoWeb icon on the left side of this paragraph to access the online InfoWeb links. Otherwise, use your Web browser and type in the address of the New Perspectives site: www.cciw.com/np3. At the New Perspectives site you'll find up-to-date links to the topics covered in this chapter.

1 Technology in the News

You can find more news stories and analysis about the impact of technology in *The New York Times*, *The San Jose Mercury News*, and other major newspapers. At *The New York Times* Web site, **www.nytimes.com**, read the Technology section for breaking news, commentary, and in-depth analysis of critical technology issues. To keep informed about the computer industry in general, read *The San Jose Mercury News*'s "Good Morning, Silicon Valley" at **www.mercurycenter.com/gmsv/**. *Wired* magazine focuses on how technology and the information revolution are changing our society. Visit *Wired*'s companion Web site at **www.hotwired.com**. Nicholas Negroponte of the Media Lab at MIT created commentary on the technology and information landscape and speculations about the future, which continues to be current even three years after its original publication. You can read a collection of his articles written for *Wired* in *Being Digital* (Knopf, 1995).

2 Labor Statistics

The single best source for historical and current labor statistics and projected trends for the future is the Bureau of Labor Statistics (BLS) at **www.bls.gov**. This site also contains a national compensation survey, an occupational compensation survey, and occupational employment statistics. If you are examining labor statistics with an eye toward making career choices, you should also look at how much you can earn in an occupation. You can find historical earnings data on the Web at **govinfo.kerr.orst.edu/earn-stateis.html**. If you are beginning a job search, you will want to know the current state of the economy. The Dismal Scientist at **www.dismal.com** presents current economic indicators, forecasts, analysis, and industry-specific information. The technology industry currently has a shortage of skilled software engineers and programmers. Many analysts believe this shortage is not likely to last more than 10 years especially since enrollments in IT college programs are on the rise. Reading career articles in magazines such as *InfoWorld* (**www.infoworld.com/**) or *Computerworld* (see the IT Careers section at **www.computerworld.com/car/index.html**) will help you keep pace with the changing employment landscape.

3 Virtual Corporations

Read an interview with Ralph Ungermann, CEO of First Virtual Corporation at **www.herring.com/mag/issue30/little.html**. Browse through the Web sites of various virtual corporations to gain an in-depth understanding of their structure and operation. A few to explore are: First Virtual Corporation at **www.fvc.com**; Corporate Staffing Center at **www.corporate-staffing.com/csc/**; CStudio International at **cstudio.com/**; and The Round Table Group at **www.interaccess.com/rtg/**. The article "Virtual Corporations" from *LanTimes* at **www.wcmh.com/lantimes/97/97aug/708b089a.html** gives some good examples of how virtual corporations are well poised to capitalize on the current trend to outsource IT functions. BRINT's (A Business Researcher's Interests) section on virtual corporations and outsourcing at **www.brint.com/EmergOrg.htm** provides a wealth of links to information on virtual corporations. Virtual corporations provide special challenges to people working in teams. In *Virtual Teams* (John Wiley & Sons, 1997), Jessica Lipnack and Jeffrey Stamps detail those challenges and describe how best to meet them with lively discussions and case studies.

4 Online Job Hunting

With so many online job sites to choose from, where should you begin? One good starting point is with index or gateway sites—Web sites that gather and present information about other Web sites. One such site, JobSmart at **www.jobsmart.org/** offers sections on how to write resumes and where to send them, career guides, links to 150 salary surveys, and information on how to find unadvertised jobs (the hidden job market). The *Washington Post* hosts the Web site of job/career guru Richard N. Bolles, author of *What Color is Your Parachute?* at **www.washingtonpost.com/wp-adv/classifieds/careerpost/ parachute/front.htm**. In addition to finding annotated links to Web sites containing job openings, many sites offer excellent advice about organizing and conducting your job search, including sections on creating and posting resumes, career counseling, networking, and research. Some of the top job search Web sites are America's Job Bank at **web.ajb.dni.us/**, CareerMosaic at **www.careermosaic.com/**, CareerPath at **www.careerpath.com**, Career Magazine at **www.careermag.com/**, JobNet at **www.jobnet.com/**, Online Career Center at **www.occ.com**, E-Span Job Search at **www.espan.com/**, and iVillage's StudentCenter.com at **aboutwork.com/indexsc.html**.

5 Technology and Education

Engaged learning, educational reform, and technology-in-education initiatives all share in common the view that our current educational system neither meets the needs of students nor realizes its own potential. You can learn about engaged learning and why many educators believe it is critical by reading the article "Meaningful, Engaged Learning" at **www.ncrel.org/sdrs/engaged.htm** from the North Central Regional Educational Laboratory (NCREL). Explore NCREL's Web site at **www.ncrel.org/** to find how technology can improve learning, and how schools are currently using technology. A good resource for learning about educational technology plans is Pitsco's Launch to Technology Plans at **www.pitsco.com/p/techplans.html**. *Reinventing Schools: The Technology is Now!* at **www.nap.edu/readingroom/books/techgap/navigate.cgi** tracks the evolution of the technology and school reform movement. Not everyone, however, agrees that technology holds the answer to our educational system's problems. In "The Computer Delusion," from *The Atlantic Monthly* at **www.theatlantic.com/issues/97jul/computer.htm** Todd Oppenheimer makes a well-researched and well-argued case that computers do not necessarily enhance teaching and learning. Two e-zines which can help you explore more issues surrounding engaged learning and technology in education are *From Now On: The Educational Technology Journal* at **www.fromnowon.org/** and *T.H.E. Online* at **www.thejournal.com/**.

6 Distance Learning

Creating a Virtual Classroom for Interactive Education on the Web at **www.igd.fhg.de/ www/www95/papers/62/ctc.virtual.class** is a great place to start for an in-depth look at issues underlying distance learning and online instruction. The Online Distance Education FAQ at **129.7.160.115/ COURSE/DISTEDFAQ/Disted_FAQ.html** answers basic questions about distance learning, identifies different types of distance learning, and provides links to other Web resources. Distance Learning on the Net at **www.hoyle.com/distance.htm** has an extensive database of information on distance learning for K-12, colleges, and training. Another excellent gateway site is The Comprehensive Distance Education List of Resources at **www.online.uillinois.edu/ramage/disted.html**. Here you can find links to papers, research, information, contact names; businesses, organizations, service providers, K-12 and higher education programs; as well as other index sites. If you are interested in taking a distance learning course, Globewide Network Academy at **www.gnacademy.org** provides a catalog of over 15,000 courses from kindergarten through doctoral programs.

7 Online Universities

Models for structuring an online university exist, ranging from the ambitious Western Governors University, which exists solely online, to distance education offerings from traditional universities such as the New School for Social Research. The *Chronicle of Higher Education* article "Western Governors U. Takes Shape as a New Model for Higher Education" at **chronicle.com/data/articles.dir/art-44.dir/issue-22.dir/ 22a02101.htm** outlines the scope of Western Governors University and discusses the challenges such an enterprise faces. You can visit the University's Web site at **www.westgov.org/smart/vu/vu.html**. More traditional universities offering online education include California Virtual University at **www.california.edu/**;

DIAL—The New School's Cyberspace Campus at **www.dialnsa.edu/home.html**; and University of California Berkeley Online at **www.learn.berkeley.edu/**. Magellan University at **magellan.edu/magellan/ default.htm** focuses only on calculus, differential equations, and preparation for MCSE certification. National Technological University at **www.ntu.edu/** also has a relatively narrow focus, offering degree, certificate, and non-credit courses in engineering, computer science, information systems, and other technical areas. The Graduate School of America at **www.tgsa.com/** offers degree programs in education, human services, organization and management, and communications technology. For more information read *The Virtual University: The Internet and Resource Based Learning* by Howard Freeman, Tom Routen, Daxa Patel, Steve Ryan, and Bernard Scott (Stylus Pub Lic, 1998).

8 Public Information Resources

A wealth of government information—both federal and state—exists on the Internet. The single best index to federal government Internet resources is the Federal Web Locator at **www.law.vill.edu/ fedagency/fedwebloc.html**. This Web site has a search engine that uses agency or organization names for keywords. Here you will find links to the legislative, judicial, and executive branches of government; executive agencies and departments; government corporations; consortia and quasi-official agencies; federal boards, commissions, and committees; international sites; and other federally-related sites. Another helpful index to government sites is the University of California's Infomine section on Government Information at **lib-www.ucr.edu/govpub/**. This searchable index can also be browsed by an alphabetized table of contents. Finally, FedWorld at **www.fedworld.gov/** is a searchable online database of information disseminated by the federal government.

9 Politics and Media

In *Electronic Whistle-Stops: The Impact of the Internet on American Politics* (Praeger, 1998), author Gary W. Selnow argues that bringing messages directly to voters has always been a part of the politician's toolkit and that the modern use of the Internet is merely an extension of this tradition. You can find the Republican National Party Web site at **www.rnc.org/** and the Democratic National Committee Web site at **www.democrats.org/index.html**. The Web sites of individual members of congress are listed at **www.house.gov/** (the House of Representatives) and **www.senate.gov/** (the Senate). For state legislative news, check out **www.policywonk.com/**. Commentary and analysis are an important part of the political process in the U.S. One of the best newspapers for Washington insider politics is the *Washington Post* at **www.washingtonpost.com/**. CNN and *Time* magazine have created the online feature All Politics at **allpolitics.com/1998/ index.html** where you can find the latest political headlines. Roll Call Online at **www.rollcall.com/** includes policy briefings, roll call files, news scoops, commentary, a 1998 election map, and fun contests and quizzes. You can find insightful discussions of political issues from race to foreign policy at the *Atlantic Unbound*'s Politics page at **www.theatlantic.com/atlantic/election/connection/**. Policy.com at **www.policy.com/** features political news headlines, a policy calendar, and a discussion of the "issue of the week." A well-rounded guide to politics on the Internet is The Jefferson Project at **www.voxpop.org/jefferson/**. For a more humorous take on politics, check out the antics of The Capitol Steps at **www.capsteps.com/**.

10 Public Interest and Special Interest Groups

In today's political landscape, special interest groups seem to have more say in the political process than individual voters. The Internet has become a powerful tool for revealing the activities of special interest groups and clarifying public interest issues. The non-partisan Web site FecInfo at **www.tray.com/fecinfo/** provides information about money contributed to federal political campaigns. The Center for Responsive Politics at **www.crp.org/** provides a lobbying database, information on individual donors to political parties and candidates, a separate database on special interests, information on campaign finance law and regulations, information on money in state politics, and analyses of the impact of money on elections. Project Vote Smart at **www.vote-smart.org/** makes information on the voting records of over 13,000 political leaders from national and state governments easily available to the public. The Public Agenda Foundation's goals include educating politicians about the public's point of view on policy issues and educating citizens so that they can make more informed decisions. Visit **www.publicagenda.org/** to learn more. The Cato Institute at **www.cato.org/** promotes "public policy based on individual liberty, limited government, free markets, and peace." The League of Conservation Voters at **www.lcv.org/** cuts across the political spectrum and aims "to elect a pro-environment majority to Congress." For a conservative view, visit the Media Research Center at **www.mediaresearch.org/**—its goal is to bring balance to political reporting by identifying sources of liberal bias.

11 Internet Enabled Political Activity

Some experts believe that our political system is failing because many people don't vote or participate in political discussions. The Internet is often presented as a vehicle for increasing political activity and improving the political process. Costa Rica has been experimenting with online voting. In November 1997, John McChesney of *HotWired* interviewed three of the leaders of Costa Rica's voting experiment; you can read a transcript of the interview at **www.hotwired.com/synapse/hotseat/97/47/transcript2a.html**. Some people are even promoting direct democracy (implemented through online voting) as an alternative to our current representative democracy. You can read about the idea of direct democracy at The Direct Democracy Center site, **www.primenet.com/~conduit/**. The article "Machine Politics" from *Forbes* magazine at **www.forbes.com/tool/html/97/july/angles0702/voting.htm** discusses the pros and cons of online voting—be sure to read the sidebar "Who Will Go First" at **www.forbes.com/tool/html/97/july/angles0702/firstside.htm**. For a deeper look at the issues of democracy and the Internet, read Alinta Thornton's thesis, "Does Internet Create Democracy?" at **www.wr.com.au/democracy/**. *The Electronic Republic: Reshaping Democracy in the Information Age* (Penguin USA, 1996) by Lawrence K. Grossman presents an optimistic view of how the Internet could transform politics and our method of government.

12 Virtual Communities and Relationships

The classic book on virtual communities is Howard Rheingold's *Virtual Communities: Homesteading on the Electronic Frontier* (HarperPerennial, 1993). It is available online at **www.rheingold.com/vc/book/**. The advent of virtual communities and relationships inspired William J. Mitchell, dean of the School of Architecture and Planning at MIT, to speculate on the impact of the new digital culture on traditional structures of society. You can read his ideas online at **www.mitpress.mit.edu/e-books/City_of_Bits/index.html**, or in *City of Bits: Space, Place, and the Infobahn* (MIT Press, 1996). In an online community, some information that you normally count on is missing. For example, online you cannot be sure of a person's gender or if an online person is real. Check out the Web site of Virtual Personalities at **www.vperson.com/** to learn about Verbots—artificially intelligent entities who are beginning to populate some areas of cyberspace. See also "Bots are Hot" from *Wired* magazine at **www.wired.com/wired/4.04/netbots/index.html**.

13 Technorealism

In cyberspace you often find extreme ideas of how technology will improve everything in our society from education to government, or how it will lead to class warfare, creating a schism of technological haves and have-nots. The new movement of technorealism takes a critical look at the benefits and costs of technology. Learn more at **www.technorealism.org/** and in the magazine *Dialog* at **www.feedmag.com/html/dialog/98.03dialog/98.03dialog_master.html**.

Review

1   Below each heading in this chapter is a focus question. Look back through the chapter and answer each question in your own words.

2   What are the major challenges facing today's employees in the workplace?

3   If you want to choose a career that offers the potential for growth in the future, what types of professions might you consider?

4   Describe the advantages and disadvantages that dial-up networking, intranets and extranets can have on the way in which you work.

5   List three advantages of a virtual corporation.

6   What types of services might you expect to find at an online job search Web site?

7   What are the advantages of an interactive learning environment?

8   How might you use the Internet to engage in lifelong learning or supplement your current education?

9   What do you think of the idea of participating in an electronic town hall meeting of candidates for local office?

10 In what ways might computer-mediated communication change democracy in the United States?

11 What is Thomas, and why is it important to you as a citizen?

12 If you want to make your opinion heard at the highest levels in the land, how would you express those opinions?

13 What do you feel are the advantages and disadvantages of meeting other people online?

14 Have you ever participated in a virtual community? If so, what individuals did that community include?

15 Locate and describe places in your community that provide free or low-cost access to computers and the Internet. Who is allowed to use that access?

Projects

1

Virtual Corporations As the number of households that have computers and Internet access increases, the World Wide Web will provide opportunities for new businesses that use online technologies as the medium for developing, promoting, and conducting a business. You will also find more and more traditional companies selling products or providing services online. Using your Web browser and a search engine, look for information on virtual corporations. From the list of search results, examine a Web site that provides an overview of virtual corporations, and save the document to disk as a text file. Find another Web site that provides information on a specific virtual corporation. Using this information, prepare a three- to five-page, double-spaced, word-processed paper that contains the following sections:

- **Overview of Virtual Corporations**. Describe how a virtual corporation differs from a traditional corporation, list the advantages of forming a virtual corporation, and identify the types of resources that you need to form a virtual corporation.

- **A Virtual Corporation on the World Wide Web**. Describe the features, organization, products, and services of a virtual corporation that you found on the World Wide Web.

- **Ideas for a Virtual Corporation**. Using what you have learned about virtual corporations, describe a business venture that you could develop as a virtual corporation. Also describe how you might fund the business venture, the backgrounds of individuals needed for this business venture, the services you might need to contract, and the alliances this company might form with other companies.

- **Resources**. List the addresses, or URLs, of the Web sites, the names and authors of any online documents that you used as references, and any other resources that you used to prepare the paper.

- **Documentation**. Print a copy of the home page of the virtual corporation you found on the Web.

2 Online Learning Communication technologies and the World Wide Web can extend educational opportunities to everyone. Using the World Wide Web or an online service, search for a virtual or online university, college, school, or continuing education program. Prepare a three- to five-page, double-spaced, word-processed paper that contains the following sections:

- **Educational Facility**. Identify the name of the virtual or online educational institution and its affiliation, if any, with existing educational institutions.

- **Programs and Degrees**. Describe the types of programs and degrees or certificates this virtual or online educational institution offers.

- **Courses**. Assume you are interested in taking a course at this online educational institution. List the name of the course, the structure of the course (content, prerequisites, duration, online interaction with the instructor, and so on) and the costs of the course.

- **Documentation**. List the address, or URL, of the educational institution's Web site, and print a copy of the home page of the educational institution.

3 Computers in Your Schools Computers are being used in administration, classroom teaching, lab environments, and in many other ways at all levels of education. Using library resources, choose a topic in any area of computers in K-12 education that interests you. Research and explore it enough that you can talk comfortably about it. Then call your local school board, parent-teacher's organization, a teacher at a local school, or the local

school's computer specialist to find someone who you can interview about how computers are being used in the school system or at a local school. Find out how many computers are being used in the school, the basic specifications that are representative of the majority of those computers, how the school is using the computers, how important a role the person thinks that computers should play in education, and where the inspiration for getting computers into the school came from. If you can, go to the local school and observe students using computers in the classroom or a computer lab. Write a five-page paper that describes what you learned. Be sure your paper includes the names and positions of the people with whom you spoke and the title, author, and source of any written documents you used as resources.

4 State and Local Politics Using the World Wide Web, you can easily locate information on state and local issues, candidates, and elections in your home state and voting district. Open your Web browser, and using a search engine, locate the home page for the Secretary of State in the state where you live, the home page of a local, nonpartisan organization like the League of Women Voters, and one other site that provides information on an important issue in your state or local district. Using the information at these Web sites, prepare a three- to five-page, double-spaced, word-processed paper that contains the following sections:

- **State Resources**. Describe the types of resources your Secretary of State's home page makes available on the Web and the links it has to other sites.

- **Local Resources**. Describe the types of resources a local, nonpartisan organization provides on the Web.

- **State or Local Issue**. Describe an issue of concern to the voters in your state or local district, a Web site dedicated to that, and perhaps other issues, and the types of information that you can draw on to make an informed decision.

- **Resources**. List the addresses, or URLs, of the Web sites and any other resources you used to prepare the paper.

- **Documentation**. Print a copy of the home page of the Secretary of State's office in your home state and a copy of the home page of a local, nonpartisan organization that discusses either state or local issues.

5 **Voting Options** Local communities are using technology to expand the options available to people at election time, whether they are voting in their local precinct or using an absentee ballot. Communities are also using technology to change the way that people learn about candidates, issues, and referendums. Use library resources, particularly local newspapers, to learn about any new voting technologies that your community is introducing. Then call your local election commission or division, the town clerk's office, or the League of Women Voters to find out what specific new technology is being used in elections, what the components of that technology are and how it functions, what impact the technology is having on the election process, and how easy or difficult it has been to implement the new technology. Write a three- to five-page paper describing what you learned. Be sure your paper includes the names and positions of the people with whom you spoke and the title, author, and source of any written documents you used as resources.

6 **Online Magazines** *Internet World* contains articles on the latest changes in computer and communication technologies as well as those for the Internet and World Wide Web. Examine the recent issues of *Internet World* either at **www.iw.com** or in your college library, and look for a feature article on technology. Prepare a three- to five-page, double-spaced, word-processed paper that describes the technology and its anticipated impact on society. At the beginning of your paper, list the title of the article, the name of the author, the issue (date and month), and the page numbers.

7 **Virtual Communities** Members of local communities around the world are creating virtual communities that mirror a physical community in their makeup and layout. Using the World Wide Web, search for information on a virtual community in the United States or overseas. Prepare a three- to five-page, double-spaced, word-processed paper that contains the following sections:

- **The Virtual Community**. Identify the name of the proposed or actual virtual community, describe how it corresponds to a physical community (if applicable), and describe the organization of the virtual community.

- **User Interface**. Describe the nature of the user interface, how you navigate in this virtual community, and what types of sites are available.

- **Goals**. Describe how this virtual community will change the interaction among people and businesses in the real community.

- **Resources**. List the addresses, or URLs, of the Web sites and any other resources that you used to prepare the paper.

- **Documentation**. Print a copy of the home page of the virtual community.

COMPUTERS AND PRIVACY

When the Founding Fathers drafted the Bill of Rights, they could not have foreseen the world of computers. The Information Age brings a host of new concerns and challenges to our traditional notions of privacy and personal freedom. Some of the information about us—from our driving histories to the price we pay for our homes—constitutes public record information maintained by the government. Other information about us—including our spending habits, our medical histories, and our incomes—is collected by businesses and organizations.

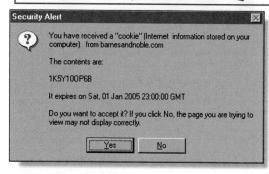

Computers and the Internet make it possible for more data to be gathered and distributed faster than ever before. Concerns arise not only about the fact that data is being gathered, but also about *how* the data and what kind of data is collected. Some Web sites create "cookies," which are packets of information sent by a server to a browser and then sent back by the browser each time it accesses that server. Cookies track a particular user's access to a site and they can track the data that was requested during the visit. Once the cookie is downloaded and installed on your computer, the site will automatically recognize your computer each time you revisit the site. The information in the cookies can be gathered into databases and analyzed to report on the site's effectiveness. It is the widespread use of these databases that impacts your privacy because data about you is recorded there. This is only one of many concerns that are being debated by computer professionals, government agencies, and public interest groups concerning the need for new laws to control the distribution of personal data.

This chapter begins with a description of various databases maintained by government and business and the privacy concerns they raise. The section on cryptography shows how the technology of public-key cryptography can be used to ensure privacy and to permit secure electronic commercial transactions. You will explore the government's concerns about the unrestricted use of this technology. This chapter concludes with a discussion about ways to discover what information is contained about you in several important databases and ways to help avoid the dissemination of your personal information.

CHAPTER**PREVIEW**

In this chapter you will see how computer technology has implications for your privacy and personal freedom. After you have completed this chapter, you should be able to:

- Identify the databases that contain personal information about you
- Describe how computer technology affects the level of personal privacy you enjoy
- Describe the level of privacy you should expect when communicating on the Internet or when using an e-mail system at work
- Explain how public-key encryption works
- Explain how you can ensure the privacy and accuracy of your personal information

A Databases and Personal Privacy

Record keeping is a traditional and necessary function of both government and business. Every major lifestyle change—the purchase or sale of a home, marriage, divorce, birth, and death—is recorded by the government. These records are traditionally open and available for public inspection. Record keeping is a necessary part of running a profitable business—from maintaining inventories, account transaction records, and employee histories to compiling customer lists and market research.

The Information Age has witnessed the migration of these records from paper to computerized databases. Computer technology makes managing, searching, copying, comparing, and sharing such records easy and inexpensive. In recent years, the development of digital databases and inexpensive, high-speed data networks for the sharing of digital information offers new opportunities for the exchange of ideas as well as new challenges for the protection of personal privacy. As a result, an entire industry of information gatherers and sellers has arisen. These entrepreneurs collect data from various digital sources. They can construct a seemingly detailed (and sometimes inaccurate) portrait of any of us, based on the data trail that we each leave behind in everyday life.

Government Databases

What kinds of information do government databases contain about me? The 178 largest federal agencies maintain approximately 2,000 databases, each containing millions of records. Many of these federal databases contain highly personal and confidential information about each of us. See Figure 1. For example, the Social Security Administration maintains welfare benefit and eligibility records about you; the Internal Revenue Service (IRS) keeps income and tax records about you; the Department of Defense has records about your military service. If you were ever arrested, the FBI maintains records about you, regardless of whether you were found guilty of a crime. As you'll learn in Section B, federal law usually places certain restrictions on the release of information from these confidential databases to the general public. However, the protection from disclosure of such confidential information is far from complete.

Figure 1

The U.S. federal government gathers information about each citizen.

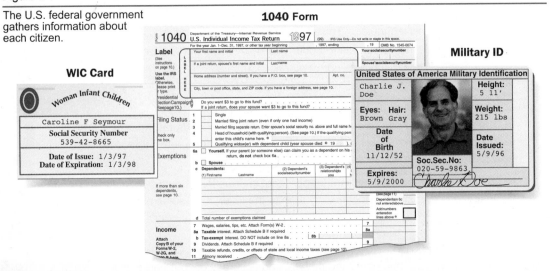

InfoWeb

Computer
Matching
& Profiling
1

Some experts worry about the ways in which the information in these databases can be shared between various federal agencies through the federal government's practice of computer matching and computer profiling. **Computer matching** involves acquiring, comparing, and consolidating data from multiple databases. Generally, an individual's Social Security number provides the match between records in different databases. For example, the IRS might use computer matching to detect under-reported income by comparing its own records with those of other government agencies, credit card companies, and financial institutions. New York and New Jersey have used computer matching to identify hundreds of welfare recipients who were receiving benefits from both states, a practice called "double-dipping."

Computer profiling is the use of records from many different databases to identify individuals who fit a predetermined model, or "profile." For example, the **National Crime Information Center (NCIC)** was started by the FBI in 1967 and is the primary criminal justice database in the United States. The NCIC contains information about stolen vehicles and other valuables, wanted individuals, missing persons, unidentified persons, and the Interstate Information Index (III). The **Interstate Information Index** contains the criminal records (including arrest records) of more than 13 million people. The NCIC is a dynamic database in that its records are continually updated by both federal authorities and the thousands of local law enforcement agencies that supply information to it. Local police departments equip their officers with wireless mobile computer terminals located in police vehicles to directly access its records, as shown in Figure 2. The NCIC has proven extremely effective for the apprehension of criminals and for other uses such as investigating potential employees prior to hiring.

Figure 2

A police officer checks the NCIC for warrants during a routine traffic stop.

InfoWeb

Public
Records
Online
2

State and local government agencies have traditionally kept administrative records of births, marriages, deaths, land ownership records, court files, driving histories, and other information specific to individuals. These are referred to as **public records** because they are generally open to public inspection. Because of digital technology, many of these records have found their way into computer databases. It is now easy for government, business, and the public at large to access and search public records. Government agencies frequently offer remote access to their public record information to business and the public at little or no charge.

Figure 3 illustrates how easily governments grant access to public records in digital form. In 1996, Aaron Nabil's Web page permitted users to look up the name and address of the owner of any Oregon vehicle at no charge, based on the license plate number. Mr. Nabil was able to create the page after purchasing Oregon's entire database of licensed vehicles for $220. To search this page, you simply needed a computer equipped with a modem. Despite the public outcry that followed, Mr. Nabil's Web page was perfectly legal under both federal and Oregon law. After a polite telephone request from the governor of Oregon, Mr. Nabil disabled the page.

Figure 3

| In August of 1996, Mr. Nabil demonstrated how accessible state government information can be when he started the Oregon License Plate Query page on the World Wide Web. | 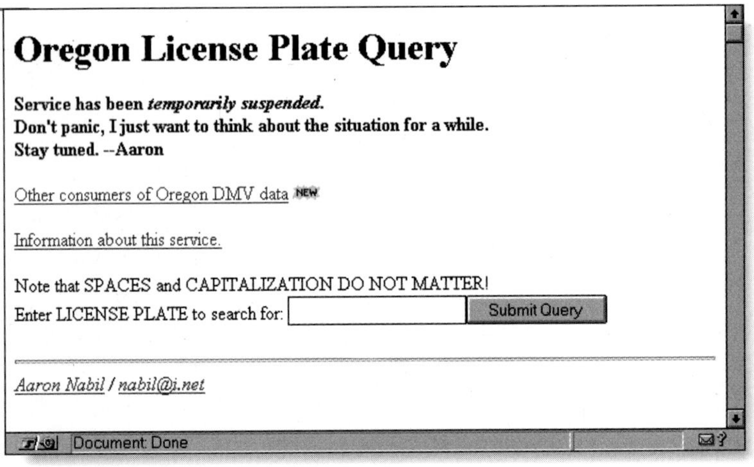 **Oregon License Plate Query**

Service has been *temporarily suspended*.
Don't panic, I just want to think about the situation for a while.
Stay tuned. --Aaron

Other consumers of Oregon DMV data `NEW`

Information about this service.

Note that SPACES and CAPITALIZATION DO NOT MATTER!
Enter LICENSE PLATE to search for: [_____] [Submit Query]

―――――――――――――――――――

Aaron Nabil / *nabil@i.net* |

Document Done

Private Databases

What kinds of information do business databases contain about me? Modern databases are vital to the business world. It's probably not too long since you received a form letter advertising some new product designed especially for your needs or announcing that you are a sweepstakes finalist, or offering you a new credit card at no charge. Businesses gather and share personal information in search of new markets and customers. Magazine publishers, mail-order retailers, and many nonprofit and political organizations use computerized mailing lists to target the right consumers.

Any business you come into contact with maintains in-house computer databases of their own. Banks and other financial institutions maintain databases of information about your money transactions and account balances. Telephone companies maintain records of your long distance calls. The local video store will usually have a database containing a history of the films you rent. Similarly, most libraries have records about the books you have checked out. Medical insurance providers maintain records of the claims you submit to them for payment and the health conditions that give rise to those claims. Manufacturers and retailers compile mailing lists based on information they receive from their customers through mail-in warranty registrations, surveys, or other contacts.

Businesses commonly sell these lists to each other for use in mail and telephone advertising. This means that once you are on one business's list of customers, you are likely to receive similar mail advertisements from other related businesses and organizations. Thus, if you subscribe to a magazine for hunting enthusiasts, you might also receive unsolicited catalogs of hunting equipment. If you make a donation to your favorite environmental organization, you will likely receive catalogs for outdoor products and mail from other sources, inviting you to give to other, similar organizations. The extent to which they share their information with other businesses often depends on the limits set by federal and state laws.

Many employers and industries collect data on employees and share that information with others. For example, the Employers Information Service in Louisiana tracks information such as which construction, oil, or gas employees have made worker's compensation claims. Potential employers in those industries can avoid hiring individuals with too many claims.

In addition, nearly all businesses that extend loans or credit accounts to individuals rely on credit reports, such as the one shown in Figure 4 on the next page, to decide whether to extend credit to a customer. Credit reports are provided by **credit reporting agencies**—businesses that maintain gigantic databases of information about individuals' credit histories. If you have ever used a credit card, you will be listed in the databases of credit reporting agencies. They are able to maintain this information through the cooperation of creditors who supply payment histories and other data, such as date of birth and residential addresses, found on credit applications. They also gather information from sources such as public record databases and court records. When you request a credit report, your credit history will be covered going back seven years.

Figure 4

An example of a credit report

TRANS UNION
CONSUMER RELATIONS DISCLOSURE
NOT TO BE USED AS A CREDIT REPORT

FILE NUMBER			
91BJ9023-001	ZB232	01	DR
DATE 8/17/97	INDIVIDUAL		13SD

AMOUNT RECEIVED   PAYMENT TYPE

CREDIT CARD NO.   EXP. DATE

DEAR CONSUMER
THIS IS A COPY OF THE CURRENT CONTENTS OF YOUR CREDIT FILE. IT IS BEING FURNISHED TO YOU BASED ON THE INFORMATION YOU HAVE PROVIDED IN ACCORDANCE WITH THE "FAIR CREDIT REPORTING ACT". PLEASE PROVIDE THE FILE NUMBER SHOWN ON THIS REPORT ON ALL CORRESPONDENCE. REFER TO THE REVERSE SIDE FOR EXPLANATIONS OF CODES AND ABBREVIATIONS IN THIS DISCLOSURE.

IN FILE SINCE: **10/87**   **BIRTH DATE 7/29/65**

CONSUMER NAME AND ADDRESS
BENNETT, ANGELA S.
1234 RIVER OAKS CIR
SAN JOSE, CA 95134

SSN **987-65-4329**   DATE RPTD **7/95**

SPOUSE NAME/SSN
MILES DYSON
987-65-4323

TEL **408-555-1212**

FORMER ADDRESS
18145 ROLLINS VIEW DR, GRASS VALLEY, CA 95945
2828 S MEMORIAL DR, GREENVILLE, NC 27834

DATE REPORTED:
2/93
5/88

PRESENT EMPLOYER AND ADDRESS
CATHEDRAL SYSTEMS
22100 STEVENS CREEK, CUPERTINO, CA 95014

POSITION/INCOME
SYSTEMS ANALYST
$53.6K

EMPL DATE **5/94**   DATE VERIF **11/96**

SPOUSE'S EMPLOYER AND ADDRESS
CYBERDYNE TECHNOLOGIES
BURBANK, CALIFORNIA

ELECTRICAL ENGINEER
$127.6K

10/91   **9/96**

SUBSCRIBER NAME	SUBSCRIBER CODE	DATE OPENED	HIGH CREDIT	DATE VERIFIED	BALANCE OWING	AMOUNT PAST DUE	PAYMENT PATTERN 1-12 MONTHS / 13-24 MONTHS	TYPE ACCOUNT & MOP
ACCOUNT NUMBER		TERMS	CREDIT LIMIT	DATE CLOSED	MAXIMUM DELINQUENCY DATE / AMOUNT / MOP			
ECOA COLLATERAL				REMARKS	TYPE LOAN		HISTORICAL STATUS NO. MONTHS / 30-59 / 60-89 / 90+	
SEARS D 1131833		4/88	$2000	9/96	$197	$0		R01
428015711223								
C								
COMMERCE BK B LA 1234		8/96	$9500	10/96	$9150	$0	1111111	I01
54603982101	M60							
I 1996 NISSAN			/AUTOMOBILE					

Besides supplying credit reports about specific individuals to businesses that extend credit to their customers, credit reporting agencies also sell mailing lists of potential customers to banks and credit card companies. For example, VISA can ask for a list of all professional people over the age of 30 who live in a specific area code, and the credit reporting agency will sell it the list of names and addresses.

Financial institutions and credit card companies share data about their mutual customers. In 1992, American Express cancelled a customer's card because it had determined that the customer didn't have enough in his bank balance to pay his bill. You might be surprised to know who has access to your financial records.

The information contained in your credit report not only affects your ability to receive credit but might even influence your prospects for future employment or promotion. Credit reporting agencies often supply detailed information to employers. Because this information is not always accurate, it is very important that you are aware of the information contained in your credit report.

Privacy Concerns

Why should I be concerned about the existence of these databases? In the past, if someone wanted to compile a detailed profile about you, they had to visit various government offices and manually search through paper-based public records. See Figure 5. If they wanted to know about the real estate you bought or sold, they had to search through land transfer and mortgage records in the local office of the Recorder of Deeds. To find out if you have ever been sued or divorced, that information was in files maintained by court clerks. To learn what kind of car you own and the value of your home, they had to review files held by the local tax collector. Searching was costly in both time and effort, and the probability that someone would spend time looking for information about you was relatively low. Therefore, before the use of computers to store and search data became widespread, personal information was relatively secure, even if it was not entirely private.

Figure 5

Searching paper government records can be time-consuming.

Today computerized databases greatly reduce the time and costs of retrieving personal information. In general, more types of databases are accessible to everyone from market researchers to nosy strangers. Often the data that was once scattered throughout remote locations is now stored on one database. Or, if it is not stored in one place, data can be retrieved from a single remote location. Because these databases contain information that is a matter of public record, anyone sitting at a computer equipped with a modem can easily access these records.

The ease with which this information can be accessed and shared has led to the rise of **information entrepreneurs**—businesses that collect and sell information. Businesses that do this type of searching are flourishing and are making the information available for a variety of purposes. These businesses generally charge a fee for access to a wide array of personal information that is not usually available to the public. One example is Executive Marketing Services, Inc., which provides accurate contact information such as telephone numbers of likely customers to direct marketers. Thomas Staffing Services maintains an extensive database of information about job applicants' skills, work experience, education, and other information that will assist employers in selecting qualified potential employees without advertising for them. In some cases, it is to a person's benefit to be included in such databases, but the disadvantage is that some information entrepreneurs gather personal information without notifying you or even asking your permission.

Social Security Numbers

| How is my Social Security number useful to others? | Easy accessibility of private information through computer databases is compounded by the increasing use of the Social Security number as a national identification number. Figure 6 shows a sample Social Security card. The number was originally intended only for the purpose of keeping track of our Social Security benefits and IRS tax records. Now, Social Security numbers are used widely and routinely by other federal agencies, state and local governments, financial institutions, schools, and other businesses as unique personal identifiers.

Figure 6

Social Security card

Information from many different sources can be collected and matched to any individual simply by using his or her Social Security number. Therefore, whenever you disclose your Social Security number, you have lost control over the personal information that can be obtained by using it.

Social Security numbers are favorite targets of individuals who engage in various kinds of fraud. An impostor who knows your name and Social Security number can assume your identity and file claims for Social Security benefits based on your contributions to the fund. An impostor can also use your Social Security number to receive extensions of credit based on your good credit history. Once credit is granted, the creditor holds you—the person legally associated with the Social Security number—responsible for debts incurred by the impostor. Victims of this type of fraud have to hire legal representation, and sometimes private investigators, to prove their innocence when creditors sue to collect the unpaid debt. Even though they don't have to pay the original debt, the victims suffer financial loss and permanent damage to their credit histories.

As an extra precaution, most businesses now also require a personal identification number (PIN) or a password that only the individual would know, like your mother's maiden name. However, even this information can be discovered by an impostor who is determined to use your identity for illegal purposes. Therefore you should be careful about when and to whom you divulge your Social Security number. The *User Focus* section at the end of this chapter discusses when you are obligated to give your Social Security number, when you are not obligated to release it, and guidelines for monitoring the information retained and disclosed about you.

Database Disasters

What can happen when database information is inaccurate? There are many examples of the invasions of privacy that result from the release of personal information in databases, including the problems of junk mail and telemarketing. A far greater problem is the tendency of business and government to treat the information in their databases as unalterable truth. This view ignores the fact that data entry clerks and designers of databases are both human and prone to error. Database errors can be the result of programming mistakes, data entry mistakes, data matching mistakes, or data tampering, for example, by hackers.

InfoWeb

Personal
Database
Disasters
3

People have been arrested as the result of mistaken identities caused by erroneous information in government databases. Others have been denied credit when their credit histories have been damaged by impostors who have used stolen Social Security numbers to receive extensions of credit. However, credit histories are more frequently damaged by data entry mistakes than by the deeds of impostors.

The term "database disaster" can refer to a range of problems from minor errors or incidents that cause inconvenience to major mistakes that permanently damage lives. In one case, a 36-year-old father of four was fired from his $70,000-a-year sales job for a cable television company after only six weeks on the job. A background check by a credit bureau revealed to the employer that the new employee had once been convicted for cocaine possession. The credit bureau mistook the innocent employee for someone else with a similar name, damaging his career and livelihood.

In another case, an individual was the victim of numerous arrests over a 14-month period after his wallet was stolen. The NCIC had identified him as a criminal. The thief who adopted his identity was a prison escapee who committed a robbery and murder. It took five years for the federal court to rule that the victim's constitutional rights had been violated by local police who arrested him. His record was cleared, and he was awarded compensatory damages.

In 1992, the Associated Press (AP) reported that residents of Hartford, Connecticut had been passed over for jury duty in federal courts because they were all reported as deceased. How did the existence of so many people disappear? In the database that identifies potential jurors, the City field containing "Hartford" overflowed into the Status field so that all the records looked like the sample in Figure 7. The data value for City became "Hartfor" and the data value for Status appeared as "d", which the computer interpreted as "deceased"!

Figure 7

A database disaster was caused by data overflow from one field into the next.

First Name	Last Name	City	Status
Susan	Moore	Hartfor	d
John	Smith	Hartfor	d
Mary	Jones	Hartfor	d
Thomas	Smith	Hartfor	d
Susan	Smith	Hartfor	d
John	Jones	Hartfor	d
Henry	Moore		

Dataveillance

Should I be concerned about the government monitoring my activities? Another problem is the impact of databases on a free society. **Dataveillance** is the systematic use of personal data systems in investigating or monitoring the actions or communications of one or more persons. Unlike traditional forms of surveillance, which involve watching and listening, dataveillance merely requires the collection and matching of personal information from various databases. Dataveillance is less expensive and time-consuming than surveillance, and it is far less likely to be detected by the person being monitored.

InfoWeb

Dataveillance
4

Some social commentators view the government's ever-increasing power to examine our personal lives using computerized records as a threat to both privacy and freedom. In fact, dataveillance provides both benefits and dangers to the individual and to society. The physical security of persons and property is made more efficient and cost-effective than the traditional forms of physical surveillance. Information about the location of individuals who pose a potential threat to others is easier to locate and distribute.

However, you have seen how easily one's identity can be assumed by anyone with access to information about you. The possibility of errors in your data grows exponentially with the amount of data that is stored about you. The responsibility for error-free data begins with the clerk who first enters it and continues throughout the data-gathering system. Ultimately, it becomes your responsibility to continuously check for errors in your own "digital identity." The *User Focus* section will give you some tips on how to do that.

QuickCheck A

1. _____ involves acquiring, comparing, and consolidating data from multiple databases to provide a match between records in different databases.

2. _____ is the use of records from many different databases to identify individuals who fit a predetermined model.

3. True or false? The FBI's National Crime Information Center (NCIC) database is continually changing, based on new information supplied by local law enforcement agencies.

4. State and local records that have historically been available for inspection are known as _____ records.

5. Two examples of private institutions or businesses that maintain and share information about you are _____ and _____.

6. True or false? Computerized databases have increased the cost of finding and retrieving personal information.

7. People who collect and sell information are information _____.

8. The primary privacy concerns with the use of the _____ as a personal identifier is the loss of personal control over private information and unrestricted data matching.

9. The systematic collection and comparison of database information to monitor the activities of a person or group is called _____.

B Privacy Law

A 1994 Equifax-Louis Harris poll found that 84 percent of Americans are concerned about threats to their personal privacy in the Information Age, and 51 percent of these described themselves as "very concerned." Technologies are emerging faster than the laws can evolve to meet the concerns of our citizens. A body of law is developing gradually to address these concerns. These laws have various sources, including the U.S. Constitution and various federal and state statutes.

Privacy Under the Constitution

Don't I have a constitutional right to privacy? | The first 10 amendments to the U.S. Constitution known as the Bill of Rights do not specifically mention a right to privacy. The drafters of our Bill of Rights lived in a world without electricity, motorized travel, or the tools of modern industry. The economy was primarily agricultural, travel was either by foot or by horse, and long-distance communication was exclusively written.

It is not surprising that the Bill of Rights addresses issues of privacy that would have been of special concern in the late 1700s, even though the word "privacy" is not specifically mentioned in the Constitution. In particular:

InfoWeb

The Bill of Rights
5

- The First Amendment protects freedom of speech and thought, freedom of the press, and freedom of religious choice.

- The Third Amendment prohibits the peacetime quartering of soldiers "in any house" without the owner's consent.

- The Fourth Amendment protects the "right of the people to be secure in their persons, houses, papers and effects against unreasonable searches and seizures."

- The Fifth Amendment protects an individual from being deprived of "liberty" without due process of law, and the right not to be "compelled in any criminal case to be a witness against himself."

- The Ninth Amendment provides that other rights not listed in the Bill of Rights are "retained by the people."

The U.S. Supreme Court serves as the final interpreter of the Constitution and the final guardian of our rights and liberties specified in the Bill of Rights. In addition to the specific protections these Amendments provide, the Supreme Court has recognized that Amendments 1, 3, 4, 5, and 9 address concerns about personal privacy as well as personal freedom. The Court has held that these five Amendments create "zones of privacy" for the individual into which the government may not intrude and that, taken together, these Amendments may be said to create a "right to privacy."

The decisions of the Supreme Court that specifically discuss the constitutional right to privacy fall into three general areas. These cases declare the right to privacy to include the following:

- The right to make personal choices about intimate matters—such as decisions about contraception, abortion, marriage, medical care, childrearing, and education

- The right to make personal choices about non-intimate matters—such as what kind of clubs you may join or the kind of people you associate with

- The right to be left alone—such as the right to possess pornographic materials in one's home or the right not to have to register with the government in order to receive Communist magazines in the mail

Unfortunately, as new technologies emerge, our Supreme Court has difficulty applying the Bill of Rights to new situations. Not long after the invention of the telephone, the Court was called upon to decide whether the Fourth Amendment right against unreasonable searches and seizures applied to private telephone communications. Could the government tap a private telephone call without obtaining a search warrant first? In the 1928 case of *Olmstead v. United States*, the Court held that the government could engage in wiretapping without a warrant because the Fourth Amendment was written to prohibit "physical invasions" by the police into one's "houses, papers and effects." Because the wiretap could be done remotely, there was no *physical* intrusion into the individual's home and therefore no Fourth Amendment violation.

It was not until 1967 in *Katz v. United States* that the Court finally recognized that the Fourth Amendment protects "people, not places" and that people have a "reasonable expectation of privacy" in their telephone communications. In that case, the Supreme Court threw out evidence gathered through a wiretap of a public phone booth used by the defendant to place illegal bets. The decision stated that warrantless wiretaps did violate the Fourth Amendment because its "search and seizure" clause protects us from government searches that violate a person's "reasonable expectation of privacy." Someone who makes a phone call, even from a public telephone, has a "reasonable expectation of privacy" in the telephone call. See Figure 8.

Figure 8

The right to private telephone conversations is protected by the Fourth Amendment.

So far, the Supreme Court has not recognized an individual's right to prevent the collection and dissemination of personal data by the government as part of any right of privacy. In the 1976 case of *Paul v. Davis*, the Supreme Court held that a state is free to publish its record of an "official act," such as an arrest record. In the 1977 case of *Whalen v. Roe*, the Court held that a state could require pharmacists to submit confidential information about individuals who receive certain prescription medications, which the state would then maintain in a central database. According to the Court, this scheme did not violate any constitutional right to privacy of the patients or their doctors.

William Brennan, shown in Figure 9, was one of the more liberal Supreme Court Justices who often wrote opinions critical of privacy invasions by the government. Justice Brennan retired from the Court in 1990. In his opinion of the Whalen case, Justice Brennan wrote:

What is more troubling about this scheme, however, is the central computer storage of the data thus collected ... [A]s the example of the Fourth Amendment shows, the Constitution puts limits not only on the types of information the State may gather, but also on the means it may use to gather it. The central storage and easy accessibility of computerized data vastly increase the potential for abuse of that information, and I am not prepared to say that future developments will not demonstrate the necessity of some curb on such technology.

Figure 9

Justice William Brennan

Legal commentators have pointed to this case, and especially Justice Brennan's comments, as evidence that the Supreme Court might, some day, apply constitutional restrictions on the gathering and distribution of personal information in computer databases.

It is important to understand that the guarantees contained in the Bill of Rights are actually special rules that prohibit certain conduct by the government toward its citizens. As a general rule, the Bill of Rights does not protect you from similar conduct by private individuals, businesses, or other institutions. For example, the Fourth Amendment's prohibition against "unreasonable searches and seizures" prevents a policeman from entering and searching your home without a warrant, except in certain emergency situations. However, this same Amendment does not prevent an intruder from entering and searching your home without your permission. To protect against privacy invasions by businesses and others (or to provide additional privacy protection against governmental conduct not prohibited by the Bill of Rights), we must rely on other laws enacted by Congress or the states.

Federal Legislation

Are there any federal laws to protect the privacy of my personal information? Although there is no clearly defined national computer privacy policy, Congress has enacted several laws to prevent unwarranted distribution of information stored in both government and private databases. These laws were enacted on a piecemeal basis as the need for privacy protection was perceived by Congress or demanded by citizens. Figure 10 lists some of these laws.

Figure 10

Federal privacy laws

The Fair Credit Reporting Act

Establishes certain rules that private consumer reporting agencies must follow in collecting and distributing credit reports, gives consumers the right to obtain a copy of their report, and establishes procedures for consumers to challenge incorrect information. This act also regulates the distribution of investigative consumer reports and requires that consumers be notified whenever an investigative consumer report is requested by someone other than his or her current employer.

The Privacy Act of 1974

Prohibits the disclosure of government records about individuals to anyone except the individual concerned, except for certain purposes such as law enforcement. This is the primary federal law dealing with the use and disclosure of Social Security numbers.

The Family Educational Rights and Privacy Act of 1974
(*also called the* **Buckley Amendment**)

Prohibits the unauthorized release of student records by schools that receive any form of federal funding. In addition, schools are required to establish procedures for students or their parents to challenge erroneous records.

The Electronic Communications Privacy Act of 1986

Prohibits federal or state law enforcement officials from accessing, intercepting, or disclosing e-mail or other electronic communications without first obtaining a search warrant. This act also imposes criminal fines and/or imprisonment for individuals who access, intercept, or disclose the private e-mail communications of others. The act includes numerous exceptions, however, and exempts systems operators from liability for accessing others' communications in specific cases, such as those that prevent harm to the system or to other users.

Computer Matching and Privacy Protection Act of 1988

Limits the use of computer matching between various agency databases by requiring that matching of records be done under a special agreement to be approved by each agency's "Data Integrity Board."

Video Privacy Protection Act of 1988

Imposes privacy requirements on video rental establishments and permits a customer to sue a video rental or sales establishment if it discloses what tapes a person borrows or buys. This law is significant in that it was passed in direct response to such records being published about a candidate for the Supreme Court in 1987.

Section 502 of The Telecommunications Act
(*also called the* **Communications Decency Act of 1996**)

Imposes criminal fines and/or imprisonment for individuals who make available any indecent communications to any person under 18 years of age. This act also prohibits an individual from sending indecent communications with the intent to annoy, abuse, threaten, or harass another person. This act was struck down as unconstitutional by a Supreme Court decision in June, 1997. Portions of the rest of the telecommunications law are also being reconsidered.

These and other federal statutes that regulate the gathering and distribution of personal information are as important for what they do not protect as for what they do. Most of the federal privacy protection statutes contain exceptions that permit the gathering, sharing, and distribution of personal information under certain circumstances. Although these federal laws go a long way toward protecting individual privacy from *governmental* intrusions, only a few of the many *businesses* that gather and share personal information are currently subject to federal privacy laws.

InfoWeb

Privacy
Rights and
Censorship
6

There is growing concern that federal regulation of privacy infringes on the individual's constitutional rights. For instance, if the Communications Decency Act prohibits the use of lewd language in an e-mail message to a bulletin board, can the same law prohibit your right to speak the same words? What happens to your First Amendment right to free speech?

The legal debate about Internet censorship continues in the U.S. Congress and in the federal courts. For instance, the Communications Decency Act was ruled unconstitutional in a Supreme Court decision made in June, 1997. The constitutionality of some of these federal laws will ultimately be decided by the Supreme Court. The American Civil Liberties Union (ACLU) maintains a Web site that posts updates and discussions pertaining to these and other cases. See Figure 11.

Figure 11

The Cyber-
Liberties page
at the ACLU
Web site

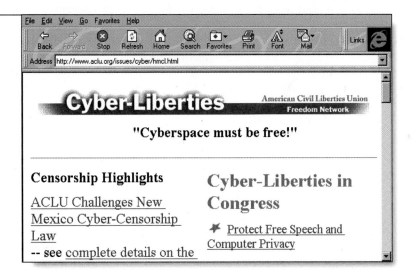

Current debate centers around filtering and blocking software, also called **censorware**, that prevents a receiving computer from accessing or downloading questionable data from another computer. In 1998, a Senate committee approved a bill that requires schools and libraries to employ censorware to prevent persons under 18 years of age from accessing adult material on the Internet.

The ACLU argues that censorware requires voluntary self-labeling of data, similar to the ratings that tell us whether movies and television shows are suitable for young viewers. However, the Internet is a worldwide system of networks that is not regulated by United States laws. Will students and library patrons be denied access to Web servers in other countries because they do not participate in the self-labeling program?

State Legislation

What is my state doing about protecting me from invasions of privacy? State laws protecting privacy vary widely. As a general rule, the states are free to provide greater protection for individual privacy rights than the U.S. Constitution or federal statutes do. Unlike the federal Bill of Rights, the constitutions of 10 states contain an explicit right to privacy. The courts of many other states have found that an implied constitutional right to privacy exists, similar to the one found by the U.S. Supreme Court. See Figure 12.

Figure 12

The constitutions of 10 states specifically protect a right to privacy (shown in green), while most other states have recognized an implied right to privacy or have enacted other laws to protect the privacy right (shown in blue). Only Minnesota rejects a right to privacy (shown in white).

One area of special concern to privacy interests is the confidentiality of medical records. Every state recognizes the confidentiality of communications between doctors and their patients, but our medical histories are stored in various databases maintained by our health insurers. The largest of these is the **Medical Information Bureau (MIB)**, a nonprofit association made up of 650 insurance companies that maintains a database containing the summaries of health conditions of more than 14 million Americans. Insurance underwriters can request a report based on MIB records to help them determine how much to charge for a policy or whether to deny coverage.

InfoWeb

Confidentiality of Medical Records

7

Because health insurers are not doctors or health care providers, the information in their databases is not subject to confidentiality. Without other legal restrictions, the personal medical information about you contained in insurance industry databases could be supplied to your employer, to government agencies, or to other businesses and individuals without your knowledge or consent. Because Congress has been unable to enact legislation that addresses the problem of insurance industry databases, this problem is currently up to the various state legislatures to remedy.

Federal laws have a direct impact on state regulations. For instance, the 1984 Budget Deficit Reduction Act mandates that all states must use computer matching to compare state and federal welfare recipients. If they do not, the state cannot receive federal social-welfare funds. Although this prohibition was intended to reduce welfare fraud, it also created a nationwide data network of individuals who receive assistance, which some critics claim is a violation of the welfare recipients' right to privacy.

Privacy at Work: Interoffice E-Mail

Is my employer permitted to read my e-mail? Monitoring employees in the workplace is a time-honored custom of many employers, and most employees recognize workplace monitoring as a legitimate business practice. While a telephone recording advises you that your call might be monitored for quality control, another purpose is to monitor the employee's performance while handling the customer's telephone call.

Computers offer another means by which employee monitoring can be conducted. Manufacturers will often track individual productivity over time through the use of computer records that track assembly line output and downtime. Software is sometimes used to count the number of keystrokes made by an employee at a computer terminal. At least one major software company requires employees to wear a special pin that allows management to know where to find any employee at any time of the day. Figure 13 shows employee badges that track employee movements as well as grant access to special areas.

Figure 13

Employee identification cards produced by Sensormatic Electronics Corporation

A more difficult problem is employer monitoring of employees' personal e-mail on the company network. Employers view their computer equipment and the data they carry as company property. They argue for the need to monitor employee e-mail to prevent employee harassment or other illegal conduct, to protect employer trade secrets from unauthorized transmission, and to ensure that their systems are not being used for recreation on company time. At the same time, employees often view e-mail as providing the same level of privacy as sending a letter or making a telephone call. Because of its efficiency and ease of use, office e-mail provides the illusion of privacy to those who use it.

InfoWeb

Employee Rights 8

Remember that e-mail transmitted across a local area network first resides on a server before it arrives on your hard drive, and servers are subject to backups. Even though you believe you have deleted a message, it might still exist on a company backup. The **systems operator**, also known as a **sysop**, is responsible for maintaining access to the computer system and for the integrity of all data stored on that system, including its backups. The sysop's responsibilities might include monitoring employees' use of e-mail.

Three court cases have upheld the right of an employer to archive and review employee e-mail and to terminate employees based on the contents of their e-mail messages. In the 1993 California case of *Bourke v. Nissan Motor Company*, an employee who wrote e-mail critical of management was fired when the sysop showed the offending e-mail to corporate managers. In another California case the same year, *Shoars v. Epson America, Inc.*, an e-mail administrator was asked to assist management in monitoring company e-mail, even though it had been management's stated policy to treat employee e-mail as private. When the sysop refused, she was fired.

In both cases, the fired employees sued their employers. The courts in both cases dismissed their claims, based on the fact that California's privacy law did not specifically extend to e-mail in the workplace and on the belief that the computer systems were company property and were properly subject to monitoring.

In a 1996 case, *Smyth v. Pillsbury Company*, a U.S. district court in Pennsylvania threw out a suit by a former employee who was fired when management read through system archives of his e-mail and found a message that referred to management in uncomplimentary terms. As in *Shoars*, the employer in *Smyth* had a stated company policy of respecting the privacy of employees' e-mail. However, the federal trial court decided that an employee has no "reasonable expectation of privacy" in company e-mail, even where the employer's stated policy was to regard such communications as confidential.

While there have been various attempts to introduce federal legislation enhancing the privacy protection of e-mail at work, none have met with much enthusiasm by Congress. In the meantime, both employers and Internet service providers (ISPs) have been held liable for illegal activities that occurred through access to their systems. In some cases, their computer equipment has been confiscated. As a result, most businesses monitor employee e-mail, and most ISPs require new users to sign an agreement that waives their privacy rights. The ACLU advises against this in a 1996 report. This practice has been legally interpreted as meaning that the privacy rights of the online system are based on the privacy rights of its users. Instead of increasing security as intended, less privacy for the users has decreased the level of protection against government seizure of the entire online system.

Until the law changes, you should assume that your employer is legally entitled to examine your e-mail, regardless of any stated policy to consider e-mail as private. It is always wiser to use your company-supplied e-mail account for company business only and to establish a private account of your own for personal e-mail to be used at home.

QuickCheck B

1. Although the Bill of Rights does not specifically mention a right to privacy, the Supreme Court has recognized that the Amendments create _____ for individuals.

2. Guarantees contained in the Bill of Rights are rules that prohibit conduct by the government towards its citizens but do not necessarily protect individuals from similar conduct by _____.

3. The Electronic Communications Privacy Act prohibits the unauthorized interception of _____ on public networks by federal or state authorities without a warrant.

4. _____ prevents a receiving computer from downloading or accessing data that is stored on another computer that might store questionable data.

5. True or false? Even when an employer's stated policy is to respect the privacy of employees' e-mail and to treat e-mail as confidential, an employer is legally permitted to monitor employee e-mail.

C Privacy and Cryptography

The explosion in the use of computers as personal communications devices is primarily due to the Internet's increasing popularity as a global medium for the exchange of information, including confidential information. We live in a time when more and more banks and private companies send information that must remain private over the Internet. Figure 14 shows a company that conducts business on the Internet.

Figure 14

An example of the electronic marketplace

There is a growing awareness about the inherent insecurity of Internet communications. It is widely recognized that e-mail can easily be intercepted and read by any individual who has access to an Internet site between the originating and receiving points.

Internet e-mail is commonly regarded as providing about as much privacy as the contents of a postcard in the mail system. Although there are far too many postcards to be read by a nosy postmaster, any mail handler along the way might read the message on the card. This poses special problems when the information being transmitted might include a credit card number. Savvy programmers can write routines that detect just such information making its way to a known commercial site.

Concerns such as these, along with the desire to ensure privacy in personal communications, generally have encouraged common use of public-key cryptography on the Internet. However, public-key cryptography is so secure that it has worried certain sectors of the U.S. government, which view its widespread use as a very real threat to national security.

The Technology of Public-Key Cryptography

What is public-key cryptography? **Cryptography** is the science of keeping messages secret by encoding them so that only the intended recipient can decode and understand them. It has traditionally been a secret science practiced by government-employed mathematicians to exchange private messages between the government and its intelligence officers, military personnel, and ambassadors overseas.

The process of encoding the data is usually referred to as **encryption**, and the process of decoding is called **decryption**. Data that has not been encrypted is referred to as **plaintext**, and the encrypted plaintext is called **ciphertext**. Cryptography generally makes use of an algorithm for combining the plaintext with a **secret key** (a sequence of numbers or characters) to produce the ciphertext, as shown in Figure 15. An **algorithm** is a step-by-step procedure for solving a problem or accomplishing a specific task.

Figure 15

Basic cryptography

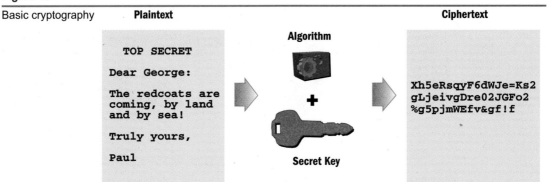

Encryption: A plaintext is encoded using a secret key and an algorithm.

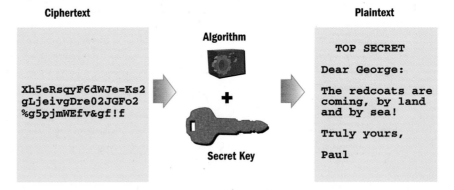

Decryption: The recipient of the message uses the same algorithm and secret key to decode the message back to its plaintext form.

One problem that has historically plagued cryptography is the difficulty in communicating the secret key to the intended recipient of a ciphertext who is located far away. If the key were to fall into the wrong hands, ciphertexts created using that key would no longer be secret.

During World War II, the Allies tried to overcome the problem of secret keys falling into enemy hands by using a two-step approach to cryptography. Besides encrypting their messages using a special code and frequently changing secret keys, plaintext messages were first translated into the native language of the Navajo Indians. The Navajo communications experts became vital links in military communications all around the world.

In 1976, Whitfield Diffie and Martin Hellman developed a new form of cryptography that did not require the exchange of secret keys between parties. Their invention, called **public-key cryptography**, involves a scheme where each person gets two keys, a **public key** and a **private key**. The public and private keys have a special mathematical relationship to one another. A plaintext that is encrypted with the *one* key can be decrypted *only* using the *other* key. At the same time, however, simply knowing the contents of one of the keys provides almost no clues about the contents of the other key. Figure 16 illustrates the basics of public-key cryptography.

Figure 16

Public and private keys

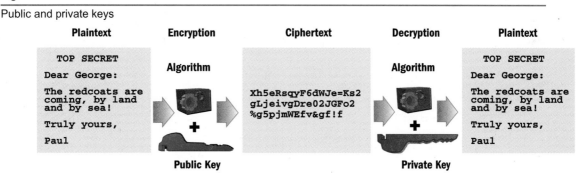

| Plaintext | Encryption | Ciphertext | Decryption | Plaintext |

The message is encrypted using a public key. This way, the sender is assured that only the intended receiver will be able to decrypt the message, using its private key.

Several public-key encryption programs are available for use on the Internet. Figure 17 illustrates how these programs work. All public-key encryption programs use algorithms that are based on the difficulty of solving a particularly complex mathematical problem. The algorithm used by a particular encryption program will generally not be secret because knowing the algorithm does not reduce the mathematical difficulty of decrypting the ciphertexts it generates.

Figure 17

Public-key cryptography

The Steps of Public-Key Encryption
1. A typical public-key encryption program is first used to generate a key pair for the user—one public key and its mathematically related private key. Once you have generated the key pair, you will never need to repeat this step again.

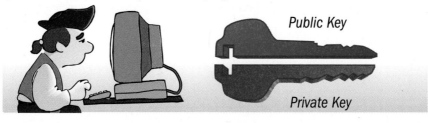

Figure 17

(continued)

2. You then distribute your public key to the world (or to those individuals from whom you wish to receive encrypted e-mail). Your private key remains private, kept in a safe place where others will not have access to it. In addition, because of the strength of the algorithm used, no one will be able to deduce your private key by examining your public key.

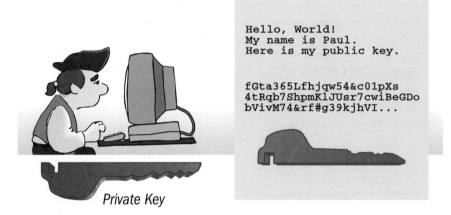

Hello, World!
My name is Paul.
Here is my public key.

fGta365Lfhjqw54&c01pXs
4tRqb7ShpmKlJUsr7cwiBeGDo
bVivM74&rf#g39kjhVI...

Private Key

3. Another user (George) who wishes to send you an encrypted message will then use your public key to encrypt the message. Once George has encrypted the message using your public key, the only key capable of decrypting the ciphertext is your private key.

Ciphertext

fj-9HF9jf)8gp0
a0I*(6HFs3ki8-0
jba(OH17&e3\Gjg
0ku3Usg3%i*fnbG

Algorithm

Your Public Key

Plaintext

Hello, Paul

Please let me know
when the redcoats
are coming, and
whether by land
or by sea.

Regards,

George

4. George then sends the ciphertext to you, assured that his message to you will be absolutely private because you are the only person capable of decrypting his message—using your private key.

Plaintext

Hello, Paul

Please let me know
when the redcoats
are coming, and
whether by land
or by sea.

Regards,

George

Algorithm

Ciphertext

fj-9HF9jf)8gp0
a0I*(6HFs3ki8-0
jba(OH17&e3\Gjg
0ku3Usg3%i*fnbG

Your Private Key

Using this method, George is assured of the **secrecy** of his message to you—which is the first level of protection afforded by public-key encryption. One problem for you, however, is assuring that the message you received from George is actually from George. The problem arises because your public key has been released to the world; therefore, someone pretending to be George could have sent you the ciphertext.

Ciphertext

Algorithm

Plaintext

```
fj-9HF9jf)8gp0
aOI*(6HFs3ki8-0
jba(OH17&e3\Gjg
0ku3Usg3%i*fnbG
```

+

Your Public Key

```
Hello, Paul

Take a vacation.
We won't be
seeing any
redcoats for at
least six months.

Regards,

George
```

Authentication refers to the problem of assuring that a message has been sent by the person who claims to have sent it. This problem is particularly important in commercial transactions because the seller will need assurance that the buyer is who he says he is or that his written promise to pay is not a forgery.

Public-key encryption addresses the problem of authentication by providing George with a way to sign the message using his private key before encrypting it with your public key. This is called creating a **digital signature**. The signing is a two-step process, although the encryption software will generally perform both steps with a single command.

The creation of a digital signature begins with a second software algorithm referred to as a **hash function**. The purpose of the hash function is to generate a fingerprint based on the exact contents of the plaintext, but that is much smaller than the original plaintext. A hash function produces a fingerprint that is mathematically impossible to reproduce using any other message. See Figure 18.

Figure 18

Creating a digital
signature

1. George runs a hash function to create a unique fingerprint, which is attached to the bottom of his message.

Document Fingerprint

Hash Function

Plaintext

```
fHy7rj9XsiL38op
```

```
Hello, Paul

Please let me know
when the redcoats
are coming, and
whether by land
or by sea.

Regards,

George
```

Figure 18

(continued)

2. The second part of George's signing involves the use of his private key to encrypt the document fingerprint to be appended to the bottom of the plaintext. This two-step process results in a digital signature to the document.

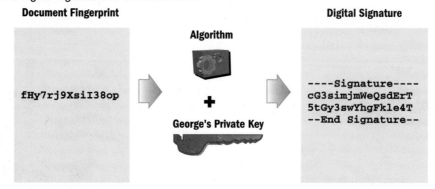

Document Fingerprint

fHy7rj9XsiI38op

Algorithm

+

George's Private Key

Digital Signature

----Signature----
cG3simjmWeQsdErT
5tGy3swYhgFkle4T
--End Signature--

3. George then encrypts the entire message (including his digital signature) with your public key.

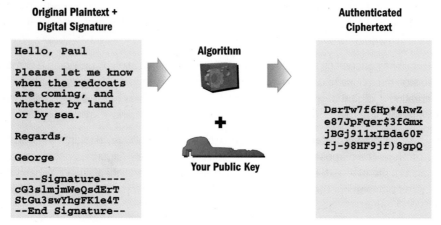

Original Plaintext +
Digital Signature

Hello, Paul

Please let me know
when the redcoats
are coming, and
whether by land
or by sea.

Regards,

George

----Signature----
cG3slmjmWeQsdErT
StGu3swYhgFKle4T
--End Signature--

Algorithm

+

Your Public Key

Authenticated
Ciphertext

DsrTw7f6Hp*4RwZ
e87JpFqer$3fGmx
jBGj911xIBda60F
fj-98HF9jf)8gpQ

4. After you receive the message, you will be able to decrypt it using your private key and then check the integrity of George's digital signature using George's public key. If George's digital signature properly decrypts, the authenticity of the message is ensured.

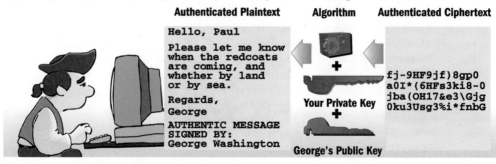

Authenticated Plaintext

Hello, Paul

Please let me know
when the redcoats
are coming, and
whether by land
or by sea.

Regards,
George

AUTHENTIC MESSAGE
SIGNED BY:
George Washington

Algorithm

+

Your Private Key

+

George's Public Key

Authenticated Ciphertext

fj-9HF9jf)8gp0
aOI*(6HFs3ki8-0
jba(OH17&e3\Gjg
0ku3Usg3%i*fnbG

Encryption in Electronic Commerce

The
Electronic
Marketplace
9

How secure is public-key encryption? The security offered by public-key cryptography depends on how difficult it is for someone to intercept and to decode a ciphertext without having the necessary key. The method used to decode a ciphertext without the key is referred to as **brute-force cryptanalysis**—which involves using one or more computers to try every possible key until the ciphertext is converted to its original plaintext. How long a brute-force cryptanalysis will take depends on how much computing power the person who intercepted the cipher text has at his or her disposal *and* the key length. **Key length** is the number on which the public and private keys are based.

The greater the key length, the more time is required to break the code. Using $1 million worth of specialized computer hardware in 1995, a 40-bit key message could be broken in two-tenths of a second, a 64-bit key message could be broken in 38 days, and a 1028-bit key message literally could take more time to break than it would take for the sun to burn out.

Businesses, such as the bank shown in Figure 19, are now making use of public-key encryption technology to provide their customers with secure transactions through the Internet. The groups responsible for setting common standards are working to establish encryption technology for use in all electronic transactions. In August 1996, a consortium of businesses that included MasterCard, Visa, IBM, Microsoft, and Netscape Communications released technical standards for Secure Electronic Transactions (SET) that would serve as a single industry standard for conducting secure financial transactions on the Internet.

Figure 19

Online banking is one example of secure electronic commerce.

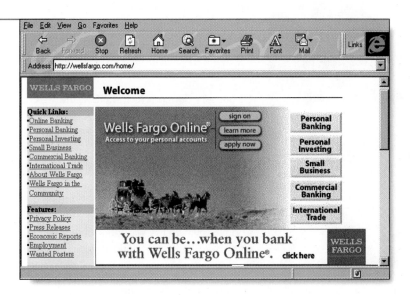

Encryption and the widespread use of SET make it relatively safe to order merchandise from commercial Web sites. The development of a fully functional electronic marketplace also depends on Web merchants who maintain a level of responsibility toward Web customers. In turn, Web customers must demand that Web merchants be responsible. In reality, using your credit card to purchase from a Web site is just as safe as using it in a store at the mall or to order merchandise over the telephone. In either place, someone could steal your card or account number. Experts contend that it is slightly more likely to happen on the telephone than on the Web.

The Debate over Privacy, Freedom, and National Security

Does public-key encryption technology pose a threat to national security? At the present time, no federal laws restrict the use of public-key encryption programs within the United States. However, the export of this technology to other countries is prohibited by State Department regulations. Specifically, the State Department regulations known as **ITAR** (**International Traffic in Arms Regulations**) treat public-key encryption software as a "munition" if the software uses an algorithm in excess of a 40-bit key. Although the *software* may not be exported, export of an encrypted *message* or ciphertext is not prohibited, and there is no restriction on the export of books containing the source code used to create the software.

The State Department regulations were created in response to the release, in June 1991, of an encryption software package for Internet use called PGP, which stands for "Pretty Good Privacy." **PGP** is public-key encryption software that uses a 1028-bit key. Phil Zimmerman, shown in Figure 20, is a consultant and programmer who released the product for free to make military-grade encryption available to the masses. At the time of PGP's release, Congress was considering legislation that would have outlawed the use and distribution of this kind of public-key software as a threat to national security. Before they could do so, PGP software became widely available at various sites in Europe and Australia.

Figure 20

Phil Zimmerman

PGP is now the most popular and widely used encryption software on the Internet. Its release highlights a debate over the appropriate limits to be placed on encryption technologies that defy the government's own abilities to crack. At one end of this debate is the U.S. National Security Agency (NSA), which views the wide availability of this technology as a serious threat to national security.

Of primary concern to the NSA, the FBI, and the Department of Justice is the problem this technology poses to national and international law enforcement efforts to prevent terrorism and other crimes. Software like PGP gives criminals the ability to communicate with each other in almost absolute secrecy. Authorities would still have the ability to intercept their communications, but the contents of the messages themselves would be useless without the private key of the intended recipient. The NSA views the wide use of this technology as threatening **crypto-anarchy**—a world in which criminals are free to conduct conspiracies without fear of detection or prosecution.

 At the other end of the debate are the **cypherpunks**—individuals who view the government's desire to be able to eavesdrop on private, digital communications as a threat to personal freedom. The cypherpunks point to the government's past abuses in its surveillance of citizens as evidence that it cannot be trusted. In their view, the public's unrestricted access to this technology is their last, great safeguard from the increasing ability of Big Brother to watch us in the Digital Age.

The
Privacy
Debate
10

The ITAR regulations have been strongly criticized—in part because PGP-like products are already available worldwide and also because these restrictions prohibit American companies from developing the Internet's commercial promise. Development of the encryption technologies needed to make commerce on the Internet practical is delayed, while competitors overseas are given a decided advantage. The ITAR regulations were relaxed somewhat in 1996 when the State Department announced that it would allow the export of 64-bit encryption software for the personal use of Americans while overseas. This personal-use exemption still prohibits delivery of the software to foreigners while overseas, and it requires the software to be kept in the personal possession of the user or at least safely under lock and key.

Several public interest groups have joined the debate over public-key encryption and other privacy issues involving computers. These include the Electronic Frontier Foundation (see Figure 21), The Center for Democracy and Technology, Computer Professionals for Social Responsibility (CPS), the Electronic Privacy Information Center, and the Internet Privacy Coalition. These groups uniformly favor relaxing the restrictions on the wide use of public-key cryptography.

Joining the debate in recent years are the commercial interests on the Internet who are interested in using encryption technology to ensure their customers' security. In addition, various software companies that specialize in developing cryptography programs have begun to complain that the U.S. government's current restrictions on the export of this technology is giving a commercial advantage to their competitors in Europe and Japan that are not subject to such export restrictions. As one possible solution to these concerns, the Clinton Administration has encouraged the use of an escrowed encryption scheme.

Figure 21

The Electronic
Frontier Foundation
is one of many
public interest
groups on the Web.

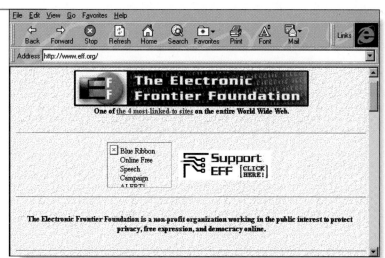

Escrowed Encryption: The Clipper Chip

What is escrowed encryption? **Escrowed encryption** is an encryption scheme that permits the unrestricted use of public-key encryption, using devices or programs in which either the private key or a special third key can be used to decrypt any ciphertext. The third key is held "in escrow" for possible future use by the government.

In 1993, the Clinton Administration introduced an escrowed encryption scheme called the **Clipper chip**. The Clipper chip, shown in Figure 22, is an integrated circuit that implements a public-key encryption algorithm called the SkipJack algorithm, which uses an 80-bit key. Under this proposal, every telecommunications device that could be used for encrypted communications—including computers and telephones—would be manufactured with the Clipper chip as part of its circuitry.

Figure 22

Clipper chips

At the time of the chip's manufacture, a user's secret key is permanently stored on the chip, and a special code for unlocking the secret key is generated. The special code would be divided into two parts, with one part placed "in escrow" with the Treasury Department and the other part placed with the Commerce Department. The two parts could be joined together at a later time to decrypt communications that were encrypted using the Clipper chip. According to the Clinton Administration, the two parts would be joined only on the order of a court in a process similar to the application for a search warrant. See Figure 23.

Figure 23

Escrowed encryption

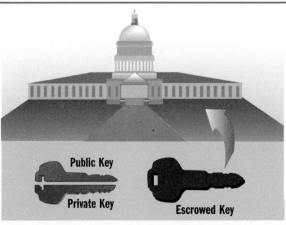

Under an escrowed encryption scheme such as the Clipper chip, a third key is generated which is held by the government. The third, or "escrowed key," can be used at a later time to access the user's private key stored on the Clipper chip.

InfoWeb

Clipper
Chip
Update
11

The Clipper chip solution to the encryption debate has met with wide criticism from cypher-punks, interest groups, and industry leaders alike. Critics charge that Clipper is not appropriate for Internet communications because those outside the United States have no interest or incentive to use a technology that permits the U.S. government to access their private messages. In addition, the Clipper scheme does not address the problem of users who will continue to use their own preferred public-key encryption.

Finally, many are suspicious of allowing the government to hold the keys to unlock their private communications. According to Clipper's supporters in the government, unrestricted public-key cryptography diminishes the power of law enforcement to do its job, and Clipper maintains the government's ability to perform useful wiretaps or examine digital evidence that agents seize as part of their investigations. Supporters of Clipper argue that escrowed encryption does not increase the power of the government to monitor its citizens because government agents would still be required to obtain a search warrant before using the escrowed keys to unlock private communications. The government views Clipper chip technology as a way to ensure its continued ability to eavesdrop on communications between known or suspected criminals and terrorists.

The most vocal opposition comes from the public interest group, Computer Professionals for Social Responsibility (CPSR), who petitioned the President directly since proposals to changes in national security policy do not require Congressional approval. The petition states concern that the Clipper proposal was developed in secret by federal agencies (including the NSA and the FBI) with the sole intent of surveillance, not to promote privacy. Required use of the Clipper chip, according to the petition, would also discourage competition in international markets where it would not be required. Finally, the CPSR voices concern that privacy protection would actually be diminished if the Clipper chip proposal were adopted.

QuickCheck C

1 _____ is the science of keeping messages secure by encoding them so that only the intended recipient can decode them.

2 Data that has not been encrypted is referred to as _____.

3 Encrypted data is called _____.

4 Public-key cryptography requires each user to have two keys, which are called the _____ and the _____.

5 The two-step process that is used to authenticate a message creates a _____.

6 _____ is the number on which the public keys and private keys are based.

7 True or false? Even though it is not illegal to use public-key encryption software in the United States, it may be illegal to export some encryption software.

8 Individuals who actively oppose the government's desire to eavesdrop on private digital communications are known as _____.

9 In escrowed encryption, a third key is held in escrow by the _____.

◌ Protecting Your Privacy

Computer technology poses many different challenges to your personal privacy. In particular, you learned how the release of your Social Security number can lead to the disclosure of much of your personal information that exists in various databases, and how it increases the chances for fraud and abuse of your credit history by others. You have also seen how inaccurate or erroneous information about you in various databases can result in the unfair denial of credit, employment opportunities, or medical insurance coverage, to name a few. In this section, you will learn ways in which you can reduce these risks and enhance your personal privacy in the Information Age.

Protecting Your Social Security Number

How do I protect my Social Security number from unauthorized disclosure? You should supply your Social Security number only when it is absolutely required. When you deal with a government agency, the agency will often have a legitimate need for your Social Security number. In such circumstances, there will generally be a law that authorizes the agency to request the number from you. The Privacy Act of 1974 requires that any federal, state, or local government agency that requests an individual's Social Security number must supply the individual with a Privacy Act notice. That notice must inform the individual about the following:

- Whether the individual's disclosure of his or her Social Security number is optional or required

- What law authorizes the agency to request the individual's Social Security number

- How the individual's Social Security number will be used by that agency

- What the consequences are if the individual refuses to supply the number

If you are not offered a Privacy Act notice like the one shown in Figure 24 at the time your number is requested, you should demand one. When you receive the notice, be sure to read it over carefully to determine whether your disclosure of the number is required or optional. If disclosure is optional, you should not disclose the number.

Figure 24

Part of a
typical
Privacy Act
notice

Privacy Act and Paperwork Reduction Act Notice

The Privacy Act of 1974 and Paperwork Reduction Act of 1980 say that when we ask you for information we must first tell you our legal right to ask for the information, why we are asking for it, and how it will be used. We must also tell you what could happen if we do not receive it and whether your response is voluntary, required to obtain a benefit, or mandatory under the law.

This notice applies to all papers you file with us, including this tax return. It also applies to any questions we need to ask you so we can complete, correct, or process ~~collect~~

We ask for tax return information to ca~~rry~~ out the tax laws of the United States. ~~We~~ need it to figure and collect the right am~~ount~~ of tax.

We may give the information to the ~~De~~partment of Justice and to other Fe~~deral~~ agencies, as provided by law. We may ~~also~~ give it to cities, states, the District of Co~~lum~~bia, and U.S. commonwealths or pos~~ses~~sions to carry out their tax laws. And we m~~ay~~ give it to foreign governments because of t~~ax~~ ~~they~~ have with the United States.

The Privacy Act notice requirements do *not* apply to private businesses or other organizations. In addition, state tax, welfare, and drivers license agencies were exempted from the Privacy Act notice requirements with the passage of the Tax Reform Act of 1976. That is one reason why some states are able to use Social Security numbers as the identifier on driver's licenses. If you live in one of those states, you are allowed to request that a random number be generated as your identification number instead of carrying around a card with your Social Security number on it.

Often, businesses have an obligation to obtain your Social Security number. Employers are required by the IRS to obtain the Social Security numbers of their employees, to report their income, and to identify the amounts withheld for federal and Social Security taxes. Therefore, you must supply your number to your employer. If you are being considered for employment but have not yet been hired, you generally should not supply your number to the potential employer because it might be used to conduct credit checks, look for criminal histories, or otherwise delve into your personal affairs. Instead, offer to supply the number after being hired.

Banks are also required by the IRS to obtain the Social Security numbers of their depositors for the purpose of reporting interest income. In addition, mortgage companies are also required to obtain your number to report the interest you pay to them on your home loan.

When you deal with other business establishments, there is generally no need for them to have access to your Social Security number. You should firmly but politely decline to reveal the number. If the person you are dealing with insists on the number, you should ask to speak with a supervisor. Most businesses are prepared to do without your Social Security number if you insist on it.

You should also be concerned about the appearance of your Social Security number on your transcript or student records. Your professors, for example, might use a portion of it to post your grades. It might be automatically used as a password on your campus computer system. The possibility that your name and Social Security number might appear on a printout can be diminished if you ask your professor to use telephone numbers or randomly generated numbers instead. You can also protect your privacy by never using passwords or personal identification numbers (PINs) for anything other than their originally intended use. You should never give your password or PIN to anyone else. They are intended for your personal use and can only remain so if you keep them private.

Ensuring the Accuracy of Personal Information

How do I find and correct inaccurate information about me that is stored in databases?

Perhaps the most important sources of personal information about you are your credit report and your Social Security benefits information. You should examine both of these important records periodically. Examine your credit report at least once a year. To obtain a copy of your report, you can send a letter that includes your full name, address, Social Security number, and date of birth, or you can call and request your credit report over the phone. Most of the large credit bureaus will allow you one free copy each year, or a free copy if you have been denied credit for any reason.

InfoWeb

Credit
Reporting
Agencies
12

Your report will contain your name, your address, recent previous addresses, information about your employment, and your Social Security number. It will also show a history of most of your credit transactions. Information obtained from public record sources might also be included, including judgments, liens, lawsuits, divorces, and bankruptcy filings. Anyone who has requested a copy of your credit report in the previous six months will also be listed near the end of the report.

You should examine this information carefully. If creditors are listed with whom you have not had dealings, or if you find other incorrect information, you should write or call the credit bureau immediately and ask that the information be changed. Remember that the credit reporting agency must re-verify any disputed information and must permit you to include a statement with your report if the disputed information is not changed to your satisfaction.

You can obtain a copy of your Social Security Earnings and Benefits Statement by filling out a form available from the Social Security Administration. You should obtain a copy of your Earnings and Benefits Statement at least once every three years. It should accurately list your contributions and include references only to employers for whom you have worked. With a careful and periodic monitoring of these reports, you can be aware of any damaging information and should be able to control potential problems.

EndNote

As you have learned in this chapter, various interested parties have voiced competing concerns in the debates over the privacy invasions of the Information Age and the legal means to address them. Consider to what extent governmental regulation is needed to protect society from the potential abuses of computer technology. When should the government be involved and what should be regulated? Where should the line be drawn between personal privacy and free enterprise? Between personal privacy and government efficiency? Between personal privacy and the protection of society from criminal conduct?

InfoWeb

InfoWeb

**Chapter
Links**

The InfoWeb is your guide to print, film, television, and electronic resources. Use it to obtain updates on quickly changing technical information and to locate information for research papers. If you're using the New Perspectives CD-ROM, click the InfoWeb icon on the left side of this paragraph to access the online InfoWeb links. Otherwise, use your Web browser and type in the address of the New Perspectives site: www.cciw.com/np3. At the New Perspectives site you'll find up-to-date links to the topics covered in this chapter.

1 Computer Matching & Profiling

The report *Electronic Records Systems and Individual Privacy* (Office of Technology Assessment, 1986) at **www.wws.princeton.edu/~ota/disk2/1986/8606_n.html** helped set the stage for current Congressional discussions of and federal laws on the use of computer matching in our government. It contains an overview of how federal government used computer matching and profiling during the 1980s. See "Personal Privacy Protection versus Your Right to Know: How the Use of GIS in This Computer Age Has Overtaken Your Individual Rights" at **www.esri.com/base/common/userconf/proc96/ TO200/PAP173/P173.HTM** for a review of the current state of laws affecting computer matching and profiling and how powerful geographic information systems (GISs) can invade people's privacy. Roger Clarke is a world renowned expert on computer matching, computer profiling, and data surveillance. His Web site at **www.anu.edu.au/people/** presents an excellent collection of articles on these topics. For an example of how colleges use computer matching and profiling to recruit students, read "Case Study: Hendrix College" at **www.acxiom.com/cip-cs-g.htm**. The Web site Data Matching, Consolidation, and Integration at **ourworld.compuserve.com/homepages/DataFarm/DATAMATC.HTM** illustrates one way in which businesses use these techniques. Recently, a Mexican dignitary, on his way to deliver a speech at Harvard University, was detained at Chicago's O'Hare International airport because he fit an airline's security risk profile. To learn more about new airline passenger profiling practices check out the Electronic Privacy Information Center's (EPIC) Air Travel Privacy pages at **www.epic.org/privacy/faa/**.

2 Public Records Online

Business and government collect vast amounts of information about individuals. Government Records and Your Privacy at **www.guess-what.com/files.htm** provides an overview of the types of information that can be found in public government databases and how easy it is to access that information. "Individual reference services" is the business of locating, identifying, or verifying the identity of individuals through information in computerized databases. Due to public concern about these practices, the Federal Trade Commission (FTC) studied the Individual Reference Services industry. You can read a copy of the resulting report at the FTC's Consumer Information Privacy Workshop at **www.ftc.gov/bcp/privacy2/ index.html** (see Individual Reference Services: A Federal Trade Commission Report to Congress). You can see examples of companies that offer individual reference services at the CDB Infotek site at **www.cdb.com/public/**, and the Information America site at **www.infoam.com/**. One of the most notorious corporate databases is Lexis-Nexis's P-trak. You can find an index to information on P-trak at **rom.oit.gatech.edu/~willday/ptrak/**. At the Privacy Info Source Web page, **www.eff.org/pub/ Privacy/HTML/monroe_priv.html**, you can find an index to businesses and other organizations involved in creating databases of personal information; the index is organized into sections on credit, personal information, medical information, criminal information, and private investigators. To observe one aspect of the debate about databases and invasion of privacy, check out the video tape *For Sale: Government Information* (Computers, Freedom & Privacy Video Library, ISBN 1-57844-019-X).

3 Personal Database Disasters

The Stalker's Home Page at **www.glr.com/stalk.html** demonstrates how easy it is for anyone to discover private information about you, from your telephone number to your Social Security number. You can read more examples of how organizations and criminals can harm consumers in the report "Identity Theft II: Access to Private and Public Databases Made Easier" from the Public Interest Research Group (PIRG) at **www.pirg.org/pirg/consumer/xfiles/page3.htm**. PIRG also conducts studies of credit report accuracy and privacy. Their sixth report on the industry, *Mistakes Do Happen: Credit Report Errors Mean Consumers Lose* (Public Interest Research Group, March 1998) is also available online at **www.pirg.org/consumer/credit/mistakes/index.htm**. Read about the extent of identity theft crimes, the current state of protection offered to consumers, and pending legislation in California in the article "Identity Theft a Big Business" from ZDNet, at **www.zdnet.com/zdnn/content/zdnn/0414/306824.html**. The Privacy Rights Clearinghouse at **www.privacyrights.org/index.html** offers fact sheets about identity theft and other violations of consumer privacy. *The Privacy Rights Handbook: How to Take Control of Your Personal Information* by Beth Givens and the Privacy Rights Clearinghouse (Avon Books, 1997) is packed with information about protecting yourself from privacy disasters. For more advice about how to avoid becoming a victim of "cybercrime," read the article "CyberCrime Prevention Kit: Get Them Before They Get You" from ZDNet's Anchordesk at **www.zdnet.com/anchordesk/story/story_2022.html**.

4 Dataveillance

Dataveillance is closely allied to—even dependent on—computer matching and profiling. The leading expert in this area is Roger Clarke. His Web site at **www.anu.edu.au/people/Roger.Clarke/** has a number of excellent articles on dataveillance and related topics. These articles include "Reasonably Easy Reading about Dataveillance and Privacy" (**www.anu.edu.au/people/Roger.Clarke/DV/Popular.html**), "Chip-Based ID: Promise and Peril" (**www.info-sec.com/crypto/crypto_090897d.html-ssi**), and "Dataveillance: Delivering 1984" (**www.anu.edu.au/people/Roger.Clarke/DV/PaperPopular.html**). David Banisar's article "Big Brother Goes High-Tech" from *CovertAction Quarterly* magazine at **www.worldmedia.com/caq/articles/brother.html** describes a variety of technologies that governments and corporations are either using or plan to use for dataveillance and surveillance of private individuals. Read a review of *Computers, Surveillance, and Privacy* by David Lyon and Elia Zureik (University of Minnesota Press, 1996) at **instruct.comm.cornell.edu/pub/comm626/reviews/reports/freeze4.html**.

5 The Bill of Rights

The First, Third, Fourth, Fifth, Ninth, and Fourteenth Amendments in the Bill of Rights have been used to establish legal and constitutional precedents that protect an individual's right to privacy. You can find a transcription of the Bill of Rights (and an image of the original) at the National Archives and Records Administration Web site, **www.nara.gov/exhall/charters/billrights/billmain.html**. The paper "Computer Privacy vs. First and Fourth Amendment Rights" at **www.eff.org/pub/Privacy/comp_privacy_4th_amend.paper** shows how to apply the rights established by the Bill of Rights to questions of privacy.

6 Privacy Rights and Censorship

The U.S. House of Representatives hosts a comprehensive index to privacy and information access law at **law.house.gov/107.htm**. The Federal and State Freedom of Information Resources site at **www.missouri.edu/~foiwww/laws.html** includes links to the Federal Privacy Act, the Freedom of Information Act and guidelines on how to use it. You can find the complete text of the 1996 Telecommunications Act, including the Communications Decency Act at **ftp.loc.gov/pub/thomas/c104/s652.enr.txt**. You can find materials on the entire Internet censorship case at the American Civil Liberties Union's Web site, **www.aclu.org/issues/cyber/trial/appeal.html**. *The Electronic Privacy Papers: Documents on the Battle for Privacy in the Age of Surveillance*, edited by Bruce Schneier and David Banisar (John Wiley & Sons, 1997) provides accounts of the legal issues involved in the current privacy debate.

7 Confidentiality of Medical Records

The Electronic Privacy Information Center (EPIC) at **www.epic.org/privacy/medical/** provides an excellent overview of the current state of medical records privacy law and policy. The article "Information Policy for the U.S. Health Sector: Engineering, Political Economy, and Ethics" at **www.med.harvard.edu/publications/Milbank/art/index.html** examines the policy tradeoffs we currently face in the debate over protecting healthcare data and medical records. The National Coalition for Patient Rights at **www.tiac.net./users/gls/cprne.html** is a grassroots organization that assesses the impact of proposed healthcare legislation on consumers' rights to privacy. You can read a transcript of Senate hearings on the privacy of medical records and learn about the Medical Information Privacy and Security Act at Senator Patrick Leahy's site, **www.senate.gov/~leahy/s971028.html**. The Clinton Administration established a President's Advisory Commission on Consumer Protection and Quality in the Health Care Industry. You can learn about the commission and read its final report at **www.hcqualitycommission.gov/**. To see an example of the type of information system that is helping to provoke the medical records privacy debate, take a look at the Los Alamos National Laboratory's TeleMed Web site at **www.acl.lanl.gov/TeleMed/**.

8 Employee Rights

The Web page "Electronic Interaction in the Workplace: Monitoring, Retrieving and Storing Employee Communications in the Internet Age" at **www.mlb.com/speech1.htm** provides a good summary of employee rights issues from an employer's point of view. The article "Employee Rights of Free Speech and Privacy in Cyberspace" at **www.collegehill.com/ilp-news/overly3.html** summarizes recent legal decisions. For information about employee privacy rights from a business's point of view check out Privacy & American Business at **idt.net/~pab/**. You can find sample e-mail and voice-mail policies at **www.cpsr.org/program/emailpolicy.html**. You can find fact sheets on employee monitoring and employment background checks at the Privacy Rights Clearinghouse site, **www.privacyrights.org/** (click on the "Fact Sheets" link). The ACLU's briefing on workplace rights, "Privacy in America: Electronic Monitoring" at **www.aclu.org/library/pbr2.html** is another excellent source of information. Also worth looking at is the Anchordesk article "The Boss Is Watching! Jesse's Privacy Self-Defense Lesson" at **www.zdnet.com/anchordesk/story/story_1951.html**.

9 The Electronic Marketplace

The National Institute of Standards and Technology hosts a computer security resource clearinghouse at **csrc.ncsl.nist.gov/** where you can find information on authentication, digital certificates and signatures, and encryption—all the current technologies that provide for secure financial transactions over the Internet. You can find a good overview of how Web browsers use encryption to create secure transaction environments in the article "Internet Security Standards: How Safe Is It to Send Your Credit Card Number Over the Internet to Make Purchases?" from *PC Magazine* at **www.zdnet.com/products/content/articles/199801/net.security/**. VeriSign makes digital authentication products, and its "Digital ID Overview" at **www.verisign.com/about/id_over.html** is a good introduction to this technology. You can find information on different types of digital cash and the security technology that enables them at **www.ssc.com/websmith/issues/i3/ws40.html**. *CIO* magazine's Electronic Commerce Research Center at **www.cio.com/forums/ec.html** includes articles and white papers, lists of vendors and industry groups, and an online forum. You can learn about secure electronic transaction (SET) technology at **www.mastercard.com/set/** and at **www.visa.com/cgi-bin/vee/nt/ecomm/main.html?2+0**. You'll find a handy and readable introduction to electronic commerce risks and security technology in *Web Security & Commerce* by Simson Garfinkel and Gene Spafford (O'Reilly & Associates, 1997).

10 The Privacy Debate

The Berkman Center for Internet and Society offers a free online course called Privacy in Cyberspace at **www.berkmancenter.org/index.html** that discusses key topics of the privacy debate. *The Nation* article "Privacy for Sale: Peddling Data on the Internet" at **www.newmedium.com/nation/html/issue/970623/0623shap.htm** introduces the idea of a market for privacy as an alternative to broad federal legislation. If you search *Wired* magazine's archives (**www.wired.com**), you'll find a variety of articles on privacy. You can learn how Canada and other countries are approaching privacy issues at the Freedom of Information and Individual Privacy from Access to Justice Network site, **www.acjnet.org/resource/primary.html**. "The Anti-Privacy Lobby" from *Mother Jones* magazine at **www.motherjones.com/news_wire/privacy.html** describes why corporations are so keen on having the right to collect and sell information about you. At the InfoWar.com site, **www.infowar.com/**, you can find links to privacy and security resources from the conservative to the paranoid *Privacy in the Information Age* by Fred H. Cate (Brookings Institute, 1997) discusses the technology, issues, values, and legal landscape surrounding the privacy debate.

11 Clipper Chip Update

The term "Clipper chip" currently refers to the U.S. government's policy on security and encryption, but in the past it had a narrower meaning. You can learn about the original meaning of Clipper chip and about the cryptography policy debate in the interview "Cryptography Renegades: On Big Brother" from ZDTV at **www.zdnet.com/products/content/articles/199801/crypto.renegade/4.html**. The ACLU's March 1998 special report *Big Brother in the Wires: Wiretapping in the Digital Age* at **www.aclu.org/issues/cyber/wiretap_brother.html** provides a complete summary of the current state of the encryption policy debate. In January 1998 the U.S. Senate held hearings on threats to national security. Louis J. Freeh, Director of the Federal Bureau of Investigation, made a statement that best expresses the administration's current position on encryption. You can read the text of Freeh's statement at **www.fbi.gov/congress/threats/threats.htm**. *The New York Times* has an excellent collection of news articles and a discussion forum on encryption at **www.nytimes.com/library/cyber/week/encrypt-index.html**. You can find an online course on encryption and the Clipper chip at **www2.ncsu.edu/eos/info/computer_ethics/www/encryption/index.html**. The Americans for Computer Privacy site at **www.computerprivacy.org/** can help you keep current with the encryption debate.

12 Credit Reporting Agencies

The three major credit reporting agencies are Equifax, Experian (formerly TRW), and TransUnion. You can request your credit report from these companies for a nominal fee; an annual report is free on request for residents of Colorado, Georgia, Massachusetts, Maryland, New Jersey, and Vermont. Free personal credit reports are available if you have been denied credit within the past 60 days. Write to Equifax at Equifax Information Service Center, P.O. Box 740241, Atlanta, Georgia 30374-0241 or call 1-800-997-2493. You can also order your credit report from a secure section of Equifax's Web site at **www.equifax.com**. You can contact Experian at Experian National Consumer Assistance Center, P.O. Box 2104, Allen, TX 75013-2104 or call 1-888-397-3742. Their Web site is at **www.experian.com/** where you can find an order form only. Write to Trans Union at Trans Union Corporation, Consumer Disclosure Center, P.O. Box 390, Springfield, PA 19064-0390 or call 1-800-888-4213. You can order a credit report online from Trans Union's Web site at **www.transunion.com/**.

Review

1 Below each heading in this chapter is a focus question. Look back through the chapter and answer each question in your own words.

2 List and describe some of the different government databases that contain personal information about you.

3 Describe how it is that the U.S. Supreme Court was able to find a "right to privacy" in the Bill of Rights even though the term "privacy" is never used in that document.

4 List at least three federal laws that are intended to protect your personal privacy, and describe what each of these laws is intended to do.

5 List three different kinds of databases maintained by private businesses that might pose a threat to personal privacy, and describe the threats they pose.

6 In your own words, describe the concerns raised by the government about the widespread and unrestricted use of public-key cryptography.

7 In your own words, describe the concerns raised by the opponents of the government's Clipper chip proposal.

8 Describe three ways to help preserve your privacy in the Information Age.

Projects

1 **Personal Profile** Visit your local government center (city or county), and try to compile a computer profile of yourself, using publicly available information. Using only information contained in government databases, see whether you can find:

a. What kind of car you own (if you own one)

b. Who owns the property where you live, what was the purchase price, and when was it purchased

c. How much was paid in personal property taxes on the place where you lived last year

d. Whether you have been named in a lawsuit, either as plaintiff or defendant, in the past five years

e. What your Social Security number is

How accurate is the information you found? What clues about you would this profile provide to a stranger?

2 **Your Credit History** Contact your nearest major credit reporting company, and request a copy of your credit report. You should be aware that some bureaus will charge you for a copy.

a. What does this report reveal about you?

b. What inaccuracies did you find, if any?

3 **INTERNET Required** **Data Collection on the Internet** Point your World Wide Web browser to the following URLs: **http://anonymizer.cs.cmu.edu:8080/** or **www.13x.com/cgi-bin/cdt/snoop.pl**

a. What does this information reveal about you?

b. Of what use would this information be to a business on the Web?

c. Under what circumstances would this information be useful to the government?

4 **Junk Mail Comparison** Instead of throwing away that junk mail in your mailbox, try saving it for two weeks. Ask two of your friends or relatives who live in other households and are not the same age as you to do the same with their junk mail. At the end of the two-week period, compare the junk mail you and your friends received.

a. In general terms, how was this mail different for you and your friends? What kinds of products were being promoted?

b. What do these differences suggest about each of your ages? Your spending habits? Your income? Your interests? Your profession or jobs?

5 **Information Entrepreneurs on the Internet** Information entrepreneurs are increasingly finding their way onto the Internet. An example of one of these is the American Information Network, which can be found on the World Wide Web at **www.ameri.com/intro.htm**. Using your Web browser, visit this site.

a. What kinds of personal information can be obtained from this service?

b. What costs are charged for the different kinds of information?

c. Does this service mention any restrictions or rules about the release of this information, and, if so, what are they?

d. In your opinion, who should have access to this kind of information, and why?

e. In your opinion, should there be any restrictions on the public availability of this information? Why or why not?

6 **Responsibility as a Sysop** Imagine that you have a great job as the sysop for a large corporation. The company has a stated policy respecting the privacy of employee e-mail. Your supervisor asks you to monitor the e-mail of particular employees and report back to him with what you learn. You know that if you refuse to comply with his request you will probably be fired.

a. Look up the Association for Computing Machinery Code of Ethics. (The ACM Code of Ethics can be found at several locations on the Internet.) Are there guidelines for this situation?

b. If you had to make the decision between doing something you don't consider ethical and losing your job, discuss how you would go about resolving the conflict.

c. Assuming that you decide not to comply with the supervisor's request, what legal protections do you have under the state law? Under federal law?

7 **Encryption Software** Encryption software packages are available on the Internet, through computer magazines, or through mail-order catalogs.

a. Create a table that compares features and prices.

b. Which packages can be legally exported?

8 **Escrowed Encryption Debate Continued** The Clinton Administration has proposed other escrowed encryption schemes besides Clipper, including a plan to require users to register their private keys with the government. At the same time, certain members of Congress have become increasingly friendly to the idea of lifting restrictions on the export of public-key cryptography. Visit the Internet Privacy Coalition at **www.privacy.org/ipc/**, a site maintained by individuals and public interest groups concerned with these issues.

a. What is the Administration's latest escrowed encryption proposal?

b. Is there any legislation pending before Congress that would implement the Administration's latest proposal, and, if so, what is the status of the bill?

c. Is there any legislation pending in Congress that pulls in the other direction by relaxing or lifting restrictions on the export of public-key cryptography? If so, what is it?

d. Take a position either for or against government regulation of encryption technologies. Provide supporting details for your arguments.

COMPUTERS, INTELLECTUAL PROPERTY, AND ETHICS

Every day, individuals are engaged in a creative process that will convert their ideas and emotions into physical objects—a work of art, a musical score, printed words on a page. Copyright law assures that they will be paid for their efforts. Our current legal system was developed to protect working machines through patents or works of authorship through copyrights. In the age of computers, an individual's work is often stored in digital form—where it can be copied infinitely and transmitted around the world inexpensively and quickly. Software also needs protection under the law to ensure that those who write programs will continue to develop new software. More than two decades of legal experimentation have led to a system that extends both patent and copyright protection to digitally stored creations. However, there is ongoing debate in the courts about how much protection existing laws provide.

This chapter introduces you to the system our society uses to encourage and reward creativity and inventiveness. You will learn how that system applies to the world of computers and how it is being redefined in light of the challenges brought by the Digital Age. You will learn some ground rules for respecting the intellectual property rights of others as you surf the World Wide Web, gather materials stored in digital form in libraries, participate in on-line discussions, and send e-mail.

CHAPTER**PREVIEW**

As you read this chapter, you should consider the competition among society's need for the creations of artists, authors, programmers, and inventors, the need of the creators to be rewarded for their work, and your right to the free flow of information. Think about how the law tries to balance these competing interests, and consider whether new proposals for changes in the law strike the proper balance. After you have completed this chapter, you should be able to:

- Describe the purposes of intellectual property law
- List the three major areas of intellectual property law, and what each area protects
- Explain the unique challenges cyberspace and the Digital Age pose to intellectual property law
- Describe how courts determine when unauthorized use of copyrighted material is a permissible fair use
- Discuss the different protection software receives under copyright law and patent law
- Explain the ethical considerations raised by the unauthorized copying of software
- Discuss under what circumstances you may use another person's work as part of your Web page, e-mail, or software program

Ⓐ Intellectual Property in the Digital Age

Imagine for a moment what your world would be like without any of the modern conveniences we take for granted—a world without telephones, copy and fax machines, computers, VCRs and televisions, radios, airplanes and automobiles, plastics, or light bulbs. Each of these products owes its existence to an idea in the mind of its inventor. The value given to the idea behind an invention cannot be measured as easily as the cost of its materials, its production, its marketing, or its distribution. However, ideas have value to manufacturers, to others who profit from those ideas, and to society as a whole. Clearly, if our system failed to reward inventors and artists for their intellectual efforts, the incentive to invent or create would be lost.

The U.S. Constitution includes language that invites Congress to pass laws that "promote the Progress of Science and useful Arts, by securing for limited Times to Authors and Inventors the exclusive Right to their respective Writings and Discoveries." However, creative works are not protected by U.S. law when they are transmitted to other countries. There are treaties and trade agreements among nations that promise to uphold each others' laws and work to protect the rights of inventors and artists.

Purpose of Intellectual Property Law

What is intellectual property?   **Intellectual property** refers to the special "rights" to which inventors, authors, and artists are entitled for their ideas and inventions, their writings, and their works of art. The law of intellectual property is the set of statutes, regulations, and court decisions that has gradually developed to define those rights and the legal protection they receive.

In particular, there are two types of court decisions that apply to intellectual property, case law and common law. **Case law** consists of the opinions that judges write when they are presented with disputes about the meaning of particular statutes. Case law is sometimes called "judge-made law." **Common law** refers to the legal principles and doctrines developed in the courts where no specific statute has been written to address a particular problem or issue.

Intellectual property law is generally divided into three major areas:

- patents, which protect ideas in inventions,

- copyrights, which protect works of art and authorship, and

- trademarks, which protect brand names and logos.

In this chapter, you will learn about each and how they apply to digital property.

Patents

What rights do inventors have in their inventions? An inventor's ideas have very limited protection until the invention is patented. This is done by filing an application for a patent with the U.S. Patent and Trademark Office in Washington, D.C. A **patent** amounts to an agreement by the inventor to reveal to the world the details of his invention in return for a 20-year monopoly on the invention. A **monopoly** is a grant from the government that gives the inventor the right to prevent all others from making, using, or selling the patented invention during the term of the patent. The process to apply for a patent is lengthy and requires that detailed plans be filed and carefully reviewed by patent examiners.

InfoWeb
Inventions
1

If the patent is issued, anyone else who copies or creates the same invention during the 20-year period without the patent owner's permission is considered an **infringer**. However, it is up to the owner of the patent to monitor compliance. If infringement is found, the owner of the patent can sue the infringer for money damages, even if the infringement was unintentional or the infringing invention was created without any knowledge of the patented invention. This right has been particularly difficult to apply to software. The patent owner may also receive an **injunction**, a special order from a court prohibiting further infringement by a particular person or company.

During the monopoly period, the inventor usually allows others to use the invention for an agreed **royalty payment** or sells the patent outright to a willing buyer. For instance, N. Joseph Woodland and Bernard Silver invented the Universal Product Code, also known as bar code, in the late 1940s. The patent was granted in 1952 when Woodland was an employee of IBM. Although computer and laser technologies were not mature enough to make the bar code as important as it has become, IBM thought it might work well with the cash registers they were building and offered to buy the patent. The two partners declined, however, and later accepted a much higher amount from Philco, another electronics company.

At the end of the 20-year period, the patent expires and then anyone may use the invention or process described in the patent application, free of any claim of infringement. In the case of the bar code, laser readers were invented about the time the code's patent expired, and a whole new way of controlling retail business became available.

The Patent Act provides that patents are available for "any new and useful process, machine, manufacture or composition of matter," or "improvement thereof." Figure 1 shows an excerpt from a patent application. Patents are generally not available to protect works of art, music, drama, poetry, or prose—collectively referred to as "works of authorship." These kinds of intellectual property receive their protection through copyright laws.

Figure 1

Patents protect inventions and ideas

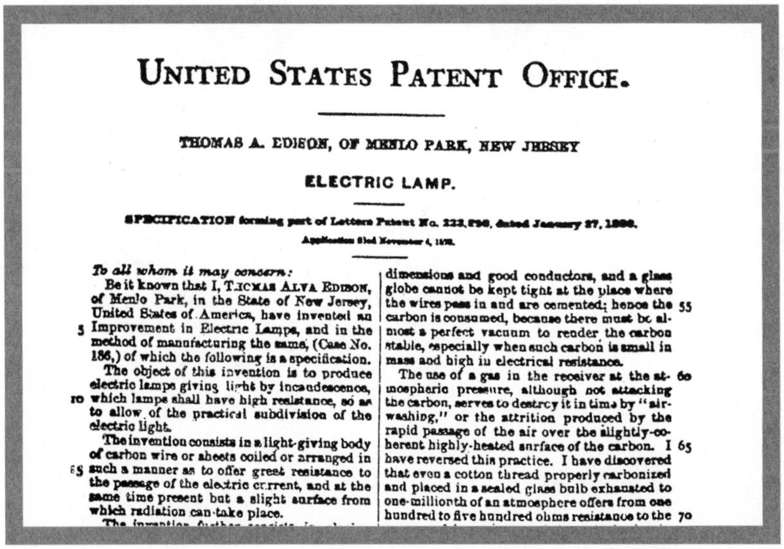

UNITED STATES PATENT OFFICE.

THOMAS A. EDISON, OF MENLO PARK, NEW JERSEY

ELECTRIC LAMP.

SPECIFICATION forming part of Letters Patent No. 223,898, dated January 27, 1880.

Application filed November 4, 1879.

To all whom it may concern:

Be it known that I, THOMAS ALVA EDISON, of Menlo Park, in the State of New Jersey, United States of America, have invented an Improvement in Electric Lamps, and in the method of manufacturing the same, (Case No. 186,) of which the following is a specification.

The object of this invention is to produce electric lamps giving light by incandescence, which lamps shall have high resistance, so as to allow of the practical subdivision of the electric light.

The invention consists in a light-giving body of carbon wire or sheets coiled or arranged in such a manner as to offer great resistance to the passage of the electric current, and at the same time present but a slight surface from which radiation can take place.

dimensions and good conductors, and a glass globe cannot be kept tight at the place where the wires pass in and are cemented; hence the carbon is consumed, because there must be almost a perfect vacuum to render the carbon stable, especially when such carbon is small in mass and high in electrical resistance.

The use of a gas in the receiver at the atmospheric pressure, although not attacking the carbon, serves to destroy it in time by "air-washing," or the attrition produced by the rapid passage of the air over the slightly-coherent highly-heated surface of the carbon. I have reversed this practice. I have discovered that even a cotton thread properly carbonized and placed in a sealed glass bulb exhausted to one-millionth of an atmosphere offers from one hundred to five hundred ohms resistance to the

Copyrights

What kinds of intellectual property are protected by copyright? Copyright is a form of legal protection that grants certain exclusive rights to the author of a program or the owner of the copyright. Copyright protection is available to any "original work of authorship" as soon as it becomes "fixed in a tangible medium of expression." A work is considered fixed in any tangible medium of expression when it is in a form sufficiently permanent or stable to permit it to be perceived, copied, or communicated. As soon as the artist's brush hits the canvas, the photographer's finger clicks the shutter, or the graphic artist clicks the Save button, a work of authorship has been created that is fixed in a tangible medium of expression. The work is automatically protected by copyright law.

Copyrights and patents differ in many ways. Patents give the inventor a 20-year monopoly on his patented invention or process; copyright merely gives the copyright owner certain rights to prevent others from copying or distributing work. Patents protect functioning *ideas*; copyrights only protect the way an idea is *expressed*, not the idea itself.

However, copyrights never prevent others from using the ideas embodied or revealed in a work of authorship. Eddie Murphy's hit movie *Coming to America* was based on columnist Art Buchwald's story, "It's a Crude, Crude World." See Figure 2. Buchwald sued Paramount Studios for a portion of the proceeds when Murphy and Paramount based the movie on his story. Copyright law did not prevent Paramount from using the ideas presented in Buchwald's humorous story about a third world leader's visit to America. Buchwald was able to win his suit only because Paramount had signed a contract with Buchwald in 1985 to use his story in a film and to pay him royalties from the film.

Figure 2

The story line of the hit movie *Coming to America* was based on the work of columnist Art Buchwald.

InfoWeb

Plagiarism and Copyright Infringement 2

In a similar case, Barbara Chase-Riboud sued Steven Spielberg and the DreamWorks SKG studio for illegally copying "themes, dialogue, characters, relationships, plots, scenes and fictional inventions" from her 1989 book *Echo of Lions* when they created the movie *Amistad* in 1997. She dropped her suit when the defendants were able to show that *Amistad* was an original work, based on historical facts and a historical novel called *Black Mutiny*, which was owned by DreamWorks.

While an inventor may accidentally infringe the patent of an invention unknown to him and be required to pay damages, these cases show that copyright infringement occurs only when someone purposely copies all or a portion of the original work. If an author unknowingly creates a work that is substantially similar to an existing copyrighted work, copyright infringement will not be found unless it can be shown that the infringer actually copied from the original work.

Trademarks

What is a trademark? Both federal and state law provide protection for trademarks. A **trademark** is any word, name, symbol, or device used to distinguish the goods or services of one business from those of another. The purpose of trademark law is to protect the consumer good will that a business builds up in its products or services. Trademark law prohibits a competitor from using the same word, name, symbol, or device to confuse consumers or to take unfair advantage of the other business's good reputation and customer loyalty.

Kimberly-Clark Corporation was awarded a trademark in the 1930s for the exclusive use of the brand shown in Figure 3. However, most consumers continue to use the word "kleenex" to refer to other brands of facial tissue. Other manufacturers, however, must use the term "facial tissue" on their packaging and in their advertisements.

Figure 3

The trademark "Kleenex" refers only to Kimberly-Clark Corporation's brand of facial tissue.

InfoWeb

Trademark Development 3

Trademarks are subject to legal protection as soon as they are used to identify a product or service. In most states, a trademark owner may receive an injunction preventing a competitor from unfairly using the trademark. The owner of a trademark can also receive monetary damages for infringement or for unfair competition. In addition, federal law allows trademarks to be registered with the U.S. Patent and Trademark Office in Washington, D.C. Federal registration provides the added benefits of nationwide protection of the trademark.

In 1998, for example, Microsoft Corporation settled a legal battle over trademark with SyNet Inc. The argument started in 1994 when SyNet applied for the registration of a trademark for its software called "Internet Explorer." Shortly thereafter, SyNet went out of business. Their trademark application was still valid; However, the U.S. Patent and Trademark Office decided to begin registration of its trademark in early 1998. By that time, Microsoft was in the news because of a related legal battle over the use of its Web browser, also called Internet Explorer, and tried to block the registration of SyNet's trademark. They argued that the name was not a brand name, but merely two words that describe a function, exploring the Internet. To settle the suit, Microsoft agreed to pay $5 million to the defunct SyNet Inc. to purchase the rights to use the name Internet Explorer.

New Challenges of Cyberspace and the Digital Age

What does intellectual property have to do with the world of computers? The works produced by human intellect are typically rendered into some tangible, material form—such as the pages of books and journals, frames of film on videotape, or yards of audiocassette tape. Creators of intellectual property receive their financial rewards by selling physical objects to willing consumers. A portion of the cost you pay for these works compensates the creators.

Before the age of computers, illegal copies were fairly easy to detect. The counterfeit copy seldom approached the quality of the original. Recordings copied using analog technology always show a loss in quality—unless the counterfeiter invests in copying equipment that is too expensive to make it a profitable venture. The physical distribution of analog counterfeits is complicated, with many opportunities for detection by the authorities, which makes counterfeiting a risky and expensive enterprise.

Figure 4 illustrates how machine-to-machine copying of a video results in a copy that cannot match the quality of the original due to the limitations of the equipment and the nature of analog signals. However, copying a digital work produces an exact, digital copy of the original. Transmission of digital copies across the Internet is almost instantaneous and almost impossible to detect. As a result, distribution of digital counterfeits is cheap and almost risk-free. Therefore, as more intellectual products are stored digitally, they become much more difficult to protect.

Figure 4
_____

Unlike works that are recorded on audio or video tape or printed on paper, digital works can be identically copied and easily transmitted.

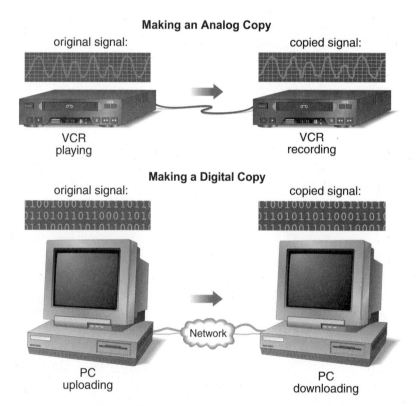

Making an Analog Copy

original signal: copied signal:

VCR   VCR
playing   recording

Making a Digital Copy

original signal: copied signal:

PC   PC
uploading   downloading

Network

Proposals for Changes in the Law

Can intellectual property law really work in cyberspace? The realities of digital reproduction and distribution have fueled an intense debate between commentators and policy makers over the future of intellectual property law. At one end of the debate are those who believe that traditional intellectual property law simply cannot meet the challenges of the Digital Age. Author, lyricist, and cyber-rights activist John Perry Barlow predicted the imminent collapse of intellectual property law as we now know it in his 1994 paper, "The Economy of Ideas." He foresaw a system that relies more on technology and ethics than law.

At the other end of the debate are those who argue for changes in the law to address these new challenges. In September 1995, the Working Group on Intellectual Property of the National Telecommunications and Information Agency issued a report entitled "Intellectual Property and the National Information Infrastructure," more commonly referred to as the **NII White Paper** or The White Paper on Copyright. Many of its recommendations have been proposed as modifications to existing law, both in the House of Representatives and the Senate. Computer Professionals for Social Responsibility (CPSR) supports such legislation as long as it protects intellectual property rights without infringing upon the public's right to access information. Another group that supports modified legislation on an international basis is the World Intellectual Property Organization (WIPO) who passed the WIPO Copyright Treaty that protects software, databases, and the distribution of digital intellectual properties, based on existing agreements that protect physical works.

InfoWeb

Current
Intellectual
Property Law
4

The provisions of the NII White Paper have been criticized by legal scholars and concerned groups such as the American Library Association, the National Education Association, and the Digital Future Coalition. These groups represent a third voice in the debate over the state of intellectual property law in cyberspace. They are ardent advocates for caution before Congress enacts wholesale changes in the law. They argue that the changes suggested in the NII White Paper go too far and would have the effect of stifling the Internet as a new medium for global information exchange and public discourse. They claim that the NII White Paper ignores the broader purpose of copyright law—to promote the progress of useful arts—in favor of turning the Internet into a toll road for the benefit of traditional mass media.

QuickCheck A

1. The special rights that both authors and inventors have in their creations are referred to as _____.

2. A _____ is a 20-year monopoly on the right to use an invention, in return for disclosing the invention's secrets to the world.

3. Copyrights protect works of authorship that are _____ in any tangible medium of expression.

4. True or false? Copyrights do not protect ideas, only the way those ideas are expressed by the author.

5. The purpose of trademark law is to protect consumer _____ that a business builds up over time and to prevent unfair _____.

6. _____ technology makes it easier to create and distribute counterfeit works, especially if the copies are transmitted over the Internet.

7. In September 1995, a government agency issued a report entitled "Intellectual Property and the National Information Infrastructure," more commonly referred to as the _____.

B Legal Protection of Creative Works

Whenever you turn on the television, visit a bookstore, attend a concert, or visit an art museum, you receive information that is protected by copyright. By the same token, whenever you visit a site on the World Wide Web, you view and receive information that is entitled to the same copyright protection. However, unlike watching television or browsing through a book, the act of browsing on the World Wide Web automatically involves receiving a digital copy of the copyrighted work onto your computer or workstation. Furthermore, the digital copy you receive is identical to the original and can be easily saved, copied, printed, and republished. This means that the opportunities for abuse of copyrights in the digital environment are far greater and much more difficult to detect. This basic difference between works in traditional media and works in the digital world is at the heart of much of the debate over copyright protection in cyberspace and whether changes are needed in the law to protect digital works.

The Nature of Copyright Protection

What kind of protection does copyright law give me? Copyright law covers more than unauthorized copying by an infringer. Copyright law gives the creator of a copyrighted work five exclusive rights in the work created. Whenever any one of these exclusive rights is violated, **copyright infringement** occurs. These rights are:

InfoWeb

Basics of
Copyright
Law
5

- **Reproduction right**—the exclusive right to *reproduce* or copy the work

- **Adaptation right**—the exclusive right to prepare *derivative works* based on the original copyrighted work (also known as the exclusive right to *adapt* the work)

- **Distribution right**—the exclusive right to *distribute* copies or phonorecords of the work to the public

- **Performance right**—the exclusive right to *perform* the work publicly (except for pictorial, graphic and sculptural works, architectural works, and sound recordings)

- **Display right**—the exclusive right to *display* the work to the public (except for architectural works or sound recordings)

The exclusive right to reproduce protects against even minor copying of a copyrighted work by another. An infringing work need not be a verbatim copy of the copyrighted work in order to violate the copyright owner's exclusive right to reproduce a work. If there is "substantial similarity" between the copyrighted work and the infringing work—referred to as **unlawful appropriation**—infringement may be found. Therefore, if someone copies an essay you wrote for a history class, makes minor changes to it, and then turns it in as his or her own work, that person has violated your copyrights in the work through unlawful appropriation.

Plagiarism and unlawful appropriation are very similar, but they are not the same thing. **Unlawful appropriation** violates the author's copyrights in a work. **Plagiarism** is an ethical concept that appears in the honor codes of most schools, but is not a concept used in copyright law. A student who copies the work of another and then passes it off as his own work is committing both plagiarism and unlawful appropriation.

The exclusive right to adapt a work covers the creation of "derivative works" such as musical arrangements, dramatizations, art reproductions, and motion picture versions, among others. It also covers the translation of a work from one media to another. Therefore, when a lithographer wishes to make printed copies of a painting, he must pay the artist-copyright owner a licensing fee or make other arrangements with him or her to make and sell the prints. If you use a computer scanner to convert a photograph from a magazine into digital form, like the person in Figure 5 is doing, but without obtaining the permission of the magazine's publisher, you have "adapted" the photograph in violation of the publisher's copyrights.

Figure 5

An image being scanned into a digital form is an "adaptation" of the original work.

The copyright owner's exclusive right to distribute—sometimes referred to as the exclusive right of publication—prohibits the unauthorized transfer of a work to the public. One important exception to the right of publication is the **first sale doctrine**, which permits the purchaser of a copy of a work to lend, rent, resell, or give away his copy, free of any claim of copyright infringement. Your ability to borrow books from the library is a direct result of the first sale doctrine. Without that doctrine, a library would be in violation of the author's exclusive right of distribution every time it loaned a book.

The first sale doctrine allows you to purchase a video cassette or a book, then give, lend, or sell your copy to another individual without obtaining the permission of the copyright owner. When you purchase a copyrighted work such as a book, album, or video cassette, you are receiving title to that copy *only* and not to the copyrights that underlie the work. You may own the copy, but you must still respect its copyrights.

When copyright infringement occurs, the owner of the copyrighted work may bring a lawsuit against the infringer to receive an injunction and an award of actual damages against the infringer. The author or creator of the copyrighted work has the right to pursue or not to pursue infringers. Generally, before an infringement suit may be filed, the copyright owner must register his or her work with the Copyright Office of the Library of Congress in Washington, D.C. In addition, under certain circumstances the infringer's conduct will violate federal criminal laws and result in a fine or prison sentence.

Obtaining Copyright Protection

How can I get copyright protection for the things I write or create? As you learned in the opening section of this chapter, copyright protection applies to any *original work of authorship* as soon as it becomes *fixed in a tangible medium of expression*. Figure 6 shows how a work in digital form receives copyright protection—as soon as it is fixed in a tangible medium of expression—by being saved to disk. Before your work is saved, it exists only in the computer's random access memory (RAM) and as momentary pixels on the display screen—both of which are too short lived to be considered fixed in a tangible medium.

Figure 6

The digital equivalent of "fixing" a work is the process of saving the work to disk.

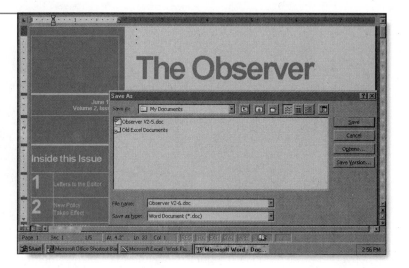

Contrary to popular belief, no special words or notices are required to create a copyright in a work. Prior to 1976, words such as "Copyright" or the © symbol, the year of creation, and the author's name were required to preserve a copyright. Amendments to the Copyright Act in 1976 did away with these requirements. After 1976, these **copyright notices** are merely a method copyright owners use to let the world know that they intend to protect their copyrights in case of infringement, but such notices technically are not required at all. Including the copyright notice prevents an infringer from claiming that he was unaware he was violating the author's copyright.

Figure 7

An anthology

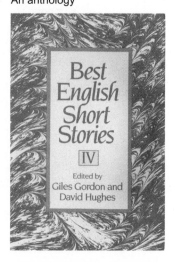

A work is considered an "original work of authorship" when the work is the product of the author's own creative labors. However, a collective work of other copyrighted works such as the literary anthology shown in Figure 7, may also qualify for copyright protection. Even though the individual stories in the literary collection or the songs in a musical collection have copyright protection, the collection itself may also be entitled to copyright protection in its own right as the result of a substantial, original, creative effort by the creator of the anthology.

One type of Web page design can be considered similar to an anthology. A **composite Web page** incorporates the graphics or other elements of a remote Web page without actually copying those elements. Composite Web page design depends on the work of other Web page designers, so the protection of copyright law for these pages is complicated. The presentation of graphics and other elements on a Web page does not amount to a license to use those individual, copyright-protected elements. It has been argued that composite Web pages probably violate the copyright owner's exclusive right to *display* these works, as well as the right to *distribute* them. In addition, the owner's exclusive *adaptation* right may have been violated as well. Any composite Web page, such as the NWBuildNet site shown in Figure 8, should obtain permission from each source to display its many elements or to provide links to each respective site.

Figure 8

NWBuildNet provides a comprehensive online guide to construction resources in the Pacific Northwest at **www.nwbuildnet.com.**

International Copyright Law 6

Similarly, a compilation of facts, such as a database, may also be protected by copyright because the arrangement and presentation of the data may be sufficiently original to enjoy copyright protection. However, a new debate arose about parts of the Copyright Treaty passed by the WIPO in 1996. The Electronic Frontier Foundation (EFF) maintains that the treaty undermines a 1991 Supreme Court decision which states that facts cannot be copyrighted, even when they are rearranged into a new collection.

Although the international treaty was intended to protect databases, the EFF and others who oppose it believe that the data within the database may be public information, even if the database is owned and maintained by a private contractor. The U.S. Congress has considered several acts that amend existing U.S. copyright laws to guarantee that government collections of information would still be available for educational and scientific research or reporting purposes. Although each proposed act varies in wording and emphasis, they all clearly state that facts are not copyrightable, as opposed to the WIPO Copyright Treaty which implies they are.

Length of Copyright Protection

How long is my work protected by copyright? A copyright lasts for the lifetime of its author plus 50 years from the date of the author's death. In the case of anonymous or pseudonymous works or works created by an employee on behalf of a corporation, the copyright extends 75 years from the date of first publication or 100 years from the date of creation, whichever is shorter. After a copyright has expired, the work is considered to be in the **public domain**—which means that you are free to use or copy the work without fear of infringing the copyright.

Public Domain and Fair Use 7

Most works written before 1920 are now in the public domain. Sound recordings and motion pictures first displayed more than 75 years ago, such as the one in Figure 9, are also in the public domain. If you wanted to make use of excerpts from Mary Shelley's novel *Frankenstein*, which was written in 1818, or if you plan to include a film clip in a multimedia presentation and you know that the clip was first displayed more than 75 years ago, you are free to do so.

Figure 9

This film clip of Buster Keaton avoiding a collision with a train was first displayed more than 75 years ago and is now in the public domain.

The definition of public domain, however, is currently being reconsidered because some familiar characters could be used in unacceptable ways when their copyright protection expires. For instance, when the copyright of Walt Disney's Mickey Mouse expires, the character could be drawn by anyone and could be portrayed engaging in unpleasant, or even illegal, activities. An extension of Mickey's copyright would require a change in U.S. copyright law.

Besides works for which the copyrights have expired, the works of the federal government such as statutes, court opinions, agency regulations, government records, and works that specifically disclaim any copyright interest are also considered to be in the public domain and not subject to copyright protection. In addition, the Copyright Act includes a specific and limited list of exceptions to copyright protection.

These exceptions include the right of a public or educational library to make limited archival copies of works, the right of public television stations to broadcast certain works, and the right of nonprofit and government institutions to make copies of certain public television transmissions for instructional purposes. However, the most important and least understood exception to copyright protection is the **fair use defense**—which excuses certain copyright infringements under special circumstances.

Fair Use Defense

When my professor copies articles for handouts, is she violating copyright law? Not every case of copyright infringement will lead to liability for the infringer. In certain cases, even though an infringement technically has occurred, a court may find that, as a matter of fairness and common sense, the infringement should be excused. The Copyright Act refers to this as the **fair use defense**. The Supreme Court has described the fair use defense as a means "to avoid rigid application of the copyright statute when, on occasion, it would stifle the very creativity the law is designed to foster." The Copyright Act describes fair use of a copyrighted work to include the use of works "for purposes such as criticism, comment, news reporting, teaching (including multiple copies for classroom use), scholarship or research."

There is no clear distinction for what constitutes fair use of copyrighted works. Instead, the Copyright Act requires courts to apply the fair use defense on a case-by-case basis, considering four factors listed in the Act:

1. The purpose and character of the use, including whether such use is of a commercial nature or is for nonprofit educational purposes

2. The nature of the copyrighted work

3. The amount and substantiality of the portion used in relation to the copyrighted work as a whole

4. The effect of the use upon the potential market for, or value of, the copyrighted work

Whenever the fair use defense is raised in an infringement suit, a court will explore each of these factors and weigh the results in light of the copyright law's purpose "to promote the progress of science and useful arts." How the fair use defense test will be applied by a court in a particular case is often difficult to predict.

In 1985, the Supreme Court held that the unauthorized printing of brief excerpts of President Ford's memoirs prior to their publication by Harper & Row was not a fair use by the news magazine *The Nation*, even though *The Nation* used the excerpts as part of its news report about the Nixon pardon. See Figure 10. In 1994, the Supreme Court held that the band 2 Live Crew's parody of Roy Orbison's song "Pretty Woman" was a fair use, despite its obvious commercial purpose. In both cases, the effect on the market value of the infringed work was an important factor.

Figure 10

The news magazine *The Nation* could not rely on the fair use defense when it published excerpts from President Ford's memoirs contained in *A Time to Heal*.

The difference between fair use and infringement is often unclear and not easily defined. There is no specific number of words or lines of text that may be taken without the owner's permission, and merely acknowledging the source of the copyrighted material is not a substitute for obtaining permission. The Copyright Office has listed the following situations where courts have excused copyright infringement as a fair use:

- Quotation of excerpts in a review or criticism for purposes of illustration or comment

- Quotation of short passages in a scholarly or technical work, for illustration or clarification of the author's observations

- Use in a parody of some of the content of the work parodied

- Summary of an address or article, with brief quotations, in a news report

- Reproduction by a library of a portion of a work to replace part of a damaged copy

- Reproduction by a teacher or student of a small part of a work to illustrate a lesson

- Reproduction of a work in legislative or judicial proceedings or reports

- Incidental reproduction, in a newsreel or broadcast, of a work located in the scene of an event being reported

In the 1996 case of *Princeton University Press v. Michigan Document Services, Inc.*, the Sixth Circuit Court of Appeals considered a case in which course materials containing other copyrighted works had been prepared and duplicated by University of Michigan professors through a local off-campus copying service and then distributed to students. Even though as much as 95 pages of certain books were included in these materials, no permission to copy or distribute these works had been sought from their publishers. In their finding that this was a fair use, the court noted that the excerpts were for educational use, that the professors did not make any money from creating these anthologies, and that the anthologies would likely trigger greater interest in the infringed works. In fact, the authors whose works were infringed had filed affidavits stating they were more interested in sharing their knowledge than in making a profit.

Princeton University Press succeeded in convincing the court to rehear the case. In their second decision, the Sixth Circuit Court of Appeals reversed itself and found that the unauthorized copying did not qualify as fair use. In particular, the court noted that Michigan Document Services made a profit when it sold its coursepacks to students, that publishers like Princeton University Press held the true copyrights and not the original authors, and that these publishers were being denied their usual permission fees whenever Michigan Document Services created and sold coursepacks without seeking permission from the publishers.

The Michigan Document Services case demonstrates how difficult it is to predict whether a court will excuse an infringement as a fair use in any particular case. While it is difficult to draw any specific rules of thumb from this area of the law, one clear guideline appears to be whether the potential market or value of the copyrighted work would be reduced if the infringement became widespread. Especially where profit is involved, it is unlikely that a court will find a particular instance of infringement to constitute a fair use. By the same token, merely because a copyrighted work is used for a nonprofit purpose such as education will not necessarily excuse an infringement.

Copyright in Cyberspace

What does copyright law have to do with my interactions in cyberspace? Traditional print media publishers like the *New York Times*, *The Wall Street Journal*, shown in Figure 11, and Time-Warner have begun making much of their material available on the World Wide Web. Individuals now enjoy a global platform to share their thoughts, ideas, and works with others—not only words, but also a wide array of multimedia such as images, sound, and video.

Figure 11

Traditional publishers are increasingly establishing a presence on the World Wide Web.

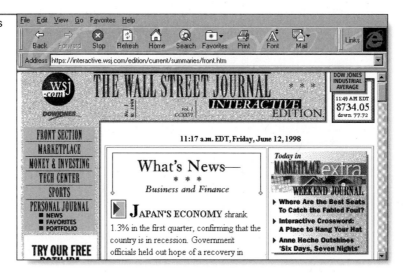

InfoWeb

Cyberspace for Sale
8

Most legal commentators agree that virtually all forms of communication on the Internet are subject to copyrights. They insist that you enjoy a copyright when you publish your words and images on Web pages, whether or not you apply for a copyright, and you still have rights to prevent its copying, distribution, or adaptation without your permission, subject to whatever fair use defenses may apply. However in late 1997, the No Electronic Theft (NET) Act (also known as the Web Copyright Law) was passed. This law is notable in that it does not permit fair use of Web-based works, even if their use is for nonprofit purposes. The argument will continue until this new law is challenged in the courts, and legal decisions are made regarding the fair use of digital works.

A similar argument concerns sending e-mail or posting a message to a Usenet group, where your words and ideas appear to have copyrights. The copyrights you have in a Usenet posting, however, are slightly different from those in an e-mail message. Because Usenet posts are automatically copied to the many news servers across the Internet and because users who post there are presumably aware that this is how the distribution system works, users who post to the Usenets grant an **implied license** for their works to be copied and distributed in that manner.

This is similar to the implied license that you give to your local newspaper when you send them your letter for publication, as shown in Figure 12. When an author writes and submits a letter to the editor for publication in a local newspaper, he or she grants the newspaper an implied license to *adapt* the work so that it fits within the paper's columnar format, to *reproduce* the work by printing multiple copies of it, and to *distribute* the work to the public at local news stands.

Beyond this limited license, the author still retains full copyrights in the work. The license between the author and the newspaper is said to be *implied* because it is not in writing, but is the result of a mutual, unspoken understanding between them.

Figure 12

A letter to the editor is considered to have an implied license.

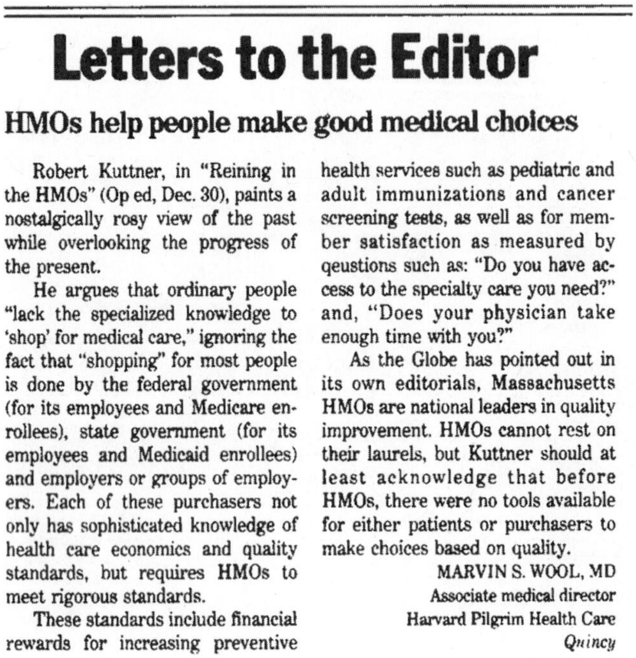

Letters to the Editor

HMOs help people make good medical choices

Robert Kuttner, in "Reining in the HMOs" (Op ed, Dec. 30), paints a nostalgically rosy view of the past while overlooking the progress of the present.

He argues that ordinary people "lack the specialized knowledge to 'shop' for medical care," ignoring the fact that "shopping" for most people is done by the federal government (for its employees and Medicare enrollees), state government (for its employees and Medicaid enrollees) and employers or groups of employers. Each of these purchasers not only has sophisticated knowledge of health care economics and quality standards, but requires HMOs to meet rigorous standards.

These standards include financial rewards for increasing preventive health services such as pediatric and adult immunizations and cancer screening tests, as well as for member satisfaction as measured by qeustions such as: "Do you have access to the specialty care you need?" and, "Does your physician take enough time with you?"

As the Globe has pointed out in its own editorials, Massachusetts HMOs are national leaders in quality improvement. HMOs cannot rest on their laurels, but Kuttner should at least acknowledge that before HMOs, there were no tools available for either patients or purchasers to make choices based on quality.

MARVIN S. WOOL, MD
Associate medical director
Harvard Pilgrim Health Care
Quincy

Some observers of the new digital media have complained that people who provide information on the Internet have waived their copyrights because such works are automatically copied to your computer or workstation's random access memory (RAM). In addition, most Web browsers copy the work to a disk cache, which can be accessed again once the user is off-line. The courts have yet to provide a clear answer to these arguments. In the future, the courts may regard this incidental copying as part of the implied license granted by online publishers, since authors on the Internet and the World Wide Web are presumed to be aware of the distribution scheme that includes storing temporary copies in RAM or a disk cache.

By publishing on the Web, you obviously intend that your work will be viewed by others. Therefore, Web page designers give an implied license to the Web server to distribute that text to be read by individuals who browse the Web site. The same holds true for images, graphics, sound files, video files, and real-time performances of audio and video using such technology as RealPlayer®, as shown in Figure 13. The suppliers of digital works know that their works are copied onto users' machines and so grant an implied license for that copying as part of the distribution scheme, although the implied license does not cover other uses that could violate their copyrights.

Figure 13

RealPlayer®
provides live and on-
demand audio, video,
and animation on
Web pages at
http//www.real.com.

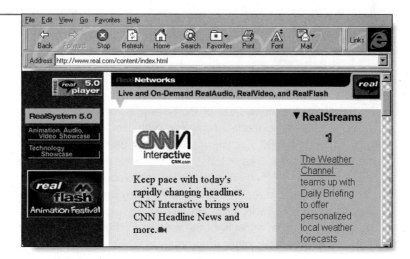

In addition, the temporary copying of a work from the Internet for either limited educational use or for private, in-home use will likely be found to be a fair use of the material. The Supreme Court has decided in several cases that private, in-home copying of a television broadcast now for viewing later constitutes a fair use of the televised broadcast. Until the Supreme Court is asked to rule on the fair use of works copied from the Internet or the World Wide Web, each charge of copyright infringement will be decided on a case-by-case basis in lower courts. In the meantime, it is best to assume that anything you see on the Internet is copyright protected and you should seek permission to reproduce it for any reason, and especially, if you will use it for financial gain.

QuickCheck B

1. True or false? Even copying small amounts from a copyrighted work can constitute copyright infringement.

2. When you purchase a book, you may then lend it to a friend without violating the copyright owner's exclusive right to distribute the work because of the _____ doctrine.

3. True or false? You must include the © symbol next to the year of creation in order to create a copyright in your work.

4. A copyright lasts for the lifetime of the author of the work plus _____ years from the date of the author's death.

5. Works in which the copyright has expired are referred to as being in the _____.

6. Copying by a teacher or student of a small portion of a copyrighted work for purposes of instruction might be excused, thanks to the _____ defense.

7. True or false? Copyright law does not apply in cyberspace because viewing any material from the Internet involves making a copy in your computer's RAM.

8. Users who post to Usenets are granting a(n) _____ for their works to be copied and distributed in that manner.

C Legal Protection of Software

Protecting software from unauthorized copying and appropriation presents special problems for intellectual property law. Recognizing how easily software may be copied, Congress extended copyright protection to software with amendments to the Copyright Act in 1980. Copyright protection is useful for prohibiting unauthorized copying and distribution of software, but it does not protect the functional aspects of a program—how it works, its method of operation, or the processes it uses—because copyrights protect *works* and not *ideas*. For this reason, many programmers prefer patent protection if it is available. If a software program can be patented, others will be prevented from duplicating the functional aspects of the patented program. At the same time, as patents are extended to programs, other programmers face the risk of liability for infringement if their programs inadvertently use processes that have already been patented.

Patent Protection

| How can I get patent protection for my work? | The granting of a patent gives an inventor a 20-year monopoly over the use of his or her invention. The patent application must include a detailed description of the invention, which is then reviewed by patent examiners to determine whether the particular invention is worthy of receiving a patent. The patent examination process is expensive and often takes a year or more to complete.

InfoWeb

Patent and
Trademark
Law
9

There are three kinds of patents: A **utility patent** protects newly invented machines and processes and is the most common form of patent. A **design patent** protects the ornamental design or appearance of a manufactured article. Its protection only lasts for 14 years. A **plant patent** protects the invention of new varieties of plant life for 17 years.

Before granting a patent, the patent examiner must find that the invention or process is new, non-obvious, and useful. An invention is new if it was not known or used by others inside the United States and was not previously patented or described in any printed literature. An invention is non-obvious if it would not be an obvious innovation to a person of ordinary skill in the pertinent field. The invention is useful if there is a current, significant, and beneficial use for the invention or product. The tests for novelty, non-obviousness, and usefulness are intended to ensure that only the most worthy inventions or processes receive patent protection.

Not all new and novel ideas may be patented. A newly discovered law of nature or mathematical truth may not be patented. Laws of nature and mathematical truths are *discovered*, not invented, and granting a patent on such discoveries would unduly hamper further scientific development. Thus, Albert Einstein, shown in Figure 14, would not be entitled to a patent on his famous formula $E = mc^2$ because this formula is a law of nature.

Figure 14

Albert Einstein

Patent Protection for Software

How does patent protection apply to software? The rule prohibiting the patent of mathematical truths has caused problems for software patent applicants whose programs, if patented, would "wholly preempt a mathematical algorithm." Because of this rule, in 1972 the Supreme Court denied patent protection to a software program that was designed to convert binary-encoded decimal numbers to pure binary numbers because it sought to patent a mathematical algorithm, which the Court defined as "a procedure for solving a given type of mathematical problem."

For nine years after this decision, the U.S. Patent and Trademark Office (shown in Figure 15) maintained that an invention or process that employs a stored program on a computer was not patentable because software programs use algorithms. In 1981, the Supreme Court revisited this issue and permitted the patenting of an invention that depended on software where the software was used as one part of a larger manufacturing process.

Figure 15

The U.S. Patent and Trademark Office

Much of the algorithm problem has been avoided in recent years through the artful drafting of patent applications that avoid use of dangerous terms such as "software" and "algorithm" in describing the invention or process. In addition, the courts have developed a variety of rather complicated tests to determine whether an invention or process that consists primarily of a software program is entitled to patent protection.

The U.S. Patent and Trademark Office has received an increasing number of patent applications relating to software-based inventions, and this trend is likely to continue. In 1996, the U.S. Patent and Trademark Office adopted new guidelines for its patent examiners in the evaluation of software patent applications. These guidelines expand the definitions of a patentable "machine," "article of manufacture," and "process" to specifically include computers and the software that operates them. They also reduce the focus on whether a particular program uses a mathematical algorithm in favor of a test that looks to the utility or usefulness of the invention or process embodied in the software.

The U.S. Patent and Trademark Office has upgraded the qualifications of its patent examiners. The entry-level requirements are a bachelor's degree or higher from an accredited four-year college or university, with preference for those with engineering degrees. In addition, a bachelor's degree in computer science, electrical engineering or computer engineering earns an additional 10% signing bonus for the newly hired patent examiner.

Patent protection gives the highest level of legal protection for the creative or functional aspects of software development. The problem with seeking a patent is that it is far more expensive and time-consuming than the automatic protection afforded by copyrights. In many cases, the software becomes obsolete before the patent is granted! It's not surprising that most software developers rely on copyright as the less expensive and less effective alternative for protecting their products. In addition, as software patents are issued to the large software development companies who can afford them, other software developers run the risk of unknowingly violating an existing patent and suffering huge infringement awards.

This danger was highlighted in August 1993, when Compton's New Media was issued a patent on its multimedia database system. The patent covered its program for simultaneously searching the text, graphics, and sound of any multimedia database. Compton's patent, which would be protected until the year 2010, had the effect of monopolizing the methods used in virtually every multimedia database product on the market. Compton's announcement of its patent and its threat to sue all other multimedia publishers who did not pay Compton a royalty enraged the software industry and led to the unusual move by the U.S. Patent and Trademark Office of reconsidering and withdrawing the patent. In spite of losing its patent, the Compton's Interactive Encyclopedia continues to be a software industry leader offering many multimedia database products. See Figure 16.

Figure 16

Compton's offers a variety of multimedia database products at its Web site.

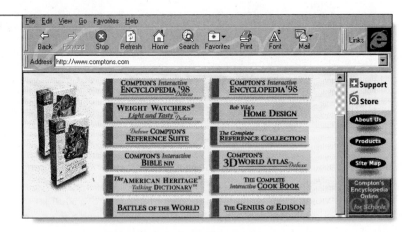

The Compton's New Media case demonstrates the difficulty patent examiners have in identifying program techniques that are not new and unique as well as the dangers patents can pose for other programmers. Following the Compton case, Congress amended the Patent Act to require patents to be open to public inspection for at least 18 months prior to the grant of a patent to aid in discovering attempts to patent processes or inventions that are already in use. This sufficiently delays the process long enough for other software developers to protest the patent, if the program contains commonly used algorithms.

Copyright Protection

When I write a program, is it protected under copyright law? When Congress amended the Copyright Act in 1980, it gave computer programs the same kind of copyright protection that other works of authorship enjoy. Thus, as soon as the program you create becomes fixed in a tangible medium of expression, whether as printed lines of source code or saved on a disk, you enjoy the exclusive right to copy, distribute, or adapt your program. The Copyright Act permits authorized users of your program to make one copy for backup or archival purposes and to copy or adapt the program if that is an essential step in using the software, such as copying it onto a hard drive or compressing it for storage.

InfoWeb

Software
Copyright
10

The Copyright Act also creates a special exception to the first sale doctrine for software. It prohibits lending, leasing, or renting computer programs, and it requires that backup or archival copies of software be destroyed by the user who gives away or resells his copy to someone else. Even though these changes address the need for some kind of intellectual property protection against software piracy, they do not answer certain issues about protecting the functional aspects of software from being copied by other programmers.

One such issue is the extent to which the copyright in a program protects the *structure* of the program. In literary works, copyright law protects only an author's *expression* and not the "idea, procedure, process, system of operation, concept, principle or discovery" that is expressed. In order to apply copyright law to software, at least two competing tests have been developed by our courts to separate a program's unique *expression* from the *ideas and concepts* behind the program. The expressive aspects of the program's structure are protected, while the ideas and concepts underlying the structure are not.

For example, if you write a database program that uses unique algorithms that you devise for faster data sorting, the algorithms themselves would be *ideas* that are not protected under copyright law, while the particular arrangement of those algorithms or other steps in your program might be protected as the *expression* of those ideas. To further complicate the issue, it is possible for a unique algorithm to be protected by a patent, in which case it might be protected by one law and not by the other.

Another issue is whether the Copyright Act prevents someone from decompiling or reverse engineering a software program. **Reverse engineering** is the process of analyzing a system, such as a machine, invention, or program, to identify the system's components and their interrelationships, with the purpose of creating a similar system in another form. Two federal appellate courts have addressed this issue and decided that decompiling or reverse engineering software is permissible.

In *Atari Games v. Nintendo* and *Sega v. Accolade*, both courts held that the owner of a legitimate copy may decompile or disassemble the program as fair use of the work, if decompiling the program is the only way to access the ideas and functionality of the program. However, fair use will not protect the programmer who incorporates protected *expression*—the program's actual code—from the reverse-engineered program into another program. Therefore, programmers are generally permitted to decompile a program to learn how the program works but then must be particularly careful not to duplicate the program's source code.

A third issue left unanswered by Congress is the extent to which the **user interface** or **status screen** that a program presents is protected by copyright. Referred to as the **look and feel issue**, this argument has been handled in different ways by different courts. In the 1987 case of *Digital Communications Associates v. Softklone Distributing*, a federal trial court in Georgia found that the appearance of the computer screen is protected by copyright law because there are various combinations of program code to design the user interface—each of which constitutes a creative *expression*.

In the case of *Apple v. Microsoft/Hewlett Packard*, a federal appellate court reached the opposite conclusion. In that case, Apple sued Microsoft for infringement of the Macintosh's graphical user interface (GUI), as shown in Figure 17. Xerox's Palo Alto Research Center developed the idea of using windows, icons, mice, and pull-down menus to create a graphical user interface in the 1960s. Apple based its GUI for the home computer market on the original Xerox design, which did not help in its copyright infringement suit against Microsoft to stop distribution of the Windows operating system. The court rejected Apple's infringement claim and found that a great majority of the screen elements had either been separately licensed by Apple to Microsoft or were "borrowed" from Xerox, so that the scope of protection Apple enjoyed was too narrow to prevent Microsoft's use of a somewhat different GUI.

Figure 17

Xerox's idea of using windows, icons, mice, and pull-down menus to create a graphical user interface or GUI was "borrowed" by both Apple (top) and Microsoft (bottom).

The look and feel issue was visited again in 1995 by another federal appellate court in *Lotus v. Borland*. In that case, Lotus sued Borland for infringement of the menu hierarchy of the Lotus 1-2-3 spreadsheet program into Borland's Quattro Pro product. The primary question was whether Lotus 1-2-3's command menu hierarchy was copyrightable as the "structure" of the program's expression—or a "method of operation" which cannot be copyrighted. See Figure 18.

Figure 18

The Lotus command menu hierarchy

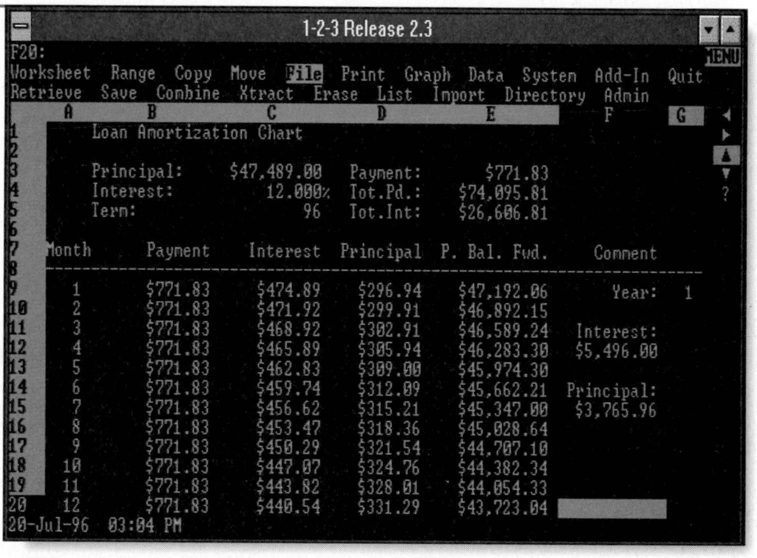

The appellate court reversed the trial court's finding of infringement. The court compared Lotus's command menu hierarchy to the arrangement of buttons on a VCR. Just as all VCRs have a play button, a stop button and a rewind button, so too all spreadsheet programs will need to have a Copy command, a Range Erase command, and a File Save command. In essence, the court noted that a copyright cannot be used to protect a "method of operation" and found that Lotus 1-2-3's command menu hierarchy was just a method of operation and, therefore, not protected.

The Supreme Court accepted the Lotus case for argument, and it was widely expected that the Court would clear up much of the confusion in this area of the law. Unfortunately, in 1996 the Court split on the Lotus case four to four, with one justice abstaining, and so issued no opinion. Since neither program is still widely used, this is considered to be a dead issue that may never be legally resolved.

These cases demonstrate the confusion and difficulty even our most experienced jurists have had in determining the proper extent and limits of copyright protection for software. Despite these difficulties and the increasing popularity of patent protection for software, copyright protection remains the primary source for preserving rights in software.

Licensing and Software

Does the law prevent me from copying or sharing software? Assume that you have a personal computer and would like to try the latest version of your favorite word processing program. Your friend recently purchased a copy of the program at a local computer store and has now offered to let you borrow his installation CD over the weekend, allowing you to install the program on your computer to check it out. You don't have the $150 to spare for purchase of the newer version. You realize that if you take your friend up on his offer to lend you the installation CD, he will expect the same generosity from you. What should you do?

The scenario described above repeats itself with surprising frequency. The Software Publishers Association estimates that software piracy costs U.S. software producers millions of dollars annually. Cyber-rights activist and lecturer John Perry Barlow is fond of asking how many in the audience can honestly say that they have no unauthorized software on their hard drives. He reports that generally less than 10% of the hands go up.

Although the rules for copyright protection of the functional aspects of software are complex and unsettled, the applicability of copyright law to the unauthorized copying and distribution of software products is not. As you have learned, the Copyright Act contains special provisions that prohibit you from lending or borrowing software and that also prohibit you from copying software except for certain limited purposes. You may recall that the fair use defense may still be available to excuse an infringement. However, a review of the four factors used by courts in applying this defense would appear to suggest that fair use will probably not be found whenever you make a copy of your friend's software or you allow your friend to copy your software, especially when the purpose of the copying is to avoid paying the purchase price.

InfoWeb

Freeware
11

There are times when it is perfectly acceptable to copy software. Certain software is distributed as **freeware**, which means that the creator of the software has either committed the software to the public domain or has elected to allow you to copy, use, and distribute the software without requiring compensation. Programmers who create freeware do so for the personal satisfaction and enjoyment of creating a program that will benefit others, without the need or desire for compensation. Usually, however, freeware is subject to licensing language such as:

```
You are free to copy and distribute this program, as long
as you do not alter this program, as long as you include
all of the files contained in this program, and as long
as this notice is included.
```

Such language has the effect of granting permission to copy and distribute the program subject to the copyright owner's adaptation right, which means you are not free to alter the program and then redistribute it without the creator's express permission. Generally, freeware of this kind may be found on many computer bulletin boards and at various locations on the Internet.

Another more common form of software encountered on the Internet, especially on the World Wide Web, is shareware. **Shareware** is software that you are free to use for a limited evaluation period, after which you must either **license** the software—in other words, pay the copyright owner for permission to use the software—or cease using the software. Shareware distributors do expect compensation for their creativity, and they are not waiving their copyrights in the software. Distributing software as shareware has the twin benefits of low distribution cost and wide distributorship. Many of the most popular client applications on the Internet are distributed as shareware, including Netscape Navigator and Trumpet Winsock. Figure 19 is an example of one of the many sites on the Web that supplies shareware and freeware.

Figure 19

Many locations on the World Wide Web offer a wide selection of both freeware and shareware products.

Microsoft
Antitrust
Case
12

The Web distribution of shareware led to one of the most famous disputes about the rights of software developers, best known as the Microsoft antitrust case. The Justice Department started getting complaints against Microsoft from rival software developers in the early 1990s. Most of these complaints centered around Microsoft's practice of requiring computer manufacturers to sign exclusive agreements to install their operating systems, DOS and Windows, on new computer systems. If the manufacturers didn't sign, they weren't allowed to sell the popular software at all. In 1994, Microsoft signed a consent decree stating that it would discontinue the practice and in 1995, a federal court order barred Microsoft from imposing such anticompetitive licensing terms on manufacturers of personal computers.

The Justice Department's Antitrust Division maintained a watchful eye on Microsoft to be sure it didn't violate its agreement. So did its competitors. Netscape Navigator was originally distributed as shareware to educators and researchers, and eventually, was publicly offered for sale. Microsoft developed its own Web browsing software, Internet Explorer, in direct competition with Netscape's browser. When Microsoft included the automatic installation of Internet Explorer with Windows 95, the Justice Department quickly imposed a $1 million a day fine against Microsoft, claiming it was violating the 1995 court order. In December 1997, a federal court entered a preliminary injuntion to halt Microsofts' distribution practice.

Early in 1998, Microsoft agreed to offer versions of Windows 95 that did not include a browser or that included a browser of the consumer's choice. Unfortunately, Microsoft's developers had already completed and were ready to distribute Windows 98 which, in order to work most efficiently, depends on the full integration of Internet Explorer. The final release of Windows 98 will be affected by the status of the government's antitrust suit against Microsoft.

Ethics and Piracy

Is it unethical to copy software?   Store-bought, **commercial software** is entitled to full copyright protection. In addition, most commercial software include shrink-wrap licenses. These licensing provisions enhance the protection the software enjoys beyond that provided under the Copyright Act. **Shrink-wrap licenses** usually forbid the resale or transfer of the software to another, thus doing away with the first sale doctrine, and often prohibit the decompiling or disassembly of the software, among other restrictions. The license goes into effect when the new owner opens the package.

InfoWeb

Software
Ethics
13

Widespread use of unauthorized software raises several ethical concerns. It is clear that if software developers believe they are receiving only 20% or so of the profits they should be receiving for their programming efforts, many will become discouraged and find other vocations that pay more fairly. This reduces the pool of programmers who will continue to contribute innovative software solutions to society. At the same time, widespread piracy has the predictable effect of increasing the price users must pay to purchase new software releases—in essence, charging the honest consumer more to compensate for some of the income lost through the software theft of others.

Commercial software sometimes appears illegally on electronic bulletin boards or on the Internet, usually at sites intended for the exchange of pirated software without regard to copyright ownership. The pirated software found at such sites is commonly referred to as **warez**. Besides detailing civil damages for infringement of copyrights, Congress has increased the criminal penalties for software piracy. It is now a felony to reproduce or distribute 10 or more copies of a copyrighted work "for purposes of commercial advantage or private financial gain" within a 180-day period, where the copies have a total retail value of more than $2,500. Those found guilty are subject to imprisonment for up to five years for the first offense or 10 years for the second or subsequent offenses.

Another troubling aspect of the pervasive copying of commercial software is the potential it may have for encouraging more stringent legal controls than are otherwise necessary. Both proponents and opponents of federal legislation to control digital works point to the 1994 case of *U.S. v. LaMacchia*. David LaMacchia was a 21-year-old student at the Massachusetts Institute of Technology (MIT), shown in Figure 20 with his attorneys.

Figure 20

David LaMacchia (right) and his attorneys successfully challenged a federal indictment for wire fraud arising from LaMacchia's distribution of commercial software on the Internet.

LaMacchia used MIT's computers to set up a bulletin board on the Internet for the purpose of encouraging others to upload and download popular commercial software packages like Excel 5.0, WordPerfect 6.0, and SimCity 2000. The activities of his bulletin board attracted the attention of federal authorities, who indicted LaMacchia under the federal wire fraud statute. The trial court threw out the indictment because his activities did not fit within that statute and because his conduct could only be prosecuted, if at all, under the Copyright Act's criminal infringement provisions. Criminal copyright infringement applies only to copyright violations "for commercial advantage or personal financial gain." Because his activities were not for "commercial advantage or personal financial gain," LaMacchia could not be criminally prosecuted for his conduct.

The outcome in the LaMacchia case was greeted with horror by business leaders in the software industry and has amounted to a rallying cry for changes in the law that go beyond a revision of the criminal copyright infringement provisions. The LaMacchia case was cited more than once in the NII White Paper as evidence that current criminal laws "do not now reach even the most wanton and malicious large-scale endeavors to copy and provide on the NII limitless numbers of unauthorized copies of valuable copyrighted works unless the copier seeks profits." Besides encouraging the consideration of new and broader criminal penalties covering LaMacchia's kind of infringement, the LaMacchia case seems to have added momentum to the movement for other copyright reforms that may have more far-reaching and negative effects on other freedoms in cyberspace.

QuickCheck C

1. The grant of a patent gives the patent owner a 20-year _____ over the use of his invention or process.

2. Copyright law has difficulty protecting the *structure* of computer programs because copyright protects _____ but not _____.

3. True or false? Disassembling or decompiling a copyrighted program is a fair use if decompilation is the only way to access the ideas that can't be protected by copyright and functionality of the program.

4. Software written and distributed by authors who do not expect compensation for their work is referred to as _____.

5. Software that is available for copying and use for a limited time but requires the payment of a licensing fee to keep is called _____.

6. Commercial software that is illegally distributed at various locations on the Internet or on certain bulletin boards is referred to as _____.

7. Commercial software often comes with licensing provisions called _____ licenses, which give even greater protection to the software than it would normally have under copyright law.

8. The _____ case is recognized as one of the reasons more stringent criminal penalties should be applied to software piracy.

D Legal Protection of Trade Names and Logos

Every business owes its success to the quality of the products and services it offers to the general public. Quality alone, however, will not win future or repeat customers unless consumers associate that quality with the name of the product or company. Businesses spend tremendous amounts of money on advertising designed to enhance the image of their products and services and the trade name that customers will associate with those products and services. The resulting good will translates into the promise of future business. Businesses are able to protect that good will only through the legal protection afforded trade names, trademarks, and service marks. As businesses expand their presence into the digital world, they bring their trademarks with them.

Legal Trademark and Trade Name Protection

What kinds of protection does trademark law give?   Trademark law is designed to protect consumer loyalty and the good reputation that businesses develop by preventing others from unfairly cashing in on the use of the distinctive names or marks that most businesses use. Trademark and trade name protection was originally developed by state courts in an attempt to prevent unfairness in business, and their holdings have developed into a separate body of law referred to as the law of "unfair competition." Many states will permit businesses to protect their marks in court if a competitor infringes the mark by using the same or a confusingly similar mark. As demonstrated in Figure 21, before trademark

Figure 21

These images are imitators of the trademark associated with a popular softdrink.

law was fully developed, it was common for some competitors to attempt to benefit from the success of others by adopting confusingly similar trademarks and trade names.

When a trademark owner sues an infringer, the bottom-line consideration is whether a particular defendant's use of his or her mark or name is likely to cause consumer confusion about the source of the defendant's goods or services. If the likelihood of confusion is present, a court may prevent continued use of the infringing mark through an injunction and may award money damages to the plaintiff to compensate for lost sales or injury to the plaintiff's business reputation.

Eventually, Congress realized the importance of protecting the trademarks of businesses and their products and services on a national scale. Congress enacted the **Lanham Act**, which provides special protection for names and marks that are registered with the U.S. Patent and Trademark Office in Washington, D.C. The Lanham Act provides for registration of four types of business marks: trademarks, service marks, certification marks, and collective marks, as explained in Figure 22.

Figure 22

These various kinds of marks, taken together, are collectively referred to as "trademarks."

Type	Use	Example
Trademarks	To identify products and the businesses that produce them	Kleenex® BRAND / Kleenex® BRAND
Service marks	To identify services and the businesses that provide them	UNITED AIRLINES / AT&T
Certification marks	Marks used by one organization to certify that certain goods or services of another business or organization have certain characteristics	UL®
Collective marks	Marks used by members of a particular trade group or organization to identify goods and services as coming from a member of the organization	AARP

To qualify for federal registration, the mark must meet certain tests for uniqueness and originality and must not have been used by someone else first. In addition, the Lanham Act lists certain kinds of marks that may not be registered, including generic terms, scandalous or immoral marks, deceptive marks, and marks consisting of the insignia of any U.S. or foreign governmental body, among others. Marks that are merely descriptive (such as Delicious Frozen Custard), or are geographical (New Jersey Auto Parts), or consist of a surname (Johnson's Car Wash) must generally have been in use for five years before they are eligible for registration.

Once a trademark has been registered under the Lanham Act, the owner of the mark may bring suit against anyone who uses the same or a confusingly similar mark or name. The owner may recover his or her lost profits and other monetary damages from the infringer if the infringer had notice of the registration of the mark. The Lanham Act provides that the owner of the mark can satisfy the notice requirement by including the words "Registered in the U.S. Patent and Trademark Office," or using the ® symbol with the trademark whenever it is displayed. The ^{TM} symbol is often associated with trademark protection. Technically, this symbol has no legal effect under the Lanham Act. When the owner of a trademark uses the ^{TM} symbol with a trademark, it usually means that the trademark is not yet registered, but that the owner still intends to protect the mark with a lawsuit if it is infringed.

Sometimes situations arise in which a confusingly similar trademark is used by a business that is not in direct competition with a trademark owner's business. For example, a chain of automobile repair shops might adopt the trade name McDonald's for obvious reasons. While the public might not be confused about the source of the services and while the McDonald's restaurant chain might not suffer lost profits due to competition, McDonald's restaurants might still prevent use of the name by suing for dilution. Most states permit trademark owners to sue for **dilution** where use of a confusingly similar name or mark by a noncompetitor could have the effect of diminishing, devaluing, or diluting the strong association that consumers have between the plaintiff and his or her distinctive mark or name.

Trademarks in Cyberspace

How are trademarks used in cyberspace? Trademarks are used on the Internet to identify and distinguish both traditional and digital goods and services. In the 1994 case of *Sega Enterprises, Ltd. v. Maphia*, a court stopped a bulletin board operator from offering unauthorized copies of Sega's video games, based on both copyright and trademark infringement.

InfoWeb

Trademarks and Domain Names
14

A bigger issue on the Internet is the use of domain names by businesses and their competitors. The Internet uses a **domain name system**, commonly referred to as the dotted quad address, that assigns a specific name to the numeric Internet Protocol (IP) address of a particular host computer on the Internet. The domain name system allows users to easily find their way to specific sites on the Internet. The user doesn't have to know that the address of Intel's host computer on the World Wide Web is "134.134.214.34." Instead, a user can more easily remember the domain name of Intel's host as "intel.com" and its Web site as "www.intel.com."

Requests for domain names are administered by Network Solutions, Inc. (NSI), which assigns names on a first-come, first-served basis. The federal registry of trademarks is not checked before domain names are issued. The result has led to legal skirmishes between businesses over domain names that would otherwise be subject to federal trademark protection. A database of U.S. domain names is maintained by the Internet Network Information Center (InterNIC) and can be accessed online with a search tool called NetFind.

In one well-publicized case, a video jockey named Adam Curry registered the name "mtv.com" while he was employed by MTV. When Curry later resigned, MTV sued to get the right to use mtv.com as its own domain name. The case was settled out of court, with MTV recovering use of the mtv.com domain name. Soon after, MTV developed its own presence on the Web at www.mtv.com. Curry changed the domain name of his site to www.metaverse.com and it remains a popular site on the Web, as shown in Figure 23.

Figure 23

After MTV reclaimed the mtv.com domain name from Adam Curry, he changed the domain name of his site to **www.metaverse.com**.

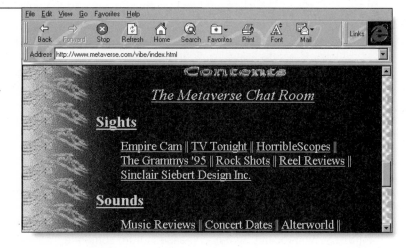

While most of these domain name disputes have been settled out of court, others are currently in litigation. Preliminary rulings in at least two federal cases suggest that businesses may be able to rely on trademark law to prevent competitors from using domain names that infringe trade names. The law in this area is still unsettled, however. Experts agree that ultimately the issue of trade name protection will come down to whether a domain name is more like a trade name or a street address. If courts treat domain names like street addresses, which are not protected by trademark law, they are unlikely to receive trademark protection.

QuickCheck D

1. _____ is designed to protect consumer loyalty and the good reputation associated with the distinctive names or marks that most businesses use.

2. The _____ provides special protection for names and marks that are registered with the U.S. Patent and Trademark Office.

3. The use of someone else's trade name in a noncompeting business, though technically not a trademark infringement, could still lead to liability for trademark _____.

4. True or false? Before authorizing the use of a specific domain name, the federal trademark registry is checked to determine whether the requested domain name might infringe a trademark.

UserFocus

E User Guidelines in Cyberspace

Cyberspace presents a wide array of intellectual property issues, problems, and traps for the unwary. The unauthorized copying, sharing, and distribution of commercial software is a violation of copyright law that could even lead to criminal liability. When downloading software of any kind, you should pay close attention to the terms of its licensing agreement. Much of the software you find will be in the form of shareware; you will occasionally come across freeware. Your use of either shareware or freeware amounts to your agreement to the licensing terms that come with it. In addition to copyright protection of software, you should also remember that practically everything communicated on a bulletin board system, online service, or the Internet is subject to copyright protection. The following are some suggestions to help you avoid infringing intellectual property rights as you interact with others in cyberspace.

Using the Words of Others

When am I permitted to copy, post, or use text found in cyberspace? Current guidelines state that nearly everything you find in cyberspace is subject to copyright protection. Whenever you receive an e-mail message from someone else, the author of the message automatically enjoys the exclusive rights to copy, adapt, distribute, and display the message. If you post the message to a Usenet, forward or display the message to others, or alter the message in some way and resend it as your own work, you have violated the sender's copyrights. Therefore, if you wish to use someone else's e-mail in these ways, you should first seek the permission of the author to do so. In addition, you could also make fair use of the message by summarizing it or by quoting small portions of it, provided that your use is for the purpose of critiquing or commenting on the message.

Posts to a Usenet group, the message bases of a bulletin board system (BBS), or the discussion areas of an online service are also entitled to copyright protection. By posting such a message, you are implicitly licensing the distribution of your post to the many news servers across the Internet that carry the particular newsgroup to which you have posted. Beyond this, however, you enjoy copyright protection from indiscriminate copying, adaptation, or distribution of your post. However, others may still make fair use of your post, such as by quoting portions of it in order to comment on it.

Just because your posts or e-mail messages are entitled to copyright protection does not mean that you are protected from an infringement claim if your post or e-mail contains the copyrighted works of others. You are not free to copy the entire text of that interesting article you just read in Newsweek and then post or e-mail it to your friends. You may still make fair use of such materials, however, by summarizing what you have read or quoting small portions as part of your message.

Certain text materials are not protected by copyright because they are in the public domain, and you are free to use these materials as you wish. In addition, you will occasionally come across messages or other materials in which the author has specifically permitted recopying and redistribution. Such materials will include licensing language like this:

> **This message may be freely copied, distributed, or otherwise transmitted.**

In this example, the copyright owner still retains the right to adapt or alter the work. Thus, you would not be permitted to make substantial changes or additions to the work and then redistribute it, unless either the version you distribute contains the entire message or you have made fair use of it by quoting portions of it or summarizing it.

Using the Graphics of Others

When can I copy graphics or other works for use in my Web page? The copyright rules applicable to text also apply to graphics, digitized images, sound files, video files, and other multimedia works that you find in cyberspace. All of these materials are considered works of authorship and are protected by copyright law. The temptation to copy a particularly attractive graphics file for use in your Web page should be avoided. You will generally need to create your own graphics elements for use in your personal pages. You will occasionally find Web pages that contain graphics images that have been specifically committed to the public domain, like those in Figure 24. The Web servers of many colleges and universities frequently provide such graphics to permit students to create Web pages without taking the time to generate their own graphics.

Figure 24

Many Web sites offer public domain graphics for use in your Web page design.

If you have access to a scanner, you may scan photographs that you have taken or that the photographer has given you permission to use in your Web pages. Remember that scanning photos from copyrighted works is an adaptation of the work and constitutes copyright infringement. The same holds true for creating collages by combining copyrighted images into a new and different image. Even though you may have a copyright in the composite image as an original compilation, this copyright interest will not aid you in defending the violation of the copyrights of others whose images you used in your collage.

Trademarks present special problems on Web pages. The trademark you decide to use on your Web page is protected both by copyright law and trademark law. Even when you are not attempting to compete with the trademark owner, you could still find yourself on the losing end of a trademark dilution suit if your use of the mark is for any commercial purpose whatsoever. Some trademark owners are willing to license the use of their mark on your page, however. For example, the HTML Writers Guild, a nonprofit educational organization (**www.hwg.org/services/logo/**), allows its members to display its logo on Web pages they design, but only if they follow very specific Logo Usage Guidelines. See Figure 25.

Figure 25

The HTML Writers Guild allows its members to display its logo if they agree to the Logo Usage Guidelines.

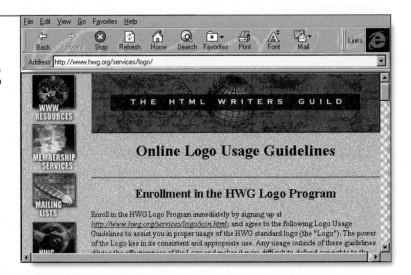

Linking and Coding on the World Wide Web

Can I use the HTML code or Java scripts I find on the Web?   It is generally permissible for your Web page to contain links to other Web sites of your choice. The very purpose of the World Wide Web is to encourage the free flow of information by encouraging hyperlinks to relevant resources. In fact, most commercial Web sites measure the success of their sites by the number of visits, or **hits**, they receive. Thus, free linking is the norm and is encouraged on the Web. By establishing a page on the World Wide Web, you are implicitly licensing others to link to your page.

The use of the hypertext markup language (HTML) code behind World Wide Web pages presents copyright problems. Generally, you are free to examine the HTML code on the pages you visit; most Web browsers are designed to allow you to do just that. You are also free to examine Java code, and then use the ideas or techniques employed in that code. **Java scripts** are special programs that create animation, moving text, or other creative interfaces that enhance Web pages. Cutting and pasting of the author's Java code into your own page is not permitted under copyright law unless the creator has granted you permission to do so.

Fortunately, Java programmers have generally adopted the widespread practice of spelling out what you can and cannot do in the comment lines of their code. Sometimes this language will commit a particular bit of Java creativity to the public domain, while at other times the author will grant permission to copy and use the code as long as his copyright and license statements are included. The comment lines may merely state that the author reserves copyrights in the code, using the traditional copyright notice provisions. When you encounter this last situation, you should contact the author and request permission to use the code. In cases where you do not find comment lines, you should avoid cutting and pasting the code because you may be infringing an author's copyright. When in doubt, you can generally reach the site administrator by e-mail and either seek permission to use the code or find out who the author is.

EndNote

The law of copyrights, patents, and trademarks has important consequences for the future growth and direction of our society in the Digital Age. Intellectual property law's complex set of rules are subject to evolution and change to meet the perceived challenges of cyberspace. In fact, intellectual property issues are complex, and readers are advised to seek the advice of an attorney competent in the field if they have legal questions. Intellectual property law's underlying purpose to "promote the progress of science and useful arts" is achieved only by maintaining a delicate balance between the needs of authors and inventors to be rewarded for their creations and the interests of society in the enjoyment of those creations and the free exchange of ideas. Users will play a critical role in the direction the law will take. Just as responsible use and respect for traditional intellectual property rights will slow the demand for legal change, so too will irresponsibility and the abuse of new freedoms encourage increasing regulation at the expense of those freedoms.

InfoWeb

Chapter
Links

The InfoWeb is your guide to print, film, television, and electronic resources. Use it to obtain updates on quickly changing technical information and to locate information for research papers. If you're using the New Perspectives CD-ROM, click the InfoWeb icon on the left side of this paragraph to access the online InfoWeb links. Otherwise, use your Web browser and type in the address of the New Perspectives site: www.cciw.com/np3. At the New Perspectives site you'll find up-to-date links to the topics covered in this chapter.

1 Inventions

The world of inventions covers all the extremes, from the useful to the humorous. Rube Goldberg was a cartoonist with a flair for drawing humorous, but seemingly useful inventions. Check out the Purdue Rube Goldberg Machine Contest at **www.purdue.edu/UNS/rube/rube.index.html**. You can view some unusual patented inventions at Wacky Patent of the Month, **colitz.com/site/wacky.htm**. Invention involves vision, insight, and real engineering skill, and many people think that Buckminster Fuller was an exemplar of all these qualities. You can learn about some of his inventions at Buckminster Fuller's Inventions Web site, **www.wnet.org/archive/bucky/invent.html**. In Japan, creating strange inventions is a pastime that many people enjoy. You can learn about the Japanese art of Chindogu in *101 Useless Japanese Inventions: The Art of Chindogu* by Kenji Kawakami (W.W. Norton & Company, 1995).

2 Plagiarism and Copyright Infringement

No creative field is safe from plagiarism and copyright infringement. The article "Plagiarism in Pop" from the Planet Sound Web site at **www1.teletext.co.uk/total/psound/song.htm** describes recent cases in which pop musicians used the work of others without acknowledgement or compensation. Professors as well as students are capable of plagiarism, as you will learn from the article "Precedent Set in Student Plagiarism Victory" at **aix2.uottawa.ca/~fulcrum/58-03/news/Psispv.html**. Are you plagiarising when you turn in a paper that you downloaded from a research paper database? The Web site Plagiarism Two: Online Paper Mills at **www.marlboro.edu/~nickc/research/cheat.html** can help you answer this question. The article "Writer Who Cried Plagiarism Used Passages From Another" at **www.ishipress.com/amistad.htm** demonstrates that distinguishing among the legal use of source material, plagiarism, and copyright infringement can be difficult. One of the most notorious Internet copyright infringement cases was that of David LaMacchia. You can learn about the case at U.S. vs. LaMacchia, **www.libraries.wayne.edu/~jlitman/majors.html**. "Three Internet Copyright Infringement Cases Settled" at **www.riaa.com/antipir/releases/massett.htm** describes the recording industry's reaction to some uses of copyright-protected music on the Internet.

3 Trademark Development

To learn more about trademarks, a good place to start is "Trademark Basics" at Identity Research Corporation, **www.idresearch.com/**. If you're not sure whether you should say "I cleaned my glasses with a Kleenex" or "I cleaned my glasses with a tissue," then you need to read the "Trademark Resources" section of the International Trademark Association Web site at **www.inta.org/**. The U.S. Patent Office's "Basic Facts About Registering a Trademark" at **www.uspto.gov/web/offices/tac/doc/basic/** will fill you in on the process of registering a trademark. In order to register a trademark, you need to make sure that no one else is already using it. This process is called trademark search, and you can learn more about it at Thomson & Thomson Trademark & Copyright Services, **www.thomson-thomson.com/**. For an example of how seriously companies take trademark rights, read the "Legal Notice" section of the LEGO Worlds Web site at **www.lego.com/worlds.asp** (click "About Us," then "Legal Notice").

4 Current Intellectual Property Law

Enter the term "intellectual property" in any Internet search engine, and you will get a list of thousands of Web sites. Two indexes that do a good job of organizing the available information are the CyberSpace Law Center: Intellectual Property Resources at **www.cybersquirrel.com/clc/ip.html**, and KuesterLaw Technology Law Resource at **www.kuesterlaw.com/** (click "IP Resources"). *Intellectual Property Magazine* at **www.ipmag.com/** can help you keep up with the latest news in intellectual property law. You can find an excellent summary of copyright and NII Issues (click "Overview"), links to current legislation and court cases, and a link to the NII intellectual property white paper (see "Overview") at the Association of Research Libraries: Copyright and Intellectual Property, **www.arl.org/info/frn/copy/copytoc.html**. John Perry Barlow, co-founder of the Electronic Frontier Foundation and former lyricist for the Grateful Dead, has written extensively on intellectual property issues in the Internet era. One of his more recent articles is "Let our Music Go!" at **www.zdnet.com/yil/content/mag/9710/barlow.html**, in which he lays out some of the issues surrounding recent efforts to redefine copyright law as it applies to the Internet.

5 Basics of Copyright Law

For a grand tour of copyright issues, check out The Copyright Web site at **www.benedict.com/**. At the U.S. Copyright Office Web site at **lcweb.loc.gov/copyright/** you can find general information about copyright law and registration, application forms, news about new and pending legislation, and more. If you are creating a Web page, and you aren't sure whether you can use that background image you found on someone else's Web site or whether you can quote your mother's favorite saying, check out The UT System Crash Course in Copyright at **www.utsystem.edu/OGC/IntellectualProperty/cprtindx.htm**. In "The Pearl of Great Price: Copyright and Authorship from the Middle Ages to the Digital Age" at **www.educom.edu/web/pubs/review/reviewArticles/30345.html** Susan Saltrick hopes history can help us begin to resolve some of the copyright issues we face in the digital era.

6 International Copyright Law

Because the Internet reaches across international barriers and the world's economies are increasingly becoming one global economy, it has become even more important than before to understand international copyright laws and conventions. The International Publishers Association at **www.ipa-uie.org/** is a good place to start learning about international copyright laws. Another excellent source of information is the World Intellectual Property Organization (WIPO) Web site at **www.wipo.org/**. WIPO is a United Nations agency, and its purpose is "to promote the protection of intellectual property throughout the world, through cooperation among States." The International Federation of Library Associations (IFLA) and Institutions wants to protect both the rights of copyright holders and the right of individual users to access information. You can read the IFLA Position Paper on Copyright in the Electronic Environment at **142.78.40.7/ifla/V/ebpb/copy.htm**, and you can find more resources on copyright and intellectual property at **ifla.inist.fr/ifla/documents/infopol2/copyright/**.

7 Public Domain and Fair Use

Determining what intellectual property is in the public domain is fairly simple: when a patent or trademark has expired, the protected material comes into the public domain. A number of people and institutions are making literature, reference materials, and historical works that are in the public domain available on the Internet. Two examples are The New Bartleby: A National Digital Library at **www.bartleby.com/**, and the Project Bartleby Archive at **www.columbia.edu/acis/bartleby/** where you can find selected works of Theodore Roosevelt, T*he Oxford Book of English Verse, Bartlett's Familiar Quotations*, W. E. B. Du Bois' *The Souls of Black Folk*, and many more significant works. The philosophy of Project Gutenberg at **www.promo.net/pg/** is "once a book or any other item (including pictures, sounds, and even 3-D items can be stored in a computer), then any number of copies can and will be available." In spite of the availability of vast amounts of literature and information in the public domain, some people propose that all information wants or needs should be free.The article "Against Intellectual Property" at **www.eff.org/pub/Intellectual_property/against_ip.article** represents one side of this debate. "Royalties, Fair Use & Copyright in the Electronic Age" at **www.educom.edu/web/pubs/review/reviewArticles/30630.html** presents another side of this debate.

8 Cyberspace for Sale

Who gets value—particularly money—from intellectual property, especially when digital media are involved? You can learn about royalties and other compensation schemes from organizations such as Publications Rights Clearinghouse (**www.nwu.org/nwu/prc/prchome.htm**), Copyright Clearance Center (**www.copyright.com/**), The Authors Registry (**www.webcom.com/registry/**), ASCAP (**www.ascap.com/**), and BMI (**www.bmi.com/**). You can find discussions of framing, linking, packaging and other economic issues at the Second International Harvard Conference on Internet and Society, **www.cybercon98.org/asp/splash.asp** (click topics, then Law). In 1997, Harvard University hosted a conference on Internet Publishing and Beyond: Economics of Digital Information and Intellectual Property. You can find copies of the conference papers, which focus on a variety of economic issues at **ksgwww.harvard.edu/iip/econ/econ.html**. Digital object identifier technology is a proposed solution to protecting copyright online. You can learn about this new technology in the article "The Digital Object Identifier: Solving the Dilemma of Copyright Protection Online," from the *Journal of Electronic Publishing* at **www.press.umich.edu/jep/03-02/doi.html**.

9 Patent and Trademark Law

The U.S. Patent and Trademark Office at **www.uspto.gov/** includes information about patent and trademark laws, regulations, rules, fees, and application forms. The Cornell Law School's Legal Information Institute contains a complete collection of information on patent law (**www.law.cornell.edu/topics/patent.html**) and trademark law (**www.law.cornell.edu/topics/trademark.html**). If you do not understand the differences among patents, trademarks, and copyright, then read the clear, brief explanations at Patent, Trademark, Copyright—What's the Difference, **www.wigman.com/art07.htm**. A very complete and well-organized index to patent resources on the Internet is The Patent Portal at **www.law.vill.edu/~rgruner/patport.htm**, created and maintained by Richard S. Gruner, Professor of Law. The Patent Resource Center at Derwent Scientific and Patent Information, **www.derwent.com/**, contains an overview and history of patents, a showcase of historically significant patents, a glossary of terms, and a patent news index.

10 Software Copyright

The search engine Lycos recently received a patent for its search engine software. Does it make sense to patent software? Is a copyright sufficient for software? Simson Garfinkel's article "Patently Absurd" at **www.wired.com/wired/2.07/features/patents.html** discusses whether it made sense for the Patent Office to grant Compton's a patent on multimedia technology. Software: Copyright or Patent? A Comparative Analysis at **www.mccutchen.com/ip/ip_2101.htm** describes the type and degree of protection of software offered by copyright and patent. In "The Blessing (or Bane) of Software Patents" at **www.educom.edu/web/pubs/review/reviewArticles/29338.html**, Edmund B. Burke points out that software copyrights are limited by nature and that a patent is a more appealing form of protection for software companies.

11 Freeware

In contrast to software companies who copyright and patent their products, McArthur award winner Richard Stallman argues that software should be free. You can learn why he makes this argument by reading his essay "If It's Not Source, It's Not Software" at **www.virtualschool.edu/mon/ElectronicProperty/StallmanSoftwareShouldBeFree**. Stallman has written and is giving away free a Unix-compatible operating system called GNU. You can learn why he gives software away in his essay, "GNU Manifesto" at **www.eff.org/pub/Intellectual_property/gnu.manifesto**. You can also find an interview with Stallman at **memex.org/meme2-04.html**. You can learn more about GNU and the idea of free software at the Free Software Foundation, **www.fsf.org/**. The League for Programming Freedom was established to "publicize the danger of interface copyrights and software patents;" it's Web site is at **lpf.ai.mit.edu/**. Can you really find free software—not shareware—on the Internet? Yes! Check out Volition Free Software (**www.volition.com/software.html**), Freeware Web (**freeware95.atlnet.com/**), and Freeware Central (**www.ptf.com/free/**).

12 Microsoft Antitrust Case

On May 18, 1998, the Justice Department filed an antitrust suit against Microsoft. Yahoo News Full Coverage Microsoft Antitrust Case at **headlines.yahoo.com/Full_Coverage/Tech/Microsoft/** will help you keep track of the news surrounding the case, the case itself, and related Senate hearings. You can learn Microsoft's side of the case at Microsoft on the Issues, **www.microsoft.com/corpinfo/**. You can learn the government's side of the case at U.S. Department of Justice Antitrust Case Filings: U.S. vs. Microsoft, **www.usdoj.gov/atr/cases/ms_index.htm**, and at the FTC Web site, **www.ftc.gov/ftc/antitrust.htm**. If you're interested in learning more about antitrust and antitrust policy, explore **www.antitrust.org/**.

13 Software Ethics

Is it okay to borrow your friend's software and install it on your computer? The article, "Why Johnny Can't Tell Copyright from Wrong" at **www.nytimes.com/library/cyber/week/0424ethics-side.html** might help you answer this question. The Educom article "Ethics Online" at **www.educom.edu/web/pubs/review/reviewArticles/31432.html** describes research conducted at Southern Illinois University that studied students' and information technology professionals' ethical decision-making. If you're not sure about the limits and range of software ethics, read the text of EDUCOM's brochure "Using Software: A Guide to the Ethical and Legal Use of Software for Members of the Academic Community" at **www.uchicago.edu/a.docs/TechSupport/software-ethics.html**. You can find a tutorial that teaches computer ethics at **www.unipa.it/~lanza/demos/EthicsDescription.html**.

14 Trademarks and Domain Names

"Chutes and Ladders" is a children's board game. Could you develop a Web site about antique fire engines, using the domain name "chutesnladders.com?" Not without invoking the ire of Hasbro, the trademark owner, and the U.S. courts. You can read about recent domain name legal cases in "Domain Name Disputes: The Recent Court Decisions" at **www.educom.edu/web/pubs/review/reviewArticles/32306.html**. "Internet Domain Names and Trademark Laws" at **www.ior.com/~malhotra/domain.html** provides a clear summary of how trademark law applies to the use of domain names. The paper "The Domain Name Versus Trademark Dilemma" at **www.intellecprop.mpg.de/Online-Publikationen/Kur-DomainNamevsTrademarkDilemma.htm** summarizes some of the history of domain name and trademark disputes, discusses some of the international issues at play, and describes several proposals for resolving some of the problems. You can learn all about the process of domain name selection, registration, buying, and selling at Domain Name News and Information, **www.igoldrush.com/**.

Review

1 Below each heading in this chapter is a focus question. Look back through the chapter and answer each question in your own words.

2 In your own words, list the three major kinds of intellectual property and what each of them is intended to protect.

3 List the five exclusive rights that copyright owners have in their work.

4 In your own words, explain why software and digital communications pose special challenges for intellectual property law.

5 Identify the four factors used by courts to determine when a particular instance of copyright infringement may be excused as fair use.

6 List at least four differences between patent and copyright protection for software.

7 In your own words, describe the difference between trademark infringement and trademark dilution.

8 List at least three kinds of intellectual property that is considered in the public domain.

9 Use your own words to describe the ethical problems involved in borrowing commercial software from others.

10 Assume that you are in the process of designing a Web page. What copyright issues should you be concerned about, and why? Explain whether and when you may use the work of others on your page.

Projects

1 **The Fair Use Defense Test** Our courts are often called on to decide whether a particular case of copyright infringement should be excused under the fair use defense. When such situations arise, a court will apply the four-factor fair use defense test to determine whether a particular instance of infringement is to be excused. Try applying the four-factor test to each of the following situations to determine whether a fair use defense might be applicable. In each example, you should consider the results of each of the four tests and then determine whether those results, taken together, indicate a fair use or inexcusable infringement. Explain why you believe each example is or is not a fair use, and include your conclusions about each of the four factors for each example.

a. Your mother sends you a clipping from a "Dear Abby" column she thinks you might be interested in reading.

b. You purchase the latest CD release of your favorite musician or band, and then you make a cassette tape recording of the CD, which you send to a friend.

c. Your cousin e-mails you a copy of a Usenet post she thinks you might be interested in reading.

d. Your friend has rented a video cassette of one of your favorite movies. Because you and he both have VCR equipment, you decide to connect them together and then make a copy of the movie for you to add to your video collection.

e. After viewing some of the scenic images available in Philip Greenspun's award winning Web novel entitled *Travels with Samantha*, you decide to save one of the images as Windows wallpaper on your PC.

f. After saving your favorite images from *Travels with Samantha* on your hard drive, you decide to use them on your own Web page.

2 **Understanding Infringement** Recall that copyright infringement occurs whenever any one of the five exclusive rights of copyright owners is violated. Consider the following situations that occur when using the World Wide Web. In each situation, identify which of the copyright owner's five exclusive rights is implicated. (*Hint*: None, one, or more than one of the exclusive rights may be involved for any particular example.) For each situation, explain whether infringement has occurred (regardless of whether the fair use defense might be available), and why you think so.

a. You click on a hyperlink, causing your browser to request a World Wide Web page from a distant host machine or server. The host machine responds by producing a digital copy of the page's elements (in this case, HTML and graphics) in its RAM, ready to be transported to your machine.

b. The host machine divides the digital copies into packets of approximately 1,500 bytes each, and then sends them on their way to your machine by passing the packets through a series of network-connected computer switches called routers.

c. Your machine receives the packets and then reassembles them into their original HTML and graphics file elements in your machine's RAM.

d. Your machine displays the completed Web page on your screen, while its HTML and graphics elements remain in your machine's RAM.

e. Your browser automatically copies the Web page elements (the HTML and graphics files) to your hard drive.

f. You decide to save some of the graphic elements of the page for future use by copying them into a separate subdirectory on your hard drive.

g. You create a Web page that uses some of the graphic elements you have saved. To do this, you must copy these images to the server machine provided by your Internet access provider, together with your own HTML text that includes image tags to incorporate the images into your page.

h. Someone else accesses your page on the World Wide Web, causing steps a, b, c and d to be repeated for that user from your server.

i. You create a composite Web page, using HTML image tags that call images from other, remote servers for display on your page, and the page is accessed by another user, causing steps a, b, c and d to be repeated for that user from the remote servers.

j. The composite Web page you created in step i is accessed by a user whose browser cannot display graphics images.

3
INTERNET Optional

Changes in Intellectual Property Law One result of the digital revolution is a series of proposals for new laws that are intended to make changes to intellectual property law to meet the challenges discussed in this chapter. Pay a visit to the home page of the Electronic Frontier Foundation (at **http://www.eff.org**). Find a discussion about any recent proposal for change in either copyright or patent law that has specific implications for computers or digital networks.

a. Describe the change under consideration.

b. Are the hosts of the site you are visiting in favor of the change or opposed to it? Why?

c. From what you have learned of this proposed change, what do you think the purposes of its proponents are?

d. In your opinion, does this proposal maintain the delicate balance between the rights of the creators of intellectual property to enjoy the fruits of their labors and the needs of society for the free flow of information? Does this proposal advance the ultimate purpose of intellectual property law—to "promote the progress of science and useful arts?" Why or why not?

e. If the site you are visiting is opposed to the change, what other alternatives are available that would satisfy both the proponents and the opponents?

4 **Confusingly Similar Trademarks** As shown in Figure 21, before passage of the Lanham Act competitors routinely sought to take advantage of their more successful rivals by using trademarks and trade names that were confusingly similar. The practice can still be seen today from time to time. Trademark infringement will be found where the infringing mark is likely to cause consumer confusion about the source of the goods or services bearing the name or mark.

a. Pay a visit to your local supermarket and find at least three products that you think are marked in such a way as to try to take unfair advantage of a larger or more successful competitor.

b. Make a list of these products and their competitors.

c. Do you think the average consumer would be confused about the source of the goods? Why or why not?

5  **The Future of Intellectual Property Law** Read the John Perry Barlow article, "The Economy of Ideas," referred to in Section A. You can find a copy of this essay at **http://www.hotwired.com/wired/2.03/ features/economy.ideas.html** or in the Intellectual Property archives at the Electronic Frontier Foundation's site on the Web at **http://www.eff.org/pub/ Intellectual_property/**.

a. Do you agree with Barlow's conclusion that intellectual property law is dead in the Digital Age? Why or why not?

b. If existing intellectual property law structures are not able to meet the challenge of digital communications, what other alternatives are there for protecting the rights of creators to enjoy the rewards of their creations?

c. Without offering any specific solutions, Barlow suggests that the present system will be replaced by one based on "ethics and technology." How could such a system work?

6 **What's in a Domain Name?** Businesses are increasingly concerned about infringement or dilution of their trade names by others who use the same or similar names as part of their Internet domain names. This problem is especially troublesome on the World Wide Web because users have come to rely on well-established domain naming conventions for finding home pages on the Web.

a. A database of U.S. domain names is maintained by the Internet Network Information Center (InterNIC). You can look up the host name of computers or sites by searching InterNIC's Netfind Server. Telnet to **ds.internic.net** and log in as "netfind." Use the "seed database lookup" function listed on the menu to find the host names of the following businesses and organizations. (Note: You may find more than one host for some of these.)

McDonnell Douglas Corporation
Ohio State University
Republican National Committee
U.S. House of Representatives
New York Times
Smithsonian Institution

b. InterNIC also maintains a database where you can learn who presently "owns" a particular domain name as well as where the host computer is located. You can access this database, known as InterNIC's "whois server," by telnetting to **rs.internic.net** and logging in as "whois". At the Whois> prompt, enter the following domain names to find out who is behind the name. For each domain name, list the name of the organization or business behind the domain name, and the name of the individual who serves as the administrative contact for the domain. (Note: The Whois server requires that you type each domain name exactly as it appears below.)

isoc.org
fsu.edu
floridastate.com
duke.edu
duke.com
stlouiscardinals.com

COMPUTERS AND INTELLIGENCE

Speculation about intelligent computers and their encroachment into our society has been a recurring theme in books, plays, and film throughout the twentieth century. As early as 1921, Karel Çapek wrote a play, *R.U.R.*, in which robots, manufactured by *Rossum's Universal Robots*, become increasingly dissatisfied with their role and with the disorder and irrationality of their inventors. The robots organize and revolt, overthrowing their masters and destroying all signs of humanity. The theme of dissident robots continues in Arthur Clarke's *2001: A Space Odyssey* and then evolves into a full society of Borg, robotic beings who share one mind, in Gene Roddenberry's *Star Trek: The Next Generation*.

Robots in
Science Fiction
1

Long before computers were invented, scientists and philosophers debated whether machines could ever achieve human intelligence. Modern computers can process huge databases of facts and apply rules of logic with impressive speed. But can computers actually think? Can computers be creative? Will computers ever have "common sense," understand emotions and beliefs, or make decisions that are contrary to logic? What would a computer have to do to convince you it is intelligent? These are some of the central questions in the field known as **artificial intelligence**, which is the study of making computers think like humans.

Although no one claims to have created a truly intelligent computer, many interesting efforts have been made. As a result, the long-standing controversy over whether a computer can have human intelligence appears to be far from settled. In this chapter you will explore the debate over artificial intelligence. You will see how even these attempts have furthered the debate about artificial intelligence and yielded some very practical results.

CHAPTER**PREVIEW**

This chapter discusses some of the different views of artificial intelligence and research into the models for intelligent machines. You will read about attempts to build intelligent machines and learn why critics claim that these machines are not truly intelligent. You will also learn about the applications of artificial intelligence that are producing useful results in business, manufacturing, medicine, and other fields. When you have completed this chapter, you should be able to:

- Describe the Turing test for artificial intelligence
- Describe current models of human intelligent behavior that researchers are applying to develop intelligent machines
- Discuss some important research in artificial intelligence
- Describe the characteristics of intelligence that are difficult to duplicate in computers
- Identify some models of artificial intelligence and describe how they work
- Describe some current and future practical applications of artificial intelligence

A Can Computers Think?

Since the early days of computer development, computers' impressive ability to calculate quickly and accurately has led many scientists to speculate that computers will someday rival humans in intelligence. If doing arithmetic, an activity formerly done only by humans, can be done by a machine, why can't a machine do other tasks considered uniquely human? Can computers relieve us of other tedious thinking tasks? Will they be able to match our capacity to solve problems? Will computers be able to imitate our human intelligence convincingly, or is there a fundamental difference between the way we think and the way computers operate? Some scientists believe that computers or intelligent machines will never behave like intelligent humans and, therefore, will never be truly intelligent. Others are convinced that computers are capable of a form of intelligence.

InfoWeb

Defining
Artificial
Intelligence
2

Although many definitions exist, a useful definition of artificial intelligence (AI) is the study of making machines behave as if they had human intelligence. Marvin Minsky, a leading researcher in the field of AI at MIT, says that intelligence is the term used to describe the processes of the human brain that aren't understood. According to him, AI is the name given to the research designed to get computers to duplicate those processes. The extent to which researchers in AI have succeeded, and will succeed, in making computers behave this way is a matter of great controversy.

There are three areas in which computers have proven capable of simulated intelligence: game-playing, solving mathematical theorems, and expert systems. In game playing, programmers have included all possible moves so that each time the computer takes its turn, it considers all of them and selects the best possible move. Computers used to solve mathematical theorems follow similar procedures. **Expert systems** are decision-making programs that, in addition to knowing all possible options, are capable of refining each task by inferring new options based on known facts. AI research centers on whether any of these computer applications make computers truly intelligent or if computers are even capable of becoming intelligent.

The Turing Test

What is an intelligent computer, and how would you prove that it is? Given the differences of opinion among the experts, how can we ever decide if a given machine is truly intelligent? Many researchers have proposed tests and criteria to determine this. The most famous of these tests was proposed by the British mathematician Alan Turing in his 1950 article, "Computing Machinery and Intelligence," in which he maintained that the question "Can machines think?" was too ambiguous to answer. Instead he proposed a simple test, now known as the Turing test, that would allow a computer to demonstrate its intelligence. His test was originally designed to see if there was any noticeable differences between the intelligence of male and female contestants. It was modified to test computer intelligence by using one human and one computer contestant.

The test, illustrated in Figure 1, requires two contestants that are segregated from the judge, who asks questions in hopes of identifying the contestants. A keyboard is used to type all questions and answers to remove all bias between the contestants and the judge. The judge can ask any question, but the contestants are not obliged to answer the questions truthfully. At the end of the questioning period, the judge must decide which of the contestants is which. AI researchers use the Turing test to decide if a computer can demonstrate intelligence. If the judge cannot decide which contestant is the computer or is convinced that the computer is the human, then the computer is declared intelligent.

Figure 1

The Turing test

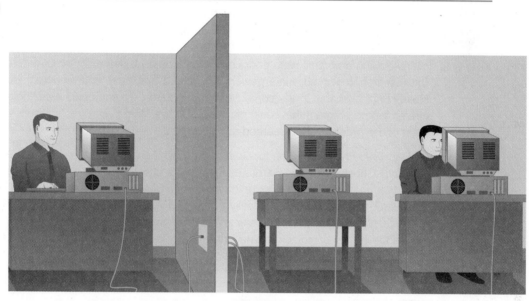

The Turing test neatly sidesteps the determination of whether the computer thinks like a human being. The computer only needs to behave so convincingly like a human being that it appears human. Critics say that this is a flaw of the test: The computer does not need to be intelligent; it needs only to appear intelligent. Critics of the Turing test stress that *appearing* intelligent is not the same as *being* intelligent. Because even though the computer may appear to be intelligent, it is simply manipulating 1's and 0's according to a set of rules. However, advocates of the Turing test say that no computer could appear so convincingly human without possessing some form of intelligence.

The Turing test is indeed a powerful test. Contests have been held and prizes offered for any computer that could pass it. No computer has yet come close to fooling human judges in a contest that uses unrestricted questions. However, some computers have arguably passed the test when the questions were restricted to a very narrow range of topics. It will undoubtedly be many years before any computer can pass the unrestricted test.

Intelligent Behavior

If we can't define human intelligence, how can we define artificial intelligence? If we are to get computers to behave intelligently, we must have a good understanding of intelligent behavior. The definition of intelligent behavior has been debated for centuries. Indeed, most AI researchers have stopped trying to define intelligence and instead have concentrated on describing the characteristics of intelligent behavior. In this way, they hope to set standards against which their attempts at creating artificial intelligence can be measured.

Defining
Intelligence
3

Critics of AI point to the game of chess as an excellent example of human intelligence. They have said that no computer would ever be able to play chess at the level of the best human players. The U.S. Chess Federation (USCF) is the official governing body in the United States. Players earn rating points based on their performance in tournament play against other rated players. A player with 2,200 or more USCF points earns the title "Master." Early chess-playing programs were poor competitors, easily defeated by amateur chess players. But research continued; more powerful hardware and more sophisticated software led to steady improvements in the computer's chess game. Tournaments were held and prizes offered for the program that could play chess at the Master level. As a result, several computer chess programs have earned ratings well above the Master level.

Early in 1996, the Association for Computing Machinery sponsored a chess match between the World Chess Champion Garry Kasparov and a chess program called Deep Blue, created by programmers at IBM. See Figure 2. When Deep Blue won the first game of the tournament, it appeared that a computer had finally achieved one of the early goals of artificial intelligence research, playing chess at the Master level. Although Kasparov ultimately won the match, four games to two, the computer had nevertheless proven itself a worthy competitor for the best human players. In a 1997 rematch, Deep Blue emerged as the victor.

Figure 2

Garry Kasparov competed with the chess-playing program Deep Blue.

The question remains: Is Deep Blue intelligent? Most people would argue that Deep Blue cannot think like a person and therefore does not have human intelligence. At best, it is a competent chess player. Given any other problem, Deep Blue would have no idea how to proceed. Yet some researchers say that Deep Blue represents one of many building blocks necessary for true artificial intelligence.

To supporters of Marvin Minsky, the fact that Deep Blue can play chess and play it almost as well as the best humans clearly demonstrates that Deep Blue has at least some kind of intelligence. If humans can create a program to play chess, it is only a matter of time before they can create programs to solve other difficult problems. Although chess is a very narrow domain of problem solving, and individual programs might solve only specific problems, the collection of these programs could resemble human intelligence.

But some people disagree and say that chess-playing programs do not bear any resemblance to human intelligence. Critics such as the philosopher Hubert Dreyfus point out that Deep Blue and all other good computer chess programs do nothing more than consider all possible moves, then all possible countermoves, and so on. The number of possible moves and countermoves is astronomical, and even Deep Blue cannot calculate more than a few moves ahead. Deep Blue is forced to select the move that is calculated to be best. These critics contend that this is not the way humans play chess.

Although it is true that the best human players look no more than two or three moves ahead, they do so by using other means—such as experience, intuition, and creativity—to play the game. Critics argue that Deep Blue's brute-force method for playing is not intelligence, just an interesting simulation. An interesting development in later matches is that Deep Blue appears to modify its programmed method of making decisions based on how Kasparov habitually plays chess. From these later matches, a new question has emerged: Does Deep Blue remember Kasparov's techniques? And if so, does that indicate the computer is capable of learning?

The philosopher John Searle offered his famous Chinese Room argument to support his claim that computers can never be truly intelligent. Suppose, he says, that a person who understands English but doesn't understand Chinese is locked in a room and given a batch of Chinese characters together with a set of rules in English for manipulating the characters and for creating new characters. By following the rules, the person manipulates and creates characters and then passes them out of the room. Suppose the original characters constituted a story and questions about the story in Chinese and that the rules actually described a method for constructing answers to the questions. The person in the room may construct correct answers and appear to be intelligent, but that person is merely manipulating symbols and still does not understand Chinese.

Searle says that a chess-playing computer is doing the same thing. The computer is playing chess by manipulating symbols, the 1's and 0's in its memory, according to a set of rules, the computer program, but it does not understand chess any more than the person in the room understands Chinese. It is merely calculating. Furthermore, critics of AI point out that chess is a game in which there is no hidden information. Both players' positions and all legal moves are completely known.

Another argument is that computers cannot account for ambiguity, emotion, motivation, or deception and will never be able to function intelligently when faced with the "irrational" components of human interaction. A computer will never truly be able to understand or participate intelligently in even simple conversation because the number of possible interpretations of words and sentences is limitless. Finally, although Deep Blue can play chess, it doesn't know it is playing chess, nor does it understand and have an emotional reaction to winning and losing. Figure 3 illustrates this critical difference between humans and computers.

Figure 3

Carl Lewis's reaction to winning his ninth Olympic gold medal compared to a computer's reaction to defeating a human player in the game of chess

Checkmate. I won.

Critics have not deterred AI researchers. Minsky and others believe that the human brain is just a very complicated machine. Emotion and motivation are simply mechanical phenomena that we do not yet, but eventually, will understand. AI researchers believe that the algorithm Deep Blue uses can be supplemented with rules of thumb and other techniques for making decisions when the number of factors to consider is too large. A **rule of thumb** is a rule that helps you solve a problem when you do not have complete information. Usually, a rule of thumb suggests an action that is likely but not guaranteed to lead you to a solution. For example, if your car won't start, one useful rule of thumb might be "Make sure there is gas in the gas tank." Critics point out that perhaps it is not necessary to duplicate human intelligence, but rather to create some form of intelligence: machine intelligence.

QuickCheck A

1 Artificial intelligence may be defined as the study of making machines behave as if they had _____ intelligence.

2 A test for machine intelligence using a human, a computer, and a judge is known as the _____ test.

3 A chess tournament between Chess Champion Garry Kasparov and a program called _____ demonstrated that chess-playing computers are capable of playing Master-level chess.

4 John Searle's argument that computers can never be intelligent because they just manipulate symbols without understanding is known as the _____ argument.

5 In Marvin Minsky's view, the human brain is nothing more than a very complicated _____.

B Teaching Computers to Think

As hardware designers and software developers improve computer technology, the possibility of intelligent computers seems more and more probable. We have seen high-tech gadgets in fiction that inspire inventors to invent real gadgets that actually work. There are many models of artificial intelligence that make computers appear to be more intelligent—character and voice recognition software, software agents and wizards, expert systems, robotics. How do they work? Why aren't they part of the standard configuration of every PC? In order to understand the barriers to developing truly intelligent computers, you need to understand some aspects of intelligence that make it difficult to duplicate in computers.

Natural Language Processing

Will you be able to speak to your computer the same way you speak to your friends?

InfoWeb

Natural Language 4

One of the most important accomplishments of human intelligence is the development of language—it is what sets us apart in the animal kingdom. The diversity and complexity of our written and spoken languages clearly distinguish us from other forms of life. For a computer to be considered intelligent, most people expect it to understand ordinary human language. The Turing test implicitly demands that the intelligent computer be able to understand the judge's questions and to reply in ordinary language.

Figure 4 shows Terry Winograd's famous program SHRDLU, a pioneering effort in natural language processing. SHRDLU (which is not an acronym for anything) inhabited a virtual world of colored blocks and boxes. The user could type instructions to SHRDLU, telling it to manipulate the blocks. The program could understand commands such as "Place the red block on the green one." When the instructions were ambiguous, SHRDLU asked questions for clarification. SHRDLU was impressive but limited. It could not understand anything outside its "micro-world" of blocks.

Figure 4

An illustration of Terry Winograd's famous program SHRDLU

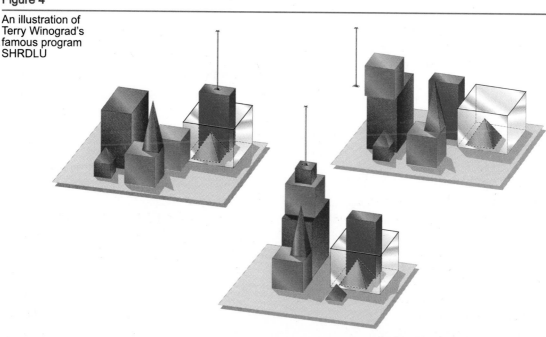

AI researchers face extremely difficult problems to get a computer to understand natural language:

- **Vocabulary, rules of grammar, and syntax.** The rules of grammar are complex and change over time. The computer must be able to recognize the correct meaning and use of words, plus the ways in which these words can be combined into appropriate sentences. The computer can store long lists of words and rules, but new words appear in our language almost daily. How will the computer learn new words?

- **Meaning.** The computer must be able to associate meaning with words and sentences. The meanings of words can be found in dictionaries, and the meanings of sentences can usually be inferred from the arrangement of words. The computer must be able to distinguish between "Tom painted the fence," which is grammatically correct and meaningful, and "Wednesday painted the determination," which is grammatically correct but nonsensical. Computers also have to be able to discriminate meanings and interpret nuance, sarcasm, and slang.

- **Ambiguity.** Looking up definitions in a dictionary is not sufficient because some words have many different meanings depending on their context. Even the speaker's intent can determine the meaning of a word, depending on whether the speaker is making a statement of fact, a pun, a sarcastic remark, or a metaphor. A classic example of ambiguity in language is the sentence, "Time flies like an arrow."

Figure 5 illustrates these possible interpretations: How will the computer interpret this sentence? Is this a comment on the swift passage of time? Does time fly in a parabolic curve as an arrow does? Are flies timed in a race the same way you might time an arrow's flight? Or are there perhaps some animals called "time flies" that enjoy arrows? All are meaningful and valid interpretations of this sentence, but most people would understand that the first interpretation is correct. How will the computer decide on that interpretation, and how will the computer decide that "Fruit flies like a banana" is not a comment on the swift passage of fruit?

Figure 5

Several interpretations of
"Time flies like an arrow"

Time moves swiftly

Time passes through air in a parabolic curve

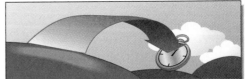

Flies in a timed race

"Time flies" enjoying their favorite arrow

In the 1960s, Joseph Weizenbaum of MIT created a program that could converse in English. The program, which he called ELIZA, was designed to imitate a psychotherapist. Figure 6 shows the kind of dialogue that ELIZA might have with a female patient.

Figure 6

Joseph Weizenbaum's program ELIZA imitated a psychotherapist.

I'm having problems with my boyfriend.

Tell me about your boyfriend.

He doesn't get along with my family.

In what way?

They get into lots of arguments.

Can you think of a specific example?

He argued with my father last night.

Tell me more about your father.

I think he is afraid of me.

Why do you think he is afraid of you?

He says I am too aggressive.

In what ways are you aggressive?

Sometimes I am angry with him and I challenge him.

Please go on.

Weizenbaum created ELIZA to demonstrate some principles of language processing. ELIZA did not understand anything about boyfriends, fathers, or aggression. It merely selected key words from the patient's sentences and repeated them in questions. To many people, ELIZA's responses were convincingly realistic. Weizenbaum was shocked to find that many patients confided in ELIZA just as they would confide in a real psychotherapist. Some patients would not allow Weizenbaum to review the conversations they had with ELIZA. Some respected scientists predicted that programs such as ELIZA would someday substitute for human therapists. However, his experience with ELIZA convinced Weizenbaum that computers would never be capable of solving truly human problems.

Problem Solving

Do humans and computers solve problems using the same methods? Humans use many different techniques to solve problems. Relatively few human problems can be solved by considering all possible solutions the way a chess-playing computer considers all possible moves and countermoves. This **algorithmic search technique**, which is a systematic approach of considering all possible solutions by looking at all moves and all countermoves, may be impractical because the number of potential solutions is too large or because all the possible steps toward a solution cannot be known. An **algorithm** is a finite sequence of instructions that define a procedure. Computer programmers usually write an algorithm as an outline for a program they plan to write. Some researchers feel that humans do most of their problem solving using **heuristics**, that is, rules of thumb that are likely, but not guaranteed, to lead to a solution.

How would you find a lost set of car keys? Few people would attempt to look exhaustively in all the places the keys might be since the number of possible locations is limitless. Instead, most people would use a heuristic such as "look in the most likely places" to guide their search. First you would check clothing pockets, the car's ignition and door locks, along the path from the car to the house, and so on. If you still did not find the keys, you would broaden the search, possibly doing a thorough room-by-room search. Eventually, either you would find the keys, or you would give up, reasoning that you searched all the likely places and searching other locations would have a low probability of success.

A computer would search differently for the lost keys. Its algorithmic search would involve a more systematic approach. If you were using an algorithm to search for your keys, you might walk into a room, turn left immediately, and scan every possible hiding place. For instance, you might start on top of the bureau, then look in the top left drawer, then the top middle drawer, and so on. If the keys were not in the bureau, you would move to the next piece of furniture and continue sequentially around the room. A human would not think this to be a very logical way to search, but a computer could do it so quickly that the keys might be found just as soon as the human, using a heuristic approach, could find them.

Scientific problems are solved by breaking them down into mathematical equations that lead to a solution. A theorem is a mathematical statement that contains a set of assumptions, called **hypotheses**, and a conclusion. If the hypotheses are true, then it can be shown, using the rules of logic, that the conclusion is true. For example, the famous Pythagorean Theorem states: "Hypothesis: IF a right triangle has sides of length A and B and hypotenuse of length C; Conclusion: THEN $A^2 + B^2 = C^2$." Both humans and computers are capable of this kind of problem solving.

Some techniques that humans use are more difficult for computers to learn. Computer programs incorporate methods of problem solving, to greater or lesser degrees. For example, **means-end analysis** is a method of trial and error. Given a goal, this method tries a possible solution, called a *candidate* solution. If the solution is correct, then the problem is solved. Otherwise, this method tries another candidate solution. Means-end analysis problem solving was incorporated in a program called the General Problem Solver (GPS) devised by Allen Newell, J.C. Shaw, and Herbert Simon in 1957. GPS proved successful at solving some problems, such as logic puzzles, and at proving mathematical theorems.

The General Problem Solver program proved adept at solving problems such as the Wolf, the Goat and the Cabbage puzzle. The puzzle, illustrated in Figure 7, consists of a trader who must transport a wolf, a goat and a cabbage from one shore of the river to another. The trader's canoe can hold the trader and two other objects. The wolf and the goat cannot be left alone on a shore because the wolf will eat the goat. Similarly, the goat and the cabbage cannot be left alone. The General Problem Solver program was able to solve problems like this; however, it proved unwieldy when faced with problems with a very large number of candidate solutions.

Figure 7

Given restrictions, how can the trader transport the three objects from one shore to another?

In addition to means-end analysis, humans solve problems in other ways—based on intuition, inspiration and creativity. Consider Archimedes, the philosopher and scientist of ancient Greece. Reportedly, Archimedes had to find a way to determine whether the king's goldsmith was using pure gold or mixing the gold with a metal of lesser value. This problem stumped Archimedes and others for a long time. One day, while bathing, Archimedes noticed that his body displaced a certain amount of water in the tub. Archimedes instantly understood that he could test the king's gold by measuring its density, that is, by comparing the amount of water it displaced with the amount displaced by an equal weight of pure gold. This discovery was so sudden and surprising that Archimedes is said to have leapt from the tub with a shout of "Eureka! (I found it!)." This famous story illustrates how humans can suddenly see a solution to a difficult problem, but no one can explain exactly how we do it.

Critics of AI contend that we will never be able to reduce this sort of inspiration to a computer program. Knowledge and understanding are not static, and an intelligent computer must be able to acquire new facts, remember them, and use them. But learning is more than just cataloging and using facts. The computer must be able to generalize and to infer new relationships and rules. It must be able to begin with the observation "I saw a car hit a wall; the car was destroyed" and reach a more general conclusion, such as "Heavy objects colliding at high speed cause extensive damage." Some computers can learn in this way, but so far they have been limited to very narrow and technical subjects.

Making Decisions Under Uncertainty

Can computers make decisions if they don't have all the facts? When you make a decision, you select a course of action from a set of alternative actions. You make decisions thousands of times a day. Some decisions, such as selecting your next move in a game of tic-tac-toe, are very easy because you have all the information necessary to select the best alternative. More difficult decisions, such as voting for a presidential candidate or choosing a college underlies most human actions. This decision-making process known as **decision making under uncertainty**, requires assessing very complex interactions or working with incomplete, contradictory, or even false information. This kind of decision making is an everyday occurrence for business managers, political leaders, teachers, and others.

Most researchers agree that for a computer to be considered intelligent, it must be able to make decisions under uncertainty and to select reasonable actions from the set of available alternatives. Some AI researchers claim that computers will be even better at this kind of decision making than humans because computers will be able to process more information more quickly and make an unemotional, rational decision. Critics point out that the unemotional, rational decision may not be the best. Humans bring to their decision making two things: experience and a sense of context that computers will never match.

Getting computers to evaluate alternative actions using ambiguous information is especially difficult because electronic switches that are either on (1) or off (0) represent all the information in a computer. In that sense, computers understand only True and False. There is no easy way to represent the concepts of Maybe, Possibly, or Probably. Humans can draw upon an enormous amount of background information when they make a decision. Your choice of college, for example, depends on more than just the number of courses it offers or the size of its faculty. In evaluating the alternatives you rely on your knowledge of schools in general, the value of education, your financial status, the job prospects upon graduation, the constraints imposed by transportation and housing, and thousands of other factors your experience suggests are important. The challenge to AI researchers is to give the computer that same sort of common-sense background knowledge and a way to evaluate it that does not depend on simple True/False logic.

QuickCheck B

1. The ability of humans to communicate with language is a characteristic of intelligence called _____.

2. Terry Winograd's famous pioneering program in natural language processing is _____.

3. Joseph Weizenbaum's famous program _____ imitated a psychotherapist and was surprisingly convincing.

4. A problem-solving method that considers all possible situations is known as a(n) _____ search.

5. A problem-solving method that uses "rules of thumb" is known as _____.

6. Making a decision with incomplete or contradictory information called _____.

⊂ How AI Works

To develop intelligent computers, researchers have created models of human intelligence. These models are descriptions, or analogies, to help visualize what cannot be directly observed. AI researchers have attempted to simplify our view of human intelligence by identifying its fundamental components and processes and ignoring the nonessential details. Different models have yielded ways of programming these models into computers. Each model has shown promise, has logged remarkable successes, and has encountered substantial, maybe insurmountable, obstacles.

Knowledge Base

What is the best way to represent human knowledge? In the most popular model, human intelligence is viewed as a way of processing symbols. Because the computer is essentially a machine for manipulating symbols (1's and 0's), many AI researchers view the computer as an excellent tool for duplicating human intelligence. This symbolic approach to AI, called **symbol processing**, attempts to embody human knowledge as a database of facts and rules of inference called a **knowledge base**. A computer program, called an **inference engine**, directs the computer to manipulate these facts according to the rules of inference to solve problems, make decisions, or direct actions.

For example, consider a typical human conversation like the one in Figure 8.

Figure 8

A typical human conversation

> **Mary: You'd better take your raincoat to work today.**
>
> **John: Why? Do you think it will rain?**
>
> **Mary: I think it might.**
>
> **John: OK. By the way, I have to stop at the library on the way home.**
>
> **Mary: What should I fix for dinner?**
>
> **John: How about hamburgers?**
>
> **Mary: Now you know that's not good for your cholesterol level. Besides, the meat seems spoiled. I think I will throw it away. How about the fish?**
>
> **John: Fine.**
>
> **Mary: I'll make it a little late since you probably won't be home at the regular time.**
>
> **John: Yeah, rain always slows up the traffic.**

Could a computer play the part of John in this conversation? Figure 9 on the next page illustrates how a computer might reason through the same human conversation. The computer would have to repeat the process to solve the second problem which is whether or not John should take his raincoat to work. The humans were able to discuss both problems concurrently.

Figure 9

A computer's attempt to interpret human conversation

Problem:	Decide whether or not to discard the spoiled hamburger.
Facts:	meat can spoil, spoiled meat can cause disease, human metabolism can be damaged by disease, etc.

Rules of inference:

IF the meat is green and it smells funny

THEN it is spoiled

IF meat is spoiled

THEN it should be discarded

Solution:	The computer decides to throw away the spoiled hamburger.

Knowledge base was one of the first general models for intelligence. Initial enthusiasm for this approach faded when it became apparent that the number of facts and rules of inference necessary to duplicate even a small portion of human intelligence is enormous. Have you ever gotten an answer wrong on a computer-based test because you left out a hyphen or didn't capitalize a word? That's because the system knows only a limited variety of answers and your answer didn't match any of those. When writing the question, the instructor must tell the system every possible correct answer that students may give, including spelling and capitalization variations. Too much of human intelligence depends on what is sometimes called **common sense**: that body of knowledge based on experience, culture, environment, and other factors that we bring to all our intellectual activities.

A remarkably ambitious attempt to build a knowledge base of common sense began at the Microelectronics and Computer Technology Corporation in 1984. The project was named CYC because of its encyclopedic nature, and was started by Doug Lenant and his team of "cyclists." It is an effort to build a knowledge base containing all the facts and rules of inference that form the basic knowledge ordinary humans have. Common sense statements, such as "no object can be in two places at the same time," form the basis of CYC's enormous and growing knowledge base. The CYC knowledge base now contains hundreds of thousands of assertions that represent, according to Lenant, only a small portion of common-sense knowledge. These assertions are facts and rules of inference. The project continues today at Cycorp, Inc., which is now responsible for its development.

Without the enormous knowledge base and rules of inference necessary to simulate common sense, computers are rigid, shortsighted, and often disappointing. Some critics contend that storing all the necessary facts and rules will never be possible. They claim that intelligence just doesn't work that way; we don't think simply by applying a set of IF-THEN rules.

Expert Systems

Can a knowledge-based system be used to create a useful intelligent computer?

Remarkably, although knowledge-based systems do not do well at imitating even childish intelligence, they are good at duplicating the specialized knowledge of technical experts. When the knowledge base is restricted to a narrow, specialized field in which the language is technical and well defined, knowledge-based systems prove adept at problem analysis and decision making.

InfoWeb

Expert
Systems
5

In the 1960s, a team headed by Edward Feigenbaum developed DENDRAL, a program for analyzing chemical compounds. DENDRAL's knowledge base embodied the expertise of chemists and, for certain classes of compounds, it performed as well as highly trained PhD's. The chemists' techniques were refined and improved in a program called MYCIN, which can diagnose infectious diseases and recommend treatments. Because programs such as these embody the knowledge of experts in technical fields, they became known as expert systems.

The success of DENDRAL and MYCIN led to the development of expert systems for commercial applications. One of the first, Digital Equipment Corporation's XCON, was used to design VAX computer systems. Roger Schank (a pioneer in AI and natural language processing) and others started companies to produce expert system shells, programs that allowed companies to develop their own expert systems.

Today expert systems are being used successfully in dozens of areas such as finance, equipment repair, and production scheduling. Computer-assisted instruction (CAI) is one application of expert systems that you may have experienced. Well-designed CAI should examine each user response to determine what further instruction the user requires. That is why you may progress differently through the instruction than another student who started the lesson at the same time. One of you may require further instruction on a particular concept while the other person may have answered correctly, causing the expert system to advance to a new concept more quickly.

Expert systems are the most successful applications of AI to practical, commercial problems. If you have ever bought insurance or taken out a loan, an expert system probably evaluated your application. Another familiar example is a software wizard that guides you through a computer process. This type of expert system quickly examines each of your answers and decides which is the most logical next question to ask you. You have probably used this type of interface to install software, for example, and noticed that if your computer doesn't include a particular hardware component, the wizard is intelligent enough to skip any steps that are not required since you don't have the necessary hardware.

Figure 10 on the next page illustrates a more complex expert system used for automotive repairs. This system is used to diagnose automotive problems and recommend repairs. The arrows represent a "caused by" relationship.

Figure 10

A portion of the
knowledge base for
Ford Motor Company's
Service Bay Diagnostic
System

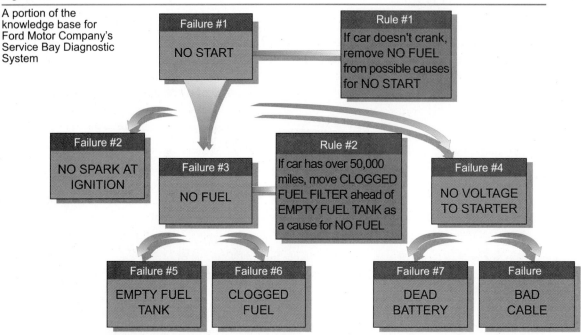

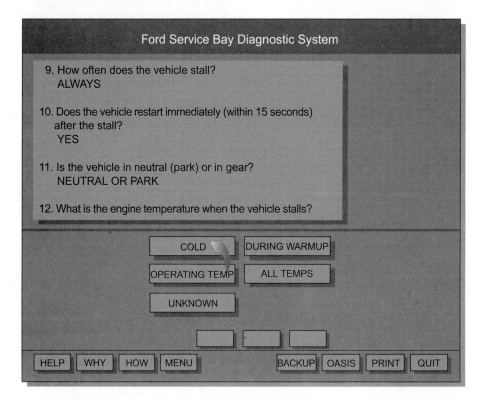

Source: Kurzweil, Raymond. *The Age of Intelligent Machines*. Cambridge, MA: The MIT Press, 1990.

Fuzzy Logic

| Can computers solve problems with information that is not exact? | The inability to deal with vague statements was an early failing of knowledge-based systems that tended to be incapable of evaluating problems and solutions where information was ambiguous or uncertain. Efforts to improve the flexibility of knowledge-based systems and other AI models led to the development of fuzzy logic. **Fuzzy logic** is a method of logic that allows the computer to express and process statements that are ambiguous. It was developed to address the ambiguity in certian decision-making situations. Despite its amusing name, fuzzy logic is no joke. It's just a way of describing a type of logic that has more than two truth values (T and F). Statements in fuzzy logic are assigned a probability of being true. Because knowledge is often uncertain, imprecise, and not reliable and because problems don't always present themselves with exact facts and figures, humans often must make decisions using information that is ambiguous or incomplete.

InfoWeb

Fuzzy
Logic
6

The computer understands only two possible states. If you think of these two possible states as True and False, then everything the computer records is either True or False; there is no Maybe. This makes a computer well suited for implementing the rules of ordinary logic in which each statement must be either true or false. This is the kind of logic used in mathematics: the statements "2 + 2 = 4" and "IF x + 2 = 7 THEN x = 5" are true, but "IF x + 2 = 7 THEN x = 1" is false.

Everyday life is not simply true or false, black or white, hot or cold. Something may be either true or false depending on the context. If I tell you that "My car is fast," the statement is true if I mean that my car is capable of exceeding freeway speeds, but the statement is false if I mean that my car is capable of competing in the Indianapolis 500 automobile race. The truth or falseness of this statement depends on the context. You must often judge that a statement is "probably true" or "could be false" when you make decisions under uncertainty.

With fuzzy logic, an extension of our system of ordinary logic, statements are assigned a probability of being true. This probability is represented as a number in the interval 0 to 1, with 0 representing False and 1 representing True. Thus, the statement "My car is fast" might be assigned a probability of .99 if my car happens to be a Ferrari or assigned a probability of .4 if my car happens to be a 1962 Volkswagen.

Fuzzy logic alone cannot learn or remember, so a great deal of research is being done on combining the rules of fuzzy logic with expert systems and other AI models. Much of this research is being done in Japan where fuzzy logic has been an integral part of the national effort to develop new computers. Fuzzy logic systems have been successfully implemented in many devices that use embedded computers. They are found most often in manufacturing processes but also in household items such as the washing machine shown in Figure 11 on the next page. In this appliance, a water sensor analyzes how dirty the water is, then decides what temperature the water should be and how much water is required to clean. For instance, if the water is still relatively clean at the end of the prewash cycle, the machine reuses the same water, rather than refilling. This fuzzy logic decision saves many gallons of water.

Figure 11

The embedded computer in this washing machine uses fuzzy logic to conserve water.

Genetic Algorithms

How can biological models help computers solve problems? Another recent approach to symbol processing is the use of **genetic algorithms**, which use rules of inference that imitate the adaptive processes of Darwinian evolution. Darwin noted that offspring are not identical to their parents. Some differences may make certain members of a species better suited to their environment than other members. Better-suited members tend to have a better chance of survival and pass on their characteristics to their own offspring through heredity. Sexual reproduction guarantees the mixing of characteristics. Over time, this process of **natural selection** causes species to become better adapted to their environment. Since Darwin's time, biologists have studied the role of heredity intensely and have augmented his theory with the concept of **mutation**: changes in genetic makeup that are spontaneous rather than inherited.

A genetic algorithm uses the principles of natural selection, crossover, and mutation to build a solution. In a simple genetic algorithm system, the genetic algorithm starts with a set of possible solutions to a given problem. It then selects the best candidates among the available solutions, imitating the Darwinian process of natural selection. From these best candidates, it selects pairs of solutions and selects parts of each solution in the pair to create a new possible solution. This is called **crossover** and imitates the process of mating and reproduction. Finally, the genetic algorithm introduces random changes to parts of candidate solutions imitating the way mutation introduces random changes in the genetic makeup of natural populations.

The exact rules for selecting the best candidates, creating offspring in the crossover process, and for introducing mutations vary from program to program, but the ultimate goal is to have the genetic algorithm evolve a good solution to the original problem. The genetic algorithm always works with a population of possible solutions. Over time, this population changes as poorly adapted candidates die out and better adapted candidates reproduce and mutate. After many generations, the population consists primarily of individual candidates that are good, if not perfect, solutions to the problem. Observers have commented that this outcome mimics the evolutionary process of biological populations and speculate that genetic algorithms hold the key to the development of **artificial life**, computer organisms that can reproduce and adapt to their environment.

A working example of a genetic algorithm is the FacePrints system, which was developed by Dr. Victor S. Johnston in the Psychology Department at New Mexico State University, and which uses a genetic algorithm to help police artists create pictures of suspects' faces. In the past, a police artist would interview the witness to a crime and develop a sketch of the suspect's face based on the witness's description. The artist sketched while the witness suggested changes, trying to remember and reconstruct the suspect's face.

An improvement in the process uses transparent overlays with which the witness builds a face from component parts. Although this is limited by the variety of overlays available, the results are often better because the witness is required only to recognize familiar features rather than reconstruct them from memory.

The FacePrints system presents the witness with a selection of several faces on a computer screen. The witness then assigns a rating from 1 to 10 for each face depending on how closely it matches the suspect's face. The genetic algorithm uses selection, crossover, and mutation to generate new faces for the witness to view and rate. By repeating the display/rating/generation cycle, the genetic algorithm actually "evolves" a face that resembles the suspect's face. The results can be remarkably accurate. An example of FacePrints is shown in Figure 12.

Figure 12

This image was created by the FacePrints system using a genetic algorithm.

The use of genetic algorithms in commercial applications is just beginning. General Electric uses genetic algorithms in the design of gas turbine engines, generators, and other machinery. Moody's Investor Services uses a genetic algorithm to develop schedules for its computer support personnel. The Prediction Company of New Mexico uses genetic algorithms for currency trading. Although genetic algorithms do not always find the best solution to a problem, in many applications they are good at finding a useful solution in a reasonable amount of time.

Neural Networks

Will computers be able to imitate the human brain and think like you? Neural networks are AI systems that attempt to duplicate the physical functioning of the human brain by using a biological model of intelligence. A neural network consists of three parts:

InfoWeb

Neural
Networks
7

- A set of input units corresponding to the five senses—sight, hearing, touch, smell, and taste

- A set of processing units called the hidden layer, corresponding to neurons in the brain

- A set of output units, corresponding to parts of the body, such as muscles, that act on signals from the brain

In your brain, neurons receive signals from senses or from other neurons. Each neuron then does or does not send an output signal, depending on the combination of input signals it receives. These signals can be sent internally to other neurons or externally to muscles or organs. Over time, the connections among neurons can be created, broken, strengthened, or weakened as your brain learns and remembers your experiences. Because this approach to AI is based on building connections rather than manipulating symbols, it is called the **connectionist approach** to AI.

Figure 13 describes the possibilities for input, processing, and output units in a neural network. In the simplest network, each input unit sends signals to each processing unit. Each processing unit gathers these signals and evaluates them. The input signals can be assigned weights or strengths, so that each processing unit responds only to the proper combination of input signals. If the sum of the input signals exceeds a certain threshold, the processing unit sends a signal to the output unit. Each output unit then reacts to the collective signals sent by the processing units.

Figure 13

Some possible
input, processing,
and output units in
a neural network

Input Layer	Hidden Layer	Output Layer
■ Cameras	■ Computer functions	■ Printers
■ Microphones	■ Computer programs	■ Screens
■ Laboratory data gathering equipment	■ Computers	■ Robot arms
		■ Chemical dispensers

An important characteristic of a neural network is its ability to learn. See Figure 14. The bottom nodes (A1, A2, ...) are the input units. These are fully connected to the processing units in the middle layer (B1, B2, ...). The processing units (hidden layer) evaluate the weighted signals from the input units to generate signals to the output units (C1, C2, ...). The lines represent the connections among the units. The connections can be weakened or strengthened over time as the neural network learns.

Figure 14

The structure
of a neural
network

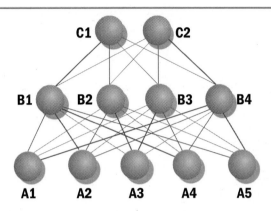

When a neural network starts operation, the weights assigned to the input signals may be completely arbitrary, and the network will send some correct and some incorrect output signals. Each time the network generates incorrect output signals, the designer can cause the network to adjust the weights of the input signals. This is how the network designer trains the network. Over time, the network adjusts the input signal weights so that the processing units generate the correct output signals. Increasing and decreasing the weights of input signals corresponds to strengthening and weakening neurons in the brain and simulates the brain's learning process. Different neural network designs allow the network to learn by observing a human doing the same task or by receiving direct feedback from each solution attempt.

Pattern Recognition

Can computers interpret the patterns in human communication? Making sense of complex patterns is one of human intelligence's most amazing skills. You recognize faces easily, understand wide varieties of speech, and perceive meaningful forms in highly abstract art, all with very little effort. Pattern recognition is essential for human interaction and communication. Making sense of patterns has posed some of the most difficult obstacles for computers. In the past, pattern recognition required that the computer be programmed to recognize every possible pattern, just like the game-playing computer has to know every possible chess move and consider them all.

Computer vision, which uses cameras for eyes, and voice recognition, which uses microphones for ears, have yielded impressive results. Computers routinely analyze visual patterns, to scan assembly line parts for defects, to interpret satellite photographs, to identify faces, as shown in Figure 15 on the next page, and to guide vehicles. **Voice synthesis**, which translates text into computer-generated speech, is common and well developed. Voice recognition systems are now capable of translating oral dictation into text with a low error rate. You must still program variations of spoken words, but neural network programs are capable of learning subtle variations.

Figure 15

The Miros TrueFace system uses pattern recognition to match the video image of a face with a stored image.

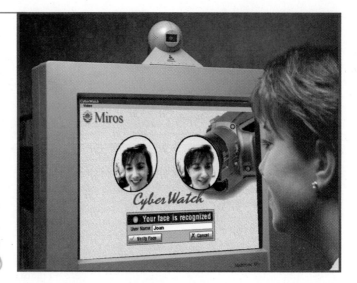

An excellent application of a neural network that uses pattern recognition is to recognize typographical characters. This was the purpose of the first neural network machine, the Perceptron, constructed by Frank Rosenblat in the 1960s. Figure 16 shows a neural network designed to recognize the 26 uppercase letters of the alphabet. A video camera plays the role of the input units; each pixel in the camera image represents the signal from an input unit to the processing units. The weighted value of each pixel is sent to each processing unit, which then sends an output signal if the combined inputs are above the unit's threshold. The output unit, such as a printer, prints the letter associated with the sum of all the output signals.

Figure 16

A neural network for recognizing typographical characters

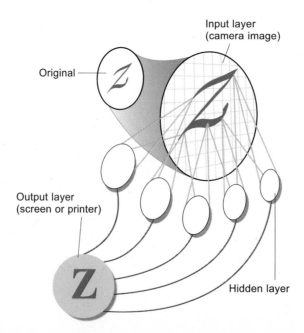

Input layer (camera image)

Original

Output layer (screen or printer)

Hidden layer

The problem with Rosenblat's process is that during the initial training period, the network might identify some characters incorrectly. The trainer's feedback then causes the network to adjust the input signal weights and try again. When the correct character is identified, the weights are not adjusted. Over time, the network gets better and better at identifying the characters. Notice that the network is perfectly capable of learning to recognize **z**, Z and z as the same letters even though their appearances differ considerably.

A newer pattern recognition process, called **optical character recognition** (**OCR**), is the use of optics to recognize written characters. An OCR system uses a neural network or another simpler algorithm to recognize only very specific character sets, such as the preprinted numbers on checks. This is the technology that makes it possible to scan a document into a word processing program. Although it may not recognize all the characters, usually enough of them are interpreted to make it possible for the user to quickly rebuild the text by replacing missing characters that were not recognized. Some new OCR programs are capable of learning to recognize characters correctly by storing the user's corrections when it inaccurately identifies a character.

Neural networks are used in all kinds of pattern recognition applications; the pattern recognition can apply to any patterns such as human faces or maps. Because of their ability to learn and to recognize patterns, neural networks are becoming increasingly popular in commercial applications. Several credit card companies use neural networks to analyze credit card transactions to detect patterns of credit card use that may indicate fraud. Telephone and computer companies use neural networks in modems to minimize the problem of echoing signals. An interesting new application is the use of neural networks to analyze noise and to generate "anti-noise" to cancel the offending sounds.

Robotics

Can intelligent computers speak, listen, move, and interact like humans? Science fiction fans have been fascinated with the notion of a computer that could not only think like a human being, but also look and act like one. Figure 17 shows an example of very well known robots from our cultural heritage. Popular fictional robots include Commander Data from the television series *Star Trek: The Next Generation*, "7 of 9" from its sequel *Star Trek: Voyager*, Robbie the Robot from *Lost in Space*, and the robot assassin from the movie *Terminator*.

Figure 17

Popular fiction has many famous fictional robots. C3PO and R2D2 from the movie *Star Wars* are shown here.

The term "robot" was coined in Karel Çapek's 1921 play *R.U.R.*, based on the Czech word "robotnik" which means *serf* or *worker* in the Czech language. From jerky-motioned automatons to human-like, super-intelligent androids, robots have appeared in innumerable novels and movies. Although the popular image of a robot is a mechanical human being, computer scientists and engineers think of a **robot** as a computer-controlled machine for manipulating objects. Thousands of robots are in use today, most in industrial applications, as shown in Figure 18. The design and development of these devices is called **robotics**.

Figure 18

A robot working
in a factory

Robots have proved to be extremely useful because they do not get tired, take vacations, or become bored with their work. They can be much more productive than human workers because they can manipulate many arms at once and lift heavy loads. Better coordination and fine motor control of robot arms and hands have allowed robots to take on more and more delicate tasks. Robots can be used in dangerous environments that would be unsafe for human workers. Robots often defuse or detonate bombs and work in radioactive or chemically contaminated environments.

Robot vision systems and sound systems use pattern recognition to identify objects. Although robots' pattern recognition systems are sophisticated, the amount of data storage and processing time required to analyze and react to images and sounds makes it difficult for them to act quickly and reliably. Engineers who design the mechanical and electronic components of robots and computer scientists who design their computer control systems are working intensely to overcome these limitations.

Most robots use a computer to operate some form of mechanical arm and hand that can grasp and lift objects or operate machinery. The simplest robots, such as the welding robots used in automobile factories, are stationary machines that move their arms in a pre-programmed path. Some robots, like the delivery robots used in hospitals, are mobile, rolling on wheels. More sophisticated robots, like exploration robots used in remote areas, walk on spider-like legs and can sense their surroundings using cameras for vision and microphones for hearing. These robots do not walk on a preprogrammed path but use their AI abilities to find a path through difficult terrain. The NASA Pathfinder mission included a rover called Sojourner, which explored Mars and broadcast visual images and data readings to scientists on earth. See Figure 19.

Figure 19

Sojourner navigated the rocky terrain of Mars as part of the Pathfinder mission.

A major stumbling block for engineers is the large size of the physical components used to build the mechanical parts of robots. Although the miniaturization of electronic components is well advanced, similar progress in the miniaturization of mechanical components has not occurred. In recent years, however, engineers have begun to build gears, motors, and other parts on a microscopic scale. Engineers are working to create mechanical components just a few micrometers in size, which they have nicknamed **nanobots**.

Robotic medical techniques and surgery are not as far-fetched as they seem. Figure 20 on the next page shows a nanobot model, built from electronic circuits and wire thread, layered on a graphic representation of blood cells and artery walls. Surgeons and medical researchers are already using surgical techniques that utilize microscopic instruments controlled by robotic arms. Scientists are able to control the movements of the tiny nanobots in the laboratory just like they controlled Sojourner on Mars. The actual use of nanobots in manufacturing and medicine is sure to happen in the near future.

Figure 20

This nanobot model appears to clean the artery wall as blood cells stream by.

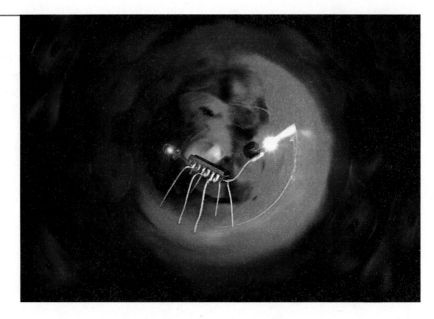

InfoWeb

Tiny Machines 8

Robotics' major challenge is to develop the computer processing power, the machine parts, and the computer programs capable of sophisticated pattern recognition so that machines can perform tasks as skillfully as humans can. A secondary challenge is to make robotic devices small and flexible enough to become an integral part of human lives. When these challenges have been met, it becomes possible to envision robotic devices that assist in everyday life.

QuickCheck C

1 In a knowledge-based system, the program that directs the computer to apply the rules of inference to data is called the _____.

2 An ongoing project to build a knowledge base of common sense is the _____ project.

3 A knowledge-based system that embodies the technical knowledge of an expert is known as a(n) _____.

4 A system of logic in which statements are assigned a probability of being true is called _____.

5 A genetic algorithm imitates the evolutionary processes of _____, mutation, and crossover.

6 A neural network is designed to emulate the function of the human _____.

7 In a neural network, the set of processing units that correspond to neurons is called the _____.

8 A computer-controlled machine for manipulating objects is called a _____.

9 _____ is the design and development of computer-controlled machines.

D AI in Your Future

Artificial intelligence is still in its infancy. The intelligent computer that Turing's judge would mistake for a human does not yet exist and does not seem close to development. For the world you live in, commercial applications of AI can excel at solving limited problems, identifying specific patterns, and performing well-defined robotic tasks.

Different AI technologies have been developed based on various characteristics of human intelligent behavior. Integrating these technologies may be the best way to produce a working intelligent computer. An expert system may employ fuzzy logic in applying its rules of inference, or a robot may use a neural network for vision processing and an expert system to direct its actions. Unless the practitioners of AI are able to develop a single, unified model of human intelligence, the continued integration of various models, each being applied to the kind of problem it addresses best, may hold the greatest promise for the development of machine intelligence.

The current theoretical and laboratory research promises to bring about a level of computer intelligence far more sophisticated than today's technology. Some obstacles that stand in the way of improvements will quickly be overcome by the increased processing power of new computer systems; however, developers are always imagining better systems that will improve the usefulness of AI technology. Three factors are important in the development of improved applications of AI systems:

Improved understanding of intelligence. The short history of AI is filled with definitions of intelligence that have been tested and then discarded as inadequate. When computers do exhibit "intelligent" behavior, such as playing Master-level chess, we sometimes conclude that that behavior is not what we really mean by intelligence. Better models of intelligence and intelligent behavior are being developed through the contributions of psychologists, biologists, computer scientists, and many other investigators.

Improved hardware. Expert systems, neural networks, and other implementations of AI take full advantage of the powerful processors and huge data storage capabilities available in today's computers. One promising avenue is **parallel architecture**, the use of many processors working on a single, complex problem. **Nanotechnology**, the design and construction of microscopic machines, has resulted in the creation of microscopic mechanical components. As these devices are refined, we will see smaller, more powerful applications of AI technology throughout our society.

Improved software. More efficient computer algorithms and more powerful computer programming languages are taking advantage of better theoretical models and improved hardware. Expert systems, for example, can recognize the limits of their expertise and hand off a problem to a more qualified expert. Genetic algorithms continue to become more sophisticated at selecting good solutions and creating mutations. Improvements in pattern recognition will make it possible for vision and speech to be processed more reliably and quickly.

The AI of Today

What are some current examples of AI in computers? There are several common applications of AI in modern application software. Wizards are expert systems that guide you through complex computer procedures, like building a spreadsheet function. They are useful the first time you do something to teach you the process, as well as when you repeat the procedure to help you through the processes that you don't use often enough to remember completely.

InfoWeb

Software
Agents
9

Software agents are another example of expert systems that are becoming increasingly popular. Microsoft introduced its Office Assistant with the software suite Office 97. It is an animated character, shown in Figure 21, that allows you to interact with the online Help system by typing questions in natural language. The Office Assistant responds by answering a question, but sometimes automatically opens a wizard that walks you through the process. You are allowed to select from several animations—the familiar Clippit shown here, as well as Dot, The Genius (resembling Einstein), Hoverbot, Mother Nature, Power Pup, Scribble (a purring digital cat), and Will (as in Shakespeare).

Figure 21

Microsoft's
Office
Assistant is a
familiar
software
agent.

Debit cards have become so commonplace that it is easy to forget how important they are in retail business. The debit card system is the first step in an intricate combination of AI tools that can manage all kinds of financial transactions. **Biometrics** is a relatively new technology that promises to replace debit and credit cards with pattern recognition devices. Developers are satisfied that a handprint or thumbprint is enough to identify you to the system, which then can deduct funds from your account, allow you to enter a secured area, or provide medical and insurance information about you.

Another alternative is the Smart Card, which replaces the credit card's magnetic strip with a microchip for the storage of vital personal, medical and insurance information. In an emergency, medical personnel can get everything they need to know about a patient from the patient's Smart Card. They are being used very effectively in hospital emergency rooms, reducing the time it takes to be treated and providing vital medical statistics about patients who are unable to communicate.

Expert systems have become commonplace in medical research, assisting in the analysis of laboratory and pharmacy data associated with almost all types of disease. They have moved into the doctor's examination room, assisting with medical diagnoses. Critics claim that this use of medical expert systems raises some serious questions about whether or not we can rely on computer-based expert systems.

Who Is
Responsible?
10

Medical misdiagnosis has become one of the strongest arguments against relying on artificial intelligence. Consider a doctor who makes a treatment decision for a patient, based on advice from a medical expert system. If the patient is harmed by the treatment, who becomes responsible? Malpractice laws protect the patient from bad decisions made by a health professional. But what protects us from "computer error" mistakes that cause harm? Is the doctor responsible or is the computer programmer responsible? Current trends in the debate indicate that this question will be answered in the courts, but unfortunately, only after a patient has been injured and sues for malpractice.

Virtual reality is an application of AI that started with helmets and data gloves designed to manipulate robotic devices in harmful environments and has evolved into an alternative for all kinds of unbelievable simulations. In manufacturing, the data glove has become an input device for testing employee skills. The employee executes a procedure—for instance, threading a weaving machine—and the glove collects data about how the task was completed, how quickly, etc.

The existence of virtual worlds such as the ones in movies like *Lawnmower Man* or television series like *ReBoot*, are not as impossible as they seem. The examples of virtual reality applications include everything from flight simulators to virtual surgery to virtual museums. All of these virtual worlds allow the user to enter a three-dimensional, graphical environment and control graphical objects there with body movements.

The cost of virtual reality technology is enormous, requiring computers that cost more than $500,000 as well as other high-tech equipment like cameras, controllers, and projection units. It is also time-consuming to develop each graphical object that makes the environment seem so real. As hardware technology improves and more computer scientists are trained to develop virtual reality, the costs will come down to affordable levels. Then the possible applications are endless. NASA used virtual reality (VR) models to design the Pathfinder mission to Mars. Figure 22 shows a VR model of the Pathfinder Landing Site.

Figure 22

The Pathfinder lander used on the Pathfinder mission was designed by Virtual Reality artists.

The AI of Tomorrow

What will computers be able to do? Some of the necessary improvements in AI technology are on the near horizon; some may never arrive. Still, it is fun to speculate about what the intelligent computers of the future may be able to do.

InfoWeb

Awesome
AI
11

- **Transportation systems.** Computers are already used to monitor traffic lights and freeway access to increase traffic efficiency. Global Positioning Systems provide information regarding your current location as well as directions to get from there to a specified location. Computers may someday operate all our transportation systems, including individual automobiles. Automobile designers have already designed a prototype that combines telecommunications and AI technologies to operate Smart Cars that literally drive themselves. While driving to the office, you drink your coffee and scan the latest news on the monitor embedded in your car's dash; the car evaluates the current traffic report and weather conditions, and follows the best route available to your office door. It even parks itself in your designated space!

- **The new infrastructure.** Machinery will fix itself, perhaps even replicate itself. Sophisticated thinking machinery will even be able to learn from its experiences and redesign itself to be more reliable and useful. Keys and locks will become obsolete as computers will recognize the faces of humans with authorized access. Our communications networks will grow and reconfigure themselves automatically.

- **The new retailers.** A comprehensive banking system with a Web-based interface in your home can make paper money and credit or debit cards obsolete. Verbally recite your grocery list into a speaker phone on your kitchen wall, your computer compares prices at several stores, faxes the list to the local grocery, and a delivery truck brings the requested items directly to your door. Based on past orders, the list can be called up by speaking its name into the system, rather than having to specify each item.

- **The new scientists.** Discoveries in mathematics, physics, medicine, and other sciences will happen quickly as tireless, intelligent experimenters learn more about our natural world. Computers will begin to design and build themselves.

- **The new leaders.** If computers are so smart, maybe they will be able to tackle some of the political and economic problems that have plagued us for centuries. Perhaps political expert systems will be able to guide stable economies and distribute food and medicine to those who need it most.

- **The new doctors.** When you feel sick or depressed, speak to your personal computer physician. The intelligent computer will diagnose and prescribe for you. Perhaps your robot doctor will also perform any necessary surgery, replacing defective organs and limbs with microscopic machines.

- **The new artists.** When computers finally have their own powerful senses of vision and hearing, they may well be able to create new art forms uniquely theirs. The fractal images in Figure 23 were drawn by computers that followed mathematical instructions created by mathematicians. They may have a sense of aesthetics completely foreign to us. Perhaps they will be able to re-create the talents of the artists and musicians of the past.

Figure 23

Although computers are not yet creating their own art, computing power is essential in creating certain forms of art, such as these fractal images.

EndNote

When computers are intelligent enough to converse with us, react with their environment in human-like ways, and provide us with leadership and intellectual challenge, we may begin to think of them in entirely different ways. Perhaps we will form friendships, loyalties, or social and emotional ties. If a computer becomes your friend, will you be able to send it to a dangerous factory to work? When your computer friend starts to act erratically, will you dismantle it for parts or offer therapy?

True artificial intelligence will present us with one of the greatest opportunities in the history of humanity. If through AI we are freed from the boring tasks of assembling machinery and keeping accounts, will we turn to art and philosophy? If intelligent computers turn out to be emotionless, will we seek to develop our emotional lives? When we acknowledge that we are no longer the only intelligent beings on earth, will we welcome the challenge and grow? How much power and responsibility will we be willing to turn over to intelligent computers? It is not too early to think about how we can best use and control intelligent machines and how they will affect our view of ourselves.

The variety of scientists who are researching intelligence is an indicator of the final impact of AI research. Biologists, neuropsychologists, neurosurgeons, and psychiatrists are continually adding to existing knowledge about intelligence and how the brain functions. Computer scientists, educators, sociologists, and even philosophers work together on the development of useful applications of AI. Roger Schank, director of the Institute for the Learning Sciences at Northwestern University, stresses the value of learning from this research and summarizes it this way:

> *"Over the past decade, AI has caused a wide range of people to ask some very interesting questions about language, reading, and understanding ... In trying to model our thought processes on a computer's, we continually learn more about what it means to be human. Far from dehumanizing us, AI research has compelled us to appreciate our human qualities and abilities."*

InfoWeb

InfoWeb

Chapter Links

The InfoWeb is your guide to print, film, television, and electronic resources. Use it to obtain updates on quickly changing technical information and to locate information for research papers. If you're using the New Perspectives CD-ROM, click the InfoWeb icon on the left side of this paragraph to access the online InfoWeb links. Otherwise, use your Web browser and type in the address of the New Perspectives site: www.cciw.com/np3. At the New Perspectives site you'll find up-to-date links to the topics covered in this chapter.

1 Robots in Science Fiction

Robots abound in fiction and film, from Asimov's R. Daneel Olivaw to *Star Wars*' R2D2 and C3PO. The Isaac Asimov Robots Page at **www.searchme.demon.co.uk/andrew/asimov.htm** documents and reviews all of Asimov's books and stories about robots. Asimov's Three Laws of Robotics at **www.sfwriter.com/rmasilaw.htm** discusses whether Asimov's three laws have an impact on modern AI research. You can learn about a real prototype humanoid robot at The Cog Shop, **www.ai.mit.edu/projects/cog/Text/cog-shop.html**. Interact with some real robots at KhepOnTheWeb, **KhepOnTheWeb.epfl.ch/**, The Telegarden, **telegarden.aec.at/**, and Where in the World is Xavier the Robot, **www.cs.cmu.edu/~Xavier/**. You can learn about the winner of the 1997 Japanese Robotics competition at the Autonomous Mobile Robotics Lab, **www.cs.umd.edu/projects/amrl/amrl.html**. You can find a list of robotics journals at **dent.ii.fmph.uniba.sk/ui/faqs/part3/faq-doc-32.html**.

2 Defining Artificial Intelligence

What exactly is artificial intelligence? The Mind and Machine Module Web site at **www.phy.syr.edu/courses/modules/MM/index.html** begins to answer this question by asking another: "To what extent can we ever expect to be able to create a machine which is 'truly' intelligent?" Sometimes the Turing test is used to define artificial intelligence. You can learn more about Turing and the Turing Test at The Alan Turing Home Page, **www.turing.org.uk/turing/**. Be sure to read about the Loebner Prize, a modern version of the Turing Test at **www.dcs.shef.ac.uk/~u6rs/turing/loebnerprize.html**. Marvin Minsky proposes that common sense is an essential component of intelligence; you can learn more about his ideas at **www.ai.mit.edu/people/minsky/minsky.html**. Rosalind W. Picard argues that emotional abilities are a critical component of intelligent behavior. You can learn more about her work at **vismod.www.media.mit.edu/~roz/**. AI on the Web at **www.cs.berkeley.edu/~russell/ai.html** has plenty of links to Web resources that will help you explore this field. How did we get from punched cards to thinking about computers with emotional abilities? The Machine That Changed the World at **ei.cs.vt.edu/~history/TMTCTW.html** can help you understand. *Mind Matters* by James P. Hogan (Del Ray, 1997) also provides an entertaining introduction to the world of artificial intelligence.

3 Defining Intelligence

A good place to learn about current theories of human intelligence is the Theories of Learning Index at **www.uwsp.edu/acad/educ/lwilson/LEARNING/index.htm**. You can find a brief introduction to Sternberg's Triarchic Theory of Intelligence at **www-cs.derby.ac.uk/tip/stern.html**; his theory proposes there are three components of intelligence: analytical, creative, and practical intelligence. Howard Gardner proposed that people have many ways of understanding the world and each contributes to intelligence. You can learn about Gardner's theory of multiple intelligences at **www.scbe.on.ca/mit/mi.htm**. An interactive checklist based on the theory of multiple intelligences is at **real.org/know/interactive.htm**. For basic information on the theory of emotional intelligence, read the interview with Daniel Goleman from the *San Francisco Chronical* at **www.sfgate.com/ea/holt/1018.html**. Does intelligence require consciousness? To learn about human consciousness, check out Going Inside: A Guide to the Dynamics of Brain Processing and Consciousness at **www.btinternet.com/~neuronaut/**.

4 Natural Language

At the Conversant Systems Web site, **www.conversantsystems.com/**, you can find an excellent overview of language processing and the sub-tasks involved in language processing. The AI Education Repository at **www.cacs.usl.edu/~manaris/ai-education-repository/nlp-tools.html** has resources on natural language processing, including information about software tools and links to other Web resources. Some of the most advanced natural language research is going on at the MIT InfoLab. You can learn about the lab's projects and explore some demos at **www.ai.mit.edu/projects/infolab/welcome.html**.

5 Expert Systems

For a quick overview of expert systems, connect to the CLIPS site at **www.ghgcorp.com/clips/ExpertSystems.html** or to MultiLogic's site at **www.multilogic.com/software/software.cfm** (click Resolver and follow the links in the left navigation bar). For additional information and links jump to the site maintained by *PC AI* magazine at **www.primenet.com/pcai**. Don't miss the Knowledge Box feature! MultiLogic's expert system shell EXSYS, runs over the Web. You can try some neat demos at **www.multilogic.com/software/software.cfm** (click Application Examples and then Internet Applications). Acquired Intelligence, Inc. also has Web-based demos—an expert system that helps you identify whales at **vvv.com/ai/demos/whale.html** and an expert system that will rate your qualifications for graduate school at **vvv.com/ai/demos/gradorig.html**. Expert Systems in Medicine at **amplatz.uokhsc.edu/acc95-expert-systems.html** presents an excellent description of medical expert systems with links to examples. Knowledge-Base Projects and Groups at **www.cs.utexas.edu/users/mfkb/related.html** provides links to Internet resources on knowledge bases.

6 Fuzzy Logic

You can find loads of information on fuzzy logic at Aptronix's FuzzyNet Online Web site, **www.aptronix.com/fuzzynet/index.htm**. Aptronix makes fuzzy logic applications that are used in washing machines, cameras, air conditioners, automobile transmissions, and automated manufacturing processes. You can find a brief course and information for beginners at Quadralay's Fuzzy Logic Archive, **www.austinlinks.com/Fuzzy/**. Be sure to read Fuzzy Environmental Control, which describes a fuzzy control unit that achieves precision temperature and humidity control. You can see an example of how fuzzy logic is being applied in research on medical imaging at **www.cs.tamu.edu/research/CFL/projects/patternid.html**. You can find a good index to fuzzy logic resources at Ortech Engineering's Fuzzy Logic Reservoir, **www.ortechengr.com/fuzzy/reservoir.html**.

7 Neural Networks

Bernard Widrow carried out the pioneering research for neural networks at Stanford University in the 1950s. It is a technology that requires massive computer capacity and, therefore, practical applications using this technology have been limited. However, it is a fascinating technology—imagine computers that function the way scientists think the brain functions! An Introduction to Neural Networks by Leslie Smith at **www.cs.stir.ac.uk/~lss/NNIntro/InvSlides.html** is a good place to begin exploring this technology. Next, check out The Artificial Brain: Neural Networks at **home.clara.net/mll/ai/nn/**. For more information and lots of links to other neural network sites, connect to the Pacific Northwest National Laboratory site at **www.pnl.gov** (click the Science link, then look for the Neural Network link).

8 Tiny Machines

Nanotechnology researchers are beginning to build tiny machines that can build other machines. You can learn about these tiny, intelligent machines and see some dramatic examples at the Sandia National Laboratories Intelligent Micromachine Initiative, **www.mdl.sandia.gov/micromachine/index.html**. The Foresight Institute at **www.foresight.org/homepage.html** has a general introduction to nanotechnology, technical information, a FAQ, and more. *Nanotechnology Magazine's* Web site at **nanozine.com/**, has a NanoMachine gallery, articles on the field's founders, and information about getting a degree in nanotechnology, among other topics.

9 **Software Agents**

For a brief introduction to software agents, read "What's an Agent?" at **foner.www.media.mit.edu/ people/foner/Yenta/agents.html**. You can find links to demonstrations of agent software at **www.isi.edu/isd/AA97/software-demo.html**. The Reader's Robot at **www.tnrdlib.bc.ca/rr.html** provides a fun way to learn what software agents can do. Firefly at **www.firefly.net** uses software agent techniques to construct a personalized Web experience and collect marketing information, while keeping personal information private. You can learn about the use of agents in business simulations and explore a demo at Thinking Tools, **www.thinkingtools.com/**. A good summary of the current state of the software agent field and links to resources is at Socially Intelligent Agents, **www.cyber.rdg.ac.uk/people/kd/WWW/aaaisocial.html**.

10 **Who Is Responsible?**

Can artificial intelligences be truly intelligent? This question is part of the Strong AI vs. Weak AI debate. "The Computer as a Metaphor for the Human Mind" at **mdr.aletheia.be/zine/issue1-96/ Mind.htm** introduces many key issues in the debate. According to "A Theology of Robots" by Edmund Furse at **www.comp.glam.ac.uk/pages/staff/efurse/Theology-of-Robots/A-Theology-of-Robots.html** eventually intelligent robots will exist and they will have a religious life. The Stanford Electronic Humanities Review special issue on AI, Constructions of the Mind: Artificial Intelligence and the Humanities at **http://shr.stanford.edu/shreview/4-2/text/toc.html** contains many interesting articles, including "Ethics and Second-order Cybernetics" by Heinz von Foerster. For an introduction to the range of ethical questions involved in the use of medical expert systems, read "Who Will Bear Moral Responsibility?" at **www.ccsr.cms.dmu.ac.uk/conferences/ccsrconf/abstracts/anderson.html**. A good book to read that considers what artificial intelligence programs can and can't do is *Fluid Concepts and Creative Analogies: Computer Models of the Fundamental Mechanisms of Thought* by Douglas Hofstadter (Basic Books, March 1996).

11 **Awesome AI**

The field of artificial intelligence is changing how we live and work in amazing ways. For example, image-guided surgery, which improves doctors' effectiveness, is based on enhanced reality technology; you can view the results at **www.ai.mit.edu/projects/vision-surgery/surgery_home_page.html**. At Intuitive Surgical, Inc., **www.intuitivesurgical.com/**, you can see how electronics, robotics, and enhanced visualization combine "to greatly improve surgical technique and take surgical precision far beyond what is possible today." Scientific American at **www.sciam.com/explorations/050596explorationsbox4.html** recently reported on the development of artificial muscles. For a practical view of what current robots can accomplish, explore the Mars Pathfinder home page and other Mars missions at **mars.sgi.com/**.

Review

1. Below each heading in this chapter is a focus question. Look back through the chapter and answer each question in your own words.

2. Write a paragraph describing why you think Searle's Chinese Room argument is or is not a good argument against the Turing test as a way of judging computer intelligence.

3. Write a statement that cannot be identified as true or false without referring to the context in which the statement is made. (*Hint:* Refer to the discussion on fuzzy logic.) Describe a context in which the statement would be true. Describe a context in which it would be false.

4. Reread the conversation between John and Mary in Figure 9. Identify at least one statement in which one of the words has several possible meanings. State which meaning you think is intended by the speaker and describe the clues in the rest of the conversation that support your interpretation.

5. List three of the researchers mentioned in this chapter and describe the importance of their work in the development of AI.

6. In your own words, briefly describe the way a genetic algorithm works.

7. List each AI model and write a brief example of each that you might encounter in everyday life.

8. In your own words, describe why knowledge-based systems seem to be better suited to imitating expert knowledge than general human knowledge.

Projects

1. **The Turing Test** Suppose you were chosen to be the judge in a Turing test. Write three questions that you would pose to the computer and to the human that would help you distinguish between them. Why did you choose the questions you did? That is, why do you think it would be difficult for a computer to answer your questions convincingly? Remember, the computer and the human do not have to answer honestly.

2.  **Acquired Intelligence, Inc.** This company is located in Victoria, B.C., Canada and publishes expert system software. To demonstrate its software's capabilities, it maintains a World Wide Web site running an expert system designed to help you identify whales. Visit the site **http://vvv.com/ai/demos/whale.html** and explore its expert system. See Figure 24.

Figure 24

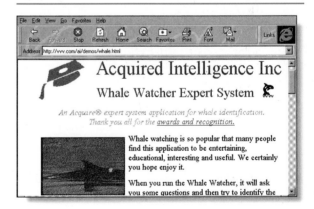

3 Asimov's Three Laws of Robotics In his 1950 novel *I, Robot*, Isaac Asimov wrote "Three Laws of Robotics" which were designed to place constraints on robots so they would not harm their inventors.

a. A robot may not injure a human being or, through inaction, allow a human being to come to harm.

b. A robot must obey the orders given it by human beings except where such orders would conflict with the first law.

c. A robot must protect its own existence as long as such protection does not conflict with the first and second laws.

Do you think these three laws are sufficient? If so, write a short paper to explain why you feel that the Three Laws of Robotics will adequately protect humans from the power of robots. If not, write a short paper describing something a robot could do to harm us without breaking the laws. Propose a fourth law to cover this possibility.

4 Problem-solving Strategies— Exhaustive Searches: Identify at least two other games in addition to chess that can be analyzed using a strategy of exhaustive search. Identify at least two games that cannot be analyzed using a strategy of exhaustive search. Give reasons why you think baseball can or cannot be analyzed using a strategy of exhaustive search.

5 Pattern Recognition: Figure 25 is a photograph of a mask. Identify the parts of the mask that make it recognizable as a human face. Identify the parts of the mask that might confuse a computer attempting to interpret the photograph.

6 Rules of Thumb Suppose you turn on your computer and it doesn't start properly. Write five heuristics (rules of thumb) that you might use to identify and correct the problem. For example: If the power light does not come on, make sure the machine is plugged in.

7 Determining Responsibility Write a short paper describing who you think is responsible when a computer makes an error. Consider the following candidates: the computer operator, the computer owner, the computer programmer, and the computer manufacturer.

8 Fuzzy Logic Fuzzy logic has been incorporated in the design of machines you encounter every day. For example, one model of television uses fuzzy logic to adjust its picture to compensate for the light level in the room. One brand of car uses fuzzy logic in its automatic transmission for more efficient shifting. Describe two machines you use that could be better, more useful, or more efficient if they used fuzzy logic as part of their control systems.

Figure 25

QuickCheck
Answers

Chapter 1

A

1. Processing (process, process data)
2. Data
3. Central
4. Memory (RAM)
5. Storage

B

1. Keyboard, monitor
2. Microcomputer (PC, personal computer)
3. Terminal
4. Mainframe
5. Compatible
6. Network

C

1. Prompt
2. Wizards
3. Enter (the Enter key)
4. Syntax
5. Submenu (sub-menu, sub menu)
6. Graphical user interfaces (GUIs)
7. Cursor, insertion point
8. Ctrl (Control)
9. Windows

Chapter 2

A

1. False (F)
2. False (F)
3. Data
4. Program
5. Software
6. Shareware
7. License (software license)
8. System, application

B

1. Multitasking (multi-tasking)
2. UNIX (VMS, MVS)
3. Micro (personal, micro-)
4. UNIX
5. Utility
6. Device driver (driver)
7. Programming language (computer programming language)

C

1. Suite (office suite)
2. Desktop publishing (DTP)
3. Vector (3-D, #D)
4. False (F)
5. Web browser (browser)
6. Vertical

D

1. True (T)

2. False (F)

3. Hypermedia (hyper-media)

4. MMX

Chapter 3

A

1. Document production

2. True (T)

3. Word wrap (word-wrap)

4. False (F)

5. Template (document template), wizard (document wizard)

6. Electronic

7. Concordance (a concordance)

8. HTML

B

1. Column, row

2. Addresses

3. Functions

4. True (T)

5. True (T)

6. False (F)

7. What if (what-if)

C

1. Database

2. Structured, free-form (free form)

3. Access (find, locate)

4. True (T)

5. Query by example (QBE)

6. Query language

7. True (T)

Chapter 4

A

1. Data, information

2. Dat (.dat)

3. Exe (.exe)

4. Logical

5. Root

6. Source (batch)

B

1. Bytes (megabytes, MB, gigabytes, GB), milliseconds (ms, ms.)

2. Magnetic, optical

3. Tracks, sectors

4. Random, sequential

5. QIC

6. Hard disk (hard disk drive)

7. FAT (file allocation table)

8. False (F)

Chapter 5

A

1. Integrate circuit (IC)
2. Bit
3. Byte
4. ASCII
5. Binary
6. Bus (data bus)

B

1. Memory (primary storage)
2. Volatile
3. Megabytes (MB, bytes)
4. Capacitors
5. Nanoseconds (ns, ns.)
6. Virtual
7. ROM (read only memory, read-only memory)
8. CMOS

C

1. Microprocessor
2. ALU (arithmetic logic unit, arithmetic-logic unit)
3. Control unit
4. Operand
5. Megahertz (MHz)
6. System clock

D

1. Expansion bus
2. Expansion card (controller card, expansion board)
3. Slot, port
4. USB (universal serial bus)

Chapter 6

A

1. Pentium
2. True (T)
3. EIDE
4. False (F)
5. LCD (liquid crystal)
6. One megabyte (1 MB, 1 megabyte)
7. PCMCIA
8. Color ink-jet (color ink jet)

B

1. Vaporware
2. True (T)
3. Competitive
4. Tiers
5. False (F)
6. VAR (value added reseller)

C

1. False (F)
2. Information systems (IS)
3. Northeast
4. Experience
5. Organizations
6. Job fairs (conferences)

Chapter 7

A

1. Server (file server)
2. Account (user account)
3. Mapped
4. True (T)
5. False (F)
6. Captured

B

1. Network interface card (NIC)
2. Non-dedicated
3. File server
4. True (T)
5. Host

C

1. Network operating
2. False (F)
3. Network license
4. Groupware
5. Workflow (document routing)

Chapter 8

A

1. Cyberspace
2. Internet
3. Terabytes
4. False (F)
5. TCP/IP (transport control protocol/Internet protocol)
6. URL (Web site)

B

1. Home
2. Streaming media
3. Plug-in (viewer)
4. False (F)
5. True (T)
6. True (T)

C

1. Links
2. False (F)
3. Body
4. False (F)
5. Web authoring
6. True (T)
7. Navigational
8. True (T)

Chapter 9

A

1. Operator
2. False (F)
3. Uninterruptible power supply (UPS)
4. Surge strip (surge suppressor, surge protector)
5. False (F)
6. False (F)
7. Backup (up-to-date backup)

B

1. Virus
2. Macro
3. Trojan horse
4. Worm
5. Virus
6. E-mail attachments
7. Signature
8. Data

C

1. Risk management
2. Policy
3. True (T)
4. Rights (user rights)
5. Trapdoor
6. Cookie
7. Downtime
8. Positive

Chapter LIF

A

1. Dial-up networking
2. Outsourcing
3. Intranets
4. Virtual corporation
5. Job hunting

B

1. Student-centered
2. Presentation graphics
3. Computer assisted instruction (CAI)
4. Distance learning
5. Virtual College
6. Video conferencing

C

1. Thomas
2. Townhall
3. Televoting
4. World Wide Web (WWW)
5. Access code

Chapter PRV

A

1. Computer matching
2. Computer profiling
3. True (T)
4. Public
5. Possible answers: banks, video stores, telephone companies, libraries, medical insurance companies
6. False (F)
7. Entrepreneurs
8. Social Security number
9. Dataveillance

B

1. Zones of privacy
2. Businesses
3. E-mail
4. Censorware
5. True (T)

C

1. Cryptography
2. Plaintext
3. Ciphertext
4. Public key, private key
5. Digital signature
6. Key length
7. True (T)
8. Cypherpunks
9. Government

Chapter IPE

A

1. Intellectual property
2. Patent
3. Fixed
4. True (T)
5. Good will, competition
6. Digital
7. NII white paper

B

1. True (T)
2. First sale
3. False (F)
4. Fifty (50)
5. Public domain
6. Fair use
7. False (F)
8. Implied license

C

1. Monopoly
2. Expression, ideas
3. True (T)
4. Freeware
5. Shareware
6. Warez
7. Shrinkwrap
8. LaMacchia

D

1. Trademark law
2. Lanham Act
3. Dilution
4. False (F)

Chapter INT

A

1. Human
2. Turing
3. Deep Blue
4. Chinese room
5. Machine

B

1. Natural language processing
2. SHRDLU
3. ELIZA
4. Algorithmic search
5. Heuristics
6. Decision making under uncertainty

C

1. Inference engine
2. CYC
3. Expert system
4. Fuzzy logic
5. Natural selection
6. Brain
7. Hidden logic
8. Robot
9. Robotics

Glossary/ Index

analog copies, counterfeit, IPE-6

Analog device A device in which continuously varying data is processed as a continuous stream of varying information (for example, a dimmer switch or a heart monitor), 5-5

analyzing information for papers, 3-40

Anderson, Harland, 1-33

animations, 2-20

Anti-virus program *See* Virus detection program, 9-12, 9-41

Apple Computer, LIF-11, 1-32, 2-30, 2-32–33, 6-20

Apple v. Microsoft/Hewlett Packard, IPE-22

Applets *See* Java applets, 9-25

Application server A computer that runs application software and forwards the results of processing to workstations, as requested, 7-15

Application software Computer programs that help the human user carry out a specific type of task (word processing, database management, etc.), 2-8, 2-10, 2-18–29. *See also* software
    accounting and finance, 2-28
    business, 2-29
    buying, 2-41
    connectivity, 2-25
    data management, 2-23
    document production, 2-19
    education and training, 2-26
    entertainment, 2-27
    graphics, 2-20
    information and reference, 2-24
    jargon, 2-18
    numeric analysis, 2-22
    operating system liaison with hardware, 2-10–11
    presentation, 2-21

Applications *See* Application software, 2-8, 2-10, 2-18

Application-specific filename extension An extension added to the name of a file, indicating that the file is associated with a particular application (for example, .wrd or .doc), 4-7

application-specific filename extensions, 4-7

.apr filename extension, 4-7

Archimedes, INT-12

Archiving The process of moving data off a primary storage device (such as a hard drive) onto a secondary storage device (such as a backup tape), for permanent storage, 4-27

ARCnet A type of network configuration, 7-11

Ariane 5 rocket, LIF-2

Arithmetic logic unit (ALU) The part of the central processing unit that performs arithmetic and logical operations, 5-15

Army Mathematics Research Center, 9-18

ARPA. *See* Advanced Research Projects Agency (ARPA)

ARPANET A project initiated in 1969 by the Advanced Research Projects Agency (ARPA) that connected computers at four universities, 8-2, 8-3

Arrow keys Keys used to move the user's position on the screen up, down, right, or left, 1-25

art, artificial intelligence, INT-32

Artificial intelligence (AI) The ability of a machine to simulate or surpass intelligent human behavior, 1-31, 1-35, INT-1–31
    current status, INT-28–29
    debate, INT-34
    decision making under uncertainty, INT-12
    definition, INT-32
    expert systems, INT-2, INT-15–16, INT-23–26, INT-29, INT-33
    future, INT-31
    fuzzy logic, INT-17–18, INT-33
    genetic algorithms, INT-18–19
    impact, INT-34
    intelligent behavior, INT-4–6
    knowledge base, INT-13–14
    natural language processing, INT-7–9, INT-33
    neural networks, INT-19–21, INT-33
    pattern recognition, INT-21–23
    problem solving, INT-10–11
    robotics, INT-23–24, INT-32
    Turing test, INT-2–3, INT-7

Artificial life Computer organisms that can reproduce and adapt to their environment, INT-18

ASCII American Standard Code for Information Interchange, the data representation code most commonly used on microcomputers, frequently used on minicomputers, and sometimes used on mainframe computers, 5-7

Asimov, Isaac, 3-5

asterisk (*), wildcard, 4-8

asynchronous communication, 8-17

Asynchronous discussion In Internet terminology, a discussion in which participants are not online at the same time, 8-17

Atari Games v. Nintendo, IPE-21

ATM (asynchronous transfer mode) A network configuration utilizing a single standard for data, video, and voice, 7-11

ATM networks, 7-11

Attachment A file, such as a word-processing document, spreadsheet, or graphic, that is sent through an e-mail system along with an e-mail message, 7-23

attachments, e-mail, 7-23

Downwardly compatible In reference to operating systems, able to use application software designed for earlier versions of the operating system, but not those designed for later versions, 2-37

Drag, Dragging Placing the mouse pointer over an object, holding down the mouse button, moving the mouse pointer to a new location, and releasing the mouse button, in order to move an object to a new location, 1-23

drawings, 2-20

DreamWorks SKG, IPE-4

Dreyfus, Herbert, INT-5

Drive hub The component of the floppy disk that the disk drive engages in order to rotate the disk, 4-17

Drive spindle The component of the hard drive that supports one or more hard disk platters, 4-20

drive(s), 5-2
    CD-ROM. *See* CD-ROM drives
    default, 5-31
    EIDE, 6-5
    floppy disk, 1-10, 4-9, 4-19, 5-2, 6-5
    hard disk. *See* hard disk(s)
    mapping, 7-4
    SCSI, 6-5
    speeds, 4-34
    tape. *See* tape drives
    testing, 5-30
    Zip, 4-9, 4-19

Drop-down list A list of options that is displayed when the user clicks an arrow button, 1-20

dual-in-line pin. *See* DIP (dual-in-line pin)

Dual-pipeline architecture A type of microprocessor chip design in which the chip can execute two instructions at one time, 6-4

dual-scan displays, 6-9

DVDs (digital video disks), 4-33

E

Earnings and Benefit Statement, examining, PRV-32

EBCDIC (extended binary-coded decimal interchange code) A method by which digital computers represent character data, 5-7

Echo of Lions (Chase-Riboud), IPE-4

economics, IPE-38

EDO (extended data out) A type of RAM technology that provides better performance than standard memory technology, 6-5

Education and training software Computer programs that help the user learn and perfect new skills, 2-26

education, computer industry careers, 6-29

educational technology, LIF-11–19, LIF-31
    distance learning, LIF-16–17, LIF-31
    K-12 education, LIF-11–13
    university classrooms, LIF-14–15, LIF-31–32
    virtual colleges, LIF-18–19

Educom, LIF-21

EduPage newsletter, LIF-21

Edutainment software Computer programs that combine elements of game software and education software, 2-26

EDVAC (Electronic Discrete Variable Automatic Computer), 1-2, 1-32

EFF (Electronic Frontier Foundation), IPE-11, PRV-26

EIDE (enhanced integrated device electronics) A type of drive that features high storage capacity and fast data transfer, 6-5

Einstein, Albert, IPE-18

electronic commerce, PRV-35

Electronic Communications Privacy Act of 1986, PRV-14

Electronic Frontier Foundation (EFF), IPE-11, PRV-26

Electronic mail (e-mail) Correspondence sent from one person to another electronically, 7-21. *See* e-mail

Electronic mail system The hardware and software that collect and deliver e-mail messages, 7-21

Electronic Privacy Information Center, PRV-26

Electronic publishing The manipulation, storage, and transmission of electronic documents by means of electronic media or telecommunications services, 3-12–13, 3-44

Electronic town hall meeting The use of voice mail, e-mail, fax, and the World Wide Web to provide for direct participation in political discourse, LIF-24

Electronic typewriter A typewriter that incorporates features of a word processor, 3-16

elementary education, LIF-11–13

ELIZA, INT-10

e-mail *See* Electronic mail, 7-21–24, 7-27
    attachments, 7-23
    composing messages, 7-23
    copyright rights, IPE-15, IPE-32
    interoffice, privacy, PRV-17–18
    managing, 7-24
    messages, 7-21

H

I

I/O (Input/Output) The collection of data for the microprocessor to manipulate, and the transportation of the results to display, print, or storage devices, 5-23

Icon A small picture on a computer screen that represents an object, 1-21, 4-3

Implied license The implicit granting of rights for works to be copied and distributed. This occurs when the creator of a work provides the work to a distribution source that he or she knows intends to distribute it (for example, posting material on a Usenet service), IPE-15–16

Importing The process by which a program reads and translates data from another source, 3-38

Inaccurate data Data that is incorrect because it was entered wrong, was deliberately or accidentally altered, or is not up to date, 9-2

Incremental backup A copy of the files that have changed since the last backup, 9-34

Index An alphabetical list of the key words in a document and the numbers of the pages on which they appear 3-15

Indicator lights Lights on the computer keyboard that indicate the status (on or off) of the toggle keys and the power switch, 1-25

Industry analysts Experts who monitor industry trends, evaluate industry events, and make prediction about what the trends may indicate, 6-25

Inference engine A program that directs a computer to evaluate facts according to a specific set of rules, in order to solve problems, make decisions, or direct actions, INT-13

Information The words, numbers, and graphics used as the basis for human actions and decisions, 4-2

Information and reference software Computer programs that provide the user with a collection of information and the means to access that information, 2-24

Information entrepreneurs Businesses that collect and sell information, PRV-7

Infringer A person who copies or constructs an invention without the owner's permission while that work is under patent, IPE-3

Injunction A special order from a court prohibiting infringement by a person or company, IPE-3

Ink-jet printer A printer that creates characters and graphics by spraying ink onto paper, 6-15

In-line spell checker A program that shows the user spelling errors, as the user types, 3-4, 3-6

In-place multimedia technology An Internet multimedia technology that plays a media element as part of a Web page, 8-12

Input Data entered into a computer system by a person, an environmental monitoring device, or another computer, 1-3

Input device A tool that gathers input and translates it into a form that the computer can process, 1-3

Insertion point A flashing vertical bar that appears on the screen, indicating where the user can begin entering text, 1-24

Installation process In reference to software, the process by which programs and data are copied to the hard disk of a computer system, 2-37

O

Q

QBE *See* Query by example, 3-35

QIC (quarter-inch cartridge) A cartridge tape that measures a quarter of an inch wide, and is used by microcomputer tape drives, 4-25

queries
    copying and printing results, 3-37
    exporting results, 3-38
    printing results, 3-37
    saving results, 3-38
    transmitting results, 3-38

Query by example (QBE) A type of database interface in which the user fills in a field with information related to the desired information, in order to initiate a search, 3-35

Query language A set of command words that the user uses to direct the computer to create databases, locate information, sort records, and change the data in those records, 3-36

R

R.U.R. (movie), INT-1, INT-25

RAID (redundant array of independent disks) A hard disk storage format, used by mainframes and microcomputers, in which many disk platters are used to provide data redundancy for faster data access and increased protection from media failure, 4-23

RAM *See* Random access memory, 5-4, 5-9

RAM address An identifying value associated with each bank of capacitors that holds information in RAM, 5-9

RAM cache *See* Cache, 5-20

Random access *See* Direct access, 4-19

Random access memory (RAM) Memory that temporarily holds data that is being processed, 5-4, 5-9–11
    capacity and speed, 5-10
    cost, 6-5
    functions, 5-10
    requirements, 6-5
    testing, 5-30
    virtual memory, 5-11

random access, floppy disk drives, 4-19

Readability formulas Instructions contained in grammar checkers that help the user to write at a level appropriate for a particular target audience, 3-14

reading ability, 3-43

Reading data *See* Loading data, 4-14

Read-only An indication that a computer can retrieve data from a storage medium such as a CD-ROM, but cannot write new data onto it, 4-27

Read-only memory (ROM) A set of chips containing permanent, nonchangeable instructions that help a computer prepare for processing tasks, 5-12

read-only storage media, 4-27

Read-write head The component of a disk drive that magnetizes particles on the storage disk surface, in order to encode data, 4-15, 4-20, 4-22

Real-time clock In a computer system, a battery-powered clock chip that maintains the current date and time, 5-4

Recycle Bin, 1-22

Redirecting Diverting data headed for a local peripheral (such as a printer) to a network peripheral (such as a network printer), 7-9

redirecting printer ports, 7-9

Reduced instruction set computer *See* RISC, 5-21

Redundancy The storage of duplicate data in more than one location, for protection against media failure, 4-23

redundancy, data security, 9-27

redundant array of independent disks. *See* RAID (redundant array of independent disks) storage devices

Reference manuals Books or online resources that describe the features of a hardware device or a software package, 1-30

reference materials, multimedia, K-12 education, LIF-12

Register A region of high-speed memory in an electronic processing device, such as an ALU, used to hold data that is being processed, 5-15
    instruction register, 5-16

Release *See* Version, 6-18

releases, software, 6-18

Remote control software Computer programs used to establish a connection, via modem, between two machines that are located at a distance from each other, 2-25

Removable hard disks Hard disk cartridges that contain platters and read-write heads, and that can be inserted into and removed from the hard drive, 4-22

Rendering In graphics software, the process of creating a 3-D solid image by covering a wireframe drawing and applying computer-generated highlights and shadows, 2-20

S

X